LOST VICTORY

The Rise & Fall of LTTE Supremo, V. Prabhakaran

The man of knowledge must be able not only to love his enemies but also to hate his friends.

– Friedrich Nietzsche (1844-1900)

STOP PRESS

Readers are informed that this book was nearing the completion of its final editing and proof reading, when it became clear that Sri Lanka was in turmoil, because of the public differences of opinion between the Rajapaksa Government and the CDS, Gen. Sarath Fonseka. This acrimony led to the General tendering his resignation on November 12, 2009, which was accepted by President Mahinda Rajapaksa, effective November 16, 2009. Gen Fonseka, post retirement, has, on his part, lost no time in announcing his candidature for the Presidential elections scheduled in end January, 2010.

The author is conscious of the readers right to be kept updated in a serious publication of this genre, on the latest developments in Sri Lanka at the time of going to press. He has therefore, added another chapter titled *Trouble in Paradise*, to update his readers on the genesis of this crisis and its possible fallouts.

LOST VICTORY
The Rise & Fall of LTTE Supremo, V. Prabhakaran

Maj. Gen. Raj Mehta
AVSM, VSM (Retired)

PENTAGON SECURITY
INTERNATIONAL
AN IMPRINT OF PENTAGON PRESS

Lost Victory: The Rise & Fall of LTTE Supremo, V. Prabhakaran / Maj. Gen. Raj Mehta

ISBN 978-81-8274-478-3

First Edition: 2010
Second Edition: 2010

Published by
PENTAGON SECURITY INTERNATIONAL
An Imprint of
PENTAGON PRESS
206, Peacock Lane, Shahpur Jat, New Delhi-110049
Phones: 011-64706243, 26491568
Telefax: 011-26490600
email: rajan@pentagon-press.in
website: www.pentagonpress.in

Printed at
Aegean Offset Printers, Geater Noida, U.P.

Contents

Part III
Miscellaneous Facets of the Conflict

Part IV
The Indian Intervention

Part V
The Way Ahead

Preface to the Second Edition

The news from the Pentagon International Publisher, Rajan Arya, that the first edition of *Lost Victory* has been sold out within three months of coming off the press, has been both pleasant and unexpected encouragement for this first time author. The reviews carried out by some respected national newspapers and military publications have also been heartening. Excerpts of some of these reviews are reproduced elsewhere in this book.

The author is now in the enviable position of writing the Preface to the Second Edition of the book. This is also, really, an opportunity for the author to take the Sri Lankan story forward in terms of the cataclysmic events that have taken place, since *Lost Victory* hit book stores country wide in January 2010. Readers will therefore benefit from the short update that follows.

Sensing that the wildly successful Sri Lankan blitzkrieg against the LTTE was going to take a huge toll on the mainstream politics of the country, the author had added a last minute chapter (Chapter 22) titled *Trouble in Paradise,* just before *Lost Victory* went into print. The chapter gave details of Gen. Sarath Fonseka's increasing unhappiness with his political masters, over the apportioning of glory and its attendant 'national war hero' halo, as the LTTE war was drawing to its spectacular closure. The chapter also recorded his feeling of being marginalized by the Governments decision to "kick him upstairs" to the largely ornamental post of CDS, and therefore away from his power base which was the largely unfettered command of the Sri Lankan Army. His subsequent, but not unexpected act of entering into the political arena to contest the Presidential elections scheduled for January 26, 2010, to cash in on his unquestioned popularity with the majority Sinhalese population, was the last nail in the coffin of his once cozy, 'blood brothers' kind of friendship with the ruling Rajapaksa combine. The chapter also explained, in some detail, how the once cozy relationship between him, the President and his brothers, Gottabhaya and Basil, had irreversibly soured over the vexed but politically exploitable issue of who was to be credited with the decisive defeat of the LTTE and the extermination of its dreaded Supremo, Prabhakaran along with most of his immediate family members and top leadership hierarchy. The chapter had presciently predicted success for Mahinda Rajapaksa, though it had expected that Gen. Fonseka would put up a spirited fight, which he did.

Much else has happened, since those tense days in July-August 2009, when open public speculation replaced the isolated murmurs that had begun surfacing in the media since March-April 2009, of the Fonseka-Rajapaksa fallout over the spoils of war; primarily the apportioning of credit for waging successful war against the LTTE. It is therefore intended to re-establish a link with the key happenings since Gen. Fonseka stepped into the fray and follow the story up to his present incarceration and commencement of dual courts martial proceedings (dual, because of the Sri Lanka Government preferring two separate sets of charges) against him. It is also intended to do a little bit of crystal gazing, especially from the Indian perspective, and look into the immediate future. [A general but necessary word of advice to readers is that, what has happened so far has *nothing* directly to do with courts martial per se, but amounts to initiation of preliminary legal actions mandated by the Army Act and Rules, under which an alleged violation of the prevalent military rules and regulations is examined for its validity and seriousness. Thus, all that has actually happened so far is that the Sri Lankan Army Headquarters, in consultation with the Sri Lankan Government, has ordered the commencement of a mandatory legal procedure called Recording of Summary of Evidence. Once this recording is over, the proceedings will be sent to the highest military (and, in this high profile case, the highest civil legal authority as well) for vetting as well as for establishing the need to proceed with the case or drop it, if the evidence on record cannot stand up to legal scrutiny or is otherwise unsustainable. It is based on this evaluation that the Convening Authority (in this case, the Army Commander, Gen. Jayasuriya) can order the assembly of a Courts Martial].

Keeping in mind the complexity and seriousness of the developments that have taken place, involving a serious military-civil Government spat round at the strategic "door step" of India, this author thus feels vindicated in adding a fresh chapter titled **Update on the Rajapaksa – Fonseka Imbroglio** as Chapter 23. The chapter will also, at its end, do a bit of crystal ball gazing on the likely fall out of the current run of events in Sri Lanka and how these could impact on India.

The author wishes his enlightened readership a thoughtful reading of *Lost Victory.*

April 18, 2010

Major General Raj Mehta
AVSM, VSM (Retired)

Preface to the First Edition

'Lost Victory' is an unabashed military book. It, however, covers a subject which is of great interest not just for military professionals the world over, but, increasingly, also the lay reader, the common citizen across gender, intellectuals across diverse disciplines, and the media, who, in these trying times, are trying to interpret terrorism as one of their key concerns. This transition from the normal span of interest of citizens has taken place in recent years because terror is now a global malady and has become the common man's concern as much as it is the concern of think tanks, members of the Fourth Estate, other professionals and for academics, in fact, just about everyone.

The key aim is not so much to 'carry coal to Newcastle' for those whose primary job it is to fight, study or research terror. There is little by way of content in these pages not already known to these experts and luminaries. There is, however, lots of information here for the lay reader, the citizen who needs to bone up on terror and its myriad dynamics.

Several thoughts arise that I have taken the liberty of sharing with my readers. Firstly (and understandably), although I have given my perception of events right through the book, there has been no effort on my part to reinvent the wheel. In other words, the substantial relevant information that was available – and an extraordinary amount is available on the subject – has been edited and reproduced with due attribution. The book has been sequenced keeping in mind the end result that I had, about sharing information on important issues of the conflict, in an objective, non-judgemental and knowledge enhancing manner.

Secondly, I see no contradiction in admiring the Tamil 'soldier' for his fighting qualities. Hyperbole aside, he (and she) must rank amongst the best in the world. This, however, has little to do with the purpose for which Prabhakaran utilized these qualities, resulting in the loss of countless lives on both sides (some say

70,000 to 100,000) in the Eelam struggle. Without denying the legitimacy of many of their demands, the book points out that the struggle for acceptance of this legitimacy could have been better orchestrated without recourse to the mindless violence that accompanied it, on both sides of the Tamil-Sinhalese divide.

Realpolitik is rather different from detached philosophical musings and this reality stands reinforced in this book. The violence went on for over 30 years, seriously challenging the sovereignty and the very existence of Sri Lanka, till it ended on May 18, 2009. One only hopes that the requisite lessons from it have been learnt by the concerned players both within and outside Sri Lanka and better sense prevails in rebuilding a proud nation to its earlier glory.

So far as military experience is concerned, my 37-plus years in uniform have given me a lot of it, including several assignments in live operations. I have had five direct exposures to counter terrorism operations between the ranks of Colonel to Major General and sustained gunshot wounds in one encounter with terrorists in January 1997, when in command of a Rashtriya Rifles Sector (Brigade) in South Kashmir.

Unrest and turbulence in Sri Lanka impinges directly on India's security. The reasons are not just demographic, but extend equally to the close cultural, religious and social contacts that the two countries have established over thousands of years. As such, peace, prosperity and wellness in the strategically located island is very desirable for India. Readers will note that Sri Lanka also dominates the key oil routes emanating from West Asia to South East Asia, East Asia and beyond, as also, in a manner of speaking, controls sea access to India's equally important neighbours, Bangladesh and Myanmar. Its stability is therefore an important consideration for India's security concerns.

This then, has been my motivation for writing the book. A professional soldier, especially when he has retired, has no axe to grind in dispassionately analyzing the flow of history. I have always viewed Sri Lanka as a friendly, peace loving country. It was, and will remain a preferred friendly foreign country for me. Her political-military synergy in the latter part of conduct of the war against terror has been world class and precedent setting; not just for the South Asian region, but also for the world at large. Yet, there was a time, not so long ago, when Prabhakaran, the iconic, ruthless LTTE supremo, was close to achieving what generations of Tamils had only dreamt of.

In analyzing a conflict, objectivity does not allow the identification of a victor or vanquished, especially where supreme national interest is at stake. Declaration of the Government forces as the victor and the LTTE as the vanquished is a superficial, jingoistic exercise which has few takers in Sri Lanka or elsewhere. The real facts are sombre. Terrorism has savagely set back a once flourishing country. A country, that, at one time was seen as an Asian Tiger for its astute policies and prosperity is limping back to normalcy after over 30 years of strife.

Similarly, LTTE supporters can grieve over their lost cause but only up to a point. On the contrary, they have all the time to rue what could have been, had sense and sensibility prevailed with its apex leadership. They also have the time, and, hopefully, the urge to let the past be forgotten and create for themselves an identity without challenging the supremacy and sovereignty of the state. This book will examine all aspects of the conflict and end with suggestions on the way forward.

Finally, all writing is essentially subjective because all authors have an aim in mind, stated or unstated, and 'Lost Victory' is no different in this respect. The writer's aim was to dispassionately examine the conflict and suggest a way forward. The reader is left free at the end to exercise his or her judgement on the value or otherwise of the book.

December 3, 2009

Maj. Gen. Raj Mehta
AVSM, VSM (Retired)

Acknowledgements

It is an irony that it was in the month of May, in 1976; May 5, 1976, to be precise, that Velupillai Prabhakaran had baptised his Tamil New Tigers (TNT) outfit as the LTTE. For all practical purposes, his organization met its effective end as a coherent terror agency in the month of its birth, 33 long years ago; at about 5.30 a.m., on the morning of May 18, 2009.

Thanks are due to the Ministry of Defence, Sri Lanka, for their detailed inputs on the conflict, including, in particular, their synergized conduct of war against the LTTE and their assessment of the assassination of Rajiv Gandhi by the LTTE.

The Centre for Land Warfare Studies (CLAWS), New Delhi, is an autonomous think-tank dealing with national security and conceptual aspects of land warfare, including conventional and sub-conventional conflicts and terrorism. CLAWS conducts research that is futuristic in outlook and policy oriented in approach. The author is indebted to Director, CLAWS, Brigadier Gurmeet Kanwal (Retired), Dr. N. Manoharan, his Managing Editor, as well as Dr. SinhaRaja Tammita-Delgoda, for according permission to reproduce his paper, 'Sri Lanka: The Last Phase in Eelam War IV – From Chundikulam to Pudumattalan' in this book.

This paper is based on his field observations, together with interviews and conversations with serving Sri Lankan officers and men in the field who participated in the dramatic final countdown leading to the death of Prabhakaran, along with most of his family and key operatives. The paper has been produced by CLAWS as Manekshaw Paper No. 13, 2009.

Thanks are also due to Brig. Gurmeet Kanwal and Dr. N. Manoharan, in their personnel capacities as authors of substance, as several articles written by them have been referred to in the text. In the case of Brig. Gurmeet Kanwal, the thanks are also in acknowledgement of a recent brief but perceptive conversation on Sri Lanka and access to his very regular, prescient, fortnightly email updates via articles, comments, views on India and its overall security concerns. A particular discussion he has held at CLAWS on Sri Lanka has, in particular, been extensively quoted being a very relevant article..

A debt of gratitude is owed to *Lankapuvath*, which is Sri Lanka's national news agency and is the only one in the country. It was created in 1978 to publish and distribute news. It is a company of five partners, national dailies and main national electronic media institutions and was read regularly by the author as well as occasionally quoted in this book.

Among the most useful and extensively quoted sites in the book is that of the Ministry of Defence, Public Security and Law and Order (MoD) (http://www.defence.lk/english.asp) and Government of Sri Lanka, particularly, its Media Centre for National Security (http://www.nationalsecurity.lk/), which must rate as one of the best informed and structured security sites in Asia, if not the world. It was a learning experience for the author to see the extraordinary detail that was and continues to be posted on this site regarding what is termed as '*The Final Countdown*' including interactive, well annotated maps that give the progress of Sri Lankan military operations on a date and time line.

The Media Centre for National Security is considered to be a brainchild of the Defence Secretary, Dr. Gotabhaya Rajapaksa, and is doing a fine job of perception management of the Sri Lankan Government's take on the Eelam War. The MoD site permits reproduction of its web content with attribution.

A large number of articles, papers and interviews have been quoted in this book and all effort has been made to ensure attribution. If some error in attribution has still occurred, it may be considered as unintended and ignored.

I am also grateful to Pentagon Press for showing keen interest in the book and enabling it to get published.

On a personal level, I owe a debt of gratitude to my multi-faceted, very well read wife of 34 years standing, Kukkie, who was as encouraging as she was constructively critical of the book and its orientation. Thanks are also due to two unnamed serving colleagues who are voracious readers of military developments and keen analysts of security, for their mail forwards and general comments on security issues concerning South Asia. Special thanks are also due to a serving, far younger colleague, who critically proof read the Preface and Introductory chapter and suggested valid corrections. He also lent me two well written books on Sri Lanka and the IPKF operations.

Maj Gen. Raj Mehta, AVSM, VSM (Retired)

December 3, 2009

Introduction

Any one who has studied the over 30-year-old Sri Lankan conflict with detachment will perhaps agree that no other phrase can define the Prabhakaran conundrum better than 'Lost Victory'. He had almost succeeded in his goal of getting a Tamil Eelam with most of his conditions agreed to by the Sri Lankan Government, with the tacit approval of the international community. On the brink of success, however, he made cardinal, irreversible blunders, linked with unbridled, overweening ambition and a total misreading of the Sri Lankan Government's resolve and capability. This resulted in his inglorious death, along with most of his family members and key henchmen and supporters, and the collapse of his movement.

Seth Mydans, writing in the *New York Times* says that for years, Prabhakaran commanded what amounted to a shadow state with its own flag, police and court system. He built a fanatical army, including many child recruits, and ordered them to abstain from sex and cut themselves off from personal ties. Sri Lanka's Tamils, who make up just 12 percent of a population that is largely Buddhist and Sinhalese, have been marginalized since independence from Britain in 1948. The dominance of the Sinhalese was cemented with the declaration of Sinhala as the national language and Buddhism as the principal religion, and with privileges for Sinhalese in education and government jobs. It was, Mydans writes with candour, Prabhakaran's refusal to compromise that undermined repeated attempts at peace agreements and led to the final battles that destroyed the movement he had built.

Jeremy Page, writing for *The Times,* reinforces this impression of Prabhakaran. It was, he writes, "supposed to be the unwinnable war. For almost three decades, Sri Lanka was held up as an example of how a small democratic state with a conventional army could never defeat a well-funded and disciplined guerrilla organisation." The implication for the war being 'unwinnable' by the Sri Lankan forces has a distaff meaning; that it was certainly winnable by the opposing forces, the LTTE. The writer records that Prabhakaran's seemingly impregnable position and status started unreeling from 2004 onwards. He goes on to say that…"The Army used guerrilla tactics – moving in small groups through the jungles rather than on main roads – while the Tigers fought a conventional campaign to defend their territory. Military intelligence split the Tigers by persuading 'Colonel' Karuna, their second-in-command, to defect in 2004, allowing the army to drive the rebels out of Eastern Sri Lanka in 2007. The Navy played a crucial role by attacking the Tigers' supply ships, with help from India and the USA. In the international arena, Sri Lanka outmanoeuvred the Tamil Tigers by taking advantage of counter-terrorism legislation introduced after the attacks on the USA on September 11, 2001. It lobbied hard to have the Tigers banned as terrorists in the USA, EU, Canada and Australia, forcing those countries to crack down on their financing and arms procurement. More recently, it has cultivated ties with China, Iran and other non-Western powers to counterbalance Western criticism of its conduct of the war. It also secured tacit approval for its campaign from the ruling Congress party in India.

The writer concludes by stating that having won an unwinnable war, Sri Lanka now needs to "present a devolution package granting enough autonomy to satisfy Tamils not just in Sri Lanka but also in the large and wealthy diaspora that funded the Tigers. If it succeeds it may yet add weight to the idea that terrorists such as the Tigers can be beaten only by curbing civil liberties, keeping the media away and using brute force – just as Russia did in Chechnya. If it fails, however, it will have squandered the sympathy of the democratic world – not to mention billions of pounds – and created a new generation of Tigers."

The term 'Lost Victory' therefore truly captures what may have been as opposed to what really happened and is therefore considered an apt title for this book.

When I began, I did so on the premise that I would write a biography of Velupillai Prabhakaran and keep the focus on his tumultuous life and dramatic death (under somewhat mysterious circumstances, not yet fully revealed by the Sri Lankan Government). As I trawled into the subject, I realized, at an early stage, that it was not going to be possible to write a linear, one-dimensional book focused merely on his life, achievements, failures and contribution to the employment of a political tool of terror.

What really happened was that, in the longer term, I began to see somewhat vaguely, at first encounter, and, later with increasing clarity, how an ex-soldier should cover this fascinating subject. More importantly, I was able to establish an important connect between how the Sri Lankan Armed Forces had finally gone about their job, and the declining efficiency and absence of synergy that had made the LTTE almost unbeatable at the peak of its powers in the 2000-2004 period.

India is deeply concerned about what happens in its immediate neighbourhood, both in terms of peace and tranquillity, which it welcomes, and the rapid spread and propagation of terror, which it does not, and in fact, abhors. When the country concerned is Sri Lanka, with whom ties of friendship, religion as well as demography go back thousands of years, the concern is paramount. It was therefore clear to me that the Indian intervention under 'Operation Pawan' would have to be covered, as also the assassination of Rajiv Gandhi. I realized that our diplomacy and tacit understanding with Sri Lanka on the modus operandi of tackling a terror organization which has been proscribed in India since 1992 would also have to be covered.

The next obvious issue was, of course, the diplomatic efforts that Sri Lanka made with other countries to develop and fine tune its war waging capability and how these assisted Sri Lanka in emerging victors.

Not the least, the book simply had to examine how the nation, from a position of desperation of the extreme kind, came to a situation that allowed the most exceptional synergy to come into play, starting from the apex political level and extending through the Sri Lankan armed forces right down to the soldier at the front line. The evolution of innovative tactics created to combat specific operational challenges had to be looked at, as also synergy in carrying out a media blitz (ironically by muzzling it most effectively, when critical operations were on) in a manner never before managed in an active combat zone.

Finally, no book can be complete if it does not examine the lessons that need to be learnt as also the way ahead for the country and its people as well as the vast Sri Lankan diaspora, which must rank as one of the largest in the world.

This, then, is the reason why this book has changed its outlook from being a linear one-dimensional biography, to a multi-faceted book in five parts. The coverage of the book is as given in the succeeding paragraphs.

Part 1: This gives an overview of the conflict. It covers the battleground (the beautiful Isle of Serendip), the dramatic death of Velupillai Prabhakaran and his family members and cohorts, the roots of the conflict which actually go back thousands of years, the conflict with the LTTE being only the latest avatar of this historic struggle between the majority Sinhala and the minority Tamils. It also covers the key protagonists in the conflict; the LTTE and the Sri Lankan Armed Forces and the Eelam Wars they fought.

Part 2: This covers the life and times of the key actor in the conflict; Velupillai Prabhakaran. It covers (in his own words), how he became a fighter, his philosophical thoughts, select interviews and speeches, his health status, and, not the least, an assessment on him; successes, failings, mindsets, warts and all.

Part 3: This covers certain key, miscellaneous aspects of the conflict that would help the lay reader see the Eelam War in its myriad complexities. Thus the propaganda and LTTE funding and Tamil diaspora aspects are touched, as also the human rights violation issues raised by the Tamils in various regional and international forums.

Part 4: This part focuses on the Indian intervention (Operation Pawan) in the Sri Lanka conflict at the request of the then Sri Lankan Government. Both sides of the coin (as also the impact on the concerned players) are analysed. This part also discusses the unfortunate assassination of Rajiv Gandhi and the take of both the LTTE as well as Sri Lanka, years after the dastardly deed was executed and the secrecy on the subject lifted to a fair extent by the LTTE on the reasons why the killing was carried out. A startling input taken out publicly by the Sri Lankan Ministry of Defence (MoD) on the assassination is also shared with the lay reader.

Part 5: The last part covers several issues. It covers the diplomacy that was carried out between Sri Lanka and regional players, especially India, China and Pakistan. It also discusses the dynamic and innovative national war fighting strategy, and its execution at the delivery end by thoroughly well-trained, experienced, motivated and intelligence led Sri Lankan officers and men. Part 5 honours the 'Master Strategists' who made the Sri Lankan success possible, in terms of the Sri Lankan President, Mahinda Rajapaksa, the Defence Secretary, Dr. Gotabhaya Rajapaksa (both real brothers) and General Sarath Fonseka, RWP, RSP, VSV, USP, Chief of Defence Staff (CDS), by briefly sketching their career graphs and contribution. No military study can be complete without bringing out the lessons learnt as well as the way ahead and the part ends with coverage of these vital indices of the Eelam conflict. The recent fallout that has resulted in the resignation of General Sarath Forseka as CDS and retirement thereto is also covered, as is the possibility of his contesting for Presidential elections.

PART I

An Overview of the Conflict

CHAPTER 1

Introduction to the Battleground of *'Lost Victory'*: The Beautiful Isle of Serendip – Sri Lanka

John Burns,[1] in a thought-provoking article, writes that the word 'serendipity,' (meaning *"the making of pleasant discoveries by accident"*) was what Sri Lanka was called long back – Serendip –"by European mariners, who found on this lush, gentle island, a sanctuary from the forbidding vastness of the Indian Ocean." It is indeed ironic, he continues, that this fabled island has become synonymous with the stench of death and deprivation. He writes that apart from the thousands who died in combat, unremitting brutality and a 'take-no-prisoners tactic adopted by all sides,' thousands more civilians who had nothing to do with the war have also got decimated.

The Eelam conflict, in its latest rebirth, began in earnest in 1993. It began with the notorious 'Black July' anti-Tamil riots of July 19, 1983. The LTTE retaliation, several months later, was a well-planned, murderous attack on the Sri Lankan Army garrison of Mullaithivu. Burns recounts that "attacking from sea and land, waves of Tiger fighters; many of them young boys and girls barely into their teens, press-ganged into suicide squads known as the Black Tigers, overran the base. By dawn, at least six hundred Tigers were dead, along with thirteen hundred government soldiers, the highest single casualty toll in the history of the conflict. After the Tigers withdrew, a relief column of government forces did not find a single government soldier alive. The wounds of many of the dead, some clutching white flags of surrender, indicated they had been shot dead or blown apart by grenades at close range; hundreds of others appeared to have been herded together, doused with gasoline, and burned to death. What occurred at Mullaithivu, it seemed, was less a battle, at least in its concluding stages, than a massacre."[2] ... Serendip then, is the ironic battleground that the reader is now made familiar with, in the succeeding pages.

Sri Lanka[3] (from the Sanskrit *'Venerable Island'*), is officially called the Democratic Socialist Republic of Sri Lanka. It was known as *Ceylon* before 1972 and as *Taprobane* in ancient times. The current name is derived from the Sanskrit word, 'Lanka', meaning 'island', and has been described in the ancient Indian epics, the Mahabharata and the Ramayana. The word 'Sri' is a Sanskrit title meaning sacred.

It is an island country in South Asia, located about 31 kilometres (19.3 mi) off the southern coast of India. It is home to around twenty million people. Because of its location in the path of major sea routes, Sri Lanka is a strategic naval link between West Asia and South East Asia. It has been a centre of Buddhist religion and culture from ancient times. The Sinhalese community forms the majority of the population; Tamils, who are concentrated in the north and east of the island, form the largest ethnic minority. Other communities include Moors, Burghers, Kaffirs and the Malays.

Famous for the production and export of tea, coffee, coconut and rubber, Sri Lanka boasts a progressive and modern industrial economy and the highest per capita income in South Asia. The natural beauty of Sri Lanka's tropical forests, beaches and landscape, as well as its rich cultural heritage, make it a world famous tourist destination. After over two thousand years of rule by local kingdoms, parts of Sri Lanka were colonized by Portugal and the Netherlands beginning in the 16th century, before control of the entire country was ceded to the British Empire in 1815. During World War II, Sri Lanka served as an important base for Allied forces in the fight against the Japanese Empire. A nationalist political movement arose in the country in the early 20th century with the aim of obtaining political independence, which was eventually granted by the British after peaceful negotiations in 1948.

Geography and Climate

The island of Sri Lanka lies in the Indian Ocean, to the southwest of the Bay of Bengal and to the southeast of the Arabian Sea. It is separated from the Indian subcontinent by the Gulf of Mannar and the Palk Strait. According to Hindu mythology, a land bridge to the Indian mainland, known as Rama's Bridge, was constructed during the time of Rama by the vanara architect Nala. Often referred to as Adam's Bridge, it now amounts to only a chain of limestone shoals remaining above sea level. According to colonial British reports, this is a natural causeway which was formerly complete, but was breached by a violent storm in 1480. The width of the Palk Strait is small enough for the coast of Sri Lanka to be visible from the furthest point near the Indian town of Rameswaram The island consists mostly of flat-to-rolling coastal plains, with mountains rising only in the south-central part. Amongst these is the highest point, Mount Pedro, reaching 2,524 metres (8,280 ft) above sea level. The climate can be described as tropical and warm.

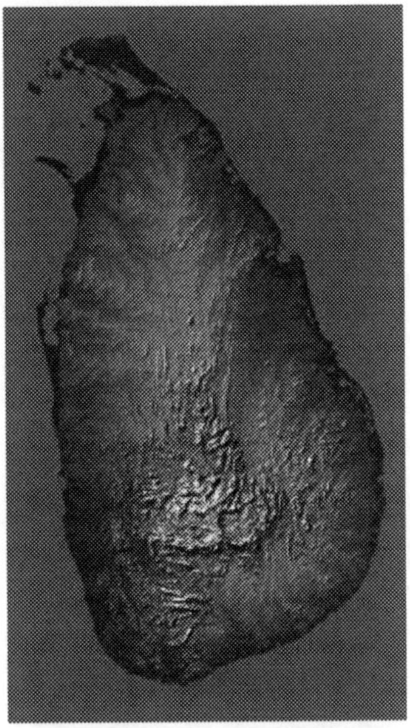

Topographical map of Sri Lanka

Flora and Fauna

Horton Plains National Park represents Sri Lanka's montane rain forests.

The mountains and the southwestern part of the country, known as the 'wet zone', receive ample rainfall at an average of 2,500 mm (98 in). Most of the east, southeast, and northern parts of the country comprise the 'dry zone', which receives between 1,200 mm (47 in) and 1,900 mm (75 in) of rain annually. Forests at one time covered nearly the entire island, but by the late 20th century lands classified as forests and forest reserves covered around 50 percent of the land. The national flower of Sri Lanka is the *Nymphaea stellata* (Sinhalese *Nil Mahanel*), the national tree is the *Ironwood* (Sinhalese *Na*), and the national bird is the Sri Lanka Jungle fowl, which is endemic to the country.

Horton Plains National Park

History: Early Periods

Anthropologists believe that some discovered burial sites and certain decorative artifacts exhibit similarities between the first inhabitants of the island and the early inhabitants of Southern India. Recent bio-anthropological studies have however dismissed these links, and have placed the origin of the people to the northern parts of India. One of the first written references to the island is found in the

Indian epic the Ramayana, which described the emperor Ravana as monarch of the powerful kingdom of *Lanka*, which was created by the divine sculptor Vishwakarma for Kubera, the treasurer of the gods. The main written accounts of the country's history are the Buddhist chronicles of Mahavansa and Dipavamsa.

The earliest-known inhabitants of the island now known as Sri Lanka were probably the ancestors of the Wanniyala-Aetto people, also known as *Veddahs.* Some remarkable archaeological sites including the ruins of Sigiriya, the so-called "Fortress in the Sky", and huge public works date back to an ancient period. Ancient Sri Lanka was also the first in the world to have established a dedicated hospital in Mihintale in the 4th century BCE. Sri Lanka was also the first Asian nation to have a female ruler in Queen Anula (47–42 BC).

Ancient Sri Lanka

Sanghamitta arriving in Sri Lanka with the Holy Bodhi Tree

Since ancient times Sri Lanka was ruled by monarchs, most notably of the Sinha royal dynasty that lasted over 2000 years. The island was also infrequently invaded by South Indian kingdoms and parts of the island were ruled intermittently by the Chola dynasty, the Pandya dynasty, the Chera dynasty and the Pallava dynasty. The island was also invaded by the kingdom of Kalinga (modern Orissa) and those from the Malay Peninsula.

Buddhism arrived from India in the 3rd century BCE, brought by Bhikkhu Mahinda, who is believed to have been the son of the Mauryan emperor Ashoka. Mahinda's mission won over the Sinhalese monarch Devanampiyatissa of Mihintale, who embraced the faith and propagated it throughout the Sinhalese population.

Colonial Era

Sri Lanka had always been an important port and trading post in the ancient world, and was increasingly frequented by merchant ships from the Middle East, Persia, Burma, Thailand, Malaysia, Indonesia and other parts of Southeast Asia. The islands were known to the first European explorers of South Asia and settled by many groups of Arab and Malay merchants. A Portuguese colonial mission arrived on the island in 1505. The Dutch arrived in the 17th century. Although much of the island came under the domain of European powers, the interior, hilly region of the island remained independent, with its capital in Kandy. The British East India Company established control of the island in 1796, declaring it a crown colony in 1802, although the island would not be officially connected with British India. The fall of the kingdom of Kandy in 1815 unified the island under British rule.

20th Century and the World Wars

European colonists established a series of tea, cinnamon, rubber, sugar, coffee and indigo plantations. The British also brought a large number of indentured workers from Tamil Nadu to work in the plantation economy. The city of Colombo was established as the administrative centre, and the British established modern schools, colleges, roads and churches that brought Western-style education and culture to the native people. Increasing grievances over the denial of civil rights, mistreatment and abuse of natives by colonial authorities gave rise to a struggle for independence in the 1930s, when the Youth Leagues opposed the 'Ministers' Memorandum,' which asked the colonial authority to increase the powers of the board of ministers without granting popular representation or civil freedoms. Buddhist scholars and the Teetotalist Movement also played a vital role in this time.

Independence

On February 4, 1948, the country won its independence as the Commonwealth of Ceylon. On July 21, 1960, Sirimavo Bandaranaike took office as Prime Minister, and became the world's first female prime minister and the first female head of government in post-colonial Asia.

Civil War

One of the aspects of the independence movement was that it was very much of a Sinhalese movement. As a result, the majority Sinhalese tried to remodel Sri Lanka as a Sinhalese nation state. The lion in the national flag is derived from the banner of the last Sinhalese kingdom, which, to the majority Sinhalese, is a symbol of their fight against British colonialism. One single strip of orange in the flag represents Tamil and is seen by many Tamils as a symbol of their marginalization (the green strip represents the Muslim community).

In 1956, the Official Language Act (commonly known as **The Sinhala Only Act**) was enacted. The law mandated Sinhala, the language of Sri Lanka's majority Sinhalese community, which is spoken by over 70 percent of Sri Lanka's population, as the sole official language of Sri Lanka. Supporters of the law saw it as an attempt by a community that had just gained independence to distance themselves from their colonial masters. The immediate (and intended) consequence of this act was to force large numbers of Tamils in civil service who could not meet this language requirement to resign. An attempt to make Buddhism as the national religion, in exclusion of Hindu and Islam was also made. Affirmative action in favour of the Sinhalese was also instituted, ostensibly to reverse colonial discrimination against them in favour of the Tamils. Many Tamils, in response to this deliberate marginalization, came to believe that they deserved a separate nation state for themselves. From 1983 to 2009, there was an on-and-off civil war against the government by the Liberation Tigers of Tamil Eelam (LTTE). On May 19, 2009, the President of Sri Lanka officially claimed the end of the insurgency and the defeat of the LTTE following the death of Velupillai Prabhakaran and much of its senior leadership.

Government and Politics

The Constitution of Sri Lanka establishes a democratic, socialist republic in Sri Lanka, which is also a unitary state. The government is a mixture of the presidential system and the parliamentary system. The President of Sri Lanka is the head of state, the commander in chief of the armed forces, as well as head of government, and is popularly elected for a six-year term. In the exercise of his duties, the President is responsible to the Parliament of Sri Lanka, which is a unicameral 225-member legislature. The President's deputy is the Prime Minister, who leads the ruling party in parliament and shares many executive responsibilities, mainly in domestic affairs. Politics in Sri Lanka are controlled by rival coalitions led by the left-wing Sri Lanka Freedom Party, headed by President Rajapaksa, the comparatively right-wing United National Party led by former prime minister Ranil Wickremesinghe and the JVP. There are also many smaller Buddhist, socialist and Tamil nationalist political parties that oppose the separatism of the LTTE but demand regional autonomy and increased civil rights. Sri Lanka receives considerable military assistance from Pakistan and China. Sri Lanka was considered one of the 'world's most politically unstable countries' by the World Bank and Asian Development Bank in 2004. The *Economist* labels Sri Lanka a 'flawed democracy' in its 2006 rankings (ranking 57 and positioned among 54 other flawed ranked ones) and *Foreign Policy* ranks Sri Lanka 25th (Alert Category) in its Failed States Index for 2007. However, Sri Lanka, according to the US State Department in 2005, was classified a 'stable democracy' amidst a ceasefire period of the long running civil war.

Military

The Sri Lanka armed forces, comprising the Sri Lanka Army, the Sri Lanka Navy and the Sri Lanka Air Force, come under the purview of the Ministry of Defence (MoD). The total strength of the three services is around 230,000 active personnel who have voluntarily joined, since military draft has never been imposed in Sri Lanka.

Economy

From 1948 to 1977, socialism strongly influenced the government's economic policies. Colonial plantations were dismantled, industries were nationalized and a welfare state established. While the standard of living and literacy improved significantly, the nation's economy suffered from inefficiency, slow growth and lack of foreign investment. From 1977 the UNP government began incorporating privatization, deregulation and promotion of private enterprise. While the production and export of tea, rubber, coffee, sugar and other agricultural commodities remains important, the nation has moved steadily towards an industrialized economy with the development of food processing, textiles, telecommunications and finance. The GDP grew at an average annual rate of 5.5 percent during the early 1990s, until a drought and a deteriorating security situation lowered growth to 3.8 percent in 1996. The economy rebounded in 1997-2000, with average growth of 5.3 percent. The year of 2001 saw the first recession in the country's history, as a result of power shortages, budgetary problems, the global slowdown, and continuing civil strife. The Colombo Stock Exchange reported the highest growth in the world for 2003, and today Sri Lanka has the highest per capita income in South Asia. According to the Sri Lankan central bank statistics, the economy was estimated to have grown by 7 percent last year, while inflation reached 20 percent.

Administrative Divisions

Sri Lanka is divided into 9 provinces and 25 districts. Each province is administered by a directly-elected provincial council:

Province	Capital	Area (km²)	Population
Central	Kandy	5,674	2,423,966
Eastern	Trincomalee	9,996	1,460,939
North Central	Anuradhapura	10,714	1,104,664
Northern	Jaffna	8,884	1,311,776
North Western	Kurunegala	7,812	2,169,892

(Contd.)

Province	Capital	Area (km²)	Population
Sabaragamuwa	Ratnapura	4,902	1,801,331
Southern	Galle	5,559	2,278,271
Uva	Badulla	8,488	1,177,358
Western	Colombo	3,709	5,361,200

Districts

The provinces of Sri Lanka are divided into 25 districts. Each district is administered under a District Secretariat. The districts are further subdivided into divisional secretariats, and these in turn to *Grama Sevaka* divisions.

Demographics

Population Growth in Sri Lanka

Sri Lanka is the 53rd most populated nation in the world, with an annual population growth rate of 0.79 percent. Sri Lanka has a birth rate of 15.63 births per 1,000 people and a death rate of 6.49 deaths per 1,000 people. The Sinhalese people form the largest ethnic group in the nation, composing approximately 81.9 percent of the total population. The Tamils are concentrated in the North, East, Central and Western provinces of the country. They are distinguished from the native Tamil population that has resided in Sri Lanka since ancient times. According to 2001 census data, Indian Tamils make up 5.1 percent of the Sri Lankan population and, Sri Lankan Tamils 4.3 percent but this figure only accounted for Sri Lankan Tamils in government-controlled areas, not accounting for those in rebel-held territories. The World Fact Book states that Sri Lankan Tamils make up 14 percent of the population. There is a significant population (8.0 percent) of Moors. There are also small ethnic groups such as the Burghers (of mixed European descent) and Malays from Southeast Asia.

Language

Sinhalese and Tamil are the two official languages of Sri Lanka. English is spoken by approximately 10 percent of the population, and is widely used for education, scientific and commercial purposes.

Religions

Sri Lanka has a multi ethnic and multi religious population. Buddhism constitutes the religious faith of about 70 percent of the population of the island, most of whom follow the Theravada school of Buddhism. According to traditional Sri Lankan chronicles, Buddhism was introduced into Sri Lanka in the 2nd century

BCE by Venerable Mahindra, the son of Emperor Ashoka, during the reign of Sri Lanka's King Devanampiyatissa. Sri Lanka has the longest continuous history of Buddhism having existed since the 2nd century BCE.

Sri Lanka Religiosity

Religion	Percentage
Buddhism	70
Hinduism	15
Christianity	8
Islam	7

Education

With a literacy rate of 92 percent, and 83 percent of the total population having had secondary education, Sri Lanka has one of the most literate populations amongst developing nations.

Media

The national radio station, Radio Ceylon, is the oldest-running radio station in Asia. It was established in 1923 by Edward Harper just three years after broadcasting was launched in Europe. Broadcast television was introduced in the country in 1979 when the Independent Television Network was launched. Initially, all television stations were state controlled, but private television networks began broadcasts in 1992. Global television networks from India, Southeast Asia, Europe and the United States are also widely popular, and cable and satellite television is gaining in popularity with Sri Lanka's middle-class. Newspapers are very well established, with popular publications being the English language *Daily Mirror, The Sunday Observer* and *The Sunday Times.*

Human Rights

The Human Rights situation in Sri Lanka has come under severe criticism by human rights groups such as Amnesty International and Human Rights Watch, as well as the United States Department of State and the European Union. They have expressed concern about the state of human rights in Sri Lanka. Both the separatist Liberation Tigers of Tamil Eelam (LTTE) and the government of Sri Lanka have been accused of violating human rights.

Sri Lanka is one of the most important, strategically located countries in the southern hemisphere. Its proximity to India and multifaceted connectivity to it through the centuries, as well as its dominant position to the critical shipping lanes emerging from West Asia make this island and its well being central to India's strategic thinking.

Endnotes

1. Burns, John. 'Giving No Quarter'. <http://www.crimesofwar.org/thebook/quarter-giving-no.html>
2. Ibid.
3. Extracted from 'Democratic Socialist Republic of Sri Lanka.' <http://en.wikipedia.org/wiki/Democratic_Socialist_Republic_of_Sri_Lanka>

References

1. 'Sri Lanka'. *undp.org*. United Nations Development Programme. 2008. http://hdrstats.undp.org/en/2008/countries/country_fact_sheets/cty_fs_LKA.html.
2. Abeydeera, Ananda. 'In Search of Taprobane: the Western discovery and mapping of Ceylon'. http://www.rootsweb.com/~lkawgw/slm-taprobane.htm.
3. Rajasingham, K.T. 'Sri Lanka: The untold story'. *Asia Times*. http://www.atimes.com/ind-pak/CH11Df02.html.
4. Zubair, Lareef. 'Etymologies of Lanka, Serendib, Taprobane and Ceylon'. http://www.glue.umd.edu/~pkd/sl/facts/name_origin.html.
5. de Silva, Colin (February 14, 1982). 'Sri Lanka, The "Resplendent Isle".' *New York Times*. http://query.nytimes.com/gst/fullpage.html?sec=travel&res=9A01EED61E38F937A25751C0A964948260.
6. Bedi, Rahul (2007-06-02). 'Sri Lanka turns to Pakistan, China for military needs'. *IANS* (Urdustan.com Network). http://www.indianmuslims.info/news/2007/jun/02/sri_lanka_turns_pakistan_china_military_needs.html.
7. http://www.economist.com/media/pdf/DEMOCRACY_TABLE _2007_v3.pdf
8. Lawlessness Grows in Strife-Torn Sri Lanka – washingtonpost.com at www.washingtonpost.com
9. Hoole, Rajan (2001). *Sri Lanka: The Arrogance of Power*. University Teachers for Human Rights (Jaffna). ISBN 978-9559447047.
10. 'The World Factbook: Sri Lanka'. *CIA World Factbook*. https://www.cia.gov/library/publications/the-world-factbook/geos/ce.html.

Chapter 2

The Death of Prabhakaran

This chapter shares with the reader in riveting detail, how the over 30 year old scourge of terrorism on an island revered for its serendipity, got a historic death blow in the early hours of May 18, 2009. The Sri Lankan Army finally managed to kill the elusive LTTE supremo, Velupillai Prabhakaran, his immediate family, body guards and key associates. They were killed in a dramatic shoot out, set out in a miniscule, 200 x 200 metre battle area, hemmed in from all sides by alert Sri Lankan troops. The site of death was by the banks of the Nandhi Kadal lagoon, near Mullaithivu town, in North East Sri Lanka.

The encounter occurred on the basis of 'hard' intelligence available to the Sri Lankan troops in contact, that Prabhakaran was finally in their net. As the desperate Prabhakaran, his family and close associates attempted an impossible break out from the tight army cordon, with the hope of melting away, out of reach, to the nearby, almost impenetrable Wanni forest area, they were shot dead. The Tamil dream of Eelam had met an inglorious end that even the most optimistic Sri Lankan across religious belief had never imagined.

The media communiqué put out by the Sri Lankan MoD[1] to announce his death, makes a departure from the stilted, unemotional, matter-of-fact language traditionally associated with military handouts. As a soldier, one understands the adrenalin driven sentiment and enormous relief of the Sri Lankan Armed Forces in issuing this extraordinary statement. Excerpts are reproduced below without change of language or syntax:

Sri Lanka MoD Communiqué

> "Commander of the army, General Sarath Fonseka who has been the nation's tower of strength and hope for eradication of LTTE terrorism right throughout

with the support of Navy, Air Force, Police and Civil Security Department a few minutes ago at about 12:15 noon on 19th May 2009 declared that the dead body of the LTTE leader Velupillai Prabhakaran has been identified and recovered.

A few hours ago on 19th May 2009,[2] our ground troops confirmed that they have recovered the dead body of the world's most ruthless terrorist leader. I make this disclosure with responsibility and pleasure as millions of Sri Lankans as well as the Army would be the most delighted at this news," General FONSEKA said.

The world's most-feared and ruthless terrorist leader, VELUPILLAI PRABHAKARAN alias THAMBI alias KIRUBAKARAN alias THURAI alias HARRY alias KARIKALAN alias ALIPHA alias JUZO alias PIRABHAHARAN, who massacred at least 30,000-40,000 human beings in the past three decades is dead and gone.

The megalomaniac PRABHAKARAN (54) sustained his bloodbaths after founding his LTTE organization on 5th May 1976, infusing eternal agony and fear-psychosis to the masses. His vicious cycle of violence commenced on 27th July 1975 after butchering Jaffna Mayor, Alfred Duraiappah in a shoot-out. As the brainchild behind all those atrocities, he engineered the assassination of a Sri Lankan President, an Indian Prime Minister, a host of Ministers, Buddhist monks, Hindu, Catholic and Muslim priests, Chiefs of the Armed Forces and the Police, Thousands of innocent villagers and almost anybody who did not tread his line. Bomb explosions, massacres, bloodbaths and heinous crimes against humanity were his bread and butter and part of the daily agenda.

He was responsible for the spate of illegal international and local rackets such as smuggling of weapons and men, money laundering, extortions, bank robberies, ransom taking, tax collections, thefts of vehicles and almost all criminal activities. PRABHAKARAN while nursing and caring for his three children, CHARLES ANTHONY and DUWARAHA and his wife MADIVADANI conscripted thousands of Tamil minors for weapon training and terrorist activities, despite protests from parents and adults. He even defied international pressure while leading a luxurious life away from others and maintained more than four security layers and protective rings. As a founder member of the LTTE, he stretched his dictatorship over his own comrades and went to the extent of decimating all those who he felt were a threat to him. MAHATTAYA was one of Prabhakaran's well-known victims.

Gaping wounds on Prabhakaran's head

He targeted not only the Sinhalese but also respected Tamil intellectuals, politicians, democrats, artists, civilians and all anti-LTTE men and women including former Foreign Minister LAKSHMAN KADIRAGAMAR, Dr. NEELAN THIRUCHELVAM, SAM THAMBIMUTTU and a host of others. Incumbent Minister DOUGLAS DEVANANDA and moderate TULF leader, V. ANANDA SANGAREE escaped LTTE death squads several times.

In addition, many more national leaders were his prey right throughout. The list included former Defence Minister RANJAN WIJERATHNA, Ministers GAMINI DISSANAYAKE, LALITH ATHULATHMUDALI, WEERASINGHA MALLIMARACHCHI, G.M. PREMARATHNA, C.V. GUNARATHNA, JEYERAJ FERNANDO PULLE, D.M. DASSANAYAKE and a large number of local politicians..."

DBS Jeyaraj, a Prabhakaran watcher of long standing, who has written at length on the life and times of Prabhakaran, compiled a well researched, informative and emotive article on Prabhakaran's last days in Transcurrents.[3] This has been extensively quoted in the succeeding paragraphs, to share the tense drama and the last minute, frantic bids by the Tigers to somehow undo their mistakes without paying the ultimate price. He writes that ... "the ephemeral nature of power was illustrated vividly by the death of Prabhakaran[4] who controlled what was perhaps the most powerful guerilla organization in the world and was raised to divine status as 'Sooriyathevan' (Sun God) by his sycophantic followers. The circumstances of his death were, just as in life, mired in controversy. His demise was anticipated before it happened. The discovery of his corpse was revealed in sections of the media even before it was found."

Gross Errors of Judgment by Prabhakaran[5]

Jeyaraj finds the LTTE leader guilty of gross errors in judgment, at a time when he had his back to the wall and attractive options to continue the struggle for Eelam were running out – with disconcerting speed. In hindsight, his biggest errors were actually two sides of the proverbial coin. This misjudgment placed the Sri Lankan forces in a win-win situation and himself and his Eelam war in a lose-all situation – he savagely underestimated his opponent, both militarily as well as politically, making small of the Government's determination and capability to bring him to book. At the same time, he equally wrongly overestimated his own capability to get out of trouble yet again, using his Tamil diaspora contacts and 'support' of countries that had, in his opinion, lent tacit and financial support to his cause over his long years of struggle.

Obviously, a part of his miscalculations was the expectation of support from some Tamil Nadu politicians who supported the LTTE cause. The arrogance of presuming that the Sri Lankan Armed Forces would tread Tiger country with great circumspection and let his cadres live to fight another day was also flawed. Jeyaraj accurately points out that the LTTE game plan focused on carving out "an area of about 350-450 sq km in Mullaithivu District, with access to the coast and then defending it strenuously. The rapid progress of the Army during this phase took the LTTE by surprise. Within a relatively quick period, the various military divisions and task forces had made sweeping strides into Tiger territory. As a result, the LTTE and hundreds of thousands of civilians were boxed into a small space that kept on shrinking as the army began advancing."...[6]

Pathmanathan (KP), Prabhakaran's vocal and well connected, charismatic man-about-town, spokesman, media handler and diaspora controller and his informally nominated successor tapped into his vast reservoir of diaspora and international contacts. Jeyaraj writes that diplomats of at least four Western nations, UN functionaries in Geneva and New York, a foreign cabinet minister, a few prominent Western journalists were all in touch with KP, trying to facilitate the LTTE bailout.[7]

LTTE's Last Attempt for a Bailout

A desperate, plan was conceived by Prabhakaran and his spin masters, with KP as the front man. The negotiation attempt was to be conducted by the LTTE political commissar Nadesan and peace secretariat director, Pulidevan. The plan envisaged the LTTE surrendering to a third party, namely the UN, but with firm guarantees from two powerful nations in the Western hemisphere. The possibility of troops from those countries landing in Mullaithivu to supervise the 'surrender' was also not ruled out. A three-tiered formula regarding the future of LTTE leaders and cadres was also mooted. The top leaders not exceeding fifty along with families were to be given safe passage outside Sri Lanka to a secret destination. The middle-level functionaries were to face trial in Sri Lanka and be given comparatively light sentences. They were to be rehabilitated after being given some vocational training. The low-level cadres particularly the new conscripts were to be given a general amnesty. They would be on parole for a period of time and be subject to monitoring.[8]

This wild hope had to die a still-born death. On the cusp of victory and with the benefit of having synergized their desired political and military end states into one seamless end state (something few democratic nations in the world have ever achieved), Mahinda Rajapaksa, Gottabhaya Rajapaksa (the President and Defence Secretary, respectively) and General Fonseka, the Army Chief, spoke with one firm voice. The expected help from Tamil Nadu in specific and the open appeal to India in general also did not materialize due to some fast paced, adroit diplomacy, on both sides of the Palk Strait, much of it behind the scenes and unannounced as well as unacknowledged till date. The die was thus cast. '*The Final Countdown*' as the MoD has put down in its well crafted web site, had begun. It was a countdown to the finish.

Broad Army Plan to Trap the LTTE

A three-pronged drive,[9] as per Jeyaraj, commenced with 58 Division led by Brig. Shavendra Silva proceeding north to south, 59 Division moving from south to north and 53 Division commanded by Maj. Gen. Kamal Gunaratne proceeding from west to east. After intense fighting resulting in thousands of civilians being killed and injured, 55 and 58 Divisions linked up along the Indian Ocean coast. 53 Division hugged the lagoon banks and moved inwards. The Tigers were well and truly trapped.

LTTE Breakout Plan[10]

When told of the situation, Prabhakaran and his commanders went into a huddle. A bold decision was reached to launch a three-pronged breakout.[11]

One group of Tigers[12] including Prabhakaran was to break out from their trapped positions and cross the lagoon and Paranthan-Mullaithivu Road or A-35 highway, with the Wanni jungles as their immediate destination. A second group of Tigers[13] would take a calculated risk and establish contact with the Sri Lankan Army to negotiate terms of surrender. The third group[14] was to engage in fierce rear guard action, as a diversionary tactic. This group, tasked to fight 'last man, last round', was led by none other than Charles Anthony, the eldest son of Prabhakaran. He was to be assisted by Special LTTE Commander (East), Ramesh. It is surmised that this was done because the criticism that Prabhakaran had sacrificed other LTTE cadre's children, while lavishing care on his own, had finally got to him, and this decision was meant to act as a final rallying call from a leader who was anxious to use all means available to him to get out of this dangerous situation.

As part of their plan, the LTTE also released seven security personnel[15] in their custody. The seven servicemen turned themselves in to 59 Division and informed them of the Tiger offer to surrender. They were advised to return and bring the tiger's political leaders. So Nadesan, Pulidevan and Vijitha, the Sinhala wife of Nadesan, came out with the released prisoners, carrying white flags. The idea was to negotiate terms of surrender with the army. Subsequently all three were found dead in mysterious circumstances. The LTTE has charged that they were shot dead in cold blood. A Tamil website[16] alleges that 35 Tigers were following Nadesan a little behind to surrender. They too were shot dead. Foreign Secretary, Palitha Kohona, has denied the allegations, stating that some Tigers who disapproved of surrendering to the Army had fired and killed Nadesan and Pulidevan.

The Phobia of 'Unlucky Eight': the LTTE's Last Attack

While these moves were on, the LTTE launched a massive attack on the SLA shortly after midnight on Sunday May 17, 2009.[17] There was a time when the LTTE would not engage in major operations on the 8th, 17th or 26th, because no. 8 was considered unlucky. These, however, were desperate times...The attack was in three directions but mainly directed towards the Nandhi Kadal lagoon area held by 53 Division. After fierce fighting led by Bhanu, the three Tiger contingents broke through. One was led by Jeyam, another by Pottu Amman and the third by Soosai. The three contingents together numbered about 250-300. Almost all military leaders were part of the three groups trying to break out while the bulk of the political wing of the Tigers stayed behind to surrender.

Jeyaraj writes that "a very large number of Black Tigers[18] (suicide squads) died in the assault as explosive-strapped boys and girls jumped on Army positions and blew themselves up. This created the 'gaps' for other Tigers to penetrate the military cordon. Though (the) Tigers breached the 53 Division defences, the soldiers began an intensive artillery barrage in which many died. Also the Army had set up layers of defence with more personnel at the back. The LTTE cadres, who broke through, were, to some extent, sandwiched and cut down. With the assault resulting in failure and many Tigers being encircled, several LTTE cadres began consuming cyanide. Similarly the Tiger 'defenders' led by Charles Anthony were also routed and several survivors swallowed cyanide to avoid capture. Charles Anthony was found dead with bullet injuries.

The group led by Soosai was initially successful in breaking out. Prabhakaran, wife Madhivadhany Erambu, daughter Duvaaraga (23) and younger son Balachandran (11) were also part of the contingent led by Soosai, who remained faithful to his leader until the last. Duvaaraga, an exceptionally beautiful girl and accomplished dancer had, for a short time, been a student abroad. She had returned after a while to be with her family and people. Duvaaraga had been a member of the Maalathi women's brigade and had fought in recent battles. The Prabhakaran family of four and forty-seven others managed to penetrate (the) Nandhi Kadal defence ring and move north to the Putumattalan area. A message sent on behalf of Prabhakaran to the remaining cadres in Mullivaaikkal stated 'udaithukondu poyitram' (we've broken through and gone).

Jeyaraj notes that "though Prabhakaran had at one time hundreds of cadres as bodyguards, only 18[19] elite fighters accompanied him on the flight from Mullivaaikkaal. It has also been said that one bodyguard had a can of gasoline with him to burn the Tiger leader's body if ever he was killed or committed suicide.[20] This was to prevent the enemy (from) seizing his body... all these expectations were belied on that fateful day. Prabhakaran's body was discovered before dawn on Tuesday, May 19, 2009, lying on the Nandhi Kadal bank. Soldiers of the 4th Vijayabâhu Infantry Regiment led by Lt.Col Rohitha Aluvihare claimed to have found it.

Prabhakaran had been shot at point blank range.[21] Four of his bodyguards were lying dead in the vicinity. Later on it was claimed that the bodies of Madhivadhany, Duvaaraga and Balachandran were found in a bushy patch about 600 metres way from where Prabhakaran's body was found. Charles Anthony's body had been found elsewhere earlier. Both these deaths were independently confirmed by KP, in an interview with the *Asian Tribune*.[22] The entire family had been wiped out. More

[Charles Anthony, Madhivadhany, Duvaaraga and Prabhakaran–undated file pic]

than 350 bodies were found. The LTTE was virtually demolished. The Army announced that the bodies of people like Soosai,[23] Bhanu, Lawrence, Pappa, Laxmanan, etc., were found. There is (however) some doubt as to whether the body of Pottu Amman or those of his family were discovered.

Duvaaraga, the daughter of Prabhakaran

The Aftermath of the Killing

Shamindra Ferdinando,[24] in his article for the Sri Lankan publication, *Island*, writes in graphic detail what happened next. "The Sri Lanka Army on Wednesday (May 20) afternoon marked the end of Eelam War with an awesome display of firepower. The army top brass involved in the Vanni campaign gathered on the Mullaithivu coast close to the Jordanian ship *Farah III* which ran aground in December 2006 to declare the war over. Two mobile multi barrel rocket launchers fired 40 rounds each over *Farah III's* wreckage as thousands of troops cheered. The MBTs (Main Battle Tanks) too, joined the firing. It marked the end of the bloodiest phase of the conflict which decimated almost the entire LTTE leadership leaving several thousand LTTE cadres in government custody."... He adds, further, that ... "Prabhakaran's body was reduced to ashes on the banks of the Nandhi Kadal lagoon. Defence Secretary Gottabhaya Rajapaksa warned that anyone trying to follow Prabhakaran would end up like the LTTE leader – shot dead. Appearing on ITN on Wednesday night, a smiling Rajapaksa said that Prabhakaran had to hide in the Nandhi Kadal lagoon area in an *amude*. He said that Prabhakaran's fate would be a clear message to anyone planning to take up arms against the State."...he adds that "Premier Ratnasiri Wickramanayake in his brief address at Friday's rally in Colombo requested the President to appoint a Special Commission to identify the sources of LTTE's arsenal. It is no secret that the bulk of arms, ammunition and equipment in their arsenal are of Chinese origin. Some of them hadn't been even available to the Sri Lankan armed forces as in the case of four barreled anti-aircraft guns."

The revelation of casualties on the Sri Lankan side in the last few years as reported by Ferdinando comes as something of a shocker. The Defence Secretary is quoted as having said that 6,260 officers and men of the armed forces were killed in action since the outbreak of the last tranche of hostilities at Mavil Aru in June 2006. A further 29,551 officers and men had been wounded in action.

Of them, 2,556 had been permanently disabled. With the LTTE accepting having lost nearly 25,000 cadres in their struggle, it is fair to accept the total losses to the nation of around 70 thousand to 1 lakh people, in the over 30 years that the conflict lasted – a huge loss, by any standards.

Different Takes on the Death of Prabhakaran

Jeyaraj writes that there was speculation that the Army had killed Prabhakaran and other top Tigers by Saturday May 16th itself. It was said that news of the killing was being withheld for President Rajapaksa to return from Jordan and make the announcement himself.[25] But Rajapaksa who returned on Sunday (May 17th) addressed the nation on Tuesday (May 19th) without announcing the death of Prabhakaran.

The fact remains that many aspects of Prabhakaran's death are controversial and can be attributable to deliberate misinformation on the part of the key players; the Sri Lankan as well as the LTTE propaganda machineries. Unsubstantiated speculation by a hyperactive and perhaps not so well informed media, as well as the natural fallouts of what the military terms as 'fog of war' are obviously contributory factors. Not the least, the Sri Lankans obviously intended to show Prabhakaran's defeat and death in a manner that depicted that finally, he had feet of clay and was rather less than the invincible 'Sun God' he was projected to be. The LTTE kept maintaining that he was alive and well, along with most of his colleagues, till reality caught up with them. Karuna, once an insider, also burst their bubble.

Sun Tzu downwards, any war veteran will tell you that truth is the first and most crippling casualty in war. No one, but no one speaks the truth, for a host of reasons. The Eelam war was no different. Thus, the initial, spaghetti Western type of escapade attributed to Prabhakaran and associates making a break for it, in an ambulance; getting shot and incinerated in the ambulance which was destroyed with rocket launchers fired by the SLA may be seen as a clumsy, initial PR effort that was aired to project Prabhakaran deserting his command to save himself; hardly a heroic act for an iconic, legendary leader, but necessary to effectively destroy his credentials. The nature of injuries on the person of the immediate family (Prabhakaran, his son, his wife and daughter) seem to indicate close range gunshot wounds, all on the head (a cynical observer might say that this was a non-negotiable compulsion, because it ensured positive identification post death; a requirement that would otherwise have got compromised, had the facial features been mutilated by burns (as in the ambulance) or by hits on the recognizable part of the visage). Similarly, no efforts were spared in informing the world that the man at whose behest hundreds of LTTE cadres, especially the Black (suicide) Tigers had bitten the bitter pill (cyanide ampoules), himself did not carry one on his person. The deduction was there for all to draw: the leader did not live by the codes he imposed so ruthlessly on his cadres; another vital step to cut Prabhakaran down to size.

War is not the domain for detached observers sitting far away from its harsh realities to sit in judgment on its rationale, logic or fall outs. War has its own dynamics; a life of its own that comes into being the moment the first bullet is fired. Military realists since ancient times, and certainly the great writers on war have candidly stated that no military plan survives the first bullet...By implication, many things happened in those last days, in fact, the last hours of this extraordinary struggle, in the confined area of Nandhi Kadal that will remain cloaked in mystery because those who could speak of the reality are either dead or bound by a covenant to keep their silence. That should not be too taxing, when tested against the reality that the period 15-18 May, 2009, however mired in controversy, was precedent setting not just for Sri Lanka, but also the world at large, especially those nations actively involved in fighting terror, starting with the USA, and obviously inclusive of India and Pakistan.

Finally, the specific date, location and manner of death of Prabhakaran seems insignificant, when viewed against the stark, incontestable fact that the world's second most wanted terror chief (after Osama bin Laden) is now confined to history. The Sri Lankans did it in a manner that will invite intense professional scrutiny of their strategy, establishment of the much needed politico-military synergy to execute it and how they now exploit the spoils of this successful war for national peace, prosperity and a return to the Serendip days of yore.

For the reader's interest, a sampling of theories/controversies surrounding the deaths of Prabhakaran, his family and cohorts, is indicated in the succeeding paragraphs.

- Dushy Ranetunge, writing from London in an article for *Transcurrents*[26] questions several assertions made by the Government. He says that the Sri Lankan State's version of the last moments of Prabhakaran is, in fact, "a clumsy and a crude execution by the Sri Lankan state... If as per the Sri Lankan state's version, Prabhakaran was fleeing in an ambulance which came under fire by troops, one would expect bullets to have ricocheted around inside the Ambulance causing far more injuries rather than one which looks like a clean single shot to the back of the head. The bodies of Madhivadhany Erambu identified as Prabhakaran's wife and a girl

Duvaaraga and a young boy, Balachandran, identified as Prabhakaran's children were reportedly found in the vicinity of the body of LTTE leader Velupillai Prabhakaran, according to a report by the army. They all had gunshot wounds on the head. It seems this ambulance was not only a crowded one, all its passengers ended up having gunshot wounds on the head[27] ..."

- He adds that, "we have been told that the UAV was used to locate the fleeing ambulance, but this footage has not been released. But above the Sri Lankan UAV's, British, American, Russian and Indian satellites are watching the crime scene with far superior technology. As I write, they are also watching the bulldozers at work at present at the crime scene, attempting to wipe it all clean and digging mass graves to bury it all, like in Srebrenica, another massacre site. These tapes were later produced during the Yugoslav war crimes trials."...
- The writer also wonders if Prabhakaran and his entire family surrendered to the Army and were (then) executed by them. He suggests that there is another possibility. "It is possible," he writes, "that Prabhakaran ordered his family and himself to be shot by his bodyguard,[28] realising the futility of the situation. The Army having recovered the bodies may have not wanted to reward Prabhakaran with any heroism in death and may have come up with the Ambulance story.
- There is another incident, which the author says has intrigued him. When President Mahinda Rajapaksa landed at Colombo from Jordan, on September 17, 2009, on alighting from the aircraft, he kissed the tarmac. The writer wonders if this "irrational and highly emotional behaviour on the part of Rajapaksa may indicate that he was aware ... that Prabhakaran was in the custody of the Sri Lankan forces,[29] either dead or alive?
- He further writes that "although Prabhakaran advocated the cult of the cyanide capsule to others, he himself would never use it at the end, and died from a 'Sinhala-Buddhist' bullet[30] on the back of the head. The ultimate humiliation to the Chola mindset, which boasted that they will not even leave the ashes of Prabhakaran to the Sinhala army. In Colombo the Sinhala Buddhist tribalists and teamsters waved their flags and celebrated..."
- There is no dearth of media reports[31] that speculated from May 16 onwards that Prabhakaran was already dead, missing in action, had perhaps already fled from the battle area or had committed suicide.

Endnotes

1. "World's Most Ruthless Terrorist Leader Prabhakaran Confirmed Dead." Communiqué put out by MoD on May 19, 2009. <http://www.army.lk/opdetail.php?id=100>
2. "Prabhakaran Was With 18 Men When He Was Killed: Karuna." Narayan Swamy, M.R. May 20, 2009.<http://www.indiaenews.com/srilanka/20090520/199022.htm> According to the above report, the fighting with Prabhakaran and his men erupted at 4 a.m. on Monday, May 18, 2009, and was over within 90 minutes, leaving the man who had terrorized the country for over a quarter century dead near a lagoon in Mullaithivu district.
3. Jeyaraj, DBS. "*The Last Days Of Thiruvenkadam Veluppillai Prabhakaran.*" May 22, 2009. <http://transcurrents.com/tc/2008/11/post_92.html>
4. "Prabhakaran's Body Was Identified By Birth Marks, Scars: Report." <http://www.indianexpress.com/news/Prabhakaran-s-body-was-identified-by-birth-marks – scars – Report/466774/>

   As per the above report, the slain LTTE supremo Velupillai Prabhakaran's body was identified by his two former aides with the help of certain scars and birth marks. Federal Minister Vinayagamoorthi Muralitharan, alias Colonel Karuna Amman, at one a time close confidante of Prabhakaran, and Daya Master, the former LTTE media spokesman who had surrendered recently, identified Prabhakaran's body after he was killed on May 18. "They identified and confirmed that the body recovered was that of Prabhakaran. Certain scars and birth marks had helped them in identification", the Sri Lankan newspaper; 'Bottomline' was quoted as saying. The newspaper further said that on the evening of May 18, a commando handed over to his CO, a pistol and a hip holster. The pistol carried the inscription T.V.P. 001, raising suspicions that it belonged to Prabhakaran. T.V.P. 001 means Thamil Vidudalai Puligal (Tamil Liberation Tigers) and Military Intelligence confirmed that it was indeed Prabhakaran's pistol.
5. "Prabhakaran Was With 18 Men When He Was Killed: Karuna." Narayan Swamy, M.R. May 20, 2009.

   http://www.indiaenews.com/srilanka/20090520/199022.htm

   The above report quotes Vinayagamurthy Muralitharan alias 'Karuna' whose 2004 revolt played a vital role in the weakening of the Liberation Tigers of Tamil Eelam (LTTE)' as saying that the Tigers would never rise again. **Karuna blamed Prabhakaran for his death saying if he had been a better strategist he should have dispersed his forces and senior leaders once the Sri Lankan military went on the offensive from late last year. Indeed if he had been a good leader he would not have insisted on an independent state for so long. He should have known it would never happen. If only he had transformed his military victories into political victories the Tamils would be holding their heads high today.** That did not happen. Karuna said the Tamil community was at a crossroads after the deaths of around 90,000 people since 1983 in the Tamil Eelam struggle. This included some 24,000 LTTE guerrillas. What did the Tamils gain after all this bloodshed, he was asked. Karuna replied: 'Nothing.'
6. Jeyaraj, DBS. "*The Last Days Of Thiruvenkadam Veluppillai Prabhakaran.*" May 22, 2009. <http://transcurrents.com/tc/2008/11/post_92.html>
7. Ibid.
8. Ibid.
9. Ibid.

10. Prabhakaran's Final Hours. May 19, 2009. <http://www.lankanewspapers. com/news/2009/5/43792.html>
    The above report states that only three LTTE leaders, other than Prabhakaran and his wife knew of his whereabouts. Other than his son Charles Anthony, the only other LTTE leaders who knew where he was were Poddu Amman, the Intelligence Chief and the head of the LTTE's Medical Unit, Reagan. The latter was taken in and detained for days until Military Intelligence got hold of him. Until then Reagan had pretended he did not know Prabhakaran's whereabouts. Thanks to Reagan's information, Sri Lankan MI officers had clearly identified the layout of Prabhakaran's lair by 16th evening/17th dawn.
11. "Prabha`s Last Night??" May 16, 2009.
    http://www.lankanewspapers.com/news/2009/5/43657_space.html
    The report suggests that, "by the time this report is being compiled, the Liberation Tigers of Tamil Eelam are preparing for its last attack...We have received HIGHLY credible reports that the SLA has located the whereabouts of Prabhakaran. This vital piece of information was received from an LTTE `Doctor` named Susiran who visited Prabhakaran on the 10th to treat Sithamparathasan, the head of the Ratha Regiment and LTTE Leader V. Prabhakaran's chief close protection officer who was injured in the Ananthapuram box-in by the Special Forces and Commandos..." Notice the contradiction in fine print between Notes 10&11.
12. Jeyaraj, DBS. "*The Last Days of Thiruvenkadam Veluppillai Prabhakaran.*" May 22, 2009. <http://transcurrents.com/tc/2008/11/post_92.html>
13. Ibid.
14. Ibid.
15. Ibid.
16. Ibid.
17. Ibid.
18. Ibid.
19. "Prabhakaran Was With 18 Men When He Was Killed: Karuna." Narayan Swamy, M.R. May 20, 2009.http://www.indiaenews.com/srilanka/20090520/199022.htm The above report confirms the assertion by DBS Jeyaraj that the Tamil Tigers chief Velupillai Prabhakaran was with 18 of his most loyal bodyguards when he was trapped and killed by the Sri Lankan military.'
20. Jeyaraj, DBS. "*The Last Days of Thiruvenkadam Veluppillai Prabhakaran.*" May 22, 2009. <http://transcurrents.com/tc/2008/11/post_92.html>
21. Ibid.
22. Murari, S. "Prabhakaran's Daughter Also Killed – Says KP." June 28, 2009. <http://asiantribune.com/06/28/prabhakarans-daughter-also-killed-says-kp/>
23. Ibid.
24. "How the War was Won." Ferdinando, Shemindra. May 24, 2009. <http://www.island.lk/2009/05/24/defence1.html>
25. Jeyaraj, DBS. "*The Last Days of Thiruvenkadam Veluppillai Prabhakaran.*" May 22, 2009. <http://transcurrents.com/tc/2008/11/post_92.html>
26. Ranetunge, Dushy. "Was Prabhakaran and His Entire Family Executed By the Army?" May 21st 2009 <http://transcurrents.com/tc/2009/05/was_prabakaran_and_his_entire.html>
27. Ibid.
28. Ibid.
29. Ibid.

30. Ibid.
31. "Breaking News: Prabhakaran Missing." Sunday, May 17, 2009 <http://www.lankanewspapers.com/news/2009/5/43743_space.html

 The above report indicates that "Prabhakaran and his clan are nowhere to be found. Clearing operations (have) started in an area 200m × 200m by the Special Forces. If Prabhakaran is hiding in this last uncleared patch or his remains are in the area, (and) they would be found..."

CHAPTER 3

The Roots of Conflict

Introduction

The roots of the Sinhala-Tamil conflict in Sri Lanka go back to antiquity, and cannot be documented with authority, at least not till the 10th century AD. In the author's perception, however, even when records are available, there is hardly a guarantee that they accurately reflect what actually happened. History is, finally, an account of events written from a certain perspective, and therefore is rarely objective. The nature and extent of subjectivity in recording or commenting on it is often a function of complex factors; amongst them, who is writing it, for whom, with what purpose and intent. Dispassionate analysis of past events is also a function of 'distance' from events that are being recorded in terms of any vested interests in projecting or suppressing the events that have occurred and the interpretation of the circumstances and culture within which these occurred.

This caution is considered before the reader is familiarized with the author's perception of the roots of conflict that is the backdrop to this Sinhala-Tamil fallout. It is intended to briefly trace the history of Sri Lanka from prehistoric times. This will include coverage of the Tamil and Sinhala people in Sri Lanka and their clashes since the early days. The contribution of the European settlers, essentially the Portuguese, the Dutch and, most importantly, the British, cannot be undermined. The issues of Sinhalese Buddhist and Tamil nationalism will also be covered. The chapter will also cover the important aspects (in terms of human loss/degradation of normal life), the riots and situations which are the milestones of the current conflict that can be traced back to 1915.

Prehistoric[1] Times

Sri Lankan Tamils, or Ceylon Tamils, are an ethnic group native to Sri Lanka, who predominantly speak Tamil. According to anthropological evidence, Sri Lankan Tamils have lived on the island since the second century BCE. Most modern Sri Lankan Tamils descend from the Jaffna Kingdom, a former kingdom in the north of the island and Vannimai chieftaincies from the east. They constitute a majority in the Northern Province, live in significant numbers in the Eastern Province, and are in the minority throughout the rest of the country.

Sri Lankan Tamils are culturally and linguistically distinct from the other two Tamil-speaking minorities in Sri Lanka, the Indian Tamils and the Moors. Genetic studies indicate that they are most closely related to the Sinhalese than any other Asian group, with the Tamil and Sinhalese population sharing a common gene pool of 55 percent. The Sri Lankan Tamils are mostly Hindus with a significant Christian population. Sri Lankan Tamil literature on topics including religion and the sciences flourished during the medieval period in the court of the Jaffna Kingdom. Sri Lankan Tamil dialects are noted for their archaism and retention of words not in everyday use in Tamil Nadu state in India.

There is, however, little scholarly consensus[2] over the presence of the Tamil people in Sri Lanka, also known as Eelam, in early Tamil literature, prior to the medieval Chola period (circa 10th century AD). One theory states that there was not an organized Tamil presence in Sri Lanka until the invasions from what is now South India in the 10th century AD; another theory contends that Tamil people were the original inhabitants of the island.

The earliest archaeological evidence of human colonization in Sri Lanka appears at the site of Balangoda. These Balangoda people arrived on the island about 34,000 years ago and are identified as Mesolithic hunter gatherers who lived in caves. The hunter-gatherer people known as the Wanniyala-Aetto or Veddahs,[3] (who still live in the central, Uva and north-eastern parts of the island), are probably direct descendants of the first inhabitants (Balangoda man). Around 400 BC, Indo-Aryan peoples emigrated from India, mixed with the Hela people and later Buddhism was established to create the Sinhalese culture in Sri Lanka. Buddhist scriptures note three visits by the Buddha to the island to see the Naga Kings. These kings are thought to be Tamil speakers, ruling kingdoms throughout North and South India prior to the Aryan invasion. The earliest surviving chronicles from the Island, the Dipavamsa and the Mahavamsa, say that tribes of Yakkhas (demon worshippers), Nagas (cobra worshippers) and devas (god worshippers) inhabited the island prior to the migration of Vijaya.

This, however, is not how the original inhabitants of Sri Lanka are viewed by the Sinhala Buddhists. According to the early chronicles relating the historical traditions of Sri Lanka, a prince named Vijaya and his followers who came from India and landed in Lanka on the day of the Parinibbaana of the Buddha were the first human inhabitants of this island. When they came the island was occupied by 'yakkhas'[4] (sprites, demons). 'Yakkhas' and 'Naagas' are also said to have inhabited Lanka in the time of the Buddha. A legend relating the existence of a great civilization before this time, under a king named Raavana is also current though the early chronicles make no mention of it. The Vijaya legend of these chronicles is taken by modern historians as a poetic expression of the actual aryanization of Sri Lanka in about the sixth century BCE. The term 'Yakkhas and Nagas' may refer to the aborigines who occupied the island before their arrival. No traces of an advanced civilization, however, have yet been discovered to support the Raavana legend. Archaeologists have discovered quartz implements and tools at various sites, believed to have been used by the aborigines of Sri Lanka, and they indicate that these people were a primitive tribe who lived by hunting. These aborigines have not left traces of a strong political organization or an advanced culture. The present Veddas are believed to be their descendants.

Mr. H.R. Perara, the author from whose book this extract is quoted, writes that "...it is evident from the chronicles relating the early history of Sri Lanka that before the introduction of Buddhism in the reign of King Devaanampiya Tissa (250-210 BCE) there was no single religion which was widely accepted as the national religion of the country. Nevertheless, there was a wide range of religious beliefs and practices, different from one another, and each individual seems to have freely observed his religion according to his belief. A noteworthy feature of the pre-Buddhist religion of Sri Lanka is that it was a mixture of the aboriginal cults and the beliefs of the aryan newcomers...Many scholars agree that these yaksas and other non-human beings are none but the spirits of the dead relatives and tribal chiefs[5] who, the people believed, were capable of helping friends and harming enemies. This belief, as is widely known, formed one of the main features of the primitive religion and is extant even today".

As per the author, "Prince Vijaya and his 700 followers are described in the Lankan chronicles as a set of adventurous young men who, when they were banished from their Indian homeland Laala (or Laata), came in search of new land for settlement. Other legends, some of which are even older, relating how the first Aryan inhabitants came to settle down in Lanka are found in several Pali and Sanskrit works. Most of them show that the settlement of early Aryan settlers is due to the enterprise of the pioneering merchant mariners who came to this island for pearls and precious stones. Historians thus do not lay much reliance on the details of the Vijaya legend but they accept Vijaya as the first traditional ruler of the newcomers – the Sinhalese."[6]

Anthropologically, however, it has been established that the indigenous Veddhas who were the original inhabitants of the Island, before the Aryan Prince Vijaya and his followers came in, are physically related to the Dravidian-speaking tribal people in South India and early populations of Southeast Asia. They no longer speak their native languages. It is believed that cultural diffusion, rather than migration of people, spread the Prakrit and Tamil languages from peninsular India into an existing Mesolithic[7] population, centuries before the Common Era. As explained above, the Veddahs continue to live in Sri Lanka even today.

It would be worth mentioning, that, in India, there is universal belief in the existence of an ancient, thriving Kingdom of Lanka, which was ruled by a powerful, enlightened, but flawed King Ravana. The epic, *Ramayana*, is centred on this well etched character from antiquity and how he became central to the main thread of narration in the *Ramayana*. There would be few takers in India, therefore, who would accept that there was never a King Ravana. What really does not matter to the average Indian is the possibility that Ravana was an Aryan or a Dravidian. In fairness, it must be stated that hard evidence to support this belief has so far not been discovered in Sri Lanka.

What would be clear to the reader is that the roots of conflict between the Sinhala Buddhists and the Tamil ancestors go all the way back to prehistoric times.

The Pali chronicles, the Dipavamsa, Mahavamsa,[8] Thupavamsa and the Chulavamsa as well as a large collection of stone inscriptions, the Indian epigraphical records, the Burmese versions of the chronicles, etc., provide an exceptional record for the history of Sri Lanka from about the 6th century BC. The Mahavamsa, written around 400 AD by the monk Nagasena, using the Deepavamsa, the Attakatha and other written sources available to him, correlates well with Indian histories of the period. Indeed, Emperor Asoka's reign is recorded in the Mahavamsa. The Mahavamsa account of the period prior to Asoka's coronation (218 years after the Buddha's death) seems to be part legend. History proper begins with the arrival of Vijaya and his 700 followers. Vijaya, is a Kalinga (ancient Orissa) prince, the eldest son of King Sinhabahu (*Man with Lion Arms*) and his sister Queen Sinhasivali. Both these Sinhala leaders were born of a mythical union between a lion and a human princess. According to the Mahavamsa, Vijaya landed on Sri Lanka near Mahathitha (Manthota or Mannar), and named the Island "Thambaparni" ('copper-colored palms). This name is attested in Ptolemy's map of the ancient world.

Devanampiya Tissa (250-210 BC) was a Sinhalese king of the Maurya clan. His links with Emperor Asoka led to the introduction of Buddhism by Mahinda (son of Asoka) in 247 BC. Sanghamitta, (sister of Mahinda) brought a Bodhi sapling via Jambukola (Sambiliturei). This king's reign was crucial to Theravada Buddhism, and for Sri Lanka.

Elara (205-161 BC), a South Indian Tamil invader ruled 'Pihiti Rata', i.e., Sri Lanka north of the Mahaweli, after killing King Asela. During Elara's time, Kelani Tissa was a sub-king of Maya Rata (south-west) and Kavan Tissa was a regional sub-king of Ruhuna (South-east). Dutugemunu (161-137 BC) – eldest son of King Kavan Tissa, who was a young man 25 years of age, defeated the South Indian Tamil Invader Elara (over 64 years of age) in single combat, described in the Mahavamsa. This may be identified as the first recorded Sinhala-Tamil clash, going back over 2000 years in history.

Dakhinathupa in Anuradhapura, currently identified as a Buddhist temple, was considered until the 1900s CE as the tomb of 2nd century BCE Tamil King Elara.[9] The identification and reclassification is considered controversial.

Dutugemunu is depicted as a Sinhala 'Asoka'. Mahasena (274-301) – Pandu (429) – the first of seven Pandian rulers, ending with Pithya, 455; Dhatusena (459-477), his uncle, Mahanama wrote the Mahavamsa and built "Kalaweva". His son Kashyapa (477-495), built the famous Sigiriya rock palace. Some 700 rock graffiti give a glimpse of ancient Sinhala.

Sinhala-Tamil Clashes from the 10th Century AD Onwards

The great Tamil king, Raja Chola I and his great son Rajendra Chola I, defeated all of the Sinhalese kings and sub-kings who ruled over Sinhala kingdoms on the island and brought the entire island under South Indian Tamil control. The Sinhala king Mahinda V and his family were captured and taken to Chola Nadu. Tamils ruled the entire island for the next 37 years (1018-1055). This is the second recorded Sinhala-Tamil clash.

King Vijayabâhu I (1055-1110), recaptured the whole Island, and established Polonnaruva as the new capital. This is the third recorded Sinhala-Tamil clash.

Sigiriya Rock Fortress

Dambadeniya is an ancient capital of Sri Lanka. Four kings ruled from here, Vijayabâhu III (1220-1236),

Parâkkamabâhu II (1236-1270), Vijayabâhu IV (1270-1272) and Bhuvanaikabâhu I(1272-1283). The Dambadeniya period is considered as the golden era of Sinhala literature. Several books in Sinhala, Pali and Sanskrit were written in this period. Among them are books of poetry such as Kausilumina, Muwadewdawatha, Sidath Sangarawa, Buthsarana, Saddharma Rathnawaliya..

The Jaffna kingdom, also known as Kingdom of Aryacakravarti came into existence after the invasion by Magha, who is said to have been from Kalinga, in South India. For a brief period, in the early to middle fourteenth century, it was an ascendant power Sri Lanka when all regional kingdoms accepted subordination. However, the kingdom was eventually overpowered by the rival Sinhala Kotte Kingdom, around 1450. This may be regarded as the fourth Sinhala-Tamil clash.

Colonial Era (1505-1948)

Portuguese Era

The first Europeans to visit Sri Lanka in modern times were the Portuguese: Francisco de Almeida arrived in 1505, finding the island divided into seven warring kingdoms and unable to fend off intruders. The Portuguese founded a fort at the port city of Colombo in 1517 and gradually extended their control over the coastal areas. In 1592 the Sinhalese moved their capital to the inland city of Kandy, a location more secure against attack from invaders. Intermittent warfare continued through the 16th century. Many lowland Sinhalese were forced to convert to Christianity while the coastal Moors were religiously persecuted and forced to retreat to the Central highlands. The Buddhist majority disliked Portuguese occupation and its influences and welcomed any power who might rescue them. In 1602, therefore, when the Dutch captain Joris van Spilbergen landed, the King of Kandy appealed to him for help.

Dutch Era

It was in 1638 that the Dutch attacked in earnest, and not until 1656 that Colombo fell. By 1660, the Dutch controlled the whole island except the kingdom of Kandy. The Dutch persecuted the Catholics but left the Buddhists, Hindus and Moslems alone. However, they taxed the people far more heavily than the Portuguese had done. A mixed Dutch-Sinhalese people known as Burgher peoples are the legacy of Dutch rule.

British Rule

In 1659, the British sea captain Robert Knox landed by chance on Sri Lanka and was captured by the King of Kandy. He escaped 19 years later and wrote an account of his stay. This helped to bring the island to the attention of the British.

During the Napoleonic Wars the United Kingdom, fearing that French control of the Netherlands might deliver Sri Lanka to the French, the British occupied the coastal areas of the island (which they called Ceylon) with little difficulty in 1796. In 1802, by the Treaty of Amiens the Dutch part of the island was formally ceded to Britain, and became a crown colony. In 1815, Kandy was occupied, finally ending Sri Lankan independence. The British found that the uplands of Sri Lanka were very suited to coffee, tea and rubber cultivation, and by the mid 19th century Ceylon tea had become a staple of the British market, bringing great wealth to a small class of white tea planters. To work the estates, the planters imported large numbers of Tamil workers as indentured labourers from South India, who soon made up 10 percent of the island's population. These workers had to work in slave-like conditions and to live in line rooms, not very different from cattle sheds. The British colonialists favoured the semi-European Burghers, certain high-caste Sinhalese and the Tamils who were mainly concentrated to the north of the country, exacerbating divisions and enmities which have survived ever since.

Modern Origins of the Sri Lankan Civil War

The origins of the Sri Lankan Civil War lie in the continuous political rancour between the majority Sinhalese and the minority Tamils. According to Jonathan Spencer, a widely read and respected social anthropologist from the School of Social and Political Studies of the University of Edinburgh, the war is an outcome of how modern ethnic identities have been made and re-made since the colonial period, with the political struggle between minority Tamils and the Sinhala-dominant government accompanied by rhetorical wars over archeological sites and place name etymologies, and the political use of the national past.

A primary contributor to the development of political awareness amongst Tamils was the advent of Protestant missionaries on a large scale from 1814. Activities by missionaries of the American Board of Commissioners for Foreign Missions, Methodists and Anglican churches led to a revival amongst Hindu Tamils who built their own schools, temples, societies and published literature to counter the missionary activities. There was initially little tension amongst Sri Lanka's two largest ethnic groups, the Sinhalese and the Tamils, when Ponnambalam Arunachalam, a Tamil, was appointed representative of the Sinhalese as well as the Tamils in the national legislative council. However, the British Governor William Manning actively encouraged the concept of 'communal representation' and created the Colombo seat which was dangled between the Tamils and the Sinhalese. Subsequently, the Donoughmore Commission strongly rejected communal representation, and brought in universal franchise. The decision was strongly opposed by the Tamil political leadership, who realized that they would be reduced to a minority in Parliament, according to the proportion of the population they make up.

Sinhala and Sri Lankan Tamil Nationalism

It is relevant at this stage to pick up the main issues involved in the nationalism that started emerging during the British period.

Sinhalese Buddhist nationalism[10] is a political ideology which combines a focus upon Sinhalese culture and ethnicity with an emphasis upon Theravada Buddhism, which is the majority belief system of most Sinhalese people in Sri Lanka. It mostly originated in reaction to the colonization of Sri Lanka by the British Empire. Dharmapala was one of the primary contributors to the Buddhist revival of the 19th century that led to the creation of Buddhist institutions to match those of the missionaries schools, (the YMCA, etc), and to the independence movement of the 20th century. It is presumed to have four main points: "(i) Praise – for Buddhism and the Sinhalese culture; (ii) Blame – on the British imperialists, including Christians; (iii) Fear – that Buddhism in Sri Lanka was threatened with extinction; and (iv) Hope – for a rejuvenated Sinhalese Buddhist ascendancy." Sinhalese Buddhist nationalism has a fractious relationship with other religious communities like Christianity and Islam in Sri Lanka, with violent protests often being organized by Buddhist nationalist organizations against the perceived interference of Christians and Muslims in the country. Relations between Buddhist nationalists and Hindus are more nuanced, with numerous Hindu figures, including Kandiah Neelakandan and T. Maheswaran working with Buddhist groups on the anti-Conversion bill.

Sri Lankan Tamil nationalism[11] is the conviction of the Sri Lankan Tamil people, that they have the right to constitute an independent or autonomous political community. This idea has not always existed. Sri Lankan Tamil national awareness began during the era of British rule during the 18th century, as Tamil Hindu revivalists tried to counter Protestant missionary activity. The revivalists, led by Arumuga Navalar, used literacy as a tool to spread Hinduism and its principles. Navalar's efforts to revive Hinduism, the predominant religion of the Sri Lankan Tamil people, influenced Tamils who built their own schools, temples, and societies. Thus, by 1925, nearly 50 schools, including the Batticotta Seminary, were fully functioning. The success of this effort led the Tamils to think confidently of themselves as a community and prepared the way for their awareness of a common cultural, religious and linguistic kinship in the mid-nineteenth century. Jaffna's history (known as Kingdom of Aryacakravarti, now northern Sri Lanka) of being an independent Tamil kingdom lends legitimacy to the political claims of the Sri Lankan Tamils, and has provided a focus for their constitutional demands.

Independence Movement

Jonathan Spencer,[12] who has written extensively on the Sri Lankan imbroglio, feels that the history of electoral politics in Sri Lanka, started in the 1930s, when "Sinhala majoritarianism, became the hegemonic political project in the island." All minorities, not just the Tamils, but minorities in general, began to see they were going to be always on the fringes of power and on the fringes of the state. The awakening of political awareness, he writes, "was an idea that was borrowed from India, where a full-fledged freedom struggle was on during the same period. …" the form that people think of, say, a 'Tamil nation' or the 'Sinhala people' or whatever, is massively shaped by the work that is being done in the political arenas, since the 1930s. My own view is that that is the single crucial factor in all of this. You can tell a story about it, and you can tell a story that makes some sense about this by comparing with Sri Lanka's giant neighbour India. In the '20s and '30s in India, the anti-colonial politicians, the Nehrus and Gandhis, were attempting to create this broadened alliance as possible in order to win political rights and to push the British out. The equivalent figures in Sri Lanka basically didn't exist, there wasn't a mass nationalist movement, and the British colonial office brought in universal adult suffrage and elections to Sri Lanka, actually in the face of reservations expressed by the only major nationalist party at the time – the Ceylon Nationalist Congress. They said that people were not ready for elections."[13] The British Soulbury Commission was the most important result of the agitation for constitutional reform in the 1930s.

Second World War

The Senanayake Government took advantage of the war to further its rapport with the commanding elite. Ceylon became crucial to the British Empire in the war, with Lord Mountbatten using Colombo as his headquarters for the Eastern Theatre. Oliver Gunatilleke successfully exploited the markets for the country's rubber and other agricultural products to replenish the treasury. Nonetheless, the Sinhalese continued to agitate for independence and Sinhalese sovereignty, using the opportunities offered by the war to establish a special relationship with Britain.

The constitutionalists, led by D.S. Senanayake, succeeded in winning independence. The Soulbury constitution was essentially what Senanayake's board of ministers had drafted in 1944. The promise of Dominion status, and independence itself, had been given by the Colonial office.

G. G. Ponnambalam[14]

The recording of Tamil activism and their demand for autonomy will be incomplete without mention of the man who can be considered to have started off the Tamil demand for a separate identity.

Ganapathipillai Gangaser Ponnambalam (8th November 1901 – 9th December 1977), known as G.G. Ponnambalam, was a Sri Lankan Tamil politician in British Ceylon, and then after independence, in Ceylon. He founded the first Sri Lankan Tamil political party, the All Ceylon Tamil Congress. Ponnambalam stood for the principle of minority representation. G.G. Ponnambalam's parents were both from the northernmost part of the island, Jaffna District; his father Gangesar was a postmaster from Alvai North, Point Pedro, and his mother was from Navali, Manipay. He received his secondary education at St. Joseph's College, Colombo, and then went to King's College, London, on a scholarship and graduated with a degree in the Natural Sciences. He went on to Fitzwilliam College, Cambridge, to study the Law Tripos. GG graduated with a BA in Law and was subsequently called to the Bar at Lincoln's Inn, London.

He was an outstanding criminal defence attorney. In the famous Ranjani taxi cab murder case, the first fingerprint case in Ceylon, he thoroughly demolished the testimony of Scotland Yard's Inspector Godsell on cross-examination. After his last (1956) term in Parliament, he migrated to Malaysia and practised law there until his death on 9th February 1977. The Sri Lankan Government honoured him by issuing a commemoration postage stamp on 22 May 1986. Ponnambalam and his colleagues stood for the principle of minority representation of the Tamils. They believed that without it the minority Tamils would become second class citizens. He rejected the 'Ceylonese identity'. Ponnambalam had declared himself a 'proud Dravidian', and attempted to establish an independent identity for the Tamils. Ponnambalam attacked the Sinhalese, and their historical chronicle known as the Mahavamsa. One such inflamed attack in Navalapitiya led to the first (modern) Sinhala-Tamil riot in 1939.[15] Ponnambalam opposed universal franchise, supported the caste system, and claimed that the protection of Tamil rights requires the Tamils (15 percent of the population in 1931) having an equal number of seats in parliament to that of the Sinhalese (~72 percent of the population). This '50-50' or 'balanced representation' policy became the hall mark of Tamil politics of the time. Ponnambalam also accused the British of having established colonization in 'traditional Tamil areas', and having favoured the Buddhists by the Buddhist temporalities act. This was immediately rejected and rebuked by the British Governor General as a 'mockery of democracy'. G.G. Ponnambalam entered the State Council of Ceylon in 1934 from Point Pedro. In 1948, Ponnambalam joined the cabinet of D.S. Senanayake of the UNP, a move seen by some as an abandonment of his principles.

All Ceylon Tamil Congress

The All Ceylon Tamil Congress (ACTC), founded by G.G. Ponnambalam in 1944, was popular among Tamils because it promoted the preservation of Tamil identity. The ACTC advocated a 'fifty-fifty' policy, in which fifty percent of the seats in Parliament would be reserved for Tamils and other minorities, the remaining fifty percent going to the Sinhalese. Which means 50 per cent of the opportunities [Education (University seats), Employment, etc.) should be allocated to minorities. D.S. Senanayake, the leader of the Sinhalese political groups, allowed Ponnambalam full control over presentations before the Soulbury Commission, prevented Sinhalese nationalists such as Solomon Bandaranaike from taking the stage, and avoided the eruption of acrimonious arguments. In 1948, Ponnambalam voted in favour of one of several bills, later known as the Ceylon Citizenship Act which disenfranchised Indian Tamils ('Hill Country Tamils'). The ACTC remained the major Tamil political party until 1956, when the Federal Party took over that position. The Tamil Congress still held parliamentary positions, however, and continued to be a force in Tamil politics. In 1976, the ACTC merged with other Tamil political factions to form a new party called the Tamil United Liberation Front (TULF).

D. S. Senanayake and the UNP[16]

At this juncture, it is necessary to mention some details of a remarkable politician whom Sri Lanka considers the 'Father of the Nation' – D.S. Senanayake.

D. S. Senanayake

Don Stephen Senanayake (October 20, 1884–22 March, 1952) was an independence activist. He was brought up in a devout Buddhist family. On his father's wishes, he converted to Christianity. He later reconverted to Buddhism in order to become a politician in the majority Buddhist Sri Lanka.

Senanayake played an active role in the independence movement first supporting his brother Frederick Richard Senanayake and after his untimely death in 1926, D.S. took his place in the Legislative Council and led the Independence movement. In 1931 he was elected to the State Council, and went on to become Minister of Agriculture and Lands. He remained a Minister for 14 years because of his competence. During World War II he was a member of the Ceylon war cabinet and established a very good relationship with Lord Mountbatten. The close collaboration of the D. S. Senanayake government with the war-time British administration led to the support of Lord Mountbatten. His despatches and a telegram to the Colonial office supporting Independence for Ceylon have been cited by historians as having helped the Senanayake government to secure the independence of Sri Lanka.[17]

He resigned in 1946 from his cabinet post to fight for Ceylon's independence. That same year he founded the United National Party (UNP) by amalgamating three right-leaning pro-dominion parties, which is still one of the main political parties and perhaps the largest single party in Sri Lanka. At the elections of 1947, the UNP won a minority of the seats in Parliament, but cobbled together a coalition with the Sinhala Maha Sabha of Solomon Bandaranaike and the Tamil Congress of G.G. Ponnambalam. The successful inclusions of the Tamil-communalist leader Ponnambalam, and his Sinhala counterpart Bandaranaike were a remarkable political balancing act by Senanayake.[18] In only a year he succeeded, and was elected as Ceylon's first Prime Minister in the general election held in 1947. D.S Senanayake is respected by Sinhalese and some Muslims. However, the Tamils were not happy with his citizenship laws that disenfranchised virtually all Tamils of recent Indian origin living in the central highlands. His bold agricultural plans and pro-Western policies, however, attracted criticism for their modern and untraditional nature. Under his family's leadership, Sri Lanka's economy flourished, and D.S. Senanayake is still known as 'The Father of Sri Lanka'.

Independence[19]

Dominion status, raised to independence itself followed for Ceylon on 4 February 1948, with military treaties with Britain (the upper ranks of the armed forces were initially British) and British air and sea bases remaining intact. Senanayake became the first Prime Minister of Sri Lanka. In 1949, with the concurrence of the leaders of the Ceylon Tamils, the UNP government disenfranchised the Indian Tamil plantation workers. This was the price that Senanayake had to pay to obtain the support of the Kandian Sinhalese who felt threatened by the demographics of the tea estates, where the inclusion of the 'Indian Tamils' would have meant electoral defeat for the Kandian leaders. Senanayake died in 1952 after falling from a horse. He was succeeded by his son, Dudley Senanayake, the Minister of Agriculture. However, in 1953 – following a massive general strike or 'Hartal' by the Left parties against the UNP, Dudley Senanayake resigned. He was followed by John Kotelawala, a senior politician and an uncle of Dudley. Kotelawala did not have the enormous personal prestige or the adroit political acumen of D.S. Senanayake. He brought to the fore the issue of national languages that D.S. Senanayake had adroitly kept on the back burner.

In 1956, the UNP was defeated at elections (being reduced to 8 seats in Parliament) by the Mahajana Eksath Peramuna, which included the Sri Lanka Freedom Party (SLFP) led by Solomon Bandaranaike and the Viplavakari Lanka Sama Samaja Party of Philip Gunawardene. Bandaranaike was a politician who had nursed the Sinhala nationalist lobby since the 1930s. He replaced English with Sinhala Only as the official language. He was the chief Sinhalese spokesmen who attempted to counter the communal politics unleashed by G.G. Ponnambalam.

Bandaranaike entered into a pact with Chelvanayagam of the Tamil-based Tamil Arasu Kachchi to secure more rights for the Tamils, but this was opposed by G.G. Ponnambalam and by J.R. Jayawardene of the UNP. The latter organised a 'March to Kandy' in protest. This triggered hostility from the Tamil minority which soon led to disturbances, culminating in serious riots in 1958. Bandaranaike was assassinated in September 1959. His successor Wijayananda Dahanayake, an ex-LSSP member from Galle, was unable to hold the government together, and elections in March 1960 brought the UNP under Dudley Senanayake back to office, but without a working parliamentary majority.

Fresh elections in July saw Bandaranaike's widow, Sirimavo Bandaranaike, lead the SLFP to power to become the world's first elected female head of government. Her government avoided further confrontations with the Tamils, but the anti socialist policies of the Republican Political Party led to a cut-off of United States aid and a growing economic crisis. Dissatisfaction with the economic situation brought the UNP under Senanayake back to office in 1965, but this government fared no better. In 1968, Bandaranaike formed a coalition, the United Front with the LSSP and the Communist Party of Sri Lanka, which swept the 1970 polls on a platform of socialism.

Republic (1970 to the Present)[20]

Under Bandaranaike the country became a republic, the Free Sovereign and Independent Republic of Sri Lanka, the Senate was abolished and Sinhala was established as the official language (with Tamil as a second language). The strongly centralized economy, functioning via a set of state corporations, grew very sluggishly.

In 1971, a group variously labelled Maoist or Guevarist, the People's Liberation Front (JVP) launched a rebellion. It was led by Rohana Wijeweera. Although the JVP rebellion was brutally suppressed, the JVP found a place in Sri Lankan politics as a voice of leftist Sinhalese nationalism, along with the right-wing movement in the UNP associated with Cyril Matthew. Militant Tamil chauvinist movements, e.g., the Pulip Padai, had been launched in Trincomalee in 1965. The Jaffna University was 'ethnically cleansed' of non-Tamils in 1976 and the city itself began to be subject to similar 'ethnic cleansing', eliminating Muslim and Sinhala residents.

The extreme-Tamil groups rejected and physically eliminated the main Colombo-Tamil leadership of the Tamil United Liberation Front (TULF). Tamil public servants or members of parliament working with the government were harassed. The mayor of Jaffna was assassinated in 1975. The militants claimed their independence, their rights, and their "traditional homeland", and formed armed separatist groups such as the Liberation Tigers of Tamil Eelam ('Tamil Tigers'), demanding an independent Tamil state called Eelam. Much of this had the implicit and material support of politicians in India.

New Constitution[21]

By 1977, the voters were tired of Bandaranaike's socialist policies and elections returned the UNP to power under Junius Jayewardene on a manifesto pledging a market economy and "a free ration of 8 seers (kilograms) of cereals". The SLFP and the left-wing parties were virtually wiped out in Parliament (although they garnered 40 percent of the popular vote), leaving the Tamil United Liberation Front, led by Appapillai Amirthalingam, as the official opposition. This created a dangerous ethnic cleavage in Sri Lankan politics. President Jayawardene had the constitution amended (one of 13 amendments during his 10 years in office) to allow Presidential elections to be held early, in 1982. The Presidential election, held amidst widespread acts of electoral malpractice, resulted in Jayewardene's re-election. He followed this with an infamous plebiscite on postponing parliamentary elections for six years.

Federal Party[22]

In 1949, a new Tamil party, called the Federal Party ('Ilankai Thamil Arasu Kadchi'), was organized by the people who broke away from the ACTC. Led by Chelvanayakam, it gained popularity among the Tamil people because it advocated Tamil rights. Its popularity was also due to the party's opposition to the Ceylon Citizenship Act and the Sinhala Only Act. As a result, the Federal Party became the dominant party in the Tamil districts after the 1956 elections. To further the new political agenda, in 1975 the Federal Party merged with the other Tamil political parties to become the Tamil United Liberation Front (TULF). In 1976, after the first national convention of TULF, the Ceylon Tamils moved toward a revised nationalism and were now unwilling to live within a confined, single-island entity.

Tamil United Liberation Front[23]

The Tamil United Liberation Front (TULF) was formed when the Tamil political parties merged and adopted the Vaddukoddai Resolution, named after the village, Vaddukoddai, where it was developed. In the 1977 election, TULF became the first Tamil Nationalist party to run on a separatist platform. It gained a majority of the votes in the north and east, won 18 seats, and became the largest opposition party in parliament. The Vaddukoddai Resolution had a profound effect on Tamil politics – the parliamentary system was soon to be replaced by guns. TULF tried to refashion itself as the political division, negotiating an agreement with the executive president of Sri Lanka at that time, J.R. Jayewardene. This agreement, known as the District Development Councils' Scheme, was passed in 1980, but TULF rejected it because J.R. Jayewardene had not agreed to let TULF have the five District Ministerships in the five Tamil districts where TULF received the most votes. The Sixth Amendment was passed in 1983, requiring Tamils in Parliament and other public offices to take an oath of allegiance to the unified state of Sri Lanka. It forbade the advocating of a separate state, and consequently TULF members were expelled from parliament for refusing to take the oath.

Militant Groups[24]

After the expulsion of TULF from parliament, militants ruled the Tamil political movement. As a result, the 1970s saw the emergence of more than 30 Tamil militant groups. Anton Balasingham, the theoretician of the Liberation Tigers of Tamil Eelam (LTTE), states that the causes of the militarization of the Tamil youth were unemployment, lack of opportunities for higher education, and the imposition of an alien language. He further alleges that the majority Sinhalese government was responsible for these problems, adding that the only alternative left for Tamil youths was a 'revolutionary armed struggle for the independence of their nation'. Only five of the militant groups – People's Liberation Organisation of Tamil Eelam (PLOTE), Tamil Eelam Liberation Organization (TELO), Eelam People's Revolutionary Liberation Front (EPRLF), Eelam Revolutionary Organisation of Students (EROS) and LTTE – remained a potent political force; the rest were flawed ideologically and therefore not strictly Tamil nationalist factions.

Of these five dominant groups, the LTTE was the most solidly nationalistic Tamil resistance organization. It had established a de facto state in the areas under its control, called Tamil Eelam, and had managed a government in these areas, providing state functions such as courts, a police force, a human rights organization, and a humanitarian assistance board, a health board, and an education board. In addition, it ran a bank (Bank of Tamil Eelam), a radio station (Voice of Tigers) and a television station (National Television of Tamil Eelam). The status has, of course, completely changed now, with the death of Prabhakaran and the near total elimination of key leaders of the LTTE.

The Civil War (1983 to 2009)[25]

In July 1983, communal riots took place due to the ambush and killing of 13 Sri Lankan Army soldiers by the Tamil Tigers. Using the voters list which contained the exact addresses of Tamils, the Tamil community faced a backlash from Sinhalese rioters including the destruction of shops, homes and savage beatings. However, quite a few Sinhalese kept Tamil neighbours in their homes to protect them from the rioters. During these riots the government did nothing to control the mob. Conservative government estimates put the death toll at 400, while the real death toll is believed to be around 3,000. Also, around 18,000 Tamil homes were destroyed, with 150,000 leaving the country resulting in a Tamil Diaspora in Canada, UK, Australia and other Western countries.

A 'stamp' issued by a Tamil militant group in 1983 representing an independent country for Tamils

Jayewardene held office until 1989, ruling as a virtual dictator under emergency powers. In 1987, following an army offensive in the Vadamarachchi peninsular, India started getting deeply involved in the ethnic conflict. A convoy sent by India was stopped in Sri

Lankan waters by the Sri Lankan Navy and the Indian Air Force retaliated with an air drop of supplies onto the Jaffna peninsula. While the UNP organised street protests against India, Jayawardene declared that he would defend the country's independence to the last bullet. However, the air drop also caused Jayawardene to reconsider his position and he then accepted the offer of Indian Prime Minister Rajiv Gandhi of a Peace Accord. Rajiv Gandhi's offer to send troops into Sri Lanka was deeply unpopular with the Sinhalese and, although initially popular with the Tamils, led to an outbreak of hostilities between the Tamil Tigers and the Indian Peace Keeping Force (IPKF) - Eelam War II.

In 1989, Jayawardene was succeeded by his own choice as President, Ranasinghe Premadasa, who asked for the Indian troops to be withdrawn – which was later done by Indian Prime Minister V.P. Singh. Premadasa was assassinated by a Tamil Tiger suicide bomber in 1993. Rajiv Gandhi had already met a similar fate (assassinated by a Tamil Tiger) in 1991. Premadasa was succeeded by Dingiri Banda Wijetunga, with Ranil Wickremesinghe as Prime Minister. In August 1994 the People's Alliance under Bandaranaike's daughter Chandrika Kumaratunga won the legislative elections on a platform of concessions to the Tamils and a 'balanced economy'. Kumaratunga became Prime Minister and in November she was elected President, appointing her 78-year-old (but still active) mother Prime Minister. A ceasefire ensued, which was broken by the Tamil Tigers after several months – the beginning of Eelam War III. Under the Bandaranaikes the war dragged on, with the military unable to defeat the separatists and the government opposed to negotiations. By 2000 an estimated 65,000 people had been killed in the conflict.

By 2005, there had been no further progress towards either a military or political solution. The assassination of Foreign Minister Lakshman Kadirgamar in August 2005 by the LTTE (although they denied responsibility), further hardened attitudes. His successor was Anura Bandaranaike, the President's brother and putative political heir. In elections held on 17th November 2005, Mahinda Rajapaksa, the son of Don Alwin Rajapaksa, was elected President, defeating Wickremesinghe. He appointed Ratnasiri Wickremanayake Prime Minister and Mangala Samaraweera Foreign Minister. Negotiations with the LTTE stalled and low-intensity conflict began. The violence dipped off after talks in February, but escalated in April and the conflict continued until the military defeat of the LTTE in May 2009.

Defeat of the LTTE

The Sri Lankan government declared total victory on Monday, 18th of May 2009. On 19th May 2009, the Sri Lankan military effectively concluded its 26-year operation against the LTTE. On 22nd May 2009, Sri Lankan Defence Secretary Gottabhaya Rajapaksa confirmed that 6,261 personnel of the Sri Lankan Armed Forces had lost their lives *The Times* newspaper of the UK accused the government of a massacre on the coastline of a refugee camp caught between the fire. This raised the estimate of deaths to 20,000; many times that of the official figures released by the government.

Recap of Major Developments that Caused the Civil War[26]

The milestones that contributed directly or indirectly to the civil war from the time the British were in power till 2006, are covered in the succeeding paragraphs.

1915 Riots

The first reported organized riots in Sri Lanka were against the minority Sri Lankan Moors in 1915.

Denial of Citizenship to Estate Tamils Act, 1949

There is a sizable population of Tamils in the Central Province, plantation labourers brought down from India by the British colonial authorities in the nineteenth and twentieth centuries. These Indian Tamils (or Estate Tamils), as they are called, still work mainly in Sri Lanka's tea plantations. They have been locked in poverty for generations and continue to experience poor living conditions. Although they speak the same language, they are usually considered a separate community from the Sri Lankan Tamils of the North and East. The government of D.S. Senanayake passed legislation stripping the estate Tamils of their citizenship in 1949, leaving them stateless.

The effect was to tilt the island's political balance away from the Tamils. In 1948, at independence, the Tamils had 33 percent of the voting power in Parliament. Upon the disenfranchisement of the estate Tamils, however, this proportion dropped to 20 percent. The Sinhalese could and did obtain more than a 2/3 majority in Parliament, making it impossible for Tamils to exercise an effective opposition to Sinhalese policies affecting them. Not content with stripping their citizenship, successive governments tried to remove the estate Tamils from the country entirely. In 1962, Prime Minister Sirimavo Bandaranaike signed an agreement with Indian Prime Minister L.B. Shastri. A second agreement was signed three years later with Indira Gandhi. These provided that 600,000 of the estate Tamils would be expelled and sent to India over a 15-year period, and 375,000 would be restored their Sri Lankan citizenship. Not all of the former group actually returned to India, and remained in Sri Lanka without the ability to vote, travel abroad, or participate fully in Sri Lankan life. It was not until 2003 that full citizenship rights were restored to the remaining Tamils in the hill country.

1953 Hartal

Hartal 1953 was a country-wide demonstration which eventually led to civil unrest.

1956 Gal Oya Riots

The first reported ethnic riots that targeted minority Sri Lankan Tamils in Gal Oya, a new settlement in the Eastern Province. The total number of deaths is reportedly 150.

1958 Riots

1958 ethnic riots popularly known also as the 58 riots was a watershed event in the race relationship of the various ethnic communities of Sri Lanka. The total number of deaths is estimated to be 300, mostly Sri Lankan Tamils, and thousands more assaulted and Tamil property looted. Over 25,000 Tamil refugees were relocated to the North.

1970 – Banning of Tamil Media and Literature Imports

Importing Tamil language films, books, magazines, journals, etc., from the cultural hub of Tamil Nadu, India was banned. Sri Lanka also banned groups such as the Dravida Munnetra Kazhagham and the Tamil Youth League. Culturally, Tamil Sri Lankans were cut off from Tamil Nadu. Foreign exchange for the long established practice of Tamil students going to India for university education was stopped. Equally, examinations for external degrees from the University of London were abolished. The government insisted this was a part of a general programme of economic self-sufficiency, part of its socialist agenda; however most of the Tamil population did not accept nor believe this.

1971 – Universities Act

During the 1970s, university admissions were standardized. This initiative took place to rectify disparities created in university enrollment during colonial rule.

Under the British, English was the state language and consequently greatly benefitted English speakers. However, the majority of the Sri Lankan populace lived outside urban areas and did not belong to the social elite, and therefore did not enjoy the benefits of English-medium education. The issue was compounded further by the fact that in the northern and eastern regions of the island, where a largely Tamil speaking populace resided, students had access to English-medium education through missionary schools regardless of their socio-economic status.

This created a situation where the large proportion of students enrolled in universities were English speaking Tamils, particularly in professional courses such as medicine and engineering.

The government policy of standardization in essence was an affirmative action scheme to assist geographically disadvantaged students to gain tertiary education. The benefits enjoyed by Sinhalese students also meant a significant fall in the number of Tamil students within the university population.

1977 Riots

The anti-Tamil riots, targeting the minority Sri Lankan Tamil people started on August 12 1977, less than a month after the United National Party came to power in 1977. Over 300 Tamils were killed during these riots.

1981 Burning of Jaffna Library

This riot involved the destruction of the Jaffna Public Library, with the loss of over 100,000 books, artifacts and palm writings. Many irreplaceable historical documents and artifacts of civilization in Sri Lanka were lost forever. Some police and army members were accused of collusion in the riots. Four Sri Lankan Tamils were killed.

1983 Riots

The ethnic riots are better known as Black July Pogrom. At least 3,000 Sri Lankan Tamil civilians were killed and many more made homeless as refugees and number of places of business destroyed.

Aranthalawa Massacre

The massacre of 31 Sinhala Buddhist Bhikkus by the LTTE on June 2, 1987, marked one of the darkest chapters in Sri Lankan history.

2000 Bandarawela Riots

In October 2000, 27 Tamil youths were massacred and 14 others seriously injured in the attack at Bandarawela detention centre housing. This massacre was carried out by the local Sinhala community with the help of the local police. Local residents assaulted the inmates with clubs and knives after reports that they had taken a security guard hostage. Some victims were said to have been burned alive. According to the Asian Centre for Human Rights no one has been prosecuted for these crimes against humanity.

2001 Mawanella riots

Also known as Mawanella riots, shops and property belonging to the Muslim minority were destroyed and a number of Muslims killed.

2006 Trincomalee

In mid 2006, a bomb blast killed 16 people, prompting a Sinhalese mob to torch Tamil-owned shops and to hunt down Tamil civilians. According to the main hospital, the blast killed 16 people, eight Tamils, five Sinhalese, two Muslims and a person who could not be identified. The reprisal attacks claimed another five: four Tamils and one Sinhalese, who were burned, stabbed and shot to death. Whether the riots were spontaneous or planned is impossible to know, although the police and the army, deployed in full force around the market, did not manage to stop them. Rohan Abeywardana, the deputy inspector general of police in charge of Trincomalee, said his forces were overpowered. Those arrested were released the next morning.

Endnotes

1. "Sri Lankan Tamil people."<http://en.wikipedia.org/wiki/Sri_Lankan _Tamil_people>
2. Ibid.
3. "History of Sri Lanka."<http://en.wikipedia.org/wiki/History_of_Sri_Lanka>
4. H.R. Perera R., "Buddhism in Sri Lanka: A Short History."<http://www.accesstoinsight.org/lib/authors/perera/wheel100.html>
5. Ibid. The author, in his Preface to the book, writes that "the present treatise, *Buddhism in Sri Lanka: A Short History* deals with the history of Buddhism in this island from the time of its introduction in 250 BCE in the reign of King Devaanampiya Tissa, up to the present time (1966). The work is the outcome of an attempt to revise Dr. W.A. de Silva's monograph entitled 'History of Buddhism in Ceylon' appearing in Buddhistic Studies of Dr. B. C. Law (Calcutta, 1931). It should be mentioned, with due respect to the great scholar and national leader, that several of the chapters of his monograph have been reproduced here while many have been revised and enlarged. A few new chapters too have been added where it was deemed necessary." The implication is clear: what the book portrays is probably what the popular Sinhala Buddhist belief is: that the history of Sri Lanka begins with the Sinhala arrival on the Island. See **Note 6** in this connection. Purely from the objectivity angle, this perception needs evidence that is currently unavailable/undiscovered.
6. Ibid.
7. "Sri Lankan Tamil people." <http://en.wikipedia.org/wiki/Sri_Lankan _Tamil_people>
8. "History of Sri Lanka." <http://en.wikipedia.org/wiki/History_of _Sri_Lanka>
9. "Sri Lankan Tamil people." <http://en.wikipedia.org/wiki/Sri_Lankan _Tamil_people>
10. "Sinhala Buddhist Nationalism." <http://en.wikipedia.org/wiki/Sinhalese _Buddhist_nationalism>
11. "Sri Lankan Tamil Nationalism." <http://en.wikipedia.org/wiki/Sri_Lankan_Tamil_nationalism>.
12. Spencer, Jonathan. "Roots of Conflict in Sri Lanka." December 12, 2006.<http://www.zmag.org/znet/viewArticle/2552>
13. Ibid.
14. "G.G. Ponnambalam." < http://en.wikipedia.org/wiki/G._G._Ponnambalam>
15. "History of Sri Lanka." <http://en.wikipedia.org/wiki/History_of_Sri_Lanka>

16. "Don Stephen Senanayake." <http://en.wikipedia.org/wiki/Don_Stephen _Senanayake>
17. "History of Sri Lanka." <http://en.wikipedia.org/wiki/History_of_Sri_Lanka>
18. "Don Stephen Senanayake." <http://en.wikipedia.org/wiki/Don_Stephen _Senanayake>
19. "History of Sri Lanka." <http://en.wikipedia.org/wiki/History_of_Sri_Lanka>
20. Ibid.
21. Ibid.
22. "Sri Lankan Tamil Nationalism." <http://en.wikipedia.org/wiki/Sri_Lankan_Tamil_nationalism>
23. Ibid.
24. Ibid.
25. "History of Sri Lanka." <http://en.wikipedia.org/wiki/History_of_Sri _Lanka>
26. "Riots and Pogroms In Sri Lanka."<http://en.wikipedia.org/wiki/riots_and_pogroms_in_sri_lanka>References

References

1. Pichumani, K.; T.S. Subramanian, S.U. Deraniyagala (05-18 June 2004). "Prehistoric basis for the rise of civilisation in Sri Lanka and southern India". *Frontline* **21** (12). http://www.lankalibrary.com/geo/prehistory.htm.
2. A Concise History of Ceylon: From the Earliest Times to the Arrival of the Portuguese in 1505, 1961, p 25; Cyril Wace Nicholas, Senarat Paranavitana – Sri Lanka; Sinhalese and Other Island Languages in South Asia: By M.W.S. de Silva, 1979, p 15, M.W. Sugathapala De Silva.
3. Mahavamsa X.90, XII.5, XII.37-39; Dipavamsa. VIII.9; Samantapasadika, (P.T.B.). I.67; See: *History of Ceylon*, Vol I, Part I, pp 88-91, Dr S. Paranavitana.
4. *History of Ceylon*, 1959, p 91, Ceylon University, University of Ceylon, Peradeniya, Hem Chandra Ray, K. M. De Silva – Sri Lanka.
5. The hidden massacre: Sri Lanka's final offensive against Tamil Tigers – http://www.timesonline.co.uk/tol/news/world/asia/article6383449.ece
6. "Two decades after the burning down of the Jaffna library in Sri Lanka". World Socialist Web Site. 30 May 2001. http://www.wsws.org/articles/2001/may2001/sri-m30.shtml.
7. Balasingham, A.S. (1983). "Liberation Tigers and Tamil Eelam Freedom Struggle". Liberation Tigers of Tamil Eelam, Jaffna.
8. McConnell, D. (2008). "The Tamil people's right to self-determination" (PDF). *Cambridge Review of International Affairs* 21 (1): 59–76. doi: 10.1080/09557570701828592. http://www.informaworld.com/index/790622093.pdf.
9. Ranganathan, M. (2002). "Nurturing a Nation on the Net: The Case of Tamil Eelam". *Nationalism and Ethnic Politics* 8 (2): 51–66. http://www.ingentaconnect.com/content/routledg/nep/2002/00000008/00000002/art00004.
10. Senewiratne, Brian (2006-07-28). "Sri Lanka's Week of Shame: The July 1983 massacre of Tamils – Long-term consequences". http://sangam.org/taraki/articles/2006/07-28_Consequences.php?uid=1866.
11. O'Ballance, Edgar (1989). *The Cyanide War: Tamil Insurrection in Sri Lanka, 1973-88.* London: Brassey's (UK). ISBN 9780080366951. p.21 see also Edgar O'Ballance.
12. Swamy, M.R. Narayan (2003). *Inside an Elusive Mind: Prabhakaran.* Literate World. ISBN 1-59121-003-8.

CHAPTER 4
The LTTE

This chapter is a natural and important progression in the reader's understanding of the Sri Lankan civil war. From the time of its creation, and, in fact, even in its baptism into terror as the Tamil National Tigers (TNT), before it coalesced into the LTTE, this organization had made a name for its exceptional brutality as well as military capability in furthering its mission of a separate homeland for the Tamils – the dream of Eelam. It has to be accepted without hesitation that, at the peak of their powers around 2004, the Tigers had successfully driven the Sri Lankan government to the negotiating table and set up a mini Eelam state covering roughly 15 percent of the country's entire geographic territory. The Government had also resigned itself to accepting their key demands, when, ironically, things started falling apart, converting a possible victory into unmitigated disaster.

It is therefore not without reason that the US State Department has termed the LTTE as one of the most sophisticated, deadly and dangerous[1] and effective terrorist insurgencies in the world. The RAND Corporation Study which has quoted the US State Department in this manner is an extremely well researched work which has made an effort to analyse, amongst other issues, **quote**: "2. *Terrorist groups that may not be formally part of al-Qaeda but that have assimilated al-Qaeda's worldview and concept of mass casualty terrorist attacks.* This, we believe, is where the center of gravity of the current global terrorist threat lies," **unquote**. Needless to say, the LTTE fits snugly into this category. The US worry level has been enhanced by the fact that Sri Lankan Intelligence agencies (quoted in the study), affirm that KP[2] had established contact on behalf of the LTTE, with the al Qaeda, in Kabul, in 2001-02.

This chapter will therefore not only study the LTTE holistically, but also see it from the perspective of the USA in particular, and the Western world in general for the terror impact that this organization has had world wide, and how important it was, not just for Sri Lanka but the world at large, to have brought its activities to a halt. In specific, the chapter will examine the founding of the LTTE and its rise to power, its conflict with the Indian Peace Keeping Force (IPKF), and how the beginning of its eventual downfall can be traced, in retrospect, to the breaking away from the LTTE of Prabhakaran's close confidant, 'Colonel Karuna' in March 2004.

Thereafter, the organizational structure (military, administrative, political) will be seen. The role of women in the LTTE will also be examined as also certain other military organizations in the LTTE such as the Black Tigers and other LTTE formations. The reader will also be apprised in clinical detail about the attacks that the LTTE has carried out from 1983. The list commences with their deadliest attacks and is followed up by a chronological sequence of their attacks since 1983. It includes a thumbnail sketch of each attack, its target, location, dates and casualties caused. This will be followed up by a detailing of the Tigers' Air Force and Navy (Sea Tigers). Their operations and tactics will next be visited, as also the linkages that LTTE had forged with terror organizations world wide will also be touched, as also their proscription as a banned terror outfit worldwide. The human rights record of the LTTE will be seen next, including their horrific use of children in war, and, lastly, their proscription.

Founding of LTTE[3]

The LTTE was founded on May 5, 1976 by Vellupillai Prabhakaran. It was a successor to the *Tamil New Tigers* (TNT), a militant group most notable for the brutal and senseless assassination of the Mayor of Jaffna, Alfred Duraiappah in 1975. Prabhakaran sought to "refashion the old TNT/new LTTE into an elite, ruthlessly efficient, and highly professional fighting force", which, as terrorism expert Rohan Gunaratne notes, he did by "keeping [his] numbers small, maintaining a high standard of training, [and] enforcing discipline at all levels". The LTTE attracted many supporters among disenchanted Tamil youth. They carried out low-key attacks against various government targets, including policemen and local politicians.

As per the RAND[4] study, the LTTE developed as an extremist outgrowth of the Tamil United Liberation Front (TULF), a socio-political movement that was prepared to advance Tamil demands through the accepted channels of the Sri Lankan state. Rejecting this stance, a hard core of militants formed a variety of underground guerrilla organizations dedicated to armed struggle against the Colombo government during the mid-1970s. Initially, 42 militant groups were created, although five quickly achieved dominance. These were: the Tamil Eelam Liberation Organisation; the People's Liberation Organisation of Tamil Eelam; the Eelam People's Revolutionary Front; the Eelam Revolutionary Organisation of Students; and the Tamil New Tigers (TNT). Of these, it was the TNT that was to assume the early mantle of the Tamil struggle. Led by Chetti Thanabalasingham, the TNT embarked on a particularly intensive campaign of assassination and violence in 1974 that was variously designed to silence pro-government Tamils, eliminate informants, and disrupt police investigations into terrorist incidents and related criminal activities perpetrated under the group's auspices. Velupillai Prabhakaran, the TNT's second in command, assumed leadership of the organization, as mentioned above, in May 1976, when Thanabalasingham was arrested. He renamed the group the Liberation Tigers of Tamil Eelam (LTTE) and set about to reconfigure it in a manner consonant with his own ambitious intentions and ideological designs. Affirming the legitimacy of the Tamil struggle for independence on the basis of the Thimphu Principles and specifying that it was only through the LTTE that these objectives could be achieved, Prabhakaran fashioned a uniquely elite, ruthlessly efficient, and highly professional fighting force[5] that emphasized selective recruitment and an institutional ethos of unswerving dedication to the Eelam cause.

The LTTE carried out their first major attack on July 23, 1983, when they ambushed a Sri Lanka Army troop transport outside Jaffna. Thirteen Sri Lankan soldiers were killed in the attack, leading to the Black July riots against the Tamil community of Sri Lanka. The subsequent anger amongst the Tamil community resulted in numerous Tamil youths joining Tamil militant groups to fight the Sri Lankan government, in what is considered the start of the current insurgency in Sri Lanka.

Rise to Power[6]

Initially, LTTE operated in cooperation with other Tamil militant groups which shared their objectives, and in April 1984, the LTTE formally joined a common militant front, the Eelam National Liberation Front (ENLF), a union between LTTE, the Tamil Eelam Liberation Organization (TELO), the Eelam Revolutionary Organisation of Students (EROS), the People's Liberation Organisation of Tamil Eelam (PLOTE) and the Eelam People's Revolutionary Liberation Front (EPRLF).

TELO usually held the Indian view of problems and pushed for India's view during peace talks with Sri Lanka and other groups. LTTE denounced the TELO view and claimed that India was only acting in its own interest. As a result, in 1986, the LTTE broke from the ENLF. Soon fighting broke out between the TELO and the LTTE and clashes occurred over the next few months. As a result, almost the entire TELO leadership and many of the TELO militants were killed by the LTTE. The LTTE attacked training camps of the EPRLF a few months later, forcing it to withdraw entirely from the Jaffna peninsula. The LTTE then demanded that all remaining Tamil insurgents join the LTTE. Notices were issued to that effect in Jaffna and in Madras, India, where the Tamil groups were headquartered. With the major groups including the TELO and EPRLF eliminated, the remaining Tamil insurgent groups, numbering around 20, were then absorbed into the LTTE, making Jaffna an LTTE-dominated city.

The LTTE's practices, such as wearing a cyanide vial for consumption, if captured, appealed to the Tamil people as an indication of dedication and sacrifice. Another practice that increased support from the Tamil people was the LTTE's practice of taking an oath of loyalty which stated LTTE's goal of establishing a state for the Sri Lankan Tamils. In 1987, LTTE established the Black Tigers, a unit of LTTE responsible for conducting suicide attacks against political, economic and military targets, and launched its first suicide attack against a Sri Lanka Army camp, killing 40 soldiers.

IPKF Period[7]

In 1987, faced with growing anger among its own Tamils, and a flood of refugees, India intervened directly in the conflict for the first time, by initially airdropping food parcels into Jaffna. After subsequent negotiations, India and Sri Lanka entered into the Indo-Sri Lanka Accord. Though the conflict was between the Tamil and Sinhalese people, India and Sri Lanka signed the peace accord instead of India influencing both parties to sign a peace accord among themselves. The peace accord assigned a certain degree of regional autonomy in the Tamil areas with Eelam People's Revolutionary Liberation Front (EPRLF) controlling the regional council and called for the Tamil militant groups to lay down their arms. India was to send a peace keeping force, named the Indian Peace Keeping Force (IPKF), to Sri Lanka to enforce the disarmament and to watch over the regional council.

Although the accord was signed between the Governments of Sri Lanka and India, and the Tamil militant groups did not have a role in the agreement, most Tamil militant groups accepted it. The LTTE, however, rejected the accord because they opposed the candidate (who belonged to the EPRLF), for the appointment of chief administrative officer of the merged Northern and Eastern provinces.

Instead, the LTTE named three other candidates for the position, which India rejected. The LTTE subsequently refused to hand over their weapons to the IPKF.

Thus LTTE found itself engaged in military conflict with the Indian Army, and launched its first attack on an Indian Army rations truck on October 8, 1987, killing five Indian Para Commandos who were on board, by strapping burning tyres around their necks. The government of India decided that the IPKF should disarm the LTTE by force, and the Indian Army launched a number of assaults on the LTTE, to win control of the Jaffna peninsula from the LTTE. The conduct of this campaign, and the Indian army's subsequent anti-LTTE operations aroused strong feelings among many Tamils in Sri Lanka and in the state of Tamil Nadu.

After the IPKF Intervention[8]

The Indian intervention created strong feelings among the Sinhalese majority, as well. After fighting with the Tamil Tigers for over 2 years, the IPKF, which was estimated to have had a strength of well over 50,000 at its peak, left the country in 1990, upon the request of the Sri Lankan government. A later chapter (Chapter 15) will discuss the IPKF operations, their highs and lows and the Machiavellian politics that compelled the IPKF to fight literally with one hand tied behind its back all the time, from induction to deinduction.

Fighting continued throughout the 1990s, and was marked by two key assassinations carried out by the LTTE, that of former Indian Prime Minister Rajiv Gandhi in 1991 (covered in detail in Chapter 16), and Sri Lankan President Ranasinghe Premadasa in 1993, using suicide bombers in both occasions. The fighting briefly halted in 1994, following the election of Chandrika Kumaratunga as President of Sri Lanka and the onset of peace talks, but fighting resumed after the LTTE sank two Sri Lanka Navy boats in April 1995. In a series of military operations that followed, the Sri Lanka Army re-captured the Jaffna peninsula, the heartland of the Tamils in Sri Lanka. Further offensives followed over the next three years, and the military captured vast areas in the north of the country from the LTTE, including an area in the Wanni region, the town of Killinochchi and many smaller towns. However, from 1998 onward, the LTTE hit back, regaining control of these areas. This culminated in the capture of the strategically important Elephant Pass base complex, located at the entrance of the Jaffna Peninsula, in April 2000, after prolonged fighting against the Sri Lanka Army.

Mahattaya, a one-time deputy leader of LTTE, was accused of treason by the LTTE and killed in 1994. He is said to have collaborated with the Indian Research and Analysis Wing (RAW) to remove Prabhakaran from the LTTE leadership.

2001 Ceasefire

In 2001, the LTTE dropped its demand for a separate state. Instead, it stated that a form of regional autonomy would meet its demands. Following the landslide election defeat of Kumaratunga and the coming to power of Ranil Wickramasinghe in December 2001, the LTTE declared a unilateral ceasefire. The Sri Lankan Government agreed to the ceasefire. In March 2002, both sides signed an official Ceasefire Agreement (CFA). As part of the agreement, Norway and the other Nordic countries agreed to jointly monitor the ceasefire through the Sri Lanka Monitoring Mission. Six rounds of peace talks between the Government of Sri Lanka and the LTTE were held, but they were temporarily suspended after the LTTE pulled out of the talks in 2003 claiming "certain critical issues relating to the ongoing peace process."

In 2003, the LTTE proposed an Interim Self Governing Authority (ISGA). This move was welcomed by the international community, but rejected by the Sri Lankan President. In December 2005, the LTTE boycotted the 2005 Presidential election. While the LTTE claimed that the people under its control were free to vote, it is alleged that they used threats to prevent the population from voting. The new Government of Sri Lanka came into power in 2006 and demanded abrogation of the ceasefire agreement, stating that the only possible solution to the ethnic conflict was a military solution, and that the only way to achieve this was by eliminating the LTTE. Further peace talks were scheduled in Oslo, Norway, on June 8 and 9, 2006, but were cancelled when the LTTE refused to meet directly with the Government delegation, stating that its fighters were not being allowed safe passage to travel to the talks. Military confrontation continued into 2007 and 2008. In January 2008, the Government officially pulled out of the Cease Fire Agreement.

Dissension[9]

In the biggest show of dissent thus far from within the organization (the earlier, much advertised case having been that of Mahattaya in 1994), a senior LTTE commander, 'Colonel Karuna' (the nom de guerre of Vinayagamurthy Muralitharan) broke away from the LTTE in March 2004 and formed the Tamil Eela Makkal Viduthalai Pulikal (TEMVP) amid allegations that the northern Tamil commanders (who were intensely loyal to Prabhakaran) were overlooking the needs of the eastern LTTE Tamils. The LTTE leadership, in its turn, accused him of mishandling of funds and questioned him about his recent personal behaviour. He tried to take control of the eastern province from the LTTE, which caused clashes between the LTTE and TEMVP. The LTTE had suggested that TEMVP was backed by the government, and the Nordic SLMM monitors have corroborated this. What is really material is that this single event became the turning point of the LTTE; the beginning of the end for it. Colonel Karuna is currently the Minister for Relief and Rehabilitation in the Mahinda Rajapaksa Government and positively identified the dead body of Prabhakaran and other top LTTE deceased, after the shoot out at Nandhi Kadal in May 2009.

Military Defeat[10]

On January 2, 2009, the President of Sri Lanka, Mahinda Rajapaksa, announced that Sri Lankan troops had captured Killinochchi, the city which the LTTE had used for over a decade as its de facto administrative capital. It was stated that the loss of Killinochchi had caused a substantial dent in the LTTE's image. On January 25, 2009, SLA troops 'completely captured' Mullaithivu town, the last major LTTE stronghold. Top LTTE leader, Cheliyan, the second-in-command of the Sea Tigers, was killed in Kariyamullivaikkal on May 8, 2009, dealing another blow to the organization.

President Mahinda Rajapaksa declared military victory over the Tamil Tigers on May 19, 2009, after over 30 years of conflict with the LTTE. State-run television interrupted its regular programming and a government information department sent a text message to cell phones across the country with the news. Shortly thereafter, LTTE spokesman and key Prabhakaran aide, Selvarasa Pathmanathan (KP) conceded defeat saying in an email statement, "This battle has reached its bitter end".

Organisation and Activities[11]

The LTTE is organized into three main divisions: a military wing, a political wing and a fund-raising wing. A central governing body oversees all of the divisions, which was headed by Velupillai Prabhakaran until his death in May 2009.

Military

In the LTTE, recruits are instructed to be prepared to die for the cause, and are issued with a cyanide capsule to be swallowed in the case of capture. The LTTE also has a special squad of suicide bombers, the Black Tigers, which it deploys for critical missions. The military wing includes the following specific subdivisions, which are directly controlled and directed by the central governing body:

- *Sea Tigers* - an amphibious warfare unit focusing on utilization of naval firepower and logistics, mainly consisting of lightweight boats.

- *Air Tigers* - an airborne group, consisting of several lightweight aircraft. It is known to be the world's first air force controlled by an organization proscribed as terrorists.
- *Black Tigers* - a suicide commando unit, known to have caused deadly aftermaths from their attacks.

Sea Tigers

Colonel Soosai of the Sea Tigers

The Naval Wing of The LTTE – the Sea Tigers

"Geographically, the security of Tamil Eelam is interlinked with that of its seas. It's only when we are strong in the seas and break the dominance our enemy now has that we will be able to retain land areas we liberated and drive our enemies from our homeland." – Prabhakaran.

N. Manoharan, now Managing Editor of the respected Delhi based think tank, CLAWS, started his 2006 article on the Naval Wing of the LTTE[12] with the above, prescient, remarkably mature statement by Velupillai Prabhakaran. He writes that this observation by the late LTTE chief succinctly encapsulates the importance of naval power for the LTTE. This realization dawned on the Tigers when the Sri Lankan Navy successfully thwarted the LTTE's attempt to capture the strategic Elephant Pass in 1991. Pursuant to the above vision, the Sea Tigers were raised in July 1992. The Tigers captured Elephant Pass nine years later, in April 2000, by extensively using their naval wing – the Sea Tigers.

Coastal Sri Lankan Tamils, especially their fishing community locally known as Kariyar (to which Prabhakaran belonged), are traditionally expert boat builders and seafarers. It is perhaps this factor which was responsible for the LTTE building its naval wing at a faster pace from scratch. The Sea Tigers became a vital part of the LTTE's combat capability.

The Sea Tigers had sea-going units, onshore marine engineering and maintenance personnel, naval communications and intelligence cadres and the commando and Black Sea Tigers units. The LTTE craft vary from heavily armed gunboats, troop carriers to ocean-going supply vessels, interestingly designed and built indigenously. Some of the LTTE vessels are capable of gaining a top speed in excess of 50 knots during combat. The Sea Tigers reportedly possess radar-evading stealth boats (perhaps North Korean built) and were suspected to be going in for submarines. Major Sea Tiger bases and facilities are situated in and around the coasts of Mullaithivu and Mannar.

The major aim of the combat arm of the Sea Tigers was to engage the Sri Lankan Navy. Its sophisticated communication systems enabled it to launch multi-vessel 'wolf pack' attacks on Sri Lankan convoys. During conflict the naval wing was tasked with ferrying the LTTE cadre to appropriate places of conflict, when land route was unavailable. The Sea Tigers also defended its coastal areas to prevent the Sri Lankan Navy from landing its troops. The Sea Tigers were skilled in rescuing LTTE militants trapped in Sri Lankan Army-held territory.

Its diving unit was tasked to infiltrate harbours to lay mines, conduct reconnaissance and recover material from sunken naval craft. Naval commandos were meant for guerrilla raids behind Sri Lankan naval lines or gather intelligence or assault coastal targets. The Black Sea Tigers (suicide unit) was the most important arm of the LTTE's naval wing. This unit was initially established to challenge the technical superiority of the Sri Lankan Navy. Its boats were specially designed with a frame in the front of the boat bearing holding grapnels that fasten the boat to its target once they have collided. As per Iqbal Ithas,[13] the JDW Correspondent, Intelligence estimates suggest that the Black Sea Tiger strength was around 100-200 suicide cadres.

Supplies[14] : The supply unit was designed to keep the marine supply lines from overseas open for the LTTE. Its ocean-going vessels were capable of delivering everything the LTTE's growing conventional army needed, ranging from surface-to-air missiles and artillery pieces to medicines and special combat kits. Most of its operations were in the Indian Ocean, especially in the waters linking Southeast Asia and Northeastern Sri Lanka. The Sea Wing was estimated to have had around 10 freighters under 'Pan-Ho-Lib' flags (Panama, Honduras, Liberia), which mostly transport legitimate commercial goods for a charge. The *modus operandi* usually was to off-load the weapons in the high seas into small high speed boats and take them to jungle hideouts in LTTE controlled areas. The procurement of arms and other military supplies were taken care of by the LTTE support network under 'KP' in Southeast Asia. The important countries of operation included Thailand, Laos, Cambodia and Myanmar.

The Sea Tigers were led by Colonel Soosai. It is believed to have about 2,000 personnel and had become a potent threat to the Sri Lankan Navy at sea. According to a 2006 publication of the Woodrow Wilson School of Politics and International Studies, the Sea Tigers had destroyed 35-50 percent of the Sri Lankan Navy's coastal craft. It was also involved in gun running, piracy, movement of LTTE cadre, ferrying of arms and ammunition by a complex arrangement involving ship transfers.

Sea Piracy[15]

The LTTE has been accused of hijacking several vessels in waters outside Sri Lanka, including the *Irish Mona* (in August 1995), *Princess Wave* (in August 1996), *Athena* (in May 1997), *Misen* (in July 1997), *Morong Bong* (in July 1997), MV *Cordiality* (in September 1997), *Princess Kash* (in August 1998) and *MV Farah III* (December 2006).

Arms Smuggling[16]

The anti-rebel Mackenzie Institute claimed that one of LTTE's secretive international operations was the smuggling of weapons, explosives, and 'dual use' technologies. The part of the LTTE responsible for these activities was nicknamed *'KP Branch'*, taking the initials of its infamous high level operative, Kumara Pathmanathan (KP). The workers for the *KP Branch* were from outside the fighting wing of the LTTE, since the identities of those fighters were recorded and available to law enforcement and counter-intelligence agencies by India's Research and Analysis Wing (RAW), which had helped train many Tiger cadres in the early 1980s. The KP Branch operated secretively by having the minimum connection possible with the LTTE's other sections for further security. It handed over the arms shipments to a team of Sea Tigers to deliver them to the LTTE-dominated areas.

The Mackenzie Institute further claimed that in order to carry out the activities of international arms trafficking, the LTTE operated its own fleet of ocean-going vessels. These vessels only operated a certain period of time for the LTTE and in the remaining time they transported legitimate goods and raised hard cash for the purchase of weapons. The LTTE initially operated a shipping base in Myanmar, but was forced to leave due to diplomatic pressure. To overcome this loss, a new base was set up on Phuket Island, in Thailand.

The LTTE Navy, as per Sri Lanka, had a rudimentary 'submarine' available to it, which may have provided Prabhakaran an escape option from the Mullaithivu coastline under water, to escape the Sri Lankan Naval dragnet that was in place to support the final Army operations. No details are available as to whether this craft was operational. The submarine, is reported by the MoD[17] to have a capacity of accommodating a crew of three to four, and was found buried at a depth of 40 feet, 500 metres from the Mullaithivu coastline. This leads one to believe that the 'submarine' was probably a LTTE propaganda creation and did not have real capability for transportation underwater as has been claimed. Following its northern offensive, the Sri Lankan military reported that it had captured the Sea Tiger main base in Mullaithivu and several boat yards. In early February 2009, the military reported once again that it had captured the last major Sea Tiger base', killing three senior commanders in the process and thus limiting Sea Tiger operations. Several days later it was claimed that Sea Tigers leader Soosai and several top aides were killed in a Sri Lanka Air Force raid on a command centre.

The Air Wing of the LTTE – The Air Tigers

According to B.Raman, a noted analyst on strategic affairs, head of a Chennai-based think tank and an ex-senior Government functionary, the Sri Lanka Government got confirmation from the LTTE on a long-held suspicion, when, on November 27, 1998, " its Voice of Tigers clandestine radio station, in a broadcast on a function held in the Wanni area in memory of its cadres killed in terrorist operations, claimed that aircraft of the 'Air Tigers' had sprinkled flowers from the air on the memorial. It did not specify the number and whether they were fixed-wing planes or helicopters. Since then, there were periodic reports that the LTTE had managed to acquire abroad and smuggle to the Wanni area at least one light aircraft, but the Sri Lankan authorities kept denying these reports. What is new now is not that the LTTE has acquired aircraft for its air wing, which is at least seven years old, but that the Sri Lankan Government has, for the first time, officially admitted it and taken up the matter with the international community."[18]

The writer in his article of March 2007[19] noted that the "LTTE had successfully launched an aerial strike using modified light aircraft and improvised payloads against strategic gas and oil facilities this past weekend, the third such attack in just under a month." This rudimentary and highly effective Tiger Air Force had sent shockwaves through the government and the military brass in Colombo.

"In a world of terrorist networks and resistance organizations, the LTTE had employed very sophisticated tactics over the years, including the formation and use of their own Navy. Today, with the addition of a Tiger Air Force, the intractable war between Tamil separatists and the government in Colombo is set to enter a new phase. In fact, the Tigers have threatened more air strikes while Sri Lankan military strategists seek new tools to "neutralize" the threat – not an easy task. Tiger military spokesman Rasiah Ilanthiraiyan laughed off the threat by telling Reuters that the Sri Lankan military, "especially the air force, are adamantly trying to prove they will always seek a military solution." He added that as a result, "we have no other way than to take our own measures…there will definitely be more. We have no choice other than striking back." Now the LTTE has gone airborne. Experts speculate that the planes purchased abroad were most likely Czech in origin, subsequently disassembled for shipment through LTTE's vast network of merchant ships, and paid for by LTTE sympathizers living in the diaspora."

The LTTE acts as a 'think tank' for terrorists worldwide, constantly inventing new tactics that are so devastatingly effective; groups like Al Qaeda, Hezbollah, Hamas, Shining Path, and Chechen fighters are eager to integrate them into their organizations. From the use of female suicide bombers (made famous with the assassination of Indian Prime Minister Rajiv Gandhi in 1991) to the deployment of suicidal naval units – the Tigers are always on the cutting edge of the advancement of non-state terror and are, in fact, the only terrorist organization that has land, sea and air capabilities.

The Air Tigers[20] were overall believed to have operated five light aircraft. With the Air Tigers, LTTE became the first non-state organization to establish an air force. Although the Sri Lankan Army captured Kilinochi on January 2, 2009, it was not able to locate the LTTE aircraft. Later, two LTTE aircraft were shot down in Colombo during a suicide attack on the Sri Lanka Air Force headquarters and the Sri Lanka Air Force base hangars in Katunayake, Colombo.

Black Tigers[21]

A Suicide Commando Unit, Black Tigers, are was for carrying deadly attacks against the Sri Lankan Army and also politicians who opposed their movement of a separate state for the minority Tamils. The Black Tigers are the first to assassinate major political figures and have been known to have carried out around 100-200 successful missions, ranging from men to women, to eliminate enemies for the LTTE to advance and control territory. The LTTE pioneered the use of concealed suicide bomb vests. According to Jane's Information Group, the LTTE carried out 168 suicide attacks between 1980 and 2000 causing heavy damage on economic and military targets.

Many of these attacks involved military objectives in the north and east of the country, although civilians have been targeted on numerous occasions, including during a high profile attack on Colombo's International Airport in 2001 that caused damage to several commercial airliners and military jets, and killed 16 people. The LTTE was also responsible for a 1998 attack on the Buddhist shrine, and UNESCO world heritage site, Sri Dalada Maligawa in Kandy that killed 8 worshippers. The attack was symbolic in that the shrine, which houses a sacred tooth of the Buddha, is the holiest Buddhist shrine in Sri Lanka. Other Buddhist shrines have been attacked, notably the Sambuddhaloka Temple in Colombo that killed 9 worshippers.. The LTTE's Black Tigers have been attributed with the assassination of Rajiv Gandhi, who was killed in 1991 using a prototype suicide vest, and Ranasinghe Premadasa, assassinated in 1993.

The BBC[22] Correspondent in Northern Sri Lanka, Francis Harrison, reporting from the war zone in Northern Sri Lanka, in November 2002, wrote that suicide bombers from the Tamil Tiger rebel group appeared in public for the first time at a parade to commemorate fallen comrades in the civil war. The Tamil Tigers pioneered the art of suicide bombing with scores of assassinations of prominent politicians in Sri Lanka, as well as former Indian Prime Minister Rajiv Gandhi. Dressed in black uniforms with their heads masked to disguise their identities, 27 suicide bombers marched in parade along with other fighters.

This was the first time the Black Tigers, as they are known, had taken part in the annual events to honour those who had died fighting in the war. Speaking to the BBC, a member of the Tigers suicide squad explained why he had pledged to give his life. He said he had seen his relatives killed and wanted to show his strength to safeguard not only his family but his community. Refusing to give his name, the suicide bomber said he was not scared to die for the cause and although his parents did not know he was a member of the Black Tigers, they would be proud of his achievements when his time came.

The BBC report states that more than 240 Tamil men and women have carried out suicide attacks for the Tigers in the war. They also mentioned that the Black Sea Tiger suicide tactic of ramming explosives laden craft into naval vessels is a tactic they believe other armed groups around the world are now copying from them. And on land they are notorious for detonating suicide belts full of explosives in front of prime ministers and presidents.[23]

Administrative[24]

- *Political Wing of LTTE:* The Chief/Leader was Anton Balasingham, who also held a key influence in major peace talks with Sri Lanka and the third-party of Norway. After his death on December 14, 2006, B. Nadesan took over as political head and led the political wing of the LTTE.
- *Tiger Intelligence:* The intelligence wing, which helped the Liberation Tigers

of Tamil Eelam with exclusive missions such as radars and more to prepare the military for an attack. Pottu Amman, the leader of the Intelligence Wing was believed to be shot by the Sri Lankan Army on May 19th, 2009.

- *International Relations:* It is believed to be the only LTTE Wing to be standing after the Sri Lankan Army's final offensive. It was led by Selvarasa Pathmanathan from an unknown location, operating outside Sri Lanka/ Tamil Eelam. KP is since in Sri Lankan custody (As of November 2009 rumours are afloat about the revival of this wing).

Tiger Courts

The LTTE implemented a judicial system that consisted of courts to adjudicate in criminal and civil matters. The Tamil Eelam judicial system consisted of district courts, high courts, a supreme court and a court of appeal. The district courts handled civil and criminal cases. The two high courts handled criminal cases such as rape, murder, treason and arson. The Supreme Court had jurisdiction over the whole of Tamil Eelam.

Tiger Police

LTTE also established a police force. The Tamil Eelam police was the other key factor in maintaining law and order. The police was formed in 1991 and, prior to the 2009 offensive, had its headquarters at Kilinochi. Police stations were established in all areas controlled by the LTTE. The LTTE claimed that its police force was the reason for the low crime rate, but critics of the LTTE claim that the police force was an integrated arm of the LTTE armed force and that the crime rate was low as a result of LTTE authoritarian rule. However, everyone agrees the police force and the judicial system was the reason for a high degree of rule of law in the areas controlled by the LTTE.

Another state function of the LTTE administration was social welfare. This humanitarian assistance arm was funded by tax collection internally. LTTE also established an education and health sector that offered services to the people under their control. It also created a human rights organization, called Northeast Secretariat on Human Rights that functioned to advocate the rights of Tamils. The Planning and Development Secretariat (PDS) was established in 2004 which acted as a needs assessment body responsible for studying the needs for people and formulating a plan for effective action in areas that needed humanitarian assistance. There were also many civil servants who worked in the LTTE-controlled areas who were directed by the LTTE but paid by the Sri Lankan government. A customs service was operated at the 'border' by the Tamil Tigers.

Voice of Tigers

In addition to the civil administration, LTTE also ran its own radio and television stations. These entities were named the *Voice of Tigers* and *National Tamil Eelam Television* respectively. Both the radio and television channels were aired from the areas under LTTE control.

Bank of Tamileelam

LTTE also ran a bank named the Bank of Tamileelam which used the Sri Lankan rupee as its currency but offered higher interest rates than any bank on the island.

Political

The 2002 Cease Fire Agreement made the LTTE shift its struggle for self-determination from militant to more political means. The LTTE's own political wing was the result of this. This political wing also played a critical role in regard to both the peace process and local state building. However, LTTE's political wing did not participate in Sri Lankan parliamentary elections. The LTTE instead openly supported the Tamil National Alliance, which won overwhelmingly in 22 out of 25 electorates in the North-east and won over 90 percent of votes in the electoral district of Jaffna.

Religion

The Liberation Tigers of Tamil Eelam purports to be a secular organization, regarding the religious beliefs of its members as a private matter.

Sothiya Regiment of the LTTE – Female Soldiers

In 1984, LTTE created an all-female unit called the Freedom Birds (*Suthanthirap Paravaikal*). This unit was the first group of women to be given military training in India. The LTTE advocates equality for women from both male oppression and social oppression. This support for equality attracted many women into the LTTE ranks. As a result LTTE became the first Tamil militant group to employ women as soldiers in the battlefield. Tamil women believed that their participation in the armed struggle would bring them advantage in a future peaceful society and allow them to take part in 'liberating' their society. The proportion of female combatants was small until June 1990, but increased rapidly afterward. Freedom Birds' first operation was in October 1987 and the first

Women Soldiers in LTTE

woman combatant to die was 2nd Lt. Maalathi, on October 10, 1987, in an encounter with the IPKF at Kopai on the Jaffna peninsula. An estimated 4,000 women cadres have been killed since then, including over 100 in 'Black Tiger' suicide squads. Apart from military roles, the female soldiers also produced numerous publications and many of them are described as rich in culture and writing.

Other Formations

Charles Anthony Brigade	Jeyanthan Brigade	Sothiya Regiment
Maalathi Regiment	Kuti Sri Mortar Unit	Victor Anti Tank and Armoured Unit
Imran Pandiyan Unit	LTTE Anti-Aircraft Unit	Kittu Artillery Unit
Ponnamman Mining Unit	Ratha Regiment	

Links to Other Designated Terrorist Organizations

As early as the mid-1970s, LTTE rebels were widely known to have trained members of the Popular Front for the Liberation of Palestine in Southern Lebanon, where concepts of suicide bombings, taxation, and war memorials were imparted to PFLP fighters. After the 1990 assassination of Rajiv Gandhi, Indian government officials claimed to have discovered a covert link between the PLO and the LTTE: the PLO had pleaded for Mr. Gandhi to accept a proposal from the LTTE. This advice raised eyebrows at the time, but was largely ignored until his assassination shortly thereafter.

As late as 1998, the Tigers clearly stated:

> ... "The LTTE has resolved to work in solidarity with the world national liberation movements, socialist states, and international working class parties. We uphold an anti-imperialist policy and therefore we pledge our militant solidarity against western imperialism, neo-colonialists, Zionism, racism and other forces of reaction.

"In this connection, The *Westminster Journal* further states:

> "Intelligence agencies are well aware that the LTTE was involved in the 1990s in training the Moro Islamic Liberation Front (MILF) and the Abu Sayyaf Group (ASG) both of which are closely linked to al-Qaeda. In 1995 and 1998, an LTTE combat tactician and an LTTE explosives expert accompanying groups of al-Qaeda Arabs was recorded training members of MILF. In 1999, an LTTE combat tactician accompanying a group of Al-Qaeda Arabs was recorded training members of the ASG. At the apparent behest of Al-Qaeda,

the LTTE is recorded training members of Al Ummah (An Islamic terrorist group formed in India in 1992, believed to be responsible for bombings in southern India in 1998) in Tamil Nadu, India."

LTTE Tactics in Other Terrorist Organizations

Operations and Tactics of the LTTE

As noted earlier by the RAND Study[25] on the LTTE, it came to the conclusion that the LTTE was one of the most adept terrorist insurgencies in the world. The group had effectively fought the Sri Lankan armed forces (SLAF) to a standstill till around 2005, after which there was a perceptible decline in their capability and a corresponding increase in efficiency, intelligence and dynamism in the SLAF. At their peak, the Tigers repeatedly demonstrated an ability to operate along the entire guerrilla conflict spectrum from selective assassinations and targeted terrorist strikes to mobile hit-and-run attacks as well as full-scale, multiple battalion-sized assaults. Much of this success was due to a highly dynamic learning process that took advantage of the inherent weaknesses in the then Sri Lankan military and security establishment.

The RAND Study in its report felt that the weaknesses and associated failings of the then Sri Lankan Armed Forces (SLAF) provided the LTTE with a useful benchmark of what *not* to do in terms of combat readiness and effectiveness. Indeed the makeup of the group's military structure is exactly contrary to that of the Sri Lankan army. Tactically, the LTTE conspicuously exploited the outmoded doctrines of the SLAF to repeatedly confound Sri Lankan military offensives. Indeed, one of the main reasons the Sri Lankan Army failed to secure much of the north and east was due to its overwhelming reliance on set-piece, trench warfare. The Tigers quickly recognized that the best way to defeat this type of warfighting stance was first to monitor the combat readiness and deployment size of known defence lines using long-range reconnaissance and sabotage teams and then, based on this intelligence, to hit them with overwhelming artillery fire and battalion sized attack forces. Between 1995 and 2002, roughly 60 percent of all Sri Lankan field casualties resulted from this adaptive combination of low- and high-level assault modalities.

On an 'unconventional' level, the LTTE had developed highly effective (and feared) suicide wings to carry out selective assassinations, urban bombings, and sea-borne attacks. Located in both the Black Tigers and Sea Tigers, these cadres were responsible for well over 200 strikes since 1987, the vast bulk of which were successful in achieving their primary aim. Indeed until recently, the LTTE was unique among militant sub state entities around the globe in specifically institutionalizing martyrdom as a signature mode of attack and establishing this form of violence as not only 'normal' and positive but also the *sine qua non* of operational effectiveness. Boosting its tactical and operational base is part of the LTTE's active and innovative R&D agenda. The group demonstrated remarkable skill in this regard, particularly in the realms of suicide devices, standoff resources, and marine attack munitions.

The Tigers developed numerous technologies to avail martyr operations, ranging from bomb vests complete with primary, secondary, and even tertiary detonation switches – including one version that explodes when the wearer raises his or her arms in surrender – to specially equipped suicide boats, bicycles, and motorbikes. These delivery media are repeatedly tested and reconfigured in secure Tiger camps and are only actively deployed after they have demonstrated a high degree of effectiveness (generally upward of 90 percent). The LTTE has been even more adroit with surface and underwater combat innovation. The group is known to have fabricated at least two types of submersible, timer-activated explosive: a cylindrical bomb (roughly 60–90 centimetres in height) that can be suspended from a ship's propeller or rudder shaft and an improvised RDX slab that can be attached to a vessel's hull with a black glycerol mixture.

The Sea Tigers also manufactured a variety of attack, logistics, personnel, and multipurpose craft as well as stealth suicide boats especially equipped with angled metallic superstructures to reduce their radar cross-section. However, perhaps the most creative R&D effort was the attempt to construct two-man mini-submarines for releasing divers inside Sri Lankan harbours. Revelations that the LTTE was making concerted moves in this direction first broke in 2000 when a partially completed prototype was discovered at a Tamil-owned shipyard in Phuket. According to informed sources, the five-metre vessel, while rudimentary, was capable of remaining submerged for up to six hours (at speeds up to five knots) and could very well have served as a prototype for more advanced versions to attack operational naval surface ships.

Similarities in Attack Patterns with Other Proscribed Groups

Some of LTTE's attacks[26] in Sri Lanka have similarities to attacks by other proscribed groups. Some examples are:

- The similarities between previous LTTE attacks against Sri Lanka Navy ships and the Al-Qaeda attack on the USS *Cole* which killed 17 US Navy sailors. The incident has raised suspicions of connections between the two groups. The 'Maritime Intelligence Group' based in Washington DC claims to have unearthed substantial evidence that the LTTE trained Indonesian Islamists in the technique of maritime suicide bombings. The group, linked to al-Qaeda, is believed to have then passed the technique it learned from the LTTE to Al-Qaeda itself.

- The website 'South Asian Terrorism Portal' claimed that the LTTE provided forged passports to Ramzi Yousef, who was one of the planners of the first attack against the World Trade Center in New York in 1993. The allegation has been backed by the *Westminster Journal* as well.
- The website 'South Asian Terrorism Portal' also states that there are increasing intelligence reports that the LTTE was smuggling arms to various terrorist organizations, including Islamic groups in Pakistan and their counterparts in the Philippines, using their covert smuggling networks. The London-based International Institute for Strategic Studies found that the LTTE was building commercial links with al-Qaeda and other militants in Afghanistan, and that several cadres were spotted in Afghan militant camps.
- India's National Security Adviser, M K Narayanan, alleges that LTTE raised money by smuggling narcotics. A recent arrest of LTTE operatives in Colombia corroborates this claim.
- According to an 'anti-LTTE' website, Glen Jenvey, a former employee of the government of Sri Lanka and a specialist on international terrorism, claimed that al-Qaeda had copied most of its terror tactics from the LTTE[. He highlighted the LTTE as the mastermind that set the pattern for organizations like Al-Qaeda to pursue. The Maritime Intelligence Group in Washington DC even states that Al-Qaeda learned the tactic through LTTE contacts teaching Indonesians the methods.
- According to *Asian Tribune*, attacks on civilians in buses and trains in Sri Lanka were copied in the attack on public civilian transport during the July 2005 bombings in London.
- The LTTE's ethnic cleansing campaigns against Muslims in northern Sri Lanka from 1985-1992 provided the inspiration for, and model by which Kashmiri separatists would evict Hindus from Kashmir in late 1989-1990.

Human Rights Violations

The United States Department of State states that its reason for banning the LTTE as a proscribed terrorist group is based on allegations that it did not respect human rights and that it did not adhere to the standards of conduct expected of a resistance movement or what might be called 'freedom fighters'. The FBI has described the LTTE as "amongst the most dangerous and deadly extremist outfits in the world". Other countries have also proscribed LTTE under the same rationale. Numerous countries and international organizations have accused the LTTE of attacking civilians and recruiting children.

Attacks on Civilians

The LTTE launched attacks on civilian targets several times. Notable attacks include the Aranthalawa Massacre, Anuradhapura massacre, Kattankudy mosque massacre, Kebithigollewa massacre and the Dehiwala train bombing. Civilians weve also killed in attacks on economic targets, such as the Central Bank bombing.

Child Soldiers

The LTTE has been accused of recruiting and using child soldiers to fight against Sri Lankan government forces. The LTTE was accused of having up to 5,794 child soldiers in its ranks since 2001.

Amid international pressure, the LTTE announced in July 2003 that it would stop conscripting child soldiers, but both UNICEF and Human Rights Watch have accused it of reneging on its promises, and of conscripting Tamil children orphaned by the tsunami.

Ethnic Cleansing

The LTTE is responsible for forcibly removing, or 'ethnically cleansing', Sinhalese and Muslim inhabitants from areas under its control, and using violence against those who refused to leave. The evictions happened in the north in 1990 and the east in 1992. Ironically, however, Muslim and Tamil communities in the North of Sri Lanka had participated together in the early days of the Tamil movement, and Muslim ironmongers in Mannar fashioned weapons for the LTTE, and local Tamil leaders were disturbed at the LTTE's call for the eviction of Muslims. However, as Tamil intellectuals began viewing Muslims as outsiders, rather than a part of the Tamil nation as they had been referred to previously, the LTTE undertook its anti-Muslim campaigns.

Beginning in 1985, the LTTE forcibly occupied 35,000 acres of Muslim-owned farmland in the north of Sri Lanka, before systematically evicting the Muslims from areas under its control. Although anti-Muslim pogroms had occurred in the north and east of Sri Lanka since 1985, the LTTE embarked on a campaign to expel Muslims from the North in 1989. The first eviction notice was sent to the

Muslims of Chavakacheri on October 15, 1989, after the LTTE had entered the local mosque and threatened Muslims a few weeks earlier. Afterward, the houses of evicted Muslims were ransacked and looted.

Ethnic cleansing culminated on October 30, 1990, when the LTTE forcibly expelled the entire Muslim population of Jaffna. LTTE commanders from the east announced at 7:30 A.M. that all Muslims in Jaffna were to report to Osmania stadium, where they were to be addressed by two LTTE leaders, Karikalana and Anjaneyar. After listening to the leaders denigrate Muslims for allegedly attacking Tamils in the east, the leaders explained to the community that they had two hours to evacuate the city. The community was released from the stadium at 10 A.M., and was only allowed to carry 500 rupees, while the rest of their possessions were seized by the LTTE after they were forced to report to LTTE checkpoints upon exiting Jaffna. In total, over 12,700 Muslim families, roughly 75,000 people, were forcibly evicted from LTTE-controlled areas in the Northern Province.

In 1992, the LTTE embarked on a campaign to create a contiguous Tamil-Hindu-Christian homeland that stretched from the north of Sri Lanka, and downwards along the Eastern Coast. A large Tamil-speaking Muslim population inhabited a narrow strip of land between the two entities, and so a pattern of 'ethnic cleansing' emerged in Eastern Sri Lanka, as was already done in the north. The LTTE unleashed violence against the Muslims of Alinchipothanai and killed 69 Muslim villagers. This led to a retaliatory violence against the Tamils in Muthugala, where 49 Tamils were killed allegedly by the Muslim home guards. Later in the year, the LTTE attacked four Muslim villages (Palliyagodalla, Akbarpuram, Ahmedpuram and Pangurana) and killed 187 Muslims. In 2002, the LTTE leader Vellupillai Prabhakaran had formally apologized for the expulsion of Muslims from the north and asked them to return. Some families have returned and re-opened the Osmaniya College and two mosques are functioning now. Since the apology, Tamil Net, which is widely seen as an LTTE mouthpiece, has featured numerous stories of Muslim civilians coming under attack from Sinhalese forces. However, the stories may simply reflect crime, and not the ethnic hatred that Tamil Net suggests.

Proscription as a Terrorist Group

32 countries have listed the LTTE as a terrorist organization. Canada (since 2006) does not grant residency to LTTE members on the grounds that they have participated in crimes against humanity.

The first country to ban the LTTE was its early ally, India. The Indian change of policy came gradually, starting with the IPKF-LTTE conflict, and culminating with the assassination of Rajiv Gandhi. India opposes the new state Tamil Eelam that LTTE want to establish, saying that it would lead to Tamil Nadu's separation from India though the leaders of Tamil Nadu opposed it. Sri Lanka itself lifted the ban on the LTTE before signing the ceasefire agreement in 2002. This was a prerequisite set by the LTTE for the signing of the agreement. The European Union banned the LTTE as a terrorist organization on May 17, 2006.

Attacks Attributed to the LTTE

The following is a list of attacks attributed to the Liberation Tigers of Tamil Eelam (LTTE), commonly known as the Tamil Tigers. The LTTE is a separatist militant group that has been fighting for a separate Tamil state in the north and east of Sri Lanka since 1976, and it has carried out numerous attacks against civilian, military, political, and religious targets. It has been banned as a terrorist organization by 30 countries, including the United States, Canada, India and the 27 member nations of the European Union.

Deadliest Attacks

Attack	Date	Location	Death Toll
2006 Digampathana truck bombing	October 16, 2006	Digampathana, Dambulla North Central Province (Army Personnel)	92–103
Kebithigollewa massacre	June 15, 2006	Kebithigollewa, Northern Province	66
Gonagala massacre	September 18, 1999	Gonagala, Eastern Province	54
Dehiwala train bombing	July 24, 1996	Dehiwala, Western Province	64
Central Bank bombing	January 31, 1996	Colombo	91
October 1995 Eastern Sri Lanka massacres	October 16, 1995	Villages in eastern Sri Lanka	120
Kallarawa massacre	May 25, 1995	Kallarawa, Eastern Province	42
Palliyagodella massacre	October 15, 1991	Palliyagodella, Eastern Province	109
Kattankudi mosque massacre	August 04, 1990	Kattankudy, Eastern Province	147
Aranthalawa Massacre	July 02, 1987	Aranthalawa, North Central Province	35
Habarana bus massacre	April 17, 1987	Habarana, North Central Province	127
Anuradhapura massacre	May 14, 1985	Anuradhapura, North Central Province	146
Kent and Dollar Farm massacres	November 30, 1984	Kent and Dollar Farm, Mullaitivu	62
Suicide Air Raid on Colombo	February 20, 2009	Colombo, Western Province	2

LTTE ATTACKS SINCE 1983 IN CHRONOLOGICAL SEQUENCE

1983

July 23 **Black July:** 13 soldiers are killed in an LTTE ambush in Jaffna, sparking anti-Tamil riots that cause the death of approximately 4000 Tamils across Sri Lanka during four days, in what would be later labeled as Black July. Jaffna, Jaffna District

1984

1984 marked the intensification of the war between the Tamil separatists and the Sri Lankan government, as well as the first reports of civilian massacres by the LTTE.

Nov 11 **Dollar Farm Massacre:** A group of armed LTTE cadres attacked the Dollar Farm village in the night and massacred at least 33 civilians including a large number of children and women. Mullaitivu District, Northern Province, Sri Lanka

Nov 30 **Kent Farm Massacre:** LTTE terrorists launched their second night raid targeting the Kent Farm village and massacred 29 civilians, including women and children, looted their belongings and set fire to their houses. Mullaitivu District, Northern Province, Sri Lanka

Dec 1 **Kokilai Massacre:** LTTE cadres kill eleven Sinhalese civilians in the fishing village of Kokilai. Kokkilai, Mullaitivu District.

1985

1985 marked a major escalation of hostilities. For the first time the LTTE attacked a major Sinhalese majority town killing 146 unarmed civilians. The impact of this attack was felt across the island and received world wide attention.

May 5 **Wilpattu Village Massacre:** A group of armed LTTE terrorists raided an ancient Sinhalese village in Wilpattu in Anuradhapura district killing 18 villagers including women and children. Wilpattu, Anuradhapura District.

May 14 **Anuradhapura Massacre:** LTTE gunmen shoot dead 146 Sinhalese civilians and injure 85 others as they were praying at a sacred Buddhist shrine in Anuradhapura. Anuradhapura, Anuradhapura District

May 14 LTTE cadres shoot dead 18 Sinhalese civilians in the Wilpattu forest reserve while they are fleeing from the massacre of 146 civilians earlier in the day (see Anuradhapura massacre). Wilpattu forest reserve.

May 30 LTTE cadres shoot and kill five Sinhalese civilians in the villages of Mahandapura and Dehiwatta. People of these villages had previously received numerous threats from the LTTE associates. This massacre was part of a series of massacres aimed at displacing Sinhalese from the North East of Sri Lanka. Mahandapura and Dehiwatta

June 4 **Dehiwatta Village Massacre:** Over 100 LTTE terrorists armed with sharp weapons butchered 15 villagers of Dehiwatta in Polonnaruwa district on their sleeping mats. Majority of the victims were women and children.
Dehiwatta, Polonnaruwa District

June 11 13 Sinhalese civilians are shot dead by LTTE gunmen in Dehiwatta.

August 2 LTTE cadres shot dead three Sinhalese Buddhist monks and three civilians, while they were worshipping at the Ruhunu Somavathiya Temple. Thrikonamadu, Polonnaruwa

August 14 **Aranthalawa Village Massacre:** A group of armed LTTE terrorists raided a Sinhalese village at Aranthalawa, in Ampara district. The terrorists butchered 7 villagers after torturing them. Aranthalawa, Ampara District.

August 18 **Namalwatta Village Massacre I:** A group of LTTE terrorists armed with sharp weapons hacked 7 innocent villagers including children after torturing them. Namalwatta, Trincomalee.

Nov 7 **Namalwatta Village Massacre II:** LTTE cadres raided Namalwatta village for the second time and executed 10 villagers including women and children. Namalwatta, Trincomalee.

Dec 20 Six Madhu pilgrims, abducted by the LTTE on 12/12/85 were executed. Mannar, Mannar District.

1986

Feb 2 **Kantale Village Massacre:** A group LTTE terrorists armed with small arms and swords raided Kantale village, the terrorists tortured and hacked 19 civilians still on their sleeping mats. Majority of the victims were women and children Kantale, Trincomalee District.

Feb 19 When refugees from Serunuwara, Dehiwatta, were being escorted by army personnel along Ella/Kantalai road, the LTTE exploded a mine killing 35 civilians and four army personnel. Sittaru Kantalai, Trincomalee District.

May 3 **Air Lanka Flight UL512:** An LTTE bomb explodes aboard an Air Lanka flight carrying mainly French, British and Japanese tourists killing 21 (including 13 foreigners – of whom 2 British, 2 German, 3 French, 2 Japanese, 1 Maldivian and 1 Pakistani) and injuring 41 at Bandaranaike International Airport. Katunayake, Western Province.

May 5 **Kinniya Village Massacre:** A group of LTTE terrorists came hunting for Muslim civilians at Kinniya village and slaughtered four civilians after brutally torturing them. Kinniya, Trincomalee District.

May 25 **Mahadivulwewa Village Massacre:** LTTE cadres shot dead 20 Sinhalese and set fire to 20 houses. Mahadivulwewa, Anuradhapura District.

June 2 **Trincomalee 3rd Mile Post:** LTTE terrorists armed with firearms, swords, and knives stormed civilian houses at 3rd Mile Post, Trincomalee, and butchered 10 civilians, including women and children. Trincomalee.

June 4 **Andankulam Village Massacre:** LTTE terrorists attacked Andankulam, a Sinhala village and 17–20 civilians, including Ven. Bakamune Subaddalanakara Thero, mostly women and children were hacked to death after undergoing brutal torture at the hands of the terrorists. Andankulam, Trincomalee District.

June 11 Trincomalee. Two bombs exploded by the LTTE almost simultaneously in two buses in front of the Bank of Ceylon and in close proximity to the SP office along Inner Harbour Road. They were on their way to Kantalai and Colombo respectively. 22 people were killed in the explosions; 75 others were injured. Trincomalee.

June 21 **Wilgamwehera Village Massacre:** LTTE terrorists stormed Wilgamwehera hamlet in Trincomalee district and butchered 9 civilians including children. Wilgamwehera, Trincomalee District.

June 25 Bomb exploded in a vehicle by the LTTE killed 16 Sinhalese. Sittaru, Kantalai.

July 8 **Monkey Bridge Village Massacre:** LTTE cadres shot dead 15 Sinhalese villagers. Monkey Bridge, Trincomalee District.

July 9 **Mullipothana Village Massacre:** LTTE terrorists armed with swords, machetes and clubs stormed Mullipothana village during night hours killing 16 civilians, largely women and children. Mullipothana, Trincomalee District.

July 13 **Pavakkulam Village Massacre:** Four LTTE cadres who had come in a jeep to tract No.16, Pavakkulam, killed eleven civilians (two Sinhalese and nine Tamils). Pavakkulam, Trincomalee District.

July 19 **Beruwil & Wadigawewa Village Massacre:** Over 100 LTTE terrorists armed with sharp weapons, clubs and small arms stormed Beruwil and Waigawewa villages. 17 villagers were killed including women and children. At least 5 others suffered serious cut wounds. Beruwil & Wilgamwehera, Trincomalee District.

July 19 LTTE cadres shot dead twelve Sinhalese villagers. Wadigawewa, North Central Province.

July 22 LTTE cadres exploded a land-mine on a civilian bus, killing 32 Sinhalese civilians and injuring 20 others. Mammaduwa, Vavuniya District.

July 24 A bomb exploded inside a bus proceeding from Vavuniya to Anuradhapura; killing 13 passengers and injuring 40 others.

July 24 About 50 LTTE cadres entered Damana, a Sinhalese village, and killed nine persons; another 13 were injured. Damana, Central Province.

Sep 17 **Massacre in the Sugar Crop:** LTTE cadres entered block No.4 Sugar Corp., Kantalai, and ten civilians were shot. Kantalai, Trincomalee District.

Sep 17 After massacring 10 villagers in Kantale, the same terrorists group attacked the village of Wadigawewa. 12 villagers including women and children were killed. Wadigawewa, Trincomalee District.

1987

Feb 07 Arantalawa, Ampara: LTTE cadres killed 28 villagers by slashing their necks.

March 07 Awarantalawa, Vavuniya: LTTE exploded a land-mine where troops were proceeding, killing seven soldiers, four NAF soldiers and six civilians.

March 22 Serunuwara Horowpathana: LTTE cadres shot dead 26 Sinhalese villagers.

April 16 Habarana, Trincomalee: LTTE cadres shot dead 127 Sinhalese civilians, including 31 police and security force personnel who were travelling in buses to Trincomalee.

April 21 Central Bus Stand, Pettah: LTTE operatives exploded a bomb, killing 113 civilians, two policemen and a soldier; 298 others were injured.

April 21 Jayanthipura Trincomalee: LTTE cadres shot dead 15 Sinhalese villagers.

May 29 Kadawathmadu, Polonnaruwa: LTTE cadres shot dead seven Sinhalese villagers.

June 02 A bus carrying Buddhist monks in Arantalawa was stopped by the LTTE who then killed 32 Buddhist monks (including Chief Priest Ven. Hegoda Indrasara) who were passengers of this bus. Only one monk survived this massacre. This was the first massacre of Buddhist monks in modern Sri Lankan history.

June 11 Veppankulam Trincomalee Private van No. 38 Sri 496 proceeding from Horowpathana to Trincomalee was blasted by a pressure mine by the LTTE, killing one soldier and 13 civilians.

June 12	Godapotta, Medirigiriya Polonnaruwa: About 175 villagers had gathered to discuss a new temple. LTTE fighters surrounded the temple and attacked them, killing eight villagers and a soldier. Six persons were injured.
July 05	In the first ever suicide attack by the LTTE Black Tigers 'Captain Miller', drives a small truck laden with explosives into a Sri Lanka Army camp in Nelliady, Jaffna peninsula, killing himself and over 50 Sri Lankan soldiers.
Oct 06	Batticaloa: LTTE cadres shot dead 18 Sinhalese civilians.
Oct 06	Sagarapura, Kuchchuveli Trincomalee: LTTE cadres shot dead 27 Sinhalese villagers.
Oct 06	Thalawai Eravur: LTTE cadres shot dead 25 Sinhalese settlers.
Oct 06	Valaichchenai Batticaloa: The night-mail train from Batticaloa was stopped by LTTE cadres and 40 Sinhalese passengers were killed.
Oct 07	Pottuvil Monargala Road: LTTE cadres shot dead 25 Sinhalese passengers, who were travelling by bus. They also killed five motor-cyclists who came along the same route.
Oct 10	Gantalawa Kantalai: LTTE cadres shot dead ten Sinhalese villagers.
Oct 15	Ella, Kantalai Road, Trincomalee: LTTE cadres shot dead 14 Sinhalese passengers travelling on two lorries.
Oct 16	Pulimodai Trincomalee: LTTE cadres stopped a private bus, took out Sinhalese persons and killed eleven of them including three policemen.
Oct 19	Kalkudah Batticaloa: Private bus 23 - 1182 transporting Tamil passengers got caught on an LTTE land-mine, killing 40 persons and an IPKF soldier.
Nov 09	Maradana, Colombo: LTTE operatives exploded a bomb in a vehicle: 23 civilians killed, 106 were injured, 15 were shot dead.
Nov 11	Kalkuda, Batticaloa: Seven Sinhalese persons selling fish were shot dead by the LTTE.
Nov 12	Cheddikulam, Vavuniya: A van transporting passengers was blasted by an LTTE land-mine explosion, killing twelve Tamil persons and 13 PLOTE members.
Dec 15	Devalagodella, Polonnaruwa: The LTTE attacked Devalagodella and Somavathiya villages, killing nine villagers.
Dec 22	Morawewa, Trincomalee: LTTE cadres abducted five Sinhalese and a Tamil, who were fishing in Morawewa Tank and subsequently killed them.
Dec 31	Mahadivulwewa Trincomalee: LTTE cadres shot dead ten villagers and burnt 15 houses.

1988

March 02	Morawewa, Trincomalee: LTTE cadres shot dead 14 Sinhalese villagers.
March 11	Suhadagama Horowpathana Anuradhapura: A group of LTTE cadres attacked a private bus, 22 Sri 2218, at Suhadagamaw with small arms and grenades, killing 19 passengers and injuring nine others.
March 14	Galmitiyawa, Kantalai: LTTE cadres shot dead 13 Sinhalese villagers at Galmitiyawa.
March 15	Kivulkade, Morawewa, Trincomalee: Two groups of LTTE operatives entered the village and killed seven Sinhalese villagers.
March 17	Deegavapiya, Damana, Ampara: LTTE cadres hacked to death 13 Sinhalese villagers.

March 22	Pudukulam, Vavuniya: Between ten and 15 LTTE cadres attacked the Sinhalese village and killed six villagers. Another three were injured.
March 22	Medavachchi-kulam Vavuniya: LTTE cadres shot dead nine Sinhalese villagers.
March 29	Wewalketiya: A LTTE bomb exploded inside CTB bus 29 Sri 9037 Anuradhapura which was proceeding from Horowpathana to Medavachchiya, killing nine passengers and injuring 14 others.
March 31	Saindamaradu, Kalmunai: LTTE cadres attacked the village, killing ten Muslims and seven Tamils.
April 08	Horowpathana, Meegaswewa, Anuradhapura: LTTE gunmen killed 14 Sinhalese.
May 01	Sittaru Kantalai, Trincomalee: LTTE cadres exploded a land-mine on a CTB bus killing twelve Sinhalese, nine Muslims and five others, who were not identified.
July 28	Ethawetunawewa, Weli Oya: LTTE operatives hacked to death 16 Sinhalese villagers.
August 16	Trincomalee (opposite Clock Tower): LTTE cadres exploded a bomb, killing six Sinhalese, two Muslims, one Tamil and a soldier; 19 persons sustained injuries.
August 25	Marawila, Polonnaruwa: LTTE cadres killed eleven civilians by cutting their necks.
September 10	16th Colony, Central Camp Ampara: LTTE cadres shot dead seven Sinhalese and four Tamils.
October 09	Mahakongaskada Medavachchiya: LTTE cadres shot dead 44 Sinhalese villagers and set fire to eleven houses.
November 14	Paniketiyawa, Gomarakadawela Trincomalee: LTTE cadres shot dead 28 Sinhalese, including two security force personnel.

1989

Jan 17	Maharambekulam Village Massacre
Feb 2	Bogamuyaya Village Massacre
Feb 11	Dutuwewa Village Massacre. Dutuwewa, Polonnaruwa District
Feb 11	Singhapura Village Massacre. Singhapura, Sri Lanka
Feb 27	Borawewa Village Bloodbath. Borawewa, Polonnaruwa District.
August 17	Nochchikulam Village Massacre: An IDE explosion, killing eight civilians and injuring four others. Nochchikulam, Vavuniya District.

1990

June 10	The LTTE signals the breakdown of ceasefire talks by overrunning police stations located throughout the North East of Sri Lanka. The LTTE massacred most of the 400 to 600 police officers captured after they had surrendered to the LTTE during this attack.
June 10	Over 400 unarmed police officers are shot dead by the LTTE in police Stations across eastern Sri Lanka.

June 15	11 soldiers are killed in Kalmunai by the LTTE and their bodies are desecrated.
July 23	Veeracholai, Batticaloa: LTTE cadres killed eight persons, thought to be Muslims and hanged them on trees.
July 24	Damminna, Aralaganvila Polonnaruwa: LTTE cadres hacked to death eight Sinhalese villagers.
July 25	Wan Ela, Trincomalee: LTTE cadres hacked to death nine Sinhalese villagers who were cutting firewood.
July 26	Thammannaelawaka, Medavachchiya: LTTE cadres hacked and shot to death 19 Sinhalese and set fire to 30 houses.
July 30	Akkaraipattu, Batticaloa: LTTE cadres shot dead 14 Muslims in the town.
July 31	Podankadu, Peraru, Kantalai: Ten Tamil civilians were killed by unidentified gunmen.
August 03	Over 30 Tamil Tiger cadres attacked four Muslim mosques in Kattankudy in Batticaloa district, killing over 147 Muslims who were praying in the mosques.
August 05	Mulliyankadu, Ampara: LTTE cadres killed 17 Muslim farmers working in a paddy-field.
August 06	Ampara: LTTE cadres killed 33 Muslim farmers working in a paddy-field.
August 07	Bandaraduwa, Uhana, Ampara: About 40 LTTE cadres went to a Sinhalese village and killed 30 Sinhalese and injured four.
August 08	Navagamuwa, Anuradhapura: LTTE cadres attacked a Sinhalese village and killed seven civilians; four persons were injured.
August 11	Division 3 & 6 Eravur: LTTE cadres attacked Div. 3 & 6, Eravur, killing 116 Muslims and injuring 20 others.
August 13	15th Mile Post, Pulmoddai, Weli Oya: Twenty-five civilians who were travelling in a lorry from Negombo at Kokuvil were ambushed by LTTE cadres, who killed 14 of them.
August 13	Awarantalawa, Vavuniya: A Muslim village adjoining a Sinhalese village was attacked by LTTE cadres; nine Muslims and one Sinhalese were killed. Three others were injured.
September 13	Poonani, Batticaloa: LTTE cadres hacked to death seven Muslim civilians and injured one.
September 19	Vellamundal, Puttalam: LTTE cadres killed 23 Sinhalese and set fire to eleven houses at the fishing village.
September 21	Pudukudiyirippu, Ampara: LTTE cadres attacked the village killing 15 Muslims and injuring eleven.
September 30	Peraweltalawa, Maha Oya, Ampara: LTTE cadres hacked to death nine Sinhalese villagers.
October	The LTTE expelled, within 48 hours, 80,000 Muslims living under their control in the northern districts of the island: Jaffna, Kilinochchi, Mullaittivu, and Mannar. Each civilian was allowed to carry only 150 Sri Lankan rupees when they were expelled from LTTE areas.

October 02 Vahalkada, Ampara: LTTE cadres shot dead seven Sinhalese.

October 11 Arugambay, Ampara: LTTE cadres shot dead nine Muslims.

October 23 Thanthirimalai, Anuradhapura: LTTE cadres killed eight Sinhalese and two home guards.

November 01 Halambawewa, Sinhapura, Weli Oya: LTTE cadres attacked the village and killed ten Sinhalese.

1991

January 23 Bogamuyaya Maha Oya, Ampara: LTTE cadres hacked to death 25 Sinhalese villagers and injured nine others; four subsequently succumbed to their injuries.

March 02 At least 19 people, including Sri Lanka's Deputy Defence Minister, Ranjan Wijeratne killed in an LTTE car bomb explosion in Colombo. A further 73 people injured.

March 24 Bogamuyaya, Akkaraipattu: Bomb explosion carried out by LTTE at Fish Market, Akkaraipattu, killing nine Muslims and injuring 32 others.

March 31 Irudayapuram, Batticaloa: LTTE cadres shot dead eight civilians at the market in the night.

April 03 Keviliya, Foul Point, Trincomalee: LTTE cadres in two boats surrounded several boats and opened fire at the fishermen. Ten dead bodies and eleven injured were found. Sixteen were missing. The missing persons were either taken away or drowned after being shot.

April 14 Ethicality, Monaragala: LTTE cadres hacked to death 17 Sinhalese villagers and injured another.

April 20 Niyadella, Okkampitiya, Moneragala: LTTE cadres attacked the village and hacked and shot to death 21 men, women and children.

May 19 Erakkamam, Ampara, LTTE cadres attacked five Muslims and two Sinhalese persons, whilst they were returning from the paddy-field, killing six persons and injuring one.

May 21 LTTE suicide bomber Thenmuli Rajaratnam assassinated former Indian Prime Minister Rajiv Gandhi while the latter was campaigning for a parliamentary candidate in Tamil Nadu, also killing an additional 13 civilians. Following the assassination, seven suspected LTTE activists committed suicide after being surrounded by police. In June 2006, the LTTE issued a formal apology for this action. However, the Indian government quickly responded saying forgiving Tamil Tigers for the 1991 killing of former Prime Minister Rajiv Gandhi would amount to endorsing their ideology of terror.

May 20 Malwatta, Sammanthurai, Ampara: LTTE cadres fired on a group of Muslims who were returning from the paddy-field in a tractor; nine Muslims were killed and two injured.

June Colombo: 12 killed and 85 civilians injured after a suicide bombing outside the Joint Operations Command (JOC) building on Flower Road, Colombo.

June 12	Kokkadicholai, Batticaloa: LTTE bomb explosion in Manmunai ferry kills ten civilians.
June 24	Weligahakandiya Batticaloa: LTTE cadres abducted and killed eight Sinhalese and injured one Tamil.
June 27	Lahugala, Ampara: LTTE cadres exploded two claymore mines and opened fire at the passengers of a private bus; 16 civilians were killed and eight wounded.
July	The army's Elephant Pass base, which controls access to the Jaffna peninsula, is surrounded by 5,000 LTTE cadres. More than 2,000 died on both sides in the month-long siege, before 10,000 government troops arrived to relieve the base.
July 06	Pudur, Jaffna: LTTE cadres cut and killed nine Muslims and moved towards the Mahaweli river bank and cut to death another eight persons, injuring four others. One of the injured succumbed to his injuries. Total killed: 16 Muslims and two Sinhalese.
July 06	Karapola, Manampitiya, Polonnaruwa: Nine Sinhala fishermen were abducted by LTTE cadres and killed.
August 08	Sammanthurai, Batticaloa: Six Muslim farmers killed by LTTE cadres.
September 19	Palliyagodella, Polonnaruwa: LTTE cadres attacked a Muslim village, killing 13 Muslims and injuring six others.
October 24	Iqbal Nagar: LTTE cadres who were in ambush, fired at a civilian van killing three Tamils and three Muslims.

1992

January 26	Between Arantalawa and Borapola, an LTTE mine explosion killed nine civilians in a bus.
April 10	Ampara Town: A LTTE bomb exploded in a bus causing the death of 25 civilians and injuring 33 civilians. One policeman was also killed and two army personnel wounded.
April 10	Maharagama: A LTTE car bomb exploded, causing the death of eight civilians; one policeman and 23 civilians were injured.
April 29	LTTE cadres kill 69 Muslim civilians including 5 infants. Reprisal attacks by Muslim civilians and home guards results in the death of 49 Tamil men.
April 29	Alinchipothana, Polonnaruwa: LTTE cadres attacked Alinchipothana village, killing 56 Muslims and injuring 15.
June 02	209th Mile Post-Ampara: A group of LTTE cadres stopped a bus, opened fire, killing 14 civilians, one policeman, and injuring two civilians and one policeman.
July 06	Parayankaulam, Vavuniya: LTTE cadres publicly shot dead ten Tamil lorry drivers and a woman, alleging that they had passed information to the security forces.
July 15	Kirankulam, Batticaloa: LTTE cadres attacked a civilian bus proceeding from Kathankudy towards Kalmunai, killing 19 Muslims and injuring seven Muslims.

July 21	Parangiyamadu, Batticaloa: LTTE cadres stopped a train, ordered the passengers to get down and opened fire at the Muslim passengers: seven Muslims were killed and four Muslims were injured.
August 30	Trincomalee Town: A LTTE bomb planted in a private bus at the bus-stand exploded, killing nine civilians and injuring 34 (including four soldiers, two reserve policemen).
September 01	Saindamaradu, Kalmunai: A LTTE bomb fixed to a push-cycle carrying an ice-cream container, exploded at the market, killing 22 Muslims and injuring 67 others.
September 10	Kiliveddi Point, Trincomalee: LTTE operatives blasted a ferry across Allai Tank and killed 22 soldiers and seven civilians, and injured one soldier and two civilians.
October 01	Konwewa Weli Oya: LTTE cadres fired and threw grenades at villagers, killing 15 civilians and injuring nine others.
October 15	Palliyagodella Polonnaruwa: LTTE cadres attacked a Muslim village and shot and hacked to death 182 civilians (171 of them were Muslims), twelve policemen and eight soldiers; 83 others were injured.
November 16	An anti-rebel website claimed that the Sri Lanka Navy Commander Vice Admiral Clancy Fernando and four others are killed by an LTTE suicide bomber.

1993

May 01	**Assassination of Ranasinghe Premadasa:** Sri Lankan President Ranasinghe Premadasa killed in LTTE suicide bomb attack at a May Day Rally. Colombo, Colombo District.
July 25	**Janakapura Village massacre:** The LTTE raids a Sinhalese village and kills nine civilians by means of stabbing, shooting and blowing up with grenades. Janakapura.
Nov 10	**Attack on Pooneryn Army Camp:** Eight officers and 233 soldiers were declared killed in action in LTTE's attack on the Pooneryn defences. The LTTE also executed 200 soldiers captured during this attack on the Pooneryn army camp. Pooneryn army camp, Pooneryn.

1994

Jan 19	**Rambewa Bus Bombing:** A LTTE bomb exploded in a private bus carrying civilians from Sripura to Anuradhapura, causing the death of ten Sinhalese civilians and injuring 51. Rambewa, Anuradhapura District.
March 16	**Kudiramalai Fishing Boats Attack:** LTTE cadres attacked about ten fishing boats, causing the death of 17 fishermen and injuring three; five fishermen were reported missing. Off Kudiramalai, Puttalam District.
Oct 24	**Assassination of Gamini Dissanayake:** Sri Lankan presidential candidate and opposition leader Gamini Dissanayake is killed by an LTTE suicide bomber who explodes herself at a campaign rally in Colombo. At least 50 others were killed in the blast and a further 75 were seriously hurt. Colombo, Colombo District.

1995

May 25	During the Kallarawa massacre 42 civilians including six children are killed by the LTTE in an attack on Kallarawa fishing village.
May 25	LTTE cadres attack a fishing village in Kallarawa, and hack and shot to death 42 civilians (22 males, 12 females and eight children).
August 07	Colombo: An LTTE suicide bomber explodes a suicide rickshaw killing 22 civilians.
October 20	Kolonnawa, Colombo: The LTTE attacked the oil storage complexes at Kolonnawa and Orugodawatta. At least three suicide bombers fought their way into the tanks and blew themselves up destroying the tanks. LTTE lost four cadres in the action while killing 22 security personnel and destroying diesel, kerosene, aviation fuel and crude oil worth over US $10 million.
October 21	Mangalagama: LTTE cadres kill 16 civilians.
October 25	Panama: LTTE cadres kill twelve Sinhala farmers.
November 11	Colombo: A LTTE suicide bomber causes an explosion near the Slave Island railway station resulting in the death of 15 children and two soldiers.
November 24	Colombo: An attack by two LTTE female suicide bombers on the Sri Lanka Army Headquarters results in the death of 16 people.
December 11	Colombo: Two LTTE suicide bombers blow themselves up at the Army Headquarters, resulting in the deaths of 15 civilians and three soldiers.
December 23	The LTTE attacked an army detachment in Batticaloa district, killing 32 troops. Military sources reported that more than 60 rebels were killed.

1996

January 31	An attack by the LTTE on the Colombo Central Bank killed 90 and injured a further 1,400 civilians, damaging other buildings in the process. It was the most deadly LTTE attack on a civilian target in the history of the group's operations.
January 31	Bombing of Sri Lanka's Central Bank resulting in 91 civilian deaths.
March 19	29 Tamil civilians killed by LTTE, as they were accused of being traitors and giving information to security forces.
June 11	Lunuoya the LTTE kills 14 civilians. According to Amnesty International, this attack was reportedly led by an LTTE member whose family had been killed in communal violence, after the LTTE attacked a police post. The main target of this appears to have been the family of those thought to have been responsible for the killing of this LTTE member's family.
July 04	Jaffna: An attack by an LTTE suicide bomber on a Sri Lankan minister results in the death of 25 people.
July 18	The LTTE overruns the Sri Lanka Army camp at Mullaitivu. The number of Sri Lankan soldiers killed in action and missing in action from this attack was over 1200. The LTTE appear to have burnt alive hundreds of Sri Lankan soldiers who had surrendered during the attack on the Mullaitivu army camp.

July 24	The LTTE bombs a passenger train killing 70 civilians.
July 24	Dehiwala train bombing where the LTTE exploded 4 bombs on Colombo-Alutgama train at Dehiwala killing between 60 and 70 civilians. The technique of simultaneously exploding multiple bombs in several carriages was used during this attack.

1997

Feb 10	**Oddamavadi Village Attack:** A group LTTE terrorists attacked Oddamavadi Muslim village in Batticaloa. The terrorists shot 5 civilians to death and wounded 3 others. Oddamavadi, Batticaloa District.
May 12	**Morawewa Village Attack:** LTTE terrorists attacked the police station of Morawewa and the village in Trincomalee. The terrorists butchered 5 civilians in this attack. Morawewa, Trincomalee District.
July 2	**Erakkandy Village Massacre:** Over 100 LTTE terrorists wielding sharp weapons, clubs and firearms stormed Erakkandy Muslim village in Trincomalee and butchered 34 civilians. Erakkandy, Trincomalee District.
Oct 15	**1997 Colombo World Trade Centre Bombing:** An LTTE bomb exploded at the Colombo World Trade Centre, killing 13 and injuring hundreds. Colombo, Colombo District.

1998

January 25	Four likely members of the Black Tiger squad drove an explosives-laden truck into the Sri Dalada Maligawa (or "Temple of the Tooth") in Kandy, a major Buddhist shrine, killing seven and injuring 25. The attack took place just days before foreign dignitaries were expected to attend celebrations of the fiftieth anniversary of Sri Lankan independence at the temple.
January 25	Four members of the Black Tiger squad drive an explosives-laden truck into a major Buddhist shrine, killing seven and injuring 25. The Maligawa is one of the most sacred Buddhist shrines in the world, and is recognized as a UNESCO World Heritage Site.
March 05	The LTTE is blamed for two bomb explosions aboard buses in Colombo killing thirty-two civilians and injuring 252 others.
May 14	A member of the Black Tiger squad jumped in front of a vehicle carrying Sri Lankan Brigadier Larry Wijeratne and detonated explosives, killing the general and two guards. Wijeratne was the commander of Sri Lankan forces in the Point Pedro area of the Jaffna peninsula in the Tamil-inhabited north of the country. Press reports described the assassination as an 'serious blow' to the government's efforts in the area.
August 29	The LTTE shoot down a AN-24 Lionair Flight 602 with 55 passengers (including 48 Tamils) and crew while it was flying over LTTE held territory. Everyone on board is killed.
September	In a massive LTTE offensive 1,500 soldiers are killed (Battle of Kilinochchi), 3,000 wounded and 500 are missing.

1999

June 02	Eleven Sinhalese civilians were murdered at Inginiyagala.
July 29	An LTTE suicide bomber killed Sri Lankan Tamil MP Dr. Neelan Thiruchelvam along with two others. Six civilians were injured. At the time of his death Dr. Neelan Thiruchelvam was working on a constitutional package aimed at ending the decades long ethnic conflict in Sri Lanka.
September 18	LTTE cadres massacre at least 50 Sinhalese civilians in three villages in Ampara District.
November 01	An LTTE attack on an army camp at Oddusuddan results in an SLA defeat with 800 soldiers killed or missing and another 1,200 deserted.
Dec.11–Jan.02, 2000	212 soldiers are killed in heavy fighting. Also another 37 are missing and 2,118 are wounded.
December 18	A LTTE suicide bomber kills 23 civilians in an attempt to kill Sri Lankan president Kumaratunga at a pre-election rally.
December 18	In Colombo, LTTE suicide bomber Skandaraja Ashoka kills eleven people and retired Sri Lanka Army Major General Lucky Algama.

2000

January 05	An LTTE suicide bomber blows herself up outside the office of the Prime Minister of Sri Lanka killing 13 civilians and three police officers.
January 07	An LTTE suicide bomber kills Sri Lankan Industrial Minister C.V. Gunaratne and 24 civilians.
January 27	LTTE bomb a post office killing 11 and injuring 70.
March 11	14 civilians and six police die when four LTTE suicide bombers attempt to assassinate the defence minister. 46 others are injured.
April 22	The LTTE overrun the most important military base in the Northern Province, the Elephant Pass base.
May 18	An LTTE bomber killed 23 and injured 70 at a Buddhist temple in Batticaloa during celebrations of the Vesak holiday.
May 17	The LTTE detonate a bomb hidden inside an ice-cream box on a bicycle during celebrations to mark the holiest day of the Buddhist calendar, Vesak, killing over 20 people and injuring 75.
June 26	LTTE suicide boats sink a chartered private ship M.V. Uhana. Five civilian crew and three navy personnel die.
September 15	An anti-rebel website claimed that in Colombo a suicide bomber explodes in front of the main government hospital in Colombo resulting in seven civilian deaths. 28 civilians are injured.
October 03	An anti-rebel website claimed that a LTTE bomb killed parliamentary candidate Mohammed Baitullah and more than twenty others in Mutur. At least 49 others were injured.
October 05	An anti-rebel website claimed that in Medawacchchiya, Anuradhapura an attack by an LTTE suicide bomber on the Health and Indigenous Medicine Deputy Minister Tissa Karaliyadda results in the death of seven civilians and injuries to 40 civilians.

2001

July 24	**Bandaranaike Airport Attack:** An LTTE 14-man suicide squad attacked a Sri Lanka Air Force base and the adjoining Bandaranaike International Airport. They destroyed many aircraft, crippling the country's economy and reducing tourism. Katunayake, Western Province.

2005

August 12	**Assassination of Lakshman Kadirgamar:** Lakshman Kadirgamar, the foreign minister of Sri Lanka and an ethnic Tamil was shot by an alleged LTTE sniper. Colombo, Colombo District.

2006

January 07	A suspected LTTE fishing boat loaded with explosives detonates and destroys a Sri Lankan navy boat as it leaves the port of Trincomalee, killing 13 sailors.
March 01	Five civilians die in suspected LTTE mine explosion.
April 23	The LTTE kill six Sinhalese civilians including two 15 year old children in the village of Gomarankadawala in the Trincomalee district.
April 25	A suicide bomber, believed to belong to the LTTE, attempts to kill Lieutenant General Sarath Fonseka, seriously injuring him while killing eight others and injuring thirty more. The explosives were disguised as the late stages of pregnancy, and the bomber was originally believed to be pregnant, although subsequent medical tests have been inconclusive.
May 11	The Liberation Tigers of Tamil Eelam Sea Tigers attacks and sink one Sri Lanka Navy vessel while seriously damaging another. The attack is ruled as a grave violation of the Cease Fire Agreement by the Sri Lanka Monitoring Mission. In response, LTTE threatened the truce monitors not to be aboard naval vessels. 18 sailors perish on the Sri Lankan patrol boat, and an unknown number of Sea Tiger cadres also die in the attack. The fact that the lives of two Sri Lanka Monitoring Mission monitors on board these ships were endangered by this attack triggered the European Union decision to ban the LTTE.
May 27	The award-winning author Nihal de Silva and seven Sri Lankan tourists were killed by a supposed LTTE land mine in Wilpattu National Park. The explosion took place near Tamil held territory in the northern part of the country. Before a 2002 cease fire agreement, rebels used the park as a hiding place. It is unclear whether the mine was planted before or after the cease fire agreement.
May 29	Thirteen farm workers were cut and shot in a village around Welikanda in Polonnaruva. The government suspected the LTTE was responsible, while the LTTE responded that they had no involvement and that they were falsely implicated. Furthermore, the LTTE condemned this attack.
May 30	An anti-rebel website claimed that the LTTE cadres killed twelve Sinhalese villagers working at an irrigation canal construction site in Omadiyamadu, close to the uncleared areas of Welikanda in Polonnaruva district.

June 15	The LTTE blow up a civilian bus killing 68, including 10 children and three pregnant women. Approximately 60 more are injured.
June 15	The LTTE bombs a bus carrying 140 civilians in Kebithigollewa, in northeastern Sri Lanka. The blast results in the death of 68 civilians including 15 school children, and injures 78 others. It was caused by two claymore mines placed side by side on the bus by LTTE cadres, which spraying the packed bus with millions of ball bearings upon manual detonation.
June 26	The third highest ranking Sri Lankan military officer, Major General Parami Kulatunga was wounded in an attack by the LTTE and died after being taken to the hospital. Two other military escorts and a passerby were also killed.
September 18	LTTE cadres massacre ten innocent Muslims at Pottuvil in the Eastern province. The sole survivor of the attack confirms it was carried out by LTTE cadres.
October 16	In the deadliest ever suicide attack by the LTTE in Sri Lanka, a suicide bomber in a truck kills 103 sailors on buses going or returning from leave at a transit point and wounds over 150 other sailors. Several civilians may also have died.
October 16	In the deadliest suicide attack in Sri Lanka to date, a suicide bomber in a truck kills 103 Sri Lanka Navy sailors on buses going or returning from leave at a transit point and wounds over 150 other sailors. Several civilians may also have died.
December 01	An LTTE suicide bomber triggers the explosives packed into a vehicle in Colombo as a five car convoy carrying Sri Lankan Defense Secretary Gotabaya Rajapaksa passes by, in an attempt to assassinate him. Secretary Rajapaksa escapes unharmed, although two people are killed and 14 others are wounded, mostly civilians who were passing by the site.

2007

January 05	Nittambuwa: The LTTE is the only suspect in bomb blast on a city bus carrying more than 80 civilians. The resulting explosion kills six civilians and wounds 63, ten of them seriously. The bus was bombed during the evening rush-hour near Nittambuwa town, 40 km (25 miles) north-east of Colombo. It followed a threat issued by the LTTE that they will carry out revenge attacks for air raids by the Sri Lanka Air Force.
January 06	Peraliya: A suspected LTTE suicide bomber detonates herself inside a Colombo–Matara passenger bus. 16 civilians are killed and more than 50 are injured. These attacks on buses appear to be a fulfillment of threats made by the LTTE.
February 07	Batticaloa: Rev. Selliah Parameswaran Kurukkal, the head priest of the Santhiveli Pilleyar Kovil and a father of three, who blessed President Mahinda Rajapaksa during the President's visit to Vakarai four days previously, is forcibly dragged out of his residence and shot dead by

gunmen from the LTTE. The gunmen had mentioned that they were from the LTTE and they needed to question the Poosari in connection with the garlanding of the President. It is also suggested he had been targeted because he had co-operated with the security forces in order to help civilians flee the fighting around Vakarai.

March 09 Puttalam: Eight people who entered the Wilpattu National Park to investigate the grievances of the local population over wild elephant attacks, including the Sri Lanka Army Area Commander, the head Park Warden and three park rangers, are ambushed and massacred by the LTTE.

March 26 The LTTE mount their first air strike, bombing a government-controlled military airbase. The attack leaves three killed and 19 wounded.

March 29 Tamil Nadu, India: LTTE cadres kill five Indian fishermen off the coast of Tamil Nadu and kidnap twelve others. An anonymous caller initially attempts to blame the incidents on the Sri Lanka Navy.

April 01 Eravur, Batticaloa: LTTE cadres massacre six aid workers who were constructing a housing scheme named '*Village of Hope*' for Tamil children orphaned by the 2004 Asian Tsunami. Another three aid workers suffer serious gunshot injuries following the shooting at close range which took place at 8.15 pm local time.

April 02 Ampara: The LTTE bombs a civilian bus in eastern Sri Lanka, killing at least 16 civilians, and wounding 25 others. Among the dead are eleven women, three men and two boys.

April 05 Polonnaruva: In the third attack on civilians in a week, LTTE cadres shoot dead four Sinhalese farmers.

April 07 Piramanalankulam, Vavuniya: In the second such incident in five days, the LTTE bomb a civilian bus travelling along the Vavuniya–Mannar main road at 7:30 am, killing eight and wounding a further 26 people.

April 12 Avarantalawa, Vavuniya: Suspected LTTE raid a village at around 4:45 pm (local time) and shoot dead seven people, six women and one man, on the eve of the traditional New Year.

April 23 Vavuniya: The Sri Lankan Defence Ministry claimed that the LTTE cadres bombed a civilian bus travelling near the town of Vavuniya killing five passengers and wounding 35.

April 24 The LTTE mounted a second air strike on Palaly, the main government-controlled military airbase in Northern Jaffna.

April 29 Two fuel facilities were bombed by the LTTE during an air raid which they said was in response to an army strike on their positions.

May 24 Colombo: The Sri Lankan Army claimed that it suspects Tamil Tigers exploded an IED fixed on a motorbike in Colombo targeting a bus transporting Sri Lankan Army personnel killing one soldier and wounding six people, including three civilians.

May 27 Thirukkovil: The Sri Lankan Military said Tamil Tiger rebels set off a road side bomb blast blowing up a truck killing three civilians.

May 28	Rathmalana: The Sri Lankan Military and a doctor claimed that the Tamil Tigers detonated a bomb targeting a truck carrying Sri Lanka Police Special Task Force (STF) personnel at Belk Kade junction, in Rathmalana during the evening, killing seven civilians and injuring more than 39 people, including seven STF personal. Amongst the dead was one pregnant mother.
July 16	Trincomalee: Suspected Tamil Tigers gunned down Eastern province chief secretary Herath Abeyweera at around 5:30 p.m. local time (12.00 GMT).
August 20	Vavuniya: Sri Lanka military claimed that Tamil Tiger rebels in a jeep opened fire on the police checkpoint in Vavuniya district, killing four home guards including three female guards and one civilian.
September 22	Trincomalee: The Sri Lankan military claimed that suspected Tamil Tigers detonate a mine targeting a bus carrying civilians in Trincomalee district killing the driver and wounding two others.
September 27	Jaffna: At least two civilians were killed and about fifteen were injured, including two policemen when LTTE rebels triggered a road side bomb targeting a police road patrol vehicle at Chunnakam, Jaffna market area around 10.30 a.m. local time (0500 GMT).
October 22	LTTE attacked Anuradhapura Airbase destroying more than 20 military aircraft.
November 26	Group of LTTE cadres shot and killed four Sinhalese farmers, including one woman, at Mahawilachchiya, Anuradhapura.
November 28	Colombo: A suspected LTTE cadre blows herself up in front of the office of Douglas Devananda, the leader of the Eelam People's Democratic Party, in an attempt to assassinate him. Devananda escapes unhurt, but his personal secretary is killed and two of his security personnel are seriously injured.
November 28	Colombo: An LTTE parcel bomb blows up a Department Store in Colombo killing 20 civilians. Amnesty International asked the LTTE to comply with international law and halt such attacks.

2008

January 01	Colombo: A former minister and a Member of Parliament belonging to the UNP for Colombo District T. Maheswaran was shot by a gunman while attending the New Year prayers at Kotahena, Sivam Kovil, around 10:35 local time (05:05 GMT) and later succumbed to his injuries at the Colombo General Hospital along with one Hindu pilgrim who was also attending the prayers. UNP parliamentarians Johnston Fernando and Dayasiri Jayasekara accused the current government as responsible by saying that T. Maheswaran's plan to reveal the Jaffna situation led to his murder. The government has denied any responsibility. However, the Council on Foreign Relations claimed that the LTTE was suspected. To the accusation that Douglas Devananda, a cabinet minister and leader of the EPDP political party was involved in his murder and had previously

threatened T. Maheswaran, Douglas had denied any responsibility. Later the government of Sri Lanka claimed that the suspected gunmen worked for the state. The suspected gunman was a security guard for Minister Douglas Devananda and for the victim – Maheswaran.

January 02 Colombo: A bomb attack outside the Nippon Hotel in the Slave Island district, aimed at a Sri Lankan Army bus, killed at least four people, including a soldier and three civilians, and injured 28 others, Sri Lankan defence and hospital officials said. The Defence Ministry blamed the rebel Liberation Tigers of Tamil Eelam for the attack.

January 08 Ja-Ela: A non-cabinet Minister of Nation Building and a Member of Parliament of Sri Lanka, D. M. Dassanayake died of injuries sustained in a roadside bomb attack in Ja-Ela, twelve miles (19 km) north of Colombo along with one of his body guards. The attack injured ten others. LTTE blamed for this assassination.

January 16 Buttala: A roadside bomb targeting a passenger bus packed with civilians, killing 27 civilians including three schoolchildren and wounding 67 others, 240 km (150 miles) south-east of the capital, Colombo. This attack took place on the same day that a ceasefire ended between the Tamil Tigers and the government of Sri Lanka. Also, after the blast, gunmen had started shooting passengers as they tried to flee. According to the Sri Lankan Defence Ministry, the bus was hit by a powerful Claymore-type mine which was packed with explosives and ball-bearings. The Sri Lankan Defence Ministry blames the LTTE.

February 02 Dambulla: A bomb blast was occurred in a passenger bus, 150 kilometres (93 miles) north of the island's capital killing 20 people and injuring 50 more. The Sri Lankan government has blamed the LTTE for this attack.

February 03 Colombo: A suicide bomber exploded herself on broad a train at the main railway station in Colombo Fort, killing eleven people and wounding 97 others. Killed in the incident were seven school children of the baseball team of D. S. Senanayake College and their coach.

February 23 Mount Lavinia: A bomb went off in a bus in the suburban town of Mount Lavinia, 10 kilometres (six miles) south of the capital of Colombo, wounding at least 18 people including seven women and an 8-month-old infant. The Government blamed the Tamil Tigers for it.

February 23 Batticaloa: A suspected Tamil Tiger suicide bomber blew himself up in east Sri Lanka on Sunday killing two members of a regional political party.

February 29 Colombo: A suicide bomber exploded himself wounding seven that included three policemen and four civilians, when Sri Lanka Police attempted to search his house during a search and cordon operation by police aimed at flushing out Tamil Tiger rebels seeking to mount attacks in the capital.

March 02	Vavuniya: A roadside bomb exploded wounding four policemen and six civilians in a northern city of Sri Lanka. Sri Lankan Military blames the LTTE.
March 10	Colombo: A bomb hidden in a roadside flowerpot in Sri Lanka's capital exploded, killing one person and injuring six others, including four children who were on their way to school. The Government blamed the Tamil Tigers.
April 06	Colombo: A suicide bomber killed 14 people at an opening ceremony for a marathon race, including a government minister who was nearing the starting line with a flag and a former Olympian. More than 90 others were wounded in the attack.
April 25	Colombo: A parcel bomb explodes inside a bus in the residential suburb of Piliyandala, killing 24 and wounding 52.
May 16	Colombo: A LTTE suicide bomber on a motorcycle packed with explosives rammed into a bus carrying a police riot squad, killing 13 people which included 11 police personnel and 2 civilians, and wounding 95.
May 26	Dehiwala: A bomb exploded inside a crowded train in Dehiwala station, killing 8 people and wounding 67. The same place or very close to that place where the LTTE's Dehiwala train bombing in 1996, which resulted in 64 deaths and 400 wounded.
June 04	Wellawatte: A bomb exploded between the railway tracks and hit a packed commuter train at 0710 local time between the Dehiwala and Wellawatte railway stations, injuring at least 24 people. The incident happened after one week in the same area. The Police said they had captured the two suspects on the same day.
June 06	Moratuwa: A roadside bomb exploded targeting a passenger bus during the rush hour, killing 23 civilians and wounding 80 more. The Sri Lankan Government blames the LTTE. Pollgolla, Kandy: A bomb blast occurred on a passenger bus, killing 2 civilians and wounding 20. The Sri Lankan Government blamed the LTTE.
June 16	Vavuniya: Suspected LTTE suicide bomber on a motorcycle detonated explosives in front of a police office killing 12 policemen including 4 female police constables and wounded 40 others including school children.

<u>2009</u>

Feb 20	**Suicide air raid on Colombo:** The LTTE launched an unsuccessful kamikaze style suicide attack targeting locations in and around Colombo. Colombo, Colombo District.
Feb 22	**Kirimetiyagara Village Massacre:** The Sri Lanka Defence Ministry claimed that 10 people were killed by LTTE. Kirimetiyagara, Gampaha District.
April 12	**Mahagodayaya massacre:** 9 people were killed including 2 children. Mahagodaya, Moneragala district.

Endnotes

1. Rabasa, Angel; Chalk, Peter; Cragin, Jim; Daly, Sara A.; Gregg, Heather S. Karasik, Theodore W. O'Brien; Kevin A.; and Rosenau, William. "Beyond Al-Qaeda: The Outer Rings of the Terrorist Universe." RAND Study Part 2. <http://www.rand.org/pubs/monographs/2006/RAND_MG430.pdf>
2. Ibid.
3. "Liberation Tigers of Tamil Eelam."<http://en.wikipedia.org/wiki/Liberation_Tigers_of_Tamil_Eelam>
4. Rabasa, Angel; Chalk, Peter; Cragin, Jim; Daly, Sara A.; Gregg, Heather S. Karasik; Theodore W. O'Brien; Kevin A. and Rosenau, William. "Beyond Al-Qaeda: The Outer Rings of the Terrorist Universe." RAND Study Part 2. <http://www.rand.org/pubs/monographs/2006/RAND_MG430.pdf>
5. Ibid.
6. "Liberation Tigers of Tamil Eelam."<http://en.wikipedia.org/wiki/Liberation_Tigers_of_Tamil_Eelam>
7. Ibid.
8. Ibid.
9. Ibid.
10. Ibid.
11. Ibid.
12. Manoharan, N. Senior Fellow, IPCS. Excerpted from "Tigers with Fins: Naval Wing of the LTTE." Article #1757. June 1, 2005. <http://www.ipcs.org/article_details.php?articleNo=1757
13. Athas, Iqbal. JDW Correspondent. Battles Highlight Sea Tigers' Capabilities. September 29, 2006.<http://www.janes.com/security/international_security/news/jdw/jdw060929_1_n.shtml>
14. Manoharan, N. Senior Fellow, IPCS. Excerpted from "Tigers with Fins: Naval Wing of the LTTE." Article #1757. June 1, 2005. <http://www.ipcs.org/article_details.php?articleNo=1757
15. "Liberation Tigers of Tamil Eelam."<http://en.wikipedia.org/wiki/Liberation_Tigers_of_Tamil_Eelam>
16. Ibid.
17. "Sri Lankan Troops Recover LTTE Submarine." July 19, 2009. <http://www.dnaindia.com/world/report_sri-lankan-troops-recover-ltte-submarine_1275399>
18. Raman, B. "The World's First Terrorist Air Force." Paper No. 1398. June 2, 2005.<http://www.southasiaanalysis.org/papers14/paper1398.html>
19. Shtender-Auerbach, Micheal. "What Happens When a 'Poor Man's Air Force' Goes Airborne?" The Century Foundation. March 5, 2007. Michael Shtender-Auerbach is a Program Officer and Associate Director of the Prospects for Peace Initiative at The Century Foundation. <http://www.tcf.org/list.asp?type=TN&pubid=1569>
20. "Liberation Tigers of Tamil Eelam."<http://en.wikipedia.org/wiki/Liberation_Tigers_of_Tamil_Eelam>
21. Ibid.
22. Harrison, Francis. BBC Correspondent. "Black Tigers Appear in Public." November 26, 2002.<http://news.bbc.co.uk/2/hi/south_asia/2516263.stm>

23. Ibid.
24. "Liberation Tigers of Tamil Eelam."<http://en.wikipedia.org/wiki/Liberation_Tigers_of_Tamil_Eelam>
25. "Beyond Al-Qaeda: The Outer Rings of the Terrorist Universe." RAND Study Part 2. the entire section titled "Operations and Tactics of the LTTE" has been updated to tune in with the current realities, but excerpted from this excellent RAND Study. <http://www.rand.org/pubs/monographs/2006/RAND_MG430.pdf>
26. "Liberation Tigers of Tamil Eelam."<http://en.wikipedia.org/wiki/Liberation_Tigers_of_Tamil_Eelam>

References

1. Tharoor, Ishaan (3 February 2009). "How Sri Lanka Tamed Its Tigers". *Time.* http://www.time.com/time/world/article/0,8599,1876556,00.html.
2. "*The Final Countdown*". Ministry of Defence.
3. Mountlake, Simon (27 January 2009). "Sri Lanka nears victory in long war with Tamil Tigers". *Christian Science Monitor.* http://www.csmonitor.com/2009/0127/p06s01-wosc.html.
4. "President to announce end of war". *Times Online.* 2009-05-17. http://www.sundaytimes.lk/090517/News/sundaytimesnews_01.html.
5. Gunaratna, Rohan, "The Rebellion in Sri Lanka: Sparrow Tactics to Guerrilla Warfare (1971–1996)," p. 13.
6. "Tamil Militant Groups". *Sri Lanka: A Country Study.* 1988. http://countrystudies.us/sri-lanka/72.htm.
7. Hellmann-rajanayagam, D. (1994). *The Tamil Tigers: Armed Struggle for Identity.* Franz Steiner Verlag. p. 164. ISBN 978-3-515-06530-6.
8. M.R. Narayan Swamy (August 1995). *Tigers of Lanka: from Boys to Guerrillas.* South Asia Books. ISBN 978-81-220-0386-4.
9. Roberts, M. (2005). "Tamil Tiger 'Martyrs': Regenerating Divine Potency?". *Studies in Conflict & Terrorism* **28** (6): 493–514.
10. "Karuna removed from the LTTE". Tamil Net report. March 6, 2004. http://www.tamilnet.com/art.html?catid=13&artid=11391.
11. Asif, Fuard (2009-09-22). "Tigers go kamikaze but attacks fail". *The Sunday Times.* http://www.sundaytimes.lk/090222/News/sundaytimesnews_02.html.
12. "Battle Progress Map". Sri Lanka Ministry of Defence. 5 February 2009. http://www.defence.lk/orbat/Default.asp.
13. "OP FOR". http://op-for.com/cia_sri_lanka.jpg.
14. Stokke, K. (2006). "Building the Tamil Eelam State: emerging state institutions and forms of governance in LTTE-controlled areas in Sri Lanka". *Third World Quarterly* **27** (6): 1021–1040. doi:10.1080/01436590600850434.
15. Ranganathan, M. (2002). "Nurturing a Nation on the Net: The Case of Tamil Eelam". *Nationalism and Ethnic Politics* **8** (2): 51–66. http://www.ingentaconnect.com/content/routledg/nep/2002/00000008/00000002/art00004.

16. Schalk, P. (1994). "Women Fighters of the Liberation Tigers in Tamil Eelam. The Martial Feminism of Atel Palacinkam". *South Asia Research* **14** (2): 163. Doi:10.1177/026272809401400203.

17. Schalk, P. (1992). "Birds of independence: on the participation of Tamil women in armed struggle". *Lanka December.*

18. "'Karuna's colleagues are returning'- Col. Ramesh". *Tamil net.* 2008-10-07. http://www.tamilnet.com/art.html?catid=13&artid=11765.

19. "Col. Ramanan". *Tamilnation.org.* 2008-10-07. http://www.tamilnation.org/tamileelam/maveerar/ramanan.htm.

20. "The taking of Elephant Pass". *Hinduonnet.* 2008-10-07. http://www.hinduonnet.com/fline/fl1710/17100100.htm.

21. "Women & the Struggle for Tamil Eelam". *Tamil Nation.* 1998. http://www.tamilnation.org/women/90womenguerillas.htm.

22. Ahmed, Rashmee Z (22 September 2001). "Osama hand in glove with LTTE". *The Times of India* (Bennett Coleman). http://timesofindia.indiatimes.com/articleshow/780319387.cms.

23. Bhattacharji, Preeti (21 July 2008 (updated)). "Does the LTTE have ties to al-Qaeda or other terrorist groups?". Council on Foreign Relations. http://www.cfr.org/publication/9242#5.

24. "al-Qaeda follows LTTE text book on terror faithfully". *Asian Tribune.* 12 February 2007. http://www.asiantribune.com/index.php?q=node/4518.

25. Nadira Gunatilleke (24 May 2007). "Aranthalawa massacre, one of the darkest chapters in Lankan history". *Daily News.* http://www.dailynews.lk/2007/05/24/news26.asp.

26. "Timeline of the Tamil conflict". BBC News. 4 September 2000. http://news.bbc.co.uk/2/hi/south_asia/51435.stm.

27. *The Hindu.* http://www.thehindu.com/holnus/001200801311401.htm.

28. "Sri Lanka (LTTE) Historical Background". *IISS Armed Conflict Database.* International Institute for Strategic Studies. 2003. http://acd.iiss.org/armedconflict/Mainpages/dsp_ConflictBackground.asp?ConflictID=174.

29. Venkataramanan, K. (24 July 2001). "LTTE Attacks Colombo Airport, Airbase". Press Trust of India. Rediff.com India. http://www.rediff.com/news/2001/jul/24ltte.htm.

30. Jeyaraj, D.B.S. (30 October 2005). "Fifteenth Anniversary of Muslim Expulsion From Jaffna". Kirushna. Archived from the original on 2007-07-30. http://www.webcitation.org/5QjPvyYV7.

Further Reading

Balasingham, Adele. (2003). *The Will to Freedom – An Inside View of Tamil Resistance.* Fairmax Publishing Ltd. 2nd ed. ISBN 1-903679-03-6.

Balasingham, Anton. (2004). *War and Peace – Armed Struggle and Peace Efforts of Liberation Tigers.* Fairmax Publishing Ltd. ISBN 1-903679-05-2.

Narayan Swamy, M. R. (2002). *Tigers of Lanka: from Boys to Guerrillas.* Konark Publishers; 3rd ed. ISBN 81-220-0631-0.

Pratap, Anita. (2001). *Island of Blood: Frontline Reports From Sri Lanka, Afghanistan and Other South Asian Flashpoints.* Penguin Books. ISBN 978-0-14-302906-9.

The Traditional Homelands of the Tamils: Separatist Ideology in Sri Lanka: An Historical Appraisal, Kandy, Sri Lanka: International Centre for Ethnic Studies, 1995.

Sri Lanka: Ethnic Conflict, Management and Resolution, Kandy, Sri Lanka: International Centre for Ethnic Studies, 1996.

Gunaratna, Rohan, *Indian Intervention in Sri Lanka: The Role of India's Intelligence Agencies,* Colombo, Sri Lanka: South Asian Network on Conflict Research, 1993a.

War and Peace in Sri Lanka, Colombo, Sri Lanka: Institute of Fundamental Studies, 1993b.

Chapter 5

The Sri Lankan Armed Forces

Having considered the LTTE at length, it is now necessary to have a holistic look at the Sri Lankan Armed Forces (SLAF). Although the SLAF have a long and chequered history, it is fascinating to watch their recent, remarkable transformation from being a staid, 'colonial hangover' force without an identifiable, worrisome threat portfolio, to a ruthlessly efficient fighting machine; one that the Sri Lankan political hierarchy has adopted as its own (a unique development in its own right, that will be examined at length in Chapters 19 of this book). The effect of this transformation is most evident in the Army and Navy, and to a lesser extent, in the Air Force. This is because the Navy, followed by the Army, has been stretched to the maximum, to almost breaking point, as it were, by the ongoing civil war against the LTTE, before emerging stronger – and better.

The indisputable credit for shaping the civil war battlefield - a vast, mind-boggling one, stretching from Sri Lanka almost up to Australian waters by the Sri Lankan Navy (SLN) – an event that, by itself, had a profound impact on the SLAF capability to call the shots in the civil war – must unhesitatingly go to the Navy's leadership. This otherwise 'silent' service, far away from the adrenalin (and challenges) of remaining in constant public gaze, as is the case with any land based force, has altered itself in an almost unbelievable, Cinderella-like transformation; from being a nobody to being someone special; from being a sleepy 'constabulary service'[1] to a 'potent counter insurgency force'[2] at a time when the inroads made on it by the LTTE, in particular, the Sea Tigers, had all but decimated it, and almost totally destroyed its professional credibility.

The transformation is eye opening and educative, as much for its short gestation period as for the clarity with which the three Services have shed inter service rivalries that are the bane of military forces world wide, and substituted these with a unified end state, in line with the expectations of the political masters.

It would appear that Henry Kissinger's sage advice:[3] "A (national) power can survive only if it is willing to fight for its interpretation of justice and its conception of vital interests," was understood by Sri Lanka's political hierarchy and successfully implemented on the ground by the SLAF, to bring the civil war to an end.

OVERVIEW OF THE SRI LANKA ARMED FORCES

The Sri Lanka Armed Forces (SLAF)[4] is the overall unified military of the Democratic Socialist Republic of Sri Lanka encompassing the Sri Lanka Army, the Sri Lanka Navy, and the Sri Lanka Air Force which comes under the purview of the Ministry of Defence (MoD). The total strength of the three services numbers around 230,000 active personnel, who have joined voluntarily since military drafts have never been imposed in Sri Lanka. The Sri Lanka Armed Forces are currently in a fully mobilized (including reserves) state due to the Sri Lankan Civil War against the Liberation Tigers of Tamil Eelam (LTTE, also known as the Tamil Tigers), proscribed as a terrorist organization by 32 countries.

History

Sri Lanka has a long military history going back 2000 years. The roots of the modern Sri Lanka military leads back to the colonial era when the Portuguese, Dutch and British established local militias to support their wars against the local kingdoms. The lineage of the Sri Lanka Armed Forces dates back to 1881, when the British created a volunteer reserve on the island, named the Ceylon Light Infantry Volunteers. Created to supplement the British garrison in Ceylon in the event of an external threat, it gradually increased in size. In 1910, it was renamed the Ceylon Defence Force (CDF) and consisted of several regiments. The CDF mobilized for home defence in World War I and again in World War II when its units were deployed along with allied forces in Asia and Africa. At the end of the war, it has grown in size of an independent Brigade, but was de-mobilized in 1946 and disbanded in 1949. In 1937, the *Ceylon Naval Volunteer Force* was established (later renamed as the *Ceylon Royal Naval Volunteer Reserve* (CRNVR), was mobilized for war in 1939 and was taken into the Royal Navy.

Gazette Extraordinary No. 10028 of October 10, 1949, marked the creation of the Ceylon Army. On December 9, 1950, the Royal Ceylon Navy (RCyN) was established. Finally, in 1951, the Royal Ceylon Air Force (RCyAF) was established as the youngest of the three forces. In the 1950s, it was mainly employed in internal security assisting the police. There was an attempted coup in 1962 by a group of reservists, which led to cuts in military spending and the disbandment of several regiments. This, together with the lack of an intelligence agency, left it ill-prepared for the insurgency launched by the Marxist JVP in April 1971. This saw the Ceylon Armed Forces mobilizing for combat operations for the first time and its size grew rapidly. The insurrection was brought under control in a few months. In 1972, Ceylon became a Republic and the Ceylon Armed Forces became the Sri Lanka Armed Forces. By the early 1980s, the Sri Lanka Armed Forces were mobilizing again as a new insurgency was begun by Tamil militant groups in the North of the island. This was the beginning of the Sri Lankan Civil War.

The size of the Armed Forces grew at a rapid rate in the 1980s. By the mid 1980s, the Armed Forces began launching operations against the LTTE. This led to the Indo-Sri Lankan Accord and the Indian Peace Keeping Force (IPKF) was sent to Sri Lanka to establish peace.

1987-89 JVP Insurrection

The SLAF was redistricted to its bases and was soon heavily involved in another insurrection by the JVP in the South of the island, from 1987 to 1989. In the North, tension increased with the LTTE and the IPKF, leading to open war, with the two suffering heavy casualties. In 1990, the IPKF pulled out and the war commenced with the Sri Lanka Armed Forces and the LTTE.

In 1994, a brief ceasefire came into place and peace talks began. But it broke down when the LTTE attacked several docked naval gunboats. The phase of the war that followed; known as Eelam War III, saw a conventional war taking place in the Northern and Eastern provinces of the island and terrorist attacks in other parts of the country. The Sri Lankan Army began deploying full divisions in offensive operations and the Navy and Air Force increased their inventory in order to support the Army.

In 2002, a new ceasefire was established with Norwegian mediation and peace talks began. The SLMM was established to monitor the ceasefire and certain progress was achieved, until the LTTE withdrew from the peace talks in 2003. Although the ceasefire continued, no peace talks took place till 2005. In April 2006, following a suicide bomb attack on the Commander of the Army, air strikes began, followed by skirmishes. An offensive was launched by the SLAF when the LTTE closed the gates of the Mavil Aru reservoir on July 21 and cut the water supply to 15,000 villages in Government controlled areas. This led to several major attacks by the LTTE in the Eastern Province and the North. The Armed Forces went on the offensive, successfully capturing LTTE controlled areas in the Eastern province during 2007.

During 2008, there was heavy fighting in the Northern Province, where the Sri Lanka Armed Forces launched major offensives and succeeded in capturing LTTE controlled areas of Mannar District, Vavuniya District and moving on to Mullaithivu District and Killinochchi District. During December 2008, the Sri Lankan Armed Forces were engaged in offensives on all fronts, with heavy fighting around Killinochchi town where the LTTE had their headquarters and close to Mullaithivu town.

In early 2009, the Armed Forces captured, in quick succession, Killinochchi town and the strategically important Elephant Pass, thus re-establishing a land route to the Government controlled Jaffna Peninsula, which had been supplied by sea and air for over 10 years after its recapture in 1995. Shortly thereafter, Mullaithivu town was captured by 59 Division of the SLA. Boxed into a small land area north of Mullaithivu, the LTTE with its remaining cardres and leadership was effectively trapped. On 19th May 2009, the SLAF claimed to have concluded its final battle against the LTTE with the death of several top LTTE leaders, including Velupillai Prabhakaran.

Strategic Importance

The posture of the SLAF has been defensive due to the nature of the strategic threats to Sri Lanka. In the short-term, internal security is considered the main threat to the nation's future. In the long-term, the threat is seen as primarily external from current and future superpowers in their quest for dominance of the Indian Ocean. Throughout the period from 2005 onwards, China has provided small arms, tanks, helicopters and howitzers, as well as mobile vehicles to the SLAF. This can be seen as China's attempt to gain leverage against other power blocs, mainly India, within the Indian Ocean. Sri Lanka also imports high-tech weapon systems from Israel and several other countries, including Pakistan.

Command Organization

As the head of state, the President of Sri Lanka is nominally the Commander-in-Chief of the Armed Forces. The National Security Council, chaired by the President, is the authority charged with formulating and executing defence policies for the nation. The highest level of military headquarters is the Ministry of Defence. The responsibility for the management of the forces is with the Ministry of Defence (MoD), while the planning and execution of combined operations is the responsibility of the Joint Operations Command (JOC). The JOC is headed by the Chief of the Defence Staff, who is the most senior officer in the Armed Forces and is an appointment that can be held by an Air Chief Marshal, Admiral, or General. The three services have their own respective professional chiefs: the Commander of the Army, the Commander of the Navy and the Commander of the Air Force, who have much autonomy.

Training

Today, the training of all armed services is carried out in Sri Lanka. With a Defence University, a Staff College, three Military Academies for the three armed services and many specialized training schools and centres, members of the Sri Lanka Armed Forces (SLAF) are considered highly trained and professional. The institutions referred to are:

- Defence University, Colombo.
- Defence Services Command and Staff College.
- Sri Lanka Military Academy, Diyatalawa.
- Naval and Maritime Academy, Trincomalee.
- Air Force Academy, SLAF, China Bay, Trincomalee.

The Sri Lankan military has received specialized training assistance from other nations such as Pakistan, Australia, the United Kingdom, Israel, the United States, India, and South Africa.

Awards and Decorations

The most prestigious decoration is the Parama Weera Vibhushanaya (PWV), a 'supreme heroism' decoration, awarded to officers, soldiers, sailors and airmen who have shown exceptional individual gallantry in the face of danger, risking their own lives to save the lives of their comrades. It is the Sri Lankan equivalent of the British Victoria Cross and the Indian Param Vir Chakra, and is very rarely awarded. So far, all awards have been posthumous, with seven being awarded to the Army and one to the Navy.

Parama Weera Vibhushanaya (PWV) Medal

Decorated Personnel

- Captain S. Aladeniya † Sri Lanka Sinha Regiment.
- Corporal Gamini Kularatne † Sri Lanka Sinha Regiment.
- Second Lieutenant K. W. T. Nissanka † Gajaba Regiment.
- Warrant Officer 2nd Class H.B. Pasan Gunasekera † Gajaba Regiment.
- Colonel A.F. Lafir † Special Forces Regiment.

- Lance Corporal W.I.M. Seneviratne † Sri Lanka Light Infantry.
- Lieutenant-Commander Jude Lakmal Wijetunga † Sri Lanka. Navy
- Major G. S. Jayanath † Commando Regiment.

THE SRI LANKA ARMY

The Sri Lanka Army (SLA)[5] is the oldest and the largest of the Sri Lanka Armed Forces and is responsible for land-based military and humanitarian operations. Established as the Ceylon Army in 1949, it was renamed when Sri Lanka became an independent republic in 1972. As of the year 2000, the Army had approximately 150,000 regular and reserve personnel and 18,000 National Guardsmen and comprised 13 operational divisions, one air-mobile Brigade, one commando Brigade, one special forces Brigade, one independent armoured Brigade, three mechanized infantry Brigades and over 40 infantry Brigades. Since the 1980s, the army has been engaged in the Sri Lankan civil war. The strength of the Army in November 2009 is 190,000 personnel.

The professional head of the Sri Lanka Army is the Commander of the Army, currently Lt Gen Jagath Jayasuriya, USP, who took over from General Sarath Fonseka, RWP, RSP, VSV, USP, on July 15, 2009. He is from the Armoured Corps. The Commander-in-Chief of the Sri Lankan Military is the President of the country, who heads the National Security Council through the Ministry of Defence, which is the highest level of military command charged with formulating and executing defence policy and procurements for the armed forces. However, operations of the Sri Lanka Army are coordinated by the Joint Operations Command, with the other two armed forces. General Fonseka, who was the CDS, retired from his appointment on November 16, 2009. His registration is being seen as the first step towards campaigning against President Nahinela Rajapaksa in the next Presidential election which, some sources say, is scheduled for end January 2010.

Organization Structure

The professional head of the army is the Commander of the Army, who is assisted by the Chief of Staff of the Army, currently Major General G.A. Chandrasiri. The Commandant of the Volunteer Force is head of the Army Volunteer Force and is responsible for the administration and recruitment of all reserve units and personnel. The Army Headquarters, situated in Colombo, is the main administrative and the operational headquarters of the Sri Lanka Army.

In late 1987, the army had a total estimated strength of up to 40,000 troops, about evenly divided between regular army personnel and reservists on active duty.

The approximately 20,000 regular army troops represented a significant increase over the 1983 strength of only 12,000. Aggressive recruitment campaigns following the 1983 riots raised this number to 16,000 by early 1985. By 2007, the Army had expanded to over 120,000 personnel.

Administration

The Army Headquarters is divided into a number of branches, namely the General Staff (GS) branch (responsible for coordination of operations and training) and the Adjutant General's (AGs) branch (responsible for personnel administration, welfare, medical services and rehabilitation). The Quarter Master General's (QMG's) branch is responsible for feeding, transport, movement and construction and maintenance. The Master General of Ordnance's (MGO's) branch is responsible for procurement and maintenance of vehicles and special equipment. The Military Secretary's Branch is responsible for handling all matters pertaining to officers such as promotions, postings and discipline. Each branch is headed by an officer in the rank of Major General who is directly responsible to the Commander of the Army for the smooth functioning of the Branch. Under each Branch, there are several Directorates, each headed by a Brigadier.

The Headquarters of field formations each have their own staff. For instance, a divisional headquarters is divided into a GS branch and an AQ branch; each headed by a Colonel and is responsible for operations and training and administration and logistics respectively. Similarly, a Brigade Major and Major AQ are responsible for operations and administration in a Brigade.

Like the Indian Army, the Sri Lanka Army has largely retained the British-style regimental system that it inherited upon independence. The individual regiments (such as the Sri Lanka Light Infantry and the Sinha Regiment) operate independently and recruit their own members. Officers tend to remain in a single battalion throughout their careers. The infantry battalion, the basic unit of organization in field operations, includes five companies of four platoons each. A typical platoon has three squads (sections) of ten personnel each. In addition to the basic infantry forces, a commando regiment was also established in 1986. Support for the infantry is provided by an armoured regiment, five reconnaissance regiments, three mechanized infantry regiments, five field artillery regiments, a rocket artillery regiment, three commando regiments, three special forces regiments, six field engineering regiments, five signals battalions, a medical corps, and a variety of logistics units.

Operational Command

Organized and controlled by the Army General Staff at Army HQ, various formations are raised from time to time to suit various security requirements and operations in the country and overseas. The Army, at present, has deployed 12 Divisions, 7 task forces and several Independent Brigades. Except for the 11 Division based at the Panagoda Cantonment which is responsible for the maintenance of capability for the defence of the capital, all other divisions, task forces and Brigades are deployed for operations in the Northern and Eastern provinces of Sri Lanka, coming under five regional commands known as *Security Forces Headquarters*, which are the Security Forces Headquarters Jaffna (SFHQ-J), Wanni (SFHQ-W), East (SFHQ-E), Killinochchi (SFHQ-KLN) & Mullaithivu (SFHQ-MLT)

Each SFHQ and most divisions are commanded by a General Officer Commanding in the rank of Major General. A SFHQ has several divisions under its command and each division is further divided into Brigades. Each Brigade is commanded by an officer in the rank of Brigadier and has a number of Infantry battalions, support arms (Artillery, Engineers and Signals) and support services (Service Corps, Engineering Services, Ordnance Corps, Electrical and Mechanical Engineers) assigned to it. There are also several independent Brigades (Air Mobile Brigade, Armoured Brigade, etc.).

In other parts of the country, there are Area and Sub-Area Headquarters. Armour, Artillery, Engineers and Signals Units are grouped under Brigade Headquarters of their own arm; Armoured Brigade, Artillery Brigade, and so on.

Combat Formations

Security Forces Headquarters – Jaffna (SFHQ-J)

- 51 Division, based in Jaffna
- 52 Division, based in the Jaffna Peninsula
- 55 Division, based in Elephant Pass, Jaffna Peninsula

Security Forces Headquarters – Wanni (SFHQ-W)

- 56 Division, operating in the Vavuniya District
- 61 Division, operating in the Vavuniya District
- 21 Division
- Area Headquarters Mannar

Security Forces Headquarters – East (SFHQ-E)

- 22 Division, based in Trincomalee
- 23 Division, based in Poonani, Batticaloa District

Regiments and Corps

Name	Headquarters	Subunits
Armoured Corps	Rock House Army Camp, Colombo	Six regular regiments and a volunteer regiment.
Artillery	Panagoda Cantonment, Panagoda	Seven regular regiments and two volunteer regiments.
Engineers	Army Headquarters, Colombo	Six regular regiments and one volunteer regiment.
Signals Corps	Panagoda Cantonment, Panagoda	Nine regular regiments and one volunteer regiment.
Light Infantry	Panagoda Cantonment, Panagoda	Ten regular battalions, five volunteer battalions.
Sinha Regiment	Ambepussa Camp, Ambepussa	Seven regular battalions, five volunteer battalions and a headquarter battalion.
Gemunu Watch	Kuruwitha Army Camp, Ratnapura	Nine regular units, four volunteer units.
Gajaba Regiment	Saliyapura Camp, Anuradhapura	Six regular battalions and five volunteer battalions.
Vijayabâhu Infantry Regiment	Boyagane Camp, Kurunegala	Eight regular battalions and four volunteer battalions.
Mechanized Infantry Regiment	N/A	Three regular battalions.
President's Guard	N/A	N/A
Commando Regiment	Ganemulla, Gampaha	Four regular regiments.
Special Forces Regiment	Seeduwa, Gampaha	Three regular regiments.
Military Intelligence Corps	Colombo	Two regular battalions.
Engineer Services Regiment	Panagoda Cantonment, Panagoda	Three regular regiments and a volunteer regiment.
Service Corps	Panagoda Cantonment, Panagoda	Four regular units and one volunteer unit.
Medical Corps	Colombo	Two regular units and one volunteer unit.

Ordnance Corps	Panagoda Cantonment, Panagoda	Three regular ordnance battalions and one volunteer ordnance battalion.
Electrical and Mechanical Engineers	Slave Island, Colombo	Three regular regiments and one volunteer regiment.
Corps of Military Police	Polhengoda, Colombo	Three regular regiments.
General Service Corps	Panagoda Cantonment, Panagoda	One regular unit and a volunteer unit.
Women's Corps	Army Headquarters, Colombo	One regular unit and 4 volunteer units.
Rifle Corps	Army Headquarters, Colombo	Two volunteer battalions.
Pioneer Corps	N/A	One volunteer unit.
National Guard	Kurunegala	32 volunteer battalions.

Security Forces Headquarters – Killinochchi (SFHQ-KLN)

- 57 Division, operating in the Killinochchi District
- Task Force 3, operating in the Killinochchi District
- Task Force 5, operating in the Killinochchi District
- Task Force 6, operating in the Killinochchi District
- Task Force 8, operating in the Killinochchi District

Security Forces Headquarters – Mullaithivu (SFHQ-MLT)

- 59 Division, operating in the Mullaithivu District
- Task Force 2, operating in the Mullaithivu District
- Task Force 4, operating in the Mullaithivu District

Independent Divisions

- 11 Division, based at the Panagoda Cantonment, Western Province
- 53 Division, based at Mankulam
- 58 Division, based at Paranthan (formally referred to as Task Force 1)

Independent Brigades

- Air Mobile Brigade
- Mechanized Infantry Brigade
- Armoured Brigade
- Special Forces Brigade

Training

General Sir John Kotelawala Defence University (KDU) formed in 1981 and situated in Ratmalana, fourteen kilometres south of Colombo, is Sri Lanka's only university specializing in defence studies. Each year, approximately 50 cadets from all three services are admitted to the university (aged 18-22) to participate in a three-year programme of academic work and basic training.

Junior field officers of the Army and their counterparts of the Navy and Air Force are given advanced training and education at the Defence Services Command and Staff College (DSCSC) at Batalanda, Makola, which was established in 1997 as the *Army Command and Staff College*.

Basic officer training is carried out at the Sri Lanka Military Academy (SLMA) (formally the Army Training Centre) situated in Diyatalawa, in Badulla District. The officer cadets graduating from the academy are commissioned as officers in the regular and volunteer forces. The course for officer cadets runs for ninety weeks and includes training in tactics and administration which helps prepare the cadets to take up the positions of platoon commanders. The course consists of military and academic subjects and also training the cadets physically. The course helps to promote leadership qualities and the understanding of each one's role as an officer and a servant of the state. Due to the lack of officers within the lower levels, the training process was speeded up in the 1980s by developing a short commission course. The cadets were given a training of fifty-six weeks and devoted themselves to continue their careers in the military with ten years of service for regular army officers and five years of service for volunteer officers.

Training for the new recruits is mostly carried out at several locations followed by additional training (both officers and other ranks) at the Infantry Training School in Minneriya, the Combat Training School in Ampara, the Army Training School in Maduru Oya while non-commissioned officers receive training at the Non Commissioned Officers Training School at Kala Oya. All these establishments come under the control of Army Headquarters. Specialist and additional training is given by specialist training schools, regimental training centres and individual field units.

As the armed forces of Sri Lanka have limited indigenous training facilities, especially in advanced roles, they have depended greatly on military training provided by foreign countries. The United Kingdom played a major role in the early years following independence and has continued to be an important source of military expertise to the Sri Lankan military. Other sources include Pakistan, Australia, Malaysia, and the United States. Additionally, in an agreement reached in 1984, Israeli security personnel (reportedly from Shin Bet, the Israeli counter-espionage and internal security organization) trained army officers in counterinsurgency techniques.

Personnel

The Sri Lanka Army presently stands at 120,000 strong including 2,960 women plus an additional 10,000 personnel in reserve.

Notable Fallen Members

- Lt. General Denzil Kobbekaduwa † Overall Operations Commander, Northern Sector.
- Lt. General Parami Kulatunga † Former Deputy Chief of Staff of the Army.
- Lt. General Nalin Angammana † Former GOC 3 Division.
- Maj. General Vijaya Wimalaratne † Former Jaffna Brigade Commander.
- Maj. General Percy Fernando † Former Deputy GOC 54 Division.

- Maj. General Larry Wijeratne † Former Brigade Commander, 51-4 Brigade.
- Maj. General Lakshman 'Lucky' Wijeratne † Former Brigade Commander, 22 Brigade.
- Maj. General Susantha Mendis † Former Brigade Commander, 51-2 Brigade.
- Maj. General Ananda Hamangoda † Former Brigade Commander, 51-2 Brigade.
- Colonel Tuan Nizam Muthaliff † Former Commanding Officer, 1st Battalion, Military Intelligence Corps.

Women in the Sri Lanka Army

The Sri Lanka Army Women's Corps (SLAWC) was formed on September 01, 1979, as an unarmed, noncombatant support unit. Set up with the assistance of the Women's Royal Army Corps, it was identical in structure to its parent organization, and its first generation of officer cadets was trained in Britain. Candidates were required to be between eighteen and twenty years old and to have passed the General Common Entrance (Ordinary level) examinations, while the Officer candidates must have passed the Advanced Level. Enlistment entailed a five-year service commitment (the same as for men), and recruits were not allowed to marry during this period. In the sixteen-week training course at the Army Training Centre at the Diyatalawa Sri Lanka Military Academy, cadets were put through a programme of drill and physical training similar to the men's programme, with the exception of weapons and battle craft training. (It may, however be noted that, "with the clearance of admittance to the Navy in 1985, they were trained in the use of weapons[6] although not assigned to any shipboard duty or combat positions"). Female recruits were paid according to the same scale as the men, but were limited to service in nursing, communications, and clerical work. In late 1987, the first classes of women graduates from the Viyanini Army Training Centre (VATC) were certified to serve as Army instructors. But, from late 1987 – after hostilities began, the first batch of women graduates from the British Army's Women's Corp Centre were certified to serve as Army instructors.

Up to now, women officers have proved their ability and serve in varied specialized fields in the service as control tower operators, electronic warfare technicians, radio material teletypists, automotive mechanics, aviation supply personnel, cryptographers, doctors, combat medics, lawyers, engineers and even aerial photographers. To meet the operational requirements in the field areas, the 2nd Volunteer Battalion of the Women's Corps was also raised. A few officers from the regular counterpart were attached to this unit to organize the command structure. They are currently employed in active combat duties in the Northern and Eastern parts of the island. Many officers commencing with Lieutenant Colonel A.W. Thambiraja were appointed to command this unit from time to time. The first women's corps officer to command the unit was Lieutenant Colonel Kumudini Weerasekara in 1992 and as of 2007 there were three female officers of the rank of Major General. At present, there is one regular regiment and four volunteer regiments in the Women's Corps.

Equipment

To meet the threat posed predominantly by the LTTE, the army purchased modern military hardware including 50-calibre Heavy Machine Guns, Rocket Propelled Grenade Launchers, Night Vision Devices, 106 mm Recoilless Rifles, 60 mm and 81 mm Mortars, 40 mm Grenade Launchers and some Sniper Rifles. Refurbished armoured personnel carriers were added to the 'A' vehicle fleet of the 1st Recce Regiment, Sri Lanka Armoured Corps. The capability of the Sri Lanka Artillery was enhanced with the introduction of Ordnance QF 25 pounders. Chinese-made 122 mm, 130 mm and 152 mm howitzers were introduced to the Sri Lankan Army in 1995 and 1998 whilst 122 mm Multi Barrel Rocket Launchers (MBRL), were first used in 2000 by the Sri Lanka Army.

Land mines proved to be the most lethal threat to the security forces, as many mines have been deployed against Government forces by the LTTE in the Northern and Eastern Provinces. These mines are deployed with normalcy against Government trucks and buses, with a high rate of casualty. They weighed approximately 50–100kgs against which no armoured vehicle that the SLA possessed was able to withstand the blast effect. Therefore the South African-made Buffel was introduced to service in 1985 to reduce damage due to land mines. By 1987, the Army's own Unicorn was also developed to a level so that they too matched the capabilities of the Buffels from South Africa, which was followed up by the newer Unibuffel class. Both the Unicorn and the Unibuffel are assembled by the Sri Lanka Electrical & Mechanical Engineers.

In recent years, Sri Lanka has become increasingly reliant on China for weapons. This is due to most European nations and the United States Governments passing regulations about the selling of weaponry to nations which are suffering from internal conflict. **China has no such regulations upon their arms producers and some see the sales as an attempt to gain political influence with the strategically-important Sri Lanka. Sri Lanka also continues to receive a variety of weapons from Britain, Pakistan, Israel and other former suppliers.**

Armour

Type	Origin	Quantity	Notes
Main Battle Tanks			
Al Khalid	Pakistan	22	On order
T-55/T-55AM2	Soviet Union	140+	
Type 69	China	20+	
Type 59	China	80+	
Light Tanks			
Type 63	China	N/A	Amphibious
Infantry Fighting Vehicles			
BMP-3	Soviet Union	145	
BMP-2	Soviet Union	52	
BMP-1	Soviet Union	12	
Armoured Personnel Carriers			
Norinco Type 89 (YW534)	China	N/A	Tracked
Type 85 (YW531H)	China	N/A	Tracked, Amphibious
Type 63 (YW531)	China	N/A	Tracked
BTR-80	Soviet Union	33	Wheeled
Type 92 (WZ551)	China	200	Wheeled
BTR-152	Soviet Union	N/A	Wheeled, operational state unknown
Unibuffel	Sri Lanka	N/A	Locally manufactured, Mine-protected APC
Unicorn	Sri Lanka	N/A	Locally manufactured, Mine-protected APC
Buffel	South Africa	N/A	Mine-protected APC
HUSSAR	United Kingdom	N/A	Wheeled, operational state unknown
Shorland S55	United Kingdom	N/A	Wheeled, operational state unknown
Hotspur	United Kingdom	N/A	Wheeled, operational state unknown
Reconnaissance Vehicles			
Alvis Saladin	United Kingdom	N/A	Wheeled
Alvis Saracen	United Kingdom	N/A	Wheeled, operational state unknown
Daimler Ferret	United Kingdom	N/A	Wheeled, operational state unknown

Engineering Support Vehicles

VT-55	Soviet Union	16	Armoured recovery vehicle
MT-55A	Soviet Union	8	Armoured vehicle-launched bridge

Artillery

Type	Origin	Quantity	Notes
Rocket Artillery			
RM-70 Multiple rocket launcher	Czechoslovakia	30+	122.4 mm Multiple rocket launcher
BM-21 Multiple rocket launcher	Soviet Union	5	122.4 mm Multiple rocket launcher
Towed Artillery			
Type 66 152 mm gun-howitzer	China	36	152 mm gun-howitzer
Type 59 130mm field gun	China	12	130 mm field gun
Type 60 122mm howitzer	China	N/A	122 mm howitzer
Ordnance QF 25 pounder	United Kingdom	N/A	field guns - Ceremonial Gun Troop
Ordnance QF 75 mm	United Kingdom	N/A	field guns - Ceremonial Gun Troop
Mortars			
Type 86 (W86)	China	55	120 mm towed mortar
Type 84 (W84)	China	N/A	82 mm mortar
Type 89	China	N/A	60 mm light mortar

Infantry Weapons

Handguns

- Beretta M9 Pistol
- Glock 17
- Enfield revolver

Assault Rifles

- AK-47 Assault rifles
- Type 56 Assault rifles
- Type 81 Assault rifles
- Heckler & Koch G3 Assault rifles
- FN FNC Assault rifles (replaced the FN FAL as far back as in 1981)
- M16 Assault rifles
- M4 Carbine
- SAR-80 Assault rifles
- Type 95 Assault rifles

Sub-Machine Guns

- H&K MP5 Submachine guns
- Uzi Submachine guns
- Sterling Submachine guns

Sniper Rifles

- Accuracy International L96A1 Sniper Rifles
- Heckler & Koch PSG1 Sniper Rifles
- Dragunov Sniper Rifles

Machine Guns

- Type 80 GPMG (Chinese version of Russian PKM)
- FN Minimi General purpose machine gun
- FN MAG General purpose machine gun
- Type 56 LMG (Chinese version of Russian RPD)
- HK21 Belt-fed light machine gun

Grenade Launchers

- Milkor MGL Grenade launcher
- HK 69 Breech-loading grenade launcher
- M203 Grenade launcher

Rocket Launchers

- RPO-A Shmel man-portable rocket launcher
- Type 69 RPG rocket launchers (Chinese version of RPG-7)

Anti-tank Missiles

- Baktar-Shikan Anti-tank guided missile

The SLA Transforms Itself

The SLA has come a long way indeed, from its laid back past. There was a time, especially in the 1980s, when the SLA (along with most conventional armies of the world) would have cheerfully subscribed to the prevailing, universal belief that terrorism could not be defeated militarily. The LTTE had, after all, effectively fought them to a standstill and seemed well on the way of achieving their Eelam dream. The Indian Army too, had had a prolonged go at them and had gone back, rapped on the knuckles savagely without achieving their mandate. The SLA had antiquated equipment which was in perpetual short supply, specially assault rifles, ammunition and combat net radio stations. Training was inadequate. Instances were reported of recruits being despatched to the battle front with barely four weeks of training. Worse, troops were operationally employed with vintage tactical doctrines that had long outgrown their utility.

The SLA's emphasis was on holding static defences as well as employment of maximum force to gain counter-insurgency objectives; an approach that was doomed to fail. The subtlety and finesse of the 'velvet glove,' (combining uncompromising military operations with 'winning hearts and minds' by facilitating development, thereby reducing the wear and tear of war on the civil populace), a tactic that the Indian Army learnt the hard way in the 1990's in Kashmir and in the North East, while combating terrorism and insurgency, was missing. Further, quite a few of the senior commanders had never seen war. The senior leadership (with some exceptions) was averse to risk taking, displaying inadequate imagination, initiative and dynamism in their thinking and functioning. Across ranks, many officers and men were willing to do their duties, but few of them sought to be heroes. Success in war is often a function of having a large number of personnel who are indoctrinated to function in the classic, heroic mould of 'Follow me!' This obviously was the exception, not the norm. The RAND Study[7] quoted earlier in Chapter 4, says, in addition, that "many officers had been promoted on the basis of seniority or as a result of political connections, personal loyalties, and friendships."[8]

In sum, the SLA had a serious problem with its higher direction of war. In addition, the troops were suffering from low morale, had taken serious casualties, were racked with desertion and indiscipline in the ranks; were finding a dire lack of recruits to join the SLA in particular and the other two services in general. In fact, just about everything that could go wrong with not just the SLA but SLAF as an entity, and even the nation in general, had gone wrong. The LTTE were on song and appeared unstoppable.

One is reminded, at this juncture, of the caustic, yet relevant remarks of a noted British historian, Corelli Barnett,[9] about the British Army. He makes a comparison in his famous book set in the North African desert in World War II, 'The Desert Generals,' between the pedestrian, steady but unimaginative British generalship exhibited by General Montgomery, vis-à-vis the brilliant, unorthodox, 'out-of-the-box German generalship', as exemplified by General Ervin Rommel. Barnett wrote that the British Army, under Montgomery, came across as hidebound and orthodox in its approach to war fighting, forever emphasizing on building up an overwhelming superiority in numbers before launching out. He notes with cynicism that one of the historical legacies of the British Army was that it had always been found *well prepared – to fight the last war*. By implication, he found Montgomery guilty of using the static, status quo, defensive 'trench warfare' strategy and tactics of World War I against the fast, mobile war that Rommel fought in the desert in World War II; a mindset that found the British repeatedly guilty of being flatfooted against the dynamic, aggressive, Afrika Corps General who had innovatively adapted to new tactics and refreshing new military thinking in his conduct of war (The strategy and tactics that the Germans employed were ironically British/Russian in origin and comprised of the British theory of Blitzkrieg and the Russian employment of Simultaneity in Battle).

A dispassionate analysis shows that the British Army mindset (that Barnett so succinctly pointed out) was fully applicable to SLAF and especially to the SLA. In fairness, it can be said without any qualification, that all ex British colonies inherited this mindset from them; with India being no exception during its starting years, extending up to conduct of the 1965 Indo-Pak War. (This period includes the disastrous Sino-Indian war of 1962 where political as well as senior military leadership failed the country.)

What the statement does reinforce is that Sri Lanka, as a nation, and certainly the SLAF, were ill equipped, both mentally and physically; in orientation, theory and in practice, to take on the bold and aggressive, unrepentant, 'out-of-the-box' operations and tactics of the LTTE, in the opening years of the civil war. The author finds a reflection of the state of the SLA in the psyche of the officers whom he saw as young officers in 1969/70 at the Armoured Corps Centre and School and at the Defence Services Staff College in 1984/85, while attending courses of instruction at these Indian military establishments. The author recalls his SLAF officer colleagues of this period, as intelligent, attentive, non aggressive and uniformly quiet and pleasant. They came across as solid, orthodox officers without any worthwhile experience of battle; officers, who, till 1985, did not really have the LTTE spell cast on them. The officers were obviously well prepared for the challenges of the course but non-committal in respect of how their war against the LTTE was progressing. Certainly, that self-confidence and euphoria that unconditional success brings was some way off from their body language...

In general, it is accepted as a universal, unchanging truth that defence forces support *status quo*; they are comfortable with orthodoxy; with the tried and tested 'beaten path' and in fact, thrive in it. They are distinctly uncomfortable with new ideas. This dislike is intense and is well articulated because execution of new ideas demands change. Accepting change is a tacit admission that you were wrong. This takes a lot of courage and guts. Thus, handling change and the subsequent management of its fallout is a complex, very demanding, long drawn out process that takes those affected by change out of their comfort zones, leaving them vulnerable and confused. Managing change therefore, needs deep insights into the dynamics of the human mind. For change to be successfully implemented, it is essential to have a clear vision and implementation roadmap.

It is also a known fact that change rarely occurs from within an organisation and often has external influences that drive in change and create an environment that allows transformation to take place as forced. This is because those within the system do not wish to be associated with the complexities of rocking the boat, and perhaps do not have the will, detachment and ruthlessness needed for transformation. The question of narrow loyalties, vested interests and a steady state of denial (no acceptance of ground realities) are never far away from institutions that resist change.

A good example of change and its management in a military context is the Goldwater-Nichols Department of Defence (DOD) Reorganisation Act of 1986[10] which was designed to improve 'jointness' in the US Armed Forces and which has been described as, "one of the landmark laws of American history. It is probably the greatest sea change in the history of the American military since the Continental Congress created the Continental Army in 1775." The trigger for the Act came on February 3, 1982. On that date, General David Jones, the sitting Chairman of the Joint Chiefs of Staff, "broke ranks" with his Pentagon colleagues and appealed to the House Armed Services Committee for reform of the joint system. General Jones confessed that he had unsuccessfully tried to reform the system from within.

In his fateful testimony, General Jones advised the House Committee, 'It is not sufficient to have just resources, dollars and weapon systems; we must also have an organisation which will allow us to develop the proper strategy, necessary planning, and full war fighting capability.' Then, with just eight words, General Jones started a profound revolution in military affairs and changed the course of American military history when he said, 'We do not have an organizational structure today'."[11] As is well known, Goldwater and Nichols were two politicians who came from outside the system to bring in change. A similar example is available closer home by the setting up of the K. Subramanyam Committee in 1999, by the Government of India, to bring in reforms in the Indian defence and security set up. Subrahmanyan, though an iconic defence analyst and ex bureaucrat, was (and is) outside the system when nominated to head the committee.

Coming back to Sri Lanka, it is a well known fact that, here too, the drivers of the change that transformed the SLAF and, in particular, the SLA, came from *outside* the system, and, like the Goldwater-Nichols Act, the change makers were politicians – the Rajapaksa brothers, Mahinda and Gottabhaya, who are President and Defence Minister, respectively. It helped that Gottabhaya is an ex Army officer of the SLA, who has excellent vibes with the Sri Lankan Chief of Defence Staff, General Sarath Fonseka, having served under and with him, when in uniform. So it was this *troika*, as the Sri Lankan media calls them, men who were 'hard of mind and hard of will' who delivered a successful change commencing with the dramatic Mavil Aru[12] sluice gate opening by SLA on August 11, 2006,(a scant two weeks after the LTTE had closed them on July 26, 2006) that brought the civil war to an end on May 18, 2009, two months short of the three year period that they had allotted themselves for completion of this task. It is not surprising, of course, almost axiomatic, that the SLA would name its transformation operation as 'Operation Watershed."[13] It was indeed a watershed. (The break up of this troika in November 2009 has serious potential fallouts which will be examined later on in this book).

As an important aside for the reader's consideration, it is important to bring in the role of the Clausewitzian elements of politico-military collusion; luck, chance and 'friction:' elements that play such a successful part in the conduct of war. Corelli Barnett notes with great prescience that Carl von Clausewitz's 'Theory of War' as a continuation of politics still holds true[14] across the continuum of recent conflicts such as the Provisional IRA's campaign ('the classic contemporary demonstration of Clausewitzian principles in action') and Yugoslavia. He could well have added Sri Lanka to this list. The election by a narrow margin of Mahinda Rajapaksa in 2005, on the focused platform of decimation of the LTTE, was the death knell of the LTTE; a realization of this fact, however, came to Prabhakaran too late for him to make amends.

So far as the elements of luck and chance are concerned, it may not have been entirely due to these factors but they definitely had a say in the manner in which, in 2004, a cataclysmic event occurred that was, from the LTTE viewpoint, the beginning of the end for them – the breaking away of the Karuna LTTE faction and his absorption into the political mainstream by Mahindra Rajapaksa. There is no doubt that this was a master stroke of intelligence to get him to do so. The element of timing is important here and this is where luck and chance played their part. Everything suddenly seemed to fall in place for Sri Lanka, much as the opposite was happening for Prabhakaran. Karuna really *knew* both Prabhakaran as well as the LTTE; did a brilliant Strengths, Weaknesses, Opportunities and Threat (SWOT) analysis of his erstwhile colleagues and leader, for the Government and the SLAF, and, thus, helped shape the transformation of the SLAF in a major way. In 2006, the LTTE assassination attempts on the Defence Minister, Gottabhaya Rajapaksa, as well as on the then Commander SLA, General Sarath Fonseka, failed to take them out. This was to prove prohibitively costly. For an organisation that had never failed in its efforts before, missing out on assassination of two key personalities was a huge and demoralizing setback for them. There was an element of luck and chance too, in the Mavil Aru incident happening in July 2006. Defeating the LTTE in their heartland, forcing the opening of the sluice gates gave the SLA a dream boost; something they otherwise could never have hoped for, in their very first anti-LTTE operation after deciding on their new strategy.

The term 'friction'[15] is used in a stunning, visionary manner by Clausewitz, in his masterly treatise, 'On War.' Clausewitz wrote in war, friction is an 'unseen, all-pervading' element. It's about how everything can and will go wrong, how things generally don't go to plan, and how simple things are difficult to do. In theory, war should end in extremes – short duration, a single decisive battle, total destruction. In practice, friction ensures that war is prolonged, confused and fails to result in some or all of the objectives set.[16] As Clausewitz adds with great sense and sensibility rare in a theorist; "the difficulties accumulate and end by producing a kind of friction that is inconceivable...". Clausewitz wrote that "great commanders understand friction and its effects. They know how to cope with friction, through courage,[17] composure, determination and grit. They are realistic about what can and can't be achieved in the face of friction. They therefore keep things simple". Let us see how this element worked for Sri Lanka (certainly for the SLA) but not so for the LTTE.

Prabhakaran started getting pilloried for leading a luxurious, safe life at a time when the suicide pill was the only way out for his cadres. He had developed a number of concurrent medical problems already made known to readers in earlier chapters, which had started affecting his abilities. He suddenly had to defend himself against the charges of saving his immediate family, particularly his son, from danger while exposing others to exceptional danger. Things had thus started going wrong for him, and, for once, he did not have the leadership resolve or the mental resolve and bandwidth to cope...friction had taken its toll after he had led his struggle for over 30 years... On the other hand, the Rajapaksa Government displayed astute leadership. Aware that friction had put paid to earlier efforts to resolve the civil war, the troika kept it simple this time: every one knew the focus was on decimation of the LTTE and at a time and pace decided by the troika; also, the aspects of the Clausewitzian formula of 'courage, composure, determination and grit' was never lost sight of. Victory had to follow.

Getting back to the key indices that defined transformation, these are as follows:

- The single point agenda and self belief for the President, Defence Secretary and SLAF rank and file was that terrorism could be defeated *militarily.* A pragmatic road plan for doing so was prepared and ruthlessly implemented.
- The need for politico-military synergy as well as inter and intra service synergy was understood and institutional corrections carried out at the

highest political levels. The SLAF was thus formally given all that the military the world over dreams of but rarely achieves: a free hand in resolving an identified problem and with unstinted political support. Retired Indian Army General, Maj Gen Ashok Mehta, a veteran of Operation Pawan and a widely read defence analyst, said, "They did everything a General dreams of: unfettered resources and no political interference."[18] The military got whatever resources it wanted simply by asking.[19]

- The *Los Angeles Times* adds that "the military budget grew by 40% a year, and the Army exploded by 70% to 180,000 troops, adding 3000 a month compared with 3000 a year previously, drawing hugely from rural Sinhalese attracted by relatively high wages in a struggling economy.[20]"The figures given by General Sarath Fonseka are a little at variance, though, but in the upward direction. These indicate that the SLA's strength "rose to 200,000 from 116,800 as some 80,000 novices joined the Army in the past few months."[21]
- The article goes on to say that the Army was finally able to invoke the Russian, tried and tested strategy of Simultaneity (referred to earlier in this chapter) and were "able to hit the Tigers on several fronts (and at varying depths – authors perception) simultaneously", making a break with years of 'hit-or-miss operations."[22] The SLA military spokesman, Brig Nayanakkara, explained this tactic to the *LA Times* Correspondent thus: "Before, the Army would take territory, then move on, allowing the LTTE to come back. That changed and we hit them on all four fronts so that they could no longer muster all their resources into one place."[23]
- Perhaps the most important aspect of the transformation that changed the profile of the SLA from a pedestrian force to a first rate one, was their development of high grade intelligence, and its subsequent, ruthless utilization. Anyone dealing with intelligence knows how its availability or absence underscores the success or failure of any operation. So it came to pass that hit-or-miss gave way to intelligence driven operations that not only led to better force utilization, but brought down casualties as much as they enhanced the morale and motivation of rank and file. Finally, intelligence, along with politico-military synergy were the key differentiators that won the war for Sri Lanka. It is surmised that Karuna's defection from the LTTE and his (presumed) SWOT analysis for the SLAF must have provided the SLAF the intelligence turnaround that it needed.
- One of the major turnarounds achieved was in the mental sphere. The SLA

rank and file was repeatedly told, ad nauseum, that the LTTE wasn't 10 feet tall; on the contrary, they were very much defeatable and in their own den. To do so, there was a need for all to do their tasks with grit, patience and determination. Perception management was, thus, very effectively reoriented to convince soldier, politician, peasant, children, young men and women, the world at large, that the State and its Army were on the right track and needed the support of all. In this connection, the blunders made by the LTTE leadership – cutting off the Mavil Aru water needed for the paddy fields of 15,000 Tamil farmer families living in Government controlled areas was one example – were broadcast far and wide and the silent Sinhala majority emotions played upon, leading to eventual vociferous public support for the Government's point of view.

- The harnessing of the enormous power of the media was intelligently thought through and a page taken from the LTTE's brilliant handling of media as a weapon of war. All mediums of media propagation; audio, video, data, print, the innovative use of cell phones and their manifold communication means, were fully and brilliantly exploited. Thus, when Prabhakaran's death was confirmed, the Government ensured that all cell phone providers carried a Government sms announcing the death to their customer bases featuring in millions, within minutes of the announcement.
- Early on, the officer cadre of the SLAF understood that if the war had to be won, it would be because they had chosen to lead. Soldiers the world over expect their officers to do that, especially if the going is tough and the simple Sinhala was no different. Post acceptance of this imperative, the SLA in particular, literally exploded. A list of officers who lost their lives in the civil war finds some of the senior most officers listed amongst the martyrs; perhaps another first for any war against insurgents. Thus you had Division commanders, Brigade commanders, Commanding Officers literally leading their men into battle, and sometimes paying the ultimate price for doing so. In fact, the pace was apparently set by the service Chiefs themselves, with Commander Army in the driver's seat. Post the aborted assassination attempt on him, he is reported to have come out all guns blazing, in that he was everywhere where the action was, goading, encouraging, sometimes using cussed soldier's language even with senior officers of the rank of Division commander (his own soldierly confession).[24] The SLA got its shot of adrenalin and got energized to deliver.

- The fact that the SLAF lost one serving Commander of the Navy, 3 Lt Gens, 7 Maj Gens (all SLA), 1 Rear Admiral, (Navy), 1 Air Commodore (Air Force) and several Brigs, Colonels and equivalent ranks, all in actual combat will make any military in the world a proud one. It may be noted that during Eelam 4, which ended in Prabhakaran's death, the SLA lost 190 officers and 5,200 soldiers, with a staggering 27,000 all ranks suffering battle injuries. For this loss, they killed 22,000 LTTE cadres and captured 9,000 of them alive.[25]
- What apparently stunned the LTTE leadership was the sudden, unexpected change in the SLA tactics. This is best explained in the words of the Commander of the Army, General Sarath Fonseka[26] himself: ... "I did not adopt traditional fighting war techniques. Sun Tzu has said `Attack the most vulnerable point first. We first launched attacks on the most difficult points. Some people in air-conditioned rooms thought we were doing the wrong thing. When the wounded numbers increased they said we were crazy, and inexperience is what made us take such measures. I had put out all three divisions from the most difficult point. It was a move made on purpose. Our priority was killing enemy numbers. To complete the operation in two to three years was our plan. We conducted the necessary operations with that in mind. It took us eight months to take Thampannai that was just four km from our front lines. On certain occasions, the Security Council asked me indirectly whether the Army was stuck? Why aren't you advancing? I knew we were on the right track with our plans to destabilise the LTTE. Once we accomplished that, the next move was advancing and capturing territory."
- The bold but well considered decision to make up for severe junior officer shortages due to battlefield losses which General Sarath Fonseka risked taking, was to promote 1,500 corporals into officer rank after exposing them to a short training capsule. Here is how he explains this issue: "There was a shortage of company leaders. I had to promote 1,500 good corporals and sergeants without any training to such positions due to urgency. They were given two months of Officer Behavioural Training only. They were fitted into companies attached to the units they were already deployed in. The most numbers in officer deaths were from this group. They were the ones who were in the forefront of operations. Their morale was also high due to their promotions. They built up their qualities in these areas."[27]
- Asked pointed questions by the interviewer about corruption in the Army

and his well known toughness, the General gave out key transformational inputs that changed the profile of his Army and made it thoroughly professional. He accepted that he was unrelenting in identifying the corrupt and inefficient and ruthlessly weeding them out. He also accepted that his reputation as a tough man had substance, as there were occasions when he had to use rough language on even his Division commanders, something previous Army Commanders had never done.[28]

SRI LANKA NAVY

The Sri Lankan Navy (SLN)[29] is the naval arm of the Sri Lankan Armed Forces and is classed as the most vital defence force of Sri Lanka, due to the country's island geography. It conducts maritime operations at sea for the defence of the Sri Lankan nation and its interests.

Sri Lanka situated in the middle of major sea lanes passing through the Indian Ocean was always a magnet for seafarers. In 1937 the Ceylon Naval Volunteer Force (CNVF) was established. After World War II, CNVF was absorbed into the Royal Navy as the Ceylon Royal Naval Volunteer Reserve (CRNVR). On 9 December 1950 the Navy Act was enacted and the Royal Ceylon Navy was formed. In 1972, with Sri Lanka becoming a Republic and the introduction of new constitution Royal Ceylon Navy was renamed as the Sri Lanka Navy. In recent years it has played a key role in the Sri Lankan civil war, conducting deep sea, costal and inshore patrols, amphibious and supply operations. The SLN has its own elite Special Forces unit, the Special Boat Squadron.

The Commander-in-Chief of the Sri Lankan Military is the President of the country, who heads the National Security Council through the Ministry of Defense, which is the highest level of military command charged with formulating, executing defence policy and procurements for the armed forces. However operations of the Sri Lanka Navy are coordinated by the Joint Operations Command, with other two armed forces. The Sri Lanka Navy numbers 48,000 people of whom approximately 15,000 are deployed for land operations and duties.

Recent History

At the beginning of the civil war in the 1980's the SLN found itself poorly equipped to face the new threats the LTTE created. But this was soon overcome by increasing the fleet of patrol boats and the introduction of fast attack craft. These proved highly successful in limiting the LTTE's use of the seas. The weapon systems on these were upgraded with time as the Sea Tigers resorted to using sophisticated suicide craft against SLN craft. In addition, two locally build Jayasagara class Off Shore Patrol Craft were added to the fleet to carry out anti-smuggling operations and coastal surveillance.

The size of the force along with the fleet increased in the years of war. In the early 80's, a land combat force was created which at first limited itself to Base defence and, as its numbers increased, took part in offensive operations against the LTTE along with the Sri Lankan Army. An Elite Naval Special Forces unit called the Special Boat Squadron was created in the late 80's, based on the British Special Boat Service. In the early 90's the SLN carried out in conjunction with the Army its first amphibious operation code named *Operation Sea Breeze* followed by the larger *Operation Balavegaya* a year later. On the seas it began an aggressive clapdown on LTTE activities including gunrunning. It was during this time in 1992, that Admiral W.W.E. Clancy Fernando, the Commander of the Navy, was assassinated by a suicide bomb attack by the LTTE. In 2000, the Navy started a fleet air arm (FAA) by acquiring a HAL Chetak from India. Currently the FAA operates from the three Offshore Patrol Vessels of the fleet. During the same timeframe, conventional warfare capability was increased by the addition of Missile Corvettes.

Following the resumption of hostilities between the Government of Sri Lanka and the LTTE since early 2006, the Navy took up an active role in limiting the LTTE's use of the seas. This resulted in several major sea battles. Most significant of these battles were the interception and sinking of several large cargo ships that were bringing illegal arms shipments to the LTTE in the Indian Ocean.

Organisation

Naval Headquarters

The professional head of the SLN is the Commander of the Navy (C of N). He is Rear Admiral Thisara Samarasinghe, and reports directly to the Minister of Defence. (Admiral Wasantha Karannagoda, RSP, VSV, USP, was the previous, distinguished Commander and is, with effect from July 15, 2009, the current National Security Advisor to the President). The Commander of the Navy exercises operational and administrative control of the Navy from Naval headquarters in *SLNS Parakrama*, Colombo. He is assisted by the Chief of Staff (C of S), at present Rear Admiral Jayanath Colombage, who along with Directors General and Directors comprise the *Board of Management* (BOM) and *Board of Directors* (BOD) of the Sri Lanka Navy.

Commands

The Navy has five commands known as Naval Area Commands, each under the control of a flag officer for effective command and administrative control. This is in order to efficiently maintain all ships, craft and vehicles; and to ensure the operational readiness of commands and units each area shall have its own harbour/ base, repair and refitting facilities, signal centres, logistic, civil engineering and medical facilities.

Units

- 3rd Fast Gun Boats Squadron (3 FGS)
- 4th Fast Attack Flotilla (4 FAF)
- 7th Surveillance Command Squadron
- Special Boat Squadron (Sri Lanka)
- Rapid Action Boat Squadron

Current Deployment

Due to the Sri Lankan Civil War the SLN has been on a constant mobilized (including reservist) state since the 1980s (except for a brief period from 2002-2005). The majority of the naval units both at sea and ground based are deployed in the North and Eastern provinces of the country, as well as in other parts of the country. The security of all major ports of the country is the responsibility of the Navy, due to terrorist activity.

Training

The basic officer training is carried out at the Naval & Maritime Academy at the SLN Dockyard in Trincomalee and short/specialized officer training is conducted at the SLNS Gemunu, Welisara. This training includes theoretical aspects covered at the training institute followed by a practical exposure on board the Sri Lanka Navy fleet at sea.

Basic training for new recruits (approximately six months) is conducted at Advanced Naval Training Centre, SLNS 'Nipuna'; Naval Artificer Training Institute, SLNS 'Thakshila', Welisara; and at Naval Recruit Training Centres at several shore establishments . This basic training will be followed by *on-the-job* training on-board fleet units and at shore establishments. Combat Training School at SLNS '*Pandukabaya*' conducts combat training for Naval Patrolmen. Additional training is carried out in UK, India, Pakistan and Australia.

Current Fleet

The Offshore Patrol Vessel SLNS Sayura

The Sri Lankan naval fleet consists of above 50 combat, support ships and inshore patrol craft.

Offshore Patrol Vessels

The Offshore Patrol Vessels (OPV) are the largest warships of the Sri Lanka Navy. There are 3 OPVs in service of the SLN; SLNS *Sayura*, SLNS *Samudura*, SLNS *Sagara* all capable of operating naval helicopters and another the locally built SLNS *Jayasagara*,. These ships are deployed in the high seas to carry out surveillance and interception of illegal arms smuggling, and also to monitor naval activity within the EEZ.

Fast Attack Vessels

The Fast Attack Vessels (FAV) were added to the SLN in 2001 when two Israeli *Saar 4* class missile boats were acquired. These vessels, which were referred to as the *Nandimithra* class and equipped with Gabriel II anti-ship missiles, increased the SLN's conventional warfare capability to provide a multi-role platform for different operations undertaken by the Navy.

Patrol Vessels

The large patrol vessels of the Sri Lankan Navy are of two categories; the Submarine Chaser and Fast Gun Boat. The SLNS *Parakramabahu* is a *Haiqing* class submarine chaser armed for anti-submarine warfare missions. Fast Gun Boats (FGB) carry out multi-role missions, from coastal patrols to shore bombardment, in support of amphibious operations. FGBs consist of ships from the Chinese *Lushun* class, *Haizhui* class and *Shanghai II* class.

Fast Attack Craft

Fast Attack Crafts (FAC) have proven to be the workhorse of the SLN in combating the Sea Tigers of the LTTE in the coastal waters of Northern and Eastern parts of the island. Attached to the 4th Fast Attack Flotilla, these boats are 25 metres in length, with around 50 tons displacement, with the ability to reach speeds of 45 knots and are armed with rapid fire weapons. Primarily deployed in offensive operations for the *denial of sea*, they are also used for defensive operations to counter the Sea Tigers' suicide craft from attacking both naval and civilian ships. There are several classes of FACs, such as the locally built *Colombo* class, the Israeli *Super Dvora* class, *Dvora* class, *Shaldag* class, British *Chevron* class and the American *Trinity Marine* class.

Inshore Patrol Craft

Inshore Patrol Craft are small, 14 metre long vessels, which are capable of operating inshore as well as for beaching. They are capable of speeds in excess of 30 knots and are used for small boat operations, harbour defence and amphibious operations.

Littoral Attack Craft

Littoral Warfare Craft are small 23 ft-long *Arrow class* attack speed boats, capable of high speed and maneuverability. These have the capability of projecting a high degree of fire power for a vessel of its size. Introduced in 2006, these boats are manufactured by SLN's own boat yard and are used by the Elite Special Boat Squadron (SBS) and the Rapid Action Boat Squadron (RABS) for small boat operations.

Amphibious Warfare Vessels

The SLN has several vessels to support amphibious operations it carries out. These include *Yuhai* class tank landing ship SLNS *Shathi*; 29 M utility landing craft (locally built); *Yunnan* class mechanized landing craft and a M-10 Utility craft air cushion.

Auxiliary Vessels

The Navy has several auxiliary vessels such as fast personnel carriers and replenishment ships. Fast personnel carriers are Catamarans which are used for both troop and civilian transport, running the gauntlet of LTTE suicide craft. SLN's fleet of non-commissioned replenishment ships have been used for different purposes, including the replenishment at sea during operations in international waters.

Equipment

- Gabriel – Anti-ship missiles.
- Typhoon – Naval Optronic Stabilized Weapon Platforms.
- M242 Bushmaster – 25 mm (25×137mm) chain-fed auto cannon.

Fleet Air Arm

With the Navy deploying offshore patrol vessels (OPV) in its fleet since 2001 when SLNS *Sayura* was commissioned, the SLN has been considering the development of a fleet air arm to operate from these offshore patrol vessels. Two types of helicopters believed to be able to operate from these ships are being tested by the Navy. They include:

- HAL Chetak.
- HH-65 Dolphin.

Special Forces

The SLN has its own Elite Special Forces unit, the Special Boat Squadron. Established in the 1980s, SBS was modelled after the Special Boat Service of the Royal Navy. It has roles in naval special operations such as amphibious raids, Maritime Counter-Terrorism, Reconnaissance and Target Indication and small boat operations. As a Special Forces Unit, its role is not limited to water-borne operations. It also conducts operations on land, either with ground combat units of the Navy and the Army, or separately.

Women in the Sri Lanka Navy

Today women are recruited to both the regular and volunteer forces. Although at first limited to the medical branch, currently both lady officers and female ratings are able to join any branch of service including the executive branch as well.

THE SLN TRANSFORMATION: BECOMING THE HUNTER, NOT THE HUNTED

The importance of the SLN transition from a *sleepy 'constabulary service' to a 'potent counter insurgency force'*, especially with its back to the wall, cannot be undermined. This change occurred under intense pressure, public scrutiny, and the pressing operational need to support the Army's operational strategy to isolate the LTTE into the chosen killing grounds – with all escape routes, supplies of war material and chances of a getaway by their elite leadership firmly closed by the SLN. This strategy was greatly successful. The aim now is to explore the dynamics of that change.

Star Player

The story of change really begins with Admiral Wasantha Karannagoda, who assumed command of the Sri Lanka Navy on the 1st of September, 2005. He left this assignment in July 2009 and is currently the NSA to President Rajapaksa. In the 59-year history of the Sri Lanka Navy, he is the only officer to be considered for the highest seat of the Commander of the Navy straight from a Naval Area Command.[30] He has commanded the four Operational Naval Commands on seven occasions – Northern, Eastern and Western Commands twice each and North Central once, for a total period spanning six years. He was the first ever Director General (Operations) at Naval Headquarters. Prior to that, he served as the Director Naval Operations, Director Naval Projects and Plans as well as Director Naval Personnel and Training.[31] After assuming command of the Navy, he changed the *modus operandi* of SLN operations by increasing deep sea operations against the LTTE Naval Wing.[32] This ensured the success of naval operations against them, with the destruction of eight of their ships within a year.

Sea Control

The Defence Secretary, Gottabhaya Rajapaksa, in an address to naval personnel at the auditorium of the SLN's Eastern Naval Command Headquarters in Trincomalee, on the 28th of August, 2009, gave the background of the Navy's transition. It started off in end 2005, he said, when the Rajapaksa Government had just taken over. A military assessment was obtained from the commanders of the three Armed Forces.[33] The country's defence policy was promulgated based on this military analysis, he said. Each commander had made an analysis of the LTTE's future plans. All these analyses revealed the LTTE's inevitable preparations for a military offensive. The President was presented with a plan containing LTTE's military preparations accordingly, the Defence Secretary further revealed. It especially showed the LTTE's attempt to take control of the Trincomalee Harbour and its environs...cripple the Navy's ships and craft movement and thereby obstruct the deployment of a substantial number of security forces in the Jaffna peninsula. If that sinister attempt was allowed to bear fruit, the entire effort in defeating LTTE terrorism would become unsuccessful. This fact alone shows how important it is militarily to retain sea control at all times and to maintain the seas and its environs safe and secure, the Defence Secretary said.[34]

Keeping Sea Routes Secure

The LTTE Sea Tigers attempted to wrest control of two-thirds of the country's coastal belt in order to exploit the sea routes for arms smuggling since they only had very little land access to the Eastern Province except via Weli Oya and to secure a link between the Northern Province and the Eastern Province. Prior to the liberation of the Wanni, the entire responsibility of transporting 40,000 to

50,000 members of the Sri Lanka Army, Sri Lanka Navy, Sri Lanka Air Force and the police to the Jaffna peninsula and providing them with food supplies and required arms and ammunitions rested with the Navy. The number of recoveries made of suicide craft, torpedoes, semi-submersibles and other underwater devices bear ample evidence to how hard the LTTE had to sweat to secure initial control of the seas.

Swarming: Paying the Sea Tigers Back with Value Added

In a detailed and fascinating 'hard talk' with Tim Fish,[35] the JNI Correspondent in March 2009, (when he was Commander SLN), then Vice-Admiral (now Admiral and NSA) Wasantha Karannagoda, says: "We found that the SLN did not have a suitable boat to stop the LTTE gunrunning and other activities. We looked around the world and saw the Israeli Navy was facing a similar threat and were using Dvora fast attack craft as a response."

Sri Lanka, the article says, bought its first pair of 47-ton Dvora-class FAC from Israel in early 1984 and another four were purchased in 1986. An upgraded version – the 54 ton Super Dvora Mk I – was ordered from Israeli Aircraft Industries (IAI) in October 1986 and delivered from 1987–88, with a further four Super Dvora Mk II-class FAC delivered in 1995–96. "We bought [the Dvoras] and first put them into action in the late 1980s, and the Sea Tigers found it very difficult to meet these Israeli-built craft," says Adm. Karannagoda. But then, to counter this, the LTTE developed very high horsepower suicide boats and used swarming tactics to overwhelm the Dvoras, which in our view could not tackle them effectively."[36] The statistics of losses incurred support his viewpoint: between 1993 and 2000, the SLN lost 6 Dvora FAC's, as well as 6 more FAC's of US and Chinese make.

"The Dvoras were finding it very difficult in battles at sea with normal fighting craft against about 15 Sea Tiger craft and another eight to 10 suicide craft, which would sometimes mingle with fishermen." Identifying the suicide boats in a swarm of Sea Tiger craft was difficult as the former appeared identical to the insurgents' regular attack boats. SLN crews would have to watch for subtle differences in the behaviour of the craft, monitoring their movements and noting if they were heavier in the water in order to identify them; this was not a skill that could be taught in the classroom. Suicide boats had to be identified and destroyed swiftly, as given time they would attack in a pack of five or six in an attempt to overwhelm the SLN crews. With a low profile and moving at 35–40 kt, the suicide craft were very difficult to engage with gunfire and some were armoured at the front, meaning small-calibre rounds would ricochet off.

Battles involved numerous small craft and intense close-quarters action between boat crews within a 2 km range. The Sea Tigers' larger craft had four 250 hp petrol outboard motors, while the small boats were equipped with two: if one motor was damaged the other could be used to effect an escape. Adm Karannagoda says: "We had to counter this situation so our engineers did some extensive research-and-development [R&D] work and developed three categories of new boats. With this we developed our Small Boats Concept, which was a major turning point in the progress of the war." The Small Boats Concept effectively copied the Sea Tigers' asymmetric tactics, but on a much larger scale."[37] Under Admiral Karannagoda and Commodore DKP Dassanayake, who was the CO of the Small Boat Squadron (SBS), the Sri Lankan Navy became the hunter and not the hunted.[38] During the 2006-2009 Eelam War IV, the Sri Lankan Navy's small boat squadron of over 200 indigenously-built boats was based in Trincomalee and was operating on the Mullaithivu coastline. The SLN developed three categories of small craft[39] and associated war fighting tactics as part of this transformation.[40] They were employed in infantry-style tactics to gain ascendancy over swarms of Sea Tiger attack craft and suicide boats. The correlation with infantry tactics is valid. In the Indian context, this is easily understood by stating that swarming was the primary tactic that the Chinese employed against the Indian Army in the 1962 Sino-Indian War. Seen in layman terms, it is the attack on the selected objective in overwhelming strength and from multiple directions, so that the target is swamped, not being able to interdict more than a portion of this multi direction attack. In the specific case of the LTTE, swarming was carried forward to a new dimension, because, for the Sea Tigers, part of the swarm cluster of boats contained suicide boats laden with explosives, which were equipped with grapnels allowing them to close up to the target and trigger an explosion, thereby destroying the target craft along with the attacking craft.

Swarming, as a military tactic, has attracted a lot of attention, especially in the USA, and is considered a Revolution in Military Affairs (RMA). It is defined[41] as "a behaviour in which autonomous, or semi-autonomous units of action, attack an enemy from several different directions and then regroup… Military swarming involves the use of a decentralised force against an opponent, in a manner that emphasises mobility, communication, unit autonomy and coordination/ synchronisation….The U.S. Joint Forces Command defined military swarming as 'a manoeuver' in which forces and firepower converge on a target force simultaneously from all directions."[42] …

The SLN thus did a 'LTTE' to the Sea Tigers, in much the same manner that the SLA had done to the LTTE's Army Wing; they replicated what the LTTE were doing, but with value addition, on a far greater scale, and with the full, unqualified support of their political masters. As Tim Fish writes in his very perceptive article, "the SLN started to use large numbers of small high-speed heavily armed Inshore Patrol Craft (IPC) to outnumber the LTTE suicide boats and overwhelm them during battle. Hundreds of indigenously produced fibre glass IPC have been built in three variants for operations in different sea states. The smallest is the 23 ft-long Arrow; a second class is 14 m long, with both types able to operate in conditions up to Sea State 3. A third variant – a 17 m command-cum fighting boat – can cope with conditions up to Sea State 4."[43] The 14 m and 17 m boats are fitted with four 250 hp engines, giving a top speed of 37 kt. Armaments include a double-barreled 23 mm gun, CIS 40 mm Automatic Grenade Launcher (AGL) acquired from Singapore Technologies Kinetics and two 12.7 mm (.50 calibre) machine guns. The smaller Arrow boats have two 250 hp engines for a top speed of 35 kt and are equipped with a single-barrel 23 mm gun (or a .50 calibre gun) and an AGL. The Dvora FAC have been upgraded with 30 mm guns and the SLN has used its own engineers to integrate the Bushmaster M242 25 mm gun on to the deck during sea acceptance and harbour acceptance trials. Bushmaster is built by US-based Alliant Techsystems, which transferred the guns to Sri Lanka under the US State Department guidelines.[44]

Destruction of Floating Arms Warehouses[45]

The Defence Secretary, in his August 28, 2009, address, said that because of the stranglehold the SLN had established, the Navy, during the past three and half years and, especially the last one year, performed its duties with utmost vigilance, never allowing the LTTE to put out any boats to sea. Because of the Navy's total sea control, the Secretary of Defence went on to add, the LTTE was forced to deploy its Sea Tigers and their leaders, not at sea but on land. While performing this onerous task, the Navy dealt the deadliest blow to the LTTE by locating and destroying their floating arms warehouses, for the first time in the naval history at great distances (2,000 nautical miles away, near Australian waters) in high seas, which was the turning point in defeating terrorism and achieving victory. "We went near (the) Australian waters and whacked the last four vessels," says then Vice-Adm Karannagoda. "Yet we are not a big Navy; we had to improvise and use innovation and ingenuity to get our job done. The SLN does not possess any frigate-sized ships, so we used offshore patrol vessels and old tankers, merchant vessels and fishing trawlers as support vessels."[46] ... After the destruction of the warehouse ships, small boats would be lowered into the water for close engagement and for the collection of debris as evidence of the ships' illicit cargos. Because the LTTE vessels were rogue ships lacking identification, the SLN forces could claim entitlement to self-defence at sea to protect themselves when they approached and came under attack.

Jet Liner – the Life Link[47]

Commending the Navy's Jet Liner Passenger Craft performance, the Defence Secretary said that it fulfilled an enormous task by transporting over three thousand security forces personnel at a time, who were going on leave as well as returning back to duty, between Trincomalee to Kankasanthurai. Had any calamity befallen on this vessel, the whole military operation would have collapsed. To make this possible, the entire Navy, from the Navy Commander down to the sailors, worked with great dedication and commitment, the Defence Secretary said. The LTTE's persistent desire to target the Jet Liner was clearly manifested in the capture of the suicide craft and underwater devices designed for such an attack, knowing very well that it would be a decisive blow to the entire effort. As such, the protection of the Jet Liner at all costs took the highest priority. The Navy rose to this challenge and maintained the sea link safe and kept the transportation of security forces personnel as well as the supplies of food and weapons uninterrupted.

SRI LANKA AIR FORCE

The Sri Lanka Air Force[48] (not abbreviated as SLAF, to avoid confusion with Sri Lanka Armed Forces) is the air arm and the youngest of the Royal Air Force (RAF). The SLAF operates more than 160 aircraft and has a projected trained strength of 27,400 airmen and 1,300 officers who are from both regular and reserve service. The Sri Lanka Air Force has expanded to specialize mainly in providing air-support to ground forces, troop landing and carrying out air strikes on rebel-held areas in the Northern and Eastern theatres, but also capable of high and low level air defence. The Commander of the Air Force is the professional head of the Sri Lanka Air Force.

Recent History

The first time the Royal Ceylon Air Force went into combat was when the Marxist JVP launched an island wide insurrection on April 5, 1971. The Ceylon Armed Forces were caught off guard, when police stations throughout the island were being attacked. Responding rapidly, the RCyAF deployed its limited aircraft, at first, to resupply besieged police stations and military outposts and patrol around major cities. The Jet Provosts were taken out of storage and put in to service in a matter of three days to carry out attacks on insurgents. During this insurgency, the left-leaning Bandaranaike Government turned to the Soviet Union for more sophisticated weaponry, and received five Mikoyan-Gurevich MiG-17F fighter bombers, a MiG-15 UTI trainer, as well as two Kamov Ka-26 helicopters meant for search and rescue and casualty evacuation. The RAF's heavy transports also flew in six Bell 47G helicopters purchased from the United States, which were put in to combat after only five days of pilot training. Air Force personnel joined the ground operations and the insurgents surrendered after about a month's fighting.

1980s & 1990s

Rapid growth of the Sri Lanka Air Force began in the mid-1980s, when the Sri Lankan civil war against Tamil separatists drew the service into a major, long-term security role. In 1982, Sri Lanka Air Force reactivated airfields (disused since World War II) in Batticaloa, Anuradhapura, Koggala and Sigiriya, all later becoming Sri Lanka Air Force Stations. During the Eelam War I conflict between 1983 and 1987, the force grew by nearly 50 percent.

After the 1983 riots, the Government worked rapidly to expand the inventory, relying largely on sources in Italy, Britain, and the United States. Because of budget constraints, the Air Force was compelled to refit a number of non-combat aircraft for military uses in counter-terrorism operations against the LTTE terrorists. From the period 1983 to 1985, the Air Force acquired 11 Bell 212 helicopters, four Bell 412 helicopters, three SIAI Marchetti SF.260s, two Cessna 337s, one Hawker Siddeley HS 748 and two Beechcraft Super King Airs. By 1985, nine more Bell 212s were added to the fleet, along with four Bell 412s. The 412s along with the SIAI Marchetti SF.260 aircraft advanced the attack capabilities of the Air Force. Central in the Government's security efforts were six SIAI Marchetti SF.260TP turboprops, which were used for rocket attacks and strafing. Additionally, the Air Force, with the help of Heli Orient of Singapore, equipped twelve Bell 212 and Bell 412 helicopters to serve as gun ships and as transport vehicles for highly successful commando assault operations. The Air Force had a fleet of approximately 80 aircraft, of which 64 were reported to be operational in early 1988.

Government forces reportedly also used helicopters on bombing missions. A more effective bombing capability was provided by a small fleet of Chinese Harbin Y-12 turboprop transport aircraft. These were equipped with bomb racks that had been fitted to carry up to 1,000 kilograms of fragmentation and antipersonnel bombs. Transport, training, and surveying functions were carried out by a variety of Cessna and de Havilland aircraft. In 1987, during the Vadamarachchi Operation, the Air Force mustered one HS 748, two Y-12s and one de Havilland Heron, all configured as improvised bombers. On 3rd September, 1987, a Women's Wing was formed and located in Colombo. The Women's Wing was set up to maintain and update all records pertaining to female officers and airwomen, prepare promotional schedules, annual assessments, issue identity cards, etc. In order to increase the attack capability, the Air Force in 1991 acquired four F-7 Sky Bolts, three FT-7s and two Shenyang J-5s from China. Later in 1993 the first of three Mil Mi-17 helicopter transports were acquired along with four FMA IA 58 Pucarás for ground attack. These proved to be effective but three of the Pucarás were lost, due to Surface-to-Air missiles launched by the LTTE. The sole remaining Pucara was retired in 1999 due to lack of spare parts. In 1995, Mil Mi-24 gun ships were acquired for close air support for the army and by 2001 Mil Mi-35s were added to the fleet. In 1996 the SLAF acquired six Kfir C.2s and a single TC.2 from Israel and a further nine of these aircrafts had been added to the inventory by 2005. This included four C.2s and four C.7s in 2001. Currently the SLAF operates two C.7s, eight C.2s and two TC.2s. The SLAF used these Kfirs to launch attacks against Tamil separatist targets in rebel-controlled areas of the island.

21st Century Developments

In 2000, new aircraft were acquired; apart from the additions of Kfir C.7s and Mi-35s, these included six Mikoyan MiG-27 dedicated ground attack aircraft (obtained due to lack of specialised ground attack aircraft since the retirement of the Pucarás), a MiG-23UB trainer and two C-130 Hercules for heavy transport. Six K-8 Karakorum trainers were soon bought from Pakistan creating the No. 14 Squadron to train pilots for the newly-expanded fleet of jets.

On 24th July 2001, thirteen aircraft including two Kfir jet fighters, one Mi-24 helicopter gunship and one MiG-27 jet fighter, were destroyed in the predawn attack by the LTTE on the Katunayake Air Base, about 35 km north of Colombo. Three military training aircraft and five civilian jets were also among the destroyed aircraft. Many of these aircraft were replaced.

Sri Lanka's airports have remained on alert for a repeat of the 2001 attack, with severe restrictions on the number of people allowed into the terminal buildings. Huge walls were also built around the terminals and the control towers to prevent impact from car bomb attacks, while a large number of sentries were placed along the approach roads to the facility. All airports including the

Katunayake International Airport are heavily guarded by members of the Sri Lankan Air Force Regiment.

In 2006, four MiG-27 were bought from Ukraine to replace two losses in crashes and one in the attack on the airport. Currently the SLAF operates three FT-7, three F-7BS, six F-7G, two Kfir TC.2, two Kfir C.7, eight Kfir C.2, seven Mig-27 and one MIG-23UB trainer. The SLAF uses these ground-attack aircraft on attacks against Tamil separatist targets in rebel-controlled areas of the island.

In the early hours of October 22, 2007, a ground attack by the LTTE on SLAF Anuradhapura at Saliyapura, which was supported briefly by its Air Wing, resulted in the destruction of eight aircraft with several others damaged. The attack only affected the SLAF's training element. Early in 2008 the Air Force received six F-7Gs; these will be primarily used as interceptors and are attached to the No.5 Jet Squadron. In October 2008 the Air Force claimed its first air-to-air kill, when it reported that one of its F-7G interceptors shot down a Zlin Z 43 of the LTTE air wing when it attempted to attack a military base in Vavuniya.

Organisation

Air Force Headquarters

The professional head of the Air Force is the Commander of the Air Force, at present Air Chief Marshal Roshan Goonatilake who reports directly to the Minister of Defence. The Commander of the Air Force exercises operational and administrative control of the Air Force from Air Force headquarters, SLAF Colombo. He is assisted by the Chief of Staff, at present Air Vice Marshal P.B. Premachandra, who along with Directors comprise the Board of Directors (BOD) of the Sri Lanka Air Force.

Commands

The Air Force has four commands known as zonal commands, each under the control of an air officer for effective command and administrative control. This is in order to efficiently command and control all flying squadrons, aircraft and air defences. Zonal Commanders are responsible for both air and ground operations that have been decided upon by the Directorate of Operations at Air Force HQ.

Air Defense Command

The Air Force is setting up an Air Defence Command. This command based at *SLAF Katunayake* is responsible for coordination of units to maintain integrated national air defence.

Aircraft Inventory

IAI Kfir of the No. 10 'Fighter' Squadron

A Mikoyan-Gurevich MiG-27 of the No. 12 Squadron

Mi-24V of No. 9 Attack Helicopter Squadron SLAF

A C-130 Hercules of No. 2 Heavy Transport Squadron SLAF

Future Equipment

Since 2007, the Sri Lanka Air Force has been planning to increase its interceptor capability with the acquisition of Mikoyan MiG-29 from Russia. Also according to the June 2009 issue of Airforce Monthly the Mig-27 and Kfir may also be retired in the near future with the winding down of combat operations and also since the aircraft are ageing. The favoured replacement will be the Mig-29; despite rumours, none have been inducted into the Air Force. The Air Force is also looking at the procurement of a dedicated maritime patrol aircraft.

Current Deployment

Due to the Sri Lankan Civil War, the Air Force has been in a constant mobilized (including reservist) state since the 1980s (except for a brief period from 2002-05).

- Air and ground operations are carried out from 20 bases around the country which includes 6 air bases with resident squadrons, 8 forward operational airfields, 4 ground stations and 2 SLAF Regiment detachments.
- Security of the Katunayake International Airport is maintained by the SLAF Regiment.

- Ground based air defence of vital infrastructure is carried out by the SLAF Regiment.

Training

Under the auspices of the British Royal Air Force, flight training was first offered to Royal Ceylon Air Force pilots at RAF Negombo, an RAF air base at Katunayake, in 1952. In addition, a number of cadet officers received flight training at the Royal Air Force College in Cranwell, England. After the British withdrew from their military facilities in Sri Lanka in 1967, the No 1 Squadron (Flight Training School) was established at the SLAF China Bay in Trincomalee. With the increase in Tamil separatist activities in the mid-1980s, the Air Force stepped up its training activities, bringing in foreign pilots to assist in the helicopter training programme.

Basic officer training is carried out at the Air Force Academy at the SLAF China Bay in Trincomalee. The academy offers a two-year programme of basic flight training and a variety of specialised courses. Pilot training is carried out at SLAF Anuradhapura by No. 1 Flying Training Wing using Cessna 150s for basic training and Nanchang CJ-6 (PT-6) aircraft for intermediate training. Advanced jet training is carried out by the No. 14 Squadron in K-8 Karakorums based at SLAF Katunayake. Specialized training for different types of aircraft is carried out by the respective squadrons; this includes MiG-23UB, FT-7 and Kfir TC.2 used by No. 5 Jet Squadron and No. 10 Fighter Squadron respectively, for this purpose at SLAF Katunayake and for training for transports, Harbin Y-12s of the No. 8 Light Transport Squadron are used along with Bell 206s for helicopter training.

Initial Ground Combat Training for both officers and other ranks of both regular and volunteer forces is carried out separately at SLAF Diyatalawa in the garrison town of Diyatalawa. It also conducts advanced training for SLAF regiment officer cadets. Following training at SLAF Diyatalawa, general pilot branch officer cadets are sent to the Air Force Academy for flight training, and airmen and airwomen are sent to Advanced & Specialized Trade Training School for specialized training in different trades. Air traffic controllers receive schooling at special facilities in Colombo as well as officer cadets from other branches. In addition, approximately twenty-five officers a year receive advanced training abroad, most commonly in Britain, India and, in recent years, at the United States Air Force Academy.

SLAF Regiment Special Force

Regiment Special Force is an elite Special Forces unit of the Sri Lanka Air Force, part of the SLAF Regiment. It provides highly effective land base defence and beyond forward defence line assault capabilities.

Women in the Sri Lanka Air Force

The first female officers to join the Air Force were in 1972, to the Volunteer Air Force. Today, women are recruited to both the regular and volunteer forces as both officers and airwomen to the SLAF Women's Wing. However there are no female pilots in the Air Force. Although female officers are not able to join the general duties pilot branch, they can join any other branch including the SLAF Regiment and the Air Force Police.

Assessment

The success of the SLA, to a fair extent, and, to a lesser extent, the SLN, has been underscored by the fact that the Sri Lanka Air Force was in support of their operations continuously; certainly during daylight hours. (No indication of night capability is available in any of the Government or think tank sites. One therefore presumes that if available, it must be restricted to a few helicopters).

Understanding the operational constraints of the Air Force are important because they serve to circumscribe what the Air Force could do and what it could not. A part of the new strategy of the SLA from 2006 onwards, was to increase their night operations. This change would almost certainly have excluded air support. Secondly, in an insurgency situation, the most difficult thing is to identify the enemy, and the location from which he /she has fired. The front line is never laid out in orderly lines so that the battle and hence its support can be templated. The ability to recognize friend or foe, a difficult situation at the best of times, becomes almost impossible for a fast flying aircraft to execute without fratricide losses. The impact of such losses due to friendly fire is heart breaking for own troops and does not promote inter-service cohesion and bonding. Not the least is the issue of the vulnerability of the flying platform to own as well as enemy fire. With the LTTE having dramatically established that they had a functional Air Force, by launching several successful air attacks on Sri Lankan Air Force assets including infrastructure, SLA could well have had trigger happy soldiers who could have taken potshots at their own aircraft, in the mistaken belief that they were those of the LTTe's. Such fratricidal losses would have proved damaging, especially since the LTTE had already imposed severe damages on the Sri Lankan Air Force.

The Navy would have had similar problems accepting air support in a swarming situation.

Aircraft	Origin	Role	Versions	In service
Attack and Offensive Support Aircraft				
IAI Kfir	Israel	fighter-bomber	C2/C7	10
		conversion trainer	TC2	2
Mikoyan-Gurevich MiG-27	Soviet Union	ground-attack aircraft	MiG-27M Flogger-D	7
Chengdu F-7 Airguard	China	interceptor	F-7GS	6
		fighter-bomber	F-7BS	3
		conversion trainer	FT-7	3
Reconnaissance and Maritime Patrol Aircraft				
Cessna 421 Golden Eagle	United States	maritime reconnaissance		1
Beechcraft 200T Super King Air	United States	maritime reconnaissance	200T	2
RQ-2 Pioneer	United States/ Israel	unmanned aerial vehicle		N/K
IAI Searcher	Israel	unmanned aerial vehicle		N/K
IAI Scout	Israel	unmanned aerial vehicle		N/K
EMIT Blue Horizon 2	Israel	unmanned aerial vehicle		N/K
Transport Aircraft				
Lockheed C-130 Hercules	United States	tactical airlift/transport	C-130K (L-382)	2
Antonov AN-32	Soviet Union Ukraine	tactical airlift/transport	AN-32B	7
Harbin Y-12	China	utility aircraft/trainer	Y-12 / Y-12(IV)	7/2
Attack Helicopters				
Mil Mi-24	Soviet Union	attack helicopter	Mi-35P/Mi-24V/ Mi-24P/Mi-24N	14

Support and Transport Helicopters				
Mil Mi-17	Soviet Union	troop transport	Mi-17	10
Bell 412	United States	utility helicopter/VIP transport	412EP	7
Bell 212 Twin Huey	United States	troop transport/MEDEVAC		9
Bell 206 JetRanger	United States	light utility helicopter/trainer	206A/B	5
Trainer Aircraft				
Hongdu K-8 Karakorum	China/Pakistan	advanced jet trainer		6
Mikoyan-Gurevich MiG-23	Soviet Union	conversion trainer	MiG-23UB	1
Nanchang CJ-6	China	Intermediate Prop Trainer	PT-6	8
Cessna 150	United States	Basic Trainer	150L	10

What remains to be seen is that the Air Force was given a free hand by the Government to carry out bombing and strafing on LTTE positions; a concession which is very rare indeed, in the conduct of anti insurgency operations; and has the contours of HR violations written into the subtext. Be that as it may, such carte blanche permission was given and had a definite impact on the end of the civil war as per the Governments road map.

Endnotes

1. Fish, Tim. "Sri Lanka Learns To Counter Sea Tigers' Swarm Tactics." *Jane's Navy International*, March 2009. <http://www.navy.lk/assets/files/pdf/2009/srilanka_jni_march2009.pdf>
2. Ibid.
3. Menezes, (Retd), Lt Gen S.L. "Fidelity and Honour: The Indian Army from the 17th to the 21st Century." UP. New Delhi, 1999. p.535.
4. The section, "Overview of SLAF" is excerpted from the article "Sri Lanka Armed Forces." <http://en.wikipedia.org/wiki/Sri_Lanka_Armed_Forces>
5. This section "Sri Lanka Army" has been excerpted from the article, "Sri Lanka Army."<http://en.wikipedia.org/wiki/Sri_Lanka_Army>
6. Aryachandra, Nisansala R. "An Officer and a Lady: You've Come a Long Way, Lass." <http://www.sundayobserver.lk/2006/10/08/zin01.asp>
7. Rabasa, Angel' Chalk, Peter; Cragin, Jim; Daly, Sara A.; Gregg, Heather S. Karasik; Theodore W. O'Brien; Kevin A. and Rosenau, William. "Beyond Al-Qaeda: The Outer Rings of the Terrorist Universe." RAND Study Part 2. <http://www.rand.org/pubs/monographs/2006/RAND_MG430.pdf>
8. Ibid.
9. "Corelli Barnett."<http://en.wikipedia.org/wiki/Correlli_Barnett>
10. Quinn, Dennis J. Editor. "The Goldwater-Nichols Department of Defence (DOD) Reorganisation Act: a Ten-Year Retrospective." National Defence University Press, Washington, D.C. 1999.
11. Ibid.
12. "Mavil Aru." <http://en.wikipedia.org/wiki/Mavil_Aru>
13. Ibid.
14. "Corelli Barnett." < http://en.wikipedia.org/wiki/Correlli_Barnett>
15. Clausewitz, Karl Von, *The Columbia Encyclopedia*, Sixth Edition. Copyright 2008. Columbia University Press. <http://www.encyclopedia.com/topic/Karl_von_Clausewitz.aspx>
16. Clausewitz "*On War*", Book 1. <http://kotare.typepad.com/thestrategist/2009/01/bourne-and-friction.html>
17. Ibid.
18. Magnier, Mark. "Sri Lanka's Victory may offer Lessons: The tactics the Government used to defeat the Tamil Tiger Rebels could help other nations grappling with insurgencies." May 23, 2009.<http://articles.latimes.com/2009.may/23/world/fg-sri-lanka-lessons23.
19. Ibid.
20. Ibid.
21. "Wanni War Heroes Given Military Honours & their Service Appreciated." <http://

www.army.lk/detailed.php?NewsId=579>; the figures given above have been extracted from a speech given by General Sarath Fonseka to his troops on May 28, 2009, at a commemoration function to honour the Wanni war heroes at Army Headquarters, Colombo.

22. Magnier, Mark. "Sri Lanka's Victory may offer Lessons: The tactics the Government used to defeat the Tamil Tiger Rebels could help other nations grappling with insurgencies." May 23, 2009.<http://articles.latimes.com/2009.may/23/world/fg-sri-lanka-lessons23
23. Ibid.
24. "Wanni War Heroes Given Military Honours & their Service Appreciated." <http:// www.army.lk/detailed.php?NewsId=579>; the figures given above have been extracted from a speech given by General Sarath Fonseka to his troops on May 28, 2009, at a commemoration function to honour the Wanni war heroes at Army Headquarters, Colombo.
25. "Wanni War Heroes Given Military Honours & their Service Appreciated." <http:// www.army.lk/detailed.php?NewsId=579>; the figures given above have been extracted from a speech given by General Sarath Fonseka to his troops on May 28, 2009, at a commemoration function to honour the Wanni war heroes at Army Headquarters, Colombo. [**Note: The figures of LTTE cadres killed are not in line with the figures of LTTE cadre strength reported in the RAND study quoted in this book and may need verification**]. The speech goes on to say that "By granting relief of death to those LTTE cadres, the Army amply depicted its discipline and dignity. More than 70 percent of the enemy's maritime and aerial resources were demolished by troops of the Army. Therefore, service and commitment, rendered by Army officers and other ranks in this battle cannot be equated to that of any other individual. As Commander of the Army, I am proud to state so, on behalf of the entire Army."
26. "Liberation of the East." Mavil Aru. July 21, 2006<http://www.lankanewspapers.com/news/ 2009/5/44102_space.html>
27. Ibid.
28. Ibid.
29. The section on the Sri Lanka Navy (SNA) has been excerpted from "Sri Lanka Navy." <http:/ /en.wikipedia.org/wiki/Sri_Lanka_Navy>
30. "Navy Commander Promoted to the Rank of Admiral." <http://www.defence.lk/ new.asp?fname=20090520_05>
31. Ibid.
32. "Wasantha Karannagoda." <http://en.wikipedia.org/wiki/Wasantha_ Karannagoda>
33. "Secretary of Defence pays glowing tribute to Sri Lanka Navy for its Decisive Role in eliminating LTTE Terrorism" <http://www.navy.lk/index.php?id =1829>
34. Ibid.
35. Fish, Tim. "Sri Lanka Learns To Counter Sea Tigers' Swarm Tactics." *Jane's Navy International*, March 2009. <http://www.navy.lk/assets/files/pdf/2009/srilanka_jni_ march2009.pdf>
36. Ibid.
37. Ibid.
38. Balachandran, PK. "India, Britain seek Lankan naval expertise." <http://www. expressbuzz.com/edition/story.aspx?>
39. Fish, Tim. IHS *Jane's Maritime Reporter*. "Other countries Could Learn from Sri Lanka

Navy's Fight Against the Tamil Tigers." August 24, 2009. <http://www.lankanewspapers.com/news/2009/8/47150_space.html>

40. Ibid. Fish writes in detail on the SBS tactics and training in his article. The SBS, he says, "was established on 22 October 2005 with 36 personnel and now numbers 600. It is the SLN's elite force, possessing high levels of physical fitness and advanced training in both land and sea warfare tactics. The SBS operates in four- to eight-man teams using the Arrow boats for rapid insertion or black rubber inflatable boats for covert approach from the sea. The teams have expertise in long-range communications and engage primarily in surveillance operations, providing a much-needed source of information on LTTE activities.
    According to one SBS operative, the completion of basic training takes a year, during which time about 60 per cent of applicants fail to make the grade or drop out. The remainder proceeds to advanced training, including paratrooper certification, diving skills and small-boat handling. The SBS is trained by the Indian Marine Commandos (MARCOS), US Green Berets and US Navy SEALs. RABS personnel are also trained to a high standard and comprise about 400 personnel, mostly those unable to make it through the selection phase for the SBS but still with sufficient levels of physical fitness and the capacity to develop their skills. The SLN uses these volunteers to man the small boats, and develops their expertise in the handling of the IPCs and fighting at sea. "Creating the two new units made a huge dent in LTTE operations as they were much better trained than previous crews," says Adm Karannagoda.
41. "Swarming (military)." < http://en.wikipedia.org/wiki/Swarming_(military)>
42. Ibid.
43. Fish, Tim. IHS *Jane's Maritime Reporter*. "Other countries Could Learn from Sri Lanka Navy's Fight Against the Tamil Tigers." August 24, 2009. <http://www.lankanewspapers.com/news/2009/8/47150_space.html>
44. Ibid.
45. "Secretary of Defence pays glowing tribute to Sri Lanka Navy for its Decisive Role in eliminating LTTE Terrorism" <http://www.navy.lk/index.php?id=1829>
46. Fish, Tim. IHS *Jane's Maritime Reporter*. "Other countries Could Learn from Sri Lanka Navy's Fight Against the Tamil Tigers." August 24, 2009. <http://www.lankanewspapers.com/news/2009/8/47150_space.html>
47. "Secretary of Defence pays glowing tribute to Sri Lanka Navy for its Decisive Role in eliminating LTTE Terrorism" <http://www.navy.lk/index.php?id=1829>
48. This section has been excerpted from "Sri Lanka Air Force." <http://en.wikipedia.org/wiki/Sri_Lanka_Air_Force>

References

1. "Sri Lanka Army Marks 50 Years". *Washington Post*, AP News. October 10, 1999. http://www.washingtonpost.com/wp-srv/aponline/19991010/aponline085414 _000.htm.
2. 'Military Balance, Sri Lanka'. *Institute of Peace and Conflict Studies*. http://www.ipcs.org/Military_militaryBalance2.jsp?database=1002&country2 =Sri%20Lanka.
3. "Training, Sri Lanka Army". *Sri Lanka Army*. http://army.lk/train.php.
4. "Sri Lanka". *Nations Encyclopedia*. http://www.nationsencyclopedia.com/Asia-and-Oceania/Sri-Lanka-ARMED-FORCES.html.
5. Kanagaraarachchi, Ramani (2007-01-20). "Heroes who made the supreme sacrifice". *Daily*

News (Associated Newspapers of Ceylon). http://www.dailynews.lk/2007/01/20/space01.asp.

6. Ratnayake, Brigadier Daya (2005-07-30). "Noble in death as in life". *The Sunday Times* (Wijeya Newspapers Ltd). http://sundaytimes.lk/050703/plus/appreciation.html.
7. "Sri Lankan Army Women's Corps". *About, Inc.* http://womenshistory. about.com/library/ency/blwh_sri_lanka_women_military.htm.
8. "Sri Lanka Army Women's Corps, Sri Lanka Army". *Sri Lanka Army.* http://www.army.lk/regiment_regular_19.php.
9. Michael K. Cecil: Sri Lanka's Military: The Search for a Mission, [1].
10. "From Unicorn to Unibuffel" (HTML). *Sunday Observer.* http://www.sundayobserver.lk/2004/04/25/fea22.html.
11. Bedi, Rahul (2007-06-02). "Sri Lanka turns to Pakistan, China for military needs". *IANS* (Urdustan.com Network). http://www.indianmuslims.info/news/2007/jun/02/sri_lanka_turns_pakistan_china_military_needs.html.
12. "Naval surveillance is the millstone around LTTE's neck". *P.K. Balachandran.* http://www.priu.gov.lk/news_update/features/20031017Naval_surveillance _millstone_LTTE.htm.
13. "Sri Lanka (LTTE)" (HTML). International Institute for Strategic Studies. March 15, 2007. http://acd.iiss.org/armedconflict/Mainpages/dsp_Conflict Weapons.asp?ConflictID=174.
14. "ZSD89 Armoured Personnel Carrier" (HTML). sinodefence.com. 2007. http://www.sinodefence.com/army/armour/zsd89.asp.
15. "Type 63" (HTML). nation.lk. //www.nation.lk/2006/10/15/newsfe1.htm.
16. "About Us". Sri Lanka Navy. http://www.Navy.lk/index.php?id=3.

CHAPTER 6

The Eelam Wars

With the roots of the conflict as also the key protagonists having been adequately covered in the preceding chapters, it is axiomatic that Part 1 of the book should end with a brief review of the wars they fought.

EELAM WAR I

Eelam War I is the name given to the initial phase of the armed conflict between the government of Sri Lanka and the LTTE.[1] Although tensions between the government and Tamil militant groups had been brewing since the 1970s, a full scale war did not break out until an attack by the LTTE on a Sri Lanka Army patrol in Jaffna, in the North of the country, on July 23, 1983, which killed 13 soldiers. The attack, and the subsequent riots in the South (dubbed Black July) are generally considered as the real start of the conflict. This fighting continued until 1985, when peace talks were held between the two sides in Thimphu,[2] Bhutan, in hopes of seeking a negotiated settlement. The Thimphu Principles affirm the following five non-negotiable demands: (1) recognition of Tamils as a nation; (2) recognition of the existence of an identified homeland for the Tamil people; (3) recognition of the right of the Tamil people to self-determination; (4) recognition of the right of the Tamil people to a separate citizenship; and (5) recognition of the fundamental right of all Tamils to look on the North and Eastern provinces of Sri Lanka as their country. They proved fruitless and fighting soon resumed.[3] This was only to be expected for two reasons: firstly, the demands were too steeply pitched for any sovereign nation to accept. Secondly, the LTTE had anticipated that the talks would fail anyway, and were anxious to get on with the business at hand – attainment of Eelam at any cost. "We fight while others merely talk,"[4] was the differentiator that the LTTE felt made them different from the rest of the pack. To what extent the LTTE were willing to go to live by this dictum is evident from a 1998 analysis of the group by the U.S. State Department. Included within a synopsis of the Tigers' 'political objectives' was "eliminate moderate Tamils and other Tamil militant groups that compete with the LTTE for influence within the Sri Lankan Tamil community."[5]

By 1987, the Sri Lankan military had cornered the LTTE in Jaffna, on the tip of the island, and were confident of bringing an end to the conflict. However, due to internal pressure, specifically concern from the 50 million Tamils living in India, the Indian Government called for a halt to the offensive. After the request was snubbed by Sri Lanka, the Indian Prime Minister Rajiv Gandhi ordered a flotilla of ships be sent to relieve the LTTE. After the convoy was blocked by the Sri Lanka Navy, India chose to airdrop supplies to the besieged city in a mission codenamed *Operation Poomalai.*

Following the successful completion of the mission, and faced with the possibility of further involvement of the Indian military, including reports that Indian ground forces were being prepared for possible involvement in Sri Lanka, the Sri Lankan President J.R. Jayewardene held talks with the Indian Government to resolve the dispute. As a result of the negotiations, the siege of Jaffna was lifted and the Indo-Sri-Lankan accord was signed on July 29, 1987. Sri Lankan troops then withdrew from the North of the country and handed over control over the entire area to Indian peacekeeping troops named the Indian Peace Keeping Force. This brought about an end to the first stage of the ethnic conflict.

Civilian Killings

Black July

On July 24, 1983, the day the 13 SLA servicemen killed in an LTTE ambush were to be buried, some Sinhalese civilians, who had gathered at the cemetery, angered by news of the ambush, which was magnified by wild rumour, formed mobs and started killing, raping, and assaulting Tamils, while looting and burning their properties in retribution for what happened. Sinhalese civilians were equipped with voter registration lists, burning and attacking only Tamil residences and business, while Army and Government officials stood by. It is estimated that at a least 1,000 Tamil people were killed (some assessments put the figure of Tamils killed to around 3,000), tens of thousands of houses were destroyed, and a wave of Sri Lankan Tamils left for other countries.

Kent and Dollar Farm Massacres

The Kent and Dollar Farm massacres were one of the earliest massacres of Sinhalese civilians carried out by the LTTE during the Sri Lankan Civil War. The massacres took place on November 30, 1984, in two tiny farming villages in the District of Mullaithivu in North-Eastern Sri Lanka. The LTTE had claimed that the North East of Sri Lanka was the exclusive homeland of Tamils, and began their campaign of ethnic cleansing in the 1980's. The Sinhalese of the Northern Province and Eastern Province of Sri Lanka suffered severe loss of lives and property as a result of numerous civilian massacres carried out by the LTTE for the purpose of ethnically cleansing the North East of Sri Lanka.

Anuradhapura Massacre

The Anuradhapura Massacre was an incident which took place on May 14, 1985, in which the LTTE cadres killed 146 Sinhalese men, women and children in Anuradhapura. They hijacked a bus and as they entered the main bus station, they opened fire indiscriminately with automatic weapons, killing and wounding many civilians who were waiting for buses. They then drove to the Buddhist Sri Maha Bodhi shrine and gunned down nuns, monks and civilians as they prayed inside the Buddhist shrine. This incident was designed to provoke massive retaliation by the Sinhalese majority against the Tamils in order to strengthen the LTTE's position among the Tamil people. Before they withdrew, the LTTE strike force entered the national park of Wilpattu and killed 18 Sinhalese in the forest reserve.

EELAM WAR II

Eelam War II[6] is the name given to the second phase of armed conflict between the Sri Lankan military and the LTTE. The war began after the failure of peace talks between the Premadasa Government and the LTTE. As per KT Balasingham,[7] tension between the LTTE and the Army began to increase in the latter part of May 1990, with the truce being broken on June 10, 1990. The SLA, having quelled the JVP (Janata Vimukthi Perumuna) uprising in the South, was proud of its achievements. Similarly, the LTTE, which took on the Indian Army and which had been engaged in the duel for 20 long months, was celebrating its final departure, and were equally proud of their achievements.[8] The LTTE did not come forward to explain why it had launched a full scale military campaign from June 11. The exact reasons for the resumption of hostilities, the launching of Eelam War II had not been fully and officially explained by the LTTE.

When, on June 11, 1990, the LTTE broke the ceasefire (which it had entered into with the Government in June 1989), the Army camps on the mainland Northern Province were abandoned, leaving the SLA with detachments at

Mullaithivu, Mannar, Elephant Pass, Pooneryn, Vettilaikerni, Idaikadu, Jaffna Fort and Palely, and also those of Weli-Oya and later Kankesanthurai, and the islands located off the Jaffna Peninsula. The sea route became difficult for the Government, when the Sea Tigers began to sink and steal (presumably some) Sri Lankan supply and naval boats and ships. Meanwhile, Rajasingham writes, "a total of 899 police personnel were abducted by the LTTE. About 125 of them escaped. Subsequently it became clear that almost all the policemen had been killed by the Tigers in cold blood. They were lined up and shot with their hands tied behind them."[9]

The author writes about the LTTE attack on the SLA camp at Jaffna Fort on June 19, 1990. It was situated on the northern coast of Jaffna near the Pannai causeway. The attack on Jaffna Fort continued for several weeks. The LTTE fighters used earth-moving vehicles and heavy fire to break through the main entrance and armour-plated bucket scrapers and ladders to climb the ramparts. Troops and policemen inside repulsed the attacks and the Air Force caused casualties among the Tigers as well as civilians. Machetti bombers, civilian aircraft and helicopter gun ships were utilized to pound the areas surrounding the fort to break the siege. The position of the besieged soldiers inside the fort became dire.[10] Sri Lanka's Northern Armed Forces, led by Major General Denzil Kobbekaduwa, became aware of the fact that at any given moment, the fort would fall into the hands of the Tigers.

Therefore, on September 13, 1990, the SLAF launched a massive combined operation to dislodge the siege. Nearly 400 troops, with the assistance of the Air Force and the Navy, mounted an operation from Mandathievu Island to destroy the LTTE's positions, which were pounded by a barrage of bombs and artillery. Fierce fighting erupted when the Sri Lankan troops attempted a sea-borne landing across Jaffna lagoon. This spelt disaster for the Sri Lankan forces as the LTTE destroyed several naval craft and scores of soldiers were killed.

The troops trapped inside the Jaffna Fort suffered without adequate food, replenishment of ammunition and proper medical treatment. But after great efforts, Squadron Leader Lasantha Waidyaratne managed to evacuate the causalities in a daring operation code-named 'Operation Eagle'. Subsequently, two more battalions and a Special Forces regiment joined in to evacuate the trapped forces. They rescued 210 service personnel, including over 100 policemen. Besides the men, it was reported that the troops managed to save valuable military equipment and about 1,000 enemy weapons and 600,000 rounds of ammunition, cash and gold belonging to the state banks.[11]

The LTTE in October 1990, in ruthless furtherance of their ethnic cleansing programme, expelled all the 28,000 Muslims[12] residing in Jaffna. The Palliyagodella massacre is an incident in October 1991 in which LTTE cadres massacred 109 Muslim men, women and children in Palliyagodella. The background to this massacre was the growing tension between the LTTE and the Muslim community. The Palliyagodella villagers had asked the Sri Lankan military for protection from LTTE extortion. The Sri Lankan forces issued shotguns to the Muslim villagers but these were inadequate to beat off LTTE attacks. Female LTTE cadres and child soldiers were involved in this attack.

EELAM WAR III

Eelam War III[13] is the name given to the third phase of armed conflict between the Sri Lankan military and the LTTE. After a period of cease-fire, hostilities broke out on April 19, 1995. The Sea Tigers planted explosives in two gun boats known as SLNS '*Sooraya*' and '*Ranasuru*', and blew them up. Also, 'Stinger' shoulder launched anti-aircraft missiles were used in this conflict by the LTTE. They were used to down two Sri Lankan Air Force AVRO aircraft flying over the Jaffna peninsula.

Major Battles of the War

July 18, 1996: The LTTE overran the Sri Lankan military base at Mullaithivu, the attack carried out after midnight. The number of killed in action and missing in action was around 1,600 as per military sources. More than 1,500 LTTE cadres participated in the attack and captured large quantities of arms and military equipment. The base was used as Sri Lanka Army's 215 Brigade Headquarters. One of the major encounters broke out between the LTTE and the *Special Forces* (SF) Commando reinforcement led by Lt. Col. Laphir. He was posthumously awarded the nation's highest gallantry award. In this attack, 36 commandos were killed and 60 more were wounded. Sri Lanka Air Force helicopter pilots landed the second batch of commando in the same location and also winched up the dead body of Lt. Col. Laphir under heavy LTTE gunfire. The code name given by the LTTE for the operation to attack the Mullaithivu Military base was '*Oyatha Alaikal*' (Endless Waves) and SLA code named its commando rescue operation as '*Operation Thrivida Pahara*.'

Civilian Killings

Kallarawa Massacre

The Kallarawa massacre is an incident on May 25, 1995, during which LTTE cadres massacred 42 Sinhalese men, women and children in Kallarawa. All the remaining civilian survivors fled the village after this incident leading to its depopulation.

Gonagala Massacre

The Gonagala Massacre was a massacre that occurred on September 18, 1999, in the small village of Gonagala, located in the Ampara District of Sri Lanka. According to reports, over 50 men, women and children were hacked to death in the middle of the night. The massacre is attributed to the LTTE. However, these murders gained notoriety because, unlike previous attacks, most of the LTTE cadres who took part in it were women. According to survivors, there was a significant presence of female cadres among the 75 LTTE cadres who took part in the killings.

Controversy over the Army's Handling of its Casualties and their Families

In August 2001, S.P. Thamilselvan, the leader of the political wing of the Tamil Tigers, accused the Sri Lankan Army of intentionally abandoning the bodies of nearly a thousand soldiers on the battlefields since May 2001, despite the Tamils' request that the Red Cross act as an intermediate agency. He told visiting relatives of missing servicemen that the military had only accepted 55 bodies to return to their families, while burying the rest with full military honours on the spot. Thamilselvan did not offer a reason for the Army's refusal, but did note that several hundred decomposing bodies remained in a minefield due to the danger of extricating them. A Sri Lankan military spokesman, Brigadier Sanath Karunaratne, acknowledged that the Army cannot always retrieve a body because it might cost more lives, but denied the Tamil accusations, saying they were propaganda aimed at demoralizing the parents of the missing soldiers.

However, this was not the first time issues had arisen over reclamation of soldiers' remains and the Army's responsiveness to the requests of families of missing soldiers for information regarding their fate. In April 2003, a group of parents of some of the 619 soldiers reported missing from a battle fought on 27 September, 1998, obtained permission from the LTTE to travel to the battle site. The families' previous inquiries at the Defence Ministry, the Sri Lankan Army, and the International Committee of the Red Cross for information on their sons' fates had been fruitless. At the battlefield they learned that some 500 bodies had been piled together, doused with kerosene, and burnt on the spot by the SLA. Upon their return, a lawsuit was filed on the families' behalf requesting a mass funeral and DNA testing so that Buddhist, Muslim and Christian families could collect their sons' remains and give them proper burials. The Ministry of Defence organized the mass funeral in 2006, but declined to perform the requested DNA testing.

EELAM WAR IV

Eelam War IV[14] is the name given to the fourth phase of armed conflict between the Sri Lankan military and the LTTE. Renewed hostilities began on July 26, 2006, when Sri Lanka Air Force fighter jets bombed several LTTE camps around the Mavil Aru sluice gates (anicut). The government's causus belli was that the LTTE had cut off the water supply to surrounding paddy fields in the area. The fighting resumed after a four-year ceasefire, between the Government of Sri Lanka and the LTTE. Continued fighting led to several territorial gains for the Sri Lankan Army, including the capture of Sampur, Vakarai and other parts of the East. The war took on an added dimension when the LTTE Air Tigers bombed Katunayake Air Base on March 26, 2007, the first rebel air attack without external assistance in history.

Peace Process 2002

The elections, held on 5 December, 2001, saw a sweeping victory for the United National Front, led by Ranil Wickramasinghe, who campaigned on a pro-peace platform and pledged to find a negotiated settlement to the conflict.

On 19 December, amidst efforts by Norway to bring the government and the Tamil Tigers to the negotiating table, the LTTE announced a 30-day ceasefire with the Sri Lankan government and pledged to halt all attacks against government forces. The new government welcomed the move, and reciprocated two days later, announcing a month-long ceasefire and agreeing to lift a long-standing economic embargo on rebel-held territory.

Signing of MoU[15]

The two sides formalized a Memorandum of Understanding (MoU) on February 22, 2002, and signed a permanent ceasefire agreement (CFA). Norway was named as the mediator, and it was decided that it, together with the other Nordic countries, would monitor the ceasefire through a committee of experts named the Sri Lanka Monitoring Mission (SLMM). In August, the government agreed to lift the ban on the LTTE and paved the way for the resumption of direct negotiations with the LTTE.

LTTE Sea Tiger boat patrolling during the cessation of hostilities

Following the signing of the ceasefire agreement, commercial air flights to Jaffna began and the LTTE opened the key A9 highway, which linked the Government-controlled area in the South with Jaffna and ran through LTTE territory, allowing civilian traffic through the Vanni region for the first time in many years. Many foreign countries also offered substantial financial support if peace was achieved and optimism grew that an end to the decade long conflict was in sight.

The much anticipated peace talks began in Phuket, Thailand, on September 16 and five further rounds followed in Phuket, Norway and Berlin, Germany. During the talks, both sides agreed to the principle of a federal solution and the Tigers dropped their long-standing demand for a separate state. This was a key compromise from the LTTE, which had always insisted on an independent Tamil state and it also represented a compromise from the Government, which had seldom agreed to more than minimal devolution. Both sides also exchanged prisoners of war for the first time.

Beginning of the War

A new crisis leading to the first large-scale fighting since signing of the ceasefire occurred when the LTTE closed the sluice gates of the Mavil Aru reservoir on July 21, 2006, and cut the water supply to 15,000 villages in Government-controlled areas. After initial negotiations and efforts by the SLMM to open the gates failed, the Air Force attacked LTTE positions on July 26, and ground troops began an operation to open the gates.

Palitha Kohona, a government spokesman, stated that the government remained committed to the cease-fire. Likewise, the LTTE also claimed that they were committed to the ceasefire.

The sluice gates were eventually reopened on August 8, 2006, with conflicting reports as to who actually opened them. Initially, the SLMM claimed that they managed to persuade the LTTE to lift the waterway blockade conditionally. However, a government spokesman said that "utilities could not be used as bargaining tools" by the rebels. Government forces thus went ahead and launched fresh attacks on LTTE positions around the reservoir. These attacks prompted condemnation from SLMM Chief of Staff, who stated "(The government) have the information that the LTTE has made this offer." It is quite obvious they are not interested in water. They are interested in something else." The LTTE then claimed they opened the sluice gates "on humanitarian grounds". Eventually, following heavy fighting with the rebels, Government troops gained full control of the Mavil Aru reservoir on August 15.

War in the East

The war between the LTTE and the Sri Lankan government started after the failure of the Norway-brokered ceasefire on July 21, 2006, when the LTTE cut off the water supply to the rice growing fields in the Mavil Aru area in Eastern Trincomalee district. The government military claimed total control of the Eastern province after capturing Thoppigala (Baron's Cap) on July 11, 2007, after nearly a year of fighting.

The TMVP contested Batticaloa district local council elections on March 10, 2008, and won all 9 councils with a high majority of 70 percent of the votes. The party also contested in the Eastern Provincial Council election on May 10, 2008, under the ruling UPFA banner and the UPFA won the election. TMVP's current leader Sivanesathurai Chandrakanthan was sworn in as the Chief Minister of the Eastern Provincial Council on May 16, 2008.

Sri Lanka Pulls Out of Ceasefire[16]

On January 2, 2008, the Sri Lankan government unanimously decided to formally withdraw from the ceasefire with the separatist Tamil Tiger rebels, which had existed only on paper over the past two years. Prime Minister Ratnasiri Wickremanayake had proposed that the cabinet annul the truce after yet another bomb blast went off on January 2 in the capital, Colombo, killing five and injuring over 28.

"The Government of Sri Lanka yesterday (3rd January 2008) formally notified the Norwegian Government of its decision to terminate the Agreement on a 'Ceasefire (CFA) between the Government of the Democratic Socialist Republic of Sri Lanka and the Liberation Tigers of Tamil Eelam' concluded on 22nd February 2002. This notification was in terms of Article 4:4 of this Agreement and will take effect 14 days from the date of this notice i.e. 16th January 2008. Accordingly, the Status of Mission Agreement (SOMA) on the Establishment and the Management of the Sri Lanka Monitoring Mission (SLMM) dated 18th March 2002 between the Royal Norwegian Government and the Government of the Democratic Socialist Republic of Sri Lanka will also stand terminated with effect from 16th January 2008."

War in the North

Meanwhile, in the north of the country, some of the bloodiest fighting since 2001 took place after the LTTE launched massive attacks on Sri Lanka Army defence lines in the Jaffna peninsula on August 11. The LTTE used a force of 400 to 500 fighters in the attacks which consisted of land and amphibious assaults, and also fired a barrage of artillery at government positions, including the key military airbase at Palali. Initially, the Tigers broke through Army defence lines around Muhamalai, and advanced further north, but they were halted after 10 hours of fierce fighting. Isolated battles continued over the next few days, but the LTTE was forced to give up its offensive due to heavy casualties.

During clashes in the Forward Defence Lines, separating their forces, both sides exchanged heavy artillery fire, after which military incursions followed. By December 22, 2007, the LTTE defences at Uyilankulam and Thampanai were lost to advancing troops of the Sri Lanka Army. On December 29, 2007, the Army overran the LTTE stronghold at Parappakandal, Mannar.

On January 5, 2008, Col. Charles, Head of LTTE Military Intelligence, was killed in a Claymore mine ambush by a suspected Sri Lanka Army Deep Penetration Unit according to a pro-LTTE website.

Capture of Mannar District

On 2 August, 2008, the Sri Lankan army captured the town of Vellankulam which was the last bastion of the Tigers in the Mannar district. This marked the capture of the entire Mannar district by the Army which took eight months.

Battle at Sea

On March 22, 2008, a Navy fast attack boat was destroyed after it hit a suspected sea mine laid by Tamil Tiger rebels off the country's North-East coast.

Battle in the Air

The battle in the air was significant for both sides in this phase of the war. The Sri Lankan Air Force used their attack planes to carry out bombing campaigns on identified LTTE targets. The LTTE Air Tigers also used their light aircraft to carry out bombings on Sri Lankan military forces.

Major Air Strikes by Sri Lanka Air Force[17]

On August 14, 2006, the Sri Lankan Air Force bombed a facility in the rebel-held Mullaitivu area, Chencholai air strike. The LTTE claimed 61 girls were killed, the SLMM stated they were able to count just 19 bodies. The Government claimed that it was an LTTE training facility and that the children were LTTE child soldiers, although the LTTE claimed the victims were schoolgirls attending a course on first aid at an orphanage. A team from the UN Children's Fund (UNICEF) and the Swedish-led Sri Lanka Monitoring Mission (SLMM) visited the bombed site and said they had found no evidence to support claims the rebels had been using the facility as a military training centre. On May 7, 2007, fighter jets of the Sri Lankan Air Force bombed a strategic LTTE base and a large fuel storage at Ramanatpuram East of Iranamadu. In November 2007, Thamilselvan, along with five other high-ranking Tamil rebels were killed by a precision air strike carried out by the Sri Lanka Air Force on an undisclosed location near the rebels' stronghold town of Killinochchi.

LTTE Air Strikes

LTTE air strikes occurred for the first time in history on March 26, 2007, on an air-force base at Katunayake, killing three Air Force personnel and wounding several. LTTE aircraft attacked Palali military complex by dropping bombs on April 23, 2007, killing six soldiers and wounding 13. The LTTE attacked Katunayake Air Base on April 26, 2007, for the second time, one month after their first attack on the same location. On April 29, 2007, the LTTE aircraft bombed two fuel tanks at Kolonnawa and Muthurajawela close to Colombo around 01:45 a.m. Sri Lankan time.

Colombo Raids[18]

On April 26, Sri Lanka's air defences in Colombo fired into the sky following reports that an unidentified aircraft had been spotted on radar. No attack was reported. However, a few days later, in the early morning of April 29, while the entire nation was watching the Cricket World Cup Final, a Tiger aircraft bombed two fuel storage facilities outside Colombo. Chaos followed and electricity in the capital was shut off for nearly an hour. There were no casualties and damage was minimal. The security forces were unable to bring down the aircraft prompting much criticism from the public and opposition political parties. On October 22, 2007, Air Tigers launched a pre-dawn combined arms assault on a SLAF airbase at Anuradhapura, about 212 kilometres (132 miles) north of the capital, Colombo. According to the Ministry of Defence, the assault started at around 3:20 a.m., with LTTE ground forces attacking the airbase and overrunning key positions, including an anti-aircraft position before the Air Tiger's ultra light planes dropped bombs on government positions. This resulted in the destruction of eight aircraft and damage to several others. The attack only affected the Air Force's training element.

THE FINAL COUNTDOWN: MOD SRI LANKA VERSION[19]

The ongoing phase of the battle commenced in August 2006, when terrorists closed down the Mavil Aru sluice gates, denying water for more than 30,000 civilians. The terrorists initially had their domination over an area of 15,000 square kilometres in the Northern and the Eastern Provinces. The LTTE was eradicated from the Eastern Province by August 2007.

Land operations commenced in the Northern Province in March 2007 with the induction of the Army's 57 Division to the Vavuniya area. The second offensive division, Task Force 1, was inducted to the battlefield from Mannar in September 2007. The SLA opened its third battlefront from Welioya with the induction of the 59 Division in January 2008.

The Army employed five offensive Divisions and three Task Forces at the LTTE hiding areas in Wanni. The LTTE terrorists were boxed into a triangular shaped area marked by the A-9 road from the west, A-34 road from the south and the north eastern coast from the east.

BRIEF DESCRIPTION OF OPERATIONS

57 Division

The 57th Division (57 Div), commanded by Major General Jagath Dias, commenced its operations in March 2007 in Vavuniya. The Division was maneouvered directly at the LTTE's heartland, Killinochchi, cutting across the strategically vital north western coast and the A-9 road.

Timeline

Sl No.	Date	Area Liberated
01.	24th April 2008	Madhu Church complex
02.	16th May 2008	Palampiddi Town
03.	23rd May 2008	Mundumurippu village
04.	15th June 2008	Periyamadhu village
05.	11th July 2008	Naddankandal village
06.	13th Aug 2008	Kalvilan village
07.	22nd Aug 2008	Thunukkai and Uilankulam towns
08.	02nd Sept 2008	Mallavi town
09.	29th Oct 2008	Akkarayankulam tank bund
10.	05th Nov 2008	Akkarayankulam built-up area
11.	01st Dec 2008	Kokavil town

(Contd.)

12.	10th Dec 2008	Terumurikandy junction
13.	02nd Jan 2009	Kilinochchi town
14.	17th Jan 2009	Ramanathapuram
15.	28th Jan 2009	Visuamadu town

58 Division

The Army 58th Division, earlier known as Task Force 1, was commanded by Brigadier Shavendra Silva, and commenced its operations from Mannar in September 2007. This was the Division that maneouvred along the north western coast of the Island and denied the LTTE their lifeline that existed across the Palk Strait.

Timeline

Serial No.	Date	Area Liberated
01.	09th May 2008	Adampan town
02.	24th June 2008	Mullikkandal, Minnaniranchan and Marattikannaddi villages
03.	29th June 2008	The Mannar rice bowl – Alankulama, Andankulama, Alakaddiveli, Parappakandal, Parappukadatan, Papamoddai, Odupallam, Neduvarampu, Kannaputtukulama and Vannakulama villages
04.	30th June 2008	Linked up with 57 Div – south west of Periyamadhu
05.	16th July 2008	Vidattaltivu town
06.	02nd Aug 2008	Illuppaikkadavai town
07.	12th Aug 2008	Vellankulam town
08.	12th Aug 2008	Mulankavil and Pallavarayankaddu areas
09.	21st Aug 2008	Nachchikudha
10.	16th Oct 2008	Maniyankulama
11.	20th Oct 2008	Vannerikkulama
12.	28th Oct 2008	Nochchimodai
13.	29th Oct 2008	Jeyapuram
14.	29th Oct 2008	Nachchikuda
15.	10th Nov 2008	Kiranchi
16.	13th Nov 2008	Devil's Point and Vallaipadu
17.	15th Nov 2008	Pooneryn
18.	23rd Dec 2008	'Sinna-Paranthan'
19.	26th Dec 2008	Nalanawakulam village
20.	01st Jan 2009	Paranthan
21.	08th Jan 2009	Murasumoddai
22.	15th Jan 2009	Dharmapuram
23.	28th Jan 2009	Visuamadu town

(Contd.)

24.	20th Feb 2009	Thevipuram
25.	17th March 2009	Iranapalai junction
26.	01st April 2009	Pachchapulmuddai
27.	05th April 2009	Puthukkudiyiruppu

59 Division

The Army 59th Division, commanded by Brigadier Nandana Udawatte, commenced its operations from the WeIioya area in January 2008. Troops of this division slowly but successfully marched across the Andankulam and Nagancholai forest reserves that stood as natural defences for the LTTE's main military bastion in Mullaithivu.

Timeline

Serial No.	Date	Area Liberated
01.	30th May 2008	Munagam base
02.	04th July 2008	Michael base
03.	27th July 2008	'Sugandan' base
04.	16th Aug 2008	Jeevan base
05.	21st Aug 2008	West of Nayaroo lagoon
06.	23rd Oct 2008	Gajabapura
07.	11th Nov 2008	Kumulamunai village
08.	29th Nov 2008	Otiyamalai
09.	26th Dec 2008	Mulliyawalai
10.	25th Jan 2009	Mullaithivu town

53 Division

The Army 53rd Division, commanded by Brigadier Kamal Gunarathne, was initially manning the forward defence line at Muhamalai in the Jaffna peninsula. The Division was deployed in the area south of A-9 road and was one of the two army divisions that defended the isolated Jaffna peninsula against LTTE infiltration over the past few years. The Division shifted its mode of operations from defensive to offensive in mid November 2008.

Timeline

Serial No.	Date	Area Liberated
01.	12th March 2009	Puthukkudiyirippu hospital
02.	01st April 2009	Pachchapulmuddai
03.	05th April 2009	Puthukkudiyiruppu

55 Divison

The 55th Division, commanded by Brigadier Prasanna Silva, was initially manning the forward defence line at Muhamalai in the Jaffna peninsula. The Division was deployed in the area North of A-9 road and was one of the two Army Divisions that defended the isolated Jaffna peninsula against LTTE infiltration over the past few years. The Division shifted its mode of operations from defensive to offensive in mid November 2008.

Timeline

Serial No.	Date	Area Liberated
01.	05th February 2009	Chalai

Task Force 2

Army Task Force 2, commanded by Brigadier Rohana Bandara, commenced its operations in June 2008 from the south of Palamoddai area. This was the first Army offensive element to manoeuvre along the west-east axis across A-9.

Timeline

Serial No.	Date	Area Liberated
01.	11th July 2008	Navvi village
02.	04th Dec 2008	Puliyankulam
03.	05th Dec 2008	Kanakarayankulam
04.	21st Jan 2009	Udayarkattukulam tank bund

Task Force 3

Army Task Force 3, commanded by Brigadier Sathyapirya Liyanage, commenced its operations in November 2008 from the Vannivilankulam area. This was the second Army offensive element to manoeuvre along the west-east axis across A-9.

Timeline

Serial No.	Date	Area Liberated
01.	17th Nov 2008	Mankulama
02.	25th Nov 2008	Olumadu
03.	15th Dec 2008	Ampakamam

Task Force 4

Army Task Force 4, commanded by Colonel Nishantha Wanniarachchi, commenced its operations in December 2008 from the Nadunkerni area. This was the second offensive element inducted to the Mullaithivu battlefront after 59 Division.

Serial No.	Date	Area Liberated
01.	20th Dec 2008	Nadunkerni
02.	04th Jan 2009	Oddusuddan
03.	12th Jan 2009	Keridattadu

BATTLE PROGRESS

The Conclusion of the War[20]

On 19th May, 2009, the Sri Lankan military effectively concluded its 26-year operation against the LTTE. The 58 Division of the Sri Lankan Army led by Brig. Shavendra Silva, 59 Division led by Brig. Prasanna de Silva and 53 Division commanded by Gen. Kamal Gunaratne, after having boxed in the remaining LTTE cadres into a small area near Nandhi Kadal lagoon, linked up and eliminated the remaining cadres. This final battle claimed the lives of several top LTTE leaders, including Jeyam, Bhanu, Lawrence, Pappa, Laxmanan, Balasingham Nadesan, Pottu Amman, Soosai and, of course, velupillai Prabhakaran, who was reported to have attempted to flee from the conflict zone. On the morning of the 19th, soldiers of the 4th Vijayabâhu Infantry Regiment led by Lt. Col. Rohitha Aluvihare, claimed to have found the body of Prabhakaran, militarily ended a separatist war that had defined Sri Lanka's history for over three decades.

Sample Battle Map

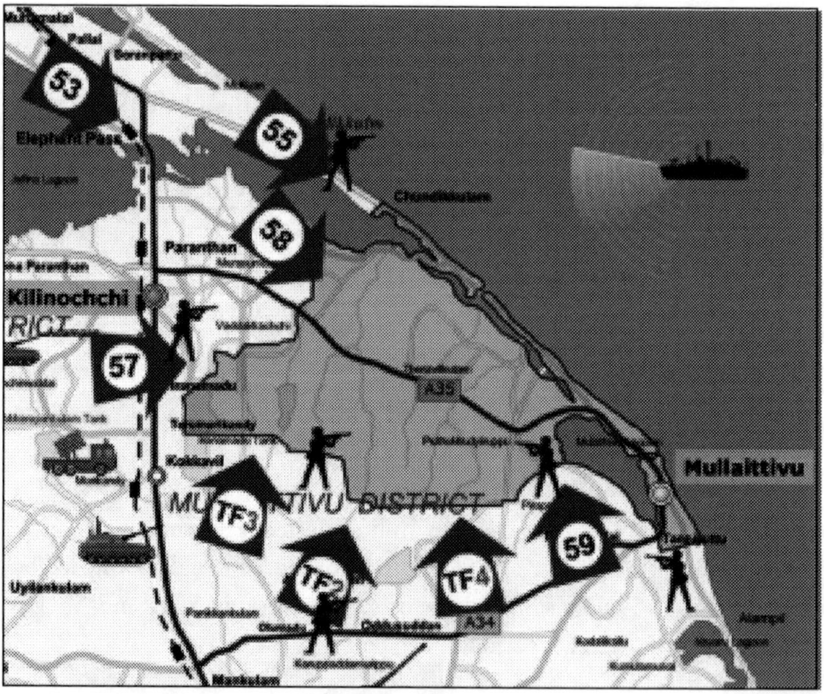

Sample Battle Graphic

On 22nd May, 2009, Sri Lankan Defence Minister Gottabhaya Rajapaksa confirmed that 6,261 personnel of the Sri Lankan Armed Forces had lost their lives and 29,551 were wounded during Eelam War IV since July 2006. Brig. Udaya Nanayakkara, the military spokesman, added that approximately 22,000 LTTE cadres had died during this period.

Impact of War on Civilian Life[21]

Since the latest upsurge in violence in April, nearly 40,000 people have been displaced in Sri Lanka. This comes amidst the government's air strikes on civilian populated areas of the east. Amnesty International quoted UN figures to say that a total of 39,883 people had been displaced in the north and east since April 7, 2009, adding that a total of 314,378 people were displaced by the conflict, while around 325,000 people were estimated to have been displaced by the tsunami.

Amnesty International has also stated that increasing violence was forcing many Sri Lankans to flee the country and that more than 2,800 people had sought shelter in India this year. The state's failure to provide adequate security and to ensure that attacks against civilians are prosecuted has resulted in widespread fear and panic. Amnesty International also accused the LTTE of breaking the international law by using civilians as buffers against the Army. A researcher for the organisation stated that there were cases where militants had forced people to stay in rebel-held areas to hamper army operations.

Endnotes

1. This section has been largely excerpted from "Eelam War 1."< http://en.wikipedia.org/wiki/Eelam_War_I>
2. Rabasa, Angel-Chalk, Peter' Cragin, Jim' Daly, Sara A.; Gregg, Heather S. Karasik; Theodore W. O'Brien; Kevin A and Rosenau, William. "Beyond Al-Qaeda: The Outer Rings of the Terrorist Universe." RAND Study Part 2. http://www.rand.org/pubs/monographs/2006/RAND_MG430.pdf **Note 21** may please be read.
3. See Kumar Ponnambala, "The Only Possible Solution to the Tamil National Problem," TamilCanadian.com (as of March 21, 2006).
4. Rabasa, Angel-Chalk, Peter; Cragin, Jim; Daly, Sara A.; Gregg, Heather S. Karasik; Theodore W. O'Brien; Kevin A. and Rosenau, William. "Beyond Al-Qaeda: The Outer Rings of the Terrorist Universe." RAND Study Part 2. http://www.rand.org/pubs/monographs/2006/RAND_MG430.pdf Notes 21 and 22 may please be read.
5. Ibid.
6. "Eelam War II."< http://en.wikipedia.org/wiki/Eelam_War_II>
7. Rajasingham, K.T. "Sri Lanka: The Untold Story. Chapter 44: Eelam War – Again." http://www.atimes.com/ind-pak/DF15Df01.html> The author has gone into great detail of the circumstances as well as key incidents that comprised Eelam War II. The excerpts quoted from the chapter have been paraphrased by this author.
8. Ibid.
9. Ibid.
10. Ibid.
11. Ibid.
12. "Eelam War II."< http://en.wikipedia.org/wiki/Eelam_War_II>
13. This section has been excerpted from "Eelam War III."< http://en.wikipedia.org/wiki/Eelam_War_III>
14. This section has been excerpted from "Eelam War IV."< http://en.wikipedia.org/wiki/Eelam_War_IV>
15. Ibid.
16. Ibid.
17. Ibid.
18. Ibid.
19. "*The Final Countdown.*" <http://www.defence.lk/new.asp?fname=20090117 _03> The Sri Lanka MoD sites are professionally engineered, use the latest technology such as interactive maps, that one is used to seeing in foreign sites such as RAND, Stratfor and BBC, and, to a large extent, are reader friendly. It is quite obvious that, being Government sites, they would espouse the Government's viewpoint, which is understandable, but also causes the reader to balance the site, where needed, with other inputs. What is important is that in the battle for perception management, the 'war on the minds' of the people, which ran coterminous with the physical war, was very intelligently fought by both sides. The LTTE, of course, led in this sphere for many years, till the Government and military (with rare synergy) decided on a unified end state – of destroying the LTTE militarily, using an array

of attrition weaponry. The new tack as it thus emerged - *of doing a 'LTTE',* – doing what the LTTE was doing in all spheres of its endeavour; in strategy, in operational art, in tactics, in perception management, in ruthlessness, but doing it better, turned out to be wildly successful. Keen observers who study war fighting, would, no doubt, note the irony that, as the war drew to a close, the Sri Lankan Armed Forces and the LTTE had, in effect exchanged roles: it was the LTTE that was mired in conventional war in the Wanni area, for which it was neither equipped, nor had the training. With supplies interdicted as far away as 2000 nautical miles away by a reborn Sri Lankan Navy, with the Sri Lankan Air Force mercilessly bombing and strafing all LTTE defences, strongholds and movements in sight, aided by UAV's for target killings, and with the Sri Lankan Army fully confident of detached, small team operations 24x7, including swarming at sea and in land operations, the LTTE found that the rules of the game had changed beyond retrieval. The only logical consequence occurred: they suffered disastrous and total annihilation. **The author has taken the liberty to edit *The Final Countdown*, including change of tense, at places, in line with the fact that the war got over a little while after the document was put out by the MoD, and reference to planned and ongoing operations had to be moderated.**

20. "Eelam War IV."< http://en.wikipedia.org/wiki/Eelam_War_IV>
21. Ibid.

References

1. "Sri Lanka forces attack reservoir". BBC News. 2006-08-06. http://news.bbc.co.uk/2/hi/South_asia/5249884.stm.
2. "Air Force jets hit LTTE targets". Sunil Jayasiri (*The Daily Mirror*). 2006-07-27. http://www.dailymirror.lk/2006/07/27/front/6.asp.
3. "'War victory party' in Sri Lanka". BBC News. 2007-07-12. http://news.bbc.co.uk/1/hi/world/South_asia/6895809.stm.
4. U.S. Department of State, 2005 Human Rights Report, March 8, 2006
5. Denyer, Simon. " 'Disappearances' on rise in Sri Lanka's dirty war". Reuters, September 14, 2006.
6. "SLMM counted 19 Bodies". monstersandcritics.com. 13 August 2006. http://news.monstersandcritics.com/Southasia/article_1190181.php/61_girls_killed_in_airstrike_8_dead_in_Colombo_blast__2nd_Roundup_.
7. "Thousands flee Sri Lanka strikes". BBC. 26 April 2006.
8. "40,000 Flee Sri Lanka Violence". *Washington Post.* 26 April 2006. http://www.washingtonpost.com/wp-dyn/content/article/2006/04/26/AR2006042600335.html.

PART II

Velupillai Prabhakaran: The Man and his Ideology

CHAPTER 7

The Life and Times of Velupillai Prabhakaran

"Few dispute that he (Prabhakaran) was one of the most effective guerrilla leaders in modern warfare – displaying the tactical prowess of Afghanistan's Ahmad Shah Masoud, the ruthlessness of Osama bin Laden and the conviction of Latin American revolutionary Che Guevara."

– *Straits Times*

This part of the book examines the life, philosophy, ideology, thoughts and times[1] of a man who rose from a humble background to meteoric heights, gave a new dimension to the meaning of terror, and brought in unprecedented ruthlessness in his effort to gain Eelam by any means and at any cost. What were the inputs that made him one of the world's most marked and feared men; his organisation proscribed in 32 countries of the world? How did the mind of this terror chief work? Did he have a life beyond the efficient spread of terror? This opening chapter makes an effort to provide an insight in this direction.

Early Life

Velupillai Prabhakaran was born in the northern coastal town of Velvettithurai on November 26, 1954, to Thiruvenkadam Velupillai and Vallipuram Parvathy. Angered by what he saw as discrimination against Tamil people by successive Sri Lankan governments, he joined the student group, TIP, during the standardization debates. In 1972, Prabhakaran founded the Tamil New Tigers (TNT) which was a successor to many earlier organizations that protested against the post-colonial political direction of the country, in which the minority Sri Lankan Tamils were pitted against the majority Sinhalese people. In 1975, after becoming heavily involved in the Tamil movement, he carried out the first major political murder by a Tamil militant group, assassinating the Mayor of Jaffna, Alfred Duraiappah, by shooting him at point-blank range, when he was about to enter the Hindu temple at Ponnaalai.[2] The assassination was in response to the 1974 Tamil conference incident, for which the Tamil radicals had blamed Duraiappah, because he backed the then ruling Sri Lanka Freedom Party. He was also seen by Tamil militants as betraying the Tamil nationalist sentiments in the Jaffna Peninsula, by allying with the Sinhalese majority government.

Young Prabhakaran. Photo courtesy Lankapuvath

Tamil Tigers: Founding of the LTTE[3]

On May 5, 1976, the TNT was renamed the Liberation Tigers of Tamil Eelam (LTTE), commonly known as the Tamil Tigers. Religion was not a major factor in Prabhakaran's philosophy or ideology, but the LTTE was characterized as anti-Buddhist. The LTTE was also an organization that did not cite any material from religion or religious texts in any of its ideological documents and propaganda, but were driven only by the idea of Sri Lankan Tamil nationalism. They focused on this single-minded approach and worked determinedly towards the attainment of an independent Tamil Eelam at all costs.

Philosophy and Ideology

Prabhakaran never expressed an all-encompassing systematic philosophy, but did declare his ideology to be driven by 'Revolutionary socialism and the creation of an egalitarian society'. He joined the Tamil nationalist movement in his youth and quickly established himself as a strong-willed militant leader by founding the LTTE. His rare interviews, his annual Tamil Eelam Heroes Day speeches, and the policies and actions of the LTTE can be taken as indicators of Prabhakaran's philosophy and ideology. The following are important areas when considering the philosophy and ideology of Prabhakaran.

Sri Lankan Nationalism

Prabhakaran's source of inspiration and direction was Sri Lankan Tamil nationalism. His stated and ultimate ideal was to get Tamil Eelam recognized as a nation as per the U.N. Charter that guarantees the right of a people to political independence which has been given in their official web page. The LTTE also proposed the formation of an Interim Self Governing Authority during peace negotiations in 2003. Former Tamil guerrilla and later turned politician Dharmalingam Sithadthan, has remarked that "his dedication to the cause of the Tamil Eelam was unquestionable. He was the only man in Sri Lanka who could decide if there should be war or peace."

Militarism of the LTTE

Prabhakaran explicitly stated that an armed struggle was the only way to resist asymmetric warfare, in which one side, that of the Sri Lankan Government is armed and the other, comparatively unarmed. He argued that he chose military means only after observing that non–violent means have been ineffectual and obsolete, especially after the Thileepan incident.[4] Thileepan, a Colonel rank officer adopted Gandhian means to protest against the IPKF killings by staging a fast unto death from September 15, 1987, and by abstaining from food or water till September 26, 1987. He died in front of thousands of Tamils who had come there to fast along with him. This further strengthened Prabhakaran's resolve that peaceful protests would either be ignored or crushed, but never heard.

Tactically, Prabhakaran perfected the recruitment and use of suicide bomber units, while his fighters usually took no prisoners, and were notorious for assaults that often left every single enemy soldier dead. Personally, Interpol described him as someone who was "very alert, known to use disguise, and capable of handling sophisticated weaponry and explosives."[5]

Press Conference at Killinochchi

Prabhakaran's first and only major press conference was held in Killinochchi on April 10, 2002. More than 200 journalists from the local and foreign media attended this event, and they had to go through a 10-hour security screening before the event in which Anton Balasingham introduced the LTTE leader as the 'President and Prime Minister of Tamil Eelam'. A number of questions were asked about LTTE's commitment towards the erstwhile peace process and Prabhakaran and Dr. Anton Balasingham jointly answered the questions. Answering a question from one of the reporters, Prabhakaran said that he had instructed the LTTE cadres to kill him if he compromised on the goal of an independent state. Repeated questions of his involvement in the Rajiv Gandhi assassination were only answered in a sober note by both Balasingham and Prabhakaran. They called it a 'tragic incident' ('Thunbiyal Chambavam', as quoted in Tamil) and they requested the press "not to dig into an incident that happened 10 years ago."

During the interview he stated[6] that the right condition has not risen to give up the demand of Tamil Eelam. He further mentioned that "There are three fundamentals. They are: Tamil Homeland, Tamil Nationality and Tamil Right to Self-determination. These are the fundamental demands of the Tamil people. Once these demands are accepted or a political solution is put forward by recognizing these three fundamentals and our people are satisfied with the solutions, we will consider giving up the demand for Eelam." He further added that Tamil Eelam was not only the demand of the LTTE but also the demand of the Tamil people. Prabhakaran also answered a number of questions in which he reaffirmed their commitment towards the peace process, quoted "We are sincerely committed to the peace process. It is because we are sincerely committed to peace that we continued a four-month cessation of hostilities" and was also firm in de-proscription of the LTTE by Sri Lanka and India. "We want the government of India to lift the ban on the LTTE. We will raise the issue at the appropriate time." Prabhakaran also insisted firmly that only de-proscription would bring forth an amenable solution to the ongoing peace process mediated by Norway: "We have informed the Government, we have told the Norwegians that de-proscription is a necessary condition for the commencements of talks".

Death

When the Sri Lankan military advanced into LTTE territory, Prabhakaran and his top leadership retreated into Mullaithivu, which became the terrorists' last stronghold. Early reports indicated that Prabhakaran was killed by a rocket attack while trying to flee the conflict zone in a captured ambulance and his body was badly burnt. But after the pro-terrorist Tamilnet claimed that he was alive, his body was shown on national TV. According to later reports, his body was found in the adjoining Nandhi Kadal lagoon north of Vellamullivaikkal near Mullaithivu. Its identity was confirmed by Karuna Amman, his former confidant, Daya Master and by DNA testing against his son's genetic material. Circumstantial evidence suggested that his death was caused by a massive head injury or he was shot dead at close range. There are also allegations that he was executed.

Criminal Indictments

Velupillai Prabhakaran was wanted by Interpol and many other organizations since 1991 for terrorism, murder, organized crime and terrorism conspiracy. He was issued a death warrant by the Madras High Court in India, for plotting the assassination of former Indian Prime Minister Rajiv Gandhi in May, 1991, and, in 2002, Judge Ambepitiya issued an open warrant to arrest him in connection with the 1996 Central Bank Bombing. The judge found him guilty on 51 counts and sentenced him to 200 years in prison.

Personal Life

Photograph showing, from right, Velupillai Prabhakaran, his wife Mathivathani, daughter Duvaaraga, son Charles Anthony and two unidentified relatives of Mathivathani

Little is known of Prabhakaran's personal life, either from his interviews or from cited media sources, although it is widely known that he was married to Mathivathani Erambu on October 1, 1984. They had a daughter (Duvaaraga) and two sons, Charles Anthony and Balachandran. Their whereabouts were not known. However, the Sri Lankan military sources stated that they had recovered the corpse of Charles Anthony. A senior Sri Lankan minister later informed that the Sri Lanka Army also found the bodies of Prabhakaran's wife, Mathivathani, his daughter, Duvaaraga, and his 13-year old son, Balachandran. However, the military spokesman Udaya Nanayakkara later stated that there was no information about the whereabouts of the remaining members of the Prabhakaran's family. "We have not found their bodies and have no information about them," he said. Yet, it is thought that Prabhakaran's entire family has been wiped out; the bodies of Mathivathani, Duvaaraga and Balachandran reportedly were found in a bushy patch about 600 metres away from where Prabhakaran's body was found. Velupillai Prabhakaran's parents, Thiruvenkadam Velupillai and Parvathi, both in their 70s, were found in the Menik Farm camp for displaced people near the town of Vavuniya. The Sri Lankan military and the government gave public assurances that they would not be interrogated, harmed or ill treated.

Health Profile of Prabhakaran[7]

The *Asian Tribune* report, claims that (in 2006, when the report on his health was filed by the paper), the health condition of Velupillai Prabhakaran had become a matter of serious concern among the inner circle of the LTTE. The *Asian Tribune* writes that it consulted various reliable sources to put this file together. The report has been largely reproduced below. There is no way that the accuracy of this report for its health or biographic details, as the paper does not identify its sources for collating the report, or comment on the veracity of their information can be verified.

Prabhakaran at age 17

Prabhakaran in 1984

Name: Prabhakaran Velupillai.
Date of Birth: 26 November 1954.
Place of Birth: Velvettithurai, Sri Lanka.
Father's Name: Thiruvenkadam Velupillai.
Mother's Name: Vallipuram Parvathy.
Brother: Manokaran (Eldest) Married to Vanajadevi.

Sisters: Jegathieswary is married to Mathiaparanam and Vinothini is married to Rasenthiran. Both sisters are elder to him. He was the youngest member in the family.

Father's Profession

Velupillai, Prabhakaran's father, was originally from Point Pedro. He started his life as a clerk in the Government Clerical Service when he was 19 years old, and retired from government service as a Land Officer when he was 58 years old.

Education: Prabhakaran studied up to G.C.E. Ordinary level at Chidampara College, Velvettithurai. It was the last school he attended.

Marriage and Family Life

Married: On 1st October 1984 at a simple temple ceremony held at Murugan Temple, Thiruporur, Chennai, Tamil Nadu, India.

Wife's Name: Mathivathani from Punguduthievu.

Name of Wife's Father: Erambu.

Name of Wife's Mother: Sinnammal.

Prabhakaran's Children: 1. Charles Anthony Seelan – Date of Birth: 18 April 1985; 2. Duvaaraga – Date of Birth: 02 June 1986; 3. Balachandran – Date of Birth: 10 January 1996.

Prabhakaran in 1987

Prabhakaran in 1989

Maladies (known)

Blood Pressure: Hypertension. His uncontrolled high blood pressure was said to be dangerous which could lead to a stroke, heart attack, heart failure or kidney failure.

Diabetes: Type 2 Diabetes, – Non-Insulin-Dependent Diabetes Mellitus (NIDDM). He was trying to control it through diet up to 2004. After that date, reports reveal that he was on pills.

Hydrocele: A collection of serous fluid that results from a defect or irritation in the tunica vaginalis of the scrotum – indirect inguinal hernia.

TIA - A Transient Ischemic Attack: This is a transient stroke that lasts only a few minutes. It occurs when the blood supply to part of the brain is briefly interrupted. TIA symptoms, which usually occur suddenly, are similar to those of stroke but do not last as long. Most symptoms of a TIA disappear within an hour, although they may persist for up to 24 hours. Symptoms can include: numbness or weakness in the face, arms, or legs, especially on one side of the body; confusion or difficulty in talking or understanding speech; trouble seeing in one or both eyes. After the TIA attack, he started wearing spectacles. There were reports that he had such mild attacks twice.

Depression: Bipolar disorder causes dramatic mood swings, often with periods of normal mood in between. Severe changes in energy and behaviour go along with these changes in mood. Instances of high and low episodes of mania and depression were observed by the doctors in Prabhakaran.

Eating Habits

He was asked to reduce fat. On Tuesdays, Fridays and Saturdays he took vegetarian meals only. He had given up eating beef, pork and mutton. He ate chicken with lots of spices, mostly as curry; and the flesh of *Lacerta Iguana* (In Tamil called Udumpu). He also ate sea food, especially sharks, crabs, prawns, shrimps. He loved to eat sea turtle flesh which was considered his favorite delicacy.

Prabhakaran in 1993

Prabhakaran in 1999

Daily Routine

He would start the day with a gentle walk for 30 minutes. His bodyguards were always present. This was followed by an oil body massage for 20 minutes by his body guards.

Breakfast

Food had to be tested before eating. His favourite menu was 'Pittu' made out of rice flour, Sambol and Murunga (drum stick) curry.

Visits

He would then visit Sencholai Girl's Home and Kantharuban Boy's Home. These were the orphanages which had a history of producing suicide bombers; mainly women suicide bombers. This was followed by a visit to the Handicap Centre for disabled ex-women cadres. A visit to the Computer Centre where there are more than 1,000 computers of all sizes and brands, followed. This centre was housed in a massive building. In some sections, entry was limited to a handful of hardcore LTTE leadership only.

Prabhakaran in 2002

Prabhakaran in 2004

Lunch: Mostly rice and curry.

Rest

This time was spent watching TV and reading South Indian weekly magazines. A siesta followed.

Evening Schedule

This involved meeting people, expatriate visitors and selected leaders in the LTTE rank and file. By 5 p.m., he started visiting building sites and training centres, followed by a 30-minute gentle walk and a 20-minute body massage thereafter.

Dinner: This comprised meals made out of wheat flour. Thereafter, he would retire to watch videos. He kept changing his sleeping place to avoid getting targeted while asleep.

Some Personality Traits of Prabhakaran[8]

Communications were his Core Concern

Prabhakaran in 2006

Shyam Tekwani writes that in November 1986, the police in Tamil Nadu, India, seized arms and sophisticated communications gear from assorted Sri Lankan Eelam or Tamil-homeland groups operating out of the state. Tamil Tigers founder Velupillai Prabhakaran – who then enjoyed the hospitality of the Indian government in Chennai – went on a much-publicised fast-to-the-death. Tellingly, he demanded the immediate return – not of his rocket launchers, surface-to-air missiles or AK-47 assault rifles – but his lifeline to the world: his wireless sets.[9] The incident showed how it was a powerful communications network and a sympathetic media that was at the core of his guerilla strategy.

Paranoid to the Core

Tekwani opines that (like others in the same category before him, one presumes) paranoia dictated his behaviour. He recalls an incident where mention by the journalist of Prabhakaran's newborn shocked him. He was less voluble, withdrawn and then, he left the room abruptly.[10] It was left to his trusted aide, Anton Balasingham, to cautiously quiz Shyam Tekwani on how and what he knew of the addition to Prabhakaran's family.

The Cult of Prabhakaran

Shyam writes that Prabhakaran, in building his force – which, at its zenith, controlled a third of Sri Lanka – adopted practices from a range of religious and political traditions and rituals, for a variety of political and publicity goals, which he changed as his awareness of their true import sank in… Tales of his marksmanship, valour and genius became commonplace. Soon, taking an oath in his name by his cadres and celebrating his birthday became mandatory. From Hinduism, he borrowed the practice of deifying martyrs and erecting shrines, to which people were expected to make offerings and pray on a day designated as holy. Hollywood taught him to produce slickly produced audio-visual presentations for profit and goodwill.[11]

Just Not When Eating[12]

"Calendars, posters, CDs, DVDs, newspapers, magazines, radio stations, TV stations – Prabhakaran had them all out years before the world had heard of the Al-Qaeda propaganda machinery. Acutely aware of the power of propaganda and his image as the most lethal weapon in his arsenal, he ensured everybody in his group understood how to use it. Cadres were not to interact with anyone outside the fold. His photo – and only his – would be the single image that hung on the walls of all denizens' homes in his territory. Every street corner would have his speeches or Eelam national songs playing from loudspeakers, at all hours. However, while Prabhakaran majestically posed for the camera with his 'cubs' (as he called the children he recruited), there were a few restrictions: He did not like being photographed while satiating his enormous appetite for food. No photos were allowed of his female cadres and none of dead or dying Tigers. These rules were later rescinded."

Learning to Befriend the Camera[13]

"During one of our initial photo sessions (in the early 1980s), Prabhakaran was awkward, uncertain of what was expected of him and very receptive to being directed. When it was suggested he change into combat fatigues, he went one step further and emerged from a room with his pistol fully loaded. Within seconds, framed by his bodyguards and a huge cut-out of a Tiger, with a huge portrait of Lenin in the background (this was before Marxism was banished from Tiger talk), he was in his element. An hour later, he eagerly asked for copies. Several photo sessions later, and in Jaffna while fighting for his supremacy against the Indian Peace Keeping Force (IPKF) that was deployed in Sri Lanka between 1987 and 1990, he revelled in playing the role of actor and director with consummate ease. He would play to the gallery with sardonic witticisms, refrain from any response in English, ponder a bit to deliver a quotable quote and strike the pose that struck him as just right for the occasion."

Cyanide Pill Myth

Tekwani writes that Prabhakaran felt it necessary to get the message across that he had a committed following – and that this commitment came from men, women and children. The cyanide pill was the emblem of commitment, and he generously arranged for Tekwani to photograph it, as his boys gamely posed with a vial containing it hung around their necks. While every instance of a cadre biting into the pill during assorted battles captured headlines, there was barely any mention of the many more who threw the vial away. Tekwani notes with irony that "recently released photos from the treasure trove of albums that Sri Lankan troops found in the fleeing Prabhakaran's house prove instructive: The black string holding the vial of cyanide disappears in a number of images where he is with his family."[14] It is of course, well documented now that neither Prabhakaran nor his immediate family members had cyanide vials on their person, when their dead bodies were examined.

Enlisting Rambo

Visiting the Tigers' training camps in the peninsula after 1991, Shyam Tekwani writes that the first thing he noticed was that the field training of the recruits (some of them very young) began with an oath to their leader: "To achieve Tamil Eelam, my life and soul, all this, I sacrifice. We'll be very faithful and trustworthy to our elder brother, Mr. Prabhakaran, the leader of our revolutionary organisation. I now begin my training. The thirst of Tigers is Tamil Eelam."[15] Their history lessons were an endless litany of hatred against the enemy – comprising only rapists, butchers and racists – and the glories of ancient Tamil kingdoms and kings. Part of the indoctrination, he noted was to show them Hollywood action films. He observed that 'Rambo' was the popular choice.[16]

Spelling of Prabhakaran's Name

There are different approaches to render his name in Latin script, which appear very different at first sight. The most straightforward option is a transliteration according to the National Library transliteration scheme. The pronunciation of the name is approximated in a spelling based on English conventions by 'Pirapakaran', 'Pirapaharan' or 'Pirabaharan'. A third option is to trace the history of the name back to its origins in Sanskrit, and then apply the National Library transliteration rules. This gives the version most often used in Western media, namely 'Prabhakaran'.

Chronological Career Graph[17]

The following is a chronological account of the life and times of Velupillai Prabhakaran, complied by the well known journalist and author, M.R. Narayan Swamy:

1954 (Nov 26):	Born in Jaffna in a Hindu middle class family, the youngest of two sons and two daughters.
1960-70s:	Takes to militancy, indulges in minor acts of violence.
1972:	Forms Tamil New Tigers (TNT); flees home for good.
1975:	Assassinates Jaffna Mayor Alfred Duraiappah at Hindu temple.
1976:	TNT becomes Liberation Tigers of Tamil Eelam (LTTE).
1978:	LTTE issues first press statement.
1982:	Arrested in Madras (now Chennai) after a shootout with a rival Tamil militant. Jailed, bailed, escapes to Sri Lanka.
1983:	Ambushes Army patrol in Jaffna, killing 13 soldiers. Anti-Tamil riots sweep Colombo, leaving hundreds dead and igniting Tamil insurgency.
1983 (Sep.):	Moves to Tamil Nadu, sets up home in Chennai. LTTE training camps come up in Tamil Nadu.
1984:	Meets Tamil Nadu Chief Minister M.G. Ramachandran and seeks support. Marries Jaffna university student, fathers two sons and a daughter.
1985 (May):	Orders massacre of Buddhists in the holy town of Anuradhapura, Sri Lanka.
1986 (April-May):	Orders slaughter of Tamil militants from rival group TELO.
1987 (January):	Quits India for good, saying there is an attempt to kill him.
1987 (July):	Meets Indian Prime Minister Rajiv Gandhi in New Delhi and says he accepts India-Sri Lanka accord meant to end Tamil separatism.
1987 (August):	Gives speech in Jaffna, saying "We love India", but tells aides he will teach India a lesson for betraying Tamil Eelam cause.
1987 (October):	Launches war against Indian troops deployed in Sri Lanka's North East.
1989 (April-June):	Goes into peace talks with Sri Lankan President Ranasinghe Premadasa, who asks Indian troops to go home.
1989 (July):	LTTE kills well known Tamil politicians A. Amirthalingam and V. Yogeswaran in Colombo.
1990 (April):	Takes control of Jaffna, addresses the media.
1990 (June):	Resumes war against Sri Lanka for Tamil Eelam, orders 100,000 Muslims living in Jaffna to quit. Rival militant K. Padmanabha and aides killed in Chennai, India.
1991 (March):	Sri Lankan Defence Minister Ranjan Wijeratne killed by car bomb.
1991 (May):	LTTE woman suicide bomber assassinates former Indian Prime Minister Rajiv Gandhi at election rally near Chennai.
1992 (August):	Sri Lanka's Northern Army command wiped out.
1992 (Nov):	LTTE suicide bomber riding motorcycle kills Sri Lanka Navy Chief Clancy Fernando.
1993:	Sri Lankan President Premadasa killed at May Day rally.
1993 (August):	Arrests LTTE Number 2, Mahattaya, on charges of being Indian spy. Executes him in December 1994.
1994:	Agrees to talk to President Chandrika Kumaratunga. Fighting halts.
1995:	Sri Lankan Presidential candidate, Gamini Dissanayake assassinated. Resumes war for Tamil Eelam.

1995 (December): Loses Jaffna to Sri Lankan troops.

1996 (July): LTTE slaughters 1,200 soldiers and policemen in military complex in just 72 hours.

1997-99: Takes control of large parts of North and East in Sri Lanka.

1999 (December): President Kumaratunga escapes assassination attempt, is blinded in one eye.

2000-01: Sri Lanka approaches Norway to facilitate peace talks with LTTE.

2001 (July): LTTE suicide cadres overrun Sri Lanka's only international airport, destroy 13 aircraft.

2002 (February): Signs Norway-brokered ceasefire agreement with Sri Lanka.

2002 (April): Addresses Sri Lankan, international media in Killinochchi, says he will never give up Tamil Eelam cause.

2003 (April): Walks out of Norway-backed peace process.

2004 (March): Faces revolt by LTTE Eastern Regional Commander Karuna and hundreds of cadres in Eastern province.

2005 (August): Sri Lankan Foreign Minister Lakshman Kadirgamar shot dead by LTTE sniper.

2006 (April): Army Chief, General Sarath Fonseka, badly hurt in attack by woman suicide bomber.

2006 (December): Defence Secretary Gottabhaya Rajapaksa, brother of President Mahinda Rajapaksa, survives assassination attempt.

2007: Launches air strike near Colombo. LTTE loses Eastern province to Sri Lanka. Prabhakaran vows to fight back.

2008 (January): Sri Lanka spikes ceasefire agreement. LTTE begins to lose territory in north.

2008 (November): Mocks President Rajapaksa says LTTE territory can never be seized.

2009 (January): Loses Killinochchi, hub of de facto Tamil Eelam state; retreats into Mullaithivu District.

2009 (May 17): Decides to 'silence' guns and end armed struggle.

2009 (May 18): Prabhakaran killed while trying to escape from war zone in Mullaithivu District. Heir apparent son and all key aides also killed.

ENDNOTES

1. This section has been excerpted from "Life and Times of Velupillai Prabhakaran." <http://en.wikipedia.org/wiki/Velupillai_Prabhakaran>
2. A Lankapuvath (official news agency of Sri Lanka) report titled "First political assassination by Prabhakaran," <http://www.lankapuvath.lk/index.php?view=article&id=273:first-political-assassination-of-prabhakaran-&option=com_content&Itemid=80> datelined January 25, 2009, suggests that Prabhakaran and Uma Maheshwaram conspired in the killing of Mayor Duraiappah.
3. "Life and Times of Velupillai Prabhakaran." <http://en.wikipedia.org/wiki/Velupillai_Prabhakaran>
4. "Thileepan." <http://en.wikipedia.org/wiki/Thileepan> The article indicates that this incident was one of the turning points of the Eelam war. Thileepan, also known as Lt. Col.

Thileepan (1962–26 September 1987), was a LTTE political wing member who died during a hunger strike during the IPKF operation of Jaffna, Sri Lanka. He was a popular student in Jaffna Hindu College, before joining the LTTE, prior to the 1983 Black July pogrom. He was given the name Thileepan. He was injured in military operations with the LTTE and was, at the time of his death, the LTTE political wing leader of the Jaffna peninsula. On the 15th of September, 1987, at 9.30 am at the Nallur Murugan Temple, Thileepan began his fast. His main objective was to bring awareness and action to a list of public demands made by himself and the Tamil Tigers, at a time when the relationship between the LTTE and the IPKF was deteriorating. The publicly stated goals of his fast were that all Tamils detained under the Prevention of Terrorism Act should be released, the colonisation of Sinhalese in Tamil areas under the guise of rehabilitation should be stopped, the Sri Lankan Government should stop opening new police stations and camps in the North Eastern province and the weapons given by the Sri Lankan government to 'Home Guards' should be withdrawn under the supervision of the Indian Army. Although several groups requested Thileepan as well as the local IPKF administration to intervene and stop the fast, Thileepan died on the 26th of September 1987. There was widespread grief in Tamil areas. Thousands of people from the north and east flooded Jaffna as news of his death spread. His death created an anti-Indian mood in Jaffna that was pro-India till then. Several days later the LTTE began hostilities against the Indian Peace Keeping Force. **The death of Thileepan was hence seen as a pivotal moment in Sri Lankan history and Sri Lankan – Indian relations for years to come.**

5. "Life and Times of Velupillai Prabhakaran."<http://en.wikipedia.org/wiki/Velupillai_Prabhakaran>
6. Ibid. Experienced and hard bitten media personalities who were present for this one off media conference of this scale noted several things. For one, the LTTE rank and file displayed an exceptional sense of security, taking nothing for granted. Their attention to even the smallest security detail impressed all present as being world class. Secondly, they noted that Prabhakaran was extremely well protected by guards who seemed to have war gamed every possible contingency. They appeared well armed, alert and very protective of him. So far as Prabhakaran himself was concerned, the media found him strangely hesitant, perhaps even overwhelmed by the gathering and its import, and largely uncommunicative. Most of the talking was done by the LTTE ideologue, Dr. Anton Balasingham, who certainly had no problem putting across his leader's thoughts. Anton shared the stage with Prabhakaran.
7. **"Health Card of Prabakaran is not so Rosy as it ought to be". July 3, 2006. <http://www.asiantribune.com/index.php?q=node/889.> Authors' Note:** *Asian Tribune* had its humble beginnings in Bangkok nine years ago. It is an epaper venture of a Sri Lanka Tamil journalist, K T Rajasingham. *Asian Tribune* moved to Sweden as the founder relocated himself in Sweden. The newspaper site says that it is owned by the "World Institute for Asian Studies (WIAS), which has been set up to bring the Asian nations closer to each other through better and in-depth understanding of regional problems. *Asian Tribune* brings to the monitor screens with breaking news and in-depth analysis of unfolding events in a package that is unique by international media standards. *Asian Tribune* has carved out a niche in the crowded net world and has succeeded in catching the eye of Presidents, Prime Ministers, law makers, chief executives, academics, students and even house wives across the nations in Asia, Europe and the Americas".
8. Tekwani, Shyam. "The Life And Times Of A Brutal Legend." <http://www.asiaone.com/News/Latest%2BNews/Asia/Story/A1Story20090520-142594.html>

   The inputs given in this section have been culled from the above article by Dr. Shyam Tekwani. He is a reputed, veteran journalist who has reported on the war in Sri Lanka for almost two decades and was one of the few Indian journalists who saw the evolution of Prabhakaran and the LTTE at close quarters. He is currently Associate Professor at Asia-Pacific Centre for Security Studies. He was previously Assistant Professor at Nanyang Technological University. He has done a portion of his education at Maryland Institute College of Art, Baltimore, USA. Dr. Tekwani has nearly two decades of experience in communications, as a reporter and photojournalist. His works have appeared in publications such as *The New York Times Magazine, Time, Newsweek, Le Figaro, Geo* and *Der Spiegel.* He is also a multimedia and web designer. He specializes on terror reportage and, besides being a journalist, has authored several monographs and books related to his specialization.

9. Ibid.
10. Ibid.
11. Ibid.
12. Quoted in the writer's own words.
13. Quoted in the writer's own words.
14. Ibid.
15. Culled from the Shyam Tekwani article.
16. Ibid. **'Rambo'** refers most commonly to the fictional character John Rambo who first appeared in the novel *First Blood,* and to the eponymous series of action films starring Sylvester Stallone: *First Blood* (1982), *Rambo: First Blood Part II* (1985), *Rambo III* (1988), *Rambo* (2008). Rambo may also refer to: *Rambo* and *Rambo III,* video games based on the films and *Rambo and the Forces of Freedom,* an animated series based on the film. **Source.** "Rambo." <http://en.wikipedia.org/wiki/Rambo>
17. Narayan Swamy, M.R. "Velupillai Prabhakaran: His Life, Times and Death." May 18, 2009. http://www.thaindian.com/newsportal/uncategorized/velupillai-prabhakaran-his-life-times-and-death_100194192.html
    The timeline has been reproduced as given, with minor syntax editing in line with the style adopted in this book.

References

1. "Tamil Tigers supreme commander Prabhakaran 'shot dead'". Times Online. May 18, 2009. http://www.timesonline.co.uk/tol/news/world/asia/article6309915.ece.
2. "War crime in the massacre of LTTE officials". http://www.tamilnet.com/art.html?catid=13&artid=29409.
3. "Tiger leader Prabhakaran killed: Sources-News-Videos – *The Times of India*". Timesofindia.indiatimes.com. http://timesofindia.indiatimes.com/videoshow/4546368.cms.
4. "Liberation Tigers of Tamil Eelam: Proscription as a Terrorist Group". http://en.wikipedia.org/wiki/Liberation_Tigers_of_Tamil_Eelam#Proscription_as_a_terrorist_group.
5. Mark Tran, Profile: Velupillai Prabhakaran, guardian.co.uk, Monday 18 May 2009.
6. "Profile of Velupillai Prabhakaran". Lankapuwath. 2009-04-22. http://www.hindustantimes.com/StoryPage/StoryPage.aspx?id=66266307-fb34-4150-b9b0-392df102e067.
7. "Asia Times: Sri Lanka: The Untold Story". Atimes.com. http://www.atimes.com/ind-pak/DA26Df04.html.
8. "Sun God's' Life of War" *Straits Times,* May 18, 2009.
9. "How it Came to This – Learning from Sri Lanka's Civil Wars By Professor John Richardson". paradisepoisoned.com. http://www.paradisepoisoned.com/PDFs/Preview21.pdf.

Chapter 8

"How I Became a Fighter..." and other Reflections

The last chapter hopefully gave rare insights into the life and times of Prabhakaran, not just to the lay reader, but also to those who have studied him in some depth. The internet is full of treasure troves of information on aspects of his life, if only one has the time and diligence to work their way through the oceans of material available.

The reader, at this stage of the book, has therefore, a fair idea, of Prabhakaran's early life and influences as also his progress as a leader of increasing importance, whose platform remained Eelam, right since the days when he was in the TNT. The human side of a public figure is always fascinating for most readers. Knowledge of the small quirks in their personalities, their peccadilloes, likes and dislikes, utilization of time, interests, strengths and weaknesses somehow make them seem more human and interesting; rather far removed from the one dimensional detail that is available for most key figures whose calling is or was terror. So we now know that Prabhakaran liked sea lobster, that he had several ailments, liked a good rub, was paranoid about security, was a computer geek and was refreshingly vain about his image and how he should be projected.

It is reassuring to know that he had fears which a man in the street also has; that he occasionally suffered from stage fright, that he changed his philosophic moorings more than once, that he was, finally, a family man who was protective about his immediate family. Seen in the context of his single track mind about Eelam and the mayhem that the LTTE under him caused in his country and the immediate neighbourhood, the LTTE head honcho acquires new overtones not available otherwise, in the bland reportage that recorded the killings, massacres and material damages engineered by both sides during their over 30-year war.

The current chapter takes up the challenge of understanding the mind and persona of Prabhakaran, thereby taking the readers' knowledge of the same a notch higher. This is made possible by focusing on extracts from some of his speeches; his surprisingly unguarded revelations during his interviews with the media on his early family life and relationships, especially his relationship with Mr. Vernugopal, a Tamil teacher from his village, Velvettithurai, who first put the idea of armed struggle in his mind. Also discernable is his world view, his early takes on the Eelam cause, which soon enough, became his idée fixe and so on. The chapter ends with some important personalities sharing their views on various facets of the Prabhakaran they saw, as leader, ideologue and ace motivator...

How I became a Freedom Fighter...[1]

"Q. *From your boyhood you have been a voracious reader. Can you tell us something about the books which instilled Tamil nationalism in you and impelled you to take up arms against oppression?*

A. From my young days, I have been a lover of books. A good part of my youth I spent reading worthwhile books. I was especially keen on reading historical novels, works of history, and biographies of heroes. The pocket money that my parents gave me I spent on books. There was a book shop in my village. It became my habit somehow or the other to buy all those valuable books there and read them. It is through books that I learnt of the heroic exploits of Alexander and Napoleon. It is through my habit of reading that I developed a deep attachment to the Indian Freedom struggle[2] and martyrs like Subhash Chandra Bose, Bhagat Singh and Bal Gangadhar Tilak. It was the reading of such books that laid the foundation for my life as a revolutionary.

"The racial riots which erupted in Sri Lanka in 1958 and the agonies that the Tamils had to endure as a result were the factors that impelled me to militancy. The reports that appeared in the dailies unleashed a hurricane of fury in me. When I read the novels of Tamil Nadu writers like Kausiyan (Paminip Pavai), Sandilyan (Kadat Pura) and Kalki (Ponniyin Selvan), I learned how our forefathers had established and ruled over great, flourishing empires. These novels aroused in me the desire to see our nation rise again from servitude and that our people should live a life of dignity and freedom in their liberated homeland."

"In my boyhood, I avidly read epics like the *Mahabharata* and the *Ramayana*; they too sparked off thoughts in me. 'Perform your duty without regard to the fruits of action', says the *Bhagavad-Gita*. I grasped this profound truth when I read the *Mahabharata*. When I read the great didactic works, they impressed on me the need to lead a good, disciplined life and roused in me the desire to be of service to the community. After I had finished reading a book, the questions 'why', 'what for', 'how did this happen this way' used to rise in my mind. I would try to connect the narrative and the characters with our life and the life of our people. At all such times, the thought that I should fight for the liberation of my people would dominate my mind."

"Q. *Your childhood must have been totally different from that of today's generation. Can you describe your childhood?*

"A. As a child, I was the pet and the darling of the family. My play-mates were the neighbours' children. My 'world' was confined to my house and the neighbours' houses. My childhood was spent in the small circle of a lonely, quiet house. When I was studying in the 8th standard, there was an institution called the 'Valvai Educational Institute' functioning in my village, Velvettithurai. Some youngster, who had had a higher education, wanted to develop my village; inspired by this ideal, they were running this institute at Sivaguru Vidyasalai (also known as Aladi School) close to my home.

Mr. Vernugopal, a Tamil teacher from my village, used to din it into our ears that the Tamils should take up arms. He was an ardent supporter of the Federal Party's Youth Front; later, feeling that the party was not militant enough, he teamed up with Mr. V. Navaratnam and was one of the founders of the 'Suyadchi Kazham' 'Self-Rule Party'. It is he who impressed on me the need for armed struggle[3] and persuaded me to put my trust in it. My village used to face military repression daily. Hence even as a child I grew to detest the Army. This hatred of military repression, combined with Mr. Vernugopal's persuasive views on armed struggle and the thirst for liberation, generated an inner dynamism within me and friends of my age flocked behind Mr. Vernugopal. The swelling thirst for freedom led me, when I was a fourteen year school boy and seven like-minded youngsters at our school, to form a movement with no name.

"Our aim was to struggle for freedom and to attack the Army. I was the leader of the movement. At that time, the idea that dominated our minds was to somehow buy a weapon and to make a bomb. Every week, the others would give me 25 cents they had saved from their pocket money. I maintained this pool of savings till we had accumulated Rs.40/-. At this time we learned that a 'Chandiyan' (thug) 'in the neighbouring village had a revolver which he was prepared to sell for Rs.150/-. Determined to buy this revolver somehow, I sold a ring which had been presented to me during my sister's wedding. It fetched Rs.70/-. Altogether we now had Rs.110/– We had then to abandon our plan to buy this revolver as we couldn't find the balance money."

"Q. *You are taking a very keen interest in the welfare of small children whose lives have been adversely affected by the ethnic war and are formulating and implementing several schemes for their welfare. What is the reason for your taking a special interest in the future of these children?*

"A. My ambition is to mould a new generation of youth who will be the architects of our country's future. This new generation will be scientific-minded, patriotic, honest, decent, heroic, and possessed of a sense of honour, self-respect and dignity. We have taken the small boys and girls who have been affected by the war into our fond embrace and are nurturing them. I do not consider them orphans or children bereft of kith and kin. They are the children of our motherland and they are flowers which have bloomed on our soil."[4]

"Nature is My Friend, Life My Philosopher and History is My Guide"[5]

"Q: *What made you opt out of a conventional system and spearhead a liberation movement which you knew would be outlawed?*

A: The democratic parliamentary system, or what you refer to as the conventional political system in Sri Lanka, has always tried to impose the will of the majority on the minority...Our just demands were totally ignored, and the oppression continued on such a scale as to threaten the very survival of the Tamils in Sri Lanka. It was these circumstances which led me to form our liberation movement. I felt that an armed struggle was the only alternative left to our people, not only to ensure our survival but ultimately to free ourselves from Sinhala oppression..."

"Q: *Could you elaborate on some of your personal experiences that compelled you to believe that an armed struggle was the only solution for the Tamils of Sri Lanka? Were you, your family members and friends, directly victimized by the discriminatory policy of the Sri Lankan government?*

"A: Once I met a widowed mother, a friend of my family, who related to me her agonizing personal experience of this racial holocaust. During the riots, a Sinhala mob attacked her house in Colombo. The rioters set fire to the house and murdered her husband. She and her children escaped with severe burn injuries...When I heard such stories of cruelty, I felt a deep sense of sympathy and love for my people...I strongly felt that armed struggle was the only way to confront a system which employs armed might against unarmed, innocent people."

"Q: *What was the reason for identifying yourselves as 'Tigers'?*

"A: I named the movement 'Liberation Tigers' since the tiger emblem had deep roots in the political history of the Tamils, symbolizing Tamil patriotic resurgence.

The tiger symbol also depicts the mode of our guerrilla warfare."

"Q: *Who is your friend, philosopher, and guide?*

"A: Nature is my friend, life my philosopher and history is my guide."

"Q: *How does it feel to be the most wanted man in Sri Lanka today?*

A: An Irish leader once remarked that when the British indict a person as a terrorist, it implied that he was a true Irish patriot. Similarly when the Sri Lanka Government refers to me as the most wanted man, it means that I am a true Tamil patriot. Hence I feel proud to be indicted as a wanted man."

"Q: *Do you experience moments of loneliness? And if you do, how do you combat it?*

"A: I have never felt lonely at any point of time. Loneliness is only a problem with those who are buried in their own individual egos. A true revolutionary transcends individuality and develops a collective, social consciousness. I live and struggle for a common collective cause."

"Q: *Do you have any regrets about not leading a normal life?*

"A: There are millions who, as you put it, lead a normal, ordinary existence. But we are fighting for a cause, for a noble ideal which gives us a profound spiritual satisfaction."

"Q: *Are you worried over the fact that most Tamil youths face a bleak future in Sri Lanka?*

"A: The youths are fighting a battle for freedom. I foresee a bright future for them."

"Q: *Would you rather die than be caught by the Sinhalese army?*

"A: I would prefer to die in honour rather than being caught alive by the enemy."

"Q: *The LTTE staged the 23rd July 1983 ambush in which 13 Sinhalese soldiers were killed. The ambush was allegedly the reason for the Sinhalese retaliation on innocent Tamils. Did you expect such a massive retaliation?*

"A: The July violence should not be assessed simply as Sinhala retaliation for the guerrilla ambush. This view is a gross oversimplification of the event. The island has been plagued with anti-Tamil racial violence which erupts periodically over the years. There were violent racial holocausts even before the emergence of our movement. Violent riots erupted in Trincomalee a couple of weeks before the ambush. Therefore, the phenomenon of anti-Tamil racial violence cannot be traced to a single event. We are engaged in protracted guerrilla warfare. There have been several guerrilla raids, several ambushes, and we have killed several Sinhala soldiers and policemen The July ambush was only a part of the warfare we are engaged in. It is incorrect to assume that one particular military operation has precipitated the entire violence. The July riots, you would have certainly observed, was not aimed at the physical extermination of our people but was also aimed at the destruction of the economic power base of the Tamils in Colombo. Our view is that the July holocaust was a pre-planned, well-orchestrated genocidal pogrom against the Tamils, carried out by the racial elements of the ruling party. Initially, these racist elements did attempt to put the whole blame on the Tigers. Then, suddenly, they blamed the left parties for the riots..."

"Q: *Why did you stage the July ambush? There are various versions afloat. According to some, it was an act of reprisal as four Tamil women had been raped. Based on my investigations I felt that, you had to prove a point to the Sinhalese army who were jubilant over the death of your close associate, Charles Anthony, leader of the LTTE military wing on 15th July, 1983. The point, I guess, that you had to assert was that the LTTE, despite the loss of one of its ablest leaders was still strong and capable of taking on the Sinhalese army. Is this theory correct?*

"A: There is an element of truth in your findings about Charles Anthony and the ambush. The attack was partly retaliation, a punishment of the Sinhala army. But still we feel that the lives of 13 soldiers cannot compensate for the life of a great revolutionary and freedom fighter like Charles. The ambush was also a part of the guerrilla warfare directed against the enemy.

"Q: *Do you have ties with other liberation movements of the world? Which are the organisations who provide training and arms to the LTTE?*

"A: We have ties with other world liberation movements. I cannot answer the second part of your question."

"Q: *Is it true that Israelis are training Sinhalese Army men on the techniques of anti-guerrilla warfare?*

"A: So far we haven't got any confirmed reports about the presence of Israeli military experts in Sri Lanka. If the reports are true I won't be surprised. Sri Lanka is turning into a base for US imperialism and its agents, whoever the trainers are or whatever their expertise may be. The Sinhala Army cannot crush the will and determination of the Tigers. We have a great moral power, a supreme sense of sacrifice, and a noble cause."

"Q: *If and when Eelam is achieved, what sort of a nation do you conceive it to be?*

"A: Tamil Eelam will be a socialist state. By socialism, I mean an egalitarian society where human freedom and individual liberties will be guaranteed, where all forms of oppression and exploitation will be abolished. It will be a free society where our people will have maximum opportunity to develop their economy and promote their culture.

"Q: *In your estimate, how long will it take to achieve this Eelam?*

"A: There cannot be a blueprint or a time limit for a freedom struggle.

Everything depends on the situation in our homeland and happenings on the international scene."[6]

Reflections of Tamil Eelam National Leader V. Prabhakaran[7]

- Nature is my friend. Life is my philosopher. History is my path-finder.
- Fear is the outcome of weakness, a coward's friend, an enemy of firmness.
- Fear of death is the cause of all human fears. One who wins the fear of death wins himself. He is the one who wins the freedom from his mental prison.
- I always give less importance to speech. It is only after growing up in action that we should begin speaking.
- We have sowed the seed of an ideal; we grow it by irrigating it with the blood of our martyrs. This seed will grow up into a luxuriant tree and make our martyrs' dreams a reality.
- The Liberation Tigers are not different from the people. The Liberation Tigers is a people movement. The people are the Tigers.
- The Tamils bowed their heads when repeatedly knocked and lived as slaves with shame. The greatness of getting them to live with self-respect was the work of out liberation movement.
- Although the Tamils live widely all over the world, it is in Tamil Eelam that there is an awakening of the national spirit. It is in Tamil Eelam that the national personality is born. It is in Tamil Eelam that there are external signs of a separate state.
- The struggle for the ideal of women's liberation is a fiery child that was born on the laps of the liberation movement.
- My comrades whom I loved as my life, my generals who have been fighting along with me shoulder to shoulder, my fighters whom I fostered for several years, when they fall in the battle field my heart bursts. Yet in that grief I do not languish. All these losses add strength to my will towards my ideal.
- A liberation warrior's death is not a normal death occurrence. This death is a historical incident. It is a miracle of high ideal becoming a reality. In fact a liberation fighter does not die.
- 'Cyanide' is the symbol to show that we are dedicated to our ideal. As long as this cyanide hangs on our neck we will not fear any force in the world.

Who Said What About Tamil National Leader V. Prabhakaran?[8]

Jyotindra Dixit, India's ex Foreign Secretary in 'Assignment Colombo', Konarak Publishers, 1998[9]

Photo from Eelamweb.com website

"The LTTE's emergence as the most dominant and effective politico-military force representing Tamil interests were due to the following factors:

- First, the character and personality of its leader V. Prabhakaran, who is disciplined, austere and passionately committed to the cause of Sri Lankan Tamils' liberation. Whatever he may be criticized for, it cannot be denied that the man has an inner fire and dedication and he is endowed with natural military abilities, both strategic and tactical. He has also proved that he is a keen observer of the nature of competitive and critical politics. He has proved his abilities in judging political events and his adroitness in responding to them.
- Secondly, he has created a highly disciplined, and dedicated cadre, a manifestation of which is inherent in what is called the 'cyanide cult.' Each regular member of the LTTE carries a cyanide pill and is pledged to committing suicide rather than being captured by the enemy.
- The third factor is the cult and creed of honesty in the disbursement and utilization of resources. Despite long years spent in struggle, the LTTE cadres were known for their simple living, lack of any tendency to exploit the people and their operational preparedness.
- The fourth factor has been the LTTE's ability to upgrade its political and military capacities including technological inputs despite the constraints imposed on it by Sri Lankan forces and later by India.
- The fifth factor is a totally amoral and deadly violent approach in dealing with those the LTTE considers as its enemies.
- The sixth factor is Prabhakaran's success in gathering around him senior advisers with diverse political, administrative and technological capacities, which contributed to effective training of his cadres and optimum utilisation of the military equipment which helped in the structuring of an efficient command and control system.

Marshall R Singer,[10] Ph.D., Professor of International and Intercultural Affairs, Graduate School of Public and International Affairs, University of Pittsburgh:

"As far as I can tell, most ordinary Tamils support the Tigers...The Tigers are ruthless and authoritarian but they are not corrupt...In fact, they are perceived as being single-minded in their defence of Tamils. They are so disciplined that when captured, they swallow cyanide capsules that they carry with them at all times, rather than risk revealing anything under torture." *(Statement before US Congress Committee on International Relations Subcommittee on Asia and the Pacific Hearing on Sri Lanka, November 14, 1995)*

Lieutenant General Depinder Singh,[11] Overall Force Commander (OFC) of the Indian Peace Keeping Force (IPKF):

"Numerous questions were to be asked as to why the IPKF could not capture or kill Prabhakaran; another equally wild allegation was that the IPKF had orders not to kill Prabhakaran. Apart from the impossibility of singling out an individual target for destruction or protection in such an environment, we must remember that by virtue of the fact that the LTTE had an effective junior leadership, the loss of Prabhakaran could never have resulted in the disintegration of the LTTE. This (book) is a left-handed salute to the LTTE whose deviousness cannot overshadow their incredible motivation and magnificent fighting prowess, for which the Indian Armed Forces will always have a healthy respect." *(Lieutenant General Depinder Singh in 'IPKF in Sri Lanka' published in 1992)*

Lieutenant General S.C. Sardeshpande,[12] IPKF Divisional Commander, Jaffna:

"I have a high regard for the LTTE for its discipline, dedication, determination, motivation and technical expertise... I was left with the impression that the LTTE was the expression of popular Tamil sentiment and could not be destroyed, so long as that sentiment remained." *(Lieutenant General S.C. Sardeshpande in 'Assignment Jaffna', published in 1992)*

ENDNOTES

1. "How I Became a Freedom Fighter". April 1994.<http://www.eelamweb.com/leader/interview/in_199404/ Tamil >National Leader Hon. V. Pirapaharan's Interview. The excerpts are from an interview given to *'Velicham'*, a Tamil language literary magazine, published in Jaffna. Velupillai Prabhakaran reflected on the events and circumstances during his early life that inspired him to take up arms and join the liberation struggle. The site does not mention the name of the interviewer. Eelamweb is considered by some observers, as favourably

disposed towards the LTTE in its coverage of the civil war.

2. Earlier chapters of '*Lost Victory*' have touched upon the influence of the Indian struggle for Independence as having motivated the founding leaders, both Tamil as well as Sinhala, to seek independence for their country as well.
3. Ibid.
4. Ibid.
5. Pratap, Anita. 'Nature is My Friend, Life My Philosopher and History is My Guide'. Interview with Tamil National Leader Hon V. Prabhakaran. Sunday Magazine, India 11-17 March 1984. Reproduced in <http://www.eelamweb.com/leader/interview/in_1984/> The excerpts that have been quoted from this in-depth and wide ranging interview of Prabhakaran cover some aspects of his intellectual leanings as well as personal admissions. The unspoken subtext for Prabhakaran to talk about the symbolism linking the Tiger with the Tamil desire for political resurgence was perhaps to indicate that a Tiger was needed to take on a Sinhala race that prided itself as being the progeny of a lion's mating with a Sinhala woman, in the days of antiquity. The interview covers the sensitive ground for the July 1983 massacre by the Tigers of 12 SLA soldiers and the retaliatory Black July action that left hundreds (some say thousands of Tamils) dead. Prabhakaran's acceptance of the massacre is startling as also his admission that the LTTE had contacts with other terror organisations. In sum, a revealing interview.
6. Ibid.
7. "Reflections of Tamil Eelam National Leader V. Pirapaharan". http://www.eelamweb.com/leader/quotes/Once again, these musings, reveal the emotional, philosophical and intellectual underpinnings of the man. The aspect of his almost genetic bitterness at being undermined as a people, the single minded focus on his desired end state of Eelam, his rationalization of loss of his leadership, his rank and file in the struggle strike the reader. His obvious passion for his dream is evident in his reflections. The reference to cyanide as a means of conquering fear (thereby making the soldier wearing it fearless of the consequences of his/her acts of terror) may make some observers feel that his idealism in this sphere underwent a change as the struggle for Eelam went on; at death, on 18 May, 2009, the Government did not hesitate to point out that Prabhakaran was not carrying his cyanide vial, neither were the members of his immediate family who also died.
8. "Who Said What About Tamil National Leader Hon. V. Pirabaharan?"< http://www.eelamweb.com/leader/about/>
   The opinions reflected are from the above quoted article put out by Eelamweb. They have been edited to an extent, but retain the essence of what the contributors have to say on the subject of their attention, Prabhakaran.
9. The quotes from the book by Mr. J.N. Dixit should be seen in the context that they were written at a time when the LTTE and its leader were, 'on song' as it were, and the troubles that overtook them later were yet to manifest themselves.
10. The comments by Marshall Singer have been edited to a fair extent as he does not appear to have any hands on knowledge of the LTTE or, for that matter, the other key players in the conflict, the SLA and the Indian Army. His mention of corruption in talking of a war where the clash of ideologies and military capability or the lack of it needed to be commented on, leaves his inputs as somewhat out of place and incomplete.
11. The comments by Lt Gen Depinder Singh, PVSM, VSM, figure (in part) on p. 127 of his book, 'IPKF in Sri Lanka', Trishul Publications, NOIDA, Third Edition, 2001. As OFC,

IPKF, his analysis carries weight. For the reader who wants an Indian perspective at the macro level of military functioning that led to the employment of the IPKF, its functioning there and areas for improvement in various aspects of politico-military synergy as well as war fighting, the book makes for essential reading.

12. The comments attributed to Lt Gen S.C. Sardeshpande, UYSM, AVSM, from his book, 'Assignment Jaffna', Lancer Publications, New Delhi, 1992, figure (again partly) on p. ix of the Preface. The General's narrative on how a Divisional Commander fought his battle during Operation Pawan; his highs and his lows, and his take on the IPKF performance makes interesting reading.

CHAPTER 9

Select Interviews of Prabhakaran

The last two chapters have essentially focused on Prabhakaran at the personal level, attempting to gain insights and knowledge about some of the lesser known details on his thoughts, life, motivation, work ethic and aspirations. This chapter shifts gears and gives the reader an insight into his development as a shrewd, astute leader who was politically savvy, street smart about developments related to terror handling world wide, and had a decided flair for interacting with the media, preferably on a one-on-one basis. [Observers have, of course, noted that this otherwise vocal and expressive leader was not at his best when in full public glare as happened in 2002, at Killinochchi, where he came across in his first mega sized media address as hesitant and unsure of himself].

The five interviews which have been excerpted here cover a wide range of responses from Prabhakaran.

"We Are Prepared to Pay for Freedom with Our Lives"[1]

"Q: *What do you hope will come out of your meeting with Prime Minister Rajiv Gandhi?*

"A: We hope to explain our problem clearly to him. Among the issues we want to raise with him is the fact that Jayewardene is using the cease-fire as a front while he goes about systematically massacring the Tamils. We want to try and convince him that what is going on in Sri Lanka is genocide of a race. We want to give him details of what exactly is going on in Sri Lanka even though there is supposed to be a cease-fire. We also want to highlight the fact that the Sri Lanka Government has so far not put forward a genuine, meaningful set of proposals.

"Q: *Do you think the PM will be sympathetic?*

"A: I trust he will be.

"Q: *Do you feel that in the last three months the Indian Government's attitude towards the militants has hardened?*

"A: In the beginning, I did not think so; but after Balasingham was deported, I am inclined to believe that the attitude has hardened."

"Q: *What do you think has caused this change in the Indian Government's stance?*

"A: I don't know what has caused this change. Perhaps, some international crisis or pressure is responsible. It is not possible for us to ascertain immediately as to what has caused this change, but with time, I am sure the reasons will come out."

"Q: *Do you think that India has become more pro-Sri Lanka?*

"A: So far, we have not thought along those lines. But certain incidents create doubts in our minds."

"We are Prepared for a Long Struggle (to Attain Eelam)"[2]

"Q: *The LTTE's general style of operation seems to be to indulge in hit-and run tactics. But after a hit-and-run attack, the Army turns on the Tamil civilians. For example, it is widely believed that your ambushing and killing the 13 soldiers presaged the 1983 riots against the Tamils. Other liberation organisations like the PLO and the IRA do not indulge in hit-and-run tactics. Further, they have expanded their base among the people. Have you expanded your base?*

"A: For the PLO, there is no room for adopting hit-and-run tactics, because they are fighting from a foreign soil. The IRA is fully indulging in hit-and-run operations. The British Army does not attack the civilians. But we work with a lot of hardship in terms of finance and resistance from (Sri Lankan) military. Yet, in Jaffna and other places, we have controlled the Army and have made them into liberated zones. This was because there is no gap between the people and us. In Jaffna, and in Nilaveli at Trincomalee, these areas are under our control. There is no Government control. We are running the civil administration. This means that we have gone a step above the hit-and-run methods. Even though we adopted hit-and-run methods in the beginning. Gradually, we have not allowed the troops to come in and as time goes on, it will become a mass struggle. Right now, in places like Jaffna, it has become a mass struggle. Besides, we are running a guerrilla force. Out of several tactics in guerrilla warfare, one is hit-and-run. In the initial development of the LTTE, we did hit-and-run operations. But now, after an attack, we give protection to the people. Without people's support, we would have been betrayed and our movement would not have been there.[3]

"Q: *Recently, you went on a tour of the Tamil areas of Sri Lanka and you also met your regional commanders. How is the morale of your cadres and what is the situation there?*

"A: There is only progress (increasing determination). There is no retardation in the struggle. There is a feeling dominant among the people that instead of slowly dying in batches, it is better to fight and die together. Our boys... comrades... are closer to the people. As a result, they are strong and firm. There cannot be any talk on morale because as long as there is one soldier (in the LTTE), they will fight for our ideal (to achieve Eelam). Till there is a last comrade, we will fight for our independence... liberation."

"I Felt Outraged at the Inhuman Atrocities Perpetrated Against My People..."[4]

"Gentleman: *You are normally projected as a symbol of Tamil militancy. Even your own organisation projects you as a big hero. As a radical, how do you justify the individual hero worship?*

"Prabhakaran: I cannot help this kind of projection and characterisation. I am only concerned with the political liberation and social emancipation of oppressed people. My people are aware of my commitment and trust me to lead them on the right path. That is why they show great affection. These projections may be expressions of people's love."[5]

"Gentleman: *How do you assess the present situation in Sri Lanka?*

"Prabhakaran: The present political situation in Sri Lanka is very critical. The Tamil nation is facing a genocide onslaught. Under the guise of a cease-fire, the Sri Lankan State has embarked on a policy of ruthless repression, military domination and annihilation of our people. Such a policy has made the present situation very critical and dangerous."

"Gentleman: *So you have nearly agreed that the talks have come to a dead end and that till they are revived, the chances of a peaceful settlement are very thin. In the interregnum, what will be your strategy? Are you planning to revive your guerrilla operations against the Armed Forces?*

"Prabhakaran: There is no war at the moment. We only defend ourselves when we are attacked. We will never go on the offensive."[6]

"Gentleman: *There were also some reports of the Sri Lankan Army's efforts to drive the Tamil peasants out of the Trincomalee district and allow Sinhalese settlements in their place. What will be your stand if these reports are true?*

"Prabhakaran: We have no other option but to fight back. We will effectively fight back and foil their plans."

"The Eye of the Tiger"[7]

For the past 14 years, Velupillai Pirabakaran (Prabhakaran) has led an armed struggle to create a separate Tamil state in Sri Lanka's volatile north-eastern region. Pirapakaran, 32, commands the Liberation Tigers of Tamil Eelam (LTTE), the strongest of Sri Lanka's numerous Tamil separatist groups. It is generally acknowledged that peace negotiations with Colombo are unlikely to prove effective without the LTTE's involvement. Shortly before his group rejected Colombo's latest proposal for peace talks, Pirapakaran spoke with NEWSWEEK'S Sudip Mazumdar in Madras. Excerpts:

"Mazumdar: *Your opponents often charge that innocent civilians are often killed in your military offensives. How do you respond?*

"Pirapaharan: The LTTE has never killed any civilians.[8] We condemn such acts of violence. There were occasions when we had to kill home guards. But they are not civilians. They are trained non-combat draftees who carry guns."

"Why do you think the LTTE has taken the lead among other groups?

"Pirapaharan: Discipline and order are most important. We emphasise personal morality and a sense of patriotism. Our cadres carry cyanide pills with them to avoid falling into enemy hands. Most of all, the people are behind us. We have imposed a strict moral code on ourselves, not to use even liquor."[9]

"Press reports say that you received military training in Cuba. How did you manage to acquire your know-how?

"Pirapaharan: Through sheer personal training. I use my natural instincts and I watch war films and western movies by [American movie actor] Clint Eastwood. If I were trained in Cuba, I would have been a better fighter."[10]

"What kind of a political system do you envisage for an independent Tamil state?

"Pirapaharan: We want to establish a socialist society. Ours will be a unique socialist model; neither Soviet nor Chinese nor any other."

The BBC Interview[11]

BBC: Prime Minister Chandrika Kumaratunga has said that she would be having talks with the LTTE. Do you think that a favourable climate has been reached for peace talks?

VP: We are ready for talks without pre-conditions. What we desire is that these talks take place in a relaxed and peaceful atmosphere. The new government has partially lifted the economic embargo. This is a positive step and an expression of its goodwill. We welcome it. However, the embargo has not been fully lifted. The ban on certain essentials still continues. That aside, the government continues to curb the free movement of people between the peninsula and the mainland by keeping the land routes closed. Aggressive acts by government forces continue; offensives by the Sri Lankan Navy in particular. These are bound to dampen peace initiatives. All in all, the situation in Tamil areas has yet to return to normalcy. It is only the government that can take constructive steps towards building up this process.

BBC: You are saying that the government must express its good intentions by announcing a cease-fire. But there is a view prevalent among the armed forces that you would make use of the cease-fire to strengthen yourself militarily. What is your response to that?[12]

VP: I must say that this is a totally erroneous assumption. Militarily speaking, a cease-fire is not advantageous for us. It is only by continuing to seize arms from the enemy, or in destroying them, that we can ensure our growth and military preparedness. That is possible only by continuing the war. To think that a cease-fire would benefit us is therefore incorrect. Despite that, if we desire a cease-fire, it is only to bring about the right climate for genuine peace, and for no other reason.[13]

BBC: You have been stressing the need for a Tamil homeland. But Prime Minister Chandrika has reportedly made it clear that she was not going to accept the concept of a Tamil homeland, nor that she is prepared for a North-East merger. What she envisages is a re-demarcation of provincial boundaries. What are your comments on that?

VP: I am not the only person to stress the need for a Tamil homeland. That had been the voice of Tamil consciousness and stressed time and again, over a long period. This is a historical fact. The areas that consist of the Northeast province had been the homeland of Tamil-speaking people. That includes the Muslims. That is our position. The government position will be known in the course of our talks. At that point of time, we can express our views.

BBC: There are allegations that the Liberation Tigers are the ones who are obstructing the opening up of land routes between the peninsula and the mainland. What is your answer to that?

VP: There is absolutely no truth in these allegations. There are two land routes between Jaffna and the Tamil mainland, that of Elephant Pass and Poonakari (Pooneryn). The Sri Lanka government forces have closed both these routes and prevented movement of people with a view to laying a military siege over the Jaffna peninsula, It is because of this that the people are using the sea route of Kilali. In the act of preventing even this, the Sinhalese armed forces have resorted to innumerable killings. To enable the people to undertake this risky journey with some safety, our Sea Tigers have made immeasurable sacrifices. Their acts of valor in this regard are legendary. Today, the Kilali sea route is under our control. People are now using the Kilali sea route without fear, under the protection of our cadres. But if the government is prepared to take steps to open up one of these land routes, and facilitate the movement of people and vehicles, we would certainly welcome it. There should be freedom of movement for the people without army checks and harassment. If the government would withdraw the remaining armed forces at Poonakari and open up the Sangupiddy pathway, our people are certain to welcome it wholeheartedly.

BBC: Recently, I visited Muslim refugee camps in Puttalam.[14] *Those Muslim people whom you had forced to evacuate from Jaffna told me that they had lived together with the Jaffna people in amity and friendship, and they were pained over what happened. They said if their protection was guaranteed, they would like to come back to Jaffna. If conditions were to return to normal, would you permit them to come back to their earlier habitats?*

VP: Those people belong to the Jaffna soil. Because of some unfortunate developments at a certain point of time, they were forced to become refugees. We express our regret over this.[15] When conditions become normal, we will permit them to come back to Jaffna. As a result of this war, there are three lakhs of Tamils living as refugees in the Jaffna peninsula alone. Because the armed forces have forcibly occupied their areas, particularly in the islands division and in Valikamam north, these people were compelled to abandon their homes, and are now living as displaced people. A considerable number of them have sought refuge in areas previously occupied by the Muslim people. If the Sinhala armed forces would withdraw from the areas they forcibly occupied, these displaced people would be in a position to get back to their original habitats. In such an event, we would permit these Muslim refugees to get back to Jaffna.

Endnotes

1. "We Are Prepared to Pay for Freedom with Our Lives". Tamil National Leader Hon. V. Prabhakaran's Interview. 'SUNDAY' Magazine, India 29 September–5 October 1985. <http://www.eelamweb.com/leader/interview/in_1985/> This interview datelined 1985, fully two years before the IPKF entered Sri Lanka at the request of the Government of Sri Lanka, to help usher the return of normalcy, gave the first pointers of the changing stance of the LTTE leader about Indian support for Tamils in Sri Lanka. Readers will note that he had still to meet the Indian Prime Minister, Rajiv Gandhi, but appeared uncertain as to the kind of response he would elicit from him.
2. "Tamil National Leader Hon. V. Pirapaharan's Interview. 'The chances of attaining Eelam are bright because the people's determination is firm. We are prepared for a long-drawn struggle (to attain Eelam)". 'Frontline' Magazine, India. 30 December 1985. <http://www.eelamweb.com/leader/interview/in_19851230/> **Note.** The 'Pirapaharan' alluded to is

the colloquial name for Prabhakaran, and has been used by Eelamweb consistently, in preference to the latter name.

3. Prabhakaran's comments about how hit-and-run tactics are employed by LTTE as opposed to the PLO or the IRA are instructive. For one they reveal him to be not only well informed but also nuanced in his understanding of the application of these tactics. The shift by the LTTE from merely hit-and-run to providing 'protection to the people' and creating liberated zones where the writ of the LTTE ran would be a fascinating study in itself for analysts who study the rise, development and fall of terror organisations. Note the absolutely correct emphasis he lays on people's support to the cause. Sun Tzu did the same, over 2000 years ago, in his masterly treatise on the 'Art of War'.
4. Singh, Jaswinder. Tamil National Leader Hon. V. Pirapaharan's Interview. "It is the plight of the Tamil people that compelled me to take up arms. I felt outraged at the inhuman atrocities perpetrated against an innocent people." 'THE WEEK' Magazine, India. March 3 1986.http://www.tamilnation.org/ltte/vp/interviews/8603%20week.htm Only small portions of the interview have been used here.
5. This comprehensive March 1986, interview with Jaswinder Singh, gave early indications of the trait that was one of the calling cards of Prabhakaran (Pirapaharan) – self projection. Like the Greek god, Narcissus; in fact like most if not all people who rose to power on a people's mandate, Prabhakaran loved the limelight. This tendency stands reinforced by an Indian journalist who covered him and the LTTE from the beginning: Shyam Tekwani. His comments have been quoted in earlier chapters and will surface again in Chapter 11, where Prabhakaran's overall assessment is intended to be carried out.
6. Readers will undoubtedly take this remark from Prabhakaran as tongue-in-cheek or the typical doublespeak of the canny, wily politician and psychological warfare expert, which he undoubtedly was. Prabhakaran was never far away from waging war against the State, and used the interregnum between sequences of war as breathing space to rearm, refit, reorient and then launch out all over again. It is debatable whether he even once strayed from his avowed intention of Eelam at all costs. His periodic, well publicised declarations of smoking a peace pipe, were of course, misunderstood and interlocutors retained the hope of getting him around. History records that their efforts were in vain.
7. Majumdar, Sudip. 'The Eye of the Tiger'. Tamil National Leader Hon. V. Pirapaharan's Interview. NEWSWEEK. August 11, 1986. <http://www.eelamweb.com/leader/interview/in_eye_1986/> Interview conducted in Madras (now Chennai). The full text of this interesting interview done when Prabhakaran was 32, is also available at http://www.tamilnation.org/forum/sachisrikantha/vp/vp42.htm Both the sites are known to support the LTTE's worldview. Only a portion of the interview has been excerpted here.
8. Readers will accept without demur, that there is little substance in this assertion of non-violence by Prabhakaran. One of the unfortunate consequences of the civil war is that thousands of civilians died on both sides of the divide.
9. The differentiators listed by Prabhakaran in response to Majumdar's question were the mainstay of the LTTE's enviable reputation as a ruthlessly efficient terror organisation that, in a way, set standards in the spread of terror world wide and was perhaps imitated for some of its innovations by the al Qaeda, PLO and others. The only thing that appears overplayed (maybe not then, but certainly later) is the issue of cyanide vials. The early fervour that was exhibited till even the late 90's, seems to have waned, as the LTTE went into a decline trajectory, certainly after 2004, when the Karuna faction broke away.

10. Prabhakaran forgot to add 'Rambo' the iconic Hollywood film series! His reflections in Chapter 8 refer.
11. Sooriyapiragasam, Ms. Aananthi. Interview of Tamil National Leader Hon. V. Pirapaharan (Prabhakaran) with assistance from BBC Tamil Section 'Tamilosai'. September 13, 1994. <http://www.eelamweb.com/leader/interview/in_1994/> It may be noted that Prabhakaran gave several such interviews to Ms Aananthi, of which the one cited has been found most relevant in the context of this book, and hence excerpted.
12. A valid and provocative question asked by the Interviewer, Ms Aananthi. The SLAF assumption was of course, correct. Each cessation in hostilities was used by the LTTE as a breather to get its voids in manpower and materials made up, as also stock up in war like stores. This was also the time to reorient operationally as also from the intelligence viewpoints. During this period, if there was a part of the LTTE that wasn't low key, it was their IT driven, well oiled, multi directional, multi channel, enormously efficient propaganda machinery. In fact their success in perception management taught a lesson or two to the SLAF, which they imbibed wonderfully from end 2005 onwards. Maybe India can take a bow for having made South Asia realize the power of the media in perception management in their precedent setting coverage of the Kargil war, in May-July, 1999.
13. Ibid.
14. The Muslim-Tamil divide is not the focus of this book but was a most serious problem. Earlier chapters have indicated that the LTTE went on an ethnic cleansing drive not just against the Sinhala population but also against the Muslims who were resident in the perceived Tamil Eelam areas. This led to horrific incidents of senseless killing. The fact that the Sinhala population in particular is also alleged to have involved in the same ethnic cleansing, this time directed mainly at the Tamils but also inclusive, in part of Muslim relocation, only adds to the complex demographic shifts that came about as a result of these drives.
15. Prabhakaran's regrets for the relocation and associated human and material losses may be a classic case of 'too little, too late'.

CHAPTER 10

Select Speeches by Prabhakaran

This chapter focuses on important extracts of six speeches/statements that Prabhakaran gave/authored, between the years 1992 and 2007. The extracts contained in this chapter have been chosen because they reveal personality details of Prabhakaran in a unique manner. As the opening sample, his views on military maters command professsional respect diverse issues. The views expressed by him for ignorance, on 'Heroes' Day (1998), are educative as he revelered revealed his understanding of intricate military matters. He termed that occasion as the first anniversary on the then ongoing SLAF operation, codenamed '*Operation Jayasikuru*' (Victory Assured).

In many ways, this operation was a landmark one, because a reoriented LTTE, operating for the first time in a conventional war fighting mode, had operated skillfully against a synchronized military operation involving all three services; in effect, SLAF, and apparently come out tops. The operation resulted in heavy casualties to the SLAF; rather more than those suffered by the LTTE. It ran from 1997 to 1999, and was launched in the Mullaithivu-Wanni areas, known to be the LTTE hotbed, with the aim of decimating the LTTE. It failed in this purpose, even though it made other incidental gains that had a long-term effect. One could go to the extent of saying, that, in losing that battle and assiduously learning from it, the SLAF, in fact won the civil war. It was after all, in the same setting that a far better prepared SLAF and correspondingly weakened and fractured LTTE fought their last war, (July 2006-May 2009) in the Wanni region, with the SLAF winning decisively this time around.

The coverage in this chapter, as stated earlier, goes well beyond the coverage of Prabhakaran's take on Operation Jayasikuru. The reader also gets familiar with his flow of thought and views on International Women's Day (celebrated as Tamil

Eelam Women's Day) on three separate occasions; 1992, 1993 and 1996. Prabhakaran's speeches on Heroes' Day (also termed Martyr's Day) in 1992 and 2007 have also been covered; adding, overall, to his views of these cataclysmic 15 years when the LTTE was not only calling the shots, but had, post 2004, started their inglorious descent as well.

The fascinating part is to track his mood swings, his highs and lows and those of the LTTE, through these 'windows' that allow the reader to look into his thoughts of that time. As has been the practice right through the book, the footnotes add value to the text, by reinforcing or giving contrary viewpoints, wherever this is considered necessary.

Tamil National Leader V. Pirapaharan's Heroes' Day Speech,[1] 1992

Today is Heroes Day. It is the sacred day when we cherish in our memory those exceptional beings that, by their sacrifice, have made our freedom struggle a heroic epic in the annals of world history.

Our heroes are supreme idealists. They loved their goal more than their lives. They embraced the liberation of their people as the highest goal in their life and they died for that ideal.

For thousands of years, since the birth of civilization, human beings have been struggling for freedom. The innumerable struggles, revolutions and wars that erupted on the face of this planet for centuries are none other than the manifestations of the human passion for freedom.

In our homeland, in the course of our struggle, extra-ordinary sacrifices have been made which have not taken place anywhere, at any time in the history of the world.

The strength of our struggle arises from the fierce determination of our fighters. Their firm commitment and their courage to act without the fear of death are the force and resource of our struggle.[2] The whole world is providing arms and funds to our enemy. We are not begging from the world. We do not depend on anybody. We stand firm on our own legs, on our own soil, on our own people and fight with our own hands. This is the specificity of our individuality. Since we are firmly rooted in our own strength, we stand upright without bowing to the pressures of others.

Today, our liberation struggle is situated in a complex historical conjuncture faced with new challenges and new crises. Our enemy, having firmly closed the doors of peace, has embarked on a course of escalating the war. The Government is not prepared to put forward any substantial proposals to resolve the Tamil national question. This year, the war has intensified on an unprecedented scale.

We were able to work out new strategies and stepped up our military assaults to foil the offensive plans of the enemy. As a consequence, the enemy suffered heavy casualties more than ever before in the history of the war. We have impressed upon the enemy that this land of ours will not tolerate the incursions of an aggressor…

We have no alternative other than to continue our struggle, to continue to intensify our struggle. We are not warmongers who love violence. In actual fact, spiritually, we love peace. We want permanent, stable and honourable peace. It is because of this reason that in spite of this bloody war, we are keeping the doors of peace open. We have not closed down the path of peace.[3] We have no such intention. One day, when our enemy knocks at our doors of peace, we will extend the hand of friendship…

Nothing and nobody can deter us any more. Let us continue our struggle with determination. History will be our guide and truth shall be our witness. Our martyrs are the pillars of our freedom movement, whose blood enriches the history of our freedom struggle, whose ideal makes our struggle supreme, whose sacrifices shape the formation of our nation, whose memories make our determination stronger. We salute our martyrs who are the architects of the freedom of our nation."[4]

National Leader V. Pirapaharan's Women's International Day Message, March 8, 1992[5]

Today is International Women's day… I am happy to see that this day of women's resurgence is celebrated all over Tamil Eelam.

The oppression of women is a mode of social injustice which was in practice for millennium, in all countries, in all social formations, in all cultures. Tamil women are subject to intolerable suffering as a consequence of the male chauvinistic oppression, violence and from the social evils of casteism and dowry.

To liberate themselves from these clutches of oppression, it is of utmost importance that women should, first of all understand the nature and structure of the modes of oppression unleashed against them. This awakening is crucial for women to rebel and re-orient their wretched conditions of existence. Women should be awakened from the darkness of an ideological world which makes them believe that their oppressive conditions are the result of their fate, of their actions of former births, of the moral laws enunciated for them, of the cultural configurations that determined their lives. Such a awakening is a necessary condition for their emancipation...

National Leader V. Pirapaharan's Women's International Day Message, March 8, 1993[6]

The historical storm of the liberation struggle is uprooting age old traditions that took root over a long period of time in our society...The ideology of women's liberation is a child born out of the womb of our liberation struggle... The Tamil Eelam revolutionary woman has transformed herself as a Tiger (sic)[7] for the liberation of our land and liberation of women."

Physical sex differences are a gift by nature to procreate the human race. Society has differentiated between men and women and created unequal relationships among them, thus defeating the objective of procreation. Gender differences and those traditional values based on them have moulded the outlook and approaches of feminism. These have placed impediments in the path of gender equality. Human dignity is beyond sexual differences. Beyond maleness and feminism there is humanism. Struggle illustrates that women can achieve anything they want to. Feminism is making a fervent appeal to maleness to honour humanism, beyond gender differences, and beyond feminism and maleness...

Tamil National Leader V. Pirapaharan's Women's International Day Message 1996[8]

Our struggle shines as a superb paradigm of women's ability to accomplish anything. So that our race may honour humanness which is beyond masculinity and femininity, womankind is extending its hand of love and friendship. Only when man as a gender grasps this loving hand with deep awareness, will equality between men and women be a reality... The Tamil Eelam revolutionary woman has transformed herself into a tigress! Fierce and fiery, she has taken up arms to fight injustice.

LTTE Leader on Sri Lanka's Military Campaign – 1998 Speech[9]

The leader of the Liberation Tigers of Tamil Eelam (LTTE) Mr. V. Pirapaharan in a statement issued today (13.05.1998) to mark the anniversary of the Sri Lankan military offensive operation called 'Jayasikuru' (Victory Assured) described the Government's military campaign as a monumental disaster. **Sri Lanka suffered unprecedented casualty rate in the year long battle with over 3,000 Sinhala soldiers killed and 7,000 injured, Mr. Pirapaharan said.** The Government of Chandrika Kumaratunga is driving the country towards the path of destruction impelled by a singular passion to dominate and subjugate the Tamil homeland by military means, he further said. Excerpts:

"Today is a significant day in the history of our national liberation struggle; it marks the end of a year during which we have resisted and fought against the biggest ever offensive operation launched by the Sri Lankan armed forces code named 'Jayasikuru', This operation has not yet come to an end but dragging on for a year though it was programmed for three months and began with much publicity and propaganda. The battle has assumed historical significance as the longest military operation, not only in the history of Eelam war, but also in the global history of armed conflict. Our liberation movement has made this remarkable military achievement by putting up fierce resistance crippling the forward mobility of the enemy forces in the Wanni jungles.

'Jayasikuru' operation is not an ordinary battle; it has been the mother of all battles that have flared up on our soil. In this confrontation, the enemy mobilized all his strength and resources at his command. We fought against a formidable force of thirty thousand troops belonging to three Army Divisions with its Special Forces and Commando units, supported in the rear by thousands of Navy and police personnel. The enemy forces used maximum fire power by utilizing heavy artillery, tanks, supersonic bombers and fighter helicopters. In the manner of an aggression on a hostile land, the Sinhala army invaded Wanni, the heart of the Tamil nation.

What is the strategic objective behind this military offensive? What are the underlying political motives of this military campaign? The Government claims that this military operation is aimed at opening the Kandy highway that will facilitate travelling of the Tamil people. But it is not the real objective. The Government has different motives which are sinister and dangerous.

The Kandy highway runs through the Wanni region. By capturing this strategic road, the Sinhala regime calculated that it could bifurcate the geographical unity of the Tamil homeland. Secondly, the Sinhala Government was well aware that Wanni was an LTTE controlled area where the headquarters as well as the military and administrative structures of our liberation movement operated. Therefore, the Government assumed that the LTTE would be compelled to confront the Sinhala army if an all-out offensive was undertaken in the Wanni heartland. In such a military confrontation the objective of the Sinhala chauvinists was to employ maximum manpower and fire power to destroy the military capability of the LTTE and to bring an end to the Tamil freedom movement.

The grand strategy of Chandrika's Government is to eliminate the Tamil Tigers and to effect a forced linkage between the North and South, thereby finding a permanent solution to the Tamil national question by military means. This is the hidden plan encapsulated in the Government's well known concept 'war for peace'.

With this sinister strategy 'Jayasikuru' offensive operation was launched on Wanni soil.

From the very beginning we realised that the offensive operation of the enemy has dangerous designs.[10] We knew that this military campaign posed a serious challenge not only to the territorial unity of the Tamil homeland but also to the very existence of our liberation movement. Therefore, we were firmly determined to fiercely resist the offensive with all our power and potential. Accordingly we worked out our strategy and tactics to thwart the forward movement of the advancing columns and to inflict heavy losses on the enemy.

Before the launching of operation 'Jayasikuru' the Sri Lankan political and military high command miscalculated the military strength and determination of the LTTE. Based on our strategic withdrawal from Jaffna Peninsula and on our non-engagement in the 'Edibala' operation, Sri Lanka Government entertained a theory that the LTTE was militarily weakened.[11] This misconception led the army high command to believe in an assured victory and made them to issue time-frames for the campaign. Ultimately the military establishment has had to face humiliation.

We were prepared to confront 'Jayasikuru' troops. We re-organised and re-structured our military machine to engage in a conventional mode of offensive.[12] Our successful campaign at Mullaithivu strengthened our fire power. On the basis of our newly acquired weaponry we built up artillery and mortar units, anti-tank and anti-aircraft units to form a well integrated military structure capable of confronting a conventional military thrust. We had a long experience about the offensive maneoeuvres of the enemy forces. On the basis of such practical experiences we devised new offensive and defensive strategies and constructed impenetrable defence lines. By such method we prepared ourselves to face the biggest ever offensive undertaken by the enemy.

In the 'Jayasikuru' military operation the Sri Lankan army has adopted various strategies and tactics. It experimented with new offensive maneoeuvres found in contemporary military sciences. Furthermore, it implemented war plans charted by foreign military experts. Yet, the armed forces could not break or weaken the LTTE's determined resistance. Rather, such offensive thrusts resulted in serious setbacks and heavy losses to the army.

In this year-long single military operation the Sri Lankan army suffered heavy causalities with over 3,000 soldiers killed and about 7,000 injured. Several specially trained commando units were annihilated and armoured units destroyed. Military stores and arsenals were wiped out. In this lengthy battle, the LTTE fighters secured huge amounts of arms and ammunition. The losses suffered by the enemy were massive. Having suffered such monumental damage, the Army has not yet achieved its strategic objective.

In every confrontation during this prolonged battle we gained new experience and learned a lot in the art of war that has helped to develop our fighting ability. It has further strengthened the commitment and dedication of our fighters. This battle was a baptism of fire through which we emerged strong with new vigour. In terms of manpower, fire-power and resources, the enemy was strong and the balance of military power was in his favour. Yet we had an extra-ordinary weapon which was not in the arsenal of the enemy. The courage and commitment of our fighters was our most powerful weapon...

Jayasikuru' military operation has plunged the Government of Chandrika Kumaratunga in to a serious crisis.[13] The Government is driving the country towards the path of destruction impelled by a singular passion to dominate and subjugate the Tamil homeland by military means.

In conclusion, Mr. Pirapaharan pledges that operation 'Jayasikuru" will not end until and unless the occupation army is driven out from Wanni soil. The LTTE leader finally pays homage to 1,300 martyrs who sacrificed their lives for the defense of their motherland."

Prabhakaran's 2007 Heroes' Day Speech[14] from LTTE Peace Secretariat, November 27, 2007

The leader of the Liberation Tigers of Tamil Eelam (LTTE), V Pirapaharan, in his annual Heroes' Day statement put a heavy responsibility on the shoulders of the international community for the breakdown of the peace process. He said that the involvement of the international community to resolve the Tamil national question has been unhelpful[15] and added that their failure to condemn unambiguously the military path of the current regime has created the present situation in the island. He asserted that the propping up of the genocidal Sinhala State by the international community through economic aid, military aid and subtle diplomatic efforts will be counterproductive.

File photo of Prabhakaran delivering Heroes' Day speech, 2007

Excerpts of the official translation of his speech follow:

Buddhism is a profound spiritual duty. Its philosophy emphasizes a life without desires, a life of love and justice. The Sinhala nation, claiming that it has followed this path for more than two thousand years, has in fact remained immersed in the poison of racism. It is unleashing unthinkable violence against another people. During the long history of the Tamil struggle, first through non-violence and later through armed struggle, the Sinhala mindset has remained unchanged. The Sinhala nation did not change even after so much destruction and lost lives. It continues on the path of violence. It only desires to find a solution to the Tamil question through military might and oppression. It cunningly evaded efforts to seek peace and is boldly taking forward its military plan. The international community's economic and military aid, its moral and political support, its diplomatic efforts, and its one-sided involvement directly aided this turn of events.

India intervened in our national question then as part of its regional expansion. India signed an accord with the Sinhala State without the consent of the Tamils. The Indo-Lanka Accord was not signed to meet the aspirations of the people of Tamil Eelam. In fact, India then attempted to force an ineffectual solution on our people – a solution which did not even devolve powers to the extent of the Banda-Chelva pact signed in the 1950's. India tried to enforce that accord with the strength of more than 100,000 Indian forces, with the power of the agreement between two countries and with the assistance of treacherous Tamil paramilitary groups. However, even this ill-considered solution, which did not even address the basic national aspirations of the Tamils, was blocked by the chauvinistic Sinhala State.[16]

Today, the international community is making the same mistake that India made many years ago. Even the countries that are the guardians of the peace efforts succumbed to the deception of the Sinhala State and listed our freedom movement as a terrorist organization. What we find most incomprehensible is the fact that these same nations, which labelled us terrorists, not so long ago fought in defence of their own freedom.

The Sinhala nation is unable to stomach the support of our diaspora for the Tamil freedom struggle; it is unable to accept the humanitarian help and the political lobbying by the diaspora to end the misery heaped on our people. That is why the Sinhala nation is trying hard to shatter the bond between our people in our homeland and our diaspora. Some countries are also assisting this amoral effort of Sinhala chauvinism. These countries are denouncing, as illegal activities, the humanitarian actions and political protests of our people abroad – actions that are carried out according to the laws of those countries. These countries have imprisoned and humiliated Tamil campaigners and representatives. These countries have ridiculed their protests and their efforts to seek justice.[17]

Operation 'Ellalan', the very first combined Black Tiger and Tamil Eelam Air Force attack[18] was a massive blow to the Sinhala military. It has disrupted the daydreams of the Sinhala nation. The Sinhala nation has not emerged from this massive shock delivered by our beloved fighters. The immeasurable dedication and sacrifice of our heroes is delivering a message to the Sinhala nation. Those who plan to destroy the Tamil nation will in the end be forced to face their own destruction...

The Rajapaksa regime, after unilaterally abrogating the ceasefire agreement, is ruthlessly implementing its military plan to remove the contiguity of the Tamil homeland. It has killed and disappeared thousands of our people. It reprimands and controls the Norwegian facilitators. It vehemently criticizes the SLMM. It even dares to brand senior UN officials as terrorists in order to hide its own terrorism. It is obscuring the ground reality in the Tamil homeland by striking fear among journalists and NGO workers.

Publicity Poster of Tamil National Leader Prabhakaran

Yet the actions of the international community with respect to our own national question are unjust. The confidence our people placed in the international community has been eroded. By only paying lip-service to peace the international community has contributed to the killing of an extraordinary son of our nation, Tamilselvan. It has stopped the heartbeat of a light that walked the path of peace. I will be lighting the lamp for my dear brother, Tamilselvan, who until last year was with me every time we, with a burning desire to reach our goal, lit the lamps for our fallen heroes. The international community has made the entire Tamil world drown in its tears. Had the international community firmly and unambiguously condemned the anti-peace activities and the war mongering of the Sinhala regime, Tamilselvan would be alive today. A huge blow would not have fallen on peace efforts"[19] ...

ENDNOTES

1. Tamil National Leader Hon. V. Pirapaharan's Heroes' Day Speech. Excerpted. <http://www.eelamweb.com/leader/messages/herosday/1992/> This speech is a fine example of Prabhakaran's erudition and fine turn of phrase. It is, in effect, a realistic backgrounder on the philosophic basis of the Eelam struggle.
2. Ibid. One more indication of his ability (an attribute that is almost a must, in the repertoire of tricks that a leader/ideologue must have) to use words as weapons, to fire up the imagination of his rank and file.
3. Ibid. Prabhakaran never lost track of his compulsion, his pressing need as a terror leader of substance, to sound optimistic for the record about "peace for our time", even when he was involved in waging unremitting war. This was obviously intended to make him come across in public scrutiny, as a reasonable person who had been wronged, but was open to peace overtures even when he was using war to redress his grievances. One is reminded of the mindset and optimism that Neville Chamberlain, then Prime Minister of UK, displayed on September 30, 1938. He is famously recorded in photos of those times, waving the folded page from which he made his brief, (eventually infamous) statement. He made it outside 10, Downing Street, after meeting the German Chancellor, Adolf Hitler, on September 29, 1938, at Berlin, to resolve the crisis triggered by the German invasion of the Low countries, starting with Czechoslovakia. "I believe it is peace for our time…Go home and get a nice, quiet sleep", he is reported saying. See <http://www.guardian.co.uk/world/1938/oct/01/germany.secondworldwar> and <http://eudocs.lib.byu.edu/index.php/Neville_ Chamberlain%27s_%22Peace_For_Our_Time%22_speech> in this connection. History of course, records that German intransigence led to the start of World War II, barely a year later. Relating the incident to Prabhakaran, it has been stated earlier in the book that his offer of peace was, for him, an important ideological tool, to be used on requirement, but not to be taken up seriously, unless it was on his terms.
4. Ibid. Another example of good use of word imagery by Prabhakaran.
5. Tamil National Leader Hon. V. Pirapaharan's Women's International Day Message. Excerpted. <http://www.eelamweb.com/leader/messages/women/1992/> This is a relevant and topical message advocating women's liberation; a missive that would have drawn plaudits at any forum, national or International. He has raised issues that any one pursuing equal rights for women and their need for emancipation would welcome. The need to shed the emotional and social baggage of fatalism, freedom from violence, chauvinism, social evils such as dowry and casteism, sound perfectly rational and well argued. So also is the need for men and women across the gender divide to "recognize each other's liberty, equality and dignity, enter into a cordial relationship based on mutual understanding and share the responsibilities of family life and also contribute to the development of society".

   The reality check is, however, different and sobering. Readers will recall that the LTTE brought in the 'innovation' of employing women for suicide bombing; a development that is now followed by terror organisations worldwide. It is indeed regrettable, that, amongst the earliest targets of high visibility assassinations of a national leader, was that of Indian Prime Minister, Rajiv Gandhi, at Sriperumbudur, outside Madras (now Chennai), on May 21, 1991. The suicide bomber who blew herself up, using an explosive belt, was a woman LTTE operative, Thenmuli Rajaratnam a.k.a. Gayatri, a.k.a. Dhanu.
6. Tamil National Leader Hon. V. Pirapaharan's Women's International Day Message. <http:/

/www.eelamweb.com/leader/messages/women/1993/> Excerpted. Any psychologist or Organisational Behaviour (OB) expert will tell you how clever placement of words and their repetition can affect young minds, especially women, who lay more store by emotions than men do.

7. Ibid. Calling women Tigresses and suggesting that they can set out to achieve anything they wish to, once they've set their minds to reach that milestone, are actually universally true statements. This powerful imagery also acts as strong motivation for someone already suffering from deprivation, perceived or actual. Small wonder that, (as this book has recorded elsewhere, that over 4,000 women cadres of the LTTE have lost their lives in combat; no doubt swayed by such motivation. Notice that the message has started becoming repetitive. It may well be a deliberate ploy.

8. Tamil National Leader Hon. V. Pirapaharan's Women's International Day Message. Excerpted. <http://www.eelamweb.com/leader/messages/women/1996/> Readers will notice that the aspect of repetition is very pronounced here. The issues being repeated are women's ability to achieve what they want; invoking the symbolism of a Tamil woman as a LTTE Tigress, and subtly bringing out the need for LTTE men and women to bridge the gender divide. Anyone would support the premise that this amounts to skilled motivation of the LTTE serving as well as potential rank and file to do their bit for the cause of Eelam. Prabhakaran, being well read, well informed and very observant of human relationships, is subtly promoting the reality that when you educate a woman, you are educating a generation. It is another matter that, in this instance, the women were being motivated to embrace death for the cause of Eelam, without giving their sacrifice a second thought. The irony is that many of them did just that; those who gave birth to life and were genetically programmed to cherish and nurture life were sufficiently brainwashed by Prabhakaran's powerful messages (the Chinese call it *hsi nao* or wash brain) to throw it all away.

9. LTTE Leader on Sri Lanka's Military Campaign – 1998 Speech. <http://www.eelamweb.com/leader/messages/military/1998/> As mentioned earlier in this chapter, Operation Jayasikuru (Victory Assured) was a somewhat optimistically worded, synchronized military operation, involving all three services; in effect, the SLAF. It ran from 1997 to 1999. Apparently, the Tigers came out tops. The operation resulted in heavy casualties to the SLAF; rather more than those suffered by the LTTE (1,300, as per their admission). It was launched in the Mullaithivu-Wanni areas, known to be the LTTE hot bed, with the aim of decimating the LTTE. In this objective, the SLAF failed significantly.

   See "Operation Jayasikuru (Victory Assured) 1997-1999's. Operation Jayasikuru was the Longest, Costliest and the Most Disastrous Operation in Sri Lanka's Military History". <http://www.lankalibrary.com/phpBB/viewtopic.php?f=66&t=3421>

   The site writes that, "After a few limited operations in the North and East, the Sri Lanka Army launched its longest and largest operation code named 'Operation Jayasikuru' on 13 May 1997. The aim of the operation was to regain the LTTE-held Wanni and Mullaithivu areas and subsequently to open a land route through Wanni and Killinochchi districts to link up with the Jaffna Peninsula. The operation was conducted in four stages… The Sri Lankan Army's most elite divisions and brigades were involved in this operation throughout, and turned the pages of Sri Lanka Army history by launching divisions in multi-directional, wider frontages and gaining territory from the enemy, causing heavy damage and casualties to the LTTE. The Army were able to capture the strategic towns which were the strongholds of the LTTE such as Omanthai, Kanagarayankulam and Mankulam. Sri Lanka Navy and Sri

Lanka Air Force, too, were involved in the operation over and above their organic tasks by deploying troops in a ground role to man the forward defence Lines. During the operation, ground troops monitored terrorist radio transmissions and other intelligence sources confirmed that 3,614 terrorists were killed in action and (KIA) 1,899 wounded in action (WIA)... Though the operation was terminated in 1999, without completion of its prime aim, it was able to force the LTTE to restrict their freedom of action only to Mullaithivu area. The Army concentrated on capturing LTTE bases in Mullaithivu and in Pudukudirippu, thereafter". **Readers will note that calling the operation "longest, costliest and most disastrous in Sri Lanka's military history" in the preamble; then claiming the death of 3,614 terrorists with injury to 1,899 of them (over 5500 in all) in the same breath appears to be a debatable way of defining success.**

10 Ibid. This paragraph shows that Prabhakaran had a clear idea of the military strategy that SLAF had intended to employ. In hindsight, one could hazard a guess and say that he was well served by his Intelligence Wing, as well as perhaps by his instinct and acquired military knowledge.

11 Ibid. Judging from other accounts of this operation, it does appear that the SLAF were guilty of over estimation of their capability as much as they were guilty of considering the LTTE weakened after its (Prabhakaran terms it strategic) withdrawal from Jaffna Peninsula.

12 Ibid. Prabhakaran deserves full credit here for having structured his guerilla warfare force into a conventional war fighting force, which used all the force multipliers of this new kind of warfare better than its veteran practitioners in the form the SLAF did, in this battle. The astute reader will note that conversion from guerilla to open warfare also meant a diametrically opposite set of tactics to absorb and employ on the ground; at best a most difficult transition for men in uniform. By any yardstick of measurement, its successful application was an astonishing military feat of arms.

13 This statement by Prabhakaran may have been correct, but only in the short term. This chapter earlier on has alluded to the incidental gains from this operation for the SLAF in specific and the Sri Lanka Government at large. These were hinged on the fact that the SLAF, as an entity, had got familiarized with the battle space where years later, commencing the from Mavil Aru reservoir operations in July 2006, it would commence its final countdown to decimate the LTTE. The fact also remains that the LTTE's wings got clipped, though not in a spectacular manner. It probably realized that, more than ever before, it was henceforth fighting for survival in what it has earlier considered its inviolable homeland. The enemy had come to roost in the Wanni region and that was a harsh reality for the LTTE to cope with.

14 Tamil National Leader Hon. V. Pirapaharan's Heroes' Day Speech. <http://www. eelamweb. com/leader/messages/herosday/2007/> Also see "Ilankai Tamil Sangam. Association of Tamils of Sri Lanka in the USA (13th Year on the Web)". http://www.sangam.org/2007/11/ HeroesDay_Speech _2007.php?uid=2646 Readers will note that two different sites have been listed, both of whom have covered the speech. The first one is of course, that of Eelamweb, with whom readers are quite familiar by now. The second one is that of the Tamil diaspora in the USA. It indicates how well the LTTE had evolved their perception management, of which a stellar role was played by the Tamil diaspora world wide.

15. Prabhakaran's anger against the international community, an issue that rises repeatedly in this landmark speech, has several components. First and foremost is his barely concealed anger at being proscribed by 32 foreign countries with warrants put out for him by Interpol, India and other nations. Next is his annoyance at seeing the Sri Lanka stranglehold on him

tightening with his diaspora contacts abroad, as well as countries friendly to his cause being unable to do much about it except mouthing platitudes. Note that it is November 2007. His infectious enthusiasm and optimism of the 90's has given way to bitterness, rancour and great frustration (the benefits of following chronology!). SLAF is achieving success after military success at this time, with Prabhakaran's world, both real and virtual, diminishing by the day. We already know how his health has taken a setback at this time. Karuna has of course joined the Government and is actively assisting in the war against the LTTE; a development which is the cause of no joy to Prabhakaran. He now really needs peace, but the Rajapaksa Government, whose election platform in 2005 was the defeat of the LTTE, is in evidently no mood to hold out the olive branch, regardless of his posturing. Prabhakaran's mood is therefore grim and sombre.

16. Ibid. It is clear, by reading this paragraph, that his angst is directed towards India as well. The support he was hoping for, is not available.
17. Ibid. The marginalization of the Tamil Diaspora has hurt Prabhakaran savagely and his bitterness comes out quite clearly here. Readers will recall that this was the time at which the SLN had come of age. The Navy had started interdicting the LTTE supply line of war like material, which was largely diaspora fund managed, as far away as 2,000 nautical miles away from the war zone in Sri Lanka. Thus, both funding and supplies had become an issue of grim portent, for which, besides the Sri Lankan Government, he found the international community and SLAF to blame.
18. Ibid. The joint Black Tiger/LTTE attacks came as a very nasty shock indeed, not just to the LTTE Government, which suffered huge collateral losses and a dramatic drop in tourism, but also the Sri Lankan Air Force in particular. In fact, the world over, governments and intelligence agencies were rattled and numbed. The Sri Lanka Government recovered, however, as did SLAF from this serious setback. They did not abandon their mission; if anything, speeded it up. Finally therefore, the final battle got prolonged but still went on to its logical conclusion.
19. Chandrasekharan, Dr. S, Sri Lanka: Heroes Day Speech by LTTE Leader (Prabhakaran): A Commentary: Update No. 132. Note No. 419. November 30, 2007. http://www.southasiaanalysis.org/%5Cnotes5%5Cnote419.html The author has, in his Note, carried out a detailed analysis on the speech which is worth perusing. He opines that the main emphasis was on taking the international community to task for continuing to support the Sri Lankan Government with war like material and financial support. The author also talks of the changing perceptions that Prabhakaran has had on his India connection, alternating between extremes of welcoming their help to condemning them for the way things worked out on the ground. (This author would like to add that engineering the killing of Prime Minister Rajiv Gandhi and later regretting the killing (in his press conference in Killinochchi in April 2002 is indicative of his blow hot blow cold behaviour towards India). Dr. Chandrasekharan also covers the Tamil diaspora aspect and suggests that Prabhakaran had focused too much on the military side of the LTTE to use this resource to its potential. He also comments constructively on the Rajapaksa stance of no talks, as he had sensed victory, the issue of the Thimphu accord, and the spread of Sinhalisation.

CHAPTER 11

Recap of Velupillai Prabhakaran's Legacy

"Few dispute that he (Prabhakaran) was one of the most effective guerrilla leaders in modern warfare – displaying the tactical prowess of Afghanistan's Ahmad Shah Masoud, the ruthlessness of Osama bin Laden and the conviction of Latin American revolutionary Che Guevara."[1]

– Straits Times

"Prabhakaran had everything: territory, international support and committed fighters. Senior Journalist Shyam Tekwani, who has covered the LTTE and Sri Lanka for almost three decades tracks the alarming rise and astonishing fall of a man who sought to live to fight another day, but found only death at the hands of his nemesis."[2]

"Velupillai Prabhakaran, the terrorist leader whom the whole world thought invincible, was found dead on a small island, surrounded by the muddy waters of the Nandhi Kadal lagoon at Vellamullivaikkal, in Puthumatalan. The man, who had control of over 15,000 square kilometres of land, but lost his domination inch by inch, breathed his last by fire in a tiny patch of land.[3] Prabhakaran, who was neck deep in the lagoon water when his loyal escorts were fighting with the elite commandos and the soldiers of the 4th Vijayabâhu Infantry Regiment (VIR), at last met death from a bullet fired by a soldier who joined the clearing of the island where there had been an indication of yet another terrorist movement.

Sergeant H.P Wijesinghe from Allawwa is the happiest soldier among thousands. He was the first to identify Prabhakaran's body lying near the dirty waters of the small islet. "We were ordered to go forward, as some terrorists were firing from 8.30 a.m. today. We were able to kill the remaining terrorists and started clearing the area. The body found dead was lying on the banks and I informed the

Commanding Officer of 4 VIR, Lt. Col. Rohitha Aluvihare, about the body and, under his command, we brought the body here," he said, adding with pride and glee that, 'I am happy that I was the first to identify Prabhakaran's body. For this is the man (who was) most wanted and who made our lives a misery. This is the man whom we fought to capture for decades.' Sgt. Wijesinghe says that he did not have words to express his happiness. With no cyanide (vial) hanging around him, his dog tag TT 3 bearing the number 001 and dated 16.09.95 hung around the monster killer's neck. His Eelam identity card with his picture bearing number 01543301002 issued on 01.01.2007 and with his personal details like date of birth – 26.11.1954, place of birth – Velvettithurai and occupation – Leader of the LTTE (was also found)."[4]

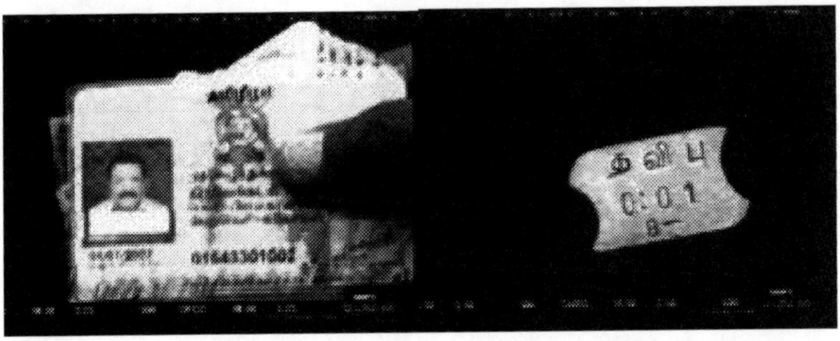

The identity card of Prabhakaran along with his dog tag bearing Number 001

The three statements, quoted above, are in themselves, a holistic, eloquent epitaph to the rise and fall of one of the world's most feared terror leaders, Velupillai Prabhakaran. The recap will conclusively explain why a leader who had everything; a man who rose meteorically from being a nonentity, a disaffected high school dropout to the undisputed, Pol Pot like Supreme Commander of the LTTE, eventually faltered at the doorstep of victory and lost all that he had gained.

The Mystique of Prabhakaran

It is educative to see how two very different people – different in age, profession, experience and outlook, recall their first impressions of Prabhakaran and how these coincide in a disturbing, almost sinister manner on the issue of understanding his psyche. Lt Gen Depinder Singh, PVSM, VSM (Retd), was the OFC of the IPKF, and a very senior army officer in his late 50's. He notes, in his book, *The IPKF in Sri Lanka*,[5] (pp. 47-48) that he met Prabhakaran for the first time at Madras, in 1987, when he was enroute from Delhi to Palaly and had stopped for a transit halt at Madras. The General was staying at the Area Headquarters Officers Mess, Guest Suite, and recalls that "before entering my room, he removed his chappals outside, in the verandah. He was dressed in a bush-shirt and trousers, and turned out to be a short, well built and handsome man, edging slightly on obesity with a strong face, stubborn chin and a diffident but pleasant presence".

He did not know till later, that, while at Delhi, Prabhakaran's phone calls had been tapped. He had reportedly remarked that "he was waiting to get out from Delhi and would then teach Rajiv (Gandhi) a lesson."[6] The General mentions that Prabhakaran did state, during the course of their discussion, that he would "never again trust the External Affairs Ministry and RAW again". Considering the time and place, the General writes that he chose not to respond.[7]

The second person, who recalls his first contact with Prabhakaran (sometime around 1985), is Shyam Tekwani, the then young photo-journalist. The meeting took place, once again at Madras. The journalist commences his article with this chilling recall: "Then more vividly than anything that came afterwards in the Sri Lanka war, I remember his first handshake. The hand was soft, the grip delicate and limp. On that occasion in Madras, as he contentedly claimed credit for assassinating the Tamil Mayor of Jaffna and later, the slaughter of 13 Sri Lankan soldiers that ignited the conflict following the anti-Tamil riots of 1983, Velupillai Prabhakaran's dainty handshake seemed in harmony with his soft voice.

These two[8] memories define, at any rate, through all my experiences over the last 25 years in Sri Lanka, the man who has finally destroyed the dream he almost made true. Both the memories give a certain insight into the mind of the man. First, deceive all into believing the contrary about your capabilities – deception is the core of all his strategies. Second, never trust your own shadow – paranoia dictates his behaviour. These traits contributed to the amazing rise – and eventually the astonishing fall – of the leader of the most ruthless terrorist organisation in the world."[9]

Readers would not have failed to make the connect between these two examples – the man who, in personal contact, came across as soft spoken, well mannered, diffident and amiable, was, in fact, ruthless and cold blooded; a man who had a dream and who had the resilience, staying power, band width, the capacity, the orientation and the focus to spare no effort to achieve it – regardless of its human and material costs. Ross James, in his article in the *NYT* has a slightly different take, though. He says that "The Tamil Tigers were never about nihilistic violence[10] (violence aimed at overturning social institutions). They had a clear agenda: to create a Tamil state, 'Tamil Eelam'. Their selling point was their claim that they were the 'sole representative' of Sri Lanka's Tamils. This guiding principle had been the group's greatest strength and weakness".

Thus a picture emerges of a man, who, to all intents and appearances, was the very picture of normalcy and bonhomie. Behind that screen, however, lay a warped genius, a person who had programmed himself to stop at nothing en route to achieving Eelam. It is noticeable that, after floundering for over two decades in their efforts to nail this Scarlet Pimpernel, the SLAF finally decided to do a 'Prabhakaran' to get at him: their methods in doing so were eventually as reprehensible as his.

Rare Organisational Ability

Mark Tran, writing for *The Guardian,* UK notes that "Prabhakaran created a powerful guerrilla force of about 30,000 fighters, backed up by a sophisticated worldwide support network for money and arms. To his followers, Prabhakaran was a dedicated freedom fighter, struggling for the emancipation of his people. Others, however, considered him to be a power-hungry maniac with no regard for human life. Under his leadership, the Tamil Tigers fought for self determination from Sri Lanka's Sinhalese majority, declaring their own state of Tamil Eelam stretching from Jaffna in the north to Batticaloa in the east[11] ... That goal came tantalisingly close as the Supreme Commander of the LTTE, at one stage, presided over what was in effect a rebel mini-state in Northern Sri Lanka. The Tigers ran their own law courts, police force and Tamil Eelam banks and even their own time zone – half an hour behind the Sri Lankan capital, Colombo."[12]

Shyam Tekwani writes that Prabhakaran's implementation of his idea of a 'Tamil' state, received a huge boost with the departure of the IPKF and his boast that the LTTE had "vanquished the fourth largest Army in the world."[13] He adds that it was at this stage that he set about the task of 'constructing a state within a state'. The task of doing so could only have been done by a man with great organisational and motivational capability; a man who clearly saw what he wanted and was clear about the path he needed to take to reach there. The fact that he was not formally educated or trained to do so; had had no formal military training to do so, underscores the reality that he was, indeed, a very gifted man; a man with a calling and the passion to achieve it.

Tekwani adds that Prabhakaran "reintroduced taxation on his population, decreed the LTTE flag as the Tamil national flag, set up courts, police stations and 'ministries' that oversaw agriculture, education, rehabilitation and economic development. But his main preoccupation was in developing a conventional armed force. Military traditions – a formal ranking system, uniforms, gun salutes, parades, ceremonial funerals of flag draped cadres killed in action – became the norm. Sarongs and flip-flops gave way to smartly pressed uniforms and spit-and polish boots. Twenty years before he acquired the half-a-dozen ZLIN-143 aircraft to boast of being the only terrorist group in the world to possess an air wing, I was led to the LTTE's 'ordnance factory' in Manipay in 1985 to witness and photograph the aircraft his 'aeronautical engineers' were assembling. The fact that it had a 200cc motorcycle engine to power it did not mask his intent to attempt building a conventional Armed Force, with its land, air and sea wings"[14] ...

The core organisation that Prabhakaran created, evolved and fine tuned for the LTTE amply reinforces his organisational genius. Speaking about the structure of the LTTE, Lt Gen S.C. Sardeshpande, UYSM, AVSM (Retd), who commanded the Jaffna Division, as part of the IPKF, writes that it comprised of four major echelons.[15] The top echelon was the hardest core, "seldom seen but always listened to". The second rung comprised "regional commanders, heads of training, logistics and communication, political go-betweens and coordinators across the Island as well as well as with India (Tamil Nadu). The third rung comprised of "area commanders, high command representatives, experts in weapons, explosives and communications, tax collectors, special guards, expert guides and navigators. This was the fighting core". Last were the "helpers, '*Podians*' as they were referred to. This was a far deadly commodity than the name suggests. Depending on need and circumstances, some of them could and did wield weapons, assassinate, abduct, behead, blow up, collect tax, carry stores and messages, treat patients, organize supplies, issue and implement threats, collect information and disseminate instructions". Need to know, school children...

The General comments that the "LTTE cadres had anticipation, opportunism and orchestration[16] of a very high order... . In particular, their ability to integrate psychological aspects, public relations, singular pursuance of the overall aim and unshakable faith in themselves and their methods stood out prominently...There was apparently method in its madness. It is this, coupled with aggressive spirit, which carries a sense of readiness to sacrifice to levels difficult to comprehend. It has thus practiced surprise at tactical, strategic and socio political levels, with consummate efficiency"[17] ... He adds that the LTTE was logistically well supported in coastal Tamil Nadu and as deep as Madurai, Trichy and Salem, as also in Jaffna and Wanni areas. Financial and material supply bases were established in Western Europe and SE Asia.

Prabhakaran created "caches, labs, workshops, pioneered coded, cipher led communications"[18] with a lot of redundancy built in so that if a channel was interdicted, some other channel could be used. Overall, he set up excellent logistics and communications, both of which were gridded, giving him enormous flexibility.

Organisationally too, he was able to create and sustain high morale and motivation with iron discipline.

Given the span of his interests and his ability to go into the fine print of what actually makes organisations work, one gets the impression of a wired up, intelligent brain, that had the capacity as well as the motivational ability to make a pronounced impact on both extremes of the learning and execution continuum: get the complex framework right and have the ability to make each subcomponent fit into the jigsaw puzzle and do its work properly as part of the larger whole. All this as a high school dropout.

He Mastered Communications, and Through Them, the Weapon of Propaganda

Shyam Tekwani quotes former US Secretary of State, Donald Rumsfeld, before highlighting how Prabhakaran took on to this sphere of activity with extraordinary prescience. "Today we're engaged in the first war in history – unconventional and irregular as it may be – in an era of e-mails, blogs, cell phones, Blackberries, instant messaging, digital cameras, a global internet with no inhibitions, cell phones, hand-held video cameras, talk radio, 24-hour news broadcasts, satellite television. There's never been a war fought in this environment before."[19] (He was speaking in the context of the Iraq war).

Tekwani continues: "Central to Prabhakaran's guerilla strategy – over two decades before Rumsfeld made his observation – was a powerful communications network and a sympathetic media. Hence, his exclusive interviews to handpicked influential publications while he was enjoying the hospitality of the Indian government in Madras during the mid-80s, when I first got to shake his hand. From the outset, it was not difficult to win the support of the media, particularly in the West. Prabhakaran played his underdog cards adroitly with the help of his advisor Anton Balasingham and his Australian born wife, Adele and the LTTE's media headquarters in London[20] ..."

"The LTTE's powerful communications network transmitted daily situation reports (sitreps) from Jaffna to its media headquarters in a Western capital where the sitreps were distributed as press releases though telex machines (later with the introduction of fax machines and the internet, it was able to readjust its media budget) to media and governments in Western capitals. Printed material was a prime means of LTTE propaganda till the early 1990s, when the group went to great expense to publish multilingual and expensively produced four-colour booklets and pamphlets with profuse illustrations. These publications were distributed to the local and international media and select government organisations[21] ..."

"The LTTE's high degree of familiarity with modern telecommunications enabled it to occupy a very definitive niche in the international public eye, in spite of the fact that it is party to a conflict in a small south Asian nation, largely ignored by the West, and the fact that its acts of violence have impacted only Sri Lanka and occasionally India...

The LTTE had its first website running on the server of a university in the United States. This conveniently coincided with an increasingly unfriendly media following the assassination of Rajiv Gandhi. A computer academy funded and run by professionals from among the diaspora in the Wanni region ensured that the 'brains trust' of the LTTE kept abreast with the latest know-how...

A wing of the group (Internet Black Tigers) is credited with the first ever cyber attack (1997) known to the world when it downed the networks of Sri Lankan embassies across the world for a fortnight. In the same year, it was able to hack into a university in the United Kingdom, steal legitimate email IDs and solicit funds for a fictitious hospital in Colombo. And as recently as last week, (mid May 2009) a group calling itself Kalai Amman Electronic Warfare Unit hacked into the Sri Lanka Army website and defaced its home page. Social network sites were quickly adopted and a search on You Tube yields several hundred videos of the group...

Prabhakaran quickly developed a media unit – photographers and videographers – which documented every battle and assassination that the group conducted. This served two purposes – as a teaching aid, it came closest to the real thing next to classroom simulations. Besides, it provided archival material for the history books that would be written once Eelam became a reality. This obsession for a visual record proved disastrous for the LTTE – it led the investigators of Rajiv Gandhi's murder right to its doorstep."[22]

It is not very often that the creator of world class, secure, cipher driven communications that breathe life into his terror organisation; a person who not only fiendishly comprehends what cutting edge computer driven technologies are all about, but also sets standards in their exploitation; a person who is a pioneer in slaving emerging digital and voice technologies to conduct a stunning propaganda campaign for three decades; a person who takes the lead in conduct of unethical hacking and other forms of cyber warfare, actually happens to be an 8th standard passed, eventual high school dropout. This, in a way, underscores the genius of the man.

One is reminded of the German propaganda minister, the infamous Joseph Goebbels[23] in this regard. His propaganda techniques were totally cynical: "That propaganda is good which leads to success, and that is bad which fails to achieve the desired result," he wrote. "It is not propaganda's task to be intelligent, its task is to lead to success." Goebbels also had a unique talent for oratory,[24] and was soon second in the Nazi movement only to Hitler as a public speaker. Where Hitler's style was hoarse and passionate, Goebbels' was cool, sarcastic and often humorous: he was a master of biting invective and insinuation, although he could whip himself into a rhetoric frenzy if the occasion demanded. Unlike Hitler, however, he retained a cynical detachment from his own rhetoric. He openly acknowledged that he was exploiting the lowest instincts of the German people – racism, xenophobia, class envy and insecurity. He could, he said, play the popular will like a piano, leading the masses wherever he wanted them to go. "He drove his listeners into ecstasy, making them stand up, sing songs, raise their arms, repeat oaths – and he did it, not through the passionate inspiration of the moment, but as the result of sober psychological calculation."[25]

If there is one thing most, if not all, Prabhakaran watchers will agree on, it is his Goebbels-like propaganda and oratory skills, which swayed the Tamil masses to his school of thought. He mesmerized a generation of Tamils to do his bidding, regardless of cost, in much the same manner as Goebbels did.

Unlike Goebbels, he did not always have things his way, and, in fact, appears to have been at his motivational best as a speaker, in front of smaller audiences. Shyam Tekwani records that his 'first and only international' press conference (April 2002) at his administrative headquarters in Killinochchi was a disaster. His experience with the media, confined to a few one-on-one interviews with select journalists, had not prepared him for this. He seemed bewildered and clearly out of his depth facing a mixed pack of journalists whose two-day uncomfortable wait was alleviated only by the non-stop screening of LTTE propaganda videos. His image makeover, as a clean-shaven, safari-suited statesman, failed to impress anyone. Announcing his idea of peace involving the Norwegians as peacemakers, he first fumbled and then chose the safer option of avoiding all questions – mostly related to the murder of Rajiv Gandhi and his own demand for a separate state – and passed on the microphone to his interpreter Balasingham."[26]

Impact on LTTE and Terror Organisations World Wide

General Depinder Singh points out early on in his book, that the very first organisation that Prabhakaran was associated with; the Tamil National Tigers (TNT) had an acronym, TNT,[27] which also stands for one of the world's premier military explosives,Tri Nitro Toluene (TNT), next in lethality only to RDX. One would like to believe that this precocious youth, even at that young age, had an instinctive feel for leadership and knew a thing or two about the intelligent use of word imagery and about motivation.

The General goes on to speak about the impact that Prabhakaran had on the then fledgling LTTE. He recounts that "LTTE cadres male and female, led lives of spartan simplicity, had a very strict code of conduct and discipline.[28] (They) were also inflexible, intolerant, and uncompromising, intolerant of dissent and the dispensation of justice was generally swift and almost always ruthless. In sum, they created the most fearsome militant group in the world has ever seen, with each member possessing an extraordinary fanaticism. They have also been eminently successful in maintaining an aura of mystery, which, in turn, has nourished their mystique". Lt Gen S.C. Sardeshpande reinforces this opinion of the former OFC, by stating that "I have a high regard for the LTTE for its discipline, dedication, determination, motivation and technical expertise; but find little justification in its senseless, mulish, destructive insistence on continuation of military means in the search of an honourable solution to the Tamil problem in Sri Lanka.[29]

General Depinder continues to add that, to Prabhakaran's credit, despite the vast powers that Prabhakaran had enjoyed, he had successfully managed to create successive tiers of junior leadership thus ensuring the prompt and effective filling of every void created. Reflecting on the atmosphere prevalent during meetings with Prabhakaran, the General opines: "What struck a visitor most forcefully was the efficiency that prevailed; noise was completely absent; and everything gone through with clockwork precision."[30]

What disturbed the world was the slow realization that the LTTE, which the West, in particular, was quite happy to dismiss initially, as a South Asian phenomenon, upsetting the peace and tranquillity of a small island nation, and to an extent, India, began taking the lead as a 'as a 'think tank'[31] for terrorists worldwide, constantly inventing new tactics that (were) devastatingly effective; groups like Al Qaeda, Hezbollah, Hamas, Shining Path, and Chechen fighters (were) eager to integrate them into their organizations. From the use of female suicide bombers [made famous with the assassination of the (former) Indian Prime Minister, Rajiv Gandhi, in 1991] to the deployment of suicidal naval units – the Tigers (were) always on the cutting edge of the advancement of non-state terror and were, in fact, the only terrorist organization that had land, sea and air capabilities."[32]

Relationship with Subordinates

Shyam Tekwani writes that, "in a move that stunned his followers,[33] Prabhakaran struck against Mahattaya, who he had anointed as his deputy during the war against the IPKF in 1987. Accusing him of treachery and collaborating with the Indians against him, Prabhakaran placed Mahattaya in custody, liquidated most of Mahattaya's troops and decisively crushed a potential rival to his supremacy as leader... Mahattaya was executed after a prolonged period of torture in December 1994." The journalist also writes about the travails of the suave Yogi, who, after fearing that he would meet with the fate of Mahattaya, was "subsequently rehabilitated to his current position as military advisor in the Vann."[34] Balasingham, the LTTE ideologue, and his wife Adele, "rose even more higher in their leader's estimate. The Balasinghams – who posed no threat of any sort to their master – became the face of the organisation across Western capitals and were an essential part of all negotiating teams at various times."[35]

Blunders that Paved the Way to Prabhakaran's Destruction

The mistake that haunted him was the assassination of Rajiv Gandhi. He found a forum to publicly accept that it was a horrifying mistake to have done so.[36] The Al Jazeera correspondent notes that he "looked distinctly uncomfortable when asked about the assassination of the former Indian Prime Minister Rajiv Gandhi, who was blown up by a female LTTE suicide bomber in 1991, describing it as a 'tragic incident'."

The most telling part of Shyam Tekwani's article on Prabhakaran's destruction of Eelam is concerning the mistakes Prabhakaran made, that actually paved his way to destruction. This is what he has to say: "Chandrika Kumaratunga, then heading the government after having survived a suicide bomber attack, quickly learnt from Prabhakaran's successful diplomatic offensives. She despatched her Tamil Foreign Minister, Lakshman Kadirgamar, to world capitals on a mission to get the international community to act against the LTTE's interests in their respective countries. Kadirgamar was beginning to notch up diplomatic successes, having got the United Kingdom to proscribe the group in 2001. He was killed by a LTTE sniper in August 2005[37] just when he seemed on the verge of getting some more countries to proscribe the group.

In his 2006 November annual speech, after his attempts to assassinate the Chief of the Army and the Secretary of Defence in Colombo, he rued, "We postponed our plan to advance our freedom struggle twice to give even more chances to the peace efforts, once when the tsunami disaster struck and again when President Rajapaksa was elected.

He set out to reassert his authority over the East – and faced an Army that was well-armed and well-trained and motivated as never before and one that was working with unprecedented intelligence provided by his breakaway commander, Karuna. Prabhakaran lost the East – and from there on, he lorded over an unending series of military defeats. For the sanguinary among us – the chief reason for his downfall was the failure of his legendary Black Tiger suicide bombers and his celebrated Intelligence chief, Pottu Amman.

For someone who pioneered the use – and masterminded remarkable innovations – of suicide bombers, Prabhakaran's Black Tigers seemed to have reached a dead-end. **President Chandrika Kumaratunga was the first miracle of the Eelam war – as the first ever survivor of a Black Tiger attack, at an election rally in December 1999.**

Then came the failures in 2006 that cost him everything – General Sarath Fonseka, Commander of the Sri Lanka Army, became the second survivor of a suicide attack in April. Prabhakaran's trusted tool of political persuasion, the Black Tiger, was beginning to let him down. And when Gottabhaya Rajapaksa, the Secretary of the Defence and the brother of the President escaped a suicide attack in December, it was curtains for Prabhakaran. The last two failures led to his destruction. Clearly, Prabhakaran was facing a short supply of efficient Black Tigers. He was desperate enough to use recruits whose mental aptitude didn't match their ferocious commitment. A woman bomber sent to kill the Tamil Cabinet Minister, Douglas Devananda, in his Colombo office in November 2007, triggered her bra bomb when she discovered her target was not available for the day, killing herself and the Minister's secretary."[38]

The Narcissus in Prabhakaran

Narcissus is a legendary Greek god who is believed to have fallen in love with his image, when seeing his reflection in a pool of water. As Prabhakaran evolved, he slowly but surely succumbed to this oldest of weaknesses. In a way, his focus on promoting himself is part of the suite of qualities that most leaders the world over have, particularly those who rise outside the pale of democracy. In part, it must have risen out of his belief that he had untrammelled power; power of life and death over all he surveyed. Since he was paranoid, brooked no competition whatsoever, and was driven by the belief that it was he alone who could represent Tamil interests with all interlocutors, it was inevitable that he would merge his identity with the LTTE and the other way around. And so it came to pass that "Prabhakaran became the symbol of militant Tamil nationalism, appearing on posters, calendars, watches and the placards waved by his supporters around the world, even if they had misgivings about some of the Tigers' tactics[39] ...he was visible on all media projections, digital, voice, data, as the sole face of the LTTE and his followers fanatically sold this ephemeral packaging to the world."

The Troika Has the Last Say...

The other factor that Shyam Tekwani believes, "led to his precipitous defeat is that Prabhakaran did not count on the troika (the President, the Army Chief and the Defence Secretary) calling his bluff. His elaborate deceptions of invincibility had begun cracking – first, with the exit of Karuna and then by the steady inroads that the specially trained units of the Sri Lankan Army's commandos were making. The chronic political one upmanship in Colombo over the Eelam war between the two national parties – the UNP and the SLFP – which had contributed largely to the growth of the LTTE and the prolongation of the war, was contained by the Rajapaksa administration. The Rajapaksa brothers pulled out a page from the Bush counter-terrorism doctrine – niceties be damned."[40] **The last word on this issue is justifiably left to Dr. Tekwani: "With international assistance – material and moral – for the war on terror pouring in, (Prabhakaran met his match) in the Rajapaksa brothers, Prabhakaran finally met with an enemy as ruthless and unswervingly committed in their goal as he."[41]**

Prabhakaran's Legacy

Seth Mydans of the *NYT* feels that Prabhakaran's "insurgency held the country hostage to terrorism, holding back social and economic development, heightening violent ethnic divisions and pushing the Government toward a more repressive posture.[42] This is a correct assessment, as far as it goes. He indeed, set back Sri Lanka savagely; a situation from which the country will take long years to recover.

There is another side to this, though. By means of his hard-line methods, which used death and destruction as negotiating ploys, Prabhakaran drew attention to the marginalisation of the largest minority in Sri Lanka that has suffered from the Sinhala only beliefs that have driven most governments in Sri Lanka, since Independence in 1948. No one will support the methods that Prabhakaran used to seek justice. That said, Sri Lanka's quest for peace and tranquillity will have to include the need to look after the nations tamil minorities in a manner that satisfies all communities and promotes unity between all communities. The sword of Damocles that hangs tenuously over Sri Lanka is the possibility of revival of the LTTE, in case the island nation cannot handle its minorities in a wise, pragmatic, accommodative and nation building manner.

Endnotes

1. This statement from the *Straits Times* was first quoted at the beginning of Chapter 7 and has been replicated here, because of its relevance.
2. Tekwani, Shyam. "The Man Who Destroyed Eelam". <http://www.tehelka.com/story_main41.asp?filename=Ne230509coverstory.asp>
The blurb preceding this article has been reproduced in italics. Dr. Tekwani's strongly worded and revealing article must rank amongst the most comprehensive coverages of Prabhakaran, the 'Supreme Leader of the LTTE', as he chose to be called, in his ending years; having gravitated there from his humbler *Thambi (younger brother)* or *Anna (elder brother)* halcyon days, as Tekwani notes acidly in the article. The coverage is by an Indian journalist, who, in the course of his almost 30-year coverage of Prabhakaran was 'embedded' into the LTTE. This gave him a rare insight into the persona of Prabhakaran, and, by extension, the LTTE and its key cast of characters, like no one else whom this author has come across, during his research. Readers are forewarned (they are already familiar with quotes from Dr. Tekwani's Prabhakaran coverage earlier on, in Chapter 7) that some of his (scathing) observations, starting with the title of the article, may arouse strong feelings. Whether these observations are positively or negatively oriented or are to be taken dispassionately, as the personal opinion of an experienced, '*hands on*' journalist, will, of course, depend upon the reader's worldview. The latter course of action is recommended. Readers may also see a huge irony in the run of events as they unfolded over these 30 years: the journalist, who had covered the early years of the LTTE, was on hand to write the epitaph of its charismatic though Goebbelisian leader; a classic case of the creator becoming his own destroyer.
3. Shanika Sriyananda, "Monster Meets His Waterloo". Sunday Observer Correspondent reporting from Vellamullivaikkal. <http://www.sundayobserver.lk/2001/pix PrintPage.asp?REF=/2009/05/24/sec06.asp>
4. Ibid.
5. Singh, PVSM, VSM (Retd), Lt Gen Depinder. "The IPKF in Sri Lanka". Trishul Publications, Third Edition. May 2001.
6. Ibid, p.48.
7. Ibid, p.48.
8. Tekwani, Shyam. "The Man Who Destroyed Eelam". <http://www.tehelka.com/story_main41.asp?filename=Ne230509coverstory.asp> (**Author's Note**: Tekwani's *second* memory is that of an unfortunate encounter in 1987, of which he was a witness and which he photo documented. It does not bear recall here.)
9. Ibid.
10. Ross, James. "Tiger by the Tail". Op-ed writer for the *New York Times*. May 20, 2009. <http://www.nytimes.com/2009/05/21/opinion/21iht-edross.html?_r=1>
11. Tran, Mark. Profile: "Velupillai Prabhakaran: Tamil Tigers Founder Who Led 25-Year War Against Sri Lankan Government". Monday 18 May 2009. <http://www.guardian.co.uk/world/2009/may/18/tamil-tigers-sri-lanka-prabhakaran> Excerpts have been used.
12. Ibid.
13. Tekwani, Shyam. "The Man Who Destroyed Eelam". <http://www.tehelka.com/story_main41.asp?filename=Ne230509coverstory.asp>
14. Ibid.
15. Sardeshpande, UYSM, AVSM (Retd), Lt Gen S.C. "Assignment Jaffna". Lancer Publications

Private Limited. New Delhi. 1992. pp. 25-26.

16. Ibid. p. 27.
17. Ibid. p. 28.
18. Ibid. p.28.
19. Tekwani, Shyam. "The Man Who Destroyed Eelam". <http://www.tehelka.com/story_main41.asp?filename=Ne230509coverstory.asp> The comprehension that Dr. Tekwani has of Prabhakaran's mastery of communications and propaganda is brilliant and not found in any of the countless other inputs available on Prabhakaran and his modus operandi. Thus, **Notes 19 to 22** make for riveting reading; in fact, the whole article.
20. Ibid.
21. Ibid.
22. Ibid.
23. "Joseph Goebbels".<http://en.wikipedia.org/wiki/Joseph_Goebbels>
24. Ibid.
25. Ibid.
26. Tekwani, Shyam. "The Man Who Destroyed Eelam". <http://www.tehelka.com/story_main41.asp?filename=Ne230509coverstory.asp>
27. Singh, PVSM, VSM (Retd), Lt Gen Depinder. "The IPKF in Sri Lanka". Trishul Publications, Third Edition. May 2001. p. 16. Reference to TNT as explosive.
28. Ibid, pp. 21-22.
29. Sardeshpande, UYSM, AVSM (Retd), Lt Gen S.C. "Assignment Jaffna". Lancer Publications Private Limited. New Delhi. 1992. Preface, p. ix.
30. Singh, PVSM, VSM (Retd), Lt Gen Depinder. "The IPKF in Sri Lanka". Trishul Publications, Third Edition. May 2001. p. 22.
31. Shtender-Auerbach, Michael. "What Happens When A 'Poor Man's Air Force' Goes Airborne?" The Century Foundation, March 5, 2007. <http://www.tcf.org/list.asp?type=TN&pubid=1569> Michael Shtender-Auerbach is a Programme Officer and Associate Director of the Prospects for Peace Initiative at The Century Foundation.
32. Ibid.
33. Tekwani, Shyam. "The Man Who Destroyed Eelam". <http://www.tehelka.com/story_main41.asp?filename=Ne230509coverstory.asp>
34. Ibid.
35. Ibid.
36. Obituary: Velupillai Prabhakaran. <http://english.aljazeera.net/news/asia/2009/04/20094217815538234.html>
37. Tekwani, Shyam. "The Man Who Destroyed Eelam". <http://www.tehelka.com/story_main41.asp?filename=Ne230509coverstory.asp>
38. Ibid.
39. Tran, Mark. Profile: "Velupillai Prabhakaran: Tamil Tigers founder who led 25-year war against Sri Lankan government". Monday 18 May 2009. <http://www.guardian.co.uk/world/2009/may/18/tamil-tigers-sri-lanka-prabhakaran>
40. Tekwani, Shyam. "The Man Who Destroyed Eelam". <http://www.tehelka.com/story_main41.asp?filename=Ne230509coverstory.asp>
41. Ibid.
42. Mydans, Seth. "Velupillai Prabhakaran". May 18, 2009. <http://topics.nytimes.com/topics/reference/timestopics/people/p/velupillai_prabhakaran/index.html>

PART III

Miscellaneous Facets of the Conflict

Chapter 12

The Propaganda War

We must remember that in times of war, what is said on the enemy's side of the front is always propaganda, and what is said on our side of the front is truth and righteousness, the cause of humanity and a crusade for peace – *Walter Lippmann.*[1]

In wartime, truth is so precious that she should always be attended by a bodyguard of lies – *Winston Churchill, British Prime Minister during World War II.*

All propaganda must be so popular and on such an intellectual level, that even the most stupid of those towards whom it is directed will understand it.... Through clever and constant application of propaganda, people can be made to see paradise as hell, and also the other way around, to consider the most wretched sort of life as paradise. – *Adolf Hitler.*

Naturally the common people don't want war: Neither in Russia, nor in England, nor for that matter in Germany. That is understood. But, after all, it is the leaders of the country who determine the policy and it is always a simple matter to drag the people along, whether it is a democracy, or a fascist dictatorship, or a parliament, or a communist dictatorship. ... Voice or no voice, the people can always be brought to the bidding of the leaders. That is easy. All you have to do is tell them they are being attacked, and denounce the peacemakers for lack of patriotism and exposing the country to danger. It works the same in any country – *General Herman Goering, President of German Reichstag and Nazi Party, April 18, 1946.*

When a country goes off to war, so goes its media with it. – *Mirren Guiterrez, The 'Prop-Agenda' at War, Inter Press Service.*

Part 3 has three chapters, which focus on Propaganda, the LTTE funding for its Eelam struggle and the issue of Human Rights violations. It is felt that are all three issues have an umbilical connection with the civil war. Their knowledge will assist in understanding the complex rubric of the conflict.

Propaganda is defined as "communication aimed at influencing the attitude of a community toward some cause or position. As opposed to impartially providing information, propaganda in its most basic sense, presents information primarily to influence an audience. Propaganda often presents facts *selectively* (thus lying by omission) to encourage a particular synthesis, or uses loaded messages to produce an emotional rather than rational response to the information presented. The desired result is a change of the attitude toward the subject in the target audience to further a political agenda."[2]

Anup Shah writes perceptively that "probably every conflict is fought on at least two grounds: the battlefield and the minds of the people via propaganda. The 'good guys' and the 'bad guys' can often both be guilty of misleading their people with distortions, exaggerations, subjectivity, inaccuracy and even fabrications, in order to receive support and a sense of legitimacy.

Common tactics in propaganda often used by either side include:

- Using selective stories that come over as wide-covering and objective.
- Partial facts, or historical context.
- Reinforcing reasons and motivations to act due to threats on the security of the individual.
- Narrow sources of 'experts' to provide insights into the situation. (For example, the mainstream media typically interview retired military personnel for many conflict-related issues, or treat official government sources as fact, rather than just one perspective that need to be verified and researched).
- Demonizing the 'enemy' who does not fit the picture of what is 'right'.
- Using a narrow range of discourse, whereby judgments are often made while the boundary of discourse itself, or the framework within which the opinions are formed, are often not discussed. The narrow focus then helps to serve the interests of the propagandists."[3]

It is clear that, in the Sri Lankan civil war, both the 'good' as well as the 'bad' guys (depending on whose side the reader is tilted) have used propaganda extensively. Though the LTTE took an early lead and remained dominant in the propaganda as well as the actual war for long years, the Sri Lanka propaganda machinery began catching up from 2005 onwards. Their coming of age in the rarefied discipline of 'war on the minds' was coterminous with the decline of the LTTE on the war front, both actual as well as metaphysical.

The reader is requested, at this stage, to reflect on the five quotations given at the start of this chapter. All of them have cynical but starkly true content; content which is directly applicable in full measure to the conduct of the Eelam war. They support the timeless, eternal reality that the first casualty in war is truth. This is why this author had suggested in the Preface, that it is pointless deciding who the victor or loser was in the civil war, because that decision may be a function of the conditioning of the reader's mind. It may be more productive to focus on the use of propaganda by both the sides and see how it engineered the realities as known to the reader.

At this point, it is necessary to give a small primer about how propaganda works. No matter how it is spread, propaganda comes in four basic varieties, says Arthur Siegel, Social Science Professor at York University, in Toronto, whose 1996 book *Radio Canada International* examines World War II and Cold War propaganda:

> "The first level is the Big Lie, adapted by Hitler and Stalin.
>
> "The second layer says, 'It doesn't have to be the truth, so long as it's plausible.'
>
> "The third strategy is to tell the truth but withhold the other side's point of view.
>
> "The fourth and most productive is to tell the truth, the good and the bad, the losses and the gains.[4]

It appears that most of the inputs available from either side of the Sri Lankan civil war are in line with the first three levels. The last level is the ideal level that has rarely, if ever, been reached in any war world wide. Its application, for instance, to the 1962 Sino-Indian War is something that the common man and researchers in India have been waiting for, since the Lt Gen Henderson Brooks Report on its conduct was handed over in 1963 to the Government of India almost 56 years ago.

Shah writes that "the military control of information during war time is also a major contributing factor to propaganda, especially when the media go along with it without question. The military recognizes the values of media and information control very well. The military often manipulates the mainstream media, by restricting or managing what information is presented and hence what the public are told. For them it is paramount to control the media. This can involve all manner of activities, from organizing media sessions and daily press briefings, or through providing managed access to war zones, to even planting stories... Over time then, the way that the media covers conflicts degrades in quality, critique and objectiveness."[5] It would be patently unfair to target the SLAF alone, or even the Sri Lanka MoD on the media control issue. The LTTE was equally, if not more guilty, of media management in the manner that suited their convenience. Hence, the trend of covering victories in detail, tightening access when the situation was unfavourable, or demanding that a setback be rationalised in a manner that would conceal the reality was common to both sides.

The issue of journalistic as well as military ethics thus comes in; one the one hand, the military wish to present various aspects that would support a campaign, while on the other hand, a journalist is supposed to be critical and not necessarily fall in line. The dilemma is captured well by Jane Kirtley,[6] a professor of Media Ethics and Law:

"The military's mission is to fight, and to win, whatever conflict may present itself – preferably on the battlefield but certainly in public opinion and the history books. The journalist, on the other hand, is a skeptic, if not a cynic, and aims to seek, find and report the truth – a mission both parties often view as incompatible with successful warfare, which depends on secrecy and deception as much as superior strategy, tactics, weaponry and manpower".

It is useful to know how journalism is sometimes misled by propaganda from the perspective of Professor Johann Galtung, a professor of Peace Studies, as summarised by Danny Schechter.[7] Galtung has laid out 12 points of concern where journalism often goes wrong when dealing with violence. These are:

1. **Decontextualizing violence**: focusing on the irrational without looking at the reasons for unresolved conflicts and polarization.
2. **Dualism**: reducing the number of parties in a conflict to two, when often more are involved. Stories that just focus on internal developments often ignore such outside or 'external' forces as foreign governments and transnational companies.
3. **Manichaeism**: portraying one side as good and demonizing the other as 'evil.'
4. **Armageddon**: presenting violence as inevitable, omitting alternatives.
5. **Focusing on individual acts of violence while avoiding structural causes**, like poverty, government neglect and military or police repression.
6. **Confusion**: focusing only on the conflict arena (i.e., the battlefield or location of violent incidents) but not on the forces and factors that influence the violence.
7. **Excluding and omitting the bereaved**, thus never explaining why there are acts of revenge and spirals of violence.

8. **Failure to explore the causes of escalation and the impact of media coverage itself.**
9. **Failure to explore the goals of outside interventionists, especially big powers.**
10. **Failure to explore peace proposals and offer images of peaceful outcomes.**
11. **Confusing cease-fires and negotiations with actual peace.**
12. **Omitting reconciliation**: conflicts tend to re-emerge if attention is not paid to efforts to heal fractured societies. When news about attempts to resolve conflicts is absent, fatalism is reinforced. That can help engender even more violence, when people have no images or information about possible peaceful outcomes and the promise of healing.

– Danny Schechter, Covering Violence: How Should Media Handle Conflict? July 18, 2001

Let us now take a few examples of the use of propaganda from the Sri Lankan civil war and judge for ourselves where they stand in terms of credibility.

Report on Collateral Damage to Civilian Habitats During *The Final Countdown*

It was widely reported that as the fighting to destroy the Tigers focused on a little spit of land surrounded on three sides by water, the people who lived there were essentially trapped, and the Tamil Tigers were said to be using them as human shields. There were reportedly, 50,000 of them as of May 15, 2009. Some photos[8] from a report commissioned by Human Rights Watch (HRW) and Amnesty International (via the BBC) give a sense of the recent damage to this area:

The photos are of the same area, and were taken four days apart. That's how long it took for most of those houses – which had been set up for displaced persons – to be obliterated by SLA shelling.

Assessment. The SLA, has, of course, consistently maintained that such incidents have not occurred, nor innocents targeted except by default. The reality may however be noted; the Tigers were suspected, within Sri Lanka as well as internationally, of using the populace as shields; a charge the Government has consistently made right through the conflict.

Glowing Praise for SLN by Secretary of Defence (August 28, 2009)[9]

The Secretary of Defence said that the Sri Lanka Navy (SLN) has earned the praise and the appreciation of the world and this fact is amply evident by the numerous requests made by the countries with powerful navies for the services of SLN

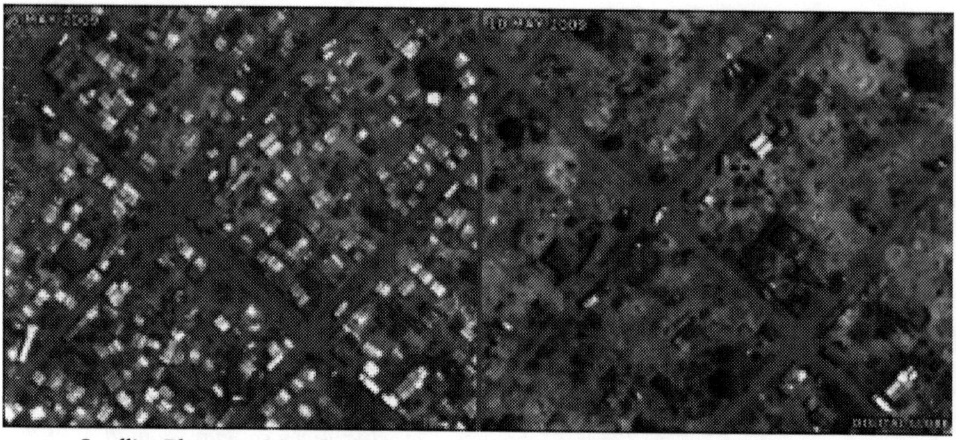

Satellite Photo on May 6, 2009

Satellite Photo of the same area on May 10, 2009

personnel and for sending their naval personnel for training with the SLN.[10] The lessons learnt in dealing with asymmetrical threats at sea have become a subject of interest for all conventional navies world-wide.

He brought out that the navy (had) played a crucial role in securing the harbours, especially the Colombo Harbour and the Trincomalee Harbour, since their protection rests with the navy, the Secretary of Defence said. The harbours had been constant targets of the LTTE and they attempted several times to attack them with the hope of inflicting damages to naval assets inside harbours since they found it difficult to take the navy head-on at sea. However, the navy skillfully defeated all such enemy attempts of causing damages to the economy and thus embarrassing the Government through their inevitable repercussions, by keeping all harbours including the strategically important Colombo Harbour safe and secure.

He further added that, going beyond its traditional roles, the navy undertook the security on land as well. The need was acutely felt to expand the army in large numbers to defeat terrorism despite the practical problems of rapid recruitment, training and arming while maintaining proper officer-soldier cadre ratios at the same time. The navy's contribution in meeting this requirement enabled the army to be deployed in full strength in operational areas to fight terrorism, the Secretary of Defence added. A large area in the Trincomalee District was protected by the navy. Similar large areas in the Wanni and from Vavuniya to Mannar were made secure through the deployment of naval troops. Security of all islets including Thalaimannar was borne by the navy. When taking into consideration all these facts, the Secretary of Defence said, it proves what a decisive role was played by the navy in defeating terrorism.

Assessment. Readers, who have followed the transformation of the SLN in earlier pages, would agree that the Secretary of Defence was, indeed, paying a handsome and well deserved, factual compliment to the navy, for having successfully transformed into an effective, aggressive, well armed and dynamic service during this conflict.

The LTTE and the Net[11]

The research article flagged at Note 11 deals with the use of the Internet to construct national identity. It uses the example of the struggle of the Sri Lankan Tamils for recognition as a nation-state, to highlight the potential of the Internet to instil a sense of nationhood among widely dispersed members and mobilize them in the struggle for transformation into a nation-state.

Assessment. Readers will realize that this experiment had a substantial propaganda component in it, but with elements of truth in it. Prabhakaran, due to his Net savvy outlook, was able to harness top quality Tamil cadres who orchestrated the Tamil nation-state identity world wide using the Tamil diaspora. The contact was also exploited to garner friends and influence in the corridors of power world wide as also elicit funds and war fighting equipment.

Misuse of Intelsat Satellite 12 for LTTE Propaganda[12]

MoD Sri Lanka said the Washington-based Intelsat Corporation had assured Sri Lanka's Ambassador in Washington DC, Bernard Goonetileke, it would take all possible steps to stop the LTTE from broadcasting its propaganda over their satellite. It said there had been a controversy on the company beaming LTTE propaganda, while the State Department considers it a foreign terrorist group. The New York-based www.tothecenter.com website published a lengthy article pointing out the fact. The Ministry quoted the Intelsat as saying, "Intelsat does not tolerate terrorists or others operating illegally on its satellites. Since we first learned of the LTTE's signal piracy, we have been actively pursuing a number of technical alternatives to halt the transmissions. We are clear in our resolve to ending this terrorist organization's unauthorized use of our satellite." Intelsat maintained that the LTTE was pirating an empty transponder frequency of their Satellite 12.

Assessment. It is the author's take that this April 2007 report appears not only credible but serves to indicate the extent to which the LTTE was prepared to go, to spread its propaganda worldwide. It is not very often that a third world terror group has the technical expertise and the vision to pirate transponders not in use to carry their propaganda gratis, and use this hi-tech enabler effectively.

Ethnic Cleansing Charge Against LTTE[13]

The Sri Lankan military alleged that at least seven persons were killed in 'ethnic cleansing raids' by the LTTE in Vavuniya district. In a statement, the Defence Ministry said the LTTE terrorists killed six women and one man. It said that the armed terrorists stormed the village around 4:30 p.m. and executed two families at two houses. "[The] LTTE is a ruthless terror group who fights for a mono-ethnic separate homeland for the Tamils living in Sri Lanka since 1983. It has been the outfit's strategy since its inception to flush out Sinhalese and Muslim people from North and East by bloody ethnic cleansing raids. Thousands of civilians, mostly women and children had perished in the most ruthless massacres during its 20 years of terror campaign," said the military.

Assessment. The reality, of course, is that ethnic cleansing charges have been traded since antiquity, between the main communities of Sri Lanka, well before the civil war began. The earlier pages of this book have given such details while covering the history of the Island. The dateline of the current Sinhala-Tamil conflict going back in time to 1915, also gives the reader a clear idea that both sides are blame-worthy. Post 1983, of course, the LTTE was the more guilty side of the two. The happenings of the last year or so, when the LTTE was rapidly folding up, seem to indicate that the SLAF were dominant in this direction. Notwithstanding the efforts of all the Human Rights organisations over the past several years, neither the LTTE nor the Government has accepted culpability. The jury is therefore still out as to apportioning of blame.

Expulsion of UN Diplomat for Rebutting Government's 'Wartime Propaganda'

A senior UN diplomat was expelled from Sri Lanka for providing detailed rebuttals of government 'wartime propaganda'[14] during the final battles against Tamil Tiger rebels...

In July, Peter Mackay, an Australian citizen, was given two weeks to leave the country, despite having a visa that ran until the summer of next year. The diplomat, who was monitoring the conflict, had put together briefings for embassies in Colombo that challenged Sri Lanka's official civilian death toll and its arrangements for relief operations...

Mr. Mackay, a field operative who worked for UNOPS – the technical arm of the UN – was less familiar to the media, but played a key role in keeping the outside world informed about the number of civilians killed in the final months of the war – a figure Sri Lanka was keen to play down. Mr. Mackay collected high-resolution satellite images showing that the number of people trapped on beaches where the Tigers made their last stand was far higher than that claimed by the Government. The data showed that not only were more people in danger than the government admitted, but that the food and medicine sent to the 'no fire zone' were inadequate.

The diplomat is seen as a legal time bomb by the Sri Lankan government, as he could take the stand and testify that the Army shelled non-combatants – a war crime. He was stranded behind Tamil lines on a mission to rescue 100 local staff and their families and endured repeated bomb attacks for 10 days in January, despite desperate calls to army commanders by his superiors..."

Assessment. The registering of protests by the international community for rebutting the official stand on civilian casualties is something that must be worrisome, if not alarming for the Sri Lankan Government. The military aspects of the LTTE attempting to gain illicit advantage by using them to shield their attempts to escape aside, the issue of perception management in your favour is an important part of the conduct of propaganda and the Government has its work cut out here, to redress the situation. With the war now over, the process of refugee screening for LTTE connectivity, and mine removal from areas where the refugees are to return, are important, but so is the need to handle the over 2.2 lakh refugees with care and consideration, and in a time sensitive manner.

Q+A: Sri Lanka's Propaganda War

COLOMBO (Reuters) – Sri Lanka and the Tamil Tiger rebels are again trading blame over reported attacks on civilians, which diplomats say sparked the U.N. Security Council and U.S. President Barack Obama to speak out.

Here are questions and answers[15] about why it is so hard to separate fact from propaganda in Asia's longest modern war:

Can Journalists or Aid Agencies Get into the War Zone?

Foreign journalists get in sometimes, mostly on guided trips chaperoned by the military. Some have been given wider access, but not as much as local and state reporters who are right on the frontline. The Tigers used to give similar guided tours. Only the International Committee of the Red Cross has consistently been inside since the government moved out foreign aid groups last year, save for their local Tamil staff.

What Role does Propaganda Play?

Given there is no unfiltered access to the war zone, an enormous one. The Liberation Tigers of Tamil Eelam (LTTE) early on recognized the power of influencing public perceptions, and have only improved during the 25-year war. They have their own cameramen to record images for propaganda and fundraising. Programming that had been carried on LTTE TV stations around the world – which the government got shut down on anti-terrorism grounds – is now carried on websites. The Voice of the Tigers radio still broadcasts. But their main outlet to the English-speaking world is the website www.TamilNet.com, which is blocked in Sri Lanka. The LTTE has media spokesmen, and activists from the Tamil diaspora who email news outlets and slip what they say are videos or pictures from the war zone to journalists.

Does Sri Lanka's Government do that Kind of Thing Too?

Yes. Since the current government came to power in 2005, it has taken the propaganda war right back to the LTTE. The defence ministry's www.defense.lk website is one of the Island's most popular and draws a third of its viewers from outside the country. It publishes videos and images from the battlefield, government statements, and pro-government news stories culled from across the world. Each page has a Facebook posting link. The government also has state-controlled TV, radio and newspapers, and a phalanx of spokesmen.

So don't the Videos and Pictures Tell the Whole Truth?

Rarely, simply because only interested parties to the conflict are vouching for their authenticity. Recent images the Tigers say are from the war zone are a good example. The bloody pictures usually come from a single e-mail, said to be that of a government doctor. There is no way to prove that or even when or where the pictures were taken. The government says the doctor is doing the LTTE's bidding. The photos almost simultaneously pop up on TamilNet and other websites sympathetic to the LTTE, and are emailed to news organizations. The government also publishes photos and videos of captured weapons, dead Tiger fighters and combat, and has its own partisans out in cyberspace who forward emails and photos and try to deconstruct LTTE images. Like the LTTE material, there is no way to prove their authenticity.

How do the Foes Try to Control the Message?

Both sides are not shy about accusing media institutions of bias or lying. The government deported a British news team for what it said was a fabricated story. Journalists in Sri Lanka throughout the war have suffered the threat of violence, arrests and harassment from both sides, according to rights groups.

Does Anyone have a Clear Idea of What is Happening?

The Tigers and the government do, as do people who are or were in the war zone. The foes will, like combatants throughout recorded history, give only their side. Refugees who have been interviewed have given harrowing narratives, and most have fallen somewhere between the extremes. (Editing by Alex Richardson)"

Assessment. As indicated at Note 15, this article captures the propaganda modus operandi of both sides brilliantly, leaving the reader in no doubt as to the cutting edge of not just the propaganda but its machinery as well, and delivery on the ground. The reader is aware that it was in 2005, when the Rajapaksa Government came into power, that the Government's propaganda started becoming effective; ironically, by modelling itself after the LTTE propaganda machinery. The role of the Sri Lanka MoD web site, which is aptly lauded here, has already been brought to the reader's attention. What is patently clear is that the propaganda was conducted with no holds barred on either side, and carried across the entire continuum of 'war on the mind,' as enunciated at the start of this chapter.

International Media and LTTE Propaganda War – An Opinion[16]

'During the Sri Lankan war, the LTTE malicious propaganda machinery worked round the clock to convince the world that the civilians held as hostage were staying willingly and certain sections of the international media sympathetic to them colluded and gave wide publicity to the LTTE stand. They were supported by countries and international organisations backing the terrorists. So, in addition to the real war fought by the forces, there was also a heavy handed propaganda war by the LTTE to demoralise the government, the forces and the people.

For example, some terminology and phrases used were, 'Un-winnable war, Invincible guerrillas...' The Sri Lankan conventional army could never ever defeat the well funded and disciplined guerrilla organisation ... Terrorism cannot be militarily defeated...' Even after Prabhakaran was killed, the Tamil website and the Tamil diaspora insisted that he was well and alive overseas. So the LTTE supporters and the international media backing them lobbied very hard to condemn Sri Lanka. Therefore, it was over to the local patriotic media to neutralise the malicious propaganda.

To thwart the efforts of the government in the war against the terrorists certain quarters from the foreign media supported the terrorists. They bowed down to pressure from various elements and gave prominence to false rumours and malicious campaigning against Sri Lanka and withheld responsibilities taking cover under a free press.

This sector of the international media aligned to the LTTE, demoralised the army and was highly critical of the military strategy and the approach of the government. They gave wide publicity to LTTE propaganda and LTTE backers such as the Tamil diaspora on the front pages or twisted stories to suit headlines. However, there were balanced views presented from others such as *The Hindu, Washington Times, Wall Street Journal, Manila Times,* etc.

Those who swallowed the LTTE propaganda pill, sided with the terrorists presenting fabricated news and unethical reporting on the Humanitarian Rescue Operation. They declined to acknowledge that the determination of the government and the security forces was not only to put an end to terrorism but also to save the civilians held as captives. Some spread blatant lies about the whole exercise to draw the attention of the UN and the Western world.

We had journalists sponsored by the LTTE to visit Sri Lanka and write adverse reports favouring their side of the story. There were also representatives from various international organisations who came as tourists and visited IDP camps and labelled them as concentration camps. A TV crew who reported about rape in IDP camps based on cooked up stories from LTTE supporters was tracked by the police. The war zone was not accessible to foreign media because of security.

So some media groups sympathetic to the LTTE became hostile to the government and presented material from the Tamil website without verification. Others from international organisations wrote reports based on data supplied by the same source. Thus these groups ganged up to mould public opinion in favour of the LTTE in an unethical manner. As such, they failed in their responsibility to preserve the canons of justice, fair play and honest commitment.

Some features (articles) highlighted to attack the Government and the forces were: withholding of the IMF loan, (the) US sending Marines, terrorist leaders to surrender to a third party, international war crimes etc. Then some terror backers hacked the Army website.

Therefore, on one side, we had the real war on the battle ground where the valiant forces were fighting tooth and nail to salvage the country from the terrorists. On the other was the propaganda war of the LTTE and their sympathisers from the international media, with whom the domestic media battled against as their attempt was to belittle the efforts of the government and the security forces and destroy the unitary state of Sri Lanka.

With colourful editorials, articles and pictures, the local media outmanoeuvred these groups and counterbalanced Western criticism of the conduct of the war. The patriotic local media played a commendable role in disseminating news on the war and the Human Rescue Operation and supported the forces to preserve the sovereignty of Sri Lanka.

Assessment. This rebuttal by the MoD covers a lot of ground in narrating the manner in which LTTE propaganda garnered a lot of international support for its cause by denigrating Sri Lanka and its forces, and spreading the canard that they were invincible. The write-up goes on to say that for a period of time, the LTTE managed to contest the death of Prabhakaran by claiming that he was alive, and found quite a few takers for its stories. What the rebuttal brings out with some bitterness, is that some Western nations, media and organisations chose to support the LTTE viewpoint over that of Sri Lanka and it was left to the local media, along with a few Western and Indian media publications (the write up names them), to report fairly on the war. That said, the point remains that propaganda on both sides was skillfully conducted, with periods of absolute dominance for either side.

Alleged Case of Extra-Judicial Killings by SLA

A video clip received from Journalists for Democracy in Sri Lanka (JDS) evidences the way extra-judicial killings[17] are executed in the Island. The video captured in January show the behaviour of Sri Lanka's soldiers during the war that is claimed 'humanitarian operation' to rescue the Tamils, JDS reported. The conversations of the killers are in Sinhala. "From the casual nature of the conversations and from the fact that it is taking place in an open area in broad daylight – it can be surmised that these are not ordinary acts by rogue elements carried out without the permission from the top leadership. The soldiers egging each other on, the insulting jokes and the laughter show that there is a consensus that these cold blooded killings should take place," JDS further reported.

As there is no reason to believe there is a change in the behaviour of the armed forces, the treatment of the 280,000 people in the internment camps kept for 'screening' and another more than 10,000 alleged to be LTTE cadres, kept in undisclosed locations, is widely feared.

The way the men are treated even in execution, shown in the video clip, is a repeatedly demonstrated feature of the chauvinism in the Island. One can imagine the treatment of women, was the observation of Tamil circles.

BBC Sinhala Service reported the trauma of the internment camp inmates about 'Dolphin vans' whisking away people, who then disappear. While some governments are sitting on indicting Colombo's war crimes and while some other governments don't want to recognise the genocidal perspectives or the need to call for the closure of internment camps, Colombo enjoys absolute impunity, Tamil circles said.

Journalists for Democracy in Sri Lanka (JDS) was founded on 18th of July in Berlin, with the participation of Tamil and Sinhala journalists coming from six

European countries, who were forced into exile. JDS aims to raise the concerns about the deteriorating conditions of democratic rights in Sri Lanka, with a special emphasis on issues related to media freedom.

Horrendous Video Images Indicate Violation of International Law – UN Expert

Philip Alston, the UN Special Rapporteur on extra-judicial, summary or arbitrary executions, commenting on the video clip aired in British Channel 4 TV, allegedly[18] showing Sri Lankan troops executing prisoners, stressed the need for an investigation, AFP reported. The images, which Alston described as 'horrendous,' indicate a serious violation of international law if found to be authentic, AFP reported Alston as saying. The video showed victims stripped naked and their hands crossed and tied behind their backs, when they were executed.

'If the government's position [of categorically denying the allegations] is validated as a result of an inquiry, the international community can rest easy and the government will have been vindicated,' AFP quoted Alston as saying.

Video grab showing alleged killings by SLA

Alston also pointed out that he had asked permission to visit Sri Lanka on several occasions in recent years, but Colombo had not given him the green light, according to the AFP report. Sri Lanka Army soldiers' action, of stripping naked the Tamil victims before summarily executing them, is more akin to what the Nazis did to the Jews, depriving their victims of the last shred of their humanity before dying, Professor Boyle of Illinois College of Law observed. In Sri Lanka's ruling party, Anura Priyadharshana Yapa, and Information Director Anusha Palpita said they had never heard of the group 'Journalists for Democracy in Sri Lanka' which sent the video clip to Channel 4, adding that it could be a front organization for LTTE remnants attempting to pump oxygen into the dying organization, according to Sri Lanka media. A UN press release issued on 9th May 2009 said: 'The current humanitarian crisis in Sri Lanka gives cause for deep concern, not only in terms of the number of civilians who have been and continue to be killed, but because of a dramatic lack of transparency and accountability.'

Philip Alston said in the same release, '[t]here is good reason to believe that thousands of civilians have been killed in the past three months alone, and the Sri Lankan Government has yet to account for the casualties, or to provide access to the war zone for journalists and humanitarian monitors of any type.'

British daily *The Times* on its 29th May issue revealed that at least 20,000 Tamil people were killed on the Mullaithivu beach by Sri Lanka Army shelling. Aerial photographs, official documents, witness accounts and expert testimony collected by the newspaper 'present clear evidence of an atrocity that comes close to matching Srebrenica, Darfur and other massacres of civilians,' the paper's editorial said. Confidential UN documents acquired by *The Times* record nearly 7,000 civilian deaths in the 'no-fire' zone up to the end of April. UN sources said that the toll then surged, with an average of 1,000 civilians killed each day until May 19.

Government Tells Channel 4: Retract Video; Scientific Evidence Proves it was a Fake

Human Rights and Disaster Management Minister Mahinda Samarasinghe said that the Government is going to ask the retraction of the controversial execution video from Channel 4, as comprehensive investigations and analysis conducted by four experts on the video have provided scientific evidence to prove that it was a fake[19] and a heavily tampered video.

Addressing the media at the Media Centre for National Security along with Defence Affairs Spokesman Minister Keheliya Rambukwella and three other experts to discuss the authenticity of the controversial video, the Minister said that he will also take up the controversial video issue with United Nations Secretary General Ban ki- Moon very soon.

The United Nations Secretary General raised the issue about this controversial execution video broadcast by UK based Channel 4 when Minister Samarasinghe met him. "We are not making a mere political statement; it is backed by scientific evidence following comprehensive investigations by well-known experts," the Minister said.

"Not only Channel 4, we will also submit scientific evidence to prove the video is a fake to Norwegian International Development Minister Erik Solheim too, to retract his statement based on the video footage," the Minister said.

Minister Rambukwella said the Government cannot easily forget the issue as a simple one because it was matter concerning the reputation and image of the country, the Government and the Armed Forces.

Minister Rambukwella said apart from the scientific evidence obtained, the Defence Ministry has also conducted investigations to ascertain whether there are Security Forces personnel similar to the people appearing in the video footage.

"It has been established with finality that the people appearing in the video are not in the Armed Forces," Minister Rambukwella added.

Minister Samarasinghe said that four experts on the subject have conducted investigations into this controversial video telecast by Channel 4 and subsequently picked up by various other international media including BBC and CNN.

"We will also raise this issue with other international media channels which had picked up the Channel 4 video and broadcast it without verifying the authenticity of the video footage provided by the so-called media organization called Journalists for Democracy in Sri Lanka," the Minister added.

He said the Journalists for Democracy in Sri Lanka or the JDS has organized and published their blogpost only on August 1, 2009.

The Minister made the statement that the video was a fake based on the findings made by Siri Hewawitharana, an international expert on the subject who is also the former head of Cisco's global broadcast and digital video practice, Dr. Chatura Ranjan de Silva, a Senior Lecturer on Computer Science and Engineering and Director of the Centre for Instructional Technology, Brigadier Prasad Samarasinghe, the Chief Signal Officer of the Sri Lanka Army and the Major P.A. Bandara attached to the Media Centre for National Security.

The four experts who analyzed the video had come to the obvious conclusion that the video footage had been filmed not by a mobile phone camera but by a digital camcorder and the sound had been dubbed separately into the video and the gun noise in the video is coming from a long distance proving the fact that the video footage was doctored.

Major P.A. Bandara making his presentation on the controversial video after playing it on normal speed and 50 percent speed, pointed out the discrepancies of the video footage and the unusual things appearing in the video.

The non-spreading blood stains, the movements of the victims while being executed, the outward appearance of the victims and the uniforms worn by the so-called soldiers executing those victims came under close study by him.

"It is not the practice of the Sri Lanka Army soldiers to wear a white coloured T-shirt with an olive green uniform," Major Bandara said making a valid point that the video was doctored.

The movements of the executed victims also came under his close scrutiny to suggest that the video was a fake.

Dr. Chatura Ranjan de Silva from the University of Moratuwa, who had earlier assisted the Government to analyse the videos of Minister Jeyaraj Fernandopulle's assassination and the suicide attempt on Minister Douglas Devananda said that the video had not been filmed by a mobile phone camera but a digital camcod.

"If it had been filmed by a mobile phone camera it should have jumping or discrete effects," he added.

He said that although the video has less colour sensitivity in the blood stains of the victims it is unusually colour sensitive and the blood stains with clear margins prove the fact that it was heavily tampered or fabricated.

"There is clear proof that the sound has been dubbed into the video separately," he added.

Dr. Chatura Ranjan de Silva made his technical analysis based on the video footage downloaded from the internet.

Chief Signal Officer of the Sri Lanka Army Brigadier Prasad Samarasinghe said that the Signal Base Workshop of the Army following a comprehensive investigation noticed a gap between the sound and the video film to suggest that the sound has been dubbed into the video footage.

The sound of gun firing had been recorded at a distance of some 102.4 metres which is quite impossible to be done by a mobile phone camera, the Brigadier added. (Courtesy: *Daily News*).

Assessment. The alleged killing is a classic case of how propaganda impacts on the minds of people (propaganda is, after all, 'war on the mind') in an amorphous war situation ruled by the Clausewitzian elements of chaos, confusion, mayhem, and, not the least, friction; factors discussed earlier in the book as attributes that define the complex nature of war. The aggressor, in this case, is the side that lost the war; the LTTE. The defender is, of course, the winning side, the Government forces. There is obviously enough in the video to disturb Human Rights watchers as much as there is substance in the Government's defence of its stand that the video is fake and is the epitome of vicious propaganda, designed to slur the image of the country in the world forum. Obviously, those agencies accused of spreading falsehoods that can damage the reputation of the SLAF and the nation will demand unqualified proof that the video was part of a malicious propaganda campaign, before they make formal amends. Judgment on this case must therefore await production of the irrefutable proof that the Government of Sri Lanka has volunteered to provide.

Custody of Pathmanathan Raises Questions about Recognition to State Terrorism

The manner in which Selvarasa Pathmanathan (KP) was 'arrested'[20] and ended up in the custody of the Sri Lankan state that is widely accused of war crimes, genocide and state terrorism, raises serious concerns about the world outlook to political justice, Tamil circles said. Mr. Pathmanathan, who denounced violence, was engaged in re-organising the LTTE and in consenting the formation of a transnational body for the Eezham Tamils. Meanwhile, acknowledging Pathmanathan's custody, Colombo's minister and spokesperson Keheliya Rambukwela said: 'There were some false hopes that after the LTTE was crushed that movement could be revived with Pathmanathan. But we have proved that we have the capability of getting to them from wherever they emerge.'[21]

Mr. Pathmanathan, a senior member of the LTTE, was appointed in January (2009) as the head of its international relations and was recently named by a committee as its chairperson. According to Tamil circles, Mr. Pathmanathan was mysteriously kidnapped in Malaysia on Wednesday (August 5, 2009) and sent to Colombo. There were earlier reports that he was arrested in Thailand but the Thai Prime Minister refuted them. Colombo refused to identify the country where he was arrested but said that its personnel were involved in the act. Meanwhile, the Sri Lankan spokesman Keheliya Rambukwella said that his government would 'allow any country to question Mr. Pathmanathan now in custody keeping with the agreements and conventions with those respective countries.' India and Sri Lanka have registered cases against him with the Interpol long back.

Assessment. The propaganda part of this otherwise factual, important development lies in doubting the manner in which the 'arrest' of Pathmanathan (KP) was carried out by Government agencies. The facts as known are that KP was very important for the continued survival of the LTTE as an entity, and is reported to have vowed to do so, post the death of Prabhakaran. His arrest in another country (Malaysia?) and quick deportation to Sri Lanka, presumably to stand trial for offences committed by him, continues to be a grey area, as the Government, besides, acknowledging that its intelligence agencies have arrested him abroad and deported him back to Sri Lanka, have chosen to throw no further light on this otherwise major development. In matters concerning national security, it is common for nations to keep a tight control on key information. This information void, has, however, given adequate grounds for TamilNet to raise the issue of 'State Terrorism' by Sri Lanka.

Endnotes

1. Shah, Anup. "War, Propaganda and the Media". <http://www.globalissues.org/article/157/war-propaganda-and-the-media>. The quotes have been excerpted from the blog run by Anup Shah.

2. "Propaganda". <http://en.wikipedia.org/wiki/Propaganda>
3. Shah, Anup. "War, Propaganda and the Media". <http://www.globalissues.org/article/157/war-propaganda-and-the-media>. The quotes have been excerpted from the blog run by Anup Shah.
4. Ibid.
5. Ibid.
6. Ibid.
7. Ibid.
8. http://obsidianwings.blogs.com/obsidian_wings/2009/05/sri-lanka.html
9. Secretary of Defence Pays Glowing Tribute to Sri Lanka Navy for its Decisive Role in Eliminating LTTE Terrorism. <http://www.navy.lk/index.php?id=1829>
10. Balachandran, PK. India, Britain Seek Lankan Naval Expertise. August 25, 2009. http://www.expressbuzz.com/edition/story.aspx?Title=India,+Britain+seek+Lankan+ naval+expertise&artid=6XtN/JuorSU=&SectionID=oHSKVfNWYm0=&MainSectionID=oHSKVfNWYm0=&SectionName=VfE7I/Vl8os=&SEO=Adm%20 Wasantha%20Karannagoda,%20D%20K%20P %20Dassanayake,%20Sri%20L The report goes on to say that India and Britain had sought Sri Lankan naval expertise in Small Boat Operations, (SBS) a Sri Lankan naval official told *Express*, thus confirming a report published in *The Island Daily* on Monday. The request was made after the Sri Lankan Navy's SBS successfully defeated the Sea Tigers, the naval arm of the LTTE, during Eelam War IV. A US naval team was already in the Island nation having joint exercises with the Sri Lankan Navy's SBS in the seas off the Eastern coast, the official added.
11. Ranganathan M. Nationalism and Ethnic Politics, Volume 8, Number 2. "Nurturing a Nation on the Net: The Case of Tamil Eelam". pp. 51-66(16). **Publisher:** Routledge. Summer 2002. <http://www.ingentaconnect.com/content/routledg/nep/2002/00000008/00000002/art00004>
12. B. Muralidhar Reddy, B. "Ethnic Cleansing: Colombo". <http://www.hindu.com/2007/04/13/stories/2007041304441600.htm>. The report that follows has been excerpted from *The Hindu* article as indicated above.
13. Ibid.
14. Ramesh, Randeep. "Sri Lanka Expelled UN Official For Disproving Propaganda". <http://www.irishtimes.com/newspaper/world/2009/0912/1224254385871.html>. Extracts from this article related to the expulsion have been used to illustrate the propaganda angle. The article also covered the tardy progress that the Government is making in returning Tamil refugees to their homes, notwithstanding its commitments to the contrary to the international community/UN aid agencies.
15. Hull, Bryson C. "Q+A: Sri Lanka's Propaganda War". May 14, 2009. <http://www. reuters.com/article/worldNews/idUSTRE54D2Z220090514>. This is a brilliant if terse summation of how propaganda was being interpreted by the two sides, as the war was drawing to a close. Note that the report is datelined May 14, 2009, just four days before the war finally got over. **All the relevant facts have been brought out and very objectively indeed, leaving the author no choice but to reproduce it in full.**
16. Samaraweera, Dr. P.A. "International Media and LTTE Propaganda war – An Opinion". <http://www.defence.lk/new.asp?fname=20090523_08>. This article has been reproduced in full from the Sri Lanka MoD website, and is a strongly worded, somewhat bitter rebuttal of both LTTE propaganda and unidentified Western nations and organisations that the writer

says became victims to the propaganda. The article, without meaning to do so, inadvertently pays a left-handed compliment to the effectiveness of the LTTE propaganda which had to be nuetralised, even as the bitter fight to the finish was carried out by the SLAF.

17. "Video Shows Style of Extra-Judicial Killings in Sri Lanka". TamilNet, August 25, 2009. http://www.tamilnet.com/art.html?catid=13&artid=30080 TamilNet is considered a part of the propaganda machinery of the LTTE. **Since this case has invited international attention, the report put out has been reproduced in full, with the precaution that the word, 'Alleged' has been added, in the heading and text, where applicable, as no conclusive proof of SLA culpability has been produced so far, which can stand up to legal scrutiny.**
18. "Horrendous Video Images Indicate Violation of International Law – UN Expert". TamilNet, August 28, 2009. **<http://www.tamilnet.com/art.html?catid=13&artid=30104>. The report is reproduced in full. Readers may note that this is a follow up report, again posted by TamilNet, which mentions that the video clip aired on British Channel 4 TV "*allegedly* shows Sri Lankan troops executing prisoners". Note too, that Philip Alston's criticism comes into play only "if the violation is found to be authentic".**
19. Wijayapala, Ranil. "Government Tells Channel 4: Retract Video; Scientific Evidence Proves it was a Fake". <http://www.army.lk/detailed.php?NewsId =1221>. The same coverage is also available at **<http://www.dailynews.lk/2009/09/08/news01.asp>. September 08**, 2009>. **Note that the report has been reproduced from the Sri Lanka MoD site in full, as was done for the TamilNet reports.**
20. "Custody of Pathmanathan Raises Questions about Recognition to State Terrorism". TamilNet, August 07, 2009. <http://www.tamilnet.com/art.html?catid=13&artid=29954>. Extracted from the above article, put out by TamilNet. Readers would be aware that Pathmanathan was a huge catch for the Government, coming on the heels of the killings of Prabhakaran and his key aides, as it were. The article conveys the shock and dismay of the LTTE organisation/its well wishers at this debilitating development.
21. Ibid.

CHAPTER 13

LTTE Funding for the 'Final War'

The last chapter covered the propaganda war in detail, and alluded several times to the fact that the LTTE funding support, particularly from its diaspora, was responsible in large measure for them waging their Eelam struggle. This chapter examines what the Tamil diaspora comprises of, and how funding from it was elicited. The points of view of Human Rights organisations in the West, specifically in Canada and UK, in terms of the use of LTTE intimidation and extortion will be discussed as also some British and American views on the subject of diaspora and funding. The US views are attributable to the US Federal Bureau of Investigation (FBI) and the US Treasury.

Sri Lankan Tamil Diaspora[1]

The Sri Lankan Tamil diaspora refers to the global diaspora of the people of Sri Lankan Tamil origin. It can be said to be a subset of the larger Tamil diaspora. Like other diasporas, Sri Lankan Tamils are scattered and dispersed across the globe, with concentrations in Canada, India, Europe, Australia, USA, Malaysia, Singapore, Seychelles and Mauritius. Readers may, however, note that when the lesser specific term, Tamil diaspora[2] is used, it is a term used to denote people of both Tamil Nadu and Sri Lanka origin who have settled in many parts of the rest of India or in other regions, particularly Sri Lanka, Malaysia, Singapore, the Middle East, Réunion, South Africa, Mauritius, Seychelles, Fiji, Guyana, Trinidad and Tobago, French Caribbean islands, Europe, Australia, United States and Canada. Thus, as noted, there are two distinct groups. The Eelam Tamil diaspora is less than 100 years old and was well established in Malaysia, Singapore and England prior to the post 1983 Black July massacre of Tamils in Sri Lanka, which induced dispersal of refugees and asylum claimants in India, Europe and Canada. Although relatively recent in origin, this subgroup had well established communities in these host countries prior to the 1983 pogroms.[3]

The Sri Lankan Tamils were quick to grab educational and economic opportunities available to them when Sri Lanka was under British colonial rule. Mostly, the Vellalar Jaffna Tamils availed themselves of the educational opportunities provided by the colonial authorities and missionaries and took up many government posts offered to locals by the British. The British themselves were said to prefer Tamils, leading to the majority Sinhalese disenchantment with the minority Tamils who felt the Tamils were much better off and the Sinhalese were deprived leading to the current ethnic conflict. In foreign lands under British rule, the British needed hardworking and skillful people to take up government posts, mainly as clerks. This led to the first wave of migrations by the Tamils to countries such as Malaysia (then Malaya), Singapore and the then Madras Presidency in India. Many of the first Asian and non-white doctors and engineers in Malaya and Singapore were of Sri Lankan Tamil descent. The world's first Asian surgeon was Dr S. S. Thiruchelvam, a Malayan of Ceylonese Tamil origin.

Former Singaporean Prime Minister Lee Kuan Yew once said:

> "In terms of numbers, the Ceylonese, like the Eurasians, are among the smallest of our various communities. Yet in terms of achievements and contributions to the growth and development of the modern Singapore and Malaysia they have done more than warranted by their numbers. In the early days of Malaysia's and Singapore's history the civil service and the professions were manned by a good number of Ceylonese. Even today the Ceylonese community continues to play a prominent role in these and other fields of civil life. For example in Singapore, today, the Speaker of Parliament is a Ceylonese. So is our High Commissioner in Great Britain. So is our Foreign Minister. In the judiciary, in the civil service, in the university, in the medical service and in the professions they continue to make substantial contributions out of all proportion to their numbers. They are there not because they are members of a minority community but on the basis of merit. The point is that the Ceylonese are holding their own in open competition with communities far larger than them. They have asked for no special favour or consideration as a minority. What they have asked for – and quite rightly – is that they should be judged on their merits and that they be allowed to compete with all other citizens fairly and without discrimination. This, as far as the Singapore government is concerned, is what is best for all of us. I believe that the future belongs to that society which acknowledges and rewards ability, drive and high performance without regard to race, language or religion."[4]

As brought out above, the eruption of the civil conflict in Sri Lanka between the Sri Lankan Government and the LTTE saw mass migration of Tamils to escape the hardships and bitter life of a country torn by war. Initially, it was professionals such as doctors and engineers who emigrated. This was followed by the poorer segments of the community who sold everything they had to be able to get a passport and ticket and seek asylum in foreign lands. The bitter ethnic fighting in Sri Lanka had driven over 800,000 Sri Lankan Tamils from their homeland, forcing them to find refuge around the globe.

Statistics[5]

The migrated Tamil population post-1983 is said to be above 1,000,000.

Country	Sri Lankan Tamils
Canada	400,000
United Kingdom	300,000
India	150,000
France	100,000
Germany	60,000
Australia	53,000
Switzerland	52,000
United States	35,000
Italy	24,000
Malaysia	20,000
Norway	13,000
Netherlands	7,000
Sweden	6,000
New Zealand	4,000
Finland	600

With the diaspora of the Sri Lankan Tamils as well as Tamils in the larger context having got established, let us recall that the LTTE obtained primary funding for their Eelam war from the Sri Lankan Tamils in particular. Obviously, some of the money collected was voluntarily donated, especially by those displaced from their homes, or those who had suffered human and/or material losses from the consequences of Black July and other pogroms where the Tamils were targeted in Sri Lanka. It is equally true that a fair amount of money came in through coercion, intimidation and extortion. These details follow.

The medium of conveying this information is a Human Rights Watch Report.[6] The report is a detailed and thorough study of the methods that the LTTE had adopted for fund collection, most of which qualified for scrutiny by this organisation for violation of human rights of those Tamils affected by the fund collection. Readers may note that only extracts relevant to our understanding have been quoted.

Extracts from the Human Rights Watch Report: The Tamil Diaspora and Support for the LTTE

Beginning in 1983, the effects of the war, including widespread Government abuses targeting the Tamil population, prompted hundreds of thousands of Tamils to flee Sri Lanka. As of 2001, the Sri Lankan Tamil diaspora was estimated at 600,000–800,000, accounting for approximately one-quarter of the global Sri Lankan Tamil population. The majority of Sri Lankan Tamils are found in Western Europe, India, Australia, and North America. The largest numbers are found in Canada (approximately 200,000–250,000), India (approximately 150,000), U.K. (approximately 110,000), Germany (approximately 50,000), Switzerland, France, and Australia (each approximately 30,000)...

The growing diaspora also became an important source of income for the LTTE. Many Tamils had suffered or witnessed abuses by Sri Lankan security forces, and gladly sent funds to support the LTTE's war against the government. There was broad support among the Tamil community in the West for the LTTE's fight for Tamil autonomy in Sri Lanka, and they saw the LTTE as a legitimate representative of the Tamil people and their interests. By the 1990s, a steady income stream flowed from the diaspora to the LTTE. By the mid-1990s, some experts believed that 80 to 90 percent of the LTTE's military budget came from overseas sources, including both diaspora contributions and income from international investments and businesses...

The exact amount of funds is impossible to determine. For example, various sources estimated the amount of money flowing from the Canadian diaspora to the LTTE in the late 1990s at anywhere between Cdn$1 million and more than Cdn$12 million a year.

Funds were raised through a variety of means, such as collections at Hindu temples and public events, including annual Heroes' Day celebrations that honour LTTE 'martyrs'. In most countries with a significant Tamil diaspora, Tamils established charitable organizations to raise funds for Tamil causes. These included the World Tamil Movement, British Tamil Association, and the Tamil Rehabilitation Organization, among others. Although the charities solicited funds to assist civilians affected by the war, numerous inquiries, including investigations by Canadian intelligence, have found that a significant amount of the funds raised were channelled to the LTTE for its military operations. The Canadian Security Intelligence Service (CSIS) concluded in 2000 that at least eight non-profit organizations and five companies were operating in Canada as fronts for the LTTE...

The LTTE and its front organizations also sought contributions by directly soliciting individuals at their homes and places of business. Human Rights Watch spoke to a Tamil who worked as a volunteer for the LTTE in London for several years in the late 1990s, going from house to house on Sundays in neighborhoods where Tamils were concentrated to collect money. He and other volunteers would often offer families pro-Tiger newspapers or books as an enticement to give. The former volunteer said that every month the regional head for the LTTE would meet with the volunteers to give a target for that month's fundraising. The instructions were often quite explicit about the funds' intended purpose. He told Human Rights Watch: "Sometimes they would say they want to form something, like a military battalion, or that they want to buy arms or an armed vehicle. They were upfront about buying weapons."...

The LTTE maintained computer records to keep track of individuals who contributed, including their addresses and telephone numbers. The former volunteer in London told Human Rights Watch: "If families didn't give money, we would keep visiting them. We would tell them we would come back next month." In addition to the monthly targets, once a year the LTTE would raise money for a special project, asking members of the Tamil community for larger amounts – £200-250 (U.S.$350-430) per family, and up to £2,000 (U.S.$3,500) from businesses. To ensure a regular flow of income, the LTTE sought pledges of regular monthly contributions from Tamil families. In London in the late 1990s, approximately 1,000 individuals reportedly were paying regular contributions of £10, £20, or £30 per month to support the London LTTE office...

Monthly pledges were encouraged in Canada and other countries as well. By the early 2000s, the system had become more sophisticated, and fundraisers in Toronto asked Tamils to sign forms authorizing automatic monthly bank transfers from their bank accounts. Such automatic transfers ensured regular payments to the LTTE and relieved volunteers of making repeated visits to Tamil homes to collect pledges. In the U.K., Canada, and elsewhere, the LTTE also used its computer database, public records, and information from supporters to keep close track of Tamils in the community, including new arrivals...

The U.K. government officially designated the LTTE as a terrorist organization in 2001, forcing the LTTE to shut down its London office. The terrorist designation and global focus on anti-terror initiatives following the September 11, 2001, Al-Qaida attacks on New York and Washington D.C. made many individuals more reluctant to give funds to the LTTE or its front groups. The rate of contributions was also affected by the February 2002 ceasefire agreement signed by the LTTE and the Sri Lankan government: with a halt in active hostilities, many in the Tamil diaspora no longer perceived a pressing need to contribute to the LTTE. Fundraising activity continued, however, and according to some accounts, became more aggressive to compensate for individuals' increasing reluctance to give...

Paying for 'The Final War': LTTE Fundraising and Extortion within the Tamil Diaspora in Late 2005 and Early 2006

Although many Tamils willingly contribute money to the LTTE, many others do so because they feel they have little choice. The same fear that silences critics of the LTTE prompts many members of the diaspora to provide financial support for the LTTE, regardless of whether they support the LTTE's cause. In late 2005, the escalation of LTTE attacks on Sri Lankan forces and the increase in rights abuses by both sides coincided with a massive LTTE fundraising drive among the Tamil diaspora. In Canada, the U.K., and other parts of Europe, LTTE representatives went house to house and visited Tamil-owned businesses, requesting substantial sums of money, often using intimidation, coercion, and outright threats to secure pledges.

LTTE representatives provided a variety of explanations for how the money would be used. In many of the cases reported to Human Rights Watch, the funds were sought for 'the final war.' Tamil families and business owners were told that the LTTE had a plan for driving out all Sri Lankan army forces from the North and East within two months, and that within that period the war would be over. Others were told that the LTTE was preparing to declare 'Tamil Eelam' (i.e. independence) and needed to build its treasury. Some members of the community were also told that the funds were needed to gain United Nations (U.N.) recognition of Tamil Eelam, and that the U.N. would subsequently provide funds to the new Tamil state...

Response from the World Tamil Movement

Sitha Sittampalam, the President of the World Tamil Movement in Canada, told Human Rights Watch that the World Tamil Movement "works for the welfare of Canadian Tamils and is also concerned with the problems we face back home in terms of suppression of rights and the freedom struggle." When asked about the World Tamil Movement's relationship to the LTTE, Sittampalan told Human Rights Watch: "We are sympathetic to our cause there and because the LTTE is fighting for our rights and in the vanguard we have always campaigned to help them." The organization's website prominently features quotes from LTTE leader Vellupillai Prabhakaran.

However, Sittampalan denies that the World Tamil Movement collects funds directly for the LTTE, or for any other organization. He told Human Rights Watch: We don't raise funds, but we canvass and advise people to help our people there [in Sri Lanka] for rehabilitation from the war and the tsunami. . . We ask them to give it to the TRO [Tamil Rehabilitation Organization] or SEDAT [Social and Economic Development Association of Tamils]. Some give to the TRO branch here, or some give bank to bank transactions. People do it individually in their own way. When asked about reports that representatives from the World Tamil Movement ask directly for money, Sittampalan responded, "I think that is not correct. We are asking them to help these people and send it [the money] themselves." He also denied that the World Tamil Movement collects money for the LTTE. "We do not say, 'Give it to the LTTE.' There are no LTTE here who are asking for money." This statement is contradicted by numerous testimonies collected by Human Rights Watch.

Extracts: Summary and Recommendations of the Human Rights Watch Study on LTTE Fund Collection by Intimidation/Extortion[7]

Ninety percent of people, even if they don't support the LTTE, are scared. The killing doesn't just happen back home in Sri Lanka. It happens even in France, Canada. Between 1983 and 2002, the armed conflict between the Sri Lankan government and the Liberation Tigers of Tamil Eelam (LTTE or Tamil Tigers) cost an estimated 60,000 or more lives, and was marked by gross human rights abuses and violations of the laws of war on both sides. The war prompted nearly one-quarter of Sri Lanka's Tamils to leave the country, many fleeing Government abuses, creating a Tamil diaspora that now numbers approximately 600,000-800,000 worldwide. As Sri Lankan Tamils established themselves in Canada, the United Kingdom (U.K.) and other Western countries, the Tamil community became a significant source of financial and political support for the LTTE in its struggle to establish an independent state, 'Tamil Eelam,' for the Tamil minority in Sri Lanka's North and East. While many members of the Tamil diaspora willingly and actively support the LTTE, others have been subject to intimidation, extortion, and physical violence as the LTTE seeks to suppress criticism of its human rights abuses and to ensure a steady flow of income...

Fundraisers for the LTTE and LTTE-linked organizations went from house to house, and approached businesses and professionals, demanding significant sums of money for their cause. In Canada, families were typically pressed for between Cdn$2,500 and Cdn$5,000, while some businesses were asked for up to Cdn$100,000. Members of the Tamil community in the U.K., France, Norway, and other European countries were asked for similar amounts...

Individuals who refused were sometimes threatened. Some were told that if they didn't pay the requested sum, they would not be able to return to Sri Lanka to visit family members. Others were warned they would be 'dealt with' or 'taught a lesson.' After refusing to pay over Cdn$20,000, one Toronto business owner said LTTE representatives made threats against his wife and children...

The LTTE identifies Tamils from the West who return to Sri Lanka to visit family members, and systematically pressures them for funds when they arrive in LTTE controlled territory in the North of Sri Lanka. The assessed 'rate' is often Cdn$1, £1, or $1 per day for the length of time they have lived in the West, so individuals who have been abroad for years may be asked for thousands, and told they may not leave until they produce the requested amount. In some cases, the LTTE may confiscate their passports until the money is paid...

Many members of the Tamil diaspora vividly remember Government abuses during the war, and willingly contribute funds to the LTTE. Other members of the Tamil community do not wish to contribute, either because of their personal economic circumstances, or because they do not believe in the LTTE's goals or methods. Some support Tamil political parties that have been decimated or marginalized by the LTTE. However, under intense pressure or outright threats, these individuals may be forced to provide financial support for LTTE operations, including its continuing pattern of child recruitment, political killings, and other human rights abuses that have continued, even during the four-year ceasefire...

The LTTE's dependence on the Tamil diaspora for financial support, and the diaspora's substantial size and influence, give the diaspora unique potential to influence the LTTE's policies and behaviour, including its human rights practices. However, that potential has been effectively neutralized by the LTTE's effective use of intimidation and extortion within the community...

Methodology of Collecting Data by Human Rights Watch

Human Rights Watch conducted research for this report from October 2005 through February 2006, conducting interviews in person and by telephone with members of the Tamil communities in Toronto, Canada; London, U.K.; Geneva, Switzerland; and Düsseldorf, Germany. The focus of the investigation was on the Tamil communities in Canada and the U.K., as together these two countries host nearly half of the global Sri Lankan Tamil diaspora. In both countries, Human Rights Watch interviewed Tamil business owners, professionals, activists, journalists, and other individuals. Most interviews were conducted in English; some were conducted with Tamil translation.

Recommendations

Take active steps to protect Tamil residents from harassment, threats, extortion and violence linked to the LTTE. Specifically

- Establish a special interagency task force, headed by the police and including other agencies as appropriate, to actively investigate intimidation and extortion in the Tamil community, and initiate prosecutions as warranted;
- Initiate a public education campaign in the Tamil community, using Tamil newspapers, radio, and other media, to publicize relevant law related to intimidation, harassment, and fundraising by the LTTE or other groups, and steps that individuals can take if they are subject to such activity;
- Establish a special hotline, staffed by Tamil speakers, to receive complaints of intimidation and extortion, and provide information as appropriate to law enforcement authorities;
- Initiate meetings with leaders in the Tamil community to discuss patterns of LTTE-related intimidation and extortion, using such meetings to communicate the government's deep concern regarding such activity, its commitment to respond, and steps that are being taken to protect members of the Tamil community;
- Take steps to inform members of the Tamil community that funds raised for the LTTE may indirectly support the commission of war crimes, including the recruitment of children as soldiers; and
- Urge the LTTE to end all use of violence, threats, intimidation, and harassment against members of the Tamil diaspora. ...

Conclusion

The LTTE's use of intimidation, harassment, extortion, and even physical violence against members of the Tamil diaspora is effectively stifling Tamil dissent regarding ongoing LTTE human rights abuses in Sri Lanka. LTTE extortion is also forcing Tamils, including those who do not support the LTTE, to provide financial support for LTTE operations, including its continuing pattern of child recruitment and political killings. Both intimidation and extortion have significantly limited the ability of Tamils in the West who do not support the LTTE's pattern of human rights abuses to effectively speak out and influence LTTE behavior. Western governments, although obliged to protect their residents and citizens from such abuses, have done too little in response to the patterns of intimidation and coercion that victimize members of the Tamil community. Governments with a significant Tamil diaspora should take stronger action to protect members of the community, ensuring their right to express themselves on issues of vital concern to their community and to

Acknowledgements (for the Human Rights Watch Study)

This report was written by Jo Becker, advocacy director of the Children's Rights Division at Human Rights Watch, based on research conducted by the author in London, U.K., and Toronto, Canada, from October 2005 through February 2006. The report was reviewed and edited by staff in Human Rights Watch's Children's Rights Division, Asia Division, Legal and Policy Department, Programme Department, and Terrorism and Counterterrorism Programme. Human Rights Watch is grateful to numerous members of the Tamil diaspora community who assisted our research and spoke with us regarding their experiences. For security reasons, their names must remain confidential."[8]

Personal Appeal to Tamil Diaspora by Prabhakaran

Shyam Tekwani, in his much quoted Prabhakaran article,[9] recalls that "in his annual Heroes Day speech, Prabhakaran, in November 2006, made his first direct appeal to the diaspora in funding the 'Final War' he had launched in July after the European Union joined a growing list of countries that had proscribed the group. Funds were drying up. 'We express our gratitude to the Tamil diaspora, our displaced brethren living all around the world, for their contribution to our struggle and ask them to maintain their unwavering participation and support.' This was in marked contrast to rebuking them for being 'quitters' and 'losers' in the late 1980s. Donations, however, have not always been voluntary (as has already been explicitly brought out).

Totalitarian Mindset

James Ross writing for the *NYT* says that the Tigers' totalitarian mind-set was also their undoing. Their use of Tamil children in military operations – including as suicide bombers – the mafia-like fund-raising tactics in Canada and Britain and their oppressive rule in the areas they controlled generated disgust among many Tamils within Sri Lanka and abroad. It also opened the door to a human rights-conscious Tamil opposition that can play a leading role in Sri Lanka's future.[10]

FBI Warning About Supporting the LTTE

"No, it's not al Qaeda or Hezbollah or even HAMAS. The group is called the Liberation Tigers of Tamil Eelam (LTTE) or the Tamil Tigers for short."[11] This is how the FBI, in October 2008, warned its clientele about the LTTE. A relevant extract follows focused on funding.

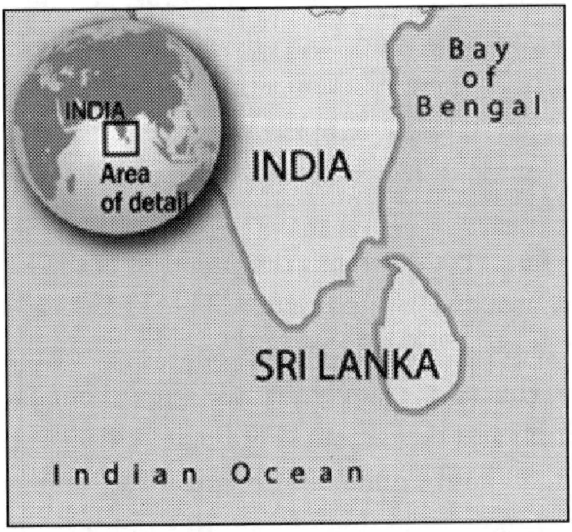

FBI Graphic on Sri Lanka's geographical location

"**Why should you care?** Certainly because of the suffering and bloodshed that the Tamil Tigers have caused. And because its ruthless tactics have inspired terrorist networks worldwide, including al Qaeda in Iraq. But also because the group has placed operatives right here in our own backyard, discreetly raising money to fund its bloody terrorist campaign overseas, including purchases of weapons and explosives. The U.S. government has designated the Tigers a foreign terrorist organization, so their activities here are illegal. And we're determined to stop them, using the full range of our investigative and intelligence capabilities.

In April, for example, we struck an important blow when our Joint Terrorism Task Force in New York arrested the alleged U.S. director of the Tigers. The man supposedly held several fundraising events at a church and various public schools in Queens and in northern New Jersey in 2004. He is also accused of arranging high-level meetings between the group's leaders and U.S. supporters. **You can help by being careful with your donations.** Like other terrorists, the Tigers have raised funds under a variety of cover organizations, often by posing as charities. A great deal of money, for example, was raised for the Tigers following the 2004 tsunami that devastated Sri Lanka and many other countries."[12]

US Treasury Department Targets the LTTE[13]

"The U.S. Department of the Treasury today targeted the support network of the Sri Lanka-based designated terrorist group Liberation Tigers of Tamil Eelam (LTTE) by designating the U.S.-based Tamil Foundation under Executive Order 13224. Executive Order 13224 targets terrorists and those providing support to terrorists or acts of terrorism. 'The LTTE, like other terrorist groups, has relied on so-called charities to raise funds and advance its violent aims,' said Adam J. Szubin, Director of the Treasury's Office of Foreign Assets Control. 'We will continue to aggressively target attempts by any terrorist group to hide behind charities, front companies, or name changes to propagate terror against innocents around the world.'

The head of the Tamil Foundation is also president of the Tamils Rehabilitation Organization (TRO) in the United States. The TRO was named a Specially Designated Global Terrorist (SDGT) under Executive Order 13224 on November 15, 2007. Over the course of many years, the Tamil Foundation and the TRO have co-mingled funds and carried out coordinated financial actions. Additional information links the Tamil Foundation to the TRO through a matching gift programme. The common leadership of the TRO and the Tamil Foundation has facilitated these activities. The TRO is a charitable organization that acts as a front to facilitate fundraising and procurement for the LTTE. Prior to its designation, Sri Lanka-based TRO operated offices in seventeen other countries worldwide, including the United States. In the U.S., TRO has raised funds for the LTTE through a network of individual representatives. According to sources within the organization, TRO is the preferred means for sending funds from the United States to the LTTE in Sri Lanka.

The LTTE is a terrorist group that seeks an independent state in northeastern Sri Lanka, where most of Sri Lanka's minority ethnic Tamil population lives. For over two decades, the LTTE has employed conventional, guerrilla, and terror tactics in a civil war that has claimed over 60,000 lives. The U.S. Department of State designated the LTTE a Foreign Terrorist Organization (FTO) on October 8, 1997. On November 2, 2001, the U.S. Department of State named the LTTE an SDGT under E.O. 13224. Under E.O. 13224, any assets the Tamil Foundation has under U.S. jurisdiction are frozen, and U.S. persons are prohibited from engaging in any transactions with the Tamil Foundation."[14]

ENDNOTES

1. "Sri Lankan Tamil Diaspora". <http://en.wikipedia.org/wiki/Sri_Lankan_Tamil_diaspora>. The details in this section have been excerpted from the above article.

2. "Tamil Diaspora". <http://en.wikipedia.org/wiki/Tamil_diaspora>.
3. Ibid.
4. Sri Lankan Tamil Diaspora". <http://en.wikipedia.org/wiki/Sri_Lankan_ Tamil_diaspora>. The details in this section have been excerpted from the above article.
5. Ibid.
6. "LTTE Intimidation and Extortion in the Tamil Diaspora. The Tamil Diaspora and Support for the LTTE". Human Rights Watch. Volume 18, No. 1(C). Canada/United Kingdom. <http://www.hrw.org/sites/default/files/reports/ltte0306webwcover.pdf>. The actual report runs into great detail and only some extracts have been used for the purposes of this chapter.
7. Ibid.
8. Ibid.
9. Tekwani, Shyam. "The Man Who Destroyed Eelam". <http://www.tehelka.com/story_main41.asp?filename=Ne230509coverstory.asp>
10. Ross, James. "Tiger by the Tail". Op-ed writer for the *New York Times*. May 20, 2009. <http://www.nytimes.com/2009/05/21/opinion/21iht-edross.html?_r=1>
11. "Taming the Tamil Tigers". Headline Archives Of The FBI. http://www.fbi.gov/page2/jan08/tamil_tigers011008.html Extracts related to LTTE funding have been quoted. The bold text is in the original article.
12. Ibid. The bold text is in the original article.
13. "Treasury Targets U.S. Front for Sri Lankan Terrorist Organization'. February 11, 2009. <http://www.ustreas.gov/press/releases/tg22.htm>. Excerpts have been used from the article.
14. Ibid.

CHAPTER 14

Human Rights Violations from the Tamil Perspective

There is, in '*Lost Victory*', deliberate 'healthy redundancy' in content, as the author terms it. This is evident from the fact that the book does not have 'stand alone' chapters which exist in their own right. The book is about war and war fighting, both of which are classic studies in complexity and inter-connectivity. Thus, any chapter of the book can be easily connected to chapters that preceded or succeeded it – and so is the case with this chapter.

Before readers get upset about the chapter's title being biased, it is reiterated that HR violations have occurred by both sides, and since antiquity at that; not just since 1915, or 1983, (depending on which date readers prefer to start their count for the modern era). One example from the article by John Burns[1] will make an immediate connect with readers.

"The war between the Government and the Tamil Tigers, with origins that go back to a savage outburst of anti-Tamil rioting that broke out in 1983, reached a cataclysmic moment in the small hours of July 19, 1996, at a remote spot in the North East of the Island in the bloodiest battle of the conflict. Desperate to regain the initiative after the loss six months earlier of their stronghold in the Jaffna Peninsula at the extreme North of the Island, the Tamil Tigers attacked a strategic base of the Government forces at Mullaithivu, a coastal outpost South East of the peninsula…

"Attacking from sea and land, waves of Tiger fighters, many of them young boys and girls barely into their teens press-ganged into suicide squads known as the Black Tigers, overran the base. By dawn, at least six hundred Tigers were dead, along with thirteen hundred Government soldiers, the highest single casualty toll in the history of the conflict. After the Tigers withdrew, a relief column of Government forces found not a single Government soldier alive...

"The wounds of many of the dead, some clutching white flags of surrender, indicated they had been shot dead or blown apart by grenades at close range; hundreds of others appeared to have been herded together, doused with gasoline, and burned to death. What occurred at Mullaithivu, it seemed, was less a battle, at least in its concluding stages, than a massacre...

"A distinguishing feature of the Sri Lankan fighting, and a cause of acute concern to international humanitarian organizations like Amnesty International and the International Committee of the Red Cross (ICRC), has been the rare occasions when the opposing forces have taken – or acknowledged having taken – prisoners. Fighters on both sides who have dared to speak candidly to human rights investigators and reporters have admitted that the rule, sometimes explicit in battle orders, more often understood, was that no enemy combatants were to be left alive...

Where prisoners have been taken, as often as not it has been to serve the ends of propaganda, not humanitarian concern, as when Government forces captured Tiger fighters as young as eleven and twelve and took them to remand homes in Colombo where foreign television crews were invited to film them as proof of the Tigers' use of children in combat. At times when they have sought respite from Government military pressures, as they did with a six-month cease-fire that they later abrogated in 1994-95, the Tigers have also held and exchanged prisoners. But overall, the Sri Lankan fighting has been a chilling demonstration of the survival of a practice going back to the earliest recorded wars – a practice that became known as 'giving no quarter' to an enemy..."[2]

The issue of HR violations has thus been a serious concern on both sides, with both unwilling to accept culpability, with rare exceptions. This book has gone over a lot of detail as to why these have occurred and, as is to be expected, a portion of this already covered ground will be reiterated in this chapter. What is new and important to note is that "the United Nations (UN) Charter of 1945 supports the view that self-determination is a legal principle, and as such the right to self-determination is placed crucially in the first article of each of the two major human rights covenants of 1966: the International Covenant on Civil and Political Rights (ICCPR) and the International Covenant on Economic, Social and Cultural Rights (ICESCR) (UN 1996)."[3] The legal recognition of this right by the UN is what the LTTE has latched on to, probably through diaspora connectivity, and this lies at the core of their planning almost since the struggle for Eelam began.

McConnell, in her comprehensive coverage of the Tamil right to self-determination, traces the historical roots of the problem back to the 5th century BC. She speaks of Jaffna, the Tamil kingdom spread over the north and east, competing historically with Kotte and Kandy, which were the two Sinhala kingdoms, spread over the south and west and how, in 1833, the British made a "unitary state,"[4] for the first time perhaps, in Sri Lankan history, calling their new possession Ceylon. The appointment of the Donoughmore and later, Soulbury Commissions did not help seal the fissures between the two communities, and, certainly, as has been brought out earlier, the sectarian policies of the founding fathers of the nation, during the final run up to Independence, did nothing to promote peace and tranquillity amongst the Tamils. Thus the colonization of Tamil areas, constitutional support to Buddhism, the citizenship laws and the Sinhala language issue helped increase the void between the two. These extended to reservation in education in favour of the Sinhala community. To add to the problem, the issue of racial superiority also came in. Anagaraka Dharmapala (1864–1933) promoted the thought that Sinhala Buddhists were racially superior to the Tamils and should vacate the Island in favour of the Sinhala. Matters came to a boil from 1983 onwards. This is also the period when the most horrendous forms of HR violations have occurred. The HR violations will now be studied from the perspective of the Tamils, and, by extension, from the perspective of HR organisations and the UN, because their analysis appears to have found some merit in the accusations made by the Tamil people, and, sometimes, on their behalf those organisations which are West Europe based.

The Tamil HR perspective is important for several reasons. Firstly, though the LTTE have decisively lost the war, the Tamils continue to be the largest minority in Sri Lanka and need rapid rehabilitation into the national mainstream. Secondly, the Sri Lanka Government, which won the conflict, now needs to be magnanimous in victory, to avoid revival of the problem as a function of continued deprivation of the Tamil minority. Thirdly, the world media, particularly Western media and the international HR community have taken serious umbrage at being sidelined by the Government in their efforts to oversee the concluding SLAF operations in order to deter HR violations. **If economic sanctions are imposed on Sri Lanka for not conforming to UN or Western expectations on HR compliance, the country will be savagely undermined and its growth will be arrested. The expectation of economic revival consequent to the victory over the LTTE has been belied thus far (end November 2009) and unless Sri Lanka cleans up its Human Rights act, expectations of western economic help are unlikely to be met.** Lastly, the nation needs peace more than it needs war. This appears to be a popular demand from within the wise counsel of the Sinhala community itself and can no longer be set aside on the grounds of military expediency. Thus, with the UN organisation and Western nations threatening to withhold financial support for the refugee camps, with sanctions looming large on their heads, the Government has to change tack, if it is to reap the full harvest from its decisive victory over the LTTE. The examples now coming up will explain how hard the country has to work to repair its international reputation as a mature and responsible democracy, which respects the international rule of law. The examples have been picked up at random and are merely illustrative of the deeper malaise that affects human rights in a war zone.

Public Display of Tamil Tigers Bodies[5]

Bodies of LTTE cadres killed in an attack on an airbase on display near Anuradhapura

... While Sri Lanka's Minister for Human Rights, Mahinda Samarasinghe, has denied allegations by a top United Nations official that torture is 'routine' in the country, there is little doubt that the renewed civil war has resulted in brutality hitting new lows. In a report on his visit to the Island in October, U.N. Special Rapporteur on torture Manfred Novak said it was 'widely practised,' and noted it was 'prone to become routine in the context of counter-terrorism operations'... Government claims and denials on the subject of torture and human rights have a hollow ring to them. For example, it first denied that the naked bodies of Tamil Tiger rebels killed in an attack on an airbase near Anuradhapura were displayed in public on Oct. 23, and then ordered an enquiry after pictures of the incident began to circulate. Novak has proposed the establishment of a field presence of the office of the U.N. High Commissioner for Human Rights with a mandate of both monitoring the human rights situation in the country, including the right of unimpeded access to all places of detention, and providing technical assistance particularly in the field of judicial, police and prison reform...

Amnesty says Sri Lanka Fails to Probe HR Abuses[6]

"The Sri Lankan Government has never seriously investigated human rights abuses allegedly committed during 25 years of civil war and needs to rapidly overhaul its justice system to bring peace to the country," Amnesty International said.

Human rights groups and diplomats accused the Government of shelling heavily populated civilian areas and said the Liberation Tigers of Tamil Eelam rebel group held thousands of civilians as human shields, shooting those who tried to flee. Both sides denied the accusations.

"If communities that have been torn apart by decades of violence and impunity are to be reconciled, the Sri Lankan Government should initiate internal reforms and seek international assistance to prevent ongoing violations and ensure real accountability for past abuses," said Sam Zarifi, Amnesty International's Asia-Pacific director.

The Government has repeatedly brushed off such calls saying it would interfere with the country's sovereignty…The Amnesty report accuses the Government of interfering with past investigations, by using bribes, threats and even murder to eliminate witnesses.

Times Online, UK, Lashes Out at UN HR Council for Ignoring Inquiry Calls[7]

"The vote by the United Nations Human Rights Council to congratulate the Sri Lanka Government on its victory over the Tamil Tigers and to ignore calls for an inquiry into possible war crimes is a disgrace.

It marks a victory for all those countries facing domestic insurgencies who fear any serious investigation into their behaviour. It gives carte blanche to armies to use whatever means available to achieve victory. And it is a terrible betrayal of the thousands of Tamil civilians who have been killed in the crossfire as the Sri Lankan Army pounded the remnants of the Tamil Tigers. The vote came after two days of heated debate in Geneva on the widespread charges that both sides committed atrocities in the final weeks of the long-running civil war on the Island...

"The European members of the 47-strong council had asked for an emergency meeting to look into what they feared were very serious abuses. But the council chose instead to debate a resolution submitted by Sri Lanka itself, which welcomed the 'liberation' of tens of thousands of the Island's citizens, condemned the defeated Tigers, made no mention of the shelling of civilians and kept silent on the desperate need to allow the Red Cross and other humanitarian groups into the camps where some 200,000 Tamil civilians have been forcibly interned...

"The vote on Sri Lanka, however, will reinforce the council's critics in the West. It was not simply that the usual suspects – China, Russia, India and Pakistan – who supported the Sri Lankan resolution, on the grounds that the conflict there was an internal matter and that the council should not intervene on the conduct of the war. A clutch of Asian and Muslim countries, also wary of outside inspection of their record, also voted not to launch an inquiry into the events in Sri Lanka..."

No Welfare for Sri Lanka's Tamils[8]

A constant stream of refugees fled the war zone in the last days of the conflict [EPA]

... "The latter stages of the war in Sri Lanka have been carefully choreographed and hidden from the outside world, with the voices of victims silenced through fear and insecurity...There are allegations of war crimes, rape and torture, summary executions and prolonged bombardments by a government which, it is believed by human rights organisations, killed thousands of its own civilian citizens. Al Jazeera has conducted its own investigation into the conflict and spoken to Tamils who have suffered and aid workers who have remained silent until now, revealing testimonies that call into question the version of events Sri Lanka's Government wants the world to believe...

After enduring months of appalling conditions in the final stages of the war between the Sri Lankan military and the Liberation Tigers of Tamil Eelam (LTTE), the suffering continues for the Tamils displaced by the fighting. One month after the government declared victory in the war, Tamils continue living in what the government calls 'welfare' camps but what critics claim are little short of the world's biggest open air prisons...

The government rejects all allegations, maintaining that it has liberated the Tamil civilians from the tyranny of the LTTE and saying the accusations are part of a propaganda campaign. "At one time it was murder. Other times it was killings. And now it has come to the extent of rape and other sexual abuses," says Rohita Bogollagama, Sri Lanka's Foreign Minister..."

Irish Congress of Trade Unions (ICTU) Supports Amnesty Call for Inquiry into War Crimes[9]

In a letter on the 29th of July (2009) to the Minister of Foreign Affairs, Micheal Martin, ICTU's General Secretary David Begg writes that he agrees with Amnesty International's call for an independent inquiry into war crimes in Sri Lanka. "The Irish Congress of Trade Unions (ICTU) hopes that the Irish Government will take initiatives on the international level, and within the European Union, for such an independent inquiry..."

'Alleged' Execution Video: Is this Evidence of 'War Crimes' in Sri Lanka?[10]

"Just three months after the Sri Lankan Government declared the country liberated from the Tamil Tigers, video footage has emerged apparently showing Government troops summarily executing Tamils. Journalists for Democracy in Sri Lanka, which obtained the material, said it was filmed in January – when the international media were prevented by the Sri Lankan Government from covering the conflict zone. The Sri Lankan High Commission denied the Government had carried out atrocities against the Tamil community. A Sri Lankan Army spokesman also called the video a 'fake...'

Video grab of 'Alleged' execution of prisoners by SLA

... Independent journalists and observers were prevented from getting anywhere near the combat. There were rumours that terrible things were happening, but this was a war without witnesses. However, one soldier we now know had a mobile phone. And eight months on, his footage of a callous execution has emerged. There is no indication of the ethnicity of the dead men, but the group which obtained the pictures claim the victims are Tamils.

Sri Lanka High Commission's Response

"The High Commission of Sri Lanka categorically denies that the Sri Lankan Armed Forces engaged in atrocities against Sri Lankan Tamil community. They were only engaged in a military offensive against the LTTE. The High Commission has noted that in many instances in the past, various media institutions used doctored videos, photographs and documents to defame the Sri Lankan Government and armed forces. Therefore, we request you to verify the authenticity of the video footage before the telecast".

Author's Note. Readers will no doubt recall that the issue of the 'alleged' execution of prisoners also came up as a function of propaganda, and was discussed at length under that heading in Chapter 12. However, since the alleged killings, if they turn out to be true, will also be a very serious breach of Human Rights, and, for that reason, this chapter has included two reports on this issue (the second one follows)

HR Violations in Sri Lanka Call for Immediate Independent Inquiry[11]

"The ('alleged' execution) video depicts disturbing and potentially incriminating footage: men dressed in what appear to be Sri Lankan military uniforms shoot two unarmed, naked, bound and blindfolded men sitting on the ground, with several other naked bodies in the background. Though the video's authenticity has yet to be independently verified, Journalists for Democracy says the video was shot in January 2009, during the Sri Lankan Army's fierce battle against the Tamil Tigers. The Sri Lankan Government has refuted that Sri Lankan troops summarily executed Tamil prisoners and claims the video was staged by Tamil supporters who wish to discredit the Sri Lankan Army...

Despite Sri Lanka's dismissal of the footage, the U.N.'s Special Rapporteur on extrajudicial, summary or arbitrary executions called for an international, independent investigation into the video's legitimacy and any possible violations of international law. The international community is right to demand an independent inquiry: any possible war crimes and human rights violations committed by either side must be immediately investigated. Extra-judicial killings as depicted in the video are considered war crimes and forbidden by the Third Geneva Convention of 1949. Both the Sri Lankan Government and the Tamil Tigers have been accused of committing human rights atrocities during the 25-year-long civil war, by the U.S. Government and international organizations alike, but an inquiry into the accusations has never been initiated."

Sri Lanka: Government Faces the Spectre of War Crimes Accusations[12]

The final phase of the war was the most brutal in Sri Lanka's modern history.

Unable to withstand the superior firepower of the Sri Lankan armed forces, the LTTE fell back deeper into its strongholds. But in their withdrawal they did an entirely unexpected thing with possibly no parallel anywhere else in the world. They took the entire civilian population with them on their retreat, and claimed that the people accompanying them did so of their own free will. This included civilians from other parts of the country who happened to be visiting their relatives in the LTTE-controlled areas at that time. A civilian population that exceeded 300,000 became hostage to the LTTE...

The dilemma to the advancing Sri Lankan military was how to get to the LTTE without harming the civilian population who were compelled to form a human shield around them. The LTTE for its part sought to provoke the Sri Lankan military to attack areas of civilian concentration by firing at them from within the civilian inhabited areas. Their hope was that the civilian casualties would bring moral and international pressure on the government to halt its military assault and give the LTTE another breather at the negotiating table...

In recent days, there has been a renewed focus on what happened in those last days of war. A part of this interest has been sparked off by the video footage of an alleged extrajudicial killing of what appears to be prisoners in the war zone by Sri Lankan military personnel. The government has strongly denied these allegations and with the backing of expert opinion has described the video footage as a fabrication. In addition, the release of displaced persons from the welfare centres back to their homes in the north and east has given the international media access to those people. Their stories have sparked fresh interest in what happened during those last days...

The government is under a great deal of pressure on the issue of human rights violations and allegations of war crimes, such as firing into civilian inhabited areas. Several months ago it was able to fend off a bid by a section of the international community led by influential Western countries to obtain a UN resolution to set up a special investigation into human rights violations in Sri Lanka. The government was able to successfully marshal the support of the majority of countries in the UN's Human Rights Council to defeat the passage of that resolution...

However, the government has not been able to stop the efforts by individual countries and blocs of countries, such as the European Union, to press on with the theme of human rights violations and possible war crimes. Some of these international efforts can have serious consequences for the well being of the entire country. The likely withdrawal of the GSP+ concession by the European Union could deal a devastating blow to the country's apparel industry in particular and to the export economy in general. This would jeopardise the livelihoods of hundreds of thousands of people...

Another source of threat to the government is the ongoing investigation by a committee appointed by the US Congress into allegations of serious human rights violations and war crimes in Sri Lanka. These investigations are only at a preliminary stage, but the report that is expected could become a launching pad for further investigations that are more detailed and specific. It is natural that government leaders would be extremely sensitive about the possibility of a US investigation into what transpired during the war. The separation of powers is so strong in the United States that those sections of the US Government that supported Sri Lanka's war effort may not be the ones to call the shots in the post-war situation...

The *Sunday Island* reported that senior Defence Ministry officials have expressed concern about my recent visit to the United States at the invitation of the US Institute of Peace, along with Dr Paikiasothy Saravanamuttu. We were invited to speak on the issue of 'Supporting Sustainable Peace and Reconciliation in Sri Lanka'. The key issues we were asked to address ourselves to were the underlying factors that led to the outbreak of war, attend to reconciliation amidst communities recovering from decades of civil war, and address post-war reconstruction, relief, and security needs. The purpose in going to the United States was this, and not to provide information on human rights violations or war crimes...

As a member of the National Peace Council, my primary mandate is to build bridges in the present and bring reconciliation in the future. It is not to break relationships and to inflict punishment for the past. From this perspective, my presentations in the United States revolved around the need for the US Government and civil society to support the positive actions of the Sri Lankan Government that were in accordance with international standards. I also made the point that, with the war ending less than four months earlier, the government was continuing to operate with a security focus, as evidenced by the security checkpoints that continue to dot the country, and pressure alone was unlikely to compel it to change...

There is indeed a way for the government to successfully cope with the looming crisis it faces. This is to step up its efforts to give justice to the Tamil people after the war. The government needs to moderate its security focus, and be more prepared to take political risks for peace and reconciliation through proposing a mutually acceptable political solution. The government's decision to facilitate the release of those displaced persons who are currently in welfare camps to their relatives outside the camps is a positive step forward that needs to be supported. A government that brings peace, justice and reconciliation to its people will be defended by its people, including those who are workers for peace, justice and reconciliation".

Analysis

This last report by Jehan Perera, a member of the Sri Lanka Government's National Peace Council, is a fit last entry for this chapter. His inputs are balanced and make it clear that human rights violations occurred on both the sides; the LTTE using civilians as a shield even as they fought the last battle. That said, the varied examples given above do indicate occasions where the State is alleged to have gone wrong in its Human Rights record. This is something that one is sure, has already invited the government's attention. It is important to note that though the battle with the LTTE has been won, the war, in a larger context, is still to be won. This will be won when, as Perera wisely suggests, the past is forgotten, bridges are built, and reconciliation is planned and executed for national good.

It does appear, therefore, that the Government of Sri Lanka has to quickly reorient itself and bring in urgent corrections before irreparable harm is done to it for openly bucking the international order.

While it is never fair or advisable to compare one set of circumstances with another, broad principles can, nevertheless be commented upon, if relevant. The conduct of the Indian Government in handling terror in J and K is, for instance, circumscribed by great restraint. The problem has run into its 20th year and is yet not resolved, though it is under control. What is important to note is that heavy weapons have not been used by the Indian Armed Forces to counter terror, for the valid fear of collateral damage involving loss of civilian lives and material damage to their property. The fact that there is consistency in exercise of restraint in conduct of war fighting is once again evident in the pronouncements of the Union Ministers of Home and Defence, who, in spite of public demands for retaliation against rapidly escalating Naxal attacks, have still not given carte blanche permission to the Indian Air Force to fire back on marauding Naxals who fire at their aircraft. The Air Force Chief has made it clear that, when permitted to retaliate, a number of checks and balances will be inbuilt into the sanction, to prevent misuse.

A parting input, as an ex soldier, is that no one, but no one; certainly none of these HR organisations, HR NGO's have ever spoken about the Human Rights of the uniformed soldier. **Few grieve for him when he sacrifices his life for the country, other than his uniformed brethren. His dependents, in general, receive**

paltry compensation for losing him (often, he is the sole bread earner of the family, besides being a husband/son/brother/father to his children if married). Post the funeral/cremation/burial and the rush of eulogies, he is quickly forgotten and his dependents ignored and more often than not, left to fend for themselves.

Ironically, a lot of tears are shed for the human rights of those who rise against the state and all kinds of protection, legal and physical is negotiated for them. The wife, the father, the mother, who lost their son, while wearing the colours of the nation remain out of sight, out of mind, their human rights never ever being aired by all those whose hearts bleed for fair play and rule compliance...

This horrifying mindset is almost universal in its application and needs to come to the attention of all those who profess to stand for the strict application of human rights in the war zone.

ENDNOTES

1. Burns, John. "Giving No Quarter". < http:// www.crimesofwar.org/thebook/quarter-giving-no.html.> Only excerpts have been quoted.
2. Ibid.
3. McConnell, Deirdre. "The Tamil People's Right to Self-Determination". Tamil Centre for Human Rights. *Cambridge Review of International Affairs.* Volume 21, Number 1, March 2008. <http://dx.doi.org/10.1080/09557570701828592>
4. Ibid.
5. "Rights – Sri Lanka: Civil War Brutality Hits New Lows". IPS Correspondents. <http://ipsnews.net/news.asp?idnews=39879> Extracts have been used from the above report.
6. "Amnesty says Sri Lanka Fails to Probe Abuses". <http://blog.taragana.com/n/amnesty-accuses-sri-lanka-of-failing-to-properly-investigate-human-rights-abuses-78201/> Excerpts from the report have been used.
7. Binyon, Michael. "A Disgraceful Vote Which Discredits the UN Human Rights Council. Internally Displaced Sri Lankans: The UNHCR Decided Not to Press for An Inquiry". May 28, 2009. <http://www.timesonline.co.uk/tol/news/world/asia/article6382331.ece> Excerpts from the Report have been used.
8. Birtley, Tony. Al Jazeera Asia Correspondent. "No Welfare for Sri Lanka's Tamils". <http://english.aljazeera.net/news/asia/2009/06/200961962329963252.html> Excerpts from the report have been used.
9. "David Begg on Sri Lanka: Support Amnesty International's Call for an Independent Inquiry into War Crimes. It is time for the International community to act". July 31, 2009. <http://www.ictu.ie/globalsolidarity/newsevents/news/2009/07/31/david-begg-on-sri-lanka-support-amnesty-Internationals-call-for-an-independent-inquiry-into-war-crimes/> Excerpts have been used from the report.
10. Miller, Jonathan. "Execution Video: Is this Evidence of 'War Crimes' in Sri Lanka?" August 25, 2009. <http://www.channel4.com/news/articles/world/asia_pacific/execution+video+is+this+evidence+of+war+crimes+in+sri+lanka/3321087 > Excerpts have been used from the report.

11. "Human Rights Violations in Sri Lanka Require an Immediate Independent Inquiry". September 4, 2009. <http://www.standnow.org/blog/human-rights-violations-sri-lanka-require-immediate-independent-inquiry > Excerpts have been used in the report.
12. Perera, Jehan. "Sri Lanka: Government Faces the Spectre of War Crimes Accusations". September 16, 2009. <http://rspas.anu.edu.au/blogs/Southasiamasala/2009/09/16/sri-lanka-Government-faces-the-spectre-of-war-crimes-accusations/ > Excerpts have been used in the report.

References

1. Amnesty International (1996) 'Sri Lanka: wavering commitment to human rights', ASA 37/08/96, August.
2. Amnesty International (1997a) 'Sri Lanka: highest number of "disappearances" reported since 1990', News Service 62/79, ASA 37/10/97, 11 April.
3. Amnesty International (1997b) 'UA 147/97 extrajudicial execution/rape', ASA 37/13/97, 21 May.
4. Amnesty International (1997c) 'Further information on UA 147/87 (ASA 37/13/97, 21 May 1997) – extrajudicial execution/rape and new concern: fear for safety', ASA 37/14/97, 13 June.
5. Amnesty International (1997d) 'Sri Lanka: Government's response to widespread "disappearances" in Jaffna', ASA 37/024/1997, 27 November.
6. Balasingham, Adele A (1993) Women fighters of Liberation Tigers (Jaffna, Sri Lanka: Thasan).
7. McDermott, Niall (1983) The Review of the International Commission of Jurists, International Commission of Jurists (Geneva), December.
8. Manogaran, Chelvadurai (1997) 'Sinhalese–Tamil relations and the politics of space', Symposium on the Plight of the Tamil Nation, London, 29 June.
9. Tamil, Nation (1995) 'Salient facts of the history of the Tamils and of the Sinhalese', *Thinakaran Daily*, 9 November.
10. Vittachi, Tarzie (1958) Emergency '58: the story of the Ceylon race riots (London: Andre Deutsch).

PART IV

The Indian Intervention

CHAPTER 15

The Indian Intervention in the Sri Lankan Civil War

Part 4 of the book deals with the Indian intervention in Sri Lanka (1987-90) followed by the assassination of Rajiv Gandhi in 1991. Knowledge of both events is commonly available as both have been well documented. The need to revisit the events is because of the manner in which they are linked to the LTTE and its leader, Prabhakaran, whose study is central to this book. To the extent possible, it is intended to present a summary of events that occurred; take a macro view of events rather than get into specific operations. A couple of landmark incidents will, however, be touched upon in some detail, because of the way in which they shaped the intervention, as well as for their overall impact. It is also intended to record the lessons that were learnt, as well as the perceptions and afterthoughts of the key players in the intervention, both diplomatic and military.

The Indian intervention in the Sri Lankan Civil War[1] (1987-90) was the deployment of the Indian military contingent, the Indian Peace Keeping Force (IPKF), which was intended to perform a peacekeeping operation in Sri Lanka. It was formed under the mandate of the Indo-Sri Lankan Accord signed between India and Sri Lanka in 1987 that aimed to end the Sri Lankan Civil War between the militant LTTE and the Sri Lankan military. The force was, initially, not expected to be involved in any significant combat by the Indian High Command. However, within a few months, the IPKF became embroiled in battle with the LTTE to enforce peace. In the two years it was in Northern Sri Lanka, the IPKF launched a number of combat operations aimed at destroying the LTTE-led insurgency and caused severe losses to them. The IPKF began withdrawing from Sri Lanka in 1989, following the election of the Vishwanath Pratap Singh Government in India and on the request of the newly-elected Sri Lankan

President Ranasinghe Premadasa. The last IPKF contingents left Sri Lanka in March 1990.

The officers of the IPKF comprising all three Services bid 'Adieu'; End another chapter in Sri Lankan History

Indian Involvement and Intervention[2]

India had, initially, under Indira Gandhi and later under Rajiv Gandhi, begun to sympathize with the Tamil insurrection in Sri Lanka due to the strong support for the Tamil cause within the Indian state of Tamil Nadu. However, this emboldened the domestic support within Tamil Nadu to include providing sanctuary to the separatists, as well as help them smuggle arms and ammunition through which the LTTE emerged as the strongest force on the island. In fact in 1982, the LTTE supremo Prabhakaran was arrested by the police in Tamil Nadu, for a shoot-out with his rival Uma Maheswaran, in the middle of the city. Both of them were arrested and later released by the police. This activity was left unchecked as India's regional and domestic interests wanted to limit foreign intervention on what was deemed as a racial issue between the Tamils and the Sinhalese. To this end, the Indira Gandhi Government sought to make it clear to Sri Lankan President Junius Richard Jayewardene that armed intervention in support of the Tamil movement was an option India would consider if diplomatic solutions should fail.

The first round of civil violence flared in 1983 when the killing of 13 soldiers of the Sri Lanka Army sparked anti-Tamil pogroms – the Black July riots – in which over 3,000 Tamils were killed. The riots only aided in the deterioration of the ethnic relations. Militant factions, including the LTTE, at this time recruited in large numbers and continued building on popular Tamil dissent and stepped up the guerrilla war. By May 1985, the guerrillas were strong enough to launch an attack on Anuradhapura, attacking the Bodhi Tree shrine – a sacred site for Buddhist Sinhalese – followed by a rampage through the town. At least 150 civilians died in the hour-long attack.

Rajiv Gandhi's Government attempted to re-establish friendly relations with the various factions in Sri Lanka while maintaining diplomatic efforts to find a solution to the conflict as well as limiting overt aid to the Tamil fighters.

The Sri Lankan Government, deducing a decline in support for the Tamil rebels from India, tried to re-arm itself extensively for its anti-insurgent role with support from Pakistan, Israel, Singapore, and South Africa. In 1986, the campaign against the insurgency was stepped up. In 1987, retaliating against an increasingly bloody insurgent movement, the Vadamarachchi Operation (Operation Liberation) was launched against LTTE strongholds in Jaffna Peninsula. The operation involved nearly 4,000 troops, supported by helicopter gun ships as well as ground-attack aircraft. In June 1987, the Sri Lankan Army laid siege to the town of Jaffna. This resulted in large-scale civilian casualties and created a condition of humanitarian crisis. India, which had a substantial Tamil population in South India, faced the prospect of a Tamil backlash at home, called on the Sri Lankan Government to halt the offensive in an attempt to negotiate a political settlement. However, the Indian efforts were unheeded. Added to this, in the growing involvement of Pakistani advisers, it was necessary for Indian interest to mount a show of force. Failing to negotiate an end to the crisis with Sri Lanka, India announced on 2nd June 1987 that it would send a convoy of unarmed ships to Northern Sri Lanka to provide humanitarian assistance but this was intercepted by the Sri Lankan Navy and they were forced to turn back.

Following the failure of the naval mission the decision was made by the Indian Government to mount an airdrop of relief supplies in aid of the beleaguered civilians over the besieged city of Jaffna. On 4th June 1987, in a bid to provide relief, the Indian Air Force mounted Operation Poomalai. Five Antonov AN-32s under fighter cover flew over Jaffna to airdrop 25 tons of supplies, all the time keeping well within the range of Sri Lankan radar coverage. At the same time the Sri Lankan Ambassador to New Delhi, Bernard Tilakaratna, was summoned to the Foreign Office to be informed by the Minister of State, External Affairs, K. Natwar Singh, of the ongoing operation and also indicated that the operation was expected not to be hindered by the Sri Lankan Air Force. The ultimate aim of the operation was both to demonstrate the seriousness of the domestic Tamil concern for the civilian Tamil population and reaffirm the Indian option of active intervention to the Sri Lankan Government.

The Indo-Sri Lanka Accord

Following Operation Poomalai, faced with the possibility of an active Indian intervention and lacking any possible ally, the President, J. R. Jayewardene, offered to hold talks with the Rajiv Gandhi Government on future moves. The siege of Jaffna was soon lifted, followed by a round of negotiations that led to the signing of the Indo-Sri Lankan Accord on July 29, 1987, that brought a temporary truce. Crucially however, the negotiations did not include the LTTE as a party to the talks.

The signing of the Indo-Sri Lankan Accord on 29 July 1987 brought a temporary truce to the Sri Lankan Civil War. Under the terms of the Agreement, Colombo agreed to devolution of power to the provinces. The Sri Lankan troops were withdrawn to their barracks in the North, and the Tamil rebels were to disarm.

The Indian Intervention

The LTTE had enjoyed support from India till the IPKF started getting inducted. However, not having been party to the negotiations leading up to the accord, it agreed to the truce only reluctantly. The Tigers had rejected the Provincial Council framework as inadequate and Prabhakaran had protested against the Indian military intervention. The Tigers resisted the spread of what was deemed India's self-serving aim of binding Sri Lanka into India's geo-political sphere of influence, as well as sympathy for Sri Lanka's ruling Sinhala community in India, outside the support-base in Tamil Nadu. With the induction of the Indian troops, the Tigers initially complied by surrendering arms along the terms of the truce. However, the opposition to the induction of Indian troops soon flared into active confrontation. Along with this, there developed an increasingly brutal confrontation within Tamil factions, with allegations that the LTTE, predominantly a Northern Tamil powerbase, was attempting to destroy both the PLOTE and the EPRLF, which represented more of the Eastern provinces. The LTTE boycotted the elections that were held in October and November 1988 along the lines outlined in the Accord. The Indian administration had not expected opposition from the Tigers and was initially taken unawares. The support for Tamil nationalism in India also raised a spectre for the Indian Government of a possible situation of a Tamil secessionist movement in Tamil Nadu However, faced with growing diligence from her erstwhile partner, India adopted a strategy of aiding alternative Tamil power bases, including the Eelam People's Revolutionary Liberation Front (EPRLF), which ultimately emerged strong in the November 1988 elections, and, at the same time continue negotiations with the LTTE.

The Mandate for the IPKF[3]

Among the provisions undersigned by the Indo-Sri Lanka Accord was the commitment of Indian military assistance, should this be requested for by the Sri Lankan Government, as well as the provision of an Indian Peace Keeping Force that would "guarantee and enforce the cessation of hostilities". It was on these grounds, and on the request of President J. R. Jayewardene, that Indian troops were inducted to Northern Sri Lanka. J. N. Dixit, the then Indian ambassador to Colombo, in an interview to rediff.com in 2000 described that ostensibly, Jayewardene's decision to request Indian assistance, came in the face of increasing civil riots and violence within the Southern Sinhala majority areas, including the capital Colombo that were initiated by the Janatha Vimukthi Peramuna (JVP) and the Sri Lanka Freedom Party that necessitated the withdrawal of the Sri Lankan Army from the Tamil areas of Northern Sri Lanka to maintain order. It may be noted that the Sinhalese nationalists, led by the JVP, did not, however, take kindly to foreign presence on their soil.

IPKF First Day Cover Released by the Government of India

The Indian Peace Keeping Force[4]

Originally, a reinforced division with small naval and air elements, the IPKF at its peak deployed four divisions with one mountain (4) and three infantry divisions (36, 54, and 57) as well as supporting arms and services. At the peak of its operational deployment, IPKF operations also included a large Indian paramilitary force and Indian special forces elements. Indeed, Sri Lanka was also the first theatre of active operations for Indian Navy commandos. The main deployment of the IPKF was in Northern and Eastern Sri Lanka. Upon its withdrawal from Sri Lanka, the IPKF was renamed 21 Corps and was headquartered at Bhopal and became the nucleus of a strike corps for the Indian Army.

IPKF Order of Battle

Indian Army

By end 1987, the IPKF consisted of:

54 Infantry Division. (Jaffna)

10 Para Commando (Jaffna) – attached unit

65 Armoured Regiment (originally with T-54 tanks and later with T-72s), – an attached unit.
91 Infantry Brigade (Jaffna)
5 MADRAS
8 MAHAR
1 MARATHA LI
76 Infantry Brigade (Mullaithivu)
47 Infantry Brigade (Trincomalee-Batticaloa-Amparai)
36 Infantry Division.
115 Infantry Brigade (Jaffna)
5/1 GR (Battle of Urumparai, Battle of Nallur Temple Jaffna, Battle of Manipai)
72 Infantry Brigade (Jaffna)
4 /5 GR
13 SIKH LI
41 Infantry Brigade. (Jaffna)
5 RAJ RIF
57 Infantry Division
4 Mountain Division
Independent Units
340 Independent Infantry Brigade (Amphibious). (Trincomalee)
18 Infantry Brigade. (Jaffna)
5 PARA.

The Indian Marine Commandos (MARCOS*)

Indian Air Force

Soon after its intervention in Sri Lanka and especially after the confrontation with the LTTE, the IPKF received a substantial commitment from the Indian Air Force (IAF), mainly transport and helicopter squadrons, including:

*MARCOS (also the Marine Commando Force or MCF) – took part in Operation Pawan in 1988 and in the raid on an LTTE base at Guru Nagar. MARCOS operators (including Lt. Singh) boarded two Gemini rafts off the coast of Jaffna City and towed two wooden rafts of explosives into a channel leading to the city's Guru Nagar Jetty. Avoiding mines, eight men and two officers shifted to the wooden rafts and paddled to the jetty then fixed demolition charges to the jetty and LTTE speedboats. The commandos were detected but laid down suppressive fire and detonated the explosives before retreating to the Geminis without taking casualties. Two nights later, commandos swam back into the harbour amidst heavy patrolling by the LTTE to destroy the remaining speedboats. They were again detected and sustained minor injuries. These actions helped recapture Trincomalee and Jaffna harbours from the LTTE. For leading these actions the 30-year-old Lt. Singh became the youngest officer to receive the Maha Vir Chakra Award.

– Antonov AN-32s
No 109 and No. 119 Helicopter Units – Mil Mi-8 helicopters
No. 125 HU – Mil Mi-24s
No. 664 AOP Squadron Chetak and Cheetah

Indian Navy

The Indian Navy regularly rotated naval vessels through Sri Lanka waters, mostly smaller vessels such as patrol boats.

Indian Naval Air Arm

No. 321 Squadron of the Indian Navy – HAL Chetak
No. 310 Squadron of the Indian Navy – Breguet Alizé

Indian Paramilitary Forces

Central Reserve Police Force
Indian Coast Guard

Conflict with the LTTE[5]

Two incidents that occurred in September-October 1987 marked the turning point of Indo-LTTE relationship. The first of these was the hunger strike and subsequent death of Lt. Col. Thileepan, a popular political wing leader of the LTTE, on 26th September, 1987. Thileepan had begun his fast in protest against what was termed the failure of the Indian forces to satisfy the political demands of the Tamils, and his death was mourned throughout the Tamil community and fuelled a growing dissatisfaction and impatience with the pace of promised reforms. In addition, it was a huge propaganda victory for the LTTE, which started taking an increasingly hard line in the negotiations for the Interim Provincial Council. The talks broke down.

However, on 4th October, 1987, the Sri Lankan Navy captured an LTTE boat off Point Pedro with Tigers, including some high-profile leaders of the movement, on board. The Colombo Government alleged the boat was involved in smuggling arms across the Palk Strait and refused immunity to the captured Tiger rebels. The LTTE claimed that the rebels' movements were in accordance with the truce, being in the process of transferring documents for shifting the Tigers headquarters from Madras to Jaffna. The Sinhalese Government intended to bring a number of the rebels captured, including Pulendran, Kumarappa and others, to trial in Colombo for allegedly masterminding the massacre of 150 civilians. The Tigers, who were at the time, still involved in negotiations with the Indian authorities, appealed for enforcement of protection by the IPKF. The rebels were, at this time, in IPKF custody at Palaly Airbase, pending transfer to Sinhalese authorities. Although the Indian authorities insist that they had explained the possible repercussions of such an action on the fragile truce and exerted considerable pressure on the Sinhalese authorities to desist from proceeding, ultimately the IPKF withdrew, allowing the Sri Lankan forces to proceed with transferring the captured rebels to Colombo. The detainees however, attempted mass suicide by swallowing cyanide – a common LTTE practice when faced with imminent capture. This singular event marked a total break-down of the truce. The night of 5 October saw large-scale slaughter of Sinhalese people who had returned to Jaffna, including eight soldiers of the Sri Lankan Army who were being held hostage by the LTTE. These coincided with armed confrontations between the Tiger cadres and the Indian troops in and around Jaffna. On 8 October, the LTTE carried out a number of mortar attacks and ambushes on the IPKF.

In the face of this deteriorating situation, President Jayawardene threatened the visiting Indian Defence Minister and the Chief of Army Staff (COAS) and told them that he would re-induct the Sri Lankan Army (SLA) to protect Sinhala interests if the IPKF did not take action against the LTTE. The Indian Government, already accused of inaction in the face of a failing accord, was forced into a position of having to enforce peace in Jaffna by force. By 7 October, the COAS had issued directives to the IPKF, laying down its operational parameters as follows:

Revised Mandate for IPKF[6]

- Seize/destroy the LTTE radio/TV transmission equipment in the Jaffna Peninsula;
- Seize or jam LTTE communication network;
- Carry out raids on LTTE camps, caches and strong points;
- Personnel manning LTTE offices in the East be detained and interrogated to gain information. In case of resistance, force to be used; and
- Actions to further consolidate hold of IPKF in the region.

It was declared on 9th October that the IPKF was to launch a final campaign against the LTTE. This was the point of no return.

Operation Pawan

The first major IPKF operation was launched on 9th October 1987. Codenamed Operation Pawan (Hindi: Wind), it was expected to neutralize the LTTE operational capability in and around Jaffna. This included the capture or neutralization of the LTTE's chain of command which was expected to leave the rebel movement directionless in the face of the impending assault on the LTTE strongholds by the IPKF. On the nights of October 9 and October 10, the IPKF raided and captured the LTTE radio station at Tavadi and TV station at Kokkuvil, while the printing presses of two LTTE sponsored newspapers were destroyed. These operations also led to the capture of nearly 200 Tiger rebels. The tigers retaliated by attacking an IPKF post (5 MADRAS) at Tellipallai with automatic and mortar fire. Later that day, the Tigers hijacked a 10 Para Commando jeep on patrol, killing all five occupants. On October 10, Indian 91 Infantry Brigade, consisting of three battalions and led by its Commander, Brigadier J. Ralli, began its push into the city of Jaffna.

The Jaffna University Helidrop[7]

The first battle signalling the real beginning of Operation Pawan was the heliborne assault on Jaffna University Headquarters of the LTTE by a detachment of 10 Para Commandos and 13 SIKH LI on the night of 12th October, 1987. Jaffna University was the tactical headquarters of the LTTE. 'Hard' intelligence was made available to the IPKF, regarding an apex LTTE meeting on the campus, involving Prabhakaran on October 12. A Special Helicopter Borne Operation (SHBO) was therefore planned, using all of the four MI-8 helicopters then available in Sri Lanka. These, till then, were being used for administration, logistics, casualty evacuation and reconnaissance duties, and were flown by pilots assembled from different flying units. The mission was briefed personally by GOC, 54 Infantry Division, Maj Gen Harkirat Singh, and his Colonel GS, who was the senior staff officer for operations. The basic induction plan was radically changed when the pilots (readers may note that out of the eight pilots needed to fly the four helicopters, only two were available, because of urgent IPKF induction related sorties) proceeded for a day reconnaissance of the landing area on the morning of 11th October. The landing sequence was changed (after the recce showed that the space available was constricted) from the planned four to two helicopters at a time. Takeoff was fixed at 0100 hours, October 12, under good moonlight conditions. The army assessed that the landing would be essentially unopposed. The helicopters were therefore stripped of their armaments as well as additional fuel tanks, in order to accommodate more troops. An available Sri Lankan helicopter was planned to be used as a diversionary tactic, during the 90 minutes that this operation was planned.

The plan was to land a company (team) of 120 men from 10 Para Commando to secure the university football field. A second wave was to follow with a company of 13 SIKH LI for taking over the protection of the landing ground from the

Para Commandos. The heliborne troops were to link up with 4/5 GURKHA Battalion of 72 Brigade and the balance SIKH LI troops advancing on the ground.

The landing was led by Maj. Sheonan Singh of 10 PARA; a tall, well built, brilliant officer with an excellent track record and pedigree (he is the nephew of Shaheed Bhagat Singh). The gutsy pilots managed to land with all lights switched off. The LTTE was not completely taken by surprise. They had possibly picked up the information of the attack by intercepting the Indian radio traffic, and thus, instead of being surprised, appeared well deployed to cope with it. The following drop was, however, aborted due to the pilots getting disoriented. The second successful drop followed, but during it, a Para Commando was hit but courageously insisted on taking part in the operation. Both the aircraft were also hit but successfully made it to their base. The third shift was preceded by great and totally unwarranted confusion and delay. The pilots of the aborted second strike were redistributed, one each to the first mission pilots. In addition, the SIKH LI also took time as they were neither trained for SHBO operations, nor had received advance notice for operations. To carry their ponderous ammunition boxes, the stick size had to be reduced from 20 to 15 per aircraft. They were led by Maj. Birender Singh, a relative of Natwar Singh, the then Union Minister of External Affairs. The overall delay was an excruciating half an hour. The drop was, however, successful, with the 10 PARA team now at 90, and SIKH LI with 15 soldiers on the ground, even though the aircraft were hit. The last landing was also severely opposed but the troops landed, with the 13 SIKH soldiers having a serious problem with their ammunition off loading under intense ground fire.

With two aircraft riddled with hits and no longer flyworthy, the balance four flights were called off. Thus only 120 paratroopers and 30 SIKH LI soldiers were finally landed. The troops in contact were under heavy fire. With the radio operator of the 13 SIKH LI platoon shot dead at the commencement contact with the Division HQ broke down. The underlying tragedy was that the SIKH LI company commander did not know that no more troops were coming in. No one shared this information with him.

The GOC told Maj. Sheonan, on being asked on radio by him for orders, to carry on with his mission. This meant that the SIKH LI were left to fend for themselves, with no accretion in forces coming in, and the PARAS rushing towards their objective. Confusion took over as the correct messages were not relayed, or inter unit coordination done. That night, SIKH LI the company commander was killed and so was his platoon commander. By mid day, the last three soldiers had run out of ammunition, had fixed bayonets and had charged the Tigers in desperation. Only Sepoy Gora Singh lived. He was injured and taken prisoner.

The PARAS, in the meanwhile, had fought all night, but did not get the LTTE leadership. They held their nerve, though, took cover, and, asked for extraction. The next morning, the GOC himself came in a Chetak helicopter and flew over the area but was shot at, the bullet narrowly missing both the pilot and General.

The operation thus ended in disaster, being doomed to failure as the LTTE, having intercepted IPKF radio transmissions, set up an ambush. In a battle that lasted through the night, 29 of the Sikh LI platoon of thirty troops and 6 of the 120 Commandos were killed, before detachments of the 65 Armoured Regiment were able to extract the PARAS from their defensive positions. The lone survivor of the Sikh LI detachment, Sepoy Gora Singh, was taken prisoner and it was not until his release, later during the conflict, that the fate of the SIKH LI platoon and its gallant men was known.

Analysis

The primary mistakes made, were that, although the operation was risky and carried the promise of success, however remote, the risks had not been balanced by adequate planning and execution arrangements, or contingencies thought of and war gamed. Signal security also appears to have been compromised. The appreciation of LTTE capability and intent was obviously flawed. The plan itself was made on wrong presumptions of induction capability. The manner of reconnaissance was wrong as was pilot familiarization with the area. The choice of the unit that had to take on SHBO was appalling. A unit that was still en route from a peace station was inducted into fierce battle without training or awareness of SHBO techniques. It is also clear that there was no familiarization between the Base protection force and the Para commandos, nor were operational contingencies tied up between them for coming to the others' aid, for redundancy in communications, or for locally deciding when and in what manner were operations to be limited or called off.

The induction was messed up, with only 50 percent of the intended force strength landing. Lack of communication about the balance induction not taking place meant that the operation had become far riskier than before, with the SIKH LI detachment being quite out of its depth, except in cold courage. The decision to still go ahead by the GOC was a bold one, but one in which the revised calculation of risk is a moot point whose merits will always be up for discussion.

The coordination by senior staff at the higher Army and Air Force levels also comes up as an area of introspection. The Division Commander's claim that he had assurances of adequate airlift from the chain of command have been denied, but do not, in any case shift the responsibility from his shoulders for having given the go ahead; not just for the initial operation, but also when Maj. Sheonan Singh asked him for fresh orders, since only part landing had taken place, the enemy had surrounded the inducted force and no more induction was possible. Finally, it was a 'command decision'; one that would have been lauded had it succeeded, but one, that, in failure, has to cope with savage criticism. This is the perpetual dilemma senior officers face and which is part of the sting that the holding of high military office always carries as a subtext. What is encouraging to learn are the words of the OFC, Lt. Gen. Depinder Singh, who supports the decision for what it might have achieved, had things fallen into place.

The subsequent apportioning of blame between the two Services and the examination of the allegations that the SIKH LI detachment was landed away from the actual approved site, were investigated by an Inter Services Staff Court of Inquiry and correctly set aside as incorrect. Most of the key participants were subsequently honoured for their courage by issue of high awards under adverse circumstances. Gallantry awards were given to the two company commanders, all the pilots and co-pilots, some of the deceased and some brave hearts from the PARAS who lived through the debacle.

Battle for Jaffna

As the battle for Jaffna progressed, the IPKF advance came under intense and vicious opposition from the Tigers. Fighting in built-up and an as-yet unevacuated Jaffna, the Indian high command insists that the slow advance was, in addition to Tiger resistance, more a result of reluctance on the part of the IPKF to use heavy weaponry to clear LTTE defences. Furthermore all the approach roads had been armed with Claymore mines or explosives by the Tigers in its years of fighting with the Sri Lankan Army. The Tigers also made extensive use of IED's, which could be remotely detonated from over a kilometre away. During this time, the Indian Navy, supported by the Coast Guards, was a key agency in establishing a 300-mile long blockade around Northern Sri Lanka from October 1987 to disrupt the Tigers' supply and communications routes. In addition, it was around this time that MARCOS Commandos of the Navy first went into action. Detachments of the IMSF (Indian Marine Special Forces, as the MARCOS was then known), along with a battalion of 340 Independent Brigade of the Indian Army, provided beach reconnaissance around Jaffna and Batticaloa. 340 Infantry Brigade was one of the first IPKF units to be deployed, and served until operations in the Trincomalee area were complete. The IMSF, at this time, also provided security patrols along the coastal road west of Jaffna until the 41st Brigade took charge later in November.

On October 15/16, the IPKF stopped its advance to stabilize the front. In addition, Palaly, the major operations headquarters for 54 Infantry Division, was secured from Tiger attacks. At this time, the Indian Air Force undertook a massive airlift to reinforce the 91 Infantry Brigade with three brigades and heavy equipment including T-72 Tanks and BMP-1 fighting vehicles. By the end of October 1987, the IAF had flown 2,200 tactical transport and 800 helicopter sorties.

Now reinforced, the IPKF resumed the battle for Jaffna town. The tanks and armoured fighting vehicles are said to have been an effective protection against the anti-personnel mines. However, even with this protection, the IPKF advance was torturous in the face of the Tigers' sniper fire. The rebel snipers would take positions along rooftops of buildings, treetops and even coconut palms. Equipped with powerful telescopic infra-red sights, the Tiger snipers were able to selectively take out officers and radiomen, taking a heavy toll and bringing the advance to a grinding halt. In addition, helicopters flying below 2,000 feet also remained vulnerable, with at least five shot at and damaged before the Mi-25s took up their offensive role. The IPKF adapted quickly, with its officers taking off pips of their ranks, wearing slouch hats and carrying oversize back packs. However, as advances got bogged down, the battalions, instead of manoeuvring around the defenders, were forced to commit more troops under orders from New Delhi. In addition, the LTTE increasingly started the use of anti-tank mines, taking a further heavy toll on IPKF casualties. A frustrated IPKF cut off power to Jaffna to counter these. In addition, the IPKF communications lines were extensively mined by the LTTE, which further compounded the sometimes perilous situations that the Indian troops faced. It was not before the IMSF commandos broke out of the besieged Jaffna port and cleared the heavily mined Navanturai Coastal Road, that a crucial link up between 1 Maratha Light Infantry in Jaffna fort and the advancing troops of 41 Brigade could be established that secured the Nallur area. On 21 October 1987, the commandos conducted a successful amphibious raid against a LTTE base at Guru Nagar. It was also toward the end of the Jaffna campaign that the IPKF started the use of Mi-25s for close air support when they flew against LTTE positions in Chavakacheri village on October 23, 1987.

Ultimately however, after two weeks of bitter fighting, the IPKF had wrested control of Jaffna and other major cities from the LTTE, but operations were to continue well into November, with major operations coming to an end with the fall of Jaffna Fort on the 28th of November. Through the duration of Operation Pawan, the casualties suffered by the IPKF have been put at varying figures between 600 and 1,200. In addition to the LTTE's defensive tactics alluded to above, the IPKF's problems were compounded by the fact that the Tigers, using classical guerrilla strategy, blended with the local population. In addition, the IPKF came face to face with the child soldiers of the LTTE, something it had not expected.

By the time Jaffna fell, however, the LTTE had merely exfiltrated out of the town, moving south to the jungles of Vavuniya. Its hard core fighters moved to the safety of the jungles by skirting the coast of Jaffna from Point Pedro to Elephant Pass, sheltered by the impenetrable jungles and criss-cross waterways of the Nittkaikulam jungles.

This was however only the first of the IPKF's three year campaign to neutralise the LTTE. The IPKF at this point still consisted mostly of an overstretched 54 Infantry Division. Following the Jaffna Operation, the 36 Infantry Division was inducted, along with two additional brigades, to take over the Vavuniya sector and the Trincomalee-Batticaloa axis. This relieved 54 Infantry Division, which could now focus on consolidating the Jaffna sector. 4 Mountain Division and the 57 Infantry Division were inducted still later in February 1988, to take charge of Wanni and Batticaloa from 36 Infantry Division.

Within Jaffna Sector, although the LTTE had shifted out of the town itself, it nevertheless harassed the 54 Infantry Division's efforts to consolidate its positions, by using IED's and anti-personnel mines. In turn, however, the IPKF was able to disrupt the LTTE's activities with regular raids that led to the capture of large caches of rebel weaponry. Small, highly mobile units became the staple of the 54 infantry Division operations.

Operations Viraat and Trishul

The major force of the Tigers' fighting capacity had retreated to the jungles of Vavuniya following Operation Pawan. By December 1987, the LTTE was able to build up a network of a large number of camps in the jungles that allowed it to regain a position of power within the local population, instituting taxes and revenues. The Vavuniya sector was strategically and geographically the key to accessing the North-South as well as East-West communication routes.

The LTTE was able to withstand the IPKF operations here as well, owing to natural cover from the dense jungles, an intimate knowledge of the terrain, and a low density of population which also probably held sympathy for the Tigers. The Vavuniya sector remained the most active sector throughout the IPKF's deployment and its casualties in this area were the highest after those suffered during the operations in Jaffna. The LTTE also managed to carry out a large number of successful ambushes against the IPKF patrols in the dense jungles.

By summer the following year, the Indian High Command had evolved its doctrine from holding key strong points to conducting extensive search and destroy missions against LTTE strongholds and bases, denying them ground. In April 1988, the IPKF initiated two near simultaneous operations through the jungles of Northern Sri Lanka. These, codenamed Operation Viraat and Operation Trishul, were launched in the provinces of Mannar to Mullaithivu and Elephant Pass to Vavuniya and utilized approximately 15,000 troops of the IPKF, including Armoured, Para, as well as Infantry troops and Army aviation. These achieved some success in disrupting LTTE operations, seizing weaponry and inflicting casualties among the LTTE cadres. During Operation Viraat, the IPKF uncovered well prepared LTTE defences, including concrete bunkers with electric generators, as well as caches of arms and reserves. The IPKF also suffered in this unconventional warfare, with the LTTE frequently ambushing IPKF convoys and patrols. By the end of summer 1988, however, the Tigers were forced to move to another stronghold, when it started to operate out of Nithikaikulam and adjacent riverine areas.

Withdrawal from Sri Lanka by IPKF

Ranasinghe Premadasa was elected President on 2 January 1989 and, in April 1989, demanded the IPKF withdraw within three months from Sri Lanka. In the 1989 elections, both Premadasa and the SLFP wanted the IPKF to withdraw. They got 95 percent of the vote and Sinhala public opinion was against the accord.

Premadasa even opened up secret channels to the LTTE to arm them against the Indians. Premadasa demanded that the IPKF leave the island and asked the Sri Lankan Armed Forces to throw them out. Any movement of the Sri Lankan forces outside their barracks would kill the still alive ISLA. Lt. Gen. A. S. Kalkat warned that the IPKF would retaliate if fired upon by the Sri Lankans. IAF squadrons moved to the south while naval units moved off the Sri Lankan coast. Thanks to the professionalism of the Indian and Sri Lankan Armed Forces, a conflict was avoided. Rajiv Gandhi refused to withdraw the IPKF in a situation which clearly showed the failure of his Sri Lanka policy both diplomatically and militarily. Rajiv believed that the only way he could succeed was to politically force Premadasa and militarily force the LTTE to accept the accord. In the December 1989 Indian elections, V. P. Singh became the Prime Minister. He viewed Rajiv Gandhi's Sri Lanka policy as a failure as it had cost over 1,100 soldiers, and over Rs. 2,000 crore of Indian tax payers money in over 32 months, and both politically and militarily a stalemate. V. P. Singh withdrew the IPKF and the last ship left on 24 March 1990. The Tamils were now paradoxically unhappy at the IPKF's departure but had to bear the start of a new ordeal. IPKF's arrival in India was boycotted by the Tamil Nadu Government headed by Karunanidhi.

AN EXAMINATION OF THE INDIAN INTERVENTION: DIFFERING VIEWS

Totally Unprepared and Ill-equipped, that was the IPKF

Colonel John Taylor[8] (Retd), one of the first officers assigned to the IPKF, says the Army was made to fight with one hand tied behind its back. He writes that by 1987, the Tigers were in full control of the North and East, including control over the judiciary and administration. The SLAF effort to dislodge them was no holds barred and included all force multipliers of war. This genocide (Tamil perception) led to huge pressure on India to intercede. He is of the opinion that, far from being 'India's Vietnam' as claimed by the LTTE, the IPKF had successfully eliminated the middle order leadership of the LTTE and broken their stronghold over the Jaffna peninsula. The LTTE was forced to take refuge in the jungles of the North and East. The Elephant Pass was open for the first time after the LTTE had taken control of Jaffna. Movement of goods from the South, East and West was made possible after a long period of time". However, he adds, the IPKF operations were not a complete success.

Intelligence figures topmost on his list of IPKF weaknesses. He is right, because the general feeling that the left (intelligence) hand did not know what the right one was doing, regrettably holds currency till today, 10 years past the Kargil War institutionalized this feeling. The second weakness he correctly points out is related to underestimating the LTTE, their extraordinary intelligence, resourcefulness, innovative skills, and their extraordinary mass support. Their awareness of communication security was stunning, both in securing their communications and breaking into Indian communications. Taylor finds RAW blameworthy in particular, for making incorrect and optimistic intelligence analysis that were divorced from the ground reality.

He feels that, (possibly due to political considerations) the non use of standard force multipliers such as Artillery, Tanks and Armoured Personnel Carriers and even concerted use of Attack Helicopters (they were used sporadically) added to the low they performance of the IPKF.

That was not all. Taylor notes that the Army lacked everything from maps to field cooking utensils, portable radio sets, an inadequate command and control set up, that was compelled to respond to 'orders from Delhi,'[9] leaving the intermediate commanders angry and helpless. Later on, corrections were brought in, but were a case of too little, too late. The realization that the IPKF was fighting a hardcore terror organisation that had unprecedented 'people support', assisting a country that decried the assistance, and had access to genuinely poor intelligence, really added up to an unprepared and ill equipped (mentally and physically) IPKF.

Good things happened, though. The IPKF held successful provisional elections, brought out peace and order by its initial operations, effectively ran emergency services; facts that no one has really highlighted. Amongst the good things, the IAF comes in for substantial praise by him for their first rate assistance in building up and sustaining the IPKF operations from beginning to the end.

What escapes attention by think tanks as well as the lay reader is that India had projected substantial military force in an out-of-area contingency for the first time. Teething troubles and personality led problems aside, India ended up learning valueable to lessons as well as re-orienting its training and equipment in the light of deficiencies that came to light in Sri Lanka. A more important issue that could not have escaped notice in South Asia, was that India would be proactive in protection of its security environment.

The Intelligence Agencies Said, Don't Worry About The LTTE, They are Our Boys, They will Not Fight Us[10]

In the wide-ranging interview with Josy Joseph, on the 10th anniversary of the Indian intervention, Mr. J.N. Dixit, the then Foreign Secretary, says that both Intelligence and Army underestimated Prabhakaran's intentions and the LTTE's fighting capability. He suggests that the Intelligence agencies believed they knew the LTTE and other Tamil groups well because they had trained them from 1977 onwards, and felt that these groups would not fight the IPKF.

The reason for providing assistance was circumscribed by the fact that Jayawardene, the Sri Lankan President, was seeking external support. Also, Mrs. Indira Gandhi, the Prime Minister, was under pressure from 60 million Tamils, who had threatened secession over the language issue in 1967. Their sentiments therefore had to be attended to. Mr. Dixit, during the interview, also severely castigated GOC Jaffna Division, Maj. Gen. Harkirat Singh, for allowing the casualties to IPKF in the early operations to escalate. He felt that the suicide attempt by the 17 LTTE cadres and the Jaffna University Helidrop were both mishandled by him.

Shoot Prabhakaran, Shoot Mahattaya! Interview with Maj. Gen. Harkirat Singh[11]

During his interview, Gen. Harkirat spoke of how he was able to meet Prabhakaran at Jaffna Medical College over a five hour meeting and convince him that the LTTE should surrender its weapons. The meeting was arranged by Lt. Gen. Depinder Singh. He was able to get Prabhakaran's consent in writing; a feat lauded by Mr. J.N. Dixit. The surrender of weapons, he says started brilliantly, but petered out because "they (RAW) did not stop arming EPRLF… This resulted in anti IPKF demonstrations..."

The General went on to say that the death of Lt. Col. Thileepan could have been prevented if the Foreign Secretary had not dragged his feet by delaying meeting him and reassuring him. Regarding the suicide attempt, he said that Mahattaya had personally requested the General that IPKF should prevent the 17 prisoners from reaching Colombo where the SLA would torture them. As per the General, the orders of the Sri Lankan Brigade Commander were to get them there at all costs. He mentions that he finally let them go once specific orders came to him from the chain of command to do so. Thus all 17 took cyanide, of which four were saved. Attribution of blame for the incident to him by the Foreign Secretary was therefore unwarranted. Overall, he felt that the Foreign Secretary could have handled the crisis differently as he had the backing of his Prime Minister and was also respected by the Sri Lankan President.

Nobody Sounded Even A *Last Post* For Our Dead in Colombo. Interview with Maj. Gen. Harkirat Singh[12]

In this no-holds-barred interview, the General tells Josy Joseph that when the suicides happened, Jaffna erupted and his troops did not have even basic wherewithal to protect themselves, other than basic weapons and ammunition. He mentions that the only time Prabhakaran was really in danger of capture or death at the hands of the IPKF was during the Jaffna heli-landed operation. Coming out with functional details not known so far, he mentions that *nine* helicopters (not *four*) had been committed to him and confirmed as allotted. However, during the operations he was told they weren't available any longer. He also finds fault with the company commander of 13 SIKH LI for not getting his men to dig in, and refusing the PARAS offer to get into the barracks. The intercepts of Prabhakaran passing messages of being trapped came courtesy the Sri Lankans as the IPKF had no intercept equipment of its own, the General said. (This point is vociferously contested by Maj. Gen. Jaswant Deva, AVSM, in his book *Sky is the Limit – Signals in Operation Pawan.* Deva was the Chief Signal Officer (CSO) of the IPKF for most of Operaton Pawan. His views will be covered later in the book).[13]

The General also decried the commotion over the soldiers who died in the Jaffna University operation, terming casualties as part of war. When asked why he had proceeded on the operation without proper intelligence, the General said that the inputs had come to him from the highest quarters. Assisted by his Col GS, himself a Paratrooper, he "was convinced operationally and logistically" that the operation could be done. However, his aircraft requirements were not met; something for which he finds the staff at HQ Southern Command blameworthy. The General also speaks of institutional neglect and says there was callousness afoot within the military system best expressed in his statement that ... "Nobody sounded even a *Last Post.* Nobody shed tears for them..."

He also adds that the IPKF administration was not up to the mark with everything coming from the mainland, unlike the LTTE which had caches all over. He also states that his Division should never have been sent to Jaffna as it was being readied for an air assault or air landed role. Divisions from the East should have taken on this task, as they were trained to combat terrorism and insurgency situations.

Impact[14]

The IPKF mission while having gained tactical successes did not succeed in its intended goals. On May 21, 1991, the LTTE assassinated Rajiv Gandhi for his role in sending the IPKF to Sri Lanka.

The primary impact of the IPKF has been that it shaped India's counter-insurgency techniques and military doctrine. On the international scene, it does not find significant mention in national or international military history. The political fallout, the IPKF's casualties, as well as the deterioration of international relations have however shaped India's foreign policy towards the Sri Lankan conflict.

The decision to send the IPKF in Sri Lanka was taken by the then Prime Minister of India, Rajiv Gandhi, who held office until 1989. The operation in Sri Lanka was one of the factors that led to the ouster of the Rajiv Gandhi-led Government in 1989.

Examination of the incidents that led to the start of the conflict between the LTTE and IPFK, the first major operation of the IPKF at Jaffna University, as well as the varying perceptions of some of the key players in the conflict all point to serious issues that undermined the synergized use of the IPKF at most stages of its functioning. As brought out earlier, the inputs available from the OFC, Lt. Gen. Depinder Singh, and Jaffna's second GOC, Lt. Gen. S.C. Sardeshpande are generally in line with the point of view that the IPKF fought with a hand tied behind its back and therefore failed to achieve its stated objectives. The fact that the experience allowed the Indian armed forces to do internal corrections is also indisputable and to an extent, reflected in its performance in the 1999 Kargil War. The reality that the Indian armed forces have still some way to go before all the deficiencies observed during the IPKF intervention can be considered eliminated is of course equally true and needs serious consideration.

ENDNOTES

1. "Indian Intervention in the Sri Lankan Civil War". <http://en.wikipedia.org/wiki/Indian_intervention_in_the_Sri_Lankan_Civil_War>
2. "Indian Peace Keeping Force". <http://en.wikipedia.org/wiki/Indian_Peace _Keeping_Force>
3. "Indian Intervention in the Sri Lankan Civil War". <http://en.wikipedia.org/wiki/Indian_intervention_in_the_Sri_Lankan_Civil_War>
4. "Indian Peace Keeping Force". <http://en.wikipedia.org/wiki/Indian_Peace _Keeping_Force>
5. "Indian Intervention in the Sri Lankan Civil War". <http://en.wikipedia.org/wiki/Indian_intervention_in_the_Sri_Lankan_Civil_War>
6. Ibid.
7. "Jaffna University Helidrop". <http://en.wikipedia.org/wiki/Jaffna_football_ground_massacre> The entire, sordid story of how intelligence, planning and execution were messed up is available in a number of narratives, of which this article is one. It may be noted that the Intelligence and planning deficiencies had no relationship with the stark courage displayed by the officers and men; Para Commandos, SIKH LI soldiers, the pilots and crew of the helicopters and the rescue force that extricated the trapped Para Commandos. Another, more detailed account can be accessed at "Indian Air Force In Sri Lanka. Descent Into Danger – The Jaffna University Helidrop".
   <http://www.bharat-rakshak.com/IAF/History/1987IPKF/Chapter3.html> It goes into clinical detail of the whole operation from conception to disaster, followed by rescue and analyses the failures that occurred at various levels of command and control.
8. "Totally Unprepared and Ill-equipped, That was The IPKF". <http://in.rediff.com/news/2000/mar/23lanka.htm>
9. Ibid.
10. "The Intelligence Agencies Said, Don't Worry About The LTTE, They are Our Boys, They will Not Fight Us".
    <http://in.rediff.com/news/2000/mar/24lanka.htm> This is one of several, in-depth interviews that were carried out by the portal and make for stunning reading in terms of the frankness of content and the insider's viewpoint of what happened and why. The element of blameworthiness for the mess ups that occurred comes up in most interviews and is answered from the interviewed personality's perspective. Readers are, of course, free to formulate their own judgment. Strongly recommended for obtaining a ringside view of some of the fallouts of the Indian intervention. The information contained above is culled from the interviews and generally focuses on the military content.
11. "Shoot Prabhakaran, Shoot Mahattaya! Interview with Maj. Gen. Harkirat Singh". <http://in.rediff.com/news/2000/mar/31lanka.htm> This is a continuation of the interview series by the rediff.com portal. Only the gist has been taken. The full interview is worth accessing.

12. "Nobody Sounded Even A *Last Post* For Our Dead In Colombo. Interview with Maj. Gen. Harkirat Singh". <http://in.rediff.com/news/2000/apr/01lanka.htm>
13. Deva, Jaswant, Maj. Gen. (Retd.), "Sky is the Limit – Signals in Operation Pawan". First Edition. 2007. Published by Maj Gen Yashwant Deva, AVSm (Retd.), Operation Pawan Veterans. Vasant Kunj, New Delhi-110070. Printed by Pentagon Press, New Delhi. The author has written a technically brilliant and thoroughly researched book covering the Signals communication challenges, achievements and deficiencies provided by him as its Chief Signals Officer (CSO) during the IPKF foray in Sri Lanka. The General comes across as a 'hands on' Signaler of calibre who took up his assignment with skill, great seriousness and a determination to succeed, often using improvisation when all else failed or was not/ inadequately available. Though this author, having operated in an intense Signals environment as an Armoured Corps officer, with substantial additional experience in combating terrorism stretching over 37 years, is not in full agreement with some aspects of the grass roots as well as macro level aspects of Signals operations as documented by him, this has nothing to do with the obvious 'must read' quality of the book for Indian Army watchers and well wishers. He is more than right in making a basic and blunt, unerringly correct assumption: success in war always rides on brilliant, reliable, redundant, sensibly formatted and secure communications.
14. "Indian Intervention in the Sri Lankan Civil War". <http://en.wikipedia.org/wiki/Indian_intervention_in_the_Sri_Lankan_Civil_War>

References

1. J.N. Dixit (ex-Indian Ambassador to Colombo) speaking to Rediff.com
2. Research and Analysis Wing. Fas.org
3. New Delhi & the Tamil Struggle- An Amoral Role. A Post Mortem on the Indian Intervention. Tamilnation.org
4. "History of the Organisation." University Teachers for Human Rights.
5. Sri Lanka in 1987: Indian Intervention and Resurgence of the JVP. Pfaffenberger B. Asian Survey, Vol. 28, No. 2, A Survey of Asia in 1987: Part II. (Feb., 1988), pp. 137-147.
6. The Day the Elected Government was in place, the Military Role of the IPKF was over. Lt. Gen. A.S. Kalkat, speaking to rediff.com
7. Jain Commission Interim Report. Growth of Sri Lankan Tamil Militancy in Tamil Nadu. Chapter I – Phase II (1987-1988)
8. Shoot Prabhakaran, shoot Mahathiah! Gen. Harkirat Singh speaking to Josy Joseph on the IPKF role. rediff.com
9. Background to the Breakdown of the Accord. University Teachers for Human Rights (Jaffna), Sri Lanka.
10. Nobody sounded even a Last Post for our Dead in Colombo. Gen. Harkirat Singh to Josy Joseph. rediff.com
11. Crocodiles into the Attack. No. 125 Helicopter Squadron. Bharat-rakshak.com
12. Shifting to the Jungles. Bharat-rakshak.com

CHAPTER 16

The Rajiv Gandhi Assassination

This chapter is a logical follow up of the last chapter on India's intervention in Sri Lanka from 1987 to 1990. Prabhakaran has gone on record, (through the words of the LTTE ideologue and public face of the LTTE as long as he lived, Anton Balasingham) that the India-Sri Lanka Accord of July 1987, followed in late September 1987 by the death of Lt. Col. Thileepan, and, shortly thereafter, by the attempted suicide by 17 LTTE cadres, in early October 1987, queered the pitch between the LTTE and India. Matters came to a head, when, in response to a wave of killings by the LTTE, post the death of Thileepan and the suicides by the LTTE cadre, the IPKF mandate was changed to focus on bringing the LTTE to heel. These events, Balasingham is recorded as saying as well as writing in his book, *'Viduthalai'* (*Liberation*)[1] , released in London in 2003, led to the assassination of the former Prime Minister, besides, of course, the paranoid fear of his return to power.

This chapter therefore, encapsulates the assassination details as are available in the open media. Details of the suicide jacket and its constituents have been woven in, as this was the first recorded instance in recent history that a terror group had used a woman suicide bomber to target a high profile political leader. No worthwhile record has, however, been found on the life or other details of the LTTE suicide bomber, Dhanu/Tanu, who killed the former Prime Minister. What may come across as new to some readers, are the inputs from the Sri Lanka MoD website, which purports to give out the untold story of his assassination. The MoD report mentions the fears of the LTTE of the consequences of a comeback to power by Rajiv; the likelihood of his return, keeping in mind the groundswell of public opinion for him in India, and the pressure on India to do something, keeping in mind the escalating refugee problem that was flooding India, with Tamils displaced from North East Sri Lanka. The LTTE assassination conspiracy and its horrifyingly clinical and efficient execution details, as well as the technical details of the assassination are also covered briefly in this report. Readers may like to browse through the book by Dr. Subramaniam Swamy's, *The Assassination of Rajiv Gandhi: Unanswered Questions and Unasked Queries*[2] for details of the assassination report.

The chapter ends with a reference to the public confession made by the LTTE that, in retrospect, they deeply regretted the assassination of Rajiv Gandhi. The reader will of course agree that this blunder set the keel for the eventual destruction of the LTTE.

The Rajiv Gandhi Assassination[3]

The assassination of Rajiv Gandhi, the seventh Prime Minister of India, took place in Sriperumbudur in Tamil Nadu, India, on 21 May 1991. It was one of the first uses of suicide bombing worldwide for the purposes of political terror. At least 14 others were also killed. It was carried out by Thenmozhi Rajaratnam, a female member of the Liberation Tigers of Tamil Eelam (LTTE). Rajaratnam was also known as Gayatri, Tanu and Dhanu.[4] Her real name was, however, Gayatri. Her birth year has not been conclusively established.

Rajiv Gandhi's last public meeting was on 21st May, 1991, in Sriperumbudur, a town approximately 45 kilometres from Chennai, where he was assassinated, while campaigning for the Sriperumbudur Lok Sabha Congress candidate Mrs. Maragatham Chandrasekhar in Tamil Nadu. Rajiv Gandhi had arrived at Chennai about two hours earlier and then was driven by motorcade in a white Ambassador car to Sriperumbudur, stopping along the way at a few other election campaigning venues. During the drive to Sriperumbudur, he was accompanied by a foreign journalist who interviewed him in the car. When he reached the venue at Sriperumbudur, he got out of his car and began to walk towards the dais where he would deliver his speech. Along the way, he was garlanded by many well wishers, Congress party workers and school children. At 10:10 p.m., the assassin, Tanu, approached him and greeted the former Prime Minister. She then bent down to touch his feet and detonated an RDX[5] explosive laden belt[6] tucked below her dress. The former

The stone mosaic that stands at the exact location where Rajiv Gandhi was assassinated in Sriperumbudur, Tamil Nadu

Prime Minister along with 14 others (18 by some reports) was killed, and 33 injured, including 12 policemen, in the explosion that followed. Rajaratnam had the belt bomb with the explosive material in her lower back region and the power pack, two switches and the circuitry in front. One switch initiated the circuitry and the other activated the bomb. The RDX had about 10,000 steel balls (16,800 as per some reports) 2 mm in diameter embedded in it. After garlanding Rajiv, Rajaratnam evidently stooped to touch his feet and activated the explosive. Rajiv might have tried to stop her as his face bore the impact of the blast.[7] The assassination was caught on film[8] through the lens of a local photographer, whose camera and film was found at the site. The cameraman himself also died in the blast.

Supreme Court Judgement

As per the Supreme Court of India judgment, by Judge Thomas, the killing was carried out due to personal animosity of the LTTE chief Prabhakaran towards Rajiv Gandhi. Additionally, the Rajiv Gandhi administration had antagonized other Tamil militant organisations like PLOTE for reversing the military coup in Maldives back in 1988.

The judgment further cites the death of Lt Col Thileepan[9] in a hunger strike and the suicide by 12 LTTE cadres in a vessel in October 1987.

Trial

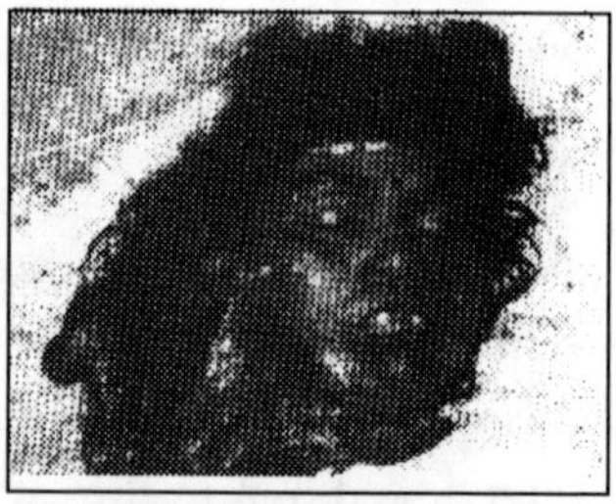

The trial was conducted under the Terrorist and Disruptive Activities (Prevention) Act (TADA). The designated TADA court in Chennai gave death sentences to all the 26 accused. The trial was held behind closed doors, in camera courts, and the non-disclosure of identity of witnesses was maintained. In the Rajiv Gandhi case confessions by the accused formed a major part of the evidence in the judgment against them which they later claimed was taken under duress. On appeal to the Supreme Court, only four of the accused were sentenced to death and the others to various jail terms.

In 2006, LTTE spokesman Anton Balasingham told the Indian television channel, NDTV, that the killing was a "great tragedy, a monumental historical tragedy which we deeply regret."[10]

Sri Lanka: The Untold Story – Rajiv Gandhi's Assassination[11]

"The political scene in India became murkier as the minority Government of

Photo of Rajiv Gandhi moments before his assassination

Prime Minister S. Chandrasekhar developed serious misunderstandings with Rajiv Gandhi, the leader of the opposition, and the latter ultimately forced Chandrasekhar to announce the resignation of his four-month-old government on March 6, 1991, from the floor of the Indian Parliament.

After Chandrasekhar's resignation, no one came forward to form a coalition government and the President dissolved Parliament and elections for the 10th Parliament were announced for June 1991. Chandrasekhar remained as the caretaker Prime Minister.

It had been reported that Rajiv Gandhi by then was already facing threats to his life from Sikh extremists, Muslim fundamentalists and a host of other militant organizations, including the Liberation Tigers of Tamil Eelam (LTTE)…

Meanwhile, the former EPRLF stalwart and the Northeast Provincial Government's Chief Minister, Varatharajah Perumal, was at the time at Chanderi, in the state of Madhya Pradesh, where he had been given refuge and protection. But he managed to break his security cordon and left for New Delhi to meet Rajiv Gandhi. Gandhi was sympathetic towards Perumal and volunteered to give him a bulletproof vest as a goodwill gesture. It was reported that whenever a Sri Lankan Tamil visited Rajiv Gandhi during this period, he appeared very concerned over the atrocities of the LTTE. Therefore, rumors were rife that, should the Congress come back to power, it would assist Sri Lankan Tamils in winning back their political rights, and would take steps to curb the LTTE in Sri Lanka.

Dr. Subramanian Swamy, who was at that time the Minister of Law and Commerce in the Chandrasekhar Government and the contact of Rajiv Gandhi in that government, wrote in his book, '*The Assassination of Rajiv Gandhi: Unanswered Questions and Unasked Queries*':[12] "In Jaffna, Prabhakaran, the LTTE supremo was monitoring the goings on in Delhi, for two reasons. The first was that he wanted Chandrasekhar's Government out because we had dismissed the DMK government in Tamil Nadu and cracked down on the LTTE in the State. He had tried, I was told, to develop contacts with Chandrasekhar just after he had taken office, but these were rebuffed…The second was that he hated R G [Rajiv Gandhi] and feared his return to office..."

On April 10, 2002, Tiger Supremo Prabhakaran met the international press at Killinochchi, located in the Wanni region of Sri Lanka. Many questions related to Rajiv Gandhi's murder.

Q: You have been indicted in the Gandhi assassination?

A: Prabhakaran: This case is going on. Four persons have been convicted. They are seeking amnesty at the moment. We do not want to make any comments at this moment.

Q: Are you denying involvement in the Rajiv Gandhi assassination?

A: (Mr. Balasingham). I know this is a sensitive issue, not only for you but for us as well. You are raising an issue that happened 10 years ago. We want to have friendly relations with India.

Q: What have you to say about the charges?

A: Prabhakaran: This is a 'tragic incident' that took place 10 years back. We cannot comment on the issue.

Q: The Rajiv Gandhi assassination...

A: (Mr. Balasingham). You are trying to dominate the press conference. You have come here when the peace process is on. You are talking of an old incident. Do not dig into the past.

At this press conference, it must be noted that Prabhakaran did not deny involvement in the assassination, opening the floodgates of positive confirmation.

Recently, Nirupama Subramaniam, an Indian woman journalist who earlier represented the *Indian Express* and who at present represents *The Hindu* of Madras, was asked by the *Sunday Observer* on June 16, 2002:

Q: What impression have you formed of Velupillai Prabhakaran?

A: He successfully led his cadres but led his people into ruin. I have not interviewed him, but I was at Killinochchi and the press conference seemed like a huge ordeal of logistical problems, security checks and catching deadlines. But you can put it down to valuable experience as to how the LTTE conduct themselves and relate to the outside world. ... When the question about Rajiv Gandhi was asked, they went into a huddle and it seemed like ages before they came out with a response and that they didn't want to comment on it because it was sub judice. But it was really post judice as the convictions had been handed out. ...

After Prabhakaran's press conference, G. Parthasarathy, who was earlier an information adviser to Rajiv Gandhi and the spokesman of the Indian Peace Keeping Forces in Sri Lanka, in a cover story in *Frontline*, the Indian fortnightly magazine, April 27-May 10, said, "There appears to be little doubt that it was the inaction on the part of the V.P. Singh government in responding to this act of terrorism on Indian soil that emboldened Prabhakaran to assassinate Rajiv Gandhi in 1991."[13]

Bala Reveals Rajiv-Prabha Secret Accord[14]

The article reveals (quoting the Liberation Tigers of Tamil Eelam (LTTE) Chief Negotiator and Political Strategist, Anton Stanislaus Balasingham) that Rajiv Gandhi and Prabhakaran had entered into a 'Gentleman's Agreement' in the early hours of July 29, 1987, in New Delhi, before the Indian Prime Minister signed the Indo-Sri Lanka Accord with the Sri Lankan President the same day, at 3 PM. As per the writer, details of the meeting have been revealed by Balasingham in his book titled 'Viduthalai' (Liberation) released in early December, 2003, in London. The book has several essays and articles, one of which covers the meeting and its conclusions. Balasingham is quoted by D.B.S. Jeyaraj as saying that the agreement was not implemented. Lt. Col. Thileepan of the LTTE (referred to at length in the last chapter) went on a fast unto death to bring out his angst against the unfulfilled commitments made to Prabhakaran. His death resulted in a major outbreak of violence which was a turning point in the civil war.

Rajiv Assassination 'Deeply Regretted': LTTE[15]

The Hindu report says that the LTTE has described the assassination of the former Prime Minister, Rajiv Gandhi, as a 'monumental historical tragedy.'[16] Anton Balasingham, LTTE's chief negotiator and ideologue, told NDTV: "As far as that event [Rajiv assassination] is concerned, I would say it is a great tragedy, a monumental historical tragedy for which we deeply regret and we call upon the Government of India and the people of India to be magnanimous to put the past behind and to approach the ethnic question in a different perspective."[17] The report quotes the LTTE ideologue as saying that the induction of the IPKF and its revised mandate of bringing the LTTE to book escalated the conflict: "...since we rejected the Sri Lankan accord, there were a lot of events that took place, creating a gulf between the LTTE and the Government of India and the Indians later sent the IPKF to disarm the LTTE and eventually (this) broke out into an open confrontation...We fought a guerrilla war against the Indian Army for two years and finally the Sri Lankans. We had a negotiation with Sri Lanka and secured the withdrawal of the Indian troops in the 90s and of course finally it was followed by the assassination of Rajiv Gandhi,"[18] he said.

Prabhakaran had Rajiv Killed for Being 'Anti-Tamil'[19]

This report suggests that Prabhakaran was afraid that Gandhi might re-induct the IPKF, what he termed the 'satanic force'[20] if he came to power again, after the 1991 election. "Gandhi's commitment to ensure Sri Lanka's sovereignty and the upswing in his poll-eve popularity, hastened the LTTE to execute its designs", the report continues.

Prabhakaran felt that India had colluded with Sri Lanka to hand over the arrested 17 LTTE rank-and-file to Sri Lanka, compelling them to attempt suicide. Later installation of an elected government in North East Sri Lanka, without involving the LTTE, added fuel to his anger against the former Indian Prime Minister. The report goes on to give details of the LTTE conspiracy as enunciated in the Sri Lanka MoD report above. It adds that "Sivarasan, who had eliminated EPRLF leader Padmanabha and 13 others in Madras in June 1990, was chosen to execute the conspiracy".

When Rajiv's tour programme was made public, the report adds that "the assassination squad met a day before the assassination at the home of Nalini's mother Padma, the twenty first accused. After giving the finishing touches, the team offered prayers for the success of the 'mission' and left for Sriperumbudur around 1700 hours by bus and reached the venue ahead of time."[21]

ENDNOTES

1. Balasingham, Anton. "Viduthalai (Liberation)". London. Fairmax Publishing Ltd, 2003.
2. Swamy, Dr. Subramaniam. "The Assassination of Rajiv Gandhi: Unanswered Questions and Unasked Queries". Konark Publishers. 2000.
3. "The Rajiv Gandhi Assassination". <http://en.wikipedia.org/wiki/Rajiv_Gandhi_assassination>
4. "Thenmozhi Rajaratnam". <http://en.wikipedia.org/wiki/Thenmozhi_Rajaratnam>
5. "Cyclotrimethylenetrinitramine (RDX)". < http://en.wikipedia.org/wiki/Cyclotrimethylene_trinitramine> Cyclotrimethylenetrinitramine, also known as RDX, cyclonite, hexogen, and T4, is an explosive nitroamine widely used in military and industrial applications. Nomenclature variants include cyclotrimethylene-trinitramine and cyclotrimethylene trinitramine. In its pure, synthesized state RDX is a white, crystalline solid. As an explosive, it is usually used in mixtures with other explosives and plasticizers, phlegmatizers or desensitizers. It is stable in storage and is considered one of the most powerful and brisant of the military high explosives. RDX forms the base for a number of common military explosives:
   - Composition A: (wax-coated, granular explosive consisting of RDX and plasticizing wax), composition A5 (mixed with 1.5% stearic acid),
   - Composition B: (castable mixtures of RDX and TNT),
   - Composition C: (a plastic demolition explosive consisting of RDX, other explosives, and plasticizers),
   - Composition D,
   - HBX: (castable mixtures of RDX, TNT, powdered aluminium, and D-2 wax with calcium chloride),

- H-6, and
- C-4.
- RDX is also used as a major component of many plastic bonded explosives used in nuclear weapons.

6. "Explosive Belt". < http://en.wikipedia.org/wiki/Suicide_belt >
An explosive belt (also called suicide belt, bomber pilot jacket, suicide vest) is a vest packed with explosives and armed with a detonator, worn by suicide bombers. Explosive belts are usually packed with nails, screws, bolts, and other objects that serve as shrapnel to maximize the number of casualties in the explosion. The explosive belt usually consists of several cylinders filled with explosive (de facto pipe bombs), or in more sophisticated versions with plates of explosive. The explosive is surrounded by a fragmentation jacket that produces the shrapnel responsible for most of the bomb's lethality, effectively making the jacket a crude body-worn claymore mine. Once the vest is detonated, the explosion resembles an omni directional shotgun blast. The most dangerous and the most widely used shrapnel are steel balls 3-7 mm in diameter. Other shrapnel material can be anything of suitable size and hardness, most often nails screws, nuts, and thick wire. Shrapnel is responsible for about 90% of all casualties caused by this kind of device. A 'loaded' vest may weigh between 5 and 20 kg and may be hidden under thick clothes, usually jackets or snow coats. Suicide vests cover the entire stomach and usually have shoulder straps. A common security drill against suspected suicide bombers is to isolate the suspect to at least 15 metres away from other people, and ask him to remove his upper clothing (coat, shirt, etc.) in order to see if there is an explosive vest strapped under them. This drill is problematic when dealing with female suicide bombers. Alternatively, an infrared detector can be used. **It may be noted that none of these precautions were put into place and reports point out that security was extremely lax at the rally site.**
7. "Thenmozhi Rajaratnam". <http://en.wikipedia.org/wiki/Thenmozhi_Rajaratnam>
8. "The Rajiv Gandhi Assassination". <http://en.wikipedia.org/wiki/Rajiv_Gandhi_assassination>
9. Developments later on in this chapter will make it clear that Thileepan was disappointed that the demands that Prabhakaran had made for Tamil Eelam had not been complied with by the Sri Lankan and Indian Governments. His fast unto death was his way of displaying his resentment. Earlier references to Thileepan's death correctly point to this event being a turning point in the civil war.
10. Ibid.
11. "Sri Lanka: The Untold Story – Rajiv Gandhi's Assassination". Ministry of Defence, Sri Lanka. July 11, 2006. <http://www.defence.lk/new.asp?fname=20060521_02> The report has been edited to keep its focus on the assassination essentials.
12. Review: "*The Assassination of Rajiv Gandhi: Unanswered Questions and Unasked Queries*". Reviewer: A.S. Paneerselvan. June 12, 2000. <http://www.outlookindia.com/article.aspx?209511>
The blurbs used by the reviewer, A.S. Paneerselvan, before getting down to the review proper say it all: **"Sleuth Without a Clue – Smug Tales, Half-Arguments, Insufficient Evidence: it's Not Elementary, Dr. Swamy"**. The review, in effect, turns out to be a savage indictment of the book.
Another review of the book, this time by the *India Today* reviewer, is not so scathing in its indictment, but conveys enough to communicate to the reader that the book does not quite have the credentials of a seriously and dispassionately researched work. The punch line, this

time is not contained in the blurbs, but in the concluding sentence. Read on.
The Assassination of Rajiv Gandhi: Tamil Tigers Trojan Horses – Book Review. "*The Assassination of Rajiv Gandhi: Unanswered Questions and Unasked Queries*". <http://www.india-today.com/itoday/20000529/books.html>
"Early in his book Subramanian Swamy recounts how he was once "watching TV news on Sri Lanka developments with Laloo Yadav". The Bihari leader, in what must rank as the most original take on the Tamil-Sinhalese ethnic conflict, remarked, *"Kya Jhagda Hai? Sub Madrasi Lagtey Hain"* (What are they fighting for? All look like Tamils)." The anecdote sets the tone for a volume that derives itself from Swamy's trademark mix of wicked humour, delicious stories and undying quest for vengeance. The central thesis of The Assassination of Rajiv Gandhi is that the killing of the former prime minister was followed by a disinformation campaign that sought to exonerate the LTTE. For this, Swamy, the Harvard-trained economist who is now President of the Janata Party blames the Tamil Tigers' 'people in high places' – a phrase borrowed from an LTTE leader (Pottu Amman). The strategy, Swamy argues, proved successful in keeping alive a contrived mystery even after the CBI and courts had done their work. It managed to "manipulate the Jain Commission" inquiring into the larger conspiracy behind the murder to the extent that it "declared open season on assassination 'theories'". Read the full review.

13. Ibid.
14. Jeyaraj, D.B.S. "Bala Reveals Rajiv-Prabha Secret Accord". *The Sunday* Leader. December 21, 2003. Volume 10, Issue 23. <http://www.thesundayleader.lk/20031221/focus.htm>
15. "Rajiv Assassination 'Deeply Regretted': LTTE. It was a 'Monumental Historical Tragedy', Anton Balasingham Tells NDTV. LTTE Prepared to Build New Understanding with India". Diplomatic Correspondent, *The Hindu.* <http://www.hindu.com/2006/06/28/stories/2006062812890100.htm>
16. Ibid.
17. Ibid.
18. Ibid.
19. "Prabhakaran Had Rajiv Killed For Being 'Anti-Tamil'." <http://www.rediff.com/news/1998/jan/28rajiv3.htm>
20. Ibid.
21. Ibid.

References

1. "1991: Bomb kills India's former leader Rajiv Gandhi". *BBC News.* 1991-05-21. http://news.bbc.co.uk/onthisday/hi/dates/stories/may/21/newsid_2504000/2504739.stm.
2. Rediff on The Net: Sonia checks her emotions, but her interpreter goes full throttle.
3. http://cbi.nic.in/Judgements/thomas.htm
4. India: The Prevention of Terrorism Bill. Past abuses revisited | Amnesty International
5. http://cbi.nic.in/Judgements/wadwa.htm
6. outlookindia.com
7. http://www.deccanherald.com/deccanherald/dec112004/i2.asp.
8. Jain Commission Report.
9. "Tamil Tiger 'regret' over Gandhi". *BBC News.* 2006-06-27. http://news.bbc.co.uk/2/hi/south_asia/5122032.stm.

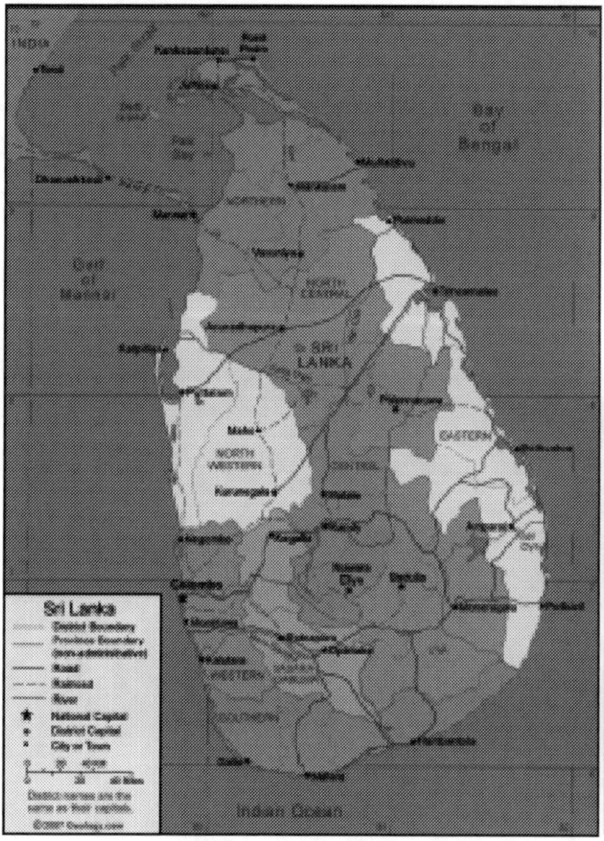

Prabhakaran

Child Soldiers

LTTE flag

Hensinger, Shane. "The Forgotten War Nears a Decisive End". <http://www.dailykos.com/story/2009/1/8/681706/-The-Forgotten-War-Nears-a-Decisive-End>

PART V

The Way Ahead

CHAPTER 17

Diplomacy During and After the Sri Lankan Conflict

Part 4 (Chapters 15 and 16) had covered the Indian intervention in Sri Lanka from 1987 to 1990) and one of its tragic fallouts; the assassination of a former Prime Minister, Rajiv Gandhi, just when it appeared that he would sweep the polls. Part 5, the concluding part of the book, starts with the diplomacy that was practised during and after the civil war, with the focus on Sri Lanka. The reader will notice that, apart from stray references to other countries, particularly those in the Western bloc, the diplomacy that was relevant from the viewpoint of Sri Lanka as well as India, being the major player in the immediate region, has been brought out. The stark fact remains that the civil war was not really of great concern in the West as their interests were hardly jeopardized by it. Their major concerns were on the issue of human rights. All efforts at the level of the UN to make the civil war a big issue, primarily on account of perceived human rights violations, were effectively put paid because of the Chinese backing to Sri Lanka. This was also the reason that the USA, UK, France, Germany and Canada, had deliberately distanced themselves from the conflict and put severe restrictions on all forms of aid to Sri Lanka, forcing it to look in other directions for the military support it needed, and the financing thereof, to win the war. The problem was thus a South Asian problem in the main, with the stand out 'external' player being China.

This chapter thus focuses on the diplomacy Sri Lanka exercised with China, Pakistan and India in the main, and their reciprocity in this respect, with other nations being mentioned et passim. The spotlight is deliberately narrow and focuses on the military side of the civil war, except in the case of India where other issues come in. The other notable exception is China, whose generous (most analysts believe opportunistic) help on several fronts besides pure military aid, has a long-term perspective that impinges on the region's security and has got the countries in the region, and especially India worried.

Notwithstanding the preamble, it would be fitting to begin with the diplomatic perceptions of the USA, if only to underscore their key worries that focus on the need for refugee care and national reconciliation on top priority, more than they concern themselves with the military part of the civil war.

The method followed thereafter will be to proceed country wise, sharing excerpted, diplomacy driven inputs from China, Pakistan and India in that order. A short analysis is dovetailed with the inputs. Readers who trawl through the exhaustive notes may find themselves benefited.

Sri Lanka Won an Important Victory over LTTE – Ambassador Blake[1]

Ambassador Robert Blake, the then new Assistant Secretary of State for South Asia and Central Asia, said at the hearing of the Congressional Subcommittee on South Asia, (June 25, 2009) that Sri Lanka won an "important victory in the North" when it defeated the LTTE.

Assistant Secretary Blake, testifying before the House of Representatives Subcommittee on the Middle East and South Asia, called on Sri Lanka to quickly resettle the 300,000 internally displaced persons in the North and to hold provincial elections. "The action the Sri Lankan government takes now," Assistant Secretary Blake said, "in the aftermath of the war, with respect to both humanitarian relief and political inclusion for minorities, will be important to securing an end to terrorism and a lasting peace."

During the hearing, Subcommittee Chairman Gary Ackerman (D-New York) said that, "I think the United States should offer its assistance to relieving the suffering of the displaced as much as we can and, while fully respecting the sovereignty of Sri Lanka, should encourage true national reconciliation."

Secretary Blake urged not only the speedy resettlement of the IDPs, but also a political process that gives the Northern Province a voice in the national government. He noted that the 13th Amendment to the Sri Lankan Constitution would do that, but that the amendment has to be fully implemented.

CHINESE MILITARY AND OTHER SUPPORT TO SRI LANKA

China a 'Stakeholder' in Sri Lanka's Development[2]

"Describing China as a 'major stakeholder' in Sri Lanka's development, Colombo has said Beijing had offered financial support and had stood by the country in 'crucial situations'... 'China has extended its support to us... despite some international pressures on Sri Lanka in recent times," senior Presidential Advisor, Basil Rajapaksa (a brother of the President, Mahinda Rajapaksa) said, while addressing a ceremony to mark the completion of the first phase of a power plant built with Chinese assistance in North-Western province. As a classic example, during the last stages of the war in Sri Lanka, some Western countries tried to throttle Sri Lanka by threatening her with stopping of aid, holding back on loans and even placing of embargoes. The USA, France, Germany and the UK were most active and were ably fooled by the protesting, LTTE supporting minority Tamil diaspora, to be negative..."

Chinese Billions in Sri Lanka Fund Battle against Tamil Tigers[3]

This perceptive report, filed by Jeremy Page, the South Asia Correspondent of *The Times*, UK, describes not just what is happening at Hambantotta Port on the south eastern coast of Sri Lanka, 240 kilometres away from Colombo, but also speculates that this seemingly commercial venture could be having a dual use military purpose. The rush of arms sales that China has given Sri Lanka since the early 1990's, when assistance from India was severely restricted, and since 2007, in the case of the USA, when it stopped military arms sales due to perceived Sri Lankan HR violations, has also been brought out. Some excerpts are reproduced:

"On the southern coast of Sri Lanka, ten miles from one of the world's busiest shipping routes, a vast construction site is engulfing the once sleepy fishing town of Hambantotta. This poor community of 21,000 people is about as far as one can get on the Island from the fighting between the Army and the Tamil Tiger rebels on the North Eastern coast...This is where China is building a $1 billion port that it plans to use as a refuelling and docking station for its Navy, as it patrols the Indian Ocean and protects China's supplies of Saudi oil. Ever since Sri Lanka agreed to the plan, in March 2007, China has given it all the aid, arms and diplomatic support it needs to defeat the Tigers, without worrying about the West...

"The Chinese say that Hambantotta is a purely commercial venture, but many US and Indian military planners regard it as part of a 'string of pearls' strategy under which China is also building or upgrading ports at Gwadar in Pakistan, Chittagong in Bangladesh and Sittwe in Burma. The strategy was outlined in a paper by Lieutenant-Colonel Christopher J. Pehrson, of the Pentagon's Air Staff, in 2006, and again in a report by the US Joint Forces Command in November. "For China, Hambantotta is a commercial venture, but it's also an asset for future use in a very strategic location," Major-General (Retd) Dipankar Banerjee of the Institute of Peace and Conflict Studies in Delhi said...

"China has no immediate plans for a fully fledged naval base but wants a similar foothold in the Indian Ocean to protect its oil supplies from piracy or blockade by a foreign power, analysts say. Beijing sent three ships on an unprecedented anti-piracy mission to the Gulf of Aden in December, and in January, a Chinese defence White Paper said that the Navy was "developing capabilities of conducting co-operation in distant waters..."

Many of the arms have been bought through Lanka Logistics & Technologies, co-headed by Gottabhaya Rajapaksa, the Defence Secretary, who is also the President's brother. In April 2007 Sri Lanka signed a classified $37.6 million (£25 million) deal to buy Chinese ammunition and ordnance for its army and navy, according to *Jane's Defence Weekly*. China gave Sri Lanka – apparently free of charge – six F7 jet fighters last year, according to the Stockholm International Peace Research Institute, after a daring raid by the Tigers' Air Wing destroyed 10 military aircraft in 2007. One of the Chinese fighters shot down one of the Tigers' aircraft a year later."

"China's arms sales have been the decisive factor in ending the military stalemate," Brahma Chellaney, of the Centre for Policy Research in Delhi, said. "There seems to have been a deal linked to Hambantotta." "That's why Sri Lanka has been so dismissive of international criticism," said B. Raman of the Chennai Centre for China Studies. "It knows it can rely on support from China.""

More Details on Hambantotta Port[4]

B. Raman the prolific security analyst writes that ... "The first stage of the 15-year (2008-2023) Hambantotta project is expected to be completed by the end of 2010. This stage envisages the construction of a 1,000-metre jetty, which will enable the harbour to function as an industrial port for the import and export of industrial chemicals, fuel and heavy machinery. By 2023, Hambantotta is projected to have a liquefied natural gas refinery, aviation fuel storage facilities, three separate docks giving the port a transshipment capacity and dry docks for ship repair and construction. The project also envisages that when completed the port will serve as a base for bunkering and refuelling...

The draught (depth) of the new harbour will be 16 metres against 15 metres in Colombo. A 230 metre passage-entrance channel will be created at the breakwater which is 988 metres long on the west end and 311 metres long on the east end. The first stage due to be ready by end 2010 will allow three ships to berth. The final stage, for which there is no offer of funding yet from China, is planned to accommodate more than 30 ships, which is the present capacity at Colombo..."

Jeremy Page adds that "China has no immediate plans to establish a fully fledged naval base at any of these sites but wants a foothold in the Indian Ocean to protect its oil supplies from piracy or blockade by a foreign power, analysts say. The Royal Navy used the Eastern Sri Lankan port of Trincomalee in the same way until 1957 and still shares a naval base with the United States on the nearby island of Diego Garcia."[5]

An authoritative Pakistani defence issue related portal supports the contention that, while seeming to assist in Sri Lanka's development, China is taking a rain cheque out to protect its energy supplies, and, of course, dominate the IOR. Excerpts: "China's massive involvement in the Hambantotta project – it has provided most of its funding and technical expertise – has provided Beijing with a 'listening post' from where it can "monitor naval activity in the Indian Ocean, and future maritime cooperation in the Indian Ocean", Zia Haider, an analyst at the Washington-based Stimson Centre, has noted. The Hambantotta port project is the latest in a series of steps that China has taken in recent years to consolidate its access to the Indian Ocean and to secure sea lanes through which its energy supplies are transported. It has adopted what analysts describe as a 'string of pearls' strategy, building strategic relationships with countries along sea lanes from the Middle East to the South China Sea...[6]

China Fuels Sri Lankan War[7]

The noted strategist, Bramha Chellaney, reinforces the conviction of most China watchers that China has mastered the art of fishing in troubled waters, by stepping into existing diplomatic voids on the grounds of providing assistance to needy nations. While appearing to meet Sri Lanka's urgent, short-term need for weapons, its far larger assistance in infrastructure development in this country has strategic nuances that have left the region, especially India, wary and unsettled. Excerpts from the article:

> ... "No sooner had the United States ended direct military aid to Sri Lanka last year over its deteriorating human rights record than China blithely stepped in to fill the breach – a breach widened by India's hands-off approach toward Sri Lanka since a disastrous 1987-90 peacekeeping operation in that Island-nation.
>
> Beijing began selling larger quantities of arms, and dramatically boosted its aid fivefold in the past year to almost $1 billion to emerge as Sri Lanka's largest

donor. Chinese Jian-7 fighter jets, antiaircraft guns, JY-11 3D air surveillance radars and other supplied weapons have played a central role in the Sri Lankan military successes against the Liberation Tigers of Tamil Eelam (or 'Tamil Tigers'), seeking to carve out an independent homeland for the ethnic Tamils in the Island's North and East.

Beijing even got its ally, Pakistan, actively involved in Sri Lanka. With Chinese encouragement, Pakistan – despite its own faltering economy and rising Islamist challenge – has boosted its annual military assistance loans to Sri Lanka to nearly $100 million while supplying Chinese-origin small arms and training Sri Lankan Air Force personnel in precision guided attacks.

China has become an enabler of repression in a number of developing nations as it seeks to gain access to oil and mineral resources, to market its goods and to step up investment. Still officially a communist state, its support for brutal regimes is driven by capitalist considerations. But while exploiting commercial opportunities, it also tries to make strategic inroads. Little surprise thus that China's best friends are pariah or other states that abuse human rights.

Indeed, with its ability to provide political protection through its U.N. Security Council veto power, Beijing has signed tens of billions of dollars worth of energy and arms contracts in recent years with such problem states – from Burma and Iran to Sudan and Venezuela.

In the case of Sri Lanka, China has been particularly attracted by that country's vantage location in the centre of the Indian Ocean – a crucial international passageway for trade and oil. Hambantotta – the billion-dollar port Chinese engineers are now building on Sri Lanka's South East – is the latest 'pearl' in China's strategy to control vital sea-lanes of communication between the Indian and Pacific Oceans by assembling a 'string of pearls' in the form of listening posts, special naval arrangements and access to ports..."[8]

The Official Chinese Take on Economic Assistance to Sri Lanka

The *China Daily* that is the mouthpiece of the Chinese Government wrote, in July 2009, that Sri Lanka has granted China an Exclusive Economic Zone[9] (EEZ) at Mirigama, near Colombo. The depth of Sri Lanka's relationship with China thus becomes clear, when one reads that China is also developing the port in the deep South, building an electricity plant, roads and so on. A follow up report from the Chinese news agency, Xinhua, gives further details. Excerpts:

"Sri Lanka has granted China an exclusive economic zone in its first post-war effort to attract more investment from the world's largest developing economy, the country's investment promotion agency said on Wednesday. Hong Kong-based conglomerate Huichen Investment Holdings Ltd. will invest $28 million to develop the zone located in Mirigama, which is 55 km (34 miles) from the main port in the capital Colombo and 40 km from the international airport. Already, China's government and Chinese firms are taking part in two major projects, building the Hambantotta port in Southern Sri Lanka and the financing of a coal-fired electricity plant. To build the second and third phases of the 900 megawatt coal-fired Norochcholai power plant, China offered an $891 million loan with a tenure of 20 years at 2 percent, media reported. China's Exim Bank also gave $360 million to finance the first phase of the Hambantotta port, in which Chinese firms are building the harbour and fuel oil bunkering terminals to service ships plying the busy sea lanes at the Indian Ocean Island's South".

Source: *Xinhua.*[10] "Li Ruogu, chairman of China's Exim Bank, and P. B. Jayasundara, Secretary to Sri Lanka's Finance Ministry, signed the agreement on behalf of the two sides. Li said his bank was very happy to support one of Sri Lanka's largest development projects and he hoped the project a success. The primary objective of the Hambantotta project is to synchronize different aspects of development such as shipping, trans-shipment, shipbuilding, and catering to increase exports and imports, for which the Port of Colombo does not have enough space and facilities".

PAKISTANI MILITARY AND OTHER SUPPORT TO SRI LANKA

A Love Triangle

Defence analysts in South Asia have noted that diplomatic ties between Sri Lanka and Pakistan started warming up in 1971, when Sri Lanka accorded transit rights to Pakistani civil aircraft carrying troops to the then East Pakistan, after India had refused overflight permission to Pakistan. A 2006 article published in Sri Lanka perhaps correctly likened the relationship between Sri Lanka, Pakistan and India lightheartedly but correctly as akin to a love triangle, with Sri Lanka being the damsel being wooed by two suitors. Excerpts:

... "There has been an Indo-Pakistan cold war over Sri Lanka. The relations involving the three nations could even be likened to a love triangle.[11] In this love triangle, Pakistan's position is that of the lover who does everything he can to woo the girl but finds that the girl loves or is compelled to love his rival.

Pakistan probably understands Sri Lanka's position, given the geo-strategic realities and domestic compulsions that have made Sri Lanka to maintain close ties with India. But it wants to be noticed more and score more points than India in Sri Lanka. This has put Sri Lanka in a diplomatically awkward position. Every time, the Sri Lanka-Pakistan relations go up a few notches, India frowns. So we prepare in advance to console or reassure India whenever Sri Lanka moves closer to Pakistan. It was Pakistan-supplied multi-barrelled rocket launchers that tilted the military balance in Sri Lanka's favour in that year when India showed reluctance to assist us militarily. Probably it was Pakistan's way of doing something in return for our favour in 1971 during the Bangladesh War. Sri Lanka defied India and allowed Pakistan civilian aircraft to fly via Colombo to Dhaka though it was aware that Pakistan was using these aircraft to transport military personnel". The significance is quite clear – Sri Lanka is acutely aware that India cannot provide the military assistance it needs beyond a point, and is increasingly looking up to Pakistan, and its strong ally, China, to get what it needs. The diplomacy is finely nuanced so that India does not get discomfited beyond a point.

Pakistan's Crucial Role[12] in the Death of Tamil Tigers

The incontestable fact is that Sri Lanka has, over the years, developed close military ties with Pakistan and the popular view in that country is that the Eelam war was won off the backs of generous military support that Pakistan and its mentor, China, provided. This is obviously not entirely true, because, as we will discover later, India contributed has also politically to the Sri Lankan success as well, but is unable to publicly claim its contribution. Let us, for the moment, see a recent Pakistani report on how they perceive the assistance they offered. Excerpts:

"It was the Pakistani defence cooperation with Sri Lanka as one of the largest suppliers of high-tech military equipment that has played a major role in the ultimate defeat of the Liberation Tigers of Tamil Eelam (LTTE) at the hands of the Lankan Army.

"According to well placed sources in the Pakistani establishment, defence cooperation between Sri Lanka and Pakistan had grown significantly in recent years as Islamabad, unlike New Delhi, had no problems supplying the Lankan Army state-of-the-art weaponry to accelerate its counter-insurgency operations against the LTTE. During his talks with Pakistani military authorities, in May 2008, Lt. Gen. Fonseka had finalised a deal according to which Pakistan sold 22 Al-Khalid tanks to Sri Lanka in a deal worth over US$100 million. General Fonseka also gave a

File Photo of Pakistani Soldiers

shopping list of weaponry worth about US$65 million to the Pakistani military authorities. While the Sri Lankan Army Chief's shopping list for the Army was pegged at $25 million, the inventory for the Lankan Air Force was worth $40 million. He had further sought diverse ammunition including grenades for urgent delivery…

"On Jan 19, 2009, Pakistani Defence Secretary Lt-Gen (Retd) Syed Athar Ali and his visiting Lankan counterpart Gottabhaya Rajapaksa in Rawalpindi had agreed to enhance cooperation in military training, exercises and intelligence sharing regarding terrorism. The agreement came amidst Sri Lankan media reports that the Pakistan Air Force (PAF) pilots had participated in several successful air strikes against several military bases of the LTTE in August 2008. Back in 2000, when the LTTE offensive code-named Operation Ceaseless Waves overran Sri Lankan military positions in the North, the Sri Lankans had sought Multi-Barrel Rocket Launcher Systems (MBRLS) and other high tech weaponry from Pakistan on an urgent basis…

Subsequently, MBRLS and weapons and ammunition, including artillery shells and multi-barrel rocket launchers, were airlifted in an emergency operation from Karachi to Colombo in May 2000. Later, in 2006, the Sri Lankan authorities had again sought Multi-Barrel Rocket Launcher Systems (MBRLS) and other advanced weapons from Pakistan when Sri Lankan President Mahinda Rajapaksa visited Pakistan in March 2006…"[13]

That the relationship between the two countries is no longer one sided, with the Sri Lankans perpetually at the receiving end, is evident from the recent media blitz in Sri Lanka, post termination of the Eelam war, that Pakistan, amongst other nations, is seeking their expertise in conduct of anti insurgency operations, as well as small team operations concerning the Navy (SBS operations). Extracts:[14] "Following the Sri Lankan Army's tremendous success against the Liberation Tigers of Tamil Eelam (LTTE), the Pakistan Government wants it to train their security personnel in counter-insurgency operations, Commander of the Sri Lankan Army, Lieutenant General Jagath Jayasuriya said. Former Sri Lanka Naval Chief, Admiral Wasantha Karannagoda, who is currently the National Security Adviser, had recently said that the strategies and tactics adopted by the Sri Lankan Navy to tackle the LTTE's Naval Arm could be very useful for other countries as well. "Future conflicts would not be like facing battleships and destroyers but small and fast boats of non-state rogue navies which could be indulging in insurgencies, piracies and trafficking of various kinds," Admiral Karannagoda had said."

TO BE OR NOT TO BE – THE SRI LANKA SECURITY CONUNDRUM FOR INDIA

Hamlet's confusion in decision making seems to be India's too at several levels of understanding and functioning with respect to her relationship with Sri Lanka. On one hand, there are traditional ties to consider, some of which can be traced beyond the pale of written records. These are historical and religious connects which have endured over thousands of years. The caution to observe here is that the ethnic tension manifest today – the Sinhala-Tamil divide – is almost as ancient and is yet to be addressed comprehensively. The economic and social ties too, extend backwards for centuries and have had periods of waxing and waning. It is reiterated earlier in this book, that when the problem erupted in the modern era, especially during the ending phases of the British era, the Indian method of non-violent protest was the preferred choice of protest, and Indian leaders struggling for Independence from the British taken to be role models.

That said, India's compulsions to look after Tamil sensitivities, whether of the Plantation Tamils or the Sri Lankan Tamils, has always been politics and vote bank driven. With 60 million Tamils in India, no Indian Government in power has dared to ignore these sensitivities, to the extent that these have seriously circumscribed the area within which India can exercise its strategic options with regard to Sri Lanka. It is therefore not a matter of surprise that India's Achilles' heel in this regard has been sensed and exploited by Sri Lanka, as well as by Pakistan and, most certainly China in pursuit of their national interests.

That notwithstanding, Indian diplomacy has still been at work, not so much in the public eye as behind the scenes. To ensure that its interests are not eroded beyond a point. Sri Lanka, in its turn, also realizes the realpolitik dictated by geographical location, size, demography and security needs. And has been careful not to stretch the diplomatic rope too tautly; thereby risking its snapping.

The functional nature of this conundrum from India's perspective is shared via a few extracts:

Sri Lanka: India's Latest Security Nightmare[15]

The writer, in this interesting article, opines that "Sri Lanka is fast emerging as a security nightmare for India. Basking in its military success against the separatist Tamil Tigers, Sri Lanka is cementing its ties with China and Pakistan, ignoring Indian security interests. By embracing India's enemies and inviting them home, treating them as guests, and doing business with them, Sri Lanka is embarking on a dangerous foreign policy that has the potential to undermine India's national security...The Chinese are building an expressway in Colombo and are also involved in an important power project in North Sri Lanka. As the two countries keep signing more collaborative projects, and the Chinese presence increases in Sri Lanka, it would bring the Chinese within breathing (or striking) distance of India's southern coast, where several sensitive installations including atomic power plants are located. Chinese personnel will be all over Sri Lanka..." The writer goes on to say that "Sri Lanka doesn't lose an opportunity to reaffirm its commitment to the one – China policy. By doing that Sri Lanka accepts Chinese claims over Taiwan. But Sri Lanka maintains a stoic silence on Kashmir and Arunachal Pradesh. It doesn't want to spoil its relations with Pakistan or China by coming out with a pro-India stand on Kashmir or Arunachal Pradesh. For all the military and financial assistance it has got from India, Colombo has done few favours in return..."[16]

Sri Lanka Turns to Pakistan, China for Military Needs[17]

Rahul Bedi, in his well researched article, says that, "Unmindful of India's opposition to Sri Lanka turning to Pakistan and China for military hardware to bolster its offensive against the Tamil Tigers, Colombo has recently inked several significant defence agreements with Beijing...

"Citing exclusive access to an internal Sri Lankan cabinet document, Britain's renowned *Jane's Defence Weekly* (JDW) reported that Sri Lanka had signed a classified $37.6 million deal with China's Poly Technologies in April to supply its defence forces with ammunition and ordnance for the Army and Navy in addition to varied small arms...

"The largest single order with Poly Technologies is for 120 mm mortar shells for the Army, of which 70,000 rounds are priced at $10.4 million. Additional imports include 68,000 rounds of varied 152 mm artillery shells worth nearly $20 million besides 50,000 81mm high-explosive mortar bombs for $3.7 million, all of which the army needs to reinforce its 'pro-active' military strategy against the LTTE. The navy's requirement valued at $ 2.7 million includes a varied range of ammunition like 100,000 14.5 mm cartridges, 2,000 RPG-7 rockets and 500 81 mm airburst mortar shells... The writer goes on to say that "Jane's declared that the China National Electronics Import Export Corp is to provide Sri Lanka a JY 11 3D radar for $5 million over the next few weeks once the site for its location near Colombo is ready. Colombo had initially ordered the JY 11 radar two years ago, making payments in advance but was forced to call off the deal following Indian protests that the system would 'over arch' into its air space...

"Thereafter, India supplied Sri Lanka two INDRA IN-PC-2D radars free of charge and is believed to have agreed to Colombo's request for at least one more following the spate of LTTE air raids. The INDRA radars have become a source of tension with India, with some Sri Lankan officials claiming they failed to detect the ingress by a Tamil Tiger propeller aircraft to an air force base outside Colombo in March… In an associated development, Sri Lanka is also planning on acquiring an unspecified number of MIG 29 fighters to boost its air power. Indian defence sources said New Delhi, which also operates at least three MIG 29 squadrons, could play an 'important' role in Sri Lanka's proposed purchase of similar fighters by agreeing to provide training, spares, servicing and other logistic back-up"…[18]

Sri Lanka – Playing Chinese Chequers[19]

N. Sathiya Moorthy, in his brilliant article, looks at the issue from a different perspective. He says that "Proximity alone is no guarantor for a better understanding of men and their methods in the evolution of bilateral relations. Moscow learnt it the hard way in Afghanistan. So did India, in the case of Sri Lanka. Both are wiser by their experiences. If anything, it is this experience that seems to be moulding the 'New Millennium' Indian approach to Sri Lanka – and possibly the rest of South Asia. He goes on to say that, "At the height of the 'Eelam War IV', India showed that it did not need veto power to bring around – or, check – emerging and more powerful adversaries of Sri Lanka on the global scene. Nor did China stop the West from a reference being made to the Sri Lankan situation in the UN Security Council, after a point. If China has the veto vote, so has Russia. In trade-offs of the kind as was witnessed in the Security Council during the closing weeks of the ethnic war, nations like Sri Lanka would continue to be treated as pawns by the 'Big Five' – and nothing more…

"India and Sri Lanka cannot shed the geographical and geological realities governing their two nations and their peoples. Nor can they wish away the geo-strategic realities on which neither has any great control after a point. Given the attendant realities, it is truer of Sri Lanka than of India – and would remain so for all times to come. By the same token, neither can Sri Lanka – nor India, for that matter – wish away the realities of Tamil Nadu politics and society in matters pertaining to the 'ethnic issue' in the island-nation. Electoral politics is a game which President Rajapaksa is as well-versed in as anyone else – and understands the compulsions of the same, as any other…[20]

The 'Tamil Nadu factor' will remain relevant to bilateral relations only until Sri Lanka finds a peaceful solution to the 'ethnic issue'. That can happen tomorrow, that can take weeks and months, if not years and decades. The other issue pertains to fishing in the Palk Bay. No Chinese presence can wish away the issue, for which peaceful solutions are already on the anvil. Negative impulses on these counts can only upset the bilateral apple-cart, where there is no need or reason…

Post-Cold War, India seems to acknowledge that Sri Lanka is the first line of strategic defence for the country in the southern seas than ever before – and that the strategic defence of Sri Lanka forms a key element to the strategic defence of India. There is more that they can do together in terms of maritime counter-terrorism and may be continued to be called upon to do so..."[21] This analysis by the writer is absolutely spot on, and is an umbilical cord that ties the two nations intimately together, regardless of their differences of perception on a host of other issues. He makes another thoughtful reflection: "China's stoic silence not to interfere in the 'Bangladesh War' of 1971, despite being plodded by (its) new-found American friend of the time, should be a case in point. More importantly, it was Pakistan, (an) ally of China that was at the receiving end at the time, yet Beijing had its role (or, non-role), well defined. So was it during the 'Kargil War' nearly three decades down the line…"[22] This remark may be the writer's way of politely expressing a contrary opinion to the escalating belief in this region, that China is preparing for a confrontation with India, in the near future.

India's Hidden Hand Behind Lanka's Victory Over LTTE[23]

Those who study Indian diplomacy, its successes and its failures, will no doubt agree that it does function rather differently than most other comparative systems. For one, access to how Indian diplomacy works is often divined by intelligent guesswork and smart reading of straws in the wind (occasional statements put out by our diplomats, in the typical bland, open-ended manner that our diplomats seem to prefer). Rarely, if ever, has there been transparency in sharing with the people what went into taking certain political decisions. Whereas this has its advantages, however obtuse these might seem in the short term, sometimes, the government refuses to share details of its dealings, no doubt keeping 'sensitivities' in mind. This is what Nitin Gokhale seems to have stumbled upon, or researched, when he suggests that, though India publicly refused to provide military support to Sri Lanka to fight the LTTE, she had a 'hidden hand' in the success of the Island nation's campaign over the terrorist outfit, says a new book, *'Sri Lanka, From War to Peace'*. Defence and Strategic Affairs Editor with NDTV, Gokhale covered the 33-month Eelam War in Sri Lanka. The book is a 'must read'.

"The MI-17s that India 'quietly gifted' to Lanka were in addition to a Sukanya class offshore patrol vessel also gifted by the Indian Coast Guard to the Sri Lankan Navy in 2002. The choppers played a major role in several daring missions launched by the Sri Lankan Air Force to rescue the Army's deep penetration units and injured soldiers from deep inside LTTE-held territory," the book says.

"Hampered by domestic compulsions, New Delhi could not go beyond such meagre and clandestine transfer of military hardware. Publicly, all India was willing to acknowledge was the supply of low-flying detection 'INDRA' radars to the Sri Lankan Air Force since this equipment was considered a defensive apparatus," the author says.[24]

Gokhale quotes senior Sri Lankan Army officers saying that "thanks to the MI-17s, the soldiers operating behind enemy lines functioned with a greater degree of confidence since they knew these choppers were always at hand to come to their rescue whenever necessary. This surely was the key factor in our Special Forces delivering spectacular results..."

Not wanting to annoy its Tamil Nadu allies like the DMK unnecessarily, New Delhi had a 'politically most important message' conveyed to Colombo to try and conclude the war against the LTTE (called Eelam War IV) before the summer of 2009 when India was expected to hold the general elections, Gokhale says.

"The Rajapaksa regime was nothing if not shrewd. Aware of the dynamics that determined India's Lankan policies, it was also conscious of India's anxiety in losing strategic space in Sri Lanka. The Rajapaksa brothers were pragmatic enough to realize that Lanka needed India's support in the war against the LTTE, total support from China and Pakistan notwithstanding…

"Colombo could ignore India but only up to a point," the author says.

"So Mahinda Rajapaksa hit upon an idea of an informal exchange mechanism between New Delhi and Colombo. He nominated both his brothers – Basil (MP and Presidential advisor) and Gottabhaya, the Defence Secretary, along with his own secretary Lalith Weeratunga...

"India too reciprocated immediately. The Indian team comprised National Security Advisor MK Narayanan, Foreign Secretary Shiv Shankar Menon and Defence Secretary Vijay Singh…

"Colombo may have been ambivalent about meeting Indian requests to end the operations before the general elections but the Sri Lankan leadership once again gratefully acknowledged the Indian Navy's contribution in locating and destroying at least 10 'floating warehouses' owned by the LTTE that were used by the Tigers to store arms, ammunition and even armoured personnel carriers…Well-coordinated operations by the two navies between 2006 and 2009 actually broke the backbone of the Sea Tigers," Gokhale says.

"Also, under an agreement between the two countries, the Indian Navy and the Coast Guard frequently sent out ships to patrol the Palk Strait and the Gulf of Mannar. The presence of warships and Indian patrol vessels acted as a firm deterrence against the Sea Tigers," the book says.

The book also notes the transformation of the Sri Lankan Air Force and Navy into lethal forces that played vital roles in victory over the LTTE. "The Sri Lankan Air Force had indeed come a long way from its inglorious days in the 1990s when it lost three aircraft to the LTTE's ground fire in the assault on Jaffna."[25]

Another review of the book[26] quotes the author as saying (with reference to the gifted helicopters) that "The ruling United Progressive Alliance (UPA) Government in New Delhi was dependent upon the DMK party from Tamil Nadu, perceived to be sympathetic to the LTTE, for its survival in Parliament. Publicly, India maintained that it would not give Sri Lanka any offensive weapons. Yet, in early 2006 India quietly gifted five Mi-17 helicopters to the Sri Lankan Air Force," Gokhale writes. "The only Indian condition was: these helicopters would fly under Sri Lankan Air Force colours. New Delhi clearly did not want to annoy UPA's Tamil Nadu allies like the DMK unnecessarily," he says. The author singles out the Indian Navy for special praise. The Indian Coast Guard gifted a Sukanya Class Offshore Patrol Vessel (OPV) to the Sri Lankan Navy in 2002, which played a major role in several daring missions launched by the Sri Lankan Air Force to rescue the Army's Deep Penetration Units when they were surrounded by LTTE's counter-infiltration units...

According to Indian and Sri Lankan Navy sources quoted by the author in his book, well-coordinated operations by the two navies between 2006 and 2009 actually broke the backbone of the LTTE's Sea Tigers. Intelligence-sharing also proved crucial. The Indian Navy's Dorniers, fitted with powerful radars, based at Ramnad in Tamil Nadu flew regular reconnaissance missions over the seas around Sri Lanka. "Whenever a suspicious ship was detected, the Indian Navy passed on the information to the Sri Lankans. The real time intelligence helped the Sri Lankan Navy to track and then destroy the LTTE arms consignments," says Gokhale, who covered the last phase of Sri Lanka's battle against Tamil Tigers for NDTV. The book also recounts vividly the last days of LTTE chief V. Prabhakaran, who pioneered the cult of suicide bombers and tormented the Sri Lankan state and people for three decades. Ordering the assassination of former Prime Minister of India Rajiv Gandhi proved to be a major strategic error on the part of the charismatic guerrilla leader, the author writes. Gokhale also provides an insight into the Sri Lankan government's winning strategy for the decimation of the LTTE that ended Asia's longest-running insurgency."[27]

Other Forms of Indian Assistance and Indian Expectations from Sri Lanka

Lest readers get the idea that Indian diplomatic assistance was restricted to undeclared transfer of arms and professional expertise, it must be reiterated that India has been both visible and vocal in declaring help to Sri Lanka in material, economic, infrastructure and political terms. This has been an ongoing process since the last few years. These meetings[28] have been held at official as well as ministerial level, extending right up to the level of the foreign ministers and a meeting between the Indian Prime Minister and the Sri Lankan President. The broad areas of concern have been the need for Tamils in Sri Lanka to "lead a life of dignity and honour"[29] within a unified Sri Lanka, the provision of substantial money for the Internally Displaced Persons' (IDP's) rehabilitation[30] and the need to start and complete the process of devolution,[31] within a period of 180 days that Sri Lanka has agreed upon. India has also provided open help for accelerating the process of demining[32] by sending trained army engineers to Sri Lanka in large numbers.

Positive Strategic Level Responses by Sri Lanka

Should the reader feel that Sri Lanka has made no reciprocal gesture towards India, this feeling may be unfounded. The Island nation is trying its best to balance its diplomacy the best way it can by having sent a proposal to India not so long back to develop Kankasanthurai (KKS) Port[33] on its east coast. India is already developing Trincomalee Port, also on its east coast.

A dispassionate overview of this chapter reveals that, notwithstanding its unavoidable constraints and historic burdens, Indian diplomacy, with reference to the Sri Lanka imbroglio, has been found sadly wanting for the over 30 years that the current crisis has lasted. There have been periods, no doubt, when India diplomacy has been vibrant, pragmatic and realpolitik driven. These occasions, however, have been few and far in between. For most of the period, we seem to have simply muddled our way through. We still lack a coherent vision; a long term perspective of what Sri Lanka means to us and how its stability and prosperity, as opposed to strife and discord impinge on our security concerns.

The blunt fact is that India is psychologically seen as the '*other*' whose publicly exhibited deriding and negation seems to be very necessary for its smaller neighbours (Sri Lanka and Nepal are prime examples) for their survival. While India does not continually have to apologise for its size and overwhelming footprint in South Asia and the Indian Ocean littoral, it certainly needs to correct the current small nation mindset of serving as the '*other*'; a nation viewed with fear, suspicion and uncertainty. This image make over is urgently needed, using wise, mature, forward looking diplomacy: not the 'on-off' effort that our diplomatic mandarins seem to be adept at. We need to wake up from our position of slumber and sloth, and may be pick up a diplomatic nuance or two from Mahinda Rajapaksa on how to win and keep 'friends' (even if these are friends of convenience) and influence nations for the supreme national interest of ones country.

India cannot claim to be happy, smug, complacent or supercilious with the visible and deep, almost insulting 'we cock-a-snook,' multi-strand relationships that both Pakistan and China have forged with Sri Lanka, at a distance of a mere 31 kilometres from India's Southern coastline. The military, political, commercial, diplomatic and strategic ties that these nations (both avowedly inimical to India's security concerns) have forged at India's door step, would not have been possible had Indian diplomacy been more proactive, watchful, visionary, and quite simply, more 'hands on'. They were not; with the result that Sri Lanka has welded ties with them that seriously militate against India's long term national interests. The shocking thing is that Sri Lanka has still managed to retain a seemingly excellent relationship with India, at least so far as public awareness goes.

There is thus no harm in accepting that the Rajapaksa clan, led by President Mahinda Rajapaksa and assisted by Gottabhaya, Basil, his two brothers and Rohitha Bogollogama, the Foreign Minister, have been far smarter and savvy in this sphere than our political and diplomatic masters and our diplomatic mandarins in South Block. From the moment he assumed office in end 2005, Mahinda had a well thought out strategic game plan to serve his short term national interest – destruction of the LTTE. This involved adroitly by passing India, to seek military assistance on ridiculously easy financial terms from Pakistan and China. His reach extended to Israel, Russia and other East European countries. Even as his policy met with thundering success, he managed to let our complacent diplomats and uncaring politicians remain assured that they need not get alarmed; that their Tamil-led worries would be attended to. The arms and ammunition imports ex China, Pakistan and others was also rationalized by Sri Lanka saying they understood why India could not help them in their time of need.

Since the real world does not believe in free lunches, and realpolitik had taught her that lesson early on in the civil war, Sri Lanka forged strong commercial relationships with both countries; the Chinese in particular. Our Foreign Office may pat itself on the back that we are likely to or are already developing KKS and Trincomalee harbours for Sri Lanka. We should however, note with deep concern that the EEZ development around Colombo has been undertaken by China. The Chinese has also been awarded the development of Hambantotta from a fishing village to a deep water world class Port on the Southern tip of Sri Lanka, *just 10 nautical miles* away from the vital oil shipping lanes linking West Asia to East and South East Asia.

It is not necessary to give the Chinese strategy (with or without Sri Lankan connivance) a name. Some analysts call it the Chinese "string of pearls" strategy on limiting Indian influence in South Asia and the Indian Ocean Region. That may or may not be the case. For the moment, it would suffice for us to accept that China will, as a consequence of this hugely important strategic development, have a **permanent naval presence** at our doorstep. If rumours (so far unconfirmed) that persist that Hambantotta Port was first offered to India for development, but was turned down only later picked up by China when offered the chance by Sri Lanka are correct, we need to be worried about the ham-handed manner in which we conduct our foreign policy. The heavy weapon supplies to Sri Lanka from Pakistan and other military, training and commercial tie ups with it can hardly also be comforting for India; empty assurances and spin doctoring by the Indian MEA notwithstanding.

Indian diplomacy therefore needs to quickly come of age, before it ends up doing untold and irreversible damage to Indian security interests in its immediate neighbourhood and in the Indian Ocean region in general. Sri Lanka is certainly India's first bulwark of defence in the south and needs nuanced, holistic and wise diplomatic handling with a long term vision and corresponding, proactive and forward looking strategy for its implementation.

Endnotes

1. "Sri Lanka Won An Important Victory Over LTTE – Ambassador Blake". Statement by Ambassador Robert Blake, New Assistant Secretary of State for South Asia and Central Asia to Congressional Sub Committee on South Asia. 25 June 2009. < http://sinhale.wordpress.com/2009/06/26/sri-lanka-won-an-important-victory-over-ltte-ambassador-blake/ > Only excerpts have been used.
2. Lalith. "China a 'Stakeholder' in Sri Lanka's Development: Sri Lanka". August 22, 2009. (Source: beta.thehindu.com).<http://www.nowpublic.com/world/china-stakeholder-sri-lanka-s-development-sri-lanka >
3. Page, Jeremy. "Chinese Billions in Sri Lanka Fund Battle against Tamil Tigers". South Asia Correspondent. *The Times*, UK. May 2, 2009. <http://www.timesonline.co.uk/tol/news/world/asia/article6207487.ece>
4. Raman, B. "The Naval Challenges". Update. <http://www.outlookindia.com/article.aspx?261008> Excerpts from his article have been used. B. Raman is Additional Secretary (Retd), Cabinet Secretariat, Govt. of India, New Delhi, and, presently, Director, Institute for Topical Studies, Chennai. He is also associated with the Chennai Centre for China Studies.
5. Page, Jeremy. "Chinese Support Crucial To Sri Lankan Victory over Tamils". South Asia Correspondent. *The Times*, UK. May 16, 2009. <http://www.timesonline.co.uk/tol/news/world/asia/article6297463.ece>
6. "Sri Lanka China Port Project". <http://www.defence.pk/forums/china-defence/22842-sri-lanka-china-port-project.html>
7. Chellaney, Bramha. "China Fuels Sri Lankan War". March 04, 2009. <http://search.japantimes.co.jp/cgi-bin/eo20090304bc.html> Brahma Chellaney is Professor of Strategic Studies at the privately funded Centre for Policy Research in New Delhi.
8. Ibid.
9. "Sri Lanka Grants China Exclusive Economic Zone". July 01, 2009. <http://www.chinadaily.com.cn/china/2009-07/01/content_8344523.htm>
10. China, Sri Lanka Sign Loan Pact on Port Project. Xinhua. October 31, 2007. http://english.people.com.cn/90001/90776/90883/6293630.html
11. The Love Triangle of Sri Lanka, India and Pakistan. April 05, 2006. http://www.lankanewspapers.com/news/2006/4/6332.html
12. Mir, Amir. "Pakistan's Crucial Role In The Death Of Tamil Tigers". Former Editor, *The*

Independent (a Lahore Weekly). May 19, 2009. <http://www.netspikes.com/news/pakistannews/pakistan%E2%80%99s-crucial-role-in-the-death-of-tamil-tigers/>

13. Ibid. The report also adds that several Pakistani officers were at hand to advise the SLAF on the actual conduct of the war. See "Military History of Pakistan: Military Assistance to Sri Lanka". http://en.wikipedia.org/wiki/Military_history_of_Pakistan#Military _assistance_ to_ Sri_Lanka in this connection. The report reiterates (in part) that "Pakistan and Sri Lanka enjoy a strong relationship and Pakistan International Airlines planes ferrying Pakistan Army reinforcements to East Pakistan, now Bangladesh, refueled in Colombo after India denied Pakistan overflight permission before the actual outbreak of the Indo-Pakistan war of 1971. Pakistan has sent military advisers, ammunition and other equipment to Sri Lanka during previous offensives against the LTTE. Many Sri Lankan officers are trained in Pakistan. The country, by supplying high-tech military equipment such as 22 Al-Khalid main battle tanks, 250,000 rounds of 60mm, 81mm, 120mm and 130mm mortar ammunition worth and 150,000 hand grenades, along with positioning some of its highly trained army officers in Sri Lanka, played a key role in the ultimate defeat of Tamil Tigers in May 2009".
14. "Pakistan Asks Sri Lankan Army to Train Its Armed Forces in Counterinsurgency Operations". ANI. August 21, 2009. <http://blog.taragana.com/n/pakistan-asks-sri-lankan-army-to-train-its-armed-forces-in-counterinsurgency-operations-145937/>
15. Kumar, P.C. Vinoj. "Sri Lanka: India's Latest Security Nightmare". August 25, 2009. Special Correspondent, Tehelka.<http://pcvinojkumar.blogspot.com/2009/08/sri-lanka-indias-latest-security.html>
16. Ibid.
17. Bedi, Rahul. "Sri Lanka Turns To Pakistan, China For Military Needs". India News. June 02, 2007. <http://www.indianmuslims.info/news/2007/jun/02/sri_lanka_turns_pakistan _china _military_needs.html>
18. Ibid.
19. Moorthy, N. Sathiya. "Sri Lanka – Playing Chinese Checkers". C3S Paper No.339. August 26, 2009. <http://www.c3sindia.org/southasia/761> (Courtesy – *Daily Mirror*, Colombo, 22, 24 and 25 August 2009.)
20. Ibid.
21. Ibid.
22. Ibid.
23. "India's Hidden Hand Behind Lanka's Victory Over LTTE". August 23, 2009. <http://in.mg50.mail.yahoo.com/dc/launch?.gx=0&.rand=ee1alls51sih9> Excerpts have been quoted from this review.
24. Ibid.
25. Ibid.
26. "Sri Lanka - From War to Peace" by Nitin A. Gokhale reveals India's 'Hidden Hand' In Sri Lanka War". IANS. August 22, 2009. http://weeksupdate.com/2009/08/sri-lanka-from-war-to-peace-by-nitin.html
27. Ibid.
28. "India Trying to Help Tamils in Sri Lanka: PM". IANS. May 9, 2009.< http://blog.taragana.com/n/india-trying-to-help-tamils-in-sri-lanka-pm-57620/> This report says (in part) that India is doing what it can to help the beleaguered Tamil community in Sri Lanka lead 'a life of dignity and honour', Prime Minister Manmohan Singh said on May 3, 2009. The Prime Minister told journalists that he was 'deeply concerned over the very difficult situation in Sri Lanka' where thousands have died in a military onslaught aimed at crushing the Tamil Tigers. Manmohan Singh emphasised that any solution to the conflict in the Island nation needed to be found 'within a unified Sri Lanka'. 'At every opportunity I have had (to interact) with the President and Prime Minister of Sri Lanka... on every occasion I have raised this issue. The Tamil people have not had a fair deal, they have justified grievances.' When it was pointed out to him that some in Tamil Nadu were glorifying the LTTE, which is outlawed in India, Manmohan Singh said: 'As far as the Government of India is concerned, the LTTE has so far been regarded as a terrorist organisation and that is the policy of the Government of India.'

29. Ibid.
30. "India Willing to Give More Money for Resettling Sri Lanka Tamils". IANS. July 30, 2009. <http://blog.taragana.com/n/india-willing-to-give-more-money-for-resettling-sri-lanka-tamils-125438/ > The report says (in part) that Prime Minister Manmohan Singh is willing to give more funds, besides the Rs.500 crores (around $100 million) which India has already pledged, for resettlement of around 300,000 civilians displaced by the conflict in Sri Lanka, External Affairs Minister S.M. Krishna said Thursday. When Manmohan Singh met Sri Lankan President Mahinda Rajapaksa on the sidelines of the Non-Aligned Movement (NAM) Summit at Sharm el-Sheikh in Egypt earlier this month, he reiterated India's willingness to enable the return of internally displaced persons (IDPs) to their homes, Krishna told Parliament.
31. Chand, Manish. "Devolution, Resettlement on Course, Sri Lanka Tells India". July 22, 2009. <http://blog.taragana.com/n/devolution-resettlement-on-course-sri-lanka-tells-india-117026/> The report says that Sri Lanka Wednesday assured India on July, 22, 2009, that the process of devolution of powers to the Tamil minority is on course as it tries to resettle over 300,000 civilians displaced by the military conflict in the shortest possible time. Indian External Affairs Minister S.M. Krishna held talks with his Sri Lankan counterpart Rohitha Bogollagama for nearly half hour on the sidelines of India-ASEAN ministerial meetings in Phuket, Thailand. This was the first high-level contact between India and Sri Lanka after Prime Minister Manmohan Singh met President Mahinda Rajapaksa on the sidelines of the Non-Aligned Summit in Egypt last week.
32. M.R. Narayan Swamy. "Post-War, India Helps Sri Lanka Rebuild Tamil Areas". September 27, 2009. http://blog.taragana.com/n/post-war-india-helps-sri-lanka-rebuild-tamil-areas-179999/The report says (in part) that, "from vocational training to mine clearing, India is providing sweeping help to Sri Lanka to rebuild vast areas after the end of a quarter-century-long Tamil separatist campaign. Already 2,600 tons of shelter materials have gone to Sri Lanka, mainly to ensure that those displaced by fighting that ended in May 2009 get a roof over the head. Another equivalent amount of 2,600 tons of shelter material are to be sent soon. After the visit by a delegation of the Indian Council of Agriculture Research (ICAR) to Sri Lanka, the Railways hope to help Colombo lay at least two rail lines in the country's north. India is going to send more de-mining teams to help Sri Lanka remove thousands of landmines buried in Sri Lanka's North and East since the war erupted in 1983. Sri Lanka is one of the world's most heavily mined areas. There are no precise estimates regarding the number of mines the military and the LTTE buried. The mines have killed and maimed thousands".
33. "In What Appears To Be A Developing Counterweight To Hambantotta: Sri Lanka Proposes India To Renovate Strategic Kankasanthurai Port". September 21, 2009. <http://www.defenceforum.in/forum/indian-strategic-alliances/6046-have-you-read-srilanka-proposes-india-renovate-strategic-kankasanthurai-port.html> As per the above report (excerpts have been quoted here), Sri Lanka has submitted a proposal to India on renovating and rehabilitating parts of the strategic Kankasanthurai (KKS) Harbour in Jaffna in North Sri Lanka. The Sri Lankan Ports Authority (SPLA) recently submitted a list of "what the Sri Lankan government expects at KKS Port" to officials of the Indian High Commission in Colombo. The meeting was attended by the SLPA chairperson P. Wickrama. The port is located at the northern tip of Sri Lanka in Jaffna, a high security zone. The Sri Lankan Army captured it from the separatist LTTE in 1995 and the SLAF continue to have heavy presence in the area. For India, presence at KKS would be important because of its proximity to its southern coast. India is also entrenched in the Trincomalee Harbour in East Sri Lanka. In the South, China has got ahead and is building the ambitious Hambantotta port project in President Mahinda Rajapaksa's home district. It was learnt that India for one could help the SLPA in salvaging wrecks of ships which sank off the KKS coast. SLPA officials estimate that at least half-dozen ships and boats belonging to the Sri Lankan Navy and the LTTE had sunk during fighting in the area.

CHAPTER 18

Dynamic and Innovative Tactics by SLA to End the War

It was an amazing, epochal transformation for an erstwhile staid, colonial mindset ridden, orthodox, conventional fighting force. This perhaps best describes the astonishing turnaround exhibited by the SLA, in the closing stages of the civil war, in specific, the last three years of the war. The transformation began, as indicated earlier in the book, with the Mavil Aru reservoir operation, and ended with the killing of Prabhakaran and his key aides in May 2009.

Casualties suffered in operations are often a clear indicator of military capability. The Secretary of Defence, MoD, Gottabhaya Rajapaksa, has said in a recent interview with Sri Lanka State television, that 23,790 Sri Lankan military personnel have been killed since 1981.[1] The corresponding casualty figures for the LTTE are 27,639. The overall figures almost match, and do not give a clear enough indication of victor or vanquished. It is the startling analysis of the casualties suffered by the opposing sides in the last three years that is both staggering as well as revealing.[2]

From the August 2006 recapture of the Mavil Aru reservoir until the formal declaration of the cessation of hostilities (on May 19, 2009), 6261 Sri Lankan soldiers were killed and 29,551 were wounded. The Sri Lankan military estimates that up to 22,000 LTTE militants were killed during the last three years of the conflict. This figure suggests a kill ratio of 1:4, that is, the SLA lost one soldier for every four LTTE cadres it killed. These are respectable figures for militaries (both developing as well as developed), involved in anti –insurgency operations. [Readers may be interested in learning that the casualty ratio in the No War No Peace (NWNP) environment in Jammu and Kashmir is 1:6 in favour of the Indian Army]. The figures given by GOC 57 Infantry Division, Maj. Gen. Jagath Dias, during a rare forward area visit by a foreign (Australian) journalist when the war was about to end, are even more startling. He claimed a kill ratio of 1:11 for his Division; a staggering figure against an enemy who, in their heyday, were one of the most feared terror outfits in the world, and who had almost broken the back of the SLA.

A great deal has already been mentioned in the book about this astonishing transformation, in particular in the SLA, and, in general, in the SLAF. It has been stated that it was driven at the macro level by the 'troika' comprising the current President, Mahinda Rajapaksa, his brother, the Defence Secretary, Gottabhaya Rajapaksa, and the Army Chief, Gen. Sarath Fonseka (now retired). The unity of politico-military objectives and intent, and the carte blanche given to the military to 'bash on regardless,' created an extraordinarily helpful and fertile platform for the military in the field, to translate strategic intent into tactical reality. With all military needs (in weapons, material and manpower) coming in practically on demand; with the needed external assistance in financial and political terms, (some visible, some invisible, as brought out in the last chapter), all that was needed was hard nosed, high quality, 'follow me' operational and tactical level military leadership to engineer the needed changes in the officers, soldiery and war fighting techniques, in order to ensure delivery as planned. This was put into place by the SLAF ruthlessly, thus succeeding in their overall design.

Perhaps the biggest change invoked was in **making the humble soldier central to the whole transformation**. A concerted, well thought-out and brilliantly executed war on the soldiers mind was carried out, using past experience, mistakes made and a most careful and detailed study of the enemy's (LTTE) tactics, capability and operational art as its foundation. The soldier's faith in his own abilities, and, thereby his confidence and his morale were targeted over time and improved. **The method used was simple but most difficult – the SLA got down to the basic building block of soldiering – the man himself. This required great moral courage of the military leadership, besides patience, perseverance and time. This was so because much of what the soldier had learnt for conventional war fighting had to be set aside for this most unconventional war against a most clever, unpredictable, tenacious and proficient enemy.**

Conventional armies preach safety in numbers. Mass in application; a strength ratio of 3:1 is the basis of a conventional attack. Command is exercised along hierarchical lines; order is the norm and disorder shunned as it leads to casualty. Individual creativity and initiative suffer savagely, because everything is programmed, with the soldier treated only as a small cog in the overall wheel of war. Orthodoxy, rigidity, predictability, slowness of response, absence of initiative, dash, innovation is the norm. In such a set up, the soldier perpetually awaits orders, is specifically told what to do, in what time frame and how. He does not have to think. That requirement is being met elsewhere, at a higher level far removed from the grime and harshness of reality. "Yours is but to do and die, yours is not to question why" is an old ditty that haunts soldiers cast in the conventional mould because it often runs true. And so it was for the SLA. They had fought in a 'brave but baffled mode' for 25 long years, picking up huge casualties along the way. It was then that the leadership, led by Gen. Sarath Fonseka decided to break the mould – and how.

He empowered the soldier. He made the soldier the most important cog of the military wheel; in fact; the soldier became the heart of the army. The army which dictated to the soldier, now listened to him – the NCO, the subaltern, the captain, the major, the colonel, the brigadier, the major general, the top-most rung in the field army all listened intently to what he had to say; a huge departure from the past where the soldier had no voice.

Thus the soldier became the focus of attention. He was taught to develop soldiering skills, both mental and physical, of the genre that is often reserved for the chosen few; the Special Forces. He thus developed as an all-rounder; capable of handling most skill requirements on his own. Map reading, self sufficiency, dash, initiative, out-of-the-box thinking added to the cold courage he already had, became his hallmarks. From being just a soldier, he converted into a thinking soldier; a person who, ironically, became like the enemy whom he needed to beat – the LTTE Tigers. General Fonseka made sure that while this mental reorientation was on, the soldiers' fitness, both mental and physical, was paid due attention. The concept of 'all round' soldier was thus taken seriously, and at all levels of functioning – and monitored, again, at all levels of command.

The next big step in empowerment that General Fonseka promoted was to institutionalize initiative and improvisational skills in the soldier. The lowest denominator for this transformation was the humble section comprising of 8/9 men. These men, who comprised the section were, in effect told, that they and their military opinions and thinking mattered to the platoon commander, who commanded three such sections; to the company commander who commanded three platoons, to the battalion commander who commanded several companies, to the brigade commander who commanded three or more battalions and to the division commander who commanded several brigades. He was their supreme field authority and answered for their military capability – or the lack of it – to the Army Chief, General Fonseka.

It is not very often in armies the world over, that a senior officer at the level of a division commander has the time, bandwidth or interest in listening to how his junior-most commanders see the war, and, if needed, learn from them. Those who do have such time or such priorities end up on the winning side, but only after a great deal of personal involvement and genuine interest in subordinate development has been invested. This is also the unglamorous recipe to winning an anti-insurgency campaign or a war, which people who are in a hurry for results have no time for. That the Sri Lankan Army realized this after 25 years of jungle and urban area bashing, and savage casualties, should be taken as a huge credit for them. Often, such radical reorientation results at an army level fail miserably because they are not followed through with patience, persistence, continuity and faith. SLA displayed this nobility and won.

Freed from the pedantry of set-piece solutions for set piece battles and encounters, the officers and men broke all the conventional templates that they could and with stunning effect. They attacked where the enemy was strong. They defied conventional military knowledge and refused massed, predictable attacks, using guile, cunning, innovation and deception in preference to frontal assaults against which the Tigers had long perfected the art of survival. They became night owls, no longer afraid of the darkness, of loss of command and control, elaborate logistics and so on. Using a unique amalgam of manoeuvre and attrition, they also brought in simultaneity, unorthodoxy and unpredictability into their functioning. They thus bettered the Tigers at their game. Ironically, as the Tigers started their decline, they did so because they chose to fight out of their comfort zone, which was stealth and surprise driven. They fought conventionally and lost decisively, in a war where convention had to be sacrificed, not sustained.

The SLA thus got into the enemy's mind at its junior-most levels and ended up doing things better than the enemy in a faster time frame and with greater consistency. Small team operations, operating at night, devolution of command and control, loads of initiative, greater self faith, confidence thereto, greater capacity for sustenance, ability to modify and change with the situation, all driven by top class 'situational awareness' as a function of top class intelligence; bridging of the officer-NCO-soldier divide by joint training and shared experiences all helped in the reorientation. Since the entire division – the senior-most field army formation of the SLA – had all ranks on one grid and knew what was to be done and how, the enemy had to lose. There was no other way out. The good thing is that the synergy did not stop at division or army level, but extended to the SLN and the Sri Lanka Air Force as well.

This, then, is the relevance of the brilliant paper by Dr. Sinharaja Tammita-Delgoda on his almost 40-day outing nearing the end of the war, with 55 Infantry Division, when it was closing in on the LTTE remnants in the Wanni region. The paper has been quoted with permission in full, to allow the reader to experience seeing a trained confident and committed army convert what was considered at one time an almost certain loss for the SLA to unexpected capitulation by the LTTE.

SRI LANKA: THE LAST PHASE IN EELAM WAR IV – FROM CHUNDIKULAM TO PUDUMATTALAN

DR. SINHARAJA TAMMITA-DELGODA

PREFACE

This is a case study of a particular area of operations during the last stages of Eelam War IV and is the result of several visits to the War Zone between 19 March and 27 April 2009. Conducted in operational conditions, it is based on the author's observations, together with interviews and conversations with serving officers and men on the field.

A portrait of the 55th Division of the Sri Lanka Army at war, its aim is to try and give an idea of the circumstances, conditions and challenges faced by the men, officers and commanders of the 55th Division and the way in which they thought about them and reacted to them.

Nearly all the information has been obtained first-hand on the field. Most of those spoken to have been named in the footnotes and, where relevant, the location of the interview has been given. There have also been exchanges with soldiers in the course of their duties but due to the circumstances, it has not always been possible to fully credit them. These have been noted as 'Conversations in the Field'.

ACKNOWLEDGEMENTS

The writer's visits to the operational areas were made possible by the permission of the Ministry of Defence of the Government of Sri Lanka. The author is grateful to the Secretary of Defence, Mr. Gottabhaya Rajapaksa, the Army Commander, General Sarath Fonseka, Major General Prasanna Dahanayake and Brigadier Udaya Nanayakkara for their support.

He would like to thank the Security Force Commander, Jaffna, Major General Mendaka Samarasinghe, Brigadier Prasanna Silva and the officers and men of the 55th Division for their hospitality, care and concern.

The author wishes to thank Major General Jagath Jayasuriya, Security Force Commander, Vanni, for his support. He would also like to express his gratitude to Major General Jagath Dias, GOC 57th Division, for his warm and generous hospitality and to Major General Kamal Gunaratne, GOC 53rd Division, for finding the time to talk in the middle of a battle.

He is particularly grateful to Brigadier Hiran Halangode (Retd) for his introduction to things military, his interest and his guidance.

He would also like to thank Major Ranjith Mallawaarachchi for all his assistance and Mr. Kapila Ariyananda and Mr. Haren Fernando for reading and commenting on this draft.

An Amphibious War

The sky arches above our heads, a sea of brilliant blue merging into an expanse of shining sand. On one side, the waters of the lagoon ripple gently on the sand; on the other, rolling breakers crash against the shore. A blazing haze of blue and yellow, it is a deceptively beautiful picture.

Eelam War IV was fought across several theatres, in the dense jungles of Mullaithivu and Madhu, in the rolling paddy lands of Mannar's rice bowl, amidst the savannah and scrub of Vanni and across the dry, arid areas of the northern peninsula. What is not known is that it was also fought across a series of beaches and lagoons. Stretching from Chundikulam to Pudumattalan, this bleached and burning landscape of sand and water represents one of the most unusual theatres of the whole conflict.

This theatre was entrusted to the 55th Division under the command of Brigadier Prasanna Silva. Alongside the 53rd Division under Major General Kamal Gunaratne, the 55th had been part of the force which had broken out of the Jaffna Peninsula. Whereas the 53rd Division attacked across the land, the 55th hugged the coast. This area had always been sparsely populated, inhabited by a straggle of fishing villages, which the Liberation Tigers of Tamil Eelam (LTTE) had converted into a string of Sea Tiger bases. The objective was to deprive the guerrillas of their access to the sea and the division's task was to work its way down the shore. It was tasked to fight on a narrow strip of land sandwiched between the sea and a series of lagoons.

This campaign was part of the multi-pronged strategy adopted by Sri Lanka's Army Commander, General Sarath Fonseka, against the LTTE. In previous wars, the Sri Lanka armed forces had attacked only from one direction. This time, several operations were launched simultaneously on various fronts, something the Tigers never thought the army was capable of. While the 55th would work its way down the coast, two other divisions, the 53rd and 58th Divisions, advanced eastwards, across the land towards Puthukudiyiruppu, the last town on the coast. Once they had taken, their objective was to link up with the 55th. Meanwhile, another infantry division, the 59th, advanced through the jungles of Mullaithivu and Oddusuddan, stopping on the edge of the Nanthi Kadal Lagoon.

Pinning the guerrillas down on many fronts, this strategy denied them the breathing space they needed to gather their resources and build up their reserves. Not only was the LTTE committed everywhere, it was always on the defensive. In the past, the Tigers had always been able to rest and regroup and they had used this opportunity to counter attack. This time, however, the momentum was never allowed to slacken. Executed with a clear vision, an overriding sense of purpose and a driving will, this approach served to drive the guerrillas back, pinning them to a tiny strip of land, with the sea at their backs.

Operating in this environment required a very different way of thinking and fighting. The Tamil Tigers had cleared the area of its fishing population; so the land was completely empty. In one way, this made the business of fighting much simpler. There were no buildings, no fields, and no people to complicate the picture. There was also scarcely any cover, just long stretches of burning sand which grew hotter and hotter as the day wore on. Dotted here and there were a few stumpy palmyra's and taller, more slender coconut palms. Further away towards the land were patches of scrub and bushes. These clumps of vegetation, however, were full of thorny thickets and bristled with sharp and vicious needles.

A test of physical endurance, thirst was a constant factor. So was exhaustion. Everybody drank more than twice his ration of water every day, depending on what he had to do. There were no wells and every drop of drinking water had to be brought up from the rear. When the vehicles could go no further, it was carried up to the line. The sand was soft and your feet sunk in with every step. Every step became an effort, requiring more and more energy. The heavier the load, the more effort it took and the more tiring it became. Sweat was always pouring down your face and the helmet became a weight, pressing down on your head, your body armour a stifling, suffocating prison. You were constantly tired.

Fighting in this terrain required a much greater level of endurance and fitness. I wondered how one could maintain concentration and sharpness of mind when all one could think of was fatigue, thirst and growing exhaustion. It required a different mentality and a very different kind of soldier.[1] I was told that in the jungle you can move much faster. It was also far less draining, for there was much more shade and you were not exposed to the same degree of heat.[2] Fighting on the sand was ideally suited to the troops from Jaffna, who had by now become accustomed to living and fighting in conditions which were very similar. However, a soldier who had fought in a different theatre could not immediately be expected to function as well and took at least a month to acclimatise.[3]

It was an infantry theatre, involving sand and water. Tracked and transport vehicles tended to plough into the sand and were constantly getting stuck. Even the tractors and their trolleys could only travel along lines of tin sheets laid out across the sand. These sheets had been cut from tin water barrels and used to create an impromptu road over the dunes.

Water was the other feature. The whole campaign was conducted across one body of water after another. It was not only a military factor, but a logistic and engineering challenge.

Here, the Tigers found themselves fighting a desperate, delaying war. Their defences were constructed so that they could be held by a minimum number of men. Commanded by Soosai, the leader of the Sea Tigers, the LTTE strategy was to slow down the army's advance and make it pay a tremendous human cost. Putting their faith in the environment and their defences, they had calculated that anyone advancing on such a narrow front could do so only at the risk of enormous casualties.

Across this narrow strip of land, from the seashore to the edge of the lagoon, the Tigers constructed a series of embankments guarded by wide ditches and swathes of mines. For the most part, however, it was a killing ground, with little cover and even less shade. The ditches were between 8-10 feet deep, while the bunds were at least 12-15 feet high. Together, they made an effective obstacle.

Earth bunds

Anyone approaching had to first come across a bare expanse of sand, where they were open targets for those who held the bund. Upon reaching the ditch, they had to go down several feet and then climb back up in full view of the defenders. At the top of the embankment was a screen of Palmyra fronds, at least five feet high. Making sure that the attackers did not have a clear view, these screens also afforded a degree of protection to the defenders.

Crowning each bund were several bunkers made from palmyra logs. Many were so covered with bushes, branches and sand that in the glaring sun they seemed to merge into the landscape. Acting as defence points, they anchored the whole position, commanding the line of fire. Despite the emptiness of the terrain, visibility was not always clear and it was difficult to spot movement and make out forms.[4]

Here, across the dunes, the Tigers erected embankment after embankment. Crossing one lagoon after another, the 55th Division found itself waging an amphibious war, attacking line after line of defences on a heavily mined front, fighting off counter-attacks at night from the sea and across the lagoon. From Chundikulam to Pudumattalan, the LTTE put up as many as 14 bunds, each with a supporting series of trenches and other defences. Each one of them was taken by the 55th Division.

Mentality

Most of the men and nearly all of the officers in the 55th Division were veterans, many of them with long years of service in the Eelam War. A seasoned force, the Sri Lankan Army had gained from their previous experiences. Not only was morale

Palmyra bunker

consistently high, the mentality was now very different. Previously hesitant, hidebound and beleaguered, they were now confident, self-reliant and resourceful; this was the new Sri Lankan Army. It had been a remarkable transformation.

As we speeded through the Vanni, rattling along in a Buffel armoured personnel carrier, I asked my escort about the change. Although he was only 26 years old, the lance corporal in charge of the Buffel was also a veteran of the Eelam War. In his eyes, the biggest difference of all was the leadership. "Now there is a proper leadership, we have confidence."[5] This was the foundation. This belief in the leadership, both political and military, ran all the way through the ranks. Breeding a sense of confidence and trust, it revolutionised the whole atmosphere. "Earlier, we did not know where we were or what we were doing. Now we know what we are doing."[6]

The other crucial factor was training. This was the general consensus amongst nearly all the senior officers spoken to. The army commander himself was a seasoned campaigner, who had fought in almost every theatre. Learning from the failures of the previous conflict, he completely overhauled the training.[7] "He was determined to fight differently, to do something which the guerrillas could not face."[8] Instead of the large formations which they had used in the past, General Fonseka adopted the idea of fighting in small groups.[9] The four-men and eight-men teams became the core of his new strategy. "Those days, we always advanced in battalion strength. We would advance for about two kilometres and then wait for artillery support. Now, we got used to going much further forward by ourselves; sometimes we would go out more than eight kilometres in a day, sometimes twelve. The enemy didn't know where we would be or what we would do."[10]

Introducing a concept known as Special Infantry Operations (SIO), General Fonseka concentrated on enhancing the skills of the ordinary infantryman and building up his confidence.[11] The infantryman was now trained in marksmanship, first aid, handling high explosives, calling in artillery support and air strikes. By developing the capability of the infantryman, SIO made him more assured and self-reliant.[12] "We do everything to build up confidence. If you are confident, you feel you can win."[13] Making the ordinary soldier fitter and stronger, it also gave him new levels of endurance.[14] This brought with it new thinking and a new way of fighting. In the past, they had relied heavily on the special forces, depending on them for reconnaissance and looking to them to make the breakthrough.[15] Now the infantry became used to going forward on its own.[16]

This process also had the effect of devolving the command process. In the past, the emphasis had been on the platoon, a unit of about 30 men.[17] As a result, everything had revolved around the platoon commander.[18] A new system –

Advanced Infantry Platoon Training (AIPT) – encouraged officers and men to work together.[19] Training was now done section-wise. As more and more emphasis was placed on the section, it was the section leader who took the responsibility.[20] This was a break with the traditions inherited from the British. Previously, it had been the officers who had made all the decisions.[21] Now everyone was involved, both men and officers.[22] Fostering a sense of participation at every level, it encouraged initiative and innovation all the way down the ranks.

As the capability of the ordinary infantrymen gradually expanded, they began to train to do things which the Sri Lankan Army had never done before. One of these was to fight at night.[23] One of the hallmarks of this theatre was that nearly all the major operations were carried out at night. From its previous experience, the LTTE had never expected Sri Lankan soldiers to fight in the dark and when they did, they were taken by surprise.[24] In the past, it had been the LTTE who had struck at night and they had come to take the army's vulnerability for granted. Now, as darkness fell, it was the guerrillas who found themselves on the defensive.

Another practice which the LTTE had come to take for granted was that any army operation would only last for a fixed period of time.[25] However, new levels of training and endurance enabled the infantrymen to sustain hostilities for much longer than before. Previously, the army had only conducted operations for a limited period; now they were able to continue for five or six days at a time.[26] This served to maintain a constant level of attrition. Wearing the guerrillas down and exhausting them, it denied them the time they needed to rest and regain their strength.

Commander

Like most of the senior commanders in the Sri Lanka Army, Brigadier Prasanna Silva was still in his mid-forties. Calm and composed, he had a reputation as a thinker. As a former special forces commander, his approach was sometimes quite unconventional. As part of his philosophy, he tried to involve everyone in his plan of operations. Determined to see things from the ground up, he made it a policy to consult with the company commanders, going right down to the section commanders when necessary.[27]

As part of his way of working, each battalion was asked to maintain a model of its own area of operations.[28] This model was updated on a daily basis as each section leader gave his input.[29] As it changed, the section leader himself could see how important his role was for the whole battalion.[30] The effect of this was radical, completely transforming the chain of command on the ground. From being merely a component in the whole process, the section leader became a vital part of it – its eyes, its ears and, sometimes, its brains.

This served to enhance the overall knowledge and combat power of the entire division.[31] As a result of the section leader's involvement, the General Officer Commanding (GOC) knew exactly what was happening on the ground. He had a specific idea of the main factors leading up to the attack on a particular area or a particular bunker, how to increase fire support, for example, when and where.[32] The GOC's involvement meant that the section leader had the maximum support and firepower behind him.[33] This enabled the GOC to deploy all the firepower, intelligence and technology at his disposal in support of the men on the ground.[34] According to Brigadier Silva, what really mattered was not the volume of fire which he was able to command, but how accurate it was. Only then was it really effective.[35]

This way of working completely changed the mentality of the Division. Giving rise to a much more unconventional and far more decentralised method of making decisions, it heightened the GOC's ability to read the battle. Not only did this prove effective in military terms, it also saw a sharp reduction in the rate of casualties, with the number of dead and wounded declining by as much as 60 per cent.[36]

Chundikulam

The Chundikulam Lagoon was the first of the lagoons which the 55th Division had to cross. A broad stretch of water more than two hundred feet across, it was one of the places where the sea flowed into the land. Cutting into the golden sands, it looked calm and tranquil in the afternoon sun. The mouth of the lagoon, however, concealed strong surging currents and, in some places, it was between 15 to 25 feet deep. Seen from one side, it was almost like a moat, guarding the LTTE defences on the other side.

The LTTE had expected an attack on a wide front, going down the side of the lagoon, where the waters were calmer and shallower. As a result, their bunkers and trenches stretched inland along the lagoon shore. To protect this line, they laid claymore mines and improvised explosive devices (IEDs). Known as 'trapping,' these were booby traps consisting of anti-personnel mines, bits of shrapnel, unexploded artillery and mortar rounds, all wired together with yards of fishing line. These lines could hardly be seen and a faulty touch or a foot misplaced was enough to set off a whole series of explosions. Living up to their name, they were veritable deathtraps, causing the largest number of casualties. Secure behind these

Teppan

natural and man-made defences, the LTTE sat and waited for the conventional attack which they felt had to come.

Instead of attacking on a wide front, the assault was launched across the narrowest and deepest part of the lagoon, the weakest point of the LTTE defences.[37] As a result of their night training, the troops felt confident enough to attack in the dark and the operation started at around 6.30 pm, the moment the light faded.[38]

Using Teppan, the light dugout canoes favoured by the fishermen, the government troops began building a bridge across the mouth of the lagoon.[39] The assault was spearheaded by the special forces, who crossed in boats. Landing on the other side, they provided cover to the men behind them. Two engineers with T-56 rifles went first, getting down into the current. Two Teppans at a time were placed in the water, then another two. With the waves swirling around their shoulders, the engineers carried on lashing the sections together, two by two.[40] As they extended the bridge further and further out into the lagoon, the current surged and eddied about them, becoming deep and shallow at turns.[41] One of the biggest challenges was anchoring the sections securely, so that they were not swept away by the tides.[42]

These activities were cloaked by the darkness and masked by heavy fire support. Mortars lining the army side of the shore opened fire. They were supported by tanks in the rear and the newly introduced multi-barrel rocket launchers (MBRL).[43] The MBRL made a huge difference in firepower, giving the Sri Lankan Army an advantage which it had not possessed before.[44]

Planks were then laid across the floats, creating a heaving, swaying and occasionally sinking bridge across the water. By midnight, they were ready to cross. It was an act of total improvisation, done under fire and executed in total darkness. With the engineers taking the lead once more, they gradually worked their way up the heavily mined beachfront. The Tiger cadres held on for 6 hours, from 8 at night until 2 in the morning before abandoning their positions. Bold, imaginative and risky, the whole operation had taken the Tigers by surprise.

Within a few days, the surging current had swept away the Teppan bridge and a new one had to be constructed. This time, they used fishing boats, but this too was washed away and another pontoon bridge was constructed. This structure, however, managed to survive.

Chalai

At Chalai too, the lagoon ran deep into the land. Although it was heavily mined, the narrowest front was chosen yet again. Once again, the crossing was made under fire and at night. Although the current here was even stronger and the water choppy, the 55th Division made the passage by foot and by boat. The whole area was heavily defended, with bunkers and trenches that they could hardly see. It was also covered with 'trapping'.

Pontoon Bridge

This time, two eight-men teams were sent forward. They were led by the team leader, who was also the section leader.[45] Before the assault, indirect fire was called in from artillery and mortars in the rear[46] and as they went forward, they were supported by heavy machine guns.[47] With an eight-men team, four men usually went ahead while the other four remained behind.[48] Acting as a reserve, their task was to supply ammunition and deal with any casualties.[49] The first two men were usually charged with the job of scouting and clearing the area.[50] The leader carried a T-56, the second a machine gun, while the remaining two fired rocket-propelled grenades. As they came closer, they hurled the grenades by hand.[51]

Advancing along an area only 20-30 metres wide, they felt their way with their hands, clearing a path in the dark.[52] Relying purely on their instincts, they moved slowly forward.[53] It was an act of sheer resolution and immense will. By morning, they had established themselves near the mouth of the lagoon, outflanking the line of defences which had been built along the shore.

The speed of the action and its boldness had succeeded. Once more, they had caught the guerrillas unawares. The roles, it seemed, were reversing. In the previous Eelam War, it had been the army that had put its faith in fixed defences. Now it was the LTTE who believed in fortifications, which they never thought could be taken.

Here, there was no bridge of boats. The tide was too deep and too strong and every attempt to construct one had been washed away. As a result, the troops were ferried to and fro in boats. All the vehicles and heavy equipment, however, were transported in makeshift rafts or ferries made up of planks, barrels and iron girders. These rafts became a lifeline, linking up the various components. As the Division advanced, everything – vehicles, supplies, men, munitions, even ambulances – had to be ferried across one stretch of water after another.

Civilians

As it advanced further and further forward, the 55th found itself having to deal with escaping non-combatants. In this theatre, people fled by sea, coming across in small boats, which put out from Tiger-controlled areas at night. The majority of these flotillas headed south towards Mullaithivu and Pulmoddai, where they were picked up by the navy boats patrolling those waters. A small number, however, turned north towards Chundikulam and Chalai.

Distinguishing between escaping civilian vessels and Sea Tiger squadrons was one of the challenges which faced the troops along the sea shore. The fact that it took place at night made this task even more difficult and dangerous. The lack of visibility, the uncertainty and the ever present threat of infiltration made the consequences of a wrong decision even more dire. The use of radar, however, allowed the army detachments to observe the speed of the oncoming vessels. This was crucial as it enabled them to decide whether the oncoming boats were Sea Tigers or civilians. Most civilian vessels had engines whose capacity was between 9-12 horsepower. As a result, their average speed was relatively slow and steady.

The Sea Tiger boats, on the other hand, had engines which ranged up to 40 horsepower. This meant that they could travel at a much greater speed, almost four times faster than the average civilian boat. As the boats approached the beach, flares were sent up. Together with the use of night vision aids, these helped establish who the occupants were. A separate unit composed of military police, intelligence personnel and women soldiers met the boats as they landed. Their task was to screen the arrivals, to talk to them, to see who they were and to find out if they were carrying any equipment.

The most urgent task was meeting the needs of these refugees. The majority were exhausted, hungry and terribly dehydrated. Many had small children with them and some were wounded and in need of medical attention. Everyone was given water or tea and the Division's supplies were used to provide a hot meal on the spot. All the injured who could be treated then and there were attended to by army medical officers. Military vehicles of all kinds were brought right down to the beach to carry the refugees inland and buses were then procured from somewhere to take them towards Jaffna. At the same time as fighting a battle, the 55th Division found itself conducting a quite separate security, logistic and administrative operation to cope with the civilian influx. As with the 58th and the 53rd Divisions, this became an essential part of their progress and perhaps, an indicator of their success.

An Infantry Operation

Once they had succeeded in crossing the lagoon, the 55th Division still faced the challenge of taking one fortified bund after another. In the past, the army had relied on the frontal assault. However, this had resulted in huge casualties.

To reduce the number of dead and wounded, Brigadier Silva adopted a new method to approach the enemy line. This was the digging of trenches. The 13th bund was taken on the morning of my arrival. The way it was done appears to have been typical. The trenches themselves were cut at an angle to the enemy bund and took the form of a zig-zag.[54] Protected by screens made from railway sleepers,[55] they would begin digging at 7.30 in the evening and continue till 2 in the morning.[56] Thirst was the biggest challenge and even at night, the diggers found themselves drinking water every 15 minutes.[57] Despite this, they were able to continue throughout the night. It was a sign of just how fit the new infantryman had become and how much he could endure.

It is an interesting historical irony. In World War I, trenches had been used as a form of defence. Almost a century later, in Sri Lanka, they were being resurrected as a form of attack.[58] By this method, the attackers were able to neutralise the effect of the enemy entrenchments and the killing field which had been created in front of them. Digging under cover of darkness, shielded by screens and backed by artillery fire, they were able to come closer and closer to the enemy line. Such was the speed at which they worked that if the soil was soft, eight men could dig a 6 foot trench in less than half an hour.[59] Although exhausting and laborious, it proved very effective, keeping casualties to a minimum.

Working their way along the sides, they did their best to outflank the LTTEpositions.[60] By dawn, they had almost reached the ditch. The men who had been digging went to the rear where they rested for five hours.[61] The fresh troops who had come to the front, now took over.[62] Seizing the edges of the bund, they forced the guerrilla cadres to withdraw.[63] The middle parts, however, remained uncleared and it was here that the attacking soldiers were most vulnerable to sniper fire from above.[64]

Trenches

Many of these lines were also linked to subsidiary trenches in the rear. They extended back into a whole series of supporting trenches, points, shelters and sub-positions. These contained first aid stations, artillery shelters and bunkers, often as not leading to the next bund. Thus, the business of driving the enemy out usually took the best part of the following day. This tended to be the general pattern. The bund was taken during the night or in the early hours of the morning, then held and gradually exploited during the day.[65]

Even after they had taken the enemy position; there was the constant danger of infiltration. This usually happened at night.[66] As they lost more and more ground, the LTTE made desperate attempts to regain the initiative. The counter-attacks came from the sea and across the lagoon. Fleets of highly charged small boats would head out from the remaining Sea Tiger bases further down the coast and speed towards the land.[67]

On one night, an attack was made by a flotilla of more than 25 boats.[68] Firing as they came, they rushed towards the shore at tremendous speed.[69] Most of them were destroyed before they reached the land by the infantry posted along the coast. The others turned and fled. However, had the landing succeeded, the entire front would have been undermined. To counter this threat, a line of points and bunkers had to be built right along the coast. As the Division forged ahead, this line gradually progressed further and further up the sea shore.

As we returned to camp, the night sky lit up with flashes of red and streaks of orange. There was the sound of firing together with the muffled burst of the heavy machine gun. Tiger boats were picked up on the radar travelling at high speed towards the land. One-by-one, they were destroyed and a voice could be heard on the radio, calling hysterically for help in Tamil. It was the voice of the commander of the last Tiger boat. His pleas became more and more frantic. Finally, he began to give up: "If you don't send help now, I am going to commit suicide."

Later that night, Soosai himself came on the radio. Although he was the commander of the entire sector, he hadn't even known that the defences had fallen. It was a sign of the growing disarray within the LTTE ranks. Here, on this front, they were finally losing control. We listened as the news was broken to him. His despair echoed that of the Sea Tiger cadre whose voice we had heard earlier. "Now we are finished," he said.

At the same time, counter-attacks were also made across the lagoon.[70] To mask the sound of their movement the LTTE used tape recordings which they played as they moved forward.[71] These gave out a series of noises, giving the impression that a large body of civilians was on the move. There would be the sound of people speaking loudly, women talking and children crying.[72] An ingenious psychological tool, it was designed to deceive the watching sentries, lulling them into a false sense of security.

To guard against this, the advancing troops often had to stand watch throughout the night, looking out from points they themselves had built during the day. As the sun set over the lagoon, a line of young soldiers stood in the shadows, looking out from newly-made sand bunkers. Although each point had two soldiers, both of them were encouraged to stay up throughout the night. "I am worried about infiltration," said the officer in charge.[73] "It's much better that both of them stay up now, that way they can keep each other awake. Otherwise, one of them might fall asleep. They can sleep tomorrow."[74]

The role of the Sri Lankan Air Force (SLAF) in this particular theatre was to support the operations on the ground. Air strikes were normally called in to take out points which could not be seen or reached from the ground.[75] In this context; the unmanned aerial vehicles (UAVs) played a vital part in locating and targeting these emplacements. [76] Whirring overhead, they provided the eyes that the troops on the ground had not possessed before.

However, the LTTE's defences were so well constructed that the SLAF's Kfir jets had to fly very low in order to be effective. Most of the time, they were flying in so low that they were exposed to small arms fire from the ground. [77] Nevertheless, by doing so, they were able to take out strong points buried deep in the scrub and sand. The targeting at times was specific. Stumbling along a line of trenches hidden in the sand, enveloped by bushes and thorny scrub, I wondered what good aircraft could do in this kind of environment. Minutes later, the scrub widened to reveal a round clearing and a crater in its middle. I was told that there had been a bunker there.

Defences

One of the problems with studying this conflict was that the situation changed so quickly. As it changed, so did the physical evidence and defences were dismantled or reoriented as one side advanced and the other withdrew. Once the Chalai Lagoon had been crossed, the troops were able to work their way into the northern reaches of Pudumattalan. Here at Pudumattalan, the line had just been taken and it was possible to see many of the defences while they were still in place.

The most striking thing about those fortifications was the tremendous ingenuity which had been exercised. Although the resources might have been limited, the thinking behind them was careful and imaginative. This was combined with a highly developed awareness of the environment, which was used for protection, disguise and surprise. Faced with a thinking enemy, who was a master of camouflage and concealment, the infantryman had to think on his feet in order to remain alive.[78] It was not always the easiest thing for a conventionally trained soldier to do.[79] However, as the Sri Lankan infantryman learned, it became the key to his survival.

Trees and bushes were also used for defence and, on some occasions, for attack. The main raw material was the palmyra tree, which was utilised in almost every conceivable way: its leaves, its trunk and sometimes even the tree itself. In some places where there were not enough palmyra logs to shore up the bunkers, boats were also used as a foundation. Positioned underneath the Palmyra logs, they added strength to the roof, which was thickly covered with sand to deaden the effect of the shelling. This ensured that the structure would not collapse under the weight of the sand.

Earthen Ditch

This ability to improvise was one of the hallmarks of the LTTE's thinking. As the scenario changed, so did their fortifications. As the guerrillas retreated, the gap between the sea and the lagoon narrowed. Adjusting to the changing circumstances, many of the ditches guarding the embankments were cut to take advantage of this fact. Some were so sited that the lagoon waters would flow in, while others were designed to join the waters from the lagoon with the incoming tide.

Armour-plated Bunkers

Armour Plated Bunker

In sharp contrast to those constructed by the army, most of the LTTE bunkers and trenches blended into the sandy environment. Some of these bunkers were little more than single manholes, carefully calculated to combat the way artillery shells fell. To add further protection, the inside of the hole was plated with strips of iron, creating a tiny armoured bunker. It was, in effect, a metal-plated box buried in the sand, with eight inches of metal plating above the surface. The top was covered with a layer of coconut fronds mixed with sand, making it almost invisible from the outside. When the artillery rounds began, the cadres would jump into these pits. Four and a half feet to five feet deep, they were so small they could only be destroyed if a shell actually fell into the hole.[80]

These defences proved to be extremely effective. "You don't know where they are, and you can't even see them until you are right on top of them."[81] Once the artillery barrage was over, the cadres emerged unscathed to fire at the advancing troops. With that type of bunker, the trajectory was so low that it was very difficult to gauge the direction of fire, let alone see it during the day-time. As long as the cadre remained where he was, he was almost invisible. As a result of defences like these, a number of troops sustained leg injuries. Nearly all of them were totally unexpected; "The first you know is when you are wounded in the leg."[82] The only thing that they could do was to crawl as close as possible, hoping that they would not touch a trip wire. All they did was to fire towards the sound, throw grenades and send off RPGs in the general direction. Only at night, when the fire flashes could be seen, did the troops have any idea of where the bunker was.[83]

Tree Bunkers

Behind the entrenchments guarding the lagoon was a patch of open land. In the midst of this expanse was a thicket. A tangled mass of branches, thorns and bushes, it was so thick at times that you could hardly put your hand in. Inside were bits of clothing, discarded wrappers, tins and empty bottles. It was a perfectly concealed defence point, commanding the open ground.[84] Designed to catch those coming through the scrub unawares, it reflected the combination of careful thinking with a painstaking use of the terrain which characterised the LTTE. The cadre who held this point could not be seen from the outside and the bush acted like an invisible bunker. Anyone coming through into the clearing relaxed momentarily, for all he could see was just another thicket.[85] Brilliantly conceived, it was a perfect utilisation of two of the principles of defence – surprise and concealment. Even when the attacker did recognise it for what it was, the approach was far from easy, for the ground in front of the thicket was set with mines.

Sniper Points in the Air

The palmyra trees which grew on the dunes also served as platforms for snipers. Commanding the space above the defensive lines of trenches, bunds and ditches, they were ideal vantage points from where one could see the whole line.[86] This was ingeniously done. The trunk of the tree acted as a shield and a chair was tied to it.[87] Sitting in the chair, the sniper's body was protected by the trunk while his legs dangled on either side.[88] A plank fixed further up the trunk acted as a platform for the sniper to rest his rifle on, while below, another plank was fixed for the cadre to place his feet.[89] Not only was the sniper hidden by the tree and the overhanging fronds, silhouetted against the glare, he was almost impossible to spot from the ground. For troops going forward, the natural tendency was to look straight ahead – it hardly ever occurred to anyone to look up as well. A tremendously inventive bit of thinking, cheap and easy to make, it was also devastatingly effective – from where a single sniper could pin down the whole line of advance.[90]

Mines and Booby Traps

As the LTTE had its own mine manufacturing plants, the Tigers were able to turn out all kinds of mines in enormous quantities. This abundance enabled them to use mines almost at will and almost every inch of land was mined. These mines – claymore mines, anti-personnel mines, booby traps – were a key element in the LTTE defences. Linking up the various lines, they delayed the pace of any advance, forcing the oncoming troops not only to fight but to clear them as they came.

The LTTE thought that this would restrict the avenues of attack, confining it to certain places and certain areas. Setting great store in this deterrent effect was how they planned their strategy. To an outsider, the part played by the engineer in this conflict was not always immediately apparent. However, as it unfolded around me, I began to realise how important it was. In this kind of warfare, with its heavily mined and booby-trapped terrain, the role of the engineer was crucial. It was the engineers who went first.[91] Clearing mines under fire, it was they who opened a path for the infantry.[92] Only when they had cleared the ground, could the infantry advance. Lacking sophisticated equipment or machinery, the 55th Division's engineers relied heavily on their experience and their instincts.[93] Depending on surprise, they worked by stealth, crawling on their bellies through the undergrowth. Most of the LTTE mines were generally hidden an inch or so below the surface.[94] While the infantry stood guard, they would first feel the surrounding area, touching very slowly with their hands.[95] Looking from the top, they would try to make out the shape and gently dig around it.[96]

In areas which had been cleared, the engineers would try to improvise a Bangalore torpedo.[97] This was the standard way of detonating mines and consisted of a long metal tube filled with explosives. However, instead of the factory-made metal pipes, they would improvise by fitting together lengths of plastic S-Lon tubes. Once it was exploded, the Bangalore torpedo would trigger off all the mines in the vicinity, creating a safe lane, two to three feet wide, for the infantry. The Bangalore torpedo normally had a 30-second fuse, enough time to get as far as 50 metres away.[98] Once it had been set, the engineers would turn around and run as fast as they could along the path which they had just cleared.[99]

As I watched this process taking place, I was reminded that it was done under fire almost every day, by men who were usually working almost 'blind.'[100] This was how the 55th Division had advanced. I was also told that of the many engineers who sustained injuries, most lost eyes, arms and legs.[101] This was the price which they had to pay.

While claymores were generally more straightforward to deal with, 'trapping' was another matter. Barely visible in the undergrowth, from a distance it looked more like discarded bits of rubbish – pieces of tin, little boxes and bits of thrown away metal. Only the lines leading into the tangle of shrubs and bushes gave them away.

An adaptation of conventional technology, utilising the debris of war, it was cheap and easy to set. It was also enormously difficult to disarm, as nobody could be sure where it began and where it ended.[102]

Immobilising large areas of territory, it made the business of moving forward painstaking and deeply fraught with danger. Fearing that detonation would lead to one explosion after another, the engineers would not touch it.[103] As a result, entire sections were just left in place, virtually rendering whole areas out of bounds. Nearly all the assaults were launched across the most heavily mined areas. Defying accepted military strategy, the Sri Lankan Army attacked the enemy's strongest points, not his weakest. This was what took the LTTE by surprise. In this theatre, they had calculated that the strength of the entrenchments would keep the army at bay. The failure to hold this northern front put enormous pressure on their other defences, enhancing the thrust of the divisions advancing towards Puthukudiyiruppu.

Conclusion

My impression of this theatre belies the general picture which has been painted of this conflict. Most authorities talk of the use of massive force and overwhelming power, [104] depicting a relentless, all-consuming bombardment, which swept away everything in its path. What I saw was a painstaking infantry operation, conducted in the face of all kinds of obstacles, by soldiers who had to think on their feet to survive.

In the final analysis, what this study proves is the continuing importance and relevance of infantry. Despite the considerable firepower which the Sri Lankan Army was able to bring to bear in terms of artillery and air power, it alone was not enough. Withstanding both artillery and aerial bombardment, the defenders remained in place, merely disappearing into their bunkers while the shelling and the bombing lasted. Against well constructed, carefully sited and heavily defended fortifications, technological supremacy and superior firepower only had a limited effect. What was required was close infantry combat. In the end, it was training, combat skill and imaginative thinking, which drove the LTTE cadres from their entrenchments.

As I stood on the wall of the 14th bund, the soldier I was with turned to me: "In this division, we are not told, go and do this, go and get this. We are asked what we can do and how we can do it. We took two bunds today without losing a single man. Where else will you see that?"[105] It was a revealing moment. An indication of morale, confidence and pride, it was also a vindication of the philosophy of command.

This Authors Note: Due to space constraints, two photos (Mine Clearance and Bangalore Torpedo [both on p. 20 of the paper] have been deleted.

Endnotes

1. Interview with Brigadier Nishanka Ranawana, Deputy GOC, 55th Division, 30-31 March 2009.
2. Ibid.
3. Ibid.
4. Conversation in the field, 30 March 2009.
5. Interview with Lance Corporal Gunatilleke, 29 March 2009.
6. Interview with Captain Warnasuriya, 2nd Mechanised Infantry, 29 March 2009.
7. Ibid.
8. Interview with Colonel Ralph Nugera, Special Forces. Kilinochchi, 31 March, 25 April 2009.
9. Ibid.
10. Interview with Captain P.K. Heenatigala, Infantry Support Battalion, 21 March 2009.
11. Interview with Major General Kamal Gunaratne, GOC 53rd Division, Puthukudiyirruppu, 20 March 2009.; 23 manekshaw Paer. 13, 2009 sri lanka: The Last Phase in Eelam war iv.
12. Ibid.
13. Interview with Brigadier Nishanka Ranawana, 30 March 2009.
14. Interview with Major General Kamal Gunaratne, 20 March 2009.
15. Ibid.
16. Interview with Brigadier Nishanka Ranawana, 30 March 2009.
17. Ibid.
18. Ibid.
19. Ibid.
20. Ibid.
21. Interview with Colonel Ralph Nugera, Special Forces, Kilinochchi, 31 March & 25 April 2009.
22. Ibid.
23. Ibid.
24. Interview with Brigadier Nishanka Ranawana, 30-31 March 2009.
25. Ibid.
26. Ibid.
27. Interview with Brigadier Prasanna Silva, GOC 55th Division, 30-31 March 2009.
28. Ibid.
29. Ibid.
30. Ibid.
31. Ibid.
32. Ibid.
33. Ibid.
34. Ibid.
35. Ibid.
36. Ibid.
37. Interview with Brigadier Nishanka Ranawana, Chundikulam, 30 March 2009.
38. Ibid.
39. Ibid.
40. Ibid.
41. Ibid.
42. Ibid.
43. Ibid.
44. Ibid.
45. Interview with Capain U. Arangala, 31 March 2009.

46. Ibid.
47. Ibid.
48. Ibid.
49. Ibid.
50. Ibid.
51. Ibid.
52. Ibid.
53. Ibid.
54. Interview with Brigadier Prasanna Silva, 30-31 March 2009.
55. Ibid.
56. Interview with Captain Prasanna Liyanagamage, 31 March 2009.
57. Ibid.
58. Interview with Mr. Kapila Ariyananda, Colombo.
59. Interview with Captain Samaradhivakara, 31 March 2009.
60. Interview with Captain Prasanna Liyanagamage, 31 March 2009.
61. Ibid. 24 manekshaw Paer. 13, 2009 sri lanka: The Last Phase in Eelam war iv
62. Ibid.
63. Ibid.
64. Ibid.
65. Conversation in the field.
66. Interview with Brigadier Prasanna Silva, 30 March 2009.
67. Ibid.
68. Ibid.
69. Ibid.
70. Interview with Captain Samaradhivakara, Pudumattalan, 31 March 2009.
71. Ibid.
72. Ibid.
73. Interview with Major Dhammika Yapa, Pudumattalan, 30 March 2009.
74. Ibid.
75. Interview with Major Senaka Premawansa, 30 March 2009.
76. Ibid.
77. Ibid.
78. Interview with Brigadier Hiran Halangode (Retd).
79. Ibid.
80. Interview with Major Dhammika Yapa, 30 March 2009.
81. Ibid.
82. Ibid.
83. Ibid.
84. Interview with Lt. Tharanga, 31 March 2009.
85. Ibid.
86. Interview with Captain Prasanna Liyanagamage, 31 March 2009.
87. Ibid.
88. Ibid.
89. Ibid.
90. Ibid.
91. Interview with Lt. Col. M.K. Jayawardene, 31 March 2009.
92. Ibid.
93. Ibid.
94. Interviews with Corporal Wasantha Kumara & Corporal Udhaya Kumara, 31 March 2009.
95. Ibid.

96. Ibid.
97. Ibid.
98. Ibid.
99. Ibid.
100. Ibid.
101. Interview with Lt. Col. M.K. Jayawardene, 31 March 2009.
102. Interview with Captain K.S. Kodikara, 31 March 2009.
103. Ibid.
104. "*Post LTTE Sri Lanka: The Way Ahead,*" Centre for Land Warfare Studies seminar report, 08 June 2009, available at www.claws.in.
105. Conversation in the field.

Chapter 19

Fighting with Exceptional Synergy: Master Strategists Who Won the War for Sri Lanka

As mentioned at several places in this book, it was the famous troika of the President, the Secretary Defence and the Army Chief (called the Army Commander in Sri Lanka), whose synergized efforts won the war for Sri Lanka; an astonishing feat that brought the whole nation succour after over 30 years of devastation. So far, the troika has been known in bits and pieces. In this chapter, their careers will be seen in thumbnail sketches, before we see how each contributed to the overall design which led to their unprecedented and unexpected success. The concluding part of the chapter will also examine whether there could be 'trouble in Paradise', consequent to the breakup of the troika and announcement by Gen. Fonseka of his running for the Presidential elections scheduled for end January 2010. The subject is treated at length in Chapter 22.

MAHINDA RAJAPAKSA

Percy Mahinda Rajapaksa is the sixth and current Executive President of Sri Lanka and Commander in Chief of the Sri Lankan Armed Forces.[1] A lawyer by profession, Rajapaksa was first elected to the Parliament of Sri Lanka in 1970, and served as Prime Minister from April 6, 2004, until his victory in the 2005 Presidential election. He was sworn in for a six-year term as president on November 19, 2005. He was conferred with the degree of Doctor of Law by the University of Colombo on September 6, 2009.

Rajapaksa was born in Weerakatiya in the southern rural district of Hambantotta. He hails from a well known political family in Sri Lanka. His father,

Mahinda Rajapaksa

D.A. Rajapaksa, was a prominent politician, independence agitator, Member of Parliament and Cabinet Minister of Agriculture and Land in Wijeyananda Dahanayake's government. D. M. Rajapaksa, his uncle, was a State Counsellor for Hambantotta in the 1930s. Rajapaksa was educated at Richmond College, Galle, before moving to Nalanda College, Colombo, and later Thurstan College, Colombo. Following the death of his father in 1967, Rajapaksa took over as the SLFP candidate for Beliatta constituency and was elected to Parliament in 1970 as the youngest Member of Parliament at the age of 24. Later he studied law at the Sri Lanka Law College. He lost his parliamentary seat in the landslide defeat of the SLFP in 1977.

In Opposition

In 1989 he was re-elected to Parliament to represent Hambantotta District under Proportional Representation. He came into prominence as a leader, together with Manorani Saravanamuttu, of the Mothers Front, which organised the mothers of the 'disappeared' in the white terror of 1988-90 instigated by a rebel group that called itself Deshapremi Jathika Vyaparaya or 'Patriotic National Movement'.

Political Career

In 1994, following the election victory of the People's Alliance, a political front led by Sri Lanka Freedom Party and headed by Chandrika Kumaratunga, Rajapaksa was appointed Minister of Labour. He held this post until 1997 when, following a cabinet reshuffle, his portfolio was changed to Minister of Fisheries and Aquatic Resources. When the United National Party (UNP) defeated the People's Alliance in the 2001 elections, Rajapaksa lost his position in the Government. He was however appointed as Leader of the Opposition in March, 2002. After the Parliamentary elections of 2004, the United People's Freedom Alliance gained a slim majority in Parliament. Rajapaksa was sworn in as Sri Lanka's 13th Prime Minister on April 6, 2004. While Rajapaksa was the Prime Minister, he also held the Ministry of Highways.

Presidency (November 2005 – Present)

Rajapaksa was chosen by the Sri Lanka Freedom Party for the Presidential election held on November 17, 2005. Rajapaksa's prime opponent was former Prime Minister and Opposition Leader, Ranil Wickremasinghe, the leader of the United

National Party in this election. Rajapaksa defeated Wickremasinghe narrowly by 190,000 votes and took office as President of Sri Lanka on November 19, 2005. After becoming President of Sri Lanka, Rajapaksa reshuffled the cabinet and took the portfolios of Defence and Finance in the new cabinet, which was sworn in on November 23, 2005.

Political Positions

Although styling himself as a man of peace and a willing negotiator, Rajapaksa signalled his intention to end the peace process once in power by forging an alliance with the Sinhalese nationalist Janatha Vimukthi Peramuna and the Jathika Hela Urumaya. The JVP had opposed the original 2002 peace process as treason. Following the closure by the LTTE of a reservoir supplying water to 15,000 people named 'Mavil Aru' in government-controlled areas on July 21, 2006, the Sri Lankan military launched an offensive against the LTTE, bringing the entire reservoir under government control.

The content of the President's historic speech in Tamil at the UN was an effort to establish that he is a people's leader representing all the peoples of Sri Lanka including the Tamil minority. "While my mother tongue is Sinhala, let me elaborate a few thoughts in Tamil. Sinhala and Tamil are the two languages of the people of Sri Lanka. Both these have been used through the centuries, are rich in literature, and are widely used in my country, with recognition as Official Languages," he said in Tamil adding, "With the widening of democracy in our country, the bonds between the Sinhala and Tamil people of Sri Lanka will grow stronger and remain a major force for its future development..."

Views on India[2]

The President has gone on record to suggest that by eliminating Prabhakaran he has fought India's war. He says that a stable relationship with India is very important to him. What appears to be a remarkable tribute to his political skills is the fact that he has adroitly managed to obtain assistance from China, Pakistan *and* India, without spoiling his relationships with any of these countries.

Family and Personal Life

He is married to former beauty queen Shiranthi Wickremasinghe, a Roman Catholic and daughter of the late Commander E. P. Wickramasinghe, SLN and Mrs. Violet Wickramasinghe and has three sons, Namal, Yoshitha and Rohitha. Namal Rajapaksa is in active politics while his brother Yoshitha was commissioned as an Acting Sub Lieutenant in the Sri Lanka Navy in March 2009 and appointed an Aide-de-Camp to the President in 2006.

Media Freedom

During the Rajapaksa administration, the *Reporters Without Borders Index*, ranked Sri Lanka 165th among 173 countries in its annual worldwide press freedom index. The Human Rights Watch research alleged that the Sri Lankan Government is responsible for widespread abductions. In sum, the Rajapaksa government is widely accused of muzzling its media, especially if the coverage by media runs counter to the governments views.

GOTTABHAYA RAJAPAKSA

Lieutenant Colonel (Retd) Nandasena Gottabhaya Rajapaksa,[3] RWP, RSP is a retired officer of the Sri Lanka Army and the current Defence Secretary of Sri Lanka. After serving through the early parts of the country's civil war with Tamil Tiger rebels, he retired from the Army in 1992. With the election of his brother Mahinda Rajapaksa as President of Sri Lanka, Gottabhaya Rajapaksa was appointed Defence Secretary in November 2005.

Gottabhaya Rajapaksa

As Defence Secretary, Rajapaksa is largely credited with masterminding the successes achieved by the Sri Lankan Military in defeating the Tamil Tigers and ending Sri Lanka's 25 year long civil war in May 2009. He was also one of the top targets of the Tamil Tigers, and survived an assassination attempt in December 2006 by a Tamil Tiger suicide bomber. He was conferred Doctor of Letters by the University of Colombo on September 06, 2009.

Early Life

Gottabhaya Rajapaksa was born in Palatuwa in the Matara District, and brought up in Weerakatiya in the southern rural district of Hambantotta. According to a writer called Narada Karunthilaka, the name Gottabhaya means 'Abhaya, the Giant' or 'fearless giant' in the Jat language. His brother, Mahinda Rajapaksa, was elected the President of Sri Lanka in 2005. Two of his other brothers, Chamal Rajapaksa and Basil Rajapaksa, are also in politics being current Members of Parliament.

Military Career

Rajapaksa joined the Sri Lanka Army as a Cadet Officer on April 26, 1971, when

Sri Lanka was still a dominion of the British Commonwealth. He was commissioned as a Second Lieutenant on May 25, 1972 and given his first command as an officer in the Ceylon Signals Corps. Thereafter he served with the Sri Lanka Sinha Regiment and the Rajarata Rifles before being transferred to the Gajaba Regiment upon its formation in 1983 with the amalgamation of the Rajarata Rifles and Vijayabâhu Infantry Regiment. He rose up the ranks in the military, serving as the second in command of the 1st Gajaba Regiment from 1983-1990. He served in the battlefronts of Jaffna, participating in Operation Liberation, the offensive mounted to liberate Vadamarachi from the LTTE in 1987. He also commanded the same battalion in Operation 'Strike Hard' and Operation 'Thrivida Balaya' in 1990. He was promoted to Lieutenant Colonel, and served as the Commandant of the Kotelawala Defence Academy at the time of his retirement in 1992.

Training Abroad[4]

Gottabhaya proceeded to Pakistan to complete the Young Officers' Course at Rawalpindi and later a mid-career course at Quetta. He had advanced training in Counter Insurgency and Jungle Warfare at Assam, India. Later in his career, Gottabhaya Rajapaksa graduated in advanced infantry training from Infantry School, Fort Benning, USA. As a staff officer, Rajapaksa completed his Staff Course at the Defence Services Staff College in Wellington, India, in 1983. He obtained his Masters degree in Defence Studies from the University of Madras in 1983. He also obtained a Postgraduate degree in Information Technology from the University of Colombo in 1992. During his 20 years of military service, Rajapaksa has received awards for gallantry from three Presidents of Sri Lanka, J. R. Jayewardene, Ranasinghe Premadasa and D. B. Wijetunga.

Life After Retirement

Upon his retirement from the army after serving for 20 years, Rajapaksa obtained a Post-Graduate Diploma in Computer Technology from the University of Colombo and was employed in the IT field of the local corporate sector. He later migrated to the United States of America, where he worked as Computer Systems UNIX Administrator at the Loyola Law School in Los Angeles. In order to assist his brother's Presidential election campaign, Rajapaksa returned to Sri Lanka in 2005. He is a naturalised US citizen.

Secretary to the Ministry of Defence

Gottabhaya Rajapaksa was appointed to the post of Permanent Secretary of the

Ministry of Defence in November 2005 by newly elected President Mahinda Rajapaksa. In this capacity he oversaw the military operation which eventually defeated the LTTE in May, 2009, after 25 years of fighting.

Attempted Assassination

On December 1, 2006, at approximately 10:35 an assassin attempted to drive an explosive-laden auto rickshaw into Rajapaksa's motorcade as it travelled through Kollupitiya, Colombo. The Sri Lanka Army commandos guarding him obstructed the vehicle carrying the explosives before it reached Rajapaksa's vehicle and two commandos were instantly killed. Rajapaksa however escaped unhurt. The LTTE were blamed for the attack.

Criticism of UN and Western countries

In June 2007, Rajapaksa was severely critical of the UN in Sri Lanka and of Western governments. He accused the UN in Sri Lanka of having been infiltrated by terrorists "for 30 years or so", and as a result the UN was fed incorrect information. He also alleged that Britain and the EU were bullying Sri Lanka, and concluded that Sri Lanka "does not need them", and that they don't provide any significant amount of aid to the country.

Controversies

Relationship with the Media[5]

Rajapaksa has been accused of threatening journalists on several occasions, including telling two journalists attached to the state-owned Lake House Publications that unless they stop criticising the armed forces "what will happen to you is beyond my control". When asked by the two journalists if he was threatening them, he replied "I am definitely not threatening your lives. Our services are appreciated by 99 per cent of the people. They love the Army Commander (General Sarath Fonseka) and the Army. There are Sri Lankan patriots who love us too and will do what is required if necessary." In April, 2007, he was accused for allegedly calling the Editor of the *Daily Mirror* Champika Liyanaarachchi and threatening her, saying that she would escape reprisals only if she resigned. He was also accused for threatening to 'exterminate' the *Daily Mirror* journalist Uditha Jayasinghe, for writing articles about the plight of civilian war casualties. Mr. Rajapaksa denied these claims. A December 5, 2008, story from *The New York Times* quoted his news reporting position as "he insists that journalists should not be allowed to report anything that demoralizes the war effort."[6]

The Karuna Link

The former LTTE commander Vinayagamurthy Muralitharan, better known as Colonel Karuna, told British authorities that Rajapaksa was instrumental in arranging for him to be issued with a false diplomatic passport so that he could flee to Britain in September 2007. These allegations were denied by the Sri Lankan Foreign Minister, Rohita.

Overall, Gottabhaya is credited for being the driving force behind the military strategy of Sri Lanka that resulted in the decimation of the LTTE. The fact that he set the strategic stage (including provision of war fighting materials) for the SLA and SLAF, and gave a free hand and unqualified support to Gen. Sarath Forseka to execute the strategy on the ground will remain his unique contribution

GENERAL SARATH FONSEKA

General Sarath Fonseka[7] RWP, RSP, VSV, USP, rcds, psc, SLSR, is a Sri Lanka Army officer and just retired Chief of Defence Staff of Sri Lanka. He previously served throughout the Sri Lankan Civil War, including as Commander of the Sri Lanka Army from December 6, 2005 - July 15, 2009. As Commander, he oversaw the final phase of the Eelam war, which resulted in the ultimate defeat of the Liberation Tigers of Tamil Eelam. Fonseka has been described as Sri Lanka's most successful Army Commander. His run of significant military victories against the LTTE during Eelam War IV led the Indian National Security Advisor (NSA) Mayankote Kelath Narayanan to describe him as the best Army Commander in the world."

On April 25, 2006, he survived an assassination attempt when an LTTE suicide bomber attacked his motorcade.

Early Life and Family

General Fonseka, a graduate of Dharmasoka College, Ambalangoda (1958-1965) and Ananda College, Colombo (1966-1969), is a top sportsman who has participated in swimming and water polo, having represented the Defence Services and the country in these events.

Military Career

Fonseka has held a large number of various staff appointments including the office of Chief of Staff of the SLA, the post he relinquished to take over as Commander of the Army.

One contribution as Deputy General Officer Commanding consisted of operation 'Riviresa', to capture Jaffna from the Tamil Tigers, in December, 1995. Later, troops commanded by Fonseka offered stiff resistance to the Tamil Tigers in 2000, following the fall of Elephant Pass, ultimately having to flee since they were unable to withstand the attack.

Fonseka was also involved in operations 'Balawegaya' and 'Jayasikuru', which led to the capture of Elephant Pass and Mankulam. The 6th Battalion of his Sri Lanka Sinha Regiment, which was under siege at Elephant Pass in 1991, repulsed the LTTE attack with reinforcements. He was wounded in 1993 in the Yaldewee operation.

As a Colonel, Fonseka commanded 23 Brigade of the Sri Lankan Army at Polonnaruwa in 1993. Among other appointments he held was Colonel, General Staff, Army Headquarters, SLA; Centre Commandant, Sri Lanka Sinha Regiment, Brigade Commander in Operation Ballavegaya, Deputy Commandant–5 Brigade Group, Mannar, and Coordinating Officer for Gampaha Gum Gumaga.

Training Abroad

The General has attended the UK-based course offered by the Royal College of Defence Studies, Infantry Officers Advanced Course (USA), Staff College Course (Bangladesh), Company Commanders Course (Pakistan), Battalion Support Weapons Course (India), Counter Insurgency Jungle Warfare Course (India), Commando Officers Course (India) and has represented Sri Lanka in a number of international seminars and conferences, including the Pacific Armies Management Seminar (Japan), Conference on fourth International Exhibition of Defence (UK) and another overseas seminar in Geneva. In what was seen a recognition of his military maturity, he was selected to undertake an inspection assignment in Iran in 1992.

'Midnight Express'

In 1993, as the Jaffna Fort was under siege for a long period, the then Colonel G. S. C. Fonseka led troops in the 'Midnight Express' (not a train name) operation to rescue the besieged troops. Incidentally, the incumbent Secretary of Defence, Lieutenant Colonel Gottabhaya Rajapaksa was with him. Several hundred soldiers were saved in this operation.

Suicide Bomb Attack

On 25th April, 2006, Lt. General Fonseka survived an LTTE suicide bomb attack by a pregnant Tamil woman who infiltrated the army base by attending the regular maternity clinic provided for civilians at the army base military hospital, in which he was seriously injured and nine others were killed. The General was later flown to Singapore for treatment, and resumed his duties in July.

Chief of Defence Staff (CDS)

He was made the Chief of Defence Staff by the President effective 15th July, 2009. After falling out with the President, he tendered his resignation effective November 16, 2009. As has been mentioned earlier, the credit of converting "Defeat into Victory" at the field levels of the SLA belongs almost exclusively to this pragmatic, ruthless, hard driving and focused, very much 'hands on' officer. Gen Sarath Fonseka took over an Army that lacked self belief, and had an institutional memory of far more defeats than success. In a short period of almost three years, he transformed it. His brutal methodology and his whiplash tongue may not have been very much appreciated by those who were at the receiving end, but it was effective and perhaps just right for the prevailing circumstances. His trump cards, learnt amidst the noise thunder and confusion of war, lay in simple as opposed to complicated plans; simple orders that were monitored and seen through; murderous but relevant training, feedback that was actually listened to and acted upon, trust building between the leader and led at all levels, and, most importantly, creating and investing in his key battle winning strategy: **empowering the soldier and enabling him in every which way to do his job regardless of the cost.**

HOW THE CIVIL WAR WAS WON

No analyst world-wide (**I am not talking of politicians yet**) will grudge the claim, if Mahinda Rajapaksa makes one, that, if one person is to be given the honours for thinking through and plotting the downfall of the LTTE, it has to be him. **The fact that, so far, he is not known to have made such a claim, and has, instead, given the credit to the team that *he personally led*, underscores the basic reason why the civil war was won by the Government:** all encompassing synergy, fuelled by a brilliant political sense; something that Capt. B.H. Liddell Hart termed as an essential quality of generalship; of being a great captain of war ... coup d'oeil (a French word implying the rarest of rare abilities of being able to presciently "look over the horizon' and see difficulties or events before they come to pass).

Few democracies in the world, (developed or developing), can lay claim to creating synergy that transcends the entire spectrum of a nation from its apex political authority; the diplomatic corps; economy; the various types of military and paramilitary forces, right down to the lowest common denominator – the citizen and the soldier. It is not that such synergy hasn't happened in the past. It happened in World Wars I and II, and, more pertinently to South Asia, it happened in India; when the country went to war in 1971 against Pakistan, and helped create a brave new nation, Bangladesh. The point made is that it happens but rarely indeed, because, most of the time, the concerned players who could contribute to the creation of synergy are dysfunctional because of narrow, sectarian span of vision, insecurity, mutual distrust and overall lack of a common end state.

Mahinda should thus be credited for putting it all together and for merging self into supreme national interest. He can also be given credit for running with the hares and hunting with the hounds, in that, by clever political management, he got on board his team, every one who mattered, whether party or individual. His single point agenda was to destroy the LTTE and he stuck to his aim through bad times and good, achieving his desired end state within the time he had allotted to himself.

To achieve his vision, he chose a brilliant team of players, who were giants in their respective fields. The focus here is primarily on his younger brother, Gottabhaya, a non-resident Sri Lankan, and a brilliant, dogged, hands-on General in Sarath Fonseka. One hallmark of a great leader is the ability to choose the right subordinate for the right job. The more challenging trait is to give them their head – within defined parameters. This is what is again Mahinda Rajapaksa's credit: he gave them their head, without once losing control or failing to remain firmly in command. Thus, the troika was formed, and with leadership zones and areas of responsibility and control clearly delineated. It must have helped that he had not one younger brother on board at the strategic level; Gottabhaya, but also a second; Basil, who became his Chief Presidential Adviser.

Let us mention another major credit that is his due: Mahinda shaped the environment both politically as well as diplomatically, to play out his game plan, and did it with stunning effect. This took huge pressure off the backs of those executing his policies and allowed them to focus on the job in hand – the destruction of the LTTE. It is not the easiest thing in the world to cock a snook at the USA, the UN, the Human Rights flag wavers and most of Europe, and get away with it, courtesy the veto powers of a friend in need, China. It isn't easy to get practically unlimited aid from China, both military as well as infrastructure oriented; from its proxy, Pakistan, without compromising on aid from India. It isn't easy either, to hunt for LTTE logistics ships in international waters and actually take them out, with scarcely a murmur from anyone. It is difficult too, to get the LTTE proscribed in 32 nations world wide, and then ensure that their funding is reduced to a trickle, so that their destruction in the field is aided. Getting aircraft from Russia, boats and UAV's from Israel, arms and ammunition from all over while denying all this to the LTTE required some doing and Mahinda Rajapaksa headed this effort.

Let us see what Gottabhaya was up to during this period. The *Manila Times* write up[8] on him deserves quoting in substantial amount because of the depth of perception of the writer, a senior journalist, who came to Sri Lanka to understand what Gottabhaya Rajapaksa stood for.

When asked (by the senior journalist of the *Manila Times*) if he felt his work was now done, the Defence Secretary (whose all encompassing brief also includes public security and law and order) notes: "To a certain extent it has. But now we have to put in place a good intelligence network to ensure that the security of our country is never again compromised by internal fighting forces."[9]

"For whilst the President played political hardball and made anyone who was willing to listen realize that the country could never defeat an enemy it wasn't prepared to fight, his Defence Secretary – with a seriousness of purpose unmatched by any previous incumbent in that key office – mapped out and unwaveringly directed the definitive final chapter of the long running saga.

Under the firm guidance of Defence Secretary Rajapaksa, the Sri Lankan military did what the Tamil Tiger leadership least expected it to do – double its manpower and bring the fight direct to the enemy and inflict decisive psychological wounds. This was all-flanks engaged warfare based on common-sense and strategic insight. It was brilliant as it was simple, making many wonder why it hadn't been instituted before.[10]

He explains: "For the first time ever in the history of Sri Lanka, we had the three commanders of the Army, Navy and Air Force working with a Defence Secretary who had served alongside them in the battlefield during the early days of the conflict. And crucially, my brother was the President which meant I could cut out the bureaucratic red-tape and, more importantly, disregard the political interference that had previously crippled this office – and invariably the war effort – and go straight to the Commander-in-Chief if and when the need arose."

Needless to say, it was a gilt-edged connection that shaped the conclusive stages of the war – especially when seeking the wherewithal to substantially boost the firepower. But in the final analysis, it was Defence Secretary Rajapaksa's depth of vision and not his scale of influence that mattered...

"What I was able to do, with the help of the Commanders (of the three services), was to professionalise the three services and change the demoralising culture where promotion was based more on political connections than merit. We instilled in our soldiers the importance of discipline and feeling of pride in wearing the uniform. We also made them understand that the cause they were fighting for was a just one. In addition, we paid special attention to their welfare and that of their families. I believe all these aspects played a vital role in helping us gain the upper hand against the enemy…

"And having been on a war footing for so long, we have to redefine the role of the Armed Forces now that peace has been restored. Also, much of the police force will have to be re-trained and re-orientated to the requirements of law and order in a post-war community setting. Beyond that, we also have to ensure peace and order in our society by disarming the many factions and individuals who, by nature of the threats they faced from the Tamil Tigers, were allowed to carry arms. We need to impress upon them that the state can now offer them adequate protection."[11]

Reading the excerpts from this brilliant coverage by the *Manila Times*, one can understand how the needed synergy was generated at the level of the Defence Secretary, aided and abetted by the fact that he had actually worn boots with the three service Chiefs, and happened to be the brother of the President. Readers will note the caution he displays in handling the victorious Army and its future role, now that victory banners have flourished. The aspect of empowering the police and other paramilitary forces and the neutralisation of those who were earlier armed by the state are indicators of political savvy that are indications of a thinking man who is looking ahead rather than behind.

So far as General Sarath Fonseka is concerned, his contribution is crystal clear and equally stunning. He revived a nearly defunct Army and gave it a kind of leadership that must rank amongst the best across generations of soldiering. His run of significant military victories against the LTTE during Eelam War IV led the Indian National Security Advisor Mayankote Kelath Narayanan to describe him as the best Army Commander in the world."[12]

It has already been stated that his revival was based on a careful study of the lessons the SLA had learnt in the preceding 25 years of civil war. He brought the humble soldier centre stage, decentralised the conduct of war, focused on small team operations, most importantly, ensured that top class strategic, operational and tactical level intelligence was created and made to deliver. Lesser known is the fact that the SLAF, not just the SLA, put its act together so far as Psychological Warfare is concerned; defeating the Tigers at their own game. The General had a hand in weaning Colonel Karuna away, thus causing discord and strife in the enemy camp (this must have been done with Government connivance and support; that is clearly obvious).

Overall, he made his soldiers better Tigers than the LTTE were, beating them at their own game with ruthlessness, courage, innovative tactics and turning known SLA operational templates on their heads. Thus the SLA now attacked the enemy by night, at places where LTTE least expected the attacks. They were shelled ruthlessly, separated from their support base; the people of the Northern Province. They were attacked by day and by night, relentlessly and simultaneously. Their codes were broken, their supplies interdicted and leaders taken out. Forced to fight a conventional war with whose nuances they were unfamiliar, they lost out.

Fonseka was there, with his commanders to ensure that. Ruthless with the weak, generous with the brave and the willing, he drove his officers and men hard and with prescience and with clarity – and succeeded. Not to be forgotten is the fact that, though, he was not the CDS then, General Fonseka was able to get the other two Chiefs to dovetail their operations into the SLA operations without visible ego or 'my service first' hassles. Defence forces and Governments the world over will gladly testify that this isn't the easiest of challenges to negotiate. The fact that during all this, the Defence Secretary was not only on board but also put his considerable muscle behind the need to suppress service egos for supreme national interest, cannot, of course, be discounted.

In sum, it is clear that the war was finally won by three strategists, who, under the leadership of Mahinda Rajapaksa, dovetailed their brilliance and skills into rare and exceptional synergy that proved unbeatable.

IS THERE "TROUBLE IN PARADISE"?

Note: This portion was written in October 2009, when the break up of the troika was merely the subject of speculation but had not actually taken place. The situation has now assumed new and potentially dangerous contours for the retention of stability in Sri Lankan politics. This, as stated is the subject of examination in Chapter 22. For the moment, the broad thrust of the October 2009 speculation has been retained.

If the latest reports[13] coming in are to be believed, it does seem like the dream run of the troika has come to an end. The report quotes the SLA spokesman as saying that rumours of a rift between the Government and the CDS, Gen. Sarath Fonseka, are unfounded. Reports that he referred to his address to the Army[14] on the occasion of the 60th anniversary of the SLA as his 'last address' hardly helped put down the rumours.

A detailed political analysis[15] in the *Sunday Times*, Sri Lanka, makes the following key points:

- Presidential elections are due early next year and the government is gearing up for that eventuality.
- The President had suggested that the CDS join him in public rallies but the CDS wasn't able to come as he was coordinating the 60th anniversary celebrations of the SLA.
- The report suggests that the promotion of the Army Commander as CDS may have been a step to limit the powers General Fonseka had as a war time commander.

- Even the suggestion that he take over as Secretary Sports in addition to being CDS was taken to be a demotion.
- The Defence Secretary had issued a circular after the war that clearance of the ministry is taken before service chiefs are interviewed.
- The Government may be of the view that the opposition may be in touch with a sidelined general, hoping to get political mileage out of this linkage.
- The general has, however, reiterated that he has no political ambition, and on retirement, will lead a civilian life.

These are straws in the wind at this moment and may well end up as much ado about nothing. The facts that speak for themselves are that with the civil war a closed chapter, the role of the SLA, and, in fact, the SLAF overall, will undergo redefinition. This is something that has to be negotiated carefully by the Government. The notional promotion of Gen. Fonseka as the CDS, has actually meant that he has lost his power base, the SLA, without much cognisable gain. This is bound to trouble him, and could be seen as an effort to limit his influence.

Endnotes

1. "Mahinda Rajapaksa". < http://en.wikipedia.org/wiki/Mahinda_Rajapaksa> Excerpts have been used from the article.
2. Narayan, Venkat S. "I Fought India's War, Too" Says President Rajapaksa. http://www.defence.lk/new.asp?fname=20090530_03 Excerpts from the report have been used.
   Sri Lankan President Mahinda Rajapaksa says he has "fought India's war" too by militarily eliminating the LTTE, which had assassinated former Prime Minister Rajiv Gandhi 18 years ago. In an interview to Indian newsmagazine "*The Week*" published in its latest issue, President Rajapaksa says: "I think my war is part of the South Asian campaign against terrorism. In fact, by eliminating the LTTE militarily, I have fought India's war." The President commended Prime Minister Manmohan Singh, ruling Congress Party President Sonia Gandhi and the Indian people for the support extended to Sri Lanka during the war. "Nothing is more important for me than what India thinks," he declared. He explained that the India-Sri Lanka Agreement of July 1987 led to the 13th amendment to the Sri Lankan Constitution. In that way, the homegrown approach covers the position of India, too. This time, a political solution will be devised after taking every shade of Sri Lankan opinion into consideration, he added.
3. "Gottabhaya Rajapaksa". http://en.wikipedia.org/wiki/Gotabhaya_Rajapaksa. Excerpts have been used from the article.
4. Rajaratnam, Dr. Levins T. C. Dr. "Gottabhaya Rajapaksa: The Man Who Tamed the Tigers". September 7, 2009. http://www.srilankaguardian.org/2009/09/dr-gotabhaya-rajapaksha-man-who-tamed.html. The author, editor of Sri Lanka Patriot [www.srilankapatriot.com].
5. "Sri Lanka Targeted for Defeating LTTE Terror – Defence Sec. International Community has Double Standards in Dealing with Terrorism" Sep 18, 2009. http://www.nationalsecurity.lk/fullnews.php?id=21522. The Defence Secretary's relationship with the media, as well as his intolerance of sections of the international community that have

held Sri Lanka guilty of human rights violations is well known. Excerpts from the article cited above support this viewpoint.

Sri Lanka was targeted by a section of the international community for being successful in her war against the LTTE, a group proscribed by India, US, UK and EU, and a section of the international community have conveniently forgotten the death and destruction caused by the LTTE, said Secretary Defence Gottabhaya Rajapaksa, in an interview with *The Island* today. Referring to a spate of recent statements attributed to Opposition politicians, INGO/ NGO activists and UN officials, he said that all this was part of a major propaganda campaign directed at the Sri Lankan government. This threat was as serious as the one posed by the LTTE a year ago. A section of the media, too, had contributed to this strategy, he said, urging the international community not to adopt double standards in dealing with the situation in Iraq and Afghanistan, where US-led allied forces were fighting terrorists and Sri Lanka's war. "Our successful war should be considered as part the global campaign against terror," he said. The comments by Defence Secretary Gottabhaya Rajapaksa came after reports that Robert O. Blake, Assistant Secretary, South and Central Asian Affairs, and former US Ambassador in Colombo, has informed Sri Lanka's Ambassador to Washington Jaliya Wickramasuriya that a report on the conduct of Government forces during the war against the LTTE would be submitted to the US Congress on Monday (September 21).

6. Rajaratnam, Dr. Levins T.C. "Dr. Gottabhaya Rajapaksa: The Man Who Tamed the Tigers". September 7, 2009. http://www.srilankaguardian.org/2009/09/dr-gotabhaya-rajapaksha-man-who-tamed.html. Note. The author is Editor of Sri Lanka Patriot [www.srilankapatriot.com]. In his article (excerpts produced below) he writes in support of the Defence Secretary in euphoric terms. This runs counter to the tone of the Wikipedia article that he has a problem with media relations.

   "He is both a historical figure and a legend – and it is sometimes difficult to separate the two. For the first time in the history of this country we have an efficient, meticulous, brilliant Secretary of Defence. As Sri Lankans we should be proud of this patriot. As a Tamil and as a citizen of Sri Lanka who owes allegiance to the Constitution of the Democratic Socialist Republic of Sri Lanka and the President, I consider it my duty to pay tribute to a worthy gentleman and hero of our times".

7. "General Sarath Fonseka". http://en.wikipedia.org/wiki/Sarath_Fonseka. Excerpts have been used.

8. "The Steely Hand Behind Demise of LTTE Terrorists". *Manila Times.* August 31, 2009. <http://www.defence.lk/new.asp?fname=20090902_08>

   Preamble to the above cited article: "Under the firm guidance of Defence Secretary Gottabhaya Rajapaksa, the Sri Lankan military did what the terrorist leadership least expected it to do – double its manpower and bring the fight direct to the enemy and inflict decisive psychological wounds. This was all-flanks engaged warfare based on common-sense and strategic insight. It was brilliant as it was simple, making many wonder why it hadn't been instituted before". So states the *Manila Times* of Aug 31, 09 in its regular column *"Open Notebook"* by Random Jottings, (a senior correspondent of the MT who was in Sri Lanka recently). Excerpts have been quoted thereafter.

9. Ibid.
10. Ibid.
11. Ibid.
12. "General Sarath Fonseka". http://en.wikipedia.org/wiki/Sarath_Fonseka. Excerpts have been used.

13. "No Fonseka-Govt. Rift says Army". <http://www.dailymirror.lk/DM_BLOG/Sections/frmNewsDetailView.aspx?ARTID=65051 > Excerpts from this startling report are quoted below:
"The Military said yesterday that there was no rift between former Army Commander and current Chief of Defence Staff (CDS) Sarath Fonseka and the Government, and that speculation to that effect was baseless and misleading...
In a statement posted on the website of the Media Centre for National Security (MCNS), Military spokesman, Brigadier Udaya Nanayakkara said that false news was being published in various print and electronic media, alleging a rift between the government and General Fonseka. Brigadier Nanayakkara said that there was no truth in the reports and insisted that General Fonseka was still the most senior officer in the Army. He went on to say that media speculation alleging differences between the Government and Gen. Fonseka had been planted deliberately, to create a rift between the Government and the Army – which had won public confidence and popularity. He said the publication of such reports on the Army was 'illegal and counterproductive' and misled the general public. The sources also stated that a near 30 year ruthless guerilla war had been effectively put to an end within a short period of two years and 10 months mainly due to Gen. Fonseka's battle strategy, intelligence and daring tactics".
14. "The Brave were Rewarded and the Weak Sidelined, General Fonseka".
http://www.spot.lk/article5555-brave-were-rewarded-weak-sidelined-general-fonseka.html
Excerpts: "This may be the last occasion that he is addressing a function of this nature, said Sri Lanka's Chief of Defence Staff (CDS) and former Army Commander General Sarath Fonseka. CDS General Fonseka was addressing Army personnel who accorded him a guard of honour at a function at Army Headquarters marking the 60th Anniversary of the Sri Lanka Army (SLA). Speaking further he said that in the 60 year history of the SLA, the past three and a half were the most difficult and demanding years. He had rewarded those who were strong and brave and others who were weak and dissatisfied were sidelined, he said. Wishing the SLA well, General Fonseka urged them to uphold the good work achieved by them in the recent past. "If you do not uphold the excellent reputation we have already gained, others will blame you for the failures," the General said.
15. "The Fonseka Factor Excites Rajapaksa Govt. Opposition Strikes Up Dialogue With Deposed Army Chief". http://sundaytimes.lk/091011/Columns/political.html

References

1. BBC NEWS | World | South Asia | Sri Lanka accuses 'bullying' West
2. The predicament of a Defence Secretary, 'srilankaguardian.org'
3. "Hardliner wins Sri Lanka election". BBC News. November 2005 18, 2005. http://news.bbc.co.uk/2/hi/south_asia/4447794.stm.
4. "How President decided on retaliation". *The Sunday Times*. April 30, 2006. http://www.sundaytimes.lk/060430/index.html.
5. "Sri Lanka President swipes at U.N. record". Reuters. September 25, 2007. http://www.reuters.com/article/worldNews/idUSCOL23239120070926?feedType=RSS&feedName=worldNews.
6. http://www.time.com/time/magazine/article/0,9171,501060508-1189385,00.html]
7. "Bomb targets Sri Lanka army chief". BBC News. 25 April 2006. http://news.bbc.co.uk/2/hi/south_asia/4941744.stm.

Chapter 20

Lessons Learnt

"I consider it an offence against the Serbian people and the betrayal of the civic notion of society when evil is identified with Serbian nationality. But I find it equally misguided when evil is not defined at all, for fear of hurting Serbian feelings. All people have their Karadzic's and Mladics, either real or potential. If such men – as the result of a mix of historical, social and cultural circumstances gain more influence than they have in other parts of the world, it does not mean that they are from a criminal people...(This) is a conflict of principles, not of nationalities.. In other words let us beware of attempts to lay the evil on whole peoples. That would be tantamount to adopting the ideologues of ethnic fanatics".

(*Former Czech President Vaclav Havel, a great visionary of Europe, from a quotation in Richard Holbrooke's book – *To End a War*)[1]

Lalin Fernando, an ex SLA officer, from whose June 2009 article in the *Asian Tribune* this quotation has been extracted, is right on target in relating the Serbian civil war to the Sri Lankan civil war. Both lasted around 30 years. The subtle message is clear for the reader to absorb and reflect upon: the Sinhala people, like their Serbian counterparts, should *not* have evil identified with them. It is equally wrong *not* to define the evil, for fear of hurting Sinhala (or Tamil) sentiments ... indeed, let us follow Vaclav Havel's sage advice and beware of attempts to lay the evil of the civil war on whole peoples, so far as the Sri Lankan civil war is concerned.

The former Czech President is right in suggesting that the conflict in the Serbian case was about principles, not so much nationalities. This may be the case in the Sri Lankan war too. The base problem, with the politics removed, was simply one of seeking an institutionalized and fair place under the Sri Lankan sun. That this was misinterpreted and made another issue altogether, is due to the short-sighted way in which the problem was tackled by sectarian rather than nation-first ideologies on the part of the warring sides.

The incontestable fact is that the 30 year war is now over. No one in their right minds wants the evil to roost yet again and ruin the peace of Serendip for generations to come. This is possible only if the correct lessons are drawn and corrections needed put into place and monitored for timely and quality implementation till completed. This chapter will seek to examine these lessons under several appropriate headings.

Developmental Issues

The first indicators that take a beating in an environment of strife and discord are developmental failures. The symptoms that indicate that a serious problem is afoot need to be identified, monitored and tackled by those in governance. Professor John Richardson, with whom the reader is already familiar,[2] says that "bewildered residents of conflict-wracked nations often ask themselves:

- How could we have come to this?
- What could we have done to prevent the conflict that has killed our family members and friends, devastated our lives, destroyed what was being so painstakingly developed?
- What can we learn and share from our experiences that may help others to avoid the path that we have trod?
- How can we share lessons from our experience most powerfully and effectively?"[3]

The symptoms, therefore, that they need to be worried about are:[4]

1. Deteriorating economic performance.
2. An increasing number of development failures.
3. Rising levels of relative deprivation manifested in heightened ethnic identities and groups mobilised around these identities.
4. Declining effectiveness in the application of state-sanctioned violence.
5. Growing strength of militant movements.

He adds further, that the following 10 development policy failures, which if avoided or corrected, could have prevented the escalation of the deadly conflict and terrorism in Sri Lanka:[5]

1. Unsustainable entitlement programmes.
2. Polarising political rhetoric and tactics.
3. 'Winner takes all' official language policies.

4. Failure to devolve power – the 'outstation' mentality in implementing Sri Lanka's development strategies and programmes.
5. Half-hearted reforms of secondary and higher education, coupled with discriminatory university admissions policies targeting Tamil youth.
6. Perpetuation of Government-controlled economic management schemes long after their economic inefficacy had been demonstrated.
7. The over-ambitious and over-politicised economic reform policies of J. R. Jayewardene.
8. Inadequate funding, Sinhalisation and politicisation of the security forces.
9. Use of repressive measures to secure the United National Party's Parliamentary majority for an additional term in 1982.
10. The attempt to restore order in the North and East (especially in volatile Jaffna province) with military forces that were clearly incapable of achieving that goal.

The issue of development is thus germane to the rise and decline of insurgency and this reality has been validated by endless successful examples. The Americans have had reasonable success in Iraq off the back of development, more than by the numbers of terrorists killed. The British were early learners of this priority in Malaya. India too, has achieved considerable success in Kashmir and in the North East, by using development as an indicator of the government's care and concern for those who feel marginalized. Insurgents and terrorists know that the coming of development is bad news for them as their psychological connect with the populace gets diluted. It thus makes them vulnerable and exposed. This is why they target development if they can. This is also the reason why the government must continue to promote it.

The Americans, currently in a logjam over their Af-Pak policies, may realise over time, that mere muscle (force accretion, offensive use of air power, Predator UAV's, may give them some success but not the kind of complete victory they are looking for. That needs time, patience and the intelligent use of development as a major weapon, in addition to their vast array of attrition weapons. This is something the USA is debating over, and one hopes they make the right choices. So far as the Sri Lanka Government is concerned, it is hoped that it has learnt its lessons and will honour its development commitments within the specified time. There is a need to be generous and accommodating in victory.

Winning a Civil War by Military Force

Peter Leitner and Rajika Jayatilake, in their examination, state that the United

States, who is the world leader in the war against terror, may have important lessons to learn from the Sri Lankan success.[6] Readers will note that these lessons appear to run counter to the suggestion given in the preceding section, that military force devoid of serious developmental content is doomed to failure. These nine lessons are:

- Perhaps the most important lesson is the debunking of the widely held belief that terrorism cannot be quelled militarily.[7] The Sri Lankan military demonstrated that professionalism, strategy, discipline and unswerving commitment can beat terrorism.

  All too often, the greatest obstacle to military success is the starry-eyed interference by third parties insisting that only diplomacy and negotiation can bring a true end to terror-based conflicts. History has demonstrated repeatedly, and Sri Lanka has just underscored, that negotiation is doomed in the face of an implacable enemy with an absolutist agenda seeking to create change by ruthless use of force.
- Terrorist outfits are highly opportunistic. They excel in politically manipulating third countries as they engage in hollow cease-fire arrangements to buy time, regroup, rearm and initiate surprise offensives. Even in defeat, terrorist operations may continue by initiating violence inside nations that house their exiles and their remaining power base.
- The terrorist support structure dies hard. Sri Lanka's Tamil Tiger terrorists were, and still are, backed by an extraordinarily sophisticated, wealthy and highly educated business and professional class. Actively preventing ex-patriot supporters of defeated terrorist organizations from funding, supplying or otherwise supporting the creation of follow-on entities that will resume the violence – albeit under different names, with different faces – must cap victory on the battlefield.

  This means, in the Sri Lankan case, that the United States, Canada, Australia, Great Britain and the rest of the Commonwealth are the front-line states in ensuring that their territories will not be used to reignite LTTE's failed but extraordinarily bloody terrorism.
- Terrorist movements rely upon the apathy of third countries toward the suffering that groups operating on their soil cause in distant nations. The hypocritical and self-serving attitude apparent in the commonly expressed "they are engaged only in fundraising here, not violence" not only rationalizes inaction, but also cripples international support for counterterrorism moves deemed vital to host nation interests.

- Even the most sophisticated and creative terror organizations make bad decisions and demonstrate self-defeating behaviour. The assassination of Rajiv Gandhi by LTTE operatives in India brought a profound backlash that saw India effectively bar its soil from being used as a staging area for operations inside Sri Lanka. Once denied physical sanctuary in neighbouring countries for combatants, logistics and training activities, terror/insurgent movements are severely crippled.
- Historical animosities do not yield to the wide-eyed 'split the difference' mentality that is the hallmark of Western diplomatic and political naiveté. Such an approach alienates all parties to a conflict and results in self-deception while exposing the incompetent middleman's own population to attack. Conflicts rooted in history are complex and should not be reduced to simplistic equations.
- If elected Western leaders actually believe their own rhetoric that all civilized nations must cooperate in this global war on terror, they must actively support the anti-terrorist initiatives of fellow democracies around the world. Ideological movements, religious cults, political insurgencies and cults of personality that employ terror to push their agenda should be eradicated as quickly, as universally and as completely as possible.

  Even leaders who hold fast to 'pragmatism' as a political creed need to be reminded that the incubation and development of terrorist activity in far-off lands will come back to haunt their own citizens sooner rather than later. The Tamil Tigers' terrorist activities went largely ignored by the West for decades. But the techniques they developed have killed thousands in unrelated terror attacks around the world.

  For instance, the use of 'boat bombs' was copied by terrorists in the October 2000 attack on the USS *Cole* in Aden Harbour. Western ambivalence toward this long-running tragedy has been costly.
- Sri Lanka's war was complex and challenging, spawning several dimensions of terrorist activity. The war was fought on the ground in Sri Lanka, while propaganda and funds for weapons were handled by LTTE supporters living in the West, and weapons were acquired from Southeast Asia and Central Europe. Although the United States designated the LTTE as a foreign terrorist organization in October 1997, it was not until November 2007 that it banned the Tamil Rehabilitation Organization as an LTTE front organization. Until then, in the guise of charity, LTTE activists were collecting funds and transferring them to the Tiger war chest. Canada

proscribed the LTTE in April 2006 and banned the World Tamil Movement (WTM) in June 2008. The banning of these front organizations was a major blow to the LTTE terrorist operations.

- Even after the unequivocal military defeat of the LTTE, its overseas supporters defiantly keep the separatist dream alive despite the annihilation of most of the LTTE's leadership and the death of founder Velupillai Prabhakaran. If unchecked, they may well transform that dream once again into virulent terrorism, and this time, the Eelam War may well be fought locally – by the diaspora in the West."[8]

As was mentioned at the start of this section, it may not always be possible to win a war with purely military means, to the exclusion of development, diplomacy, public support and so on. Readers will agree that, in Sri Lanka, what publicly appeared to be a hard-line, much advertised and widely propagated 'military solution', was, in its actual execution content, a well thought-out and complex vision of many parts, whose core lay in astute diplomacy and some exceptional perception management. This has been brought out in detail in the last chapter. Thus, the *shaping* of the military battlefield was cannily done by the adroit use of a combination of diplomacy; access to open-ended military aid from countries; (some inimical to each other) and psychological warfare, directed as much against the enemy as at the SLAF and the populace, all wrapped up in a type of synergy rarely achieved in a civil war situation.

Sri Lanka was also fortunate, in that its relative isolation, as well as being a third world country not directly threatening Western interests, allowed it to follow its chosen approach without really drawing the ire of the international community. Obviously, the tacit, understated but solid support from India, (which could have gone to town on the issue, had it wanted to, and who had the clout to interfere substantially, by exercise of diplomacy), helped enormously. However, the time-tested way of isolating the terrorists from the local population through populist WHAM (Winning Hearts And Minds) programmes does remain relevant as long as the military is given a free hand, but is monitored to ensure that its hard-nosed measures that go along with development do not affect the majority of the population.

Not surprisingly, support for this approach that lays value to the human side over brute force comes from Paul Reynolds, in his dispassionate analysis of the lessons from the Sri Lankan war.[9]

Don't Fight an Unconventional War with a Conventional Mindset and Strategy

This is a lesson that conventional armies learn, only to unlearn rather rapidly. Readers will recall that the redesigning of the SLA's operational philosophy way back when the troika assembled in 2005 after Mahinda Rajapaksa had taken over was that the SLAF must undergo grass root changes if they are to succeed. They were thus degutted of their conventional wisdom and compelled to go off the 'beaten track' into erstwhile Tiger domain, where content became more important than form. The soldier, freed of the burdens of predictability, went galactic with his now unorthodox, innovative methods of waging war. The Indian Army too, learnt this bitter lesson in its first forays with the LTTE. They encountered gigantic, improvised explosive devices (IED's) wherever they went, were fired at from behind a wall of children and women, lost lives saving women, who suddenly pulled out weapons and shot them, had their messages intercepted and traps laid, leading to casualties. They learnt rapidly but did not get a real chance to give it back, because they were pulled out. The revived SLA (and SLAF overall) learnt this lesson at huge cost, but remembered it and became masters of unorthodoxy as they advanced into their final war. As readers know, the rate, volume, focus and momentum of this sudden change and the synergy with which it was delivered caused mind paralysis in the LTTE, causing their rapid disorientation and defeat.

Converting the SLAF from its erstwhile 'War by the Rule book' mindset was an 'insider' who knew what real war was all about, the Defence Secretary. He doubled the strength of the SLA, gave a carte blanche to the Army Commander to re-engineer training, made it an 'all front's' war, instead of its earlier linear approach, had all the service Chiefs as co-passengers, and used his connectivity with the President to place change on fast track. The proverbial 'one-hand-tied-behind-the-back' syndrome that castrates most conventional armies in conduct of anti-insurgency operations was discarded and all ranks from the Chiefs downwards empowered.

Examples abound. The SLA ruthlessly isolated the LTTE into pockets, particularly in the Wanni, and having done so by use of their new tactics, literally swamping them by simultaneous attacks and surprising tempo of operations that gave no time for the LTTE to recover or react coherently, they battered them with intense, heavy shelling. This wherewithal was largely Chinese (40 massive 152mm artillery pieces, called the Type 66, a Chinese copy of a Soviet weapon)[10] but also comprised the equally devastating GRAD Multi Barrel Rocket Launcher (MBRL) system ex Pakistan. The LTTE tactic of using women and children for shelter thus did not help beyond a point, as the Wanni region closer to the sea coast had been sanitized of most of its population by the Tigers for operational purposes. Although examples exist from recent history of other nations also using heavy calibre weapons against insurgents, the reader needs to be cautioned that one country's template may not be transferable to another country. It is thus not a matter of surprise that the Government of India is hedging its bets before allowing the IAF the permission to fire if fired at by the Naxals. The Prime Minister of India is also on record to say that the Indian Army will not be used against the Naxals.

The Navy, after suffering embarrassing losses of its ships to the Sea Tigers, finally became Sea Tigers themselves; using their Dvora and indigenous Arrow boats like if not better than the LTTE. They used the SBS most effectively. Aided by the Indian Navy's considerable surveillance reach, the LTTE logistics platforms were located and destroyed, thus mercilessly cutting off imports of arms and ammunition, when they were most needed by a beleaguered LTTE.

The Sri Lankan Air Force went one better. They used the Israeli UAV's they had to deadly effect. The Air Force also made light of the LTTE air defence capability and provided intimate air support to SLA attacks, in a manner that had not happened before.

All these lessons of coping with a determined and capable enemy were well learnt by the SLAF and implemented on the ground through astute, knowledgeable and determined leadership.

Intelligence No Longer Neglected: Made Central to Conduct of Operations

This is again a lesson that blights conventional war fighting. The SLA had suffered enormously till the early 2000 period when they decided to put their act together. It was in 2004 that they managed to infiltrate the LTTE ranks and cause a schism that led to Colonel Karuna entering into the Government camp. The tactics they employed to make this possible were totally out-of-the-box and they succeeded. The LTTE were hereafter no longer considered 10 feet tall. Their strengths and weaknesses became known; and since knowledge is power, this vital inside information was of great use in planning and executing operations. More importantly, Karuna managed to disaffect a large number of his ex-colleagues. His absorption in governance gave many the hope that there was a life beyond the LTTE. Cases began coming to light that the LTTE cadre had started preferring surrender to suicide and, in certain cases, throwing away their cyanide vials. This had never happened before.

These are stray examples of success culled from an overall, implementable strategy for acquiring intelligence that was *actionable*, and using that intelligence to lethal effect. Intelligence acquisition beyond HUMINT (Human Intelligence) and extended across the complete spectrum of intelligence acquisition, including the electronic, digital and non-communication media. It included acquisition, denial, monitoring as well as suppression capability. Reports abound with transcripts of LTTE functionaries being picked up on radio in real time, expressing their frustration at the SLA actions to decimate them and their inability to do anything about it. This was one indicator of a rejuvenated intelligence set up. Intelligence also became the basis of the Sri Lanka propaganda and psychological warfare campaign, within Sri Lanka as well as globally.

Aggressive and Nuanced Psychological Warfare

The LTTE taught the world how psychological warfare and its subset, propaganda, can influence perceptions. The Al-Qaeda and the Pakistani terror groups may have learnt valuable lessons from the LTTE in this sphere, including managing perceptions about their philosophy, mission, intent, methodology, time line, plans and needs. This capability was driven by Prabhakaran, assisted by KP and Anton Balasingham amongst others. Prabhakaran gave art form status and visibility to the Internet, using it with extraordinary success right through the rise and fall of his organisation. He was not only net savvy, but extended his understanding of this form of warfare across the entire gamut of communication means; radio, television, print media, posters, give-aways, videos, everything. His responses were time sensitive, submission deadline related, focused on destroying the credibility of the government and its forces and handled by communication experts within Sri Lanka and amongst the Tamil diaspora.

This rare skill amongst terror organisations (it was certainly rare and spasmodic amongst terror organisations before 9/11) was also his key means of accessing funds and making friends or weaning support for Eelam world wide. It also opened doors for obtaining war like material that he needed for continuing his struggle. This book has mentioned that part of his inspiration may have come from the Indian handling of perceptions during the Kargil War of May-July 1999. This ability of Prabhakaran to learn lessons and adapt them for his purposes was what set the LTTE apart.

It is to Sri Lanka's credit, that, having messed up their psychological warfare campaigns earlier, they learnt a valuable lesson from the LTTE and put their act together, at the start of 2000, and slowly made their handling at par, if not better and more sophisticated than the LTTE's campaign. This contributed to their victory in a big, big way.

This capability, as mentioned earlier, was directed inwards, towards the public, the military forces and towards political forces within Sri Lanka. The soldier was told he was special. He believed it. The country was told that the situation was under control and their active support was needed to end the war. The country rallied to the call. Politicians were shown their place, with the result that the criticism of the government became muted and opposition defanged for fear of public censure.

A lesson for India and certainly its armed forces is to emulate the manner in which the Sri Lanka MoD and its constituent parts are handling information on the net. One of the smartest and most up to date sites is the MoD site itself. There are also several blogs that are obviously government sponsored that generate good information on defence activities. This is not necessarily the case with India, with a few notable exceptions. The common message seen by the author on several military sites in India, is that the site 'is under construction'. Even those that are not so tagged, have little to offer to the viewer. This needs major attention by the MoD and the services.

Coming back to Sri Lanka, the extension of their control over public perceptions also has a negative side, and amounts to 'managing' its media. This is of course something that has not gone well with the Sri Lankan Government's otherwise successful propaganda handling. The political as well as military authority have shown a marked dislike of criticism of what they do; a point that bothers the international community as well, however ineffectual their protests may be. This is a lesson that Sri Lanka has yet to learn. No government can cope with a hostile media over the long term. Also, their occasional needling and questioning of intent and execution is one of the prime indicators of a mature (maturing) democracy.

Only Professional Armed Forces Win Anti-Insurgency Wars

The Army Commander, Gen Fonseka, not only led by example, having fought the LTTE in all sectors of its operations, but also in most ranks. He led the reform process by removing politics and political patronage from the army. He went on record saying in his farewell speech that he had to punish the undeserving and reward those who delivered. He is known to have occasionally used abusive language to get his army to deliver, but that is a minor aberration, against the background of what he achieved. In his tenure as Chief, he changed the army's basic thinking and philosophy, their operating culture. This he did by empowering the soldier, and freeing him of conventional constraints. Instead of being told what to think, the soldier learnt how to think; how to optimize his performance within the existing constraints. The army, at last, got on the move professionally.

This was not all. To keep up his morale and motivation, the government gladly supported the Defence Secretary and Chief's proposals to look after the soldier's welfare in a manner that his morale shot up sky high. The soldier was thus convinced that he mattered to his army, his country. With his family and dependents cared for, it was easier to sacrifice his life for his country if that was needed. The casualty figures of over 6,000 soldiers dead and almost 30,000 wounded in the last three years alone support this thought. The lesson learnt was thus clear: be professional to the core if you want to win.

Resistance to Change Killed the LTTE

It is indeed ironical that the LTTE, which started off as an innovative, out-of-the-box organisation that owed its astounding successes to thinking on the feet, ability to learn, adapt, and be flexible in planning and execution, eventually lost out on these advantages as the Eelam struggle went on. Ironically too, there was an inexplicable role reversal, starting sometime in the early 2000 period and escalating thereafter, under which the LTTE practically became a clone of the Sri Lankan Army of old and the Sri Lankan Army became the young and enterprising LTTE in outlook and delivery.

Prabhakaran simply refused to accept the emerging realities, especially after the Mavil Aru July 2006 operation in the LTTE heartland, that the SLA had undergone a transformation and was no longer the orthodox hidebound force he was so familiar with. What was needed then was the ability to adapt and be on the ball. A tiring, sick Prabhakaran, now the 'supreme commander' (no longer Anna – elder brother or Thambi – younger brother – who was approachable, was cocooned by his own volition and by acolytes, from reality. Bereft of Mahattaya, who was executed long ago, of Karuna, who left him, he had been left pretty much on his own. He did not change his basic opinions of the SLA/SLAF and kept reinforcing failure instead of seeking success. His rigidity finally killed him. The Sri Lankans, in the meanwhile, blossomed from having learnt the lesson of adaptability.

Diaspora Management and the International Community

There is an important lesson here, that the LTTE has taught Sri Lanka, if not the world, in getting much of its vast diaspora spread all over the world, to propagate its cause and, more importantly, give funding and moral support. That a fair portion of the West, including international agencies such as the UN and Human Rights organisations believed what the Tamil diaspora and the propaganda machinery of the LTTE said about human rights violations, for instance, has caused Sri Lanka no end of trouble, forcing the nation on the defensive, time and again.

The Sri Lankan response in this context has had mixed success. Whereas they were able to get the LTTE proscribed by important nations in the region and world, and whereas, as a consequence, they were able to reduce funding support by the diaspora to a trickle by getting them picked up by Western intelligence agencies and funds frozen, they also got a lot of negative publicity from the international community on their repression of free speech and strong-arm tactics used by the government and its agencies in fighting the war.

One short-term reality that Sri Lanka has exposed and benefitted from is that if you have friends in right places (in this case, China, its economic clout and membership of the Security Council that allows any censuring of Sri Lanka for its human rights record or IDP handling to be set aside), you can ignore the international community and get away with it. The international community, in any case, will do little to quell insurgencies which are geographically isolated. The fact that Sri Lanka is an island nation in South Asia ensured this isolation.

The lesson to be learnt is that, as long as the diaspora of any nationality avoids violence on Western or any foreign shores, it can always continue to provide moral and material support to the perpetrators of violence in their home countries. This is something Sri Lanka has to learn how to handle. Obviously, the correct way is to win them over, now that the basis of their support is defunct. By extension, this implies that the government has to look after Tamil diaspora interests within the country, to remove the very basis of their angst. This is a formidable challenge for any nation.

India Remains Very Relevant for Sri Lanka and Cannot be Marginalised

This is a lesson that the Mahinda Rajapaksa Government has not forgotten; in fact, it has played the India card discreetly, in line with Indian sensitivities, and to full advantage. The demographic, religious, social, economic and historical connectivity's with India are facts that cannot be wished away. Earlier governments in Sri Lanka may have made mistakes in attempting distancing, but these have failed. The fact remains that, with 60 million Tamil citizens of its own, the handling of Tamils in Sri Lanka will always concern India. The lesson for India is its graceful acceptance of the sovereignty of Sri Lanka (never questioned in India) and its right to choose the company it keeps.

The larger lesson is more important: the defence of India starts with the defence of Sri Lanka, because of its proximity to India and to the world's oil carrying shipping traffic that passes close by. Assisting Sri Lanka in defence matters should therefore be a priority with India, as it amounts to securing a portion of its own South Eastern flanks. The distaff side for Sri Lanka in this lesson is that Indian support will always be differently packaged and should not be taken as a 'given'. Communication channels have thus to be kept unclogged, with redundancy in communication modes.

Can Sri Lanka Afford a 'Sinhala Only Army' any Longer?

This appears to be a lesson whose answer is so obvious that it does not bear statement. With substantial minorities in terms of its Tamils as well as Muslims, true, long-term integration demands that both be included in sufficiently large numbers. This will be easier said than done, because of the hurt caused by the civil war, and the historical animosity between the three communities. It is, however, an issue that cannot be ignored, if the country is to bring in long-term peace and stability, supported by all its component communities.

A Lesson that Pakistan Needs to Learn from Sri Lanka – Before it is too Late

Robert Mackay[11] has written a perceptive and compelling article in May 2009 for the *New York Times,* about the manner in which the governments of Pakistan and Sri Lanka are handling their displaced persons (called refugees in Pakistan and IDP's in Sri Lanka). His words put across his concern best: "While the Sri Lankan Government has set up internment camps and is locking up all of the Tamils that leave the battle zone in the country's northeast, to prevent Tamil Tigers militants from escaping, Pakistan's Government is simply allowing hundreds of thousands of people to drive away, with no comparable effort to ensure that members of the Taliban are not slipping away from the front lines disguised as civilians.

"On Friday, as my colleagues Dexter Filkins and Alan Cowell report, it has become clear that the scale of the displacement in Pakistan is enormous. William

Spindler, a spokesman for the United Nations High Commissioner for Refugees in Geneva, said that up to 200,000 people had arrived in safe areas over the past few days and that there could be another 300,000 on the move or about to flee areas in northwestern Pakistan.

"The numbers were in addition to 555,000 counted since last August fleeing the areas of Dir, Buner and Swat, he said in a telephone interview. 'We could be talking about a total of one million' since last (2008) August.

"In late April, my colleague Thomas Fuller reported that a spokesman for the Sri Lankan military, Brig. Gen. Udaya Nanayakkara, estimated that 'among the nearly 200,000 people who have escaped rebel-held territory since January, about 3,000 were determined to be fighters disguised as civilians.'

"If that estimate is accurate, given that the entire Taliban force in the part of Pakistan where the fighting is taking place now is estimated at 4,000 or 5,000 men, it is not hard to imagine that many Taliban fighters could take advantage of the free flow of civilians from the area to escape this battle to fight another day. In both Sri Lanka and Pakistan, the militants which the government is trying to defeat are guerrillas who use their ability to blend in with the civilian population to their advantage"[12] ...

It is quite clear that the two civil wars have different dynamics which do not bear recounting here. What is worth stating is that "the Sri Lankan government may have more secure control over its military than Pakistan's new civilian government. Sri Lanka's Defence Secretary, Gottabhaya Rajapaksa, and its President, Mahinda Rajapaksa, are brothers,"[13] as Mackay astutely observes. This line of thinking could be extended by saying that the Sri Lankans are fighting a synergised war, with the politicians and the military sharing a vision and its executing philosophy. This is certainly not the case with Pakistan which has gone to war reluctantly, after considerable goading by the USA. Mackay quotes Andrew Exum of *The Washington Post* who has correctly read the fine print and suggested that "Pakistan was simply not as consistent, or as committed, to defeating the Taliban militarily as Sri Lanka is to defeating the Tamil Tigers."[14] Exum is quoted again saying that "By alternately striking a series of deals with the Taliban from 2004 until the present in the FATA and the NWFP and also fighting the Taliban in the very same regions, the Pakistani Army and state looks schizophrenic. No wonder they're having trouble.

In stark contrast, the Sri Lankan government has brushed aside calls from the international community to put civilian safety first, and hold its military back from a final confrontation with the besieged Tamil Tiger force."[15]

Each War is Different

This is a concluding thought that the author feels obliged to bring to the reader's attention. There is a pronounced tendency to 'template' wars and use them to make recommendations for corrections that are often worse than the problem itself. The Sri Lankan civil war, was, finally, a contained and isolated war, whose only really visible face outside of the immediate region, was its proactive and hyper diaspora and Sri Lanka`s much publicised tie ups with China, not so much on the war front as in the sphere of infrastructure development and allotment of an EEZ outside Colombo. Except for the Indian intervention, that too at the then government's formal request, there was no physical outside interference, if one is willing to overlook the few Pakistani advisers who are reported to have helped them with military advice.

The war was also not on the Western world's radar except for alleged human rights violations and inadequate refugee care during and post the conflict. Thus, comparing it with the Chechen problem, the Israeli-PLO war, the Af-Pak conflict or the Kashmir problem will not pay professional dividends because each of these insurrections have totally different dynamics.

That said, there are some lessons that are indeed common, as has been brought out, and which need introspection for the extent to which these are applicable.

Endnotes

1. Fernando, Lalin. "End of the War". June 30, 2009. http://asiantribune.com/06/30/end-of-the-war/ Quotation cited at the start of the chapter is given at the end of a perceptive, pragmatic article by the writer, who is a retired SLA officer of the Gemunu Watch Regiment.
2. "How it Came to This – Learning from Sri Lanka's Civil Wars By Professor John Richardson". paradisepoisoned.com. <http://www.paradisepoisoned. com/PDFs/Preview21. pdf>.
3. Ibid.
4. Ibid.
5. Ibid.
6. Leitner, Peter and Jayatilake, Rajika. "Lessons from Sri Lanka". <http://www. centerforsecuritypolicy.org/g1.xml>
   Peter Leitner is President of the Higgins Counterterrorism Research Centre and has previously served for 31 years in various national security positions. Rajika Jayatilake is a communications specialist with expertise in international media and public relations. Excerpts (the nine lessons) have been used from their article.
7. Reynolds, Paul. "Lessons of War from Tigers' Defeat". World Affairs Correspondent. Paul.Reynolds-INTERNET@bbc.co.uk BBC News Website. <http://news.bbc.co.uk/2/hi/south_asia/8057118.stm>. Reynolds eloquently reasons that success by military means may be possible. An extract is given below:
   The defeat of the Tamil Tigers might encourage other governments to put more emphasis on

fighting insurgents by military means. This would go against the modern theory of counter insurgency, which tries to win over populations as the key to long-term peace. The modern theory has been enshrined in the US manual of counter insurgency. This was written by General David Petraeus, the man who led the surge in Iraq and brought a greater degree of stability. He is now trying to do the same thing in Afghanistan. "Counter-insurgents should prepare for a long-term commitment" is one sentence from the manual. "Offensive operations are only the beginning" is another. In Sri Lanka it was certainly a long-term counter-insurgency commitment. But offensive operations were the end as well as the beginning.

8. Leitner, Peter and Jayatilake, Rajika. "Lessons from Sri Lanka". <http://www.centerforsecuritypolicy.org/g1.xml>.
9. Reynolds, Paul. "Lessons of War from Tigers' Defeat". World Affairs Correspondent. Paul.Reynolds-INTERNET@bbc.co.uk BBC News Website. <http://news.bbc.co.uk/2/hi/south_asia/8057118.stm>. Excerpt:

   The Sri Lankan victory comes as US counter-insurgency thinking is continuing to evolve. In an article in the *Small Wars Journal*, in which such issues are discussed in detail, James A Gavrilis, who fought in Iraq as a Green Beret, wrote this month: "One of the most profound changes the US military must make to be effective at countering insurgency is to shift strategic centres of gravity from the physical to the human aspects of warfare." He notes with approval that the US now uses more civil affairs units and said: "Our military has a predisposition to focus on enemy forces and capabilities and the confrontation between friendly and enemy forces, with little emphasis on the social or political context within which the confrontation takes place."
10. Ibid.
11. Mackey, Robert. "Pakistan and Sri Lanka, a Tale of Two Counter Insurgencies". May 08, 2009. <http://thelede.blogs.nytimes.com/2009/05/08/a-tale-of-two-counterinsurgencies-in-pakistan-and-sri-lanka/>. Excerpts have been used.
12. Ibid.
13. Ibid.
14. Ibid.
15. Ibid.

CHAPTER 21

The Way Ahead in Sri Lanka

The universal, historically tested truism is that, consciously as well as inadvertently, nations commit blunders/ errors of judgment, during cataclysmic events such as wars. Post event, whether in retrospect or with the wisdom imparted by hindsight, they learn lessons that suggest why and how things got messed up. They earnestly resolve never to repeat their mistakes, only to inexplicably disregard the 'lessons learnt' when it comes down to implementation. This only reinforces the widely held belief that nations do not really learn lessons from their past mistakes. At least, most nations do not appear to undo past mistakes. Readers, who, for instance, are following the Af-Pak conundrum and US President Barack Obama's curious initiative to escalate force levels but at the same time announce withdrawal plans commencing July 2011, will probably relate the strategy to re-election compulsions and therefore the need to appease both the US left and right wings of opinion. A section of the media and Af-Pak watchers have taken such a policy to be a cardinal blunder that is destined to fail. When victory is not assured and is nowhere in sight either, they feel announcement of withdrawal intentions will only serve to strengthen the resolve of the al Qaeda/Taliban combine to not only hold on but play out the publicised period of time that the US has set aside for overwhelming victory by simply going underground. Ironically, one of the lessons that the senior most General (Gen Petraeus) overseeing the US efforts had stated a few months ago, was that if the US does not watch its step it could fail in an area known as "the graveyard of empires". The signs point ominously in that direction, especially with their key ally, Pakistan playing truant.

Progressive nations need both clarity and perseverance to set themselves a rendezvous with prosperity and peace. They can do so by shedding the historic baggage of learning only to unlearn and moving towards serious implementation of learnt lessons; thus avoiding committing the same mistakes ad nauseum. To do so, they need national will, national resolve, national character as well as a visionary implementation roadmap – a map which indicates the chosen path to progress and prosperity, with pitfalls (and their antidotes) clearly annotated. Also indicated should be a pragmatic, implementable time-space-resources continuum against which the nation's progress can be tabulated till the desired end-state is reached.

Sri Lanka is a case in point. A proud nation, it was progressive; a *Tiger* nation in economic performance till the civil war of the seventies, stymied all progress. The war has now been won at great personal, material and national cost and is over – for the moment anyway – leaving Sri Lanka face to face with a more serious challenge – winning an enduring peace and returning to its pole position economically as was once an enviable part of its DNA, when it was serenaded as the Isle of Serendip. The last chapter focused on the lessons that Sri Lanka has learnt or ought to have learnt from its fratricidal civil war. It is really not necessary to prove the cliché right that no one ever learns from history. The time is ripe for national reconciliation and national consensus in preparing and implementing a roadmap that will once again make Sri Lanka supreme amongst the nations of South Asia, if not the whole Asian continent and Indian Ocean littoral. The time to start is now.

The lessons learnt were varied – ranging from developmental, policy related, unorthodox use of the military in overwhelming force to win the war, use of path breaking strategy at all levels and spheres of functioning, the need for quality intelligence, conduct of nuanced psychological warfare, diaspora and international community management, conduct of dynamic foreign relations, and, not the least, the need for politico-military-diplomatic synergy in conduct of war. Sri Lanka has documented these lessons well enough. Now, there is clearly a need to implement those lessons which indicate an urgent need for reform and improvement. Probably the most critical of these is the need to learn from the past, that the country needs unity above all other needs. It also needs generosity and the ability to forgive and forget between the victor and vanquished. The way ahead for Sri Lanka, therefore, starts with this mandate which, purely from the national resurgence point of view, should be considered non-negotiable and binding.

Diverse sources have different takes on what the 'way ahead' could mean for Sri Lanka, as well as the penalties that may be incurred for non-compliance. These have been synthesized in this chapter, with due attribution, and are laid out in the succeeding paragraphs with the author's comments, where warranted. In several cases, the heading is clearly indicative of the key thought being propagated by these diverse sources.

President Mahinda Rajapaksa – Nationalist Avenger or Unifying Peacemaker?

Lydia Polgreen, writing in the *New York Times*, begins her excellent article by recalling a landmark event of ancient times in Sri Lanka's Sinhala -Tamil strife laden history. She writes[1]: "More than 2,000 years ago, a Sinhalese king named Dutugemunu saddled up his elephant and headed North to fight and kill Elara, an invading Tamil king from India. The battle between the men is one of the most celebrated moments in Sri Lankan history, and the last time (until two months ago), that a Sri Lankan ruler won such a decisive victory over a mortal threat. President Mahinda Rajapaksa's defeat of the Tamil Tigers has made him a hero in the eyes of many Sri Lankans, but others find his air of triumph unseemly". She continues "Perhaps it is no wonder, then, that fans of Mahinda Rajapaksa, the President of Sri Lanka, have taken to calling him a modern-day incarnation of King Dutugemunu. After all, he presided over the defeat of the Tamil Tigers, among the world's most enduring and vicious guerrilla separatists; hardened fighters who have humiliated four Presidents over nearly three decades.

Asked about this comparison earlier this month, Mr. Rajapaksa laughed it off, insisting that the legend was misunderstood as a triumph of one ethnicity over another. After his victory, the story goes: Dutugemunu made peace with the Tamils and honoured the memory of Elara, who was beloved by his people. History will decide whether Mr. Rajapaksa will be remembered as a nationalist avenger or a unifying peacemaker."[2]

She notes further that "President Rajapaksa is careful to use conciliatory language and speak about the importance of winning the peace, not just the war... But so far, talk of reconciliation has been just that, according to politicians, analysts and diplomats here and there, there have been no concrete steps toward a lasting political solution to Sri Lanka's thorny ethnic problem."[3]

There could be no better start to the 'way ahead' for Sri Lanka than Lydia Polgreen's wise and sensitive connect with the past. The war has, indeed, been won. It is now the elusive peace that needs to be won in Serendip; the sooner the better. Accommodation rather than hard line views and attitudes on the opposing sides is the requirement; more on the side of the victor than on the side that lost the war. The subtext is clear – if the current euphoria of winning is sectarian led and not national interest led, the country can get into a vicious, negative spiral again, undoing all the hard work done and the sacrifices made to reach this far; 2000 years after sectarian conflict first occurred on the island.

Sri Lanka well wishers will undoubtedly recall that the British were the first to unite the island's three warring kingdoms together, when they colonized the country in 1815, baptizing their possession as Ceylon; a name that continued from 1815 to 1972, after which it was renamed as the "Free, Sovereign and Independent Republic of Sri Lanka."[4] The implication is clear and straightforward: the country's best bet of winning the peace is to be inclusive and take its minority Tamil and Muslim populations along with the Sinhala majority. Politics that continue to profess the 'Sinhala only' line will simply not succeed. The winning (and wise) leader in the January 2010 Presidential elections will be the one who promotes or promises unity (and therefore country good) above all else. The way ahead is to drop sectarian jingoism by winning over the people to this platform. This is a formidable challenge, but is achievable by a leader who walks tall and who, over time, manages to win public support for this point of view.

Think Tank CLAWS Suggestions on the Way Ahead

The need for national unity is also one amongst several seminal observations that the erudite Brig Gurmeet Kanwal (Retd), Director CLAWS, and his distinguished panel have divined in a recent (June 2009) round table discussion organised by him at CLAWS, New Delhi, on the subject. A key point raised by him is that the military's capability to "win a stand alone war" should not be overplayed; by implication, all wars have differing dynamics and what has worked in one set of circumstances may not work in another situation.[5]

Maj. Gen. Ashok Mehta (Retd),[6] while noting the military lessons that won the war for the SLAF and, correspondingly, lost it for the LTTE, points towards the boldness and willingness of the Sri Lankan military commanders in using unorthodox tactics (and inexplicable adoption of set piece tactics by the LTTE) as well as extraordinary synergy between the three services and between the services and Government that bodes well, as a future trend for military forces combating terrorism. The role of the Navy and Air Force in limiting the area of operations and logistics reach of the LTTE also comes in for justifiable praise. What he feels must not be "templated"[7] is the savage, orchestrated emasculation of the media, both local and foreign and the cordoning off of the war zone from media scrutiny. A via media between the US practice of "embedding" and the Sri Lankan model of total exclusion may certainly be the way ahead in media handling, for countries combating terror.

Nitin Gokhale[8] stresses that so far as conduct of psychological warfare was concerned, both sides, with the LTTE initially leading, used media effectively. The smart Tamil diaspora management by the LTTE also comes in for notice. While disapproving of the "media firewall" that the government created during the concluding stages of the civil war, Nitin nevertheless lauds the idea of the Media Centre for National Security (MCNS) for single point communications with the media, which the Sri Lankan MoD created. This was a good move, he feels, which India should adopt in a crisis situation like 26/11. However, what is not worth emulating is the way the media was intimidated and controlled. During the period of operations, 14 journalists were killed; 20 fled the country; many were silenced by threats. At the same time, all pro-LTTE media, websites and blogs were barred. Simultaneously, the government catered for information hungry media through an information-rich website, but with only the government's perspective. The government for its own good, he writes, has to learn to tolerate dissent. It should throw open all Tamil-dominated areas to the media at least in a phased manner. A war-like situation cannot be allowed to remain forever.[9]

M.R. Narayan Swamy[10] focuses on the need for political resolution. Unfortunately, he says, the Tigers never acted as a political force. They either silenced or subjugated other Tamil political voices. LTTE mistakenly thought that Eelam was possible and obdurately pursued it. However, the Tamil community gained nothing even after 30 years of armed struggle and loss of over 90,000 lives. LTTE is responsible for the present sorry state of affairs of Tamils, who have been humiliated more than ever before. There are moves to bring a political package on the lines of 13th Amendment of the Constitution. But, what is required, he opines, is a 13th Amendment plus.

N. Manoharan[11] focuses on resolving the prevailing humanitarian crisis which, he feels, is vital for both military and political reasons. Military success is not complete without tending to humanitarian problems. At the same time, if the humanitarian crisis remains unaddressed, it will be difficult to arrive at a meaningful and lasting political solution for the ethnic issue. The displaced people are living in various camps in the North East. There are severe shortages of essentials like food, medicine, water, clothes and living space in relief camps. Because of stringent screening procedures to filter out possible LTTE cadres, harassments are prevalent in these camps. Above all, they are "beyond the protection of law". The Sri Lankan government has put forward a "180-day plan" to resettle all the IDPs. The pace of demining and construction of basic infrastructure, however, is not appreciable. There is also no serious thinking on providing means of livelihood to the resettled IDPs. The way ahead, he suggests, is to settle the refugees soonest and with dignity, compassion and understanding. This can only be done by the government showing resolve and will and by their not overplaying the LTTE card (fear of LTTE cadre hiding amongst the IDP's).

P. Sahadevan[12] notes that the international component in the Sri Lankan military victory is significant (and, presumably, worth emulating). Sri Lanka got as many as 31 important countries to proscribe the Tigers, resulting in their international isolation and choking of warlike supplies and logistics to them. At the same time, Colombo boosted its military supplies by truly adept diplomacy. China topped the list of military donors and Pakistan, Israel, Russia, and Ukraine also chipped in. On its part, India granted non-lethal military armaments. On the distaff side, partly due to pressure from the Sri Lankan Tamil diaspora, some Western countries including the USA turned critical of Sri Lankan military operations, citing human rights violations. Sri Lanka, however, overcame this obstacle with the help of countries like China, India, Pakistan and Russia. Nevertheless, the author suggests that, in order to regain its credibility and normalize its relationships with the Western bloc in particular, Colombo should open itself for enquiry on human rights abuses instead of talking of what Sahadevan terms as "inviolable sovereignty."

Political Sagacity Needed by the President – Look Afresh at Devolution

Lydia Polgreen's sentiment finds repetition again and again, amongst those who wish Sri Lanka well. They feel that President Rajapaksa (or his successor, should there be one post the January 2010 elections) should rise above any sectarian agenda or consideration; rise above himself for the supreme national interest of Sri Lanka, and make peace with his Tamil citizens that lasts. He has the broad support of the masses and his party (excepting hard line elements of both sides, which he has to tackle tactfully, in his trademark, politically adept and savvy manner). History will laud him if he shows that this capacity, resolve and will, say Sri Lanka watchers.

Rajapaksa is however known to have recently stated that "Federalism is out of the question,"[13] This non-negotiable start point that the President has set for himself, implies that only limited devolution may be possible. This is something that the Tamils may not look too kindly at, besides the Sinhala JVP hardliners, some of whom insist on denial of any devolution whatsoever. Ms. Green quotes Paikiasothy Saravanamuttu of the Center for Policy Alternatives, a nonpartisan research and advocacy institution in Colombo, as saying that "Peace will require a more federal power-sharing arrangement". "There has been this primordial fear that federalism is a precursor to secession." But, the opposite is true, he argues. "It is the refusal to share power that has led to the armed conflict to begin with." Saravanamuttu's take is that the Tamil king came from India and the Sinhala community fears (has perhaps always feared) getting swamped by the 60 million Tamils who reside in India. This may be their compulsion against power sharing arrangements. Readers will no doubt note that India is keen and anxious to assist in resolving the problem in a manner that satisfies both sides and can be expected to facilitate an understanding.

Reconciliation, Rehabilitation, Reintegration, Development and Unity Needed

Lalin Fernando, the ex Gemunu Watch Sinhalese SLA officer uses a different syntax which is just as profound: "Let there be reconciliation, rehabilitation, reintegration, development and unity now. Let there never be a cruel conflict like this in Sri Lanka again."[14] The general opinion is that if anyone can achieve this near state of utopia, it has to be Mahinda Rajapaksa, he says. "There could be no clearer enunciation of what the way ahead could mean for Sri Lanka or what its desired end state should be with reference to winning the peace. The way ahead is tricky and complex and has to be negotiated with great care. Let us examine what these challenges are, which need resolution before the larger issue of the return of peace to the Garden of Eden can be assured".

Establishing an Egalitarian and Plural Society the Way Ahead

The well known Tamil journalist, DBS Jeyaraj, suggests that[15] "three schools of thought have been clashing. The Sinhala hardliners want Sinhala-Buddhist domination. They see this country as theirs alone. Others are excluded in this 'Chinthana.' The Tamil hardliners want a separate state for the North East (Tamil Eelam) Just as Sinhala hawks say Sri Lanka is for the Sinhalese, these Tamil hawks say Tamil Eelam is for the Tamils...**The third idea is that of establishing an egalitarian and plural society where all children of this country can live together in amity and fraternity.** It incorporates a vision where no one will claim superior rights on the basis of belonging to the majority race/religion or claim exclusive rights to their historic habitat...The call for the third option between the hegemonistic one state and secessionist two-state schools of thought is a voice of sanity and sensibility. It is presently inaudible amidst the raucous battle-cries. I, however, firmly believe that it will be heard and heard effectively one day. Sri Lanka will then be alive with the sound of concord."[16]

Talking to Terrorists[17]

David Betz makes an insightful correlation between a new book, *Talking to Terrorists* by John Bew, Martin Frampton and Inigo Gurruchaga and the Sri Lankan situation. Let us repeat the portion of this book that interests Betz: The authors argue that what really matters is not the act of Governments talking to terrorists itself, but a range of other variables including the role of state actors, intelligence agencies, hard power and the wider democratic process. In some cases, talking can do more harm than good. But, above all, there is a crucial difference between talking to terrorists who believe that their strategy is succeeding and engaging with those who have been made to realise that their aims are unattainable by violence."

Talking now to the Tamil Tigers, after their defeat, Betz suggests, would be a good idea. If there's any chance that the insurgency cycle can be broken now would seem a crucial opportunity not to squander. He suggests that, rather than treating them as annihilated; it may be more useful to presume that they are back to Phase 1 of the insurgency, when they are willing to talk, eschewing violence, with the Government who calls all or most of the shots. Keeping in mind that reports indicate that several thousands of LTTE cadres have neither been caught nor have surrendered, (estimates vary widely from 3000 to several times that figure), he is right in suggesting that the Government should not only talk but take the under mentioned precautions:[18]

- **Control the area.** The enemy must not have any place to rest. If they cannot rest, they will lose morale. And when they lose morale, they surrender. In the terminal phase of Turkey's war, PKK terrorists surrendered en masse.
- **Offer amnesty to anyone who surrenders willingly.** Ex-terrorists can become great COINOPS assets, as they know the enemy's tactics.
- **Always target the leaders.** Without leaders, the followers surrender easily.
- **Local support is very important.** Local people generally support the side that does them less harm and also is physically closer to them.
- **A terrorist group needs outside support.** They need to have weapons and ammunition as supplies, safe resting and training facilities. This outside support is their life line. It must be severed.
- **Most important of all.** The enemy must understand that you are ready to go to the end to win the war. That means a resolve for the long slog and a stomach for attrition. If the enemy thinks that you develop feet of clay quickly, he will continue fighting."[19]

Rehabilitation of Former LTTE Cadres[20]

A logical extension of the willingness to talk is the consideration that those who consider giving up the struggle, as thousands have already done, need rehabilitation. "Leaving such young men in limbo will be counter productive if not dangerous. It could possibly lead to some of them being integrated into the Armed Services and police while the others could take part in development work depending on their aptitude and attitude. **SLAF have a golden opportunity to create themselves as true representatives of the country and change the much criticized impression of being a Sinhala only SLAF**. Former LTTE cadres have become cabinet and provincial chief ministers, thus, integrating the others should not be considered difficult or hazardous."

Such an approach will also, to a large extent, lessen the threat of LTTE revival. This is the feeling of researcher Ajit Kumar Singh.[21] SLA spokesman, Brigadier Udaya Nanayakkara said on August 12, 2009, that the LTTE operatives overseas could be keen to carry out a suicide attack to re-energize demoralized supporters. Daya Mohan, the senior-most LTTE leader to survive the military onslaught, and others, like 'Colonel' Ram, Nagulan, were still at large, according to media reports. The threat becomes more real bearing in mind the fact that there are 9,797[22] former LTTE militants, including some suicide cadres, currently detained at rehabilitation centers across the island. The vast majority of these cadres have received the LTTE's 'ten-day training' and some of these cadres had taken part in the burial of LTTE arms caches throughout the North. If any of these cadres are re-enlisted by the 'surviving LTTE leadership' after they are resettled, a potentially deadly insurgency could arise. Their rehabilitation is therefore an important way forward.

Redefining the Role of the Armed Forces

Basil Rajapaksa, the Adviser to the President, who also happens to be his brother makes an important point that reveals the thinking of the Government and may well be an important way ahead. He says that, "having been on a war footing for so long, we have to redefine the role of the Armed Forces now that peace has been restored. Also, much of the police force will have to be re-trained and re-orientated to the requirements of law and order in a post-war community setting. "Beyond that, we also have to ensure peace and order in our society by disarming the many factions and individuals who, by nature of the threats they faced from the Tamil Tigers, were allowed to carry arms. We need to impress upon them that the state can now offer them adequate protection".[23]

Intelligent Tamil Diaspora Management by Sri Lanka Needed

Robert Mackay is probably right in asserting in the *New York Times NYT)* that… "certainly anyone who has read even a few of the hundreds of comments posted on *The Lede (a NYT* blog*)* in recent weeks by Sri Lankans can see that most arguments about what is happening in Sri Lanka boil down to an exchange of these two words, "genocide" and "terrorist," which are both, in a sense, meant to close down debate and assign blame solely to one side. This polarized view of the conflict is obviously not restricted to the blogosphere."[24]

It is a foregone fact that normalization of ethnic relations in Sri Lanka must necessarily include the vast Tamil diaspora spread globally and particularly in the Americas, Canada and Europe. This is in recognition of the fact that they had a major hand in fuelling and sustenance of the Tamil Eelam movement right through the struggle. Success was achieved by the Sri Lanka government only after the diaspora was hugely marginalised by launch of a massive diplomatic campaign by the government, and the development of effective propaganda machinery belonging to the government. Small wonder that, according to a recent report, the Rajapaksa Government is seriously considering mobilizing the Sri Lankan diaspora through a governmental organization. *Asian Tribune* has suggested long ago that a separate 'Ministry for Sri Lankans abroad, be set up to look after the interest of the Diasporas in the Western Countries.[25]

There are an estimated 2.5 million plus Lankans in Europe as well as in the North America. The Gulf and West Asian countries account for a little more than 1.5 million migrant Sri Lankan workers. The LTTE received more than USD 300 million annually from the Tamil diaspora, according to a survey by Jane's Weekly. This money enabled the Tigers to acquire highly sophisticated lethal military hardware to challenge the might of the State. Also, the LTTE, managed to run an effective and efficient propaganda against the Sri Lanka Government. The campaign was so efficient and professional that it cleverly projected their terrorist activities as struggle for independence of the Tamil ethnicity. Therefore it is high time that Sri Lankan leadership considers appointing a Minister for Overseas Sri Lankans – a person of the calibre of Basil Rajapaksa, who is doer, who at present heads the Governments Reconciliation and Reconstruction Committee is apparently being thought of, as per this report by KT Rajasingham.[26]

Development Must be Done in the North

This is something that has been the biggest bone of contention for the Tamils in the period preceding as well as after Independence in 1948. Ajit Kumar reports in his article that, unsurprisingly, President Mahinda Rajapaksa, on March 23, 2009, launched the *Uturu Mithuru* (Northern Friends) Project for the development of the North. The project, under the leadership of Basil Rajapaksa, MP, brother of the President and his Senior Adviser, as well as Chairman of the Presidential Task Force for the Development of the North, emphasizes infrastructure development, electricity, water supply and sanitation, agriculture, irrigation, livestock development, inland fisheries, health, solid waste disposal, education, sports, cultural affairs and transportation.[27] He adds that, concurrent to the *Uturu Mithuru* Project, the Government has launched projects worth SLR 1.058 billion to provide higher education facilities to children of the displaced, funded by the Asian Development bank and the World Bank.[28]

In another positive, the economy is showing signs of revival. The Colombo Stock Exchange has gained more than 32 percent since the end of the war. Also, the International Monetary Fund (IMF) said its Executive Board, on July 24, approved the USD 2.6 billion, 20-month Stand-By loan that Sri Lanka had requested to support the country's economic reform program.

Enhancing Security in the North

Ajit Kumar Singh further points out that, the Police Department is to set up 21 new Police Stations in the North and a Tamil language training centre for Police personnel in Killinochchi, in addition to Tamil language training centre at Kalladi. The country has total police strength of 75,000.[29] Further, reports indicate that 18 armed groups, holding more than 400 firearms, continue to exist in the East. On July 31, the Sri Lanka Police announced that, except for the Security Forces and Police, no other party will be allowed to carry weapons in the Eastern Province. The Deputy Inspector General of Police in the East, Edison Gunathilaka, said several main Tamil political parties who bore weapons in the past would also not be allowed to carry weapons any more. According to the new rule, the Thamil Makkal Viduthalai Pulikal (TMVP), EPDP, PLOTE, and EPRLF were no longer allowed to hold weapons.[30]

A Utopian Dream?

DBS Jeyaraj, at the end of his article[31] on his country's 61st year of celebration of its Independence, shares his dream with his readers. He writes: "Let me conclude with a poem that is one of my favourites. It is from the *Gitanjali* by Rabindranath Tagore:

> "Where the mind is without fear and the head is held high; Where knowledge is free; Where the world has not been broken up into fragments by narrow domestic walls; Where words come out from the depths of truth; Where tireless striving stretches its arms towards perfection; Where the clear stream of reason has not lost its way into the dreary desert sand of dead habit; Where the mind is led forward by thee into ever-widening thought and action- Into that heaven of freedom, my Father, let my country awake".

Assessment

The core issue on which this way ahead for Sri Lanka is hinged on, is the urgent need for its leaders and people to move on with sagacity and far sightedness. They should convert the gains of the bloody, over 30 year civil war into permanent nation building assets that promote unity, peace and prosperity for all in the emerald isle, not just the majority community. Mahinda Rajapaksa came into governance with a slim majority, on the single point agenda of defeating the LTTE. He has succeeded in doing so beyond his wildest dreams. In fact, he has almost decimated them. Enough of the LTTE is, however, left on the island as well as abroad, within the diaspora, to revive as a movement, should their current annihilation not be taken political mileage of. This is something that worries the current government; something that can ruin the current state of euphoria, if mishandled and allowed to fester like a running sore. The solution is obviously political in nature. Apart from attending to the various 'ways ahead' as have been indicated in this chapter and elsewhere in the book, the nation has to accommodate the legitimate demands of its largest minority, the Tamils, without compromising on its sovereignty or the reasonable aspirations of the Sinhala majority. Failure to do so will set the clock back to the 1970's, when the problem surfaced, with its resultant chaos and mayhem.

Notwithstanding who amongst the various aspirants comes to power, post the January 2010 Presidential elections, the above considerations will have to remain central to the policies of the winning candidate, to avoid a return to the nightmarish past that resulted in the loss of countless lives lost and an end to prosperity in a once vibrant and prosperous nation. No one thinks the transition in outlook for the nation will be easy; certainly not with General Sarath Fonseka having just thrown in his hat as a serious Presidential candidate. That said, a call will still have to be taken in the supreme national interest of the country not to compromise on this key essential for peace, prosperity and tranquility to return to Sri Lanka.

Endnotes

1. Polgreen, Lydia. "Lanka Justifying a Costly War in Sri Lanka". July 18, 2009. <http://www.nytimes.com/2009/07/19/world/asia/19lanka.html?_r=1&pagewanted=2&th&emc=th>
2. Ibid.
3. Ibid.
4. "Sri Lanka". http://en.wikipedia.org/wiki/Sri_Lanka.
5. "Post-LTTE Sri Lanka: The Way Ahead". Round Table Discussion at CLAWS Conference Room Chaired by Mr. PR Chari, Research Professor, Institute of Peace and Conflict Studies (IPCS). June 08, 2009. Brig Gurmeet Kanwal (Retd), Director, CLAWS, welcomed the participants and pointed out that recent counter-insurgency effort, both in Sri Lanka and North-West Pakistan has relied on excessive use of military force and there is need to consider whether this is an emerging trend. He also expressed the hope that the Sri Lankan government would put in requisite effort since the the war against the LTTE had been won. Presentations were made by Maj Gen Ashok Mehta (Retd.), Mr. Nitin Gokhale (Defence

Editor, NDTV), Mr. M R Narayan Swamy (News Editor, IANS), Mr. Rajesh Sundaram (Headlines Today), Dr N Manoharan (Senior Fellow, CLAWS) and Prof P Sahadevan (Jawaharlal Nehru University). The round-table was attended by a select gathering of officers and members of the strategic community. The report was compiled by Dr N Manoharan, Senior Fellow, Centre for Land Warfare Studies (CLAWS), New Delhi.

6. Ibid.
7. Ibid.
8. Ibid.
9. Ibid.
10. Ibid.
11. Ibid.
12. Ibid.
13. Polgreen, Lydia. "Lanka Justifying a Costly War in Sri Lanka". July 18, 2009. <http://www.nytimes.com/2009/07/19/world/asia/19lanka.html?_r=1&pagewanted=2&th&emc=th>
14. Fernando, Lalin. "End of the War". Jun 30, 2009. <http://asiantribune.com/06/30/end-of-the-war/>.
15. Jeyaraj, DBS. "Sixty-One Years of Independence and the Tamils of Sri Lanka". February 4, 2009. <http://dbsjeyaraj.com/dbsj/archives/213>.
16. Ibid.
17. Betz, David. "The Window Opens, the Window Shuts: "When to 'Talk to Terrorists"? http://kingsofwar.wordpress.com/2009/06/17/the-window-opens-the-window-shuts-when-to-talk-to-terrorists
18. Ibid.
19. Ibid.
20. Fernando, Lalin. "End of the War". Jun 30, 2009. <http://asiantribune.com/06/30/end-of-the-war/>.
21. Singh, Ajit Kumar. "Advances and Ambiguities". Research Associate, Institute for Conflict Management. South Asia Terrorism Portal. http://www.kanglaonline.com/index.php?template=kshow&kid=1673&Idoc_Session=a6bc89ca267e4e86bb299f3a68b9b0af
22. Ibid.
23. "Basil Rajapaksa to Resign From Sri Lanka Parliament". October 15, 2009. <http://www.colombopage.com/archive_091/Oct1255608292RA.html>.
24. Mackey, Robert. "Outside Sri Lanka, Tamil Diaspora Not Ready to Surrender". May 18, 2009. <http://thelede.blogs.nytimes.com/2009/05/18/outside-sri-lanka-tamil-diaspora-not-ready-to-surrender/>
25. Rajasingham, KT. "Face the Threat from Rump Tigers in the West Politically". Jun 28, 2009. <http://asiantribune.com/06/28/face-the-threat-from-rump-tigers-in-the-west-politically/>
26. Ibid.
27. Singh, Ajit Kumar. "Advances and Ambiguities". Research Associate, Institute for Conflict Management. South Asia Terrorism Portal. http://www.kanglaonline.com/index.php?template=kshow&kid=1673&Idoc_Session=a6bc89ca267e4e86bb299f3a68b9b0af
28. Ibid.
29. Ibid.
30. Ibid.
31. Jeyaraj, DBS. "Sixty-One Years of Independence and the Tamils of Sri Lanka". February 4, 2009. <http://dbsjeyaraj.com/dbsj/archives/213>.

Chapter 22

Trouble in Paradise

"The ability to evaluate the situation objectively has always been a sign of true leadership"
– General Frido and Senger Etterlin

The unlikely troika of the suave, astute, street smart politician Mahinda Rajapaksa, his brilliant, hands-on ex Army brother, Gottabhaya Rajapaksa, and the hard bitten, mercurial but equally brilliant Gen Sarath Fonseka had got together in end 2005, to orchestrate the decimation of the LTTE. For almost three years, they made this "unattainable" charter their sole preoccupation. They succeeded in a manner that must rank as a first in the annals of the world's fight against terror. Their sterling achievement now runs the real danger of being consigned to memory and to folklore. This is because these once seemingly inseparable personalities have fallen out in a bitter, very public spat. After months of what initially appeared to be differing but manageable post victory perceptions, post battle stress, LTTE propaganda or, at best, educated media speculation, Gen Fonseka has, opted out and entered the political arena as an avowed opponent of the Rajapaksa Government.

On the Warpath: Gen Fonseka and President Rajapaksa

Ironically, the break has come within months of achieving what is arguably one of the greatest victories against terror in recent times – the clinical, near total, synergised destruction of the world's second most feared terror organisation after the al Qaeda. The greater irony is, of course, that the spat was not over substantial issues like war strategy, post conflict termination aims and methodology, IDP settlement or other equally cerebral considerations. It was over the *seemingly* trivial issue of sharing credit. The Rajapaksa's, whom no one has ever accused of suffering from humility, have never had a doubt that 'they dun it' in exclusion of everyone else. They have gone to town making sure everyone hears of their astonishing feat. They have also laboured to explain that Gen Fonseka has merely competently executed his portion of the brilliant strategy which they had evolved and presciently put into place. Gen Fonseka, on the other hand, is furious and feels he has been denied the exclusive credit that is his hard earned due. The war, he thunders was won by him – a war for which the Rajapaksa's were the supporting cast; merely providing admirable support for his stellar effort. The long knives are out.

A No-Holds-Barred Power Struggle is at the Core of the Fallout

The reader will, of course, have seen through this barely concealed façade and prudently viewed the fall out through the prism of *realpolitik.* Under the guise of credit sharing, what the world is witnessing is a no-holds-barred power struggle between a long serving, very ambitious and savvy political family and an equally ambitious, capable but politically naive ex General. At stake is the pole position for running the country, using the victory over the LTTE as the USP for garnering public support and votes.

Every wise and experienced politician knows that the issue of blind public support or gratitude should not be taken for granted. While the Sinhala majority and substantial portions of the minority communities in Sri Lanka; the Tamils, Muslims and Burghers, do appreciate the unexpected victory over the LTTE, public memory is notoriously short. Many amongst the public across race, strata of society or gender are looking beyond the victory for a fast track return to normalcy and prosperity. Above all, most Sri Lankans seem to have realized that prosperity and unity go hand in hand. What they therefore need is a leader who can steer the country to its earlier winning ways, taking all along. Are the two likely contenders to power capable of meeting this daunting challenge? Let us briefly examine the issue.

Both are Capable Men who are also Sinhala Hardliners[1]

The wily and honey tongued President Rajapaksa had promised generosity and large-hearted accommodation towards the Tamil minority,[2] even when victory against the LTTE was not on the horizon. The content of the President's historic speech in Tamil at the 63rd session of the UN General Assembly in end September 2008 was a dramatic and much applauded effort to establish that he was a people's leader representing all the peoples of Sri Lanka, including the Tamil minority. "While my mother tongue is Sinhala, let me elaborate a few thoughts in Tamil. Sinhala and Tamil are the two languages of the people of Sri Lanka. Both these have been used through the centuries, are rich in literature, and are widely used in my country, with recognition as Official Languages" he had said. He had added, "With the widening of democracy in our country, the bonds between the Sinhala and Tamil people of Sri Lanka will grow stronger and remain a major force for its future development. We will march towards a richer freedom and lasting unity that await us as a nation."[3]

In Chapter 21 of this book, Lydia Polgreen records that, like the legendary Sinhala King Dutugemunu who headed north to Jaffna to combat the invading Tamil King Elara, defeating and then magnanimously forgiving him, Mahinda Rajapaksa also plans to do as much, taking the whole country along with him. Strangely, but not unsurprisingly, this is not what has happened thus far. The north and east provinces, post the cessation of hostilities, continue to feel deprived, notwithstanding the much publicised, election driven appeasement gestures[4] that the government has very recently made. The reasons are not far to seek. Mahinda is acutely aware about the extent he can stray from his Sinhala-Buddhist roots; a realization which is evident in his recent remarks on the extent to which he is willing to accept a federal structure and consequent devolution of powers with the Tamil minority. James Ross is the legal and policy director at Human Rights Watch. A *NYT* report in May 2009 reflects his sentiment that "President Rajapaksa needs to realize that winning the war, no matter how important, is not the same as achieving peace. Alienating Tamil society will merely push the country's problems down the road for the future. If that's the case... peace and justice will continue to elude the Sri Lankan people."[5]

Gen Sarath Fonseka

On the other hand, skeptical Fonseka watchers note that he too, could also be the proverbial wolf in sheep's clothing, so far as his strong, publicly declared Sinhala-Buddhist roots are concerned. A *Lankaweb* article by Sunil Kumar notes that it was not long ago (in fact, as recently as September 23, 2008), that he, as Sri Lanka's Army Commander, had given an interview to Stewart Bell of the National Post Newspaper of Canada.[6] During this interview he had made some disquieting observations – not expected of a General, whose army has members of all ethnic groups in the country. "I strongly believe", the General told the interviewer," that this country belongs to the Sinhalese but there are minority communities and we treat them like our people...We being the majority of the country, 75 percent, we will never give in and we have the right to protect this country...We are also a strong nation ... They (the minorities) can live in this country with us. But they must not try to, under the pretext of being a minority, demand undue things..."[7] He spoke of a Sinhala nation and not as a Sri Lankan who intended to take all along with him, the report notes with obvious discomfort.

Another issue on which Fonseka has been found ambivalent and unconvincing by his critics is on his suddenly developed affinity for the Tamil refugees (IDP's) as expressed in his resignation letter. Sunil Kumar[8] quotes from the publicly available document: "The plight of the IDPs (Internally Displaced Persons) is also a point of great concern to me. Thousands of valiant soldiers sacrificed their valuable lives to liberate these unfortunate civilians from the brutality and tyranny of the LTTE in order that they could live in an environment of freedom and democracy. Yet, today many of them are continuing to live in appalling conditions due to the lack of proper planning on the part of the government. The IDPs who have friends and relatives elsewhere in the country must be given the choice to live with them until proper demining has been done in their areas." The columnist writes that "Gen Fonseka and his concern for IDPs have been cited as a joke as it was common knowledge that when President Mahinda Rajapaksa wanted to start the resettlement process much earlier, this very General Fonseka had stalled the move. Does he need reminding today that he had carried the day by claiming that more than 10,000 LTTE cadres were lurking in the midst of the IDPs and by insisting on a thorough screening before resettling them?"[9] The fact becomes relevant when it is realized that the possibility of presence of LTTE cadres in the IDP ranks is now accepted as being a fraction of what was initially projected by Gen Fonseka.

Sudha Ramachandran, an independent journalist/researcher, stresses that neither Rajapaksa nor Fonseka evokes confidence among the island's Tamils.[10] This isn't surprising, she says, given that both were part of the violence unleashed on ordinary Tamils in the name of fighting the LTTE and both are known Sinhala-Buddhist hardliners.

A Full Blown National Crisis is at Hand

What is clearly therefore on the cards is the nucleus of a full blown national crisis, with conflicting and divisive vested interests at work; none of which seem to have the supreme national interest of Sri Lanka in mind. This a far cry indeed, from the euphoria and bonhomie that engulfed the entire nation when the Sri Lanka Government declared victory over the LTTE. A sampling of the international response to the victory (reproduced below)[11] makes for interesting reading, because, hidden in the diplomatic niceties of the congratulations, are clear *suggestions-cum-politely couched warnings* to the nation on what needs to be done post war, to gain and retain the peace. These have been placed in italics to draw the readers attention to the commonality of the international concern on what Sri Lanka needs to do to ensure a return to peace and prosperity

Suggestions-cum-Couched Warnings from International Organisations

United Nations – At a press conference in Geneva on 19 May 2009, United Nations Secretary General Ban Ki-Moon said "I am relieved by the conclusion of the military operation, but I am deeply troubled by the loss of so many civilian lives. *The task now facing the people of Sri Lanka is immense and requires all hands. It is most important that every effort be undertaken to begin a process of healing and national reconciliation.* I listened very carefully to what President Rajapaksa said in his address to Parliament today. *The legitimate concerns and aspirations of the Tamil people and other minorities must be fully addressed."*

European Union – The European Council met in Brussels on 18 May 2009, during which it adopted a statement calling on *"the Government of Sri Lanka urgently to proceed towards a comprehensive political process" and "the President of Sri Lanka to outline a clear process leading to a fully inclusive political solution, based on consent, equality and the rule of law". The Council stated that such moves are the only way toward long-term security, post-conflict reconstruction and prosperity in Sri Lanka.*

Response from Selected Countries[12]

India – The Indian Ministry of External Affairs issued a statement on 18 May 2009 saying "In a telephone conversation with External Affairs Minister Shri Pranab Mukherjee earlier today, the President of Sri Lanka confirmed that armed resistance by the LTTE has come to an end and that LTTE leader Velupillai Prabhakaran is dead. India will work with the people and Government of Sri Lanka to *provide relief to those affected by the tragic conflict, and to rapidly rehabilitate all those who have been displaced, bringing their lives to normalcy as soon as possible. It is our view that as the conventional conflict in Sri Lanka comes to an end, this is the moment when the root causes of conflict in Sri Lanka can be addressed. This would include political steps towards the effective devolution of power within the Sri Lankan*

Constitution so that Sri Lankans of all communities, including the Tamils, can feel at home and lead lives of dignity of their own free will."

Canada – Canada urges the Government of Sri Lanka to begin to *find a long-term political solution that responds to the legitimate aspirations of all the people of Sri Lanka. Canada is prepared to assist Sri Lankan efforts to find political reconciliation and a lasting peace."*

Japan – *"It is now important to help internally displaced people and their resettlement as well as to start showing improvement in the political process towards peace-building".* It also outlined that poverty was one of the factors that create fertile ground for terrorism and said he would like to see Sri Lanka build infrastructure, adding that Japan would support Sri Lanka's efforts as much as possible.

Maldives -"This momentous occasion in Sri Lanka's history will pave the way towards realizing *greater equality and justice for all Sri Lankans.*"

Norway – Norwegian Foreign Minister Jonas Gahr Store said in a statement "our thoughts go to all who have lost relatives and loved ones in the war. *We must cooperate to aid the victims. People in the refugee camps must quickly be allowed to return home."* Store also said the situation in the refugee camps for internally displaced people must be improved, in line with demands made by the United Nations.

Philippines – A Department of Foreign Affairs press release dated 22 May, 2009 "welcomes the return of law and order in northern Sri Lanka and *supports the Government of Sri Lanka's search for a comprehensive, fair, and lasting political solution to the problems faced by its Tamil minority. The Philippines hopes that a lasting political solution will be crafted in order that the Tamil minority share in the fruits of peace in their country."*

Russia – "Officials from Sri Lanka's Foreign Ministry said Russia has said that it supports the fight of the Sri Lankan government against terrorism and separatism. *Russia hoped that the end to the bloody armed conflict that lasted in Sri Lanka for more than a quarter century will be a guarantee of the establishment of an enduring peace, security and stability in the country.*

South Africa – "The South African government has noted the conciliatory tone in the speech of President Mahinda Rajapaksa on 19 May 2009 and *express our hope that the end of the military campaign will result in a peaceful dialogue with all minorities to address their long standing grievances. We will continue to support any efforts aimed at bringing about peace and reconciliation between the parties"*

Singapore – "The final cessation of military operations by the Sri Lankan Government provides a short window of opportunity to close a sad chapter of history and quickly begin a process of genuine national healing and reconciliation. *A long term agreement taking into full consideration the interests of all communities within Sri Lanka must be forged and implemented to ensure a lasting peace."*

Switzerland – "Switzerland calls on all parties to refrain from incitement to hatred and to work towards reconciliation by means of unilateral or jointly agreed measures. All parties and groupings as well as members of the diaspora should work openly and in conjunction with international institutions to initiate a reconciliation process and a sustainable solution in the framework of a political dialogue."

Turkey – The president of Sri Lanka, Mahinda Rajapaksa telephoned President of Turkey, Abdullah Gül. The conversation was released by Turkish Presidency Media Center. Sri Lankan president informed Gül about the recent achievements in the fight against terrorism. The president Gül stated that he was pleased with the recent events and Turkey was ready to provide humanitarian aid, in the telephone conversation.

United Kingdom – Lord Malloch Brown, the Minister of State Foreign and Commonwealth office: *"The political solution to this must come from inside Sri Lanka from a process set up and led by President Rajapaksa."* Speaking further, Brown said, "But we also made it extremely clear to him that, whether or not that victory would be seen as the *opening of a new and happier chapter in Sri Lanka depended on whether he could now go that next step and show the statesmanship to find a political as well as humanitarian solution to this community's issues.*"

United States – At a press conference in Washington, D.C. on 18 May 2009, United States Department of State spokesman Ian Kelly said: "The Department of State welcomes the fact that the fighting has ended, and we are relieved that the immense loss of life and killing of innocent civilians appears to be over. *This is an opportunity for Sri Lanka to turn the page on its past and build a Sri Lanka rooted in democracy, tolerance, and respect for human rights. Now is the time for the government to engage the Tamils, Sinhalese, and other Sri Lankans to create a political arrangement that promotes and protects the rights of all Sri Lankans. It is also vital for the government to provide for the needs of the 280,000 civilians now living in relief camps.* Providing food, water, shelter, basic health care, and sanitation, as well as expediting their return to their homes should be a top priority for the government."

Vietnam – On 21 May 2009, Foreign Affairs Ministry spokesman Le Dung released the following statement in response to journalist inquiries: *"Vietnam welcomes the recent victory of the Government and people of Sri Lanka. This victory will create favorable conditions for Sri Lanka to concentrate on the cause of national* *construction and development, contributing to peace, stability and development in the region."*

Sri Lanka has No Option but to Comply or Get Internationally Isolated

In a way, the enormity of the challenges that lie ahead in Sri Lanka becomes clear by reading how well, and with rare unity, the international community has sensed the current deficiencies in Sri Lankan governance – deficiencies that need to be bridged before Sri Lanka can take its rightful place in the hierarchy of nations. With the world increasingly becoming a global village, there is absolutely no way for any nation, especially one that subscribes to democratic norms of functioning, such as Sri Lanka, to make worthwhile progress and return to prosperous ways unless the above international concerns are suitably addressed. Sri Lanka did manage to cock a snook at Western concerns for a limited period of time towards the ending stages of the war, but the fear of continued economic sanctions, coupled with the unending recession have dampened the governments appetite for further confrontation with the international community. Though jingoistic noises will continue to be made for internal consumption, the government of the day may not choose to buck the unified demands for improvement in governance by the international community, (especially the Western nations and India) to clean up its act and remove identified deficiencies. The last thing that Sri Lanka needs post victory is international isolation.

The world community's message to both the candidates for the Presidential elections is thus understandingly unambiguous: the Sinhala-only line is not going to cut ice with the international community and will not bring back peace and prosperity to Sri Lanka – large hearted accommodation will. Both candidates will therefore have to "walk their talk" if they are to succeed politically. They must exhibit the talent, maturity and conviction of doing so. So far, neither candidate has shown the bandwidth to take all communities of the nation along with him; may be because of the fear of antagonizing the majority Sinhala-Buddhist vote bank that both are assiduously cultivating. This is a dangerous short term gain that portends disaster in the medium and long term.

Events Leading to Gen Fonseka's Resignation

Readers will be keen on learning how it came to pass that the troika suddenly folded up. In fact, the straws in the wind had surfaced quite some time ago, but were papered over by the antagonists as well as by their supporters. The media was undoubtedly aware of the friction but understandably did not play it up, undoubtedly in exercise of the national interest as long as the war lasted. The much criticized media suppression by the Rajapaksa Government also contributed to muted local criticism of wrong doing on part of the government. It may be noted that coverage of the SLAF in the war zone was near prohibited except at MoD terms; with the opportunity of doing so available to only a few journalists.

The first warning signs of trouble came on 25 May 2009,[13] when, very soon after the victory over the LTTE, Gen Fonseka made an announcement that the Sri Lankan military was planning to boost its manpower by more than 100,000 troops, purportedly to meet any future challenge, including the resurgence of the LTTE or any other armed formation. The troop build up would raise the Sri Lankan Army strength from 200,000 to 300,000. The General emphasised at an address that "new recruits and soldiers who joined the Army en masse contributed largely to this victory. Had they failed to do so, we would not have been able to see an end to this battle. Parents and their family members who directed those heroic soldiers to join the Army also deserve our praise. The Army's strength rose to 200,000 from 116,000 as some 80,000 novices joined the Army in the past few months. Their entry helped us enormously to hold on to the territory thus captured and minimize soldier casualties."[14] Anyone listening in could easily infer that the General was very assertive about the role of the SLA, and therefore his contribution in winning the war. This was of course not what the Government publicly stated at any time. It remains to be seen whether the projected increase of the SLA is now given much publicity by the Government in the run up to the elections.

The serious nature of the rift becomes clearer by another example of the General speaking out his mind in the public domain. In a report filed by *Lanka News Web* on July 18, 2009, three days after Gen Fonseka was shifted from his appointment as Army Commander SLA to the appointment of CDS, the paper has reported that "a senior Foreign Ministry official told *Lanka News Web* that irresponsible comments made by former Army Chief General, Sarath Fonseka, in the past few days (at Ambalangoda, in presence of a civilian audience gathered to felicitate him) put Foreign Minister Rohitha Bogollagama in a difficult spot during his visit to the Non-Aligned Movement (NAM) summit in Egypt. Gen Fonseka (had) recently stated that the military had to overlook the traditional rules of war and even kill LTTE rebels who came to surrender carrying white flags during the war against the LTTE". The paper goes on to say that "Many foreign ministers and

Gen Sarath Fonseka at Ambalangoda, July 10, 2009

diplomats who attended the NAM summit had inquired after the statements made by Gen Fonseka from Rohitha Bogollagama on the sidelines of the summit. They have further said that killing those who try to surrender in a war amounts to a war crime."[15] What is more revealing is the Generals blunt and unapologetic assertion of the harsh battle field realities of Eelam IV and his thinly concealed almost direct attack on the political hierarchy, who, he says were far removed from war zone realities. The exact statement made by the General is worth recounting:

> **"I managed the war like a true soldier. I did not make decisions from A/C rooms. I was under pressure to stop the war even during the final phase. I got messages not to shoot those who are carrying white flags. A war is fought by soldiers. They do so by putting their lives on the line. Therefore, the decisions about war should be taken by the soldiers in the battlefront. Not the people in A/C rooms in Colombo. Our soldiers have seen in life the kind of destruction carried out by those people before they decided to come carrying a white flag. Therefore, they carried out their duties. We destroyed any one connected with the LTTE. That is how we won the war,"[16]**

"A senior government minister told Lanka News Web", the paper goes on to say, "that the comments made by Fonseka, which were critical of the Defence Secretary and the President, at the Ambalangoda event and another book launch added to the reasons behind the decision to send him on early retirement (the paper, by *retirement*, obviously implies, "as the CDS". The use of the word "retirement" is incidentally quite revealing, whether attributable to the spokesman or the newspaper).[17]

Most observers (including the General himself) thus very correctly saw the newly created post of CDS to which Fonseka was moved on July 15, 2009, as a ceremonial sinecure although the government has continued to deny this. The speculation increased when the news emerged that the General had been offered the job of secretary to the sports ministry, but had rejected it. It was not seen as a prestigious offer. But government ministers and deputies have been making pointed remarks of a different kind – for instance, that in Sri Lankan history it was kings, not soldiers, that won wars; or that military rule in Pakistan (a close friend of Sri Lanka) had left that country "in a total mess."[18] The fact remains that the October 16, 2009 Daily Mirror, Colombo, report which hinted at trouble in paradise (and which has been referred to in Chapter 19 of this book; in particular, at Note 13 of its End Notes) actually turned out to be accurate and prescient. It is quite another matter that the military spokesman, Brigadier Udaya

Nanayakkara, had then said[19] (rebutting news of a rift appearing in the media), that "false news was being published using various print and electronic media alleging a rift between the government (Ministry of Defence) and General Fonseka. Brigadier Udaya Nanayakkara said that there was no truth in the reports and insisted that General Fonseka is still the most senior officer serving in the Army. He went on to say that media speculations alleging differences between the government and Gen Fonseka had been planted deliberately to create a rift between the government and the army which had won public confidence and popularity. He said the publication of such reports on the army is *illegal and counter productive* and mislead the general public."[20]

Sudha Ramachandran writes that "Rajapaksa's campaign to take sole credit for the victory has ruffled feathers in the armed forces, triggering an ever-widening rift at the nation's highest levels of power. Relations between Rajapaksa and Fonseka deteriorated visibly in the weeks after the LTTE's defeat. Fonseka was a big part of the offensive, leading crucial military offensives. He was Army Commander from December 2005 to July this year, leading the planning of the final phases of the "Eelam War IV", which culminated in the final defeat of the LTTE. The Rajapaksa government has tried to downplay his contribution. "It was President Rajapaksa and his brother, Defense Secretary Gottabhaya Rajapaksa, who steered the forces to victory against the LTTE,"[21] Labor Minister Mervyn Silva said at a public rally recently, calling on General Sarath Fonseka and others not to take "personal credit" for the victory".

The facts may be that the move of Gen Fonseka as CDS was a ploy to limit the vast powers that he had exercised as a war commander, and for which he is identified as a genuine "war hero" by rapturous troops and media. A worried government had interposed itself to do damage control to its plans to make political capital of the victory, by ensuring, after the first few interviews that the service chiefs gave to media, that henceforth the Defence Secretary's clearance would have to be taken "before service chiefs could be interviewed."[22] The refusal of the General to join President Rajapaksa at political rallies on the plea that he was busy coordinating the 60th anniversary functions of the SLA, can, in retrospect, be seen not so much as the Generals effort to distance himself from politics, but an early indication that he was not going to allow the Rajapaksa's to hog the credit for winning the war, but, on the contrary, indicate his dissent with the ruling governments near total denial in accepting that the General had contributed substantially to the victory.

The General's private visit to the USA in October 2009, to spend some time with his daughters in Oklahoma, was really the straw that broke the camel's back, so far as the troika was concerned, and became a source of tremendous friction and embarrassment for the Government of Sri Lanka. It was officially reported by him, while there, that the US Department of Homeland Security was going to question him over alleged human-rights violations in the latter stages of the war. There was real fear in the Rajapaksa camp that he would give evidence against the Defence Secretary, Gottabhaya Rajapaksa, who is a US citizen. This possibility apparently resulted in the government recalling him forthwith to Sri Lanka; a direction he complied with, without demur.[23] The exhaustive *Frontline* report covering the issue gives a detailed backgrounder. It says that in a surprising "obsessive pursuit of Sri Lanka-related issues by Washington,"[24] the US, on October 21, 2009, tabled a State Department report titled "Report to Congress on Incidents During the Recent Conflict in Sri Lanka". On October 28, 2009, the US authorities, on the basis of this document, called Gen Fonseka for questioning on November 4, 2009. He was informed during this meeting with the US authorities would like to question him on November 8, 2009. He was forewarned that his statement could be used as possible evidence against the Defence Secretary, Gottabhaya Rajapaksa over charges of excesses by the security forces and LTTE during the 34-month war.

The *Frontline* article goes on to say that the General immediately informed the Sri Lanka High Commissioner in USA who reached the Defence Secretary and "all hell broke loose in Colombo."[25] ... On November 1, 2009, Rohitha Bogollagama, the Foreign Minister summoned the US Ambassador to Sri Lanka and the Maldives and conveyed that Washington should "desist from any endeavour to interview" General Fonseka.[26] The report goes on to say that the government suspected subterfuge in the episode as Gen Fonseka was being touted by the opposition parties as a possible consensus candidate. Matters were not helped by remarks made by Fonseka in USA to Sri Lankan expatriates that he would step out of uniform to bring the country back on track "if it continues to go the wrong way even after defeating terrorism."[27] As it transpired, Gen Fonseka was back in Sri Lanka on November 8, 2009; the day his statement was to have been recorded in the USA. However, what followed dramatically was that, on November 12, 2009, "within hours after former Prime Minister and Opposition leader Ranil Wickremesinghe, who heads the 12-party opposition alliance, returned to the island nation after consultations with New Delhi on the current developments in Sri Lanka,"[28] General Sarath Fonseka sent his letter of resignation to Lalit Weeratunga, the Secretary to the President.

The Resignation Letter of Gen Sarath Fonseka along with its Appendix

[**Note:** The document is available at a number of sites on the internet and is reproduced in full for information of the reader. The text reproduced below is from the *Lankatruth* site. A careful reading is recommended as the document clearly reveals the Generals angst at being sidelined and denied his due, as also raising issues of security, refusal to increase the size of the Army, and, in essence, bluntly giving the reasons why the troika fell apart. The references to India are sensational but have not been commented upon by the MEA in India either by way of confirmation or denial. Some syntax errors that have surfaced in the letter and its annexure have been removed on the presumption that these errors may not be there in the original document and are attributable to transmission inadequacies.]

CONFIDENTIAL

His Excellency the President
Through the Secretary, Ministry of Defence,
Public Security, Law and Order
Presidential Secretariat
COLOMBO

12 November 2009

Your Excellency
REQUEST TO RETIRE FROM THE REGULAR FORCE OF THE SRI LANKA ARMY

1. I, General G S C Fonseka RWP RSP VSV USP rcds psc presently serving as the Chief of Defence Staff, was enlisted to the Ceylon Army on 05th Feb 1970 and was commissioned on the 01st June 1971. On the 6th Dec 2005 due to the trust and confidence placed on me, Your Excellency was kind enough to promote me to the rank of Lieutenant General and appoint me as the Commander of the Sri Lanka Army in an era when the Country was embroiled with the menace of a bloody terrorism and was in a stalemate state after having toiled for a solution politically or otherwise for over 25 years without a success.
2. During my command of 3 years and 7 months, the Sri Lanka Army managed to eradicate the terrorist movement having apprehended an unbelievable stock

of arms and munitions and decisively defeating the LTTE and its murderous leadership which Your Excellency is obviously aware of. I would not be exaggerating to state that I was instrumental in leading the Army to this historic victory, of course with Your Excellency's political support, which helped to materialize this heroic action. Though the field commanders, men and all members of the Army worked towards this common goal, it is with my vision, command and leadership that this yeomen task was achieved.

3. I do appreciate the fact that the Country and Your Excellency did recognize my services which led to me being promoted to the first ever serving four star general to command the Army, nevertheless the courses of action which initiated subsequently greatly depressed me which I have enumerated in the Annex hereto.
4. Considering the facts mentioned in the Annex and more, which I am privy to withhold, I am compelled to believe that Your Excellency and the Government has lost your trust and faith bestowed upon me for reasons best known to Your Excellency. Hence as the senior most serving military officer in the Country with 40 years of service, such a situation does not warrant a continuation of my duties any longer, thereby I have the honour to request that I be permitted to terminate my services and retire from the Regular Force of the Army with effect from 01st December 2009.
5. Furthermore I have the honour to request that on retirement Your Excellency would be kind enough to grant me sufficient security which includes trained combat soldiers, a suitable vehicle with sufficient protection (Bullet proof) and escort vehicles for my conveyances due to the fact that I am considered as one of the highest priority targets by the LTTE, which they are yet capable of achieving. Also, I wish to bring to Your Excellency's kind notice that over 100 men, six escort vehicles and a bullet proof vehicle have been placed at the convenience of the former Commander of the Navy, Admiral WKJ Karannagoda. I presume that such arrangements would be made available to me, considering the threat factor I am facing, which Your Excellency is well aware of.
6. I would also wish to quote an example in the case of the former Indian Chief of Army Staff General A S Vaidya, instrumental in leading the Indian Army in Operation Blue Star against the Sikhs at the Golden Temple, Amritsar in 1984, was assassinated whilst on retirement in 1986 purely in revenge of his victories achieved. I do not wish to experience a similar incident as I have already sustained serious injuries after the attempt on my life by a suicide

cadre of the LTTE. Thereby, I am compelled to entrust you with my security which is requested for life.

7. Furthermore, I would like to emphasis on a statement made by me during my tenure as the Commander of the Army. In that, I mentioned my dislike to be in command forever and also I would ensure that my successor would not be burdened with the task of war fighting, which I abided with. Hence, as I have already overstayed my retirement date by 4 years, I wish to proceed on retirement without further delay.
8. Forwarded for Your Excellency's kind consideration please.

I have the honour to be
Your Excellency's
Obedient Servant

G S C FONSEKA RWP RSP VSV USP rcds psc
General
Chief of Defence Staff

The annexure sent along with the resignation letter is also reproduced on the opposite page from the same source:

Annex A

12 November 2009

FACTORS AFFECTING MY RETIREMENT FROM THE REGULAR FORCE OF THE ARMY

1. Various agencies misleading Your Excellency by stating a possible coup immediately after the victory over the LTTE which obviously led to a change of command in spite of my request to be in command until the Army celebrated its 60th Anniversary. This fear psychosis of a coup is well known among the defence circles.
2. Appointing an officer pending a disciplinary inquiry who performed duties only as a holding formation commander in the final battle as my successor, disregarding my recommendations to appoint Major General G A Chandrasiri as the Commander of the Army who was the then Chief of Staff and an officer with an exemplary service as the Security Forces Commander in Jaffna for over 3 years. This has already led to a deterioration of the high standards I was capable of introducing to the Army, to my bitter disappointment.
3. Appointing me as the Chief of Defence Staff, though a senior appointment to that of a service commander, with basically no authority, except for mere coordinating responsibilities in a manner which misled the general public of the country and most members of the Armed Forces. In that the Secretary Defence pushing me to vacate the post of the Commander in just two weeks after the victory and Your Excellency insisting on me to hand over duties in less than two months depriving me of my moral obligations in revamping the welfare and providing a sound administration to the men who fought a gallant battle.
4. Further, prior to my appointment I was misled on the authority vested with the CDS. I was made to understand that the appointment carried more command responsibilities and authority than earlier, but subsequent to my appointment a letter by the Strategic Affairs Adviser to the Secretary Defence indicated that my appointment was purely to coordinate the services and not that of overall command. The letter is attached herewith for Your Excellency's information. [**Not attached. Ed.**] Such actions clearly define Your Excellency's and the Governments unwillingness to grant me with command responsibilities which leads me to believe that there is a strong mistrust in me, which is most depressing after all what was performed to achieve war victory.

5. During a subsequent Service Commanders Meeting, the Secretary Defence was bold enough to state an unethical and uncalled statement by mentioning that "if operational control of all three services is granted to the CDS it would be very dangerous", which indeed was a loss of face to me in the presence of subordinate services commanders.
6. Your Excellency, you too made a statement at the very first security council soon after the 18th of May 09 when the battle was declared over, "that no further recruitment would be necessary" and "a strong public opinion is in the making stating that the Country is in possession of a too powerful army." It was surprising to hear such a comment from Your Excellency in spite of your repeated praise and boast of the war victory. I personally felt that Your Excellency has commenced mistrusting your own loyal Army which attained the unimaginable victory just a week ago. You again repeated the same statement even after I handed over the command. Over these comments I felt disgusted as we even insulted those who made the supreme sacrifice by such comments.
7. The present Army Commander immediately on assuming duties commenced transferring senior officers who immensely contributed to the war effort during my command tenure including those junior officers working with my wife at the Seva Vanitha Army Branch which was clearly to challenge the loyalty of officers and most discouraging to the officer corps of the Army, with a wrong signal being transmitted on my authority.
8. With a pain of mind it was noted that the same Army which gained victory for the Nation was suspected of staging a coup and thereby alerting the Government of India once again on the 15th of October 2009, unnecessarily placing the Indian Troops on high alert. This action did tarnish the image and reputation gained by the Sri Lanka Army as a competent and professional organization who was capable of defeating a terrorist group after the Malayan Emergency, in the eyes of the World. This suspicion would have been due to the loyalty of the Sri Lanka Army towards me as its past Commander who led the Army to the historic victory.
9. During my absence from the Country (23 Oct 2009 to 5 Nov 2009) being on overseas leave, the Army Headquarters was bold enough to change the security personnel deployed at the AHQ Main Entrance and the Ministry of Defence emphasizing the withdrawal of the Sinha Regiment troops who were attached to me, as you are aware is my parent regiment and supplementing them with other regimental personnel. The Sinha Regiment troops were good enough to provide security to the Ministry of Defence for 4 years and it is

surprising to note how the combat efficiency of the said troops supposed to have dropped overnight as per Secretary Defence's opinion. Further the Sinha Regiment troops numbering a mere 4, non combatants, deployed for vehicle checking duties at the AHQ Main Entrance, were replaced by 14 armed Armoured Corps personnel, whilst a further two platoons were brought in to prevent the 4 non combat Sinha Regiment personnel performing duties, creating a mockery to the general public including to some foreign missions. This clearly indicates a questionable loyalty of troops good enough for duties for over four years purely due to the fact that the troops were from my Regiment. This also indirectly reflects mistrust on me or an indication that the persons concern wish to keep a tab on my movements and visitors to my HQ/residence which is a clear display of suspicion created on me.

10. Further on instructions of the Secretary Defence, troops from the Gajaba Regiment was brought in to the MOD complex which indicated a divide loyalty within the Army and reasons to believe that the Army now being politicized. This is being encouraged by the Army Commander too who thinks that the Armoured Corp troops should over power Sinha Regiment troops.
11. Instigating malicious and detrimental news items and rumors by interested parties including several senior government politicians which led to identify me as a traitor in spite of my personal contribution of the government to change the history of our country.
12. During my absence from the Country, an acting CDS or an officer to overlook duties was not appointed which indicates that the much spoken appointment of the CDS is unimportant to the Government and the National Security Council. If the appointment was of significant importance as stated by most, it should have been imperative to appoint somebody to oversee the duties and thereby I am convinced that I have being granted with an unimportant appointment in spite of all the work done.
13. It is with sadness that I note that the ordinary Army which I toiled to transform into a highly professional outfit is now losing its way. Increased desertions, lack of enthusiasm to enlist (a drop in enlistment rate by 50% is recorded), disciplinary problems on advocating divided commands indicates an unprofessional organization is in the offing. During the last two months the members who have deserted are higher than the recruitment intake.
14. The plight of the IDPs is also a point of great concern to me. Thousands of valiant soldiers sacrificed their valuable lives to liberate these unfortunate civilians from the brutality and tyranny of the LTTE in order that they could live in an environment of freedom and democracy. Yet, today many of them

are continuing to live in appalling conditions due to the lack of proper planning on the part of the government and the IDPs who have friends and relatives elsewhere in the country must be given the choice to live with them until proper demining has been done in their areas.

15. Your Excellency's government has yet to win the peace in spite of the fact that the Army under my leadership won the war. There is no clear policy to win the hearts and minds of the Tamil people, which will surely ruin the victory, attained paving the way for yet another uprising in the future.
16. The peace dividend the whole country expected at the conclusion of the war has yet to materialize. The economic hardships faced by the people have increased while waste and corruption have reached endemic proportions; media freedom and other democratic rights continue to be curtailed. The many sacrifices the army made to end the war would not have been in vain, if we can usher in a new era of peace and prosperity to our motherland.

CONFIDENTIAL

Media Analysis of the Resignation Letter and Gen Fonseka's Candidature

Rajan Philips, a prolific Sri Lankan journalist, has carried out a thorough analysis of the letter, in particular its annexure. His key comments have been excerpted in the succeeding paragraphs; the original language being retained.

He says that the letter by the General, written with military license, is perfectly professional in tone and duly submissive to his civilian authority. The sting is in the tail annexed to the letter. Thirteen – someone is going to be unlucky here – of the sixteen points of contention, or reasons for resignation, are concerned with military organization and the rapid changes thereto so soon after victory. At this point, it is only one side of the story, but a man will not end his career and plan a future in so public a manner if what he is giving as reasons is less than true. But the thirteen reasons are not all factually verifiable, as some of them are perceptions and therefore contestable.

The fatal perception appears to have been about Sarath Fonseka becoming too big for his boots and posing a threat to the present political establishment. The perception of this threat led to paranoia of a military coup, not once but twice. First, the non-existent – according to Sarath Fonseka – the coup threat was dealt with by the changing of guards in key areas of the military and state establishments. The second time, as was also independently known, the non-existent coup threat had morphed into an irrational coup fear, and India was asked to be at the ready for any eventuality. Whether there was any truth to these coup threats, we will not know unless those whom General Fonseka is accusing begin to tell their side of the story,

The 12th of the 16 annex points in General Fonseka's resignation letter is an interesting one. He was hurt by the failure of the government to appoint an acting Chief of Defense Staff during his recent and much publicized sojourn in the US. His point is that the CDS position is a no-status position and he had been ungratefully shoved into it so soon after he had run aground the LTTE. The good General should have known better. There is no provision in our constitution or convention for an acting President or a Vice President. What is good for the presidency should be good enough for a military office. The last three points in the annex veer from the military into the political. There is the concern for the displaced people, anxiety over the failure to reach a political solution after the military victory, and criticism for the failure to capitalize on the peace dividend due to corruption and maladministration.

Sunil Kumar brings out the fact that Gen Fonseka, wrote in his letter of resignation that "Your Excellency's government has yet to win the peace in spite of the fact that the Army under my leadership won the war.[29] Nilantha Nangamuwa writes that, in Colombo, two key level officers who advocated the elimination of the Tamil Tiger rebels have been punished as a result of President Rajapaksa's ungrateful attitude. Gen Fonseka is one of them. The letter of Gen Fonseka is thus a lamentation of an officer who did his best for the regime and its leadership that entrusted him with the gigantic task to eliminate the LTTE.[30] *DNA* in its report[31] notes that, in his resignation letter, Fonseka said the Sri Lankan government had asked neighbouring India on October 15, 2009, to place its troops on alert to be deployed on the island, in the event of a coup. "This action did tarnish the image and reputation gained by the Sri Lankan army as a competent and professional organisation which was capable of defeating a terrorist group," the ex-Chief of Defence Staff said. The *DNA* in a separate coverage quotes the Sri Lanka Agriculture Development Minister, who suspects a foreign hand behind Fonseka's resignation and desire to contest elections. The report quotes him saying that "Former top Gen Sarath Fonseka, who led the army to victory over the Liberation Tigers of Tamil Eelam (LTTE), has now become a pawn in the hands of some western nations "conspiring" to bring "regime change" in Sri Lanka. The minister, Maithripala Sirisena, also alleged that "certain Western nations were trying to bring about a regime change here since the government has never given into their pressure in its fight against terrorism." The report also adds that the *Daily Mirror* newspaper quoted Sirisena as saying. "There must be an invisible foreign force behind the UNP-JVP combine to defeat this government."[32]

Gen Fonseka's own statement on his candidature is revealing. Chandani Kirinde writing from Colombo brings out in a report carried by *The Tribune*,[33] that, on announcing that he is contesting elections, Gen Fonseka has said that "we did not defeat the world's most dastardly terrorist to hand the country over to a dictator". He added that people can trust him because he made two promises when he took over as Chief – finishing off the LTTE and eliminating Prabhakaran – and delivered on both. He also brought out issues of growing corruption and the nepotism associated with the Rajapaksa family. Another separate report filed by PTI in the same newspaper says that, in his maiden press conference on November 29, 2009 at Colombo, the General said that "They (India) are the closest neighbour and powerful neighbour in the region. So we have to obviously have 100 percent best relationship with India".[34] He also added that "if someone says okay I worked in China or Pakistan, that was only for the purpose of getting approved..., the military equipment to fight the war (against the LTTE)".[35]

One issue that will undoubtedly worry the General if he chooses to be the consensus candidate of the 12- party opposition alliance headed by Ranil Wickremesinghe is that the party has sent him a set of 10 questions and will take a final call on putting him up, after studying his response to them. The details can be accessed at http://www.groundviews.org[36] as per the *Frontline* article quoted at Note 24 of this chapter. Another report says that Ranil Wickremesinghe has included questions that include giving government portfolios to the Tamil National Alliance, a pro-Tamil Tiger parliamentary group.[37] To many, such a possibility seems scarcely credible. This, in a way, raises questions on opposition support to the General, if their preconditions are not met.

The article goes on to say that those opposed to Fonseka's entry into politics say it will politicize the military and undermine Sri Lanka's democracy. Fonseka as president will spell the end of democracy, his critics say. Dire warnings are being made of what lies ahead for Sri Lanka should a former general become president. Education minister Susil Premajayantha has pointed to the "total mess" in Pakistan after General Zia-ul Haq came to power in a 1977 coup. The general died in 1988, but "the trend of destabilization continues even today,"[38] Premajayantha said

Concluding Comments from the Indian Perspective

The involvement of a serving military officer of the country's senior most rank in politics is something no democracy world wide has historically looked at kindly.

Such a development is therefore correctly within the domain of serious criticism and censure. To that extent, it is clear that Gen Sarath Fonseka has exceeded his brief as CDS in bringing out in the public domain, issues that are non-military and political in nature. The plea that he is legislating in the supreme national interest does not hold water, as the net loser is not the individual but the institution of democracy; a strictly avoidable development so far as this author is concerned.

It is clear, though, that the shabby treatment meted out to the General, post termination of hostilities and his almost immediate marginalisation was a deliberate effort on the part of the Rajapaksa Government to undermine his position in popular perception as a national "hero" who won the ground war for Sri Lanka by dint of his superior abilities, staying power, charisma and sheer professional skills and determination.

The reality is of course too well known to the reader to bear detailed recounting. When the troika worked and were on song, there was pure magic in the air. While Mahinda provided brilliant, absolutely brilliant political leadership, and looked after the diplomatic angle through his most capable foreign minister, Rohitha Bogollogama, his brother, Gottabhaya, got the military synergy both internally (between the uniformed forces) as well as in terms of military supplies sorted out in an equally brilliant manner. An ex soldier himself who had once served with distinction under General Fonseka, he had the wisdom and maturity as well as trust to allow General Fonseka a free hand in reviving a demoralised Army and getting it to deliver in an astounding manner which the military world worldwide, applauds without reservation. Gen Fonseka was truly in his elements and did a stunning job which has been truly lauded nationally as well as internationally. Gottabhaya also put military intelligence, media handling and the government propaganda machinery on track, and in his usual visionary manner. The fact that he got the Navy and Air Force to fully support the land battle is a unique credit that belongs to Gottabhaya's leadership skills, which must rank amongst the finest on display in recent times.

It is thus clear, that, in fact, neither the Rajapaksa's nor General Fonseka won the war in their individual capacities. They did so as a team of truly rare calibre, who built up on each other's strengths, laughed off weaknesses and failures, subordinated ego's and achieved two months before schedule, all that they had set out to do. This chapter's inclusion and its titling as *Trouble in Paradise* is starkly indicative of the fact that the magic moment for the Isle of Serendip is past. In the race for power, national interest has been shelved, at least temporarily, and the knives are truly out. The bonhomie that won them the war is now working in overdrive to *lose the peace*, which is a far greater dividend that winning a war could ever be.

Indian diplomacy has indeed been wayward and unfocused in its relationship with Sri Lanka since the IPKF returned in early 1990. By comparison, Sri Lanka has handled its diplomacy far better. Certainly since the Rajapaksa Government assumed office in November 2009 till date, their diplomacy has been astute, wily, forward looking and sophisticated. Our lassitude and lack of strategic culture, sense and sensibility in the diplomatic sphere has given huge operating space to Pakistan, and, of far greater security concern, to China, and that too, within 31 kilometres of our Southern shores. This was strictly avoidable by looking at Sri Lankan needs in a pragmatic manner rather than endlessly through the prism of Tamil concerns. As it has transpired, even the legitimate Tamil concerns India has, keeping in mind its huge 60 million strong population, have also not been met, starting with the poor treatment meted out to the Tamil IDP's and extending to implementation of the 13th Amendment that allows for devolution within the sovereign laws of Sri Lanka.

India is now faced with wanting mature stable and visionary relations with Sri Lanka regardless of who wins the presidential elections and needs to put its diplomatic act together soonest as also speed up all the development work that it has undertaken in the island nation.

In conclusion, Mahinda Rajapaksa, as per *The Economist*[39] has reason to be tense if his strategy of preponing the Presidential elections by two years before they were due backfires. It will, if his challenger, who like him, is very popular with the President's main support base, the country's Sinhala-Buddhist majority, wins the January 2010 elections. Straw polls indicate that though the elections could be a close run event, Mahinda Rajapaksa has his nose ahead. Whoever is the final winner, may do well to draw a parallel with the last big Sinhala winner, King Dutugemunu, and remember to forgive the loser. This will put this great nation back on the path of peace and prosperity.

Endnotes

1. Buncombe, Andrew. Asia Correspondent. "General Who Beat Tamil Tigers Quits to Challenge The President". *13 November 2009.* http://www.independent.co.uk/news/world/asia/general-who-beat-tamil-tigers-quits-to-challenge-the-president-1819929.html The report suggests that, in the perception of observers, General Fonseka is as much a Sinhala Buddhist nationalist as the Rajapaksa's are.
2. Full address by President Mahinda Rajapaksa at the UN. http://www.un.org/ga/63/generaldebate/pdf/srilanka_en.pdf
3. "Mahinda Rajapaksa". http://en.wikipedia.org/wiki/Mahinda_Rajapaksa

4. Haviland, Charles. "Sri Lanka War Displaced 'Free to Leave' Military Camps". BBC News, Colombo, Sri Lanka. November 30, 2009. The news report suggests that, more than 100,000 displaced people in military-run camps in Northern Sri Lanka will be allowed "free movement" from December 1, 2009. The government, which faces elections in January 2010, has in the past month stepped up the formal process of returning people to the villages; the numbers living in the camps have halved. The authorities have been screening them all for possible links to the Tamil Tigers.
5. Ross, James. "Tiger by the Tail". May 20, 2009. http://www.nytimes.com/2009/05/21/opinion/21iht-edross.html?_r=1
6. Kumar, Sunil. "Why Retd. Lieut.Gen.Sarath Fonseka Should Ride Out Graciously into the Sunset!" November 21, 2009. http://www.lankaweb.com/news/items/2009/11/21/why-retd-lieut-gen-sarath-fonseka-should-ride-out-graciously-into-the-sunset/
7. Ibid.
8. Ibid.
9. Ibid.
10. Ramachandran, Sudha. "Sri Lanka Split over War Honors". November 13, 2009. http://www.atimes.com/atimes/South_Asia/KK13Df04.html Sudha Ramachandran is an independent journalist/researcher based in Bangalore.
11. "Sri Lankan Civil War". http://en.wikipedia.org/wiki/Sri_Lankan_Civil_War#cite_note-275 The text has been edited and the sequence in which the countries appear, changed in the case of India. All countries given in the web article have not been listed.
12. Ibid.
13. Singh, Ajit Kumar. "Advances and Ambiguities". Research Associate, Institute for Conflict Management. South Asia Terrorism Portal. http://www.kanglaonline.com/index.php?template=kshow&kid=1673&Idoc_Session=a6bc89ca267e4e86bb299f3a68b9b0af
14. "Wanni War Heroes Given Military Honours & their Service Appreciated". http://www.army.lk/detailed.php?NewsId=579
15. Fonseka's statement puts Foreign Minister in difficulty". July 18, 2009. http://www.lankanewsweb.com/news/EN_2009_07_18_005.html
16. Ibid.
17. Ibid.
18. Haviland, Charles. BBC News, Colombo "Trouble at the top in Sri Lanka?" http://news.bbc.co.uk/2/hi/south_asia/8352676.stm
19. "No rift between Fonseka and the Government- Army Spokesman". http://www.spot.lk/article5790-no-rift-between-fonseka-government-army-spokesman.html
20. Ibid.
21. Ramachandran, Sudha. "Sri Lanka Split over War Honors". November 13, 2009. 2009.2009http://www.atimes.com/atimes/South_Asia/KK13Df04.html Sudha Ramachandran is an independent journalist/researcher based in Bangalore
22. http://www.dailymirror.lk/DM_BLOG/Sections/frmNewsDetailView.aspx?ARTID=64919
23. Ramachandran, Sudha. "Sri Lanka Split over War Honors". November 13, 2009. http://www.atimes.com/atimes/South_Asia/KK13Df04.html Sudha Ramachandran is an independent journalist/researcher based in Bangalore
24. Reddy, Muralidhar, B. "General Alert – Eelam War IV Takes a Further Toll as a US Report Upsets Colombo and a Proposed Political Line up Pits the 'War Hero' against the President". Frontline. Volume 26, Number 24. November 21-December 4, 2009.

25. Ibid.
26. Ibid.
27. Quoted from the article.
28. Quoted from the article. This is worth perusing in its full form by interested readers.
29. Kumar, Sunil. "Why Retd. Lieut.Gen.Sarath Fonseka Should Ride Out Graciously Into The Sunset!" November 21, 2009. http://www.lankaweb.com/news/items/2009/11/21/why-retd-lieut-gen-sarath-fonseka-should-ride-out-graciously-into-the-sunset/
30. Ilangamuwa, Nilantha. "SRI LANKA – Will General Sarath Fonseka become a National Leader?" Guest Column. November 25, 2009.
31. "I was replaced as army chief on fears of coup: Fonseka", PTI. November 13, 2009. http://www.dnaindia.com/world/report_i-was-replaced-as-army-chief-on-fears-of-coup-fonseka_1311069
32. "West Using Sarath Fonseka to Bring Regime Change in Lanka: Minister". PTI. December 4, 2009. http://www.dnaindia.com/world/report_west-using-sarath-fonseka-to-bring-regime-change-in-lanka-minister_1320055
33. Kirinde, Chandani. "Fonseka Jumps into Fray, Formally". The Tribune. Chandigarh. November 30, 2009. World Section. pp 13.
34. "If Elected, will Forge Best Ties with India". The Tribune. Chandigarh. PTI Report. Colombo. November 29, 2009. World Section. pp 13. No change has been made to the General's syntax.
35. Ibid. No change has been made to the General's syntax.
36. Reddy, Muralidhar, B. "General Alert – Eelam War IV Takes a Further Toll as a US Report Upsets Colombo and a Proposed Political Line up Pits the 'War Hero' against the President". Frontline. Volume 26, Number 24. November 21-December 4, 2009.
37. Haviland, Charles. BBC News, Colombo "Trouble at the top in Sri Lanka?" http://news.bbc.co.uk/2/hi/south_asia/8352676.stm
38. Ibid.
39. Reddy, Muralidhar, B. "General Alert – Eelam War IV Takes a Further Toll as a US Report Upsets Colombo and a Proposed Political Line up Pits the 'War Hero' against the President". Frontline. Volume 26, Number 24. November 21-December 4, 2009.

Chapter 23
Update on the Rajapaksa - Fonseka Imbroglio

As mentioned in the Preface to the Second Edition, beginning August 2009, there was intense media speculation about Gen. Sarath Fonseka entering politics. One of the media articles[1] put it across it as follows: "Gen. Fonseka launches political campaign – I will make a supreme sacrifice to defend my land against the politicos who ever they may be joining hands with India. Now we have a daunting task to protect our Motherland from India". In fact, it is now a well established fact that there was rising media speculation about Gen. Sarath Fonseka entering politics even during the ending stages of the war against the LTTE.

After several false starts, Gen. Fonseka was installed as the common candidate of a rag tag coalition of political parties, mainly United National Party (UNP) and Janatha Vimukthi Peramuna (JVP), termed as the New Democratic Front. Immediately after declaration that Fonseka was applying for candidacy, President Rajapaksa, sensing that a serious challenge lay ahead, chose to call for new Presidential elections two years before expiry of his term. He did so in the belief that the common man across race and ideology was beholden to him for leading the country successfully in its war against the LTTE scourge and would vote him back into office by a resounding majority.

The Gen. Fonseka, UNP and JVP combine led a fierce battle against President Rajapaksa. They claimed that Gen. Fonseka was the real hero who won the war against LTTE and, if elected, the new Government would eliminate the prevailing corruption under the Mahinda Rajapaksa Government. They also promised to change the Sri Lankan Constitution to remove executive powers from the Presidency and transfer such powers to the Parliament.

Gen. Fonseka, however, suffered a number of setbacks in his election campaign. In December 2009, a news item was published in the *"Sunday Leader"* quoting Sarath Fonseka saying that, during the final few days of the war against LTTE, Defence Secretary Gottabhaya Rajapaksa, had given orders to execute LTTE cadres who surrendered to the Army. Due to the massive publicity given in the Government media, this statement was taken by the whole country as a betrayal of Army officers by their retired Army Commander (Chief) himself. Although Gen. Fonseka later issued a statement saying that his original statement had been published by the *Sunday Leader* out of context, many analysts felt that Fonseka had committed a serious blunder that actually lost him the election. Sections of the media recalled how he had earlier justified the killings at a rally at his village, Ambalangoda, as a military inevitability, and wondered about his credibility, maturity and motives for making such an incendiary statement, quite clearly for political gain.

Meanwhile, the ruling Government raised the issue of personal corruption for financial gains against Gen. Fonseka, when he was the Commander of the Sri Lankan Army. There was evidence that he removed the Tender Board Chairman from his office and he himself became the Chairman, only to offer all the tenders for arms purchases to a company owned by his son-in-law. Gen. Fonseka subsequently claimed that the company referred to in the accusation had no connection with his son-in-law, Danuna Tilekeratne's company, *HiCorp International*.[2] There were few takers for this statement.

The Sri Lankan Government then disclosed the details of a secret agreement between TNA and Gen. Fonseka, in which he had promised merger of the North and East provinces and grant of an autonomous status for Tamils in return for the support of the North and East Tamil population in the Presidential elections. The Sinhalese reacted with anger to this agreement since the Army had fought the nearly 30 year old bloody war against LTTE only to reject the demand for a similar autonomous state, "Eelam," claimed by the LTTE. The document was later proved to be planted as reported in the popular media, but, by then, the damage had been done.[3] His credentials thus came under serious doubt.

Closer to the election, rumours began circulating about Gen. Sarath Fonseka that he intended to arrest President Mahinda Rajapaksa and execute Gottabhaya Rajapaksa and Basil Rajapaksa. Rumours (and later inputs from the Defence Secretary, Gottabhaya Rajapaksa)[4] suggested that he had booked 70 rooms each in the *Taj Samundra* and *Cinnamon* hotels close to the President's residence, for 400 supporters who were deserters from the Army, and who might have engaged in post election violence. It was later learnt that the whole allegation was unsubstantiated. The Government actually arrested only nine persons (who were not deserters but who had honourably retired from the Army) from the hotel premises, for allegedly illegally helping the General in his political machinations.

Election results were released on the morning of Jan 27, 2010. Sarath Fonseka stood defeated by a record number of 1,800,000 votes.[5] The distaff side of the coin, however, was that the General had been sufficiently credible to voters across the sectarian divide to garner *over 4 million votes.* In that context, he had succeeded in identifying himself as a politician of some substance. This is a cause of concern for the ruling Government.

Sri Lankan Presidential Election, 2010

January 26, 2010

Nominee	Mahinda Rajapaksa	Sarath Fonseka
Party	United People's Freedom Alliance	New Democratic Front
Home state	Southern Province	Southern Province
States carried	16	6
Popular vote	6,015,934	4,173,185
Percentage	57.88%	40.15%

Previous President: Mahinda Rajapaksa (United People's Freedom Alliance)

President-Elect: Mahinda Rajapaksa (United People's Freedom Alliance)

Wikipedia notes that Sri Lankan elections have a history of violence, misuse of state resources and other violations of election laws. The Sri Lankan police received nearly 975 election-related complaints, and 375 arrests were made during the run up to the January 2010 Presidential elections. The *Centre for Monitoring Election Violence* (CMEV) had recorded 809 incidents from 23 November 2009, when the elections were officially announced, to 25 January 2010. *People's Action for Free and Fair Elections* (PAFFREL) recorded 666 incidents between 17 December 2009 and 25 January 2010. The final turnout was 74.5%. Mahinda

Rajapaksa was declared elected to a second term of office with 6,015,934 votes, or 57.88% of the vote. Gen. Sarath Fonseka finished second with 4,173,185 votes, or 40.15%[6] of the votes.

Fonseka announced that he did not accept the results, and that legal action would be taken by him, challenging the election results. There were subsequent reports that said that he was seeking asylum in Australia, UK or India. Meanwhile, BBC announced that Gottabhaya Rajapaksa, the Defence Secretary, was intending to take legal action against Gen. Fonseka for leaking top secret Government information. The rumours were refuted by Gen. Fonseka. On Jan 28, 2010, the CID began its investigations on claims that Fonseka was planning a coup to remove Mahinda Rajapaksa in case of close election results. On Feb 8, 2010, the Sri Lankan Army arrested Gen. Sarath Fonseka for committing military offences. He was taken into military custody for facing Courts Martial proceedings under Army Act 57 (1) for allegedly "committing military offences" during his tenure as Chief of Defense Staff (CDS).

DBS Jeyaraj, the well known and credible political commentator on Sri Lankan affairs, and, in particular, on the LTTE War, has been quoted often and to effect in *Lost Victory*. His take on what the riveting, hidden sub text may have been, in context of the Fonseka – Rajapaksa fallout, and why the Government involved itself in the extreme step of arresting and charging its ex CDS and Army Commander with serious breaches of military and civil law, has been paraphrased for the reader in the succeeding paragraphs to give the reader an intimate view on what all could have happened behind the sensational headlines that have become routine in the coverage of this spat.

"A striking facet of Gottabhaya Rajapaksa's intriguing personality is the candour he displays in some media interviews. Instead of bluffing, sidestepping or trying to wriggle out of answering tricky questions, the (feisty) Defence Secretary responds directly and fields them in a frank, forthright manner. This characteristic was very much evident in the telephonic interview given by the Presidential sibling on February 10, 2010, to Ravi Velloor of the Singapore based *"Straits Times,"* barely 48 hours after the controversial arrest and detention of ex-Army Commander, CDS and defeated Presidential candidate, Gen. Sarath Fonseka.

Given the furore surrounding the arrest, one may have expected the Defence Secretary to be a little evasive or 'diplomatic' in commenting about the retired four–star general but Gottabhaya –true to form– was bluntly open and pulled no punches in answering.

When Velloor raised the issue of Government fears that Fonseka was conspiring to lead a coup attempt, Gottabhaya did not mince his words in replying. This is what he said – 'He was planning on military rule. It was very clear in the latter stages, in the way he had spoken and addressed the people. He said he wouldn't allow the politicians to rob the military of the victory they had achieved and offer a political solution. He was completely trying to isolate the politics and take the country on a different path. In his very last stages as Army Commander, he began bringing his people into Colombo and his Regiment, positioning his senior regiment people all over. All these things were looking like a military coup. He also took a keen interest in changing the previous Navy Commander' (who was not well inclined towards him). Whatever the merits or otherwise of the Defence Secretary's response, it certainly seemed to have impressed the newspaper concerned as the highlight of the interview. So much so that the heading given to the feature was 'He was definitely planning a coup.'

The Defence Secretary's bold assertion that his former comrade at arms was planning a *coup d'etat* is perhaps the crucial factor governing the conduct of this Government towards the former Army commander and ex – CDS. Rightly or wrongly, the Rajapaksa regime has been entertaining suspicion and fear for a long time that Sarath Fonseka was plotting a coup against it. This paranoia or reasonable caution, depending on how one perceives it, explains much of the government's rationale in dealing with the Fonseka phenomenon before and after the Presidential elections.

It remains to be seen as to whether these investigations would uncover genuine evidence about a coup being planned or not. However, the powers that beseem convinced that there really was a plot and are determined to identify and charge the culprits. On the other hand, there is much doubt about this coup conspiracy theory. Many see it as a total fabrication aimed at stifling the chief Presidential contender and his political allies. The real conspiracy they say is not the alleged coup conspiracy but that of the ruling regime planning to penalise Gen. Sarath Fonseka through false accusations.

Against that backdrop, the situation seems to be that of the Govt. procuring enough evidence through interrogation and investigation to construct an effective case against Sarath Fonseka over a *coup d'etat* conspiracy. It also appears that the Govt. will resort to both a Courts Martial by a military tribunal as well as an indictment under the penal code in a civil court. One does not know at this juncture whether the state would be able to prove charges about a coup conspiracy against Gen. Sarath Fonseka or not. However, there seems little doubt that such an attempt would definitely be made. In fact it may be the pivotal issue in any legal action contemplated.

A brief examination of the recent past concerning the coup conspiracy factor would be of relevance in understanding the current course of events.

The reducing bonhomie between the Rajapaksa's and Gen. Fonseka was aggravated by Fonseka making two 'excessive' demands. One was that the Army's strength should be raised to 400,000 and that he be made a Field Marshal. The other was that at least one battalion should be stationed or deployed in every town in Sri Lanka from Paruthithurai (Point Pedro) in the North to Devinuwara (Dondra) in the South. Both these requests aroused suspicion amidst the Rajapaksa fraternity. It was further compounded by Fonseka's elaborate plans to set up 'cantonment townships' housing soldiers' families in various parts of the Country, with particular emphasis on the North and East. He also had plans of independent economic projects capable of generating sustainable funds for maintaining these townships.

Being an adroit, seasoned politician, Mahinda Rajapaksa did not veto Fonseka's proposals when the war was on, as he did not want to alienate the General at that critical stage, but when the Army triumphed over the Tigers, he began moving deftly.

When Fonseka reiterated his twin demands in the wake of military victory, the Army Commander was given a rude shock. Both demands were turned down. Furthermore, President Rajapaksa informed him (very correctly) that there was no need of a huge army in post-war Sri Lanka and that gradual downsizing would soon be underway.

This infuriated Fonseka who openly indicated his displeasure. Thereafter, the Army Chief started making derogatory remarks about the President and the Defence Secretary. He also commenced speaking of becoming the President through elections or any means. Fonseka also effected changes within the officer echelons and moved his loyalists to Colombo and to key positions.

Disturbed by this trend, the President and Defence Secretary struck swiftly and, in July 2009, removed Fonseka as the Army chief and appointed him as the CDS. This rankled so much that when Fonseka quit his post in November 2009 he specifically referred to it in his publicized resignation letter, as a job that had neither content nor authority, and was, only notionally, a promotion.

After Fonseka was kicked upstairs as the CDS, Lt. Gen. Jagath Jayasuriya who was ranked No. 9 in seniority, was made the Army Commander. Thereafter, a number of internal appointments, transfers and changes were made within the military structure. Many of the Fonseka loyalists were moved out to non–strategic positions. The Fonseka effect was being steadily reversed. This too irritated Gen. Sarath Fonseka who mentioned it in his resignation letter. An excerpt – 'The present Army Commander immediately on assuming duties, commenced transferring senior officers who immensely contributed to the war effort during my command tenure including those junior officers working with my wife at the Seva Vanitha Army Branch which was involved in looking after the welfare of the troops. This was done … clearly to challenge the loyalty of officers and (was) most discouraging to the officer corps of the Army, with a wrong signal being transmitted on my authority.'

Gen. Fonseka is reported to have demonstrated his disregard for military discipline by encouraging desertions and accepting deserters into his campaign folds. He is alleged to have set the wrong precedent right at the start of his campaign when his earlier security contingent was reduced. Fifteen of the original were from the military intelligence. Most of these men did not report for duty when recalled, but opted to stay on with the General who, to his discredit, encouraged it. Fonseka also refused to return some of the Army vehicles allocated to him earlier. The ex–Army Chief continued to be in touch with former colleagues and subordinates. Politicisation of the military had reached peak levels and the Army as an institution was seen getting divided horizontally and vertically.

It was against this backdrop that the National Security Council met on January 22, 2010. Various issues were discussed, chief among which was a possible *coup d'etat* by Gen. Fonseka. Some pre-emptive and/or counter measures were proposed and approved. These included a plan to encircle the home and office of Fonseka in the event of violence erupting.

A crackdown amounting to a witch-hunt was on. Section 39 of Army Regulations Act of 1992 was invoked by the Army Chief to send five Major Generals, five Brigadiers, one Colonel, one Lt Col and two Captains on compulsory retirement with effect from Feb 1, 2010. This was the largest ever group of officers to be dealt with in this way. All of them were regarded as Gen. Fonseka loyalists.

However far-fetched the possibility may seem, the Government is well within its rights to investigate the matter thoroughly and discover the truth. If there has really been a conspiracy involving Gen. Sarath Fonseka, serving army officers, ex – military personnel, deserters and sections of the JVP to stage a military coup and capture state power, then those found guilty should certainly be meted out punitive justice. The Government should, however, go the extra mile in ensuring that due process is followed in probing the alleged conspiracy. Already the ways and means adopted in the investigation have caused serious doubts whether the due process (of law) is being followed."[7]

Gen. Sarath Fonseka is being tried on seven charges as per the military spokesman Maj. Gen. Prasad Samarasinghe. Gen. Fonseka would face three charges for participation in political work while on active service and four charges related to military procurements.[8] President Mahinda Rajapaksa, on recommendations by Army Commander, Lt. Gen. Jagath Jayasuriya, has appointed two separate Courts Martials to try the former Army commander and CDS. As per a later report filed by *Lanka Daily News*, proceedings of the second courts martial were in jeopardy over the composition of its panel. Gen. Fonseka appeared before the first courts martial on March 10, 2010, on charges of engaging in politics while in uniform but he disputed the proceedings as "illegal" and refused to reply to the accusations. Its next hearing has been set for May 05, 2010. "The second courts martial proceedings ... just went on for over 30 minutes and without our intervention it was decided to unanimously adjourn its sitting till a decision on its composition is taken," Fonseka's lawyer, Nuwan Popege, told PTI. The second Courts martial has now been adjourned to April 19, 2010.

In the February 25, 2010, free wheeling interview with the noted Indian journalist, Inderjit Badhwar referred to at Note 2, Defence Secretary, Gottabhaya Rajapaksa, in response to questions by Inderjit Badhwar about the specific charges under which the Government had arrested Gen. Fonseka, reiterated that Fonseka had politicised the military. "We share a proud tradition with India as the only two countries in the region that can boast about a neutral military, but when that tradition was subverted in Sri Lanka by Fonseka, there was no option but to take action against him. He should have had a clean break from the military and then entered politics. In his utter greed for power, he used his position and contacts for his own benefits. He did this while he was CDS, and also when he was Army Commander. He used the Army Commander's bungalow to conduct political activities and kept military resources made available to him in his official capacity for personal political use".[9]

In a typically informative and interesting follow up article[10] on the Fonseka incarceration and trial, DBS Jeyaraj, writes that the Governments Legal adviser, GL Peiris, held a press conference during which he stated that the Government was also preparing to file sedition charges against General Fonseka whose actions had allegedly caused unrest among the rank and file in the military and for harbouring Army deserters. He writes that Gen. Fonseka may also have to face Penal Code and Foreign Exchange Control Act violation charges. Notwithstanding Fonseka's take on the issue, that he cannot be tried under the Army Act as he has retired, Jeyaraj says that the "Governments understanding is that Fonseka is indeed subject to military law and cites related legal provisions. Basically, the Government holds that Gen. Fonseka retired only in mid-November 2009 and that he remains bound by military law until mid-May 2010. Apparently, as per Sri Lankan law, a retired officer is subject to military law up to six months after retirement... There is no doubt that Fonseka and supporters will contest the Govt. in this respect by challenging the legality and substantive basis of charges. It will be up to the courts to decide on these questions and act accordingly".

DBS Jeyaraj makes another point demanding attention. "It is interesting in a way", he says, "that the four top army officers involved in the arrest, detention and inquiry of Fonseka have a "hostile history" with him. To prove his point, Jeyaraj has clinically examined the background of the hostility between these four officers and their retired Army Commander and CDS.[11] The details will cause the reader to reflect on the possibility of a witch hunt.

What is clear to analysts and lay readers alike is that the last word has not yet been spoken or written on this ugly Fonseka-Rajapaksa saga. Much more is to come, and the portents are that Gen. Fonseka's troubles can only multiply at this point in time, considering how the dice appear loaded against him. Given his abrasive, impulsive and clearly boastful persona, it is no surprise that, in front of the wily Rajapaksa combine, he comes across as a maverick, foot-in-the-mouth politician who did not or could not play his cards with the sense and sensibility expected from someone of his experience and exposure.

Politics is neither this author's forte nor his love; the military certainly is. Purely from a military viewpoint, therefore, what DBS Jeyaraj and the Defence Secretary, (himself an ex, illustrious, war decorated Army officer), have implied, by way of military impropriety on part of Gen. Fonseka in their articles/statements, is a matter of deep concern. For a democratic Government to seriously consider pressing the ultimate anti-national charge of sedition along with charges of corruption and politicisation of the Army's rank and file against its ex CDS and iconic, path breaking Army Chief, seen till recently as a war hero in the eyes of soldiers and citizens alike, is a matter which merits serious consideration particularly if found to be substantiated. Though it seems unlikely at this moment, because what is on record so far is mere conjecture, the possibility of Gen. Fonseka having considered *coup d' etat* as an option does not make for pleasant reading. Even given the fact that Sri Lanka is no banana republic to allow its Army to write rough shod over its legitimate and well established democratic credentials, the unavoidable but harsh fact is that some of the Generals doings as well as military related demands from the Government, while he was in service as the Army Chief, and, later, as the CDS, if true, do not make much professional sense. On the contrary, they point towards a level of politicisation that is not expected of a serving Army Chief/CDS in any democracy world wide, leave alone a nascent, growing democracy like Sri Lanka, that needs all its national institutions to grow in accordance with healthy democratic practices; especially its military forces.

Seen dispassionately, the demand for a huge (over 100 percent) increase in the strength of the 1,90,000 strong Army (to 400,000); the demand for locating combat units at all important towns of the country, North and South along with their attendant cantonments, even as the war against the LTTE was raging towards its stunning closure; the demand for being appointed as Field Marshal in recognition of his personal performance, does not make military sense, unless seen through the prism of overweening personal ambition. Neither do statements attributed by the media to the General in the run up to the Presidential elections, as to what all he would do (by way of corporal punishment) and to whom, if and when elected. If all this is not a product of savvy, clever, media manipulation (something for which the ruling Government has a reputation, going by media opinion) against a pretender to the top job with a view to undermining his credibility and maturity, then it is a serious violation of democratic norms, not expected from an otherwise competent and brave officer who led his field Army in an unexpectedly wildly successful war against a ruthless and competent enemy.

DBS Jeyaraj is therefore more than right in saying that, if any of these charges stick in an impartial court of law, the due process of justice must take its toll; not just against the principal perpetrator but against all his cohorts as well. Democracy must extract this price from those privileged to serve under its flag, particularly if they are uniformed personnel.

The issue that begs consideration is that justice cannot be delivered by a court adjudged in popular perception to be a Kangaroo court. The fundamental point that therefore needs resolution is the legality involved in trying the General under military law, when his lawyers claim that, on retirement; he became a civilian and therefore needs to be tried under civil law statutes and in open court. Apparently, Sri Lankan laws do allow for a six month period commencing from the day of retirement, under which a retired military person can indeed be tried under military law. This, however, needs both confirmation as well as public declaration. Even if permitted, the conduct of the trial by Courts Martial comprising of officers who were harmed or sidelined by Gen Fonseka when he was in uniform, if true, may point towards vendetta and small mindedness, rather than towards fair play which must not be compromised if the Govt. does not want its credibility challenged.

The larger issue that the author supports without any qualification whatsoever is that the Sri Lankan military, if it is to perform in support of national interest, always and every time, must remain completely apolitical. No compromise should be made on this count under any circumstances. In this context, India's well-defined and time-tested model of apolitical armed forces and civil control of the military has served the country well; notwithstanding the dire need to improve this interface, especially in-so-far as civilian trust in the military remaining apolitical and therefore empowering it with greater Institutional say in matters of national security and national interest is concerned. It is an example Sri Lanka can and must emulate.

Besides the military developments, there has been another significant political development that has great nation building potential. The Sri Lankan political party closest to the defeated LTTE, the Tamil National Alliance (TNA), has dropped its demand for a separate Tamil homeland.[12] The TNA, which is the biggest political grouping representing the ethnic minority, has very recently said it is amenable to a "federal" solution. The party wants the two Tamil-majority provinces to be merged back into one, and significant devolution of powers. This is something that has the potential, if it is serious, to accelerate national reconciliation and allow Sri Lanka to return to its winning ways and its Asian 'Tiger' prosperity of yore. This (devolution) is also something that India has been pitching for along time. It is certainly in India's security interests that Sri Lanka returns soonest to its prosperous ways and resolves the ongoing internal spat with dispatch, impartiality and objectivity.

Even rudimentary crystal ball gazing by the author points to the fact that too much has happened for reconciliation to be a possible option for resolving the current Rajapaksa -Fonseka crisis in Sri Lanka. The fact that Gen. Sarath Fonseka has emerged as a credible opponent of Mahinda Rajapaksa and therefore needs to be publicly diminished in stature is a political imperative of which the Rajapaksa clan is well aware. The distaff side of this argument is that Mahinda Rajapaksa and his family will do all it takes to ensure that the Rajapaksa hold over Governance is strengthened to ward off any short and medium term threat to it by taking suitable political initiatives. Mahinda Rajapaksa, is, in particular, an adept exponent of *realpolitik*, and can hardly be expected to let go of his advantage in this otherwise grossly unequal struggle for power.

The military Courts Martials, followed by the arraignment of Gen. Sarath Fonseka in an appropriate civil court on charges tenable under the country's civil and penal laws can be expected to run their legal course. By implication, with the might of the country's Governance and military pitched against him at a time when he is in military custody, Gen. Sarath Fonseka is fighting a losing battle and with his back against the wall. Even if some, not all the charges (which have or which are likely to be preferred against him) are proved conclusively, he is headed for a long period of incarceration. This will effectively render him *hors de' combat* so far as his short and medium term political ambitions are concerned.

India has always stood for stability. This, notwithstanding its problems with the Rajapaksa Government and its short-term-gains-led penchant for cozying up with countries inimical to India, such as Pakistan, and, lately, China. India has thus shown its open support for the current Government by being amongst the earliest nations to compliment Mahinda Rajapaksa on his victory. Its financial help to Sri Lanka to facilitate Tamil refugee return to their homes has also been generous. The subtext of this policy is clear: Gen Sarath Fonseka's fulminations against India before and during the Presidential elections to garner hard-line Sinhala votes could hardly have endeared him to the Indian political establishment. If, subsequently, it is proved that he had harboured ambitions of overthrowing a legitimately elected Government by staging a coup, he would certainly be *persona non grata* and correctly so, as far as India is concerned. Under the current circumstances, therefore, not much sympathy for him is likely to be expended in India.

India, will, of course, not renege on its devolution/issue of 13th Amendment aims and try all it can diplomatically, to ensure that Sri Lanka deals with the Tamil problem in line with its public commitments of devolution and allowing a fair degree of autonomy. This authors value added advise to the Indian MEA will be to reclaim lost ground and try and make Sri Lanka central to the strategic defence of India, by attending to Sri Lankan security and developmental concerns with greater dispatch and understanding than hitherto fore. There is a critical need for India to ensure that Sri Lanka does not develop deeper defence, commercial and economic/infrastructure development ties with these countries than it already has. This will need concerted and synergised action by India and must be given due priority by the Indian political establishment. Sri Lanka is too closely located for India not to be very watchful of what happens on this Island country that might strain its otherwise historical and stable ties with this country of Serendip.

What has to also be kept in mind is that Sri Lanka, at its apex level, clearly realises the extent up to which it can take India and Indian support for granted. With India progressing rapidly in terms of its economic and diplomatic clout, Sri Lanka, in effect needs India and its material and moral support as much as India needs a stable Sri Lanka that understands India's security concerns and the part Sri Lanka has to play therein. It is therefore a truly symbiotic relationship that benefits both countries in implementation of which both countries must toil hard to optimize.

Not the least of the considerations that intimately concern both countries is that the spectre of terrorism that haunted Sri Lanka for well nigh 30 years and ended up souring the historically friendly relations between the two during its run must not be allowed to revive, recur or resurface. The key causes that fuelled its fires – the lot of the Tamils – must also be attended to with maturity and vision. That will need both countries to put their heads together with understanding and concern and for their common and regional good.

Endnotes

1. http://en.wikipedia.org/wiki/Sarath_Fonseka#Politics
2. Bhadwar, Inderjit. "General Fonseka was Only Member of National Security Council Who Opposed Early Re-settlement of IDPs". Gottabhaya Rajapaksa interviewed by Inderjit Badhwar. Article/Interview reprinted on website courtesy *Tehelka*, New Delhi. February 25, 2010. http://www.lankanewspapers.com/news/2010/2/54549_space.html
3. http://en.wikipedia.org/wiki/Sarath_Fonseka#Politics
4. Bhadwar, Inderjit. "General Fonseka was Only Member of National Security Council who Opposed Early Re-settlement of IDPs". Gottabhaya Rajapaksa interviewed by Inderjit Badhwar. Article/Interview reprinted courtesy *Tehelka*, New Delhi. February 25, 2010. http://www.lankanewspapers.com/news/2010/2/54549_space.html
5. "Sri Lankan Presidential Election, 2010." http://en.wikipedia.org/wiki/Sri_Lankan_presidential_election,_2010
6. Ibid.
7. Jeyaraj, DBS. "Were the General And JVP Involved in a Coup Conspiracy?" 12 February 2010. http://www.dailymirror.lk/print/index.php/opinion1/3603-were-the-general-and-jvp-involved-in-a-coup-conspiracy.html

   The full article makes for fascinating reading and comes across as an objective and in depth analysis and is strongly recommended for first hand reading and reflection. It may be observed that, even if, to an extent, the Jeyaraj analysis is weighted in favour of the Government, no indictment has been made against Gen Sarath Fonseka. What has, on the contrary, been demanded of the Govt. is the need for a fair trial in line with the military and civil laws of the country.
8. "Gen. Fonseka to be produced before Courts Martial Next Week." March 11, 2010. Source: Ada Derana. http://www.colombotoday.com/english/articles/Lite/Gen.-Fonseka-be-produced-courts-martial-week/10028.htm
9. Badhwar, Inderjit. "General Fonseka was Only Member of National Security Council who Opposed Early Re-settlement of IDPs". Gottabhaya Rajapaksa interviewed by Inderjit Badhwar. Article/Interview reprinted courtesy *Tehelka*, New Delhi. February 25, 2010. http://www.lankanewspapers.com/news/2010/2/54549_space.html
10. Jeyaraj, DBS. "The Case against Military Justice for Sarath Fonseka." February 26, 2010. http://dbsjeyaraj.com/dbsj/archives/1409
11. Ibid. **Excerpts:** "It was the Army commander Jagath Jayasuriya who ordered that Fonseka be arrested. He did so after getting the green light from the President who reportedly obtained advice to that effect from the Attorney-General. On one level there is absolutely no problem in all this. Everyone is doing their duty keeping the best interests of the country and army.

But on another level there is a problem. Fonseka displayed great hostility towards Jayasuriya while in service and even got his ADC arrested. He was apparently gunning for Jayasuriya himself. After Jayasuriya became Army Chief, Fonseka complained bitterly against him to the President. He also ridiculed him publicly as a "holding" officer unfit to lead the Army.

Now about his arrest. Who were the senior officers who arrested him? Provost Marshal Brig. Jagath Wijesiri and Colombo District Operations Commander Maj Gen Sumith Manawadu. Both were following orders. But again there is a personal element here.

Brig. Wijesiri held the post of Provost Marshal a few years ago. There was an incident where an Army vehicle driven by an officer met with an accident. In the vehicle was an attractive woman army deserter. Wijesiri, then a Colonel did his duty by investigating the incident. He discovered that the vehicle was being driven to a particular location for a rendezvous with a top army officer. The Army Commander of the day, Sarath Fonseka took keen interest in the matter and tried to suppress the investigation.Wijesiri was transferred out to Trincomalee as a transit camp commandant. A Fonseka loyalist, Brig. Bimal Dias was made Provost Marshal. The course of internal military justice was perverted...

In the case of Maj Gen Sumith Manawadu, he served as Planning Director at Army Headquarters under Sarath Fonseka. At that time he was a Fonseka favourite and appointed as GOC 57 division. But, there was some friction with Fonseka and soon Manawadu was transferred from "Command" stream to "Common" stream. Within Army circles, this was akin to a demotion. Manawadu was restricted to inconsequential administrative functions. After Fonseka quit the Army, Manawadu was promoted as Major-General. It was Manawadu who supervised the military action of surrounding Hotel Lakeside-Cinnamon where Fonseka was holed up with his associates.

Last but not least is the Chief of Staff, Major-General Daya Ratnayaka. He was tasked by the Army Commander to question Fonseka and procure a summary of evidence into charges against him. But Fonseka has refused to cooperate. Interestingly there is a history of friction between Fonseka and Ratnayaka too. Sarath Fonseka was injured seriously in April 2005 when a woman suicide bomber exploded herself within Army Headquarters premises. The doughty General fought for his life on the hospital bed and miraculously survived. It was when Fonseka was in hospital that the Maavil Aru battle took place. After protracted fighting, the Liberation Tigers of Tamil Eelam (LTTE) retreated. The entire area came under Army control. Daya Ratnayaka was responsible for publishing a special volume to mark the Maavil Aru victory. Since Nanda Mallawaratchy was the acting Army Commander in Fonseka's absence and played a part in the Maavil Aru war, he was given due recognition in the special volume.

Fonseka, upon resuming charge as Commander was livid with fury at Ratnayake for acknowledging Mallawaratchi's role. He was harassed and due promotions were withheld. Today, Fonseka has fallen from grace while Ratnayaka has got his well-deserved elevation. Fate has decreed Ratnayake being in charge of the Fonseka inquiry.

12. Haviland, Charles. "Sri Lanka Tamil Party Drops Statehood Demand." BBC News, Colombo. March 13, 2010. http://news.bbc.co.uk/2/hi/south_asia/8566114.stm